Handbook of
Psychological Assessment
(PGPS-131)

Pergamon Handbooks of Related Interest

Anchin/Kiesler HANDBOOK OF INTERPERSONAL
PSYCHOTHERAPY
Hersen/Kazdin/Bellack THE CLINICAL PSYCHOLOGY HANDBOOK
Matson/Mulick HANDBOOK OF MENTAL RETARDATION

Other Related Titles

Barlow/Hayes/Nelson THE SCIENTIST PRACTITIONER: Research
and Accountability in Clinical and Educational Settings
Barlow/Hersen SINGLE CASE EXPERIMENTAL DESIGNS: Strategies
for Studying Behavior Change, Second Edition
Hersen/Bellack BEHAVIORAL ASSESSMENT: A Practical
Handbook, Second Edition

Related Journals*

BEHAVIORAL ASSESSMENT
BEHAVIOUR RESEARCH AND THERAPY
CLINICAL PSYCHOLOGY REVIEW
JOURNAL OF BEHAVIOR THERAPY AND EXPERIMENTAL
PSYCHIATRY
PERSONALITY AND INDIVIDUAL DIFFERENCES

*Free specimen copies available upon request.

PERGAMON GENERAL PSYCHOLOGY SERIES
EDITORS
Arnold P. Goldstein, *Syracuse University*
Leonard Krasner, *SUNY at Stony Brook*

Handbook of Psychological Assessment

edited by

Gerald Goldstein

*Veterans Administration Medical Center,
Pittsburgh, PA*

Michel Hersen

University of Pittsburgh School of Medicine

PERGAMON PRESS
New York   Oxford   Toronto   Sydney   Paris   Frankfurt

Pergamon Press Offices:

U.S.A.   Pergamon Press Inc., Maxwell House, Fairview Park,
                        Elmsford, New York 10523, U.S.A.

U.K.   Pergamon Press Ltd., Headington Hill Hall,
                        Oxford OX3 0BW, England

CANADA   Pergamon Press Canada Ltd., Suite 104, 150 Consumers Road,
                        Willowdale, Ontario M2J 1P9, Canada

AUSTRALIA   Pergamon Press (Aust.) Pty. Ltd., P.O. Box 544,
                        Potts Point, NSW 2011, Australia

FRANCE   Pergamon Press SARL, 24 rue des Ecoles,
                        75240 Paris, Cedex 05, France

FEDERAL REPUBLIC   Pergamon Press GmbH, Hammerweg 6,
OF GERMANY   D-6242 Kronberg-Taunus, Federal Republic of Germany

Copyright © 1984 Pergamon Press Inc.

Library of Congress Cataloging in Publication Data

Goldstein, Gerald, 1931-
    Handbook of psychological assessment.

    (Pergamon general psychology series ; 131)
    Bibliography: p.
    Includes index.
    1. Psychometrics. 2. Psychological tests. I. Hersen,
Michel. II. Title. III. Series. [DNLM: 1. Personality
assessment--Handbooks. 2. Psychological tests--
Handbooks. BF 176 H236]
BF39.G56   1984   150'.287   84-3092
ISBN 0-08-029401-4

Printed in the United States of America

CONTENTS

PREFACE

As in many areas of psychology, the field of psychological assessment has become so specialized that it is becoming increasingly difficult to imagine a single individual composing a comprehensive textbook of the type represented by the "psychological testing" or "mental testing" texts of the past. Indeed, a multiauthored handbook such as the present one has become a necessity. One can reasonably write about some single aspect of assessment, such as intelligence testing, but the construction of a comprehensive work on psychological assessment, in general, might well strain the capacities of even an outstanding renaissance scholar. It is our view that the major source of this change has been the expansion of the testing concept to the idea of assessment. The traditional role of psychologists as testers has changed in recent years, and current psychologists do not simply give tests, but also interview, observe behavior systematically in structured and unstructured settings, measure behaviors in ways that go well beyond test administration, and become involved not only in construction, administration, and interpretation of tests, but in policy matters regarding the utilization of tests as well. Moreover, they also have had a primary role as therapists for some time.

In view of these complexities, we elected to assemble a volume of the edited type in which acknowledged experts in the major areas of psychological assessment were asked to contribute chapters. Our avowed intention was to go well beyond the traditional borders of psychological testing. In doing so, we have included the more traditional areas of intelligence, personality, achievement, aptitude, and interest testing, but have also added extensive sections on interviewing, behavioral and neuropsychological assessment, and the practical application of such assessment.

This handbook is divided into 9 major sections and contains 21 chapters. Part I (*Introduction*) considers some of the historical issues in the field. This is followed by sections on *Psychometric Foundations* (Part II), *Assessment of Intelligence* (Part III), *Achievement, Aptitude, and Interest* (Part IV), *Neuropsychological Assessment* (Part V), *Interviewing* (Part VI), *Personality Assessment* (Part VII), *Behavioral Assessment* (Part VIII), and finally *Assessment and Intervention* (Part IX).

Many individuals have taken part during the course of this lengthy process. First and foremost, we thank our eminent contributors for sharing with us and our readers their respective expertise. The senior editor would like to acknowledge the support of the Veterans Administration in the preparation of this work, as well as the following individuals: Adelaide Goertler, Lorraine Hummel, and Carolyn Shelly. The junior editor thanks Susan Capozzoli, Mary Newell, and Janet Twomey for their technical assistance. Finally, we are most appreciative of our editor at Pergamon, Jerome Frank, whose patience and good cheer was a constant source of encouragement.

Gerald Goldstein
Michel Hersen
Pittsburgh, PA

PART I

INTRODUCTION

1 HISTORICAL PERSPECTIVES

Gerald Goldstein
Michel Hersen

INTRODUCTION

"A test is a systematic procedure for comparing the behavior of two or more persons." This definition of a test, offered by Lee Cronbach many years ago (Cronbach, 1949, 1960) probably still stands as a means of epitomizing the major content of psychological assessment. The invention of psychological tests, then known as mental tests, is generally attributed to Galton (Boring, 1950) and occurred during the middle and late 19th century. Galton's work was largely concerned with individual differences, and his approach was essentially the opposite of what was the general case for the psychologists of his time. Psychologists then were largely concerned with the exhaustive study of mental phenomena in a few subjects, while Galton was more interested in somewhat less specific analyses of large numbers of people. Perhaps the first psychological test was the "Galton whistle," which evaluated high tone hearing. Galton also appeared to have the statistical concept that errors of measurement in individuals could be cancelled out through the mass effect of large samples.

Obviously, psychologists have come a long way from the simple tests of Galton, Binet, and Munsterberg, and the technology of testing has already entered the computer age, with almost science fiction-like extensions, such as testing by satellite. Psychometrics is now an advanced branch of mathematical and statistical science, and the administration, scoring, and even interpretation of tests have become increasingly objectified and automated. While some greet the news with dread and others with enthusiasm, we may be rapidly approaching the day when most or all testing will be administered, scored, and interpreted by computer. Thus, the 19th century image of the school teacher administering paper-and-pencil tests to the students in her classroom and grading them at home has changed to the extensive use of automated procedures administered to huge portions of the population by representatives of giant corporations. Testing appears to have become a part of western culture, and there are indeed very few people who enter educational, work, or clinical settings who do not take many tests during their lifetimes.

In recent years, there appears to have been a distinction made between testing and assessment, assessment being the broader concept. Psychologists do not just give tests now; they perform assessments. The title of this volume, the *Handbook of Psychological Assessment*, was chosen advisedly and is meant to convey the view that it is

3

not simply a handbook of psychological testing, although testing will be covered in great detail. The term *assessment* implies that there are many ways of evaluating individual differences. Testing is one way, but there are also interviewing, observation of behavior in natural or structured settings, and recording of various physiological functions. Certain forms of interviewing and systematic observation of behavior are now known as behavioral assessment, as opposed to the psychometric assessment accomplished through the use of formal tests. Historically, interest in these two forms of assessment has waxed and waned, and in what follows we will briefly try to trace these trends in various areas.

INTELLIGENCE TESTING

The testing of intelligence in school children was probably the first major occupation of clinical psychology. The Binet scales and their descendants continue to be used, along with the IQ concept associated with them. Later, primarily through the work of David Wechsler and associates (Wechsler, 1944), intelligence testing was extended to adults, and the IQ concept was changed from the mental age system (Mental Age/Chronological Age × 100) to the notion of a deviation IQ based on established norms. While Wechsler was primarily concerned with the individual assessment of intelligence, many group administered paper-and-pencil tests also emerged during the early years of the twentieth century. Perhaps the old Army Alpha and Beta tests, developed for intellectual screening of inductees into the armed forces during the first world war, were the first examples of these instruments. The use of these tests progressed in parallel with developments in more theoretical research regarding the nature of intelligence. The English investigators Burt, Pearson, and Spearman and the Americans Thurstone and Guilford are widely known for their work in this area, particularly with factor analysis. The debate over whether intelligence is a general ability (g) or a series of specific abilities represents one of the classic controversies in psychology. A related controversy that is still very much with us (Jensen, 1983) has to do with whether intelligence is primarily inherited or acquired and with the corollary issue having to do with ethnic-racial differences in intellectual ability.

Another highly significant aspect of intelligence testing has to do with its clinical utilization. The

IQ now essentially defines the borders of mental retardation, and intelligence tests are extremely widely used to identify retarded children in educational settings (DSM-III, APA, 1980). However, intelligence testing has gone far beyond the attempt to identify mentally retarded individuals and has become widely applied in the fields of psychopathology and neuropsychology. With regard to psychopathology, under the original impetus of David Rapaport and collaborators (Rapaport, 1945), the Wechsler scales became clinical instruments used in conjunction with other tests to evaluate patients with such conditions as schizophrenia and various stress related disorders. In the field of neuropsychology, the use of intelligence testing is perhaps best described by McFie's (1975) remark, "It is perhaps a matter of luck that many of the Wechsler subtests are neurologically relevant" (p.14). In these applications, the intelligence test was basically used as an instrument with which the clinician could examine various cognitive processes, on the basis of which inferences could be made about the patient's clinical status.

In summary, the intelligence test has become a widely used assessment instrument in educational, industrial, military, and clinical settings. While in some applications the emphasis remains on the simple obtaining of a numerical IQ value, it would probably be fair to say that many, if not most, psychologists now use the intelligence test as a means of examining the individual's cognitive processes; of seeing how he/she goes about solving problems; of identifying those factors that may be interfering with adaptive thinking; of looking at various language and nonverbal abilities in brain damaged patients; and of identifying patterns of abnormal thought processes seen in schizophrenic patients. Performance profiles and qualitative characteristics of individual responses to items appear to have become the major foci of interest, rather than the single IQ score.

PERSONALITY ASSESSMENT

Personality assessment has come to rival intelligence testing as a task performed by psychologists. However, while most psychologists would agree that an intelligence test is generally the best way to measure intelligence, no such consensus obtains within the realm of personality evaluation. In long-term perspective, it would appear that two major philosophies have emerged and perhaps three assessment methods. The two philosophies can be traced back to Allport's (1937) distinction between nomothetic versus idiographic methodologies and Meehl's (1954) distinction between clinical and statistical or actuarial prediction. In essence, some psychologists feel that personality assessments are best accomplished when they are highly individualized, while others have a preference for quantitative procedures based on group norms. The phrase "seer versus sign" has been used to epitomize this dispute. The three methods referred to are the interview, the projective, and the objective test. Obviously, the first way psychologists and their predecessors found out about people was to talk to them, giving the interview historical precedence. But following a period when the use of the interview was eschewed by many psychologists, it has made a return. It would appear that the field is in a historical spiral, with various methods leaving and returning at different levels.

The interview began as a relatively unstructured conversation with the patient and perhaps an informant, with varying goals, including obtaining a history, assessing personality structure and dynamics, establishing a diagnosis, and many other matters. Numerous publications have been written about interviewing (e.g., Menninger, 1952), but in general they provided outlines and general guidelines as to what should be accomplished by the interview. However, model interviews were not provided. With or without this guidance, the interview was viewed by many as a subjective, unreliable procedure that could not be sufficiently validated. For example, the unreliability of psychiatric diagnosis based on studies of multiple interviewers had been well established (Zubin, 1967). More recently, however, a number of structured psychiatric interviews have appeared in which the specific content, if not specific items, has been presented, and for which very adequate reliability has been established. There are by now several such interviews available including the Schedule for Affective Disorders and Schizophrenia (SADS) (Spitzer & Endicott, 1977), the Renard Diagnostic Interview (Helzer, Robins, Croughan, & Welner, 1981), the Diagnostic Interview Schedule (DIS) (Robins, Helzer, Croughan, & Ratcliff, 1981) and the Structured Clinical Interview for DSM-III (SCID) (Spitzer & Williams, 1983). These interviews have been established in conjunction with objective diagnostic criteria including DSM-III it-

self, the Research Diagnostic Criteria (Spitzer, Endicott, & Robins, 1977) and the Feighner Criteria (Feighner, Robins, Guze, Woodruff, Winokur, & Munoz, 1972). These new procedures have apparently ushered in a "comeback" of the interview, and many psychiatrists and psychologists now prefer to use these procedures rather than either the objective or projective type psychological test.

Those advocating the use of structured interviews point to the fact that in psychiatry, at least, tests must ultimately be validated against judgments made by psychiatrists. And these judgments are generally based on interviews and observation, since there really are no biological or other objective markers of most forms of psychopathology. If that is indeed the case, there seems little point in administering elaborate and often lengthy tests when one can just as well use the criterion measure itself, the interview, rather than the test. There is no way that a test can be more valid than an interview if an interview is the validating criterion. The structured interviews have made a major impact on the scientific literature in psychopathology, and it is rare to find a recently written research report in which the diagnoses were not established by one of them. It would appear that we have come full cycle regarding this matter, and until objective markers of various forms of psychopathology are discovered, we will be relying primarily on the structured interviews for our diagnostic assessments.

Interviews of the SADS or DIS type are relatively lengthy and comprehensive, but there are now several briefer and more specific interview or interview-like procedures. Within psychiatry, perhaps the most well-known procedure is the Brief Psychiatric Rating Scale (BPRS) (Overall & Gorham, 1962). The BPRS is a brief, structured, repeatable interview that has essentially become the standard instrument for assessment of change in patients, usually as a function of taking some form of psychotropic medication. In the specific area of depression, the Hamilton Depression Scale (Hamilton, 1960) plays a similar role. There are also several widely used interviews for patients with dementia, which generally combine a brief mental status examination with some form of functional assessment, particularly with reference to Activities of Daily Living. The most popular of these scales are the Mini-Mental Status Examination of Folstein, Folstein, and McHugh (1975) and the Dementia Scale of Blessed, Tomlinson, and Roth (1968). Extensive validation studies have been conducted with these instruments, perhaps the most well known one having to do with the correlation between scores on the Blessed, Tomlinson, and Roth scale during life and the senile plaque count determined on autopsy in patients with dementia. The obtained correlation of .7 quite impressively suggested that the scale was a valid one for detection of dementia. In addition to these interviews and rating scales, numerous methods have been developed for assessment of psychopathology by nurses and psychiatric aids based on direct observation of ward behavior (Raskin, 1982). The most widely used of these rating scales are the Nurses' Observation Scale for Inpatient Evaluation (NOSIE-30) (Honigfeld & Klett, 1965) and the Ward Behavior Inventory (Burdock, Hardesty, Hakerem, Zubin, & Beck, 1968). These scales assess such behaviors as cooperativeness, appearance, communication, aggressive episodes, and related behaviors, and are to be based on direct observation rather than reference to medical records or the report of others. Scales of this type supplement the interview with information concerning social competence and capacity to carry out functional activities of daily living.

Again taking a long-term historical view, it is our impression that after many years of neglect by the field, the interview has made a successful return to the arena of psychological assessment, but the interviews now used are quite different from the loosely organized, "free-wheeling," conversation-like procedures of the past. First of all, their organization tends to be structured, and the interviewer is required to obtain certain items of information. It is generally felt that the formulation of specifically worded questions is counterproductive; rather, the interviewer, who should be an experienced clinician trained in the use of the procedure, should be able to formulate questions that will elicit the required information. Second, the interview procedure must meet psychometric standards of validity and reliability. Finally, while the structured interviews tend to be atheoretical in orientation, they are based on contemporary scientific knowledge of psychopathology. Thus, for example, the information needed to establish a differential diagnosis within the general classification of the affective disorders is derived from the scientific literature on depression and the related affective disorders.

The rise of the interview appears to have occurred in parallel with the decline of projective techniques. Those of us now in a chronological category that may be roughly described as middle-aged may recall that their graduate training in clinical psychology probably included extensive course work and practicum experience involving the various projective techniques. Most clinical psychologists would probably agree that even though projective techniques are still used to some extent, the atmosphere of ferment and excitement concerning these procedures that existed during the 1940s and 1950s no longer seems to exist. Even though the Rorschach technique and Thematic Apperception Test (TAT) were the major procedures used during that era, a variety of other tests emerged quite rapidly: the projective use of human figure drawings (Machover, 1949), the Szondi Test (Szondi, 1952), the Make-A-Picture-Story (MAPS) Test (Shneidman, 1952), the Four Picture Test (VanLennep, 1951), the Sentence Completion Tests (e.g., Rohde, 1957), and the Holtzman Inkblot Test (Holtzman, 1958). The exciting work of Murray and his collaborators reported on in *Explorations in Personality* (Murray, 1938) had a major impact on the field and stimulated extensive utilization of the TAT. It would probably be fair to say that the sole survivor of this active movement is the Rorschach. Many clinicians continue to use the Rorschach, and the work of Exner and his collaborators has lent it increasing scientific respectability (See Erdberg & Exner, Chapter 17).

There are undoubtedly many reasons for the decline in utilization of the projective techniques, but in our view they can be summarized by the following points.

1. Increasing scientific sophistication created an atmosphere of skepticism concerning these instruments. Their validity and reliability were called into question by numerous studies (e.g., Swensen, 1957, 1968; Zubin, 1967), and it was felt by a substantial segment of the professional community that the claims made for these procedures could not be substantiated.

2. Developments in alternative procedures, notably the MMPI and other objective tests, convinced many clinicians that the information previously gained from projective tests could be gained more efficiently and less expensively with the objective methods. In particular, the voluminous MMPI research literature has demonstrated

its usefulness in an extremely wide variety of clinical and research settings. When the MMPI and related objective techniques were pitted against the projectives during the days of the "seer versus sign" controversy, it was generally demonstrated that sign was as good as or better than seer in most of the studies accomplished (Meehl, 1954).

3. In general, the projective techniques are not atheoretical and, in fact, are generally viewed as being associated with one or another branch of psychoanalytic theory.

While psychoanalysis remains a strong and vigorous movement within psychology, there are numerous alternative theoretical systems at large, notably behaviorally and biologically oriented systems. As is implied in the section of this chapter covering behavioral assessment, behaviorally oriented psychologists pose theoretical objections to the projective techniques and make little use of them in their practices. Similarly, the projective techniques tend not to receive high levels of acceptance in biologically oriented psychiatry departments. In effect, then, utilization of the projective techniques declined for scientific, practical, and philosophical reasons. However, the Rorschach in particular continues to be productively used, primarily by psychodynamically oriented clinicians.

The early history of the objective personality tests has been traced by Cronbach (1949, 1960). The beginnings apparently go back to Sir Francis Galton, who devised personality questionnaires during the latter part of the 19th century. We will not repeat that history here, but rather will focus on those procedures that survived into the contemporary era. In our view, there have been three such major survivors: a series of tests developed by Guilford and collaborators (Guilford & Zimmerman, 1949); a similar series developed by Cattell and collaborators (Cattell, Eber, & Tatsuoka, 1970); and the MMPI. In general, but certainly not in all cases, the Guilford and Cattell procedures are used for individuals functioning within the normal range, while the MMPI is more widely used in clinical populations. Thus, for example, Cattell's 16PF test may be used to screen job applicants, while the MMPI may be more typically used in psychiatric health care facilities. Furthermore, the Guilford and Cattell tests are based on factor analysis and are trait oriented, while the MMPI in its standard form does not make use of

factor analytically derived scales and is more oriented toward psychiatric classification. Thus, the Guilford and Cattell scales contain measures of such traits as dominance or sociability, while most of the MMPI scales are named after psychiatric classifications such as paranoia or hypochondriasis.

Currently, most psychologists use one or more of these objective tests rather than interviews or projective tests in screening situations. For example, many thousands of patients admitted to Veterans Administration psychiatric facilities take the MMPI shortly after admission, while applicants for prison guard jobs in the state of Pennsylvania take the Cattell 16PF. However, the MMPI in particular is commonly used as more than a screening instrument. It is frequently used as a part of an extensive diagnostic evaluation, as a method of evaluating treatment, and in numerous research applications. There is little question that it is the most widely used and extensively studied procedure in the objective personality test area. Even though the 566 true or false items have remained the same since the initial development of the instrument, the test's use in clinical interpretation has evolved dramatically over the years. We have gone from a perhaps overly naive dependence on single scale evaluations and overly literal interpretation of the names of the scales (many of which are archaic psychiatric terms) to sophisticated configural interpretation of profiles, much of which is based on empirical research (Gilberstadt & Duker, 1965; Marks, Seeman, & Haller, 1974). Correspondingly, the methods of administering, scoring, and interpreting the MMPI have kept pace with technological and scientific advances in the behavioral sciences. Beginning with sorting cards into piles, hand scoring, and subjective interpretation, the MMPI has gone to computerized administration and scoring, interpretation based at least to some extent on empirical findings, and even computerized interpretation (Fowler, 1979). As is well known, there are several companies that will provide computerized scoring and interpretation of the MMPI.

Even though we should anticipate continued spiraling of trends in personality assessment, it would appear that we have passed an era of projective techniques and are now living in a time of objective assessment with an increasing interest in the structured interview. There also appears to be increasing concern with the scientific status of our assessment procedures. In recent years, there has been particular concern with reliability of diagnosis, especially since distressing findings appeared in the literature suggesting that psychiatric diagnoses were being made quite unreliably (Zubin, 1967). The issue of validity in personality assessment remains a difficult one for a number of reasons. First, if by personality assessment we mean prediction or classification of some psychiatric diagnostic category, we have the problem of there being essentially no known objective markers for the major forms of psychopathology. Therefore, we are left essentially with psychiatrists' judgments. DSM-III has greatly improved this situation by providing objective criteria for the various mental disorders, but the capacity of such instruments as the MMPI or Rorschach to predict DSM-III diagnoses has not yet been evaluated and remains a research question for the future. Some scholars, however, even question the usefulness of taking that research course rather than developing increasingly reliable and valid structured interviews (Zubin, in press). Similarly, there have been many reports of the failure of objective tests to predict such matters as success in an occupation or trustworthiness with regard to handling a weapon. For example, objective tests are no longer used to screen astronauts, since they were not successful in predicting who would be successful or unsuccessful (Cordes, 1983). There does, in fact, appear to be a movement within the general public and the profession toward discontinuation of use of personality assessment procedures for decision making in employment situations. We would note as another possibly significant trend a movement toward direct observation of behavior in the form of behavioral assessment. The zeitgeist definitely is in opposition to procedures in which the intent is disguised. Burdock and Zubin (in press), for example, argue that, "nothing has as yet replaced behavior for evaluation of mental patients."

NEUROPSYCHOLOGICAL ASSESSMENT

Another area that has an interesting historical development is neuropsychological assessment. The term itself is a relatively new one and probably was made popular through the first edition of Lezak's (1976) book entitled with that term. Neu-

ropsychological assessment is of particular historical interest because it represents a confluence of two quite separate antecedents; central and eastern European behavioral neurology and American and English psychometrics. Neurologists, of course, have always been concerned with the behavioral manifestations of structural brain damage and the relationship between brain function and behavior. Broca's discovery of a speech center in the left frontal zone of the brain is often cited as the first scientific neuropsychological discovery because it delineated a relatively specific relationship between a behavioral function, speech, and a correspondingly specific region of the brain (the third frontal convolution of the left hemisphere). Clinical psychologists developed an interest in this area when they were called upon to assess patients with known or suspected brain damage. The first approach to this diagnostic area involved utilization of the already existing psychological tests, and the old literature in the area deals primarily with how such tests as the Wechsler scales, the Rorschach, or the Bender-Gestalt test could be used to diagnose brain damage. More recently, special tests were devised specifically for assessment work with patients having known or suspected brain damage.

The merger between clinical psychology and behavioral neurology can be said to have occurred when the sophistication of neurologists relative to the areas of brain function and brain disease was combined with the psychometric sophistication of clinical psychology. The wedding occurred when reliable, valid, and well-standardized measurement instruments began to be used to answer complex questions in neurological diagnosis and differential diagnosis. Thus, clinicians who ultimately identified themselves as clinical neuropsychologists tended to be individuals who knew their psychometrics, but who also had extensive training and experience in neurological settings. Just as many clinical psychologists work with psychiatrists, many clinical neuropsychologists work with neurologists and neurosurgeons. This relationship culminated in the development of standard neuropsychological test batteries, notably the Halstead-Reitan (Reitan & Davison, 1974) and Luria-Nebraska batteries (Golden, Hammeke, & Purisch, 1980), as well as in the capacity of many trained psychologists to perform individualized neuropsychological assessments of adults and children. Thus, within the history of psychological assessment, clinical neuropsychological evaluation has recently emerged as an independent discipline to be distinguished from general clinical psychology on the basis of the specific expertise members of that discipline have in the areas of brain-behavior relationships and diseases of the nervous system.

BEHAVIORAL ASSESSMENT

Over the years, behavioral assessment has been one of the most exciting developments to emerge in the field of psychological evaluation. Although its seeds were planted long before behavior therapy became a popular therapeutic movement, it is with the advent of behavior therapy that the strategies of behavioral assessment began to flourish (cf. Hersen & Bellack, 1976, 1981). As has been noted elsewhere (Hersen & Barlow, 1976a), behavioral assessment can be conceptualized as a reaction to a number of factors. Among these were the (a) problems with unreliability and invalidity of aspects of the DSM-I and DSM-II diagnostic schemes, (b) concerns over the indirect relationship between what was evaluated in traditional testing (e.g., the projectives) and how it subsequently was used in treatment planning and application, (c) increasing acceptance of behavior therapy by the professional community as a viable series of therapeutic modalities, and (d) parallel developments in the field of diagnosis in general involving greater precision and accountability (e.g., the problem-oriented record).

We will briefly consider each of the four factors in turn and see how they contributed historically to the development of behavioral assessment. To begin with, DSM-I and DSM-II had been the target of considerable criticism from psychiatrists (Hines & Williams, 1975) and psychologists alike (Begelman, 1975). Indeed, Begelman (1975), in a more humorous vein, referred to the two systems as "twice told tales." They were "twice told" in the sense that neither resulted in highly reliable classification schemes when patients were independently evaluated by separate psychiatric interviewers (cf. Ash, 1949; Sandifer, Pettus, & Quade, 1964). Problems were especially evident when attempts to obtain interrater reliability were made for the more minor diagnostic groupings of the DSM schemes. Frequently, clinical psychologists would be consulted to carry out their testing procedures to confirm or disconfirm psychiatrists' diagnostic impressions based on DSM-I and DSM-II. But in so doing, such psychologists,

operating very much as x-ray technicians, were using procedures (objective and projective tests) that only had a tangential relationship to the psychiatric descriptors for each of the nosological groups of interest. Thus, the futility of this kind of assessment strategy over time became increasingly apparent. Moreover, not only were there problems with the reliability of DSM-I and DSM-II, but empirical studies documented considerable problems as well with regard to external validity of the systems (Eisler & Polak, 1971; Nathan, Zare, Simpson, & Ardberg, 1969).

Probably more important than any of the above was the fact that the complicated psychological evaluation had a limited relationship to eventual treatment. At least in the psychiatric arena, the usual isomorphic relationship between assessment and treatment found in other branches of therapeutics did not seem to hold. The isolated and extended psychological examination frequently proved to be an empty academic exercise resulting in poetic jargon in the report that eventuated. But its practical utility was woefully limited. Treatment seemed to be unrelated to the findings in the reports.

All of the aforementioned resulted in attempts by clinical psychologists to measure the behaviors of interest in direct fashion. For example, if a patient presented with a particular phobia, the objective of evaluation was not to assess the underlying "neurotic complex" or "alleged psychodynamics." Quite the contrary, the primary objective was to quantify in distance how close our patient could approach the phobic object (i.e., the behavioral approach task) and how his heart rate (physiological assessment) increased as he got closer. In addition, the patient's cognitions (self-report) were quantified by having him assess his level of fear (e.g., on a 1–10 point scale). Thus, the behavioral assessment triad, consisting of motoric, physiological, and self-report systems (Hersen, 1973), was established as the alternative to indirect measurement.

Commenting on the use of direct measurement, Hersen and Barlow (1976b) argue that:

> Whereas in indirect measurement a
> particular response is interpreted in terms of
> a presumed underlying disposition, a
> response obtained through direct
> measurement is simply viewed as a sample of
> a large population of similar responses
> elicited under those particular stimulus

conditions. . . . Thus, it is hardly surprising that proponents of direct measurement favor the observation of individuals in their natural surroundings whenever possible. When such naturalistic observations are not feasible, analogue situations approximating naturalistic conditions may be developed to study the behavior in question (e.g., the use of a behavioral avoidance test to study the degree of fear of snakes). When neither of these two methods is available or possible, subjects' *self-reports are also used as independent criteria* and, at times, may be operating under the control of totally different sets of contingencies than those governing motoric responses. . . . (p. 116)

We already have referred to the tripartite system of direct measurement favored by the behaviorists. But it is in the realm of motoric behavior that behavior therapists have made the greatest contributions as well as being most innovative. With increased acceptance of behavior therapy, practitioners of the strategies found their services required in a large variety of educational, rehabilitation, community, and hospital settings. Very often they were presented with extremely difficult educational, rehabilitation, and treatment cases, both from assessment and therapeutic perspectives. Many of the clients and patients requiring remediation exhibited behaviors that previously had not been measured in any direct fashion. Thus, there were few guidelines with regard to how the behavior might be observed, quantified, and coded. In many instances, "seat-of-the-pants" measurement systems were devised on-the-spot but with little regard for psychometric qualities cherished by traditional testers.

Consider the following example of a measurement strategy to quantify "spasmodic torticollis," a tic-like disorder (Bernhardt, Hersen, & Barlow, 1972):

"A Sony Video Recorder model AV-5000A, an MRI Keleket model VC-1 television camera, and a Conrac 14-inch television monitor were employed in recording torticollis. A Gra Lab sixty minute Unusual Times was used to obtain percentage of torticollis. . . . A lightolier lamp served as the source of negative feedback.

Two to three daily ten minute sessions were scheduled during the experiment in which the subject was videotaped while seated in a profile arrangement. A piece of clear plastic containing superimposed Chart-Pac taped horizontal lines (spaced one-quarter to one-half inch apart) was placed over the monitor. A shielded observer depressed a switch activating the timer whenever the subject's head was positioned at an angle where the nostril was above a horizontal line intersecting the external auditory meatus. This position was operationally defined as an example of torticollis, with percentage of torticollis per session serving as the experimental measure. Conversely, when the horizontal line intersected both the nostril and auditory meatus or when the subject's nostril was below the horizontal line he was considered to be holding his head in a normal position. (p. 295)

If one peruses through the pages of the *Journal of Applied Behavior Analysis, Behaviour Research and Therapy, Journal of Behavior Therapy and Experimental Psychiatry,* and *Behavior Modification*, particularly in the earlier issues, numerous examples of innovative behavioral measures and more comprehensive systems are to be found. Consistent with the idiographic approach, many of these apply only to the case in question, have some internal or face validity, but, of course, have little generality. (We will further comment on this aspect of behavioral assessment in a subsequent section of this chapter.)

A final development that contributed to and coincided with the emergence of behavioral assessment was the problem-oriented-record (POR). This was a system of recordkeeping first instituted on medical wards in general hospitals to sharpen and pinpoint diagnostic practices (cf. Weed, 1964, 1968, 1969). Later this system was transferred to psychiatric units (cf. Hayes-Roth, Longabaugh, & Ryback, 1972; Katz & Woolley, 1975; Klonoff & Cox, 1975; McLean & Miles, 1974; Scales & Johnson, 1975), with its relevance to behavioral assessment increasingly evident (Atkinson, 1973; Katz & Woolley, 1975). When applied to psychiatry, the POR can be divided into four sections: (a) data base, (b) problem list, (c) treatment plan, and (d) follow-up data. There can be no doubt that this kind of recordkeeping promotes and enhances the relationship of assessment and treatment, essentially forcing the evaluator to crystallize his or her thinking about the diagnostic issues. In this regard, we previously have pointed out that:

Despite the fact that POR represents, for psychiatry, a vast improvement over the type of record-keeping and diagnostic practice previously followed, the level of precision in describing problem behaviors and treatments to be used remedially *does not* yet approach the kind of precision reached in the carefully conducted behavioral analysis. (Hersen, 1976, p.15)

However, the POR certainly can be conceptualized as a major step in the right direction. In most psychiatriac settings some type of POR is currently being used and, to a large extent, has further legitimized the tenets of behavioral assessment by clearly linking the problem list with specific treatment (cf. Longabaugh, Fowler, Stout, & Kriebel, 1983).

ASSESSMENT SCHEMES

Over the last two decades a number of comprehensive assessment schemes have been developed to facilitate the process of behavioral assessment (Cautela, 1968; Kanfer & Saslow, 1969; Lazarus, 1973). Although a very detailed analysis of these schemes is much beyond the scope of this historical overview, we will briefly describe the outlines of each in order to illustrate how the behavioral assessor conceptualizes his/her cases. For example, Cautela (1968) depicted in his scheme the role of behavioral assessment during the various stages of treatment. Specifically, he delineated three stages. In the *first stage* the clinician identifies maladaptive behaviors and those antecedent conditions maintaining them. This step is accomplished through interviews, observation, and self-report questionnaires. The *second stage* involves the selection of the appropriate treatment strategies, evaluation of their efficacy, and the decision when to terminate their application. In the *third stage* a meticulous follow-up of treatment outcome is recommended. This is done by examining motoric, physiologic, and cognitive functioning of the client, in addition to independent confirmation of the client's progress by friends, relatives, and employers.

A somewhat more complicated approach to initial evaluation was proposed by Kanfer and Saslow (1969), which involves some seven steps. The *first* involves a determination as to whether a given behavior represents an excess, deficit, or an asset. The *second* is a clarification of the problem and is based on the notion that in order to be

maintained, maladjusted behavior requires continued support. *Third* is the motivational analysis in which reinforcing and aversive stimuli are identified. *Fourth* is the developmental analysis, focusing on biological, sociological, and behavioral changes. *Fifth* involves assessment of self-control and whether it can be used as a strategy during treatment. *Sixth* is the analysis of the client's interpersonal life, and *seventh* is the evaluation of the patient's socio-cultural-physical environment.

In their initial scheme, Kanfer and Saslow (1969) viewed that system in complementary fashion to the existing diagnostic approach (i.e., DSM-II). They did not construe it as supplanting DSM-II. But they did see their seven-part analysis as serving as a basis for arriving at decisions for precise behavioral interventions, thus yielding a more isomorphic relationship between assessment and treatment.

More recently, Kanfer and Grimm (1977) have turned their attention to how the interview contributes to the overall behavioral assessment. In so doing, suggestions are made for organizing client complaints under five categories: "(1) behavioral deficiencies, (2) behavioral excesses, (3) inappropriate environmental stimulus control, (4) inappropriate self-generated stimulus control, and (5) problematic reinforcement contingencies" (p.7).

Yet another behavioral assessment scheme has been proposed by Lazarus (1973), with the somewhat humorous acronym of BASIC ID: B = behavior, A = affect, S = sensation, I = imagery, C = cognition, I = interpersonal relationship, and D = the need for pharmacological intervention (i.e., drugs) for some psychiatric patients. The major issue underscored by this diagnostic scheme is that if any of the elements is overlooked, assessment will be incomplete, thus resulting in only a partially effective treatment. To be fully comprehensive, deficits or surpluses for each of the categories need to be identified so that specific treatments can be targeted for each. This, then, should ensure the linear relationship between assessment and treatment, ostensibly absent in the nonbehavioral assessment schemes.

Despite development of the aforementioned schemes and others not outlined here (e.g., Bornstein, Bornstein, & Dawson, 1984), there is little in the way of their formal evaluation in empirical fashion. Although these schemes certainly appear to have a good bit of face validity, few studies, if any, have been devoted to evaluating concurrent and predictive validity. This, of course, is in contrast to the considerable effort to validate the latest edition of DSM (i.e., DSM-III, APA, 1980; Hersen & Turner, 1984).

In a somewhat different vein, Wolpe (1977) has expressed his concern about the manner in which behavioral assessment typically is being conducted. Indeed, he has referred to it as "The Achilles' Heel of Outcome Research in Behavior Therapy." He is especially concerned that too little attention has been devoted to evaluation of the antecedents of behaviors targeted for treatment, thus leading to a therapeutic approach that may be inappropriate. For example, in treating homosexuality, Wolpe (1977) rightly argues that:

> It seems obvious that each factor found operative in a particular patient needs to be treated by a program appropriate to it. Failure is predictable when homosexuality that is exclusively based on approach conditioning to males is treated by desensitization to heterosexual themes, or if homosexuality based on timidity or on fear of females is treated by aversion therapy. To compare the effects of different treatments on assorted groupings of homosexuals is about as informative as to compare the effects of different antibiotics on tonsillitis without bacterial diagnosis. (p. 2)

The same analysis, of course, holds true for other disorders, such as depression and phobia. Blanket treatment that does not take into account antecedents undoubtedly should fail. But here too, the necessary research findings to document this are as of yet forthcoming (see White, Turner, & Turkat, 1983).

CHANGES IN BEHAVIORAL ASSESSMENT

Contrasted to the field of psychological assessment in general, behavioral assessment as a specialty has had a history of less than 30 years. However, in these three decades we have witnessed some remarkable changes in the thinking of behavioral assessors. Probably as a strong overt reaction to the problems perceived by behavioral assessors in traditional psychological evaluation, many of the sound psychometric features of that tradition were initially abandoned. Indeed, in some instances they appear to have thrown out "the baby with the bath water." As we already have noted,

consistent with the idiographic approach to evaluation and treatment, little concern was accorded to traditional issues of reliability and validity. (The exception, of course, was the obsessive concern with high interrater reliability of observations of motoric behavior.) This was particularly the case for the numerous self-report inventories developed early on to be consistent with the motoric targets of treatment (e.g., some of the fear survey schedules).

There were many other aspects of traditional evaluation that also were given short shrift. Intelligence testing was eschewed, norms and developmental considerations were virtually ignored, and traditional psychiatric diagnosis was viewed as anathema to behavior therapy. However, since the late 1970s this "hard line" has been mollified. With publication of the second edition of *Behavioral Assessment: A Practical Handbook* and emergence of two assessment journals (*Behavioral Assessment* and *Journal of Behavioral Assessment*), greater attention to cherished psychometric principles has returned. For example, the external validity of role playing as an assessment strategy in the social skill area is undergoing evaluation (cf. Bellack, Hersen, & Lamparski, 1979; Bellack, Hersen, & Turner, 1979; Bellack, Turner, Hersen, & Luber, 1980) instead of being taken on faith.

Also, more recently, an argument has been made (Nelson, 1980) for use of intelligence tests within behavioral assessment. But most importantly, the relevance of the psychometric tradition to behavioral assessment has been articulated with considerable vigor (e.g., Adams & Turner, 1979; Cone, 1977; Haynes, 1978; Nelson & Hayes, 1979; Rosen, Sussman, Mueser, Lyons, & Davis, 1981). Looking at behavioral assessment today from a historical perspective, it certainly appears as though the "baby" *is* being returned from the discarded bath water.

DSM-III AND BEHAVIORAL ASSESSMENT

In the earlier days of behavioral assessment, traditional psychiatric diagnosis was for the most part eschewed. Behavioral assessors saw little relationship between what they were doing and the overall implicit goals of DSM-II. Moreover, as we have noted, categories subsumed under DSM-II had major problems with reliability and validity. So, consistent with cogent criticisms about the official diagnostic system, behavioral assessors tended to ignore it when possible. They continued to develop their strategies independently of DSM-II and the then emerging DSM-III. In fact, some (e.g., Adams, Doster, & Calhoun, 1977; Cautela, 1973) advocated totally new diagnostic formats altogether, but these never had a chance of being accepted by the general diagnostic community, given the political realities.

In spite of its problems and limitations, with the emergence of DSM-III (APA, 1980), behavioral therapists and researchers appear to have retrenched and assumed a somewhat different posture (cf. Hersen & Turner, 1984). Such positions have been articulated by a number of prominent behavior therapists, such as Nathan (1981) and Kazdin (1983). But the issues concerning DSM-III and behavioral assessment are most clearly summarized by Taylor (1983), a behavioral psychiatrist:

> The new Diagnostic and Statistical Manual of the American Psychiatric Association is a major improvement in psychiatric diagnosis over previous classification systems. Where symptomatic diagnoses are useful, as in relating an individual's problem to the wealth of clinical and research data in abnormal psychology or in identifying conditions which require specific treatments, DSM-III represents the best available system. Many conceptual and practical problems remain with DSM-III; for instance, it retains a bias toward the medical model, it includes many conditions which should not fall into a psychiatric diagnostic system, and it includes descriptive axes which have not been adequately validated. Nevertheless, behavior therapists are well advised to become familiar with and use DSM-III as part of behavioral assessment. (p. 13)

We are fully in accord with Taylor's comments and believe that if behavior therapists wish to impact on the accepted nosological system, they are urged to work from within rather than from without.

SUMMARY

We have attempted to provide a brief historical overview of several major areas in psychological evaluation: intellectual, personality, neuropsycho-

logical, and behavioral assessment. Some of these areas have lengthy histories, and others are relatively young. However, it seems clear that the tools used by psychologists as recently as 20 years ago are generally different from those used now. Behavioral assessment techniques, structured psychiatric interviews, and standard, comprehensive neuropsychological test batteries are all relatively new. Furthermore, the computer is at least beginning to make significant inroads into the assessment field, with on-line testing, scoring, and interpretation a reality in some cases. Serious efforts have been made in recent years to link assessment more closely to treatment and other practical concerns. We may also note a trend away from indirect methods to direct acquisition of information and observation. The structured interview is an example of the former approach, and many behavioral assessment techniques would exemplify the latter one. Similarly, while neuropsychological assessment is still heavily dependent on the use of formal tests, there is increasing interest in the use of those tests in rehabilitation planning and in the association between neuropsychological test results and functional activities of daily living. We also note a corresponding decrease in interest in such matters as brain localization, particularly since the CT scan and related brain imaging procedures have solved much of that problem. We would prognosticate that psychological assessment will be increasingly concerned with automation, the direct observation of behavior, and the practical application of assessment results.

REFERENCES

Adams, H.E., & Turner, S.M. (1979). Editorial. *Journal of Behavioral Assessment, 1,* 1–2.

Adams, H.E., Doster, J.A., & Calhoun, K.S. (1977). A psychologically based system of response classification. In A.R. Ciminero, K.S. Calhoun, & H.E. Adams (Eds.), *Handbook of behavioral assessment.* New York: Wiley.

Allport, G.W. (1937). Personality: *A psychological interpretation.* New York: Holt.

American Psychiatric Association (1980). *Diagnostic and statistical manual of mental disorders* (3rd ed.). Washington, DC: Author.

Ash, P. (1949). The reliability of psychiatric diagnosis. *Journal of Abnormal and Social Psychology, 44,* 272–276.

Atkinson, C. (1973). Data collection and program evaluation using the problem-oriented medical record. Miami: Association for Advancement of Behavior Therapy.

Begelman, D.A. (1975). Ethical and legal issues in be-
havior modification. In M. Hersen, R.M. Eisler, &
P.M. Miller (Eds.), *Progress in behavior modification:
Volume 1.* New York: Academic Press.

Bellack, A.S., Hersen, M., & Lamparski, D. (1979).
Role-playing tests for assessing social skills: Are they
valid? Are they useful? *Journal of Consulting and
Clinical Psychology, 47,* 335–342.

Bellack, A.S., Hersen, M., & Turner, S.M. (1979). Relationship of role playing and knowledge of appropriate behavior to assertion in the natural environment.
Journal of Consulting and Clinical Psychology, 47,
679–685.

Bellack, A.S., Turner, S.M., Hersen, M., & Luber, R.
(1980). Effects of stress and retesting on role playing
tests of social skill. *Journal of Behavioral Assessment,
2,* 99–104.

Bernhardt, A.J., Hersen, M., & Barlow, D.H. (1972).
Measurement and modification of spasmodic torticollis: An experimental analysis. *Behavior Therapy, 3,*
294–297.

Blessed, G., Tomlinson, B.E., & Roth, M. (1968). The
association between quantitative measures of dementia and of senile change in the cerebral grey matter of
elderly subjects. *British Journal of Psychiatry, 114,*
797–811.

Boring, E.G. (1950). *A history of experimental psychology.* New York: Appleton-Century-Crofts.

Bornstein, P.H., Bornstein, M.T., & Dawson, B. (1984).
Integrated assessment and treatment. In T.H. Ollendick & M. Hersen (Eds.), *Child behavioral assessment: Principles and procedures.* New York:
Pergamon Press.

Burdock, E., & Zubin, J. (in press). Objective evaluation
in psychiatry. *Psychiatric reference and record book*
(2nd ed.). New York: Roerig Laboratories, Inc.

Burdock, E.I., Hardesty, A.S., Hakerem, G., Zubin, J.,
& Beck, Y.M. (1968). *Ward behavior inventory.* New
York: Springer.

Cattell, R.B., Eber, H.W., & Tatsuoka, M.M. (1970).
*Handbook for the sixteen personality factor question-
naire.* Technical Report, Institute for Personality and
Ability Testing.

Cautela, J.R. (1968). Behavior therapy and the need for
behavioral assessment. *Psychotherapy: Theory, Research and Practice, 5,* 175–179.

Cautela, J.R. (1973, September). A behavioral coding
system. Presidential address to the seventh annual
meeting of the Association for Advancement of Behavior Therapy, Miami.

Cone, J.D. (1977). The relevance of reliability and validity for behavioral assessment. *Behavior Therapy, 8,*
411–426.

Cordes, C. (1983). Mullane: Tests are grounded. *APA
Monitor, 14,* 24.

Cronbach, L.J. (1949). *Essentials of psychological testing.* New York: Harper & Brothers (2nd ed., 1960).

Eisler, R.M., & Polak, P.R. (1971). Social stress and
psychiatric disorder. *Journal of Nervous and Mental
Disease, 153,* 227–233.

Feighner, J., Robins, E., Guze, S., Woodruff, R., Winokur, G., & Munoz, R. (1972). Diagnostic criteria for
use in psychiatric research. *Archives of General Psychiatry, 26,* 57–63.

Folstein, M.F., Folstein, S.E., & McHugh, P.R. (1975).
Mini-mental state. A practical method for grading
the cognitive state of patients for the clinician.
Journal of Psychiatric Research, 12, 189–198.

Fowler, R.D. (1979). The automated MMPI. In C.S.
Newmark (Ed.), *MMPI clinical and research trends.*
New York: Praeger.

Gilberstadt, H., & Duker, J. (1965). *A handbook for
clinical and actuarial MMPI interpretation.* Philadelphia: Saunders.

Golden, C.J., Hammeke, T.A., & Purisch, A.D. (1980).
The Luria-Nebraska Battery manual. Los Angeles,
CA: Western Psychological Services.

Guilford, J.P., & Zimmerman, W. (1949). *Guilford-Zim-
merman Temperament survey.* Los Angeles, CA:
Western Psychological Services.

Hamilton, M. (1960). A rating scale for depression.
*Journal of Neurology, Neurosurgery and Psychiatry,
23,* 56–62.

Hayes-Roth, F., Longabaugh, R., & Ryback, R. (1972).
The problem-oriented medical record and psychiatry.
British Journal of Psychiatry, 121, 27–34.

Haynes, S.N. (1978). *Principles of behavioral assessment.*
New York: Gardner Press.

Helzer, J., Robins, L., Croughan, J., & Welner, A.
(1981). Renard Diagnostic Interview. *Archives of
General Psychiatry, 38,* 393–398.

Hersen, M. (1973). Self-assessment and fear. *Behavior
Therapy, 4,* 241–257.

Hersen, M. (1976). Historical perspectives in behavioral
assessment. In M. Hersen & A.S. Bellack (Eds.), *Behavioral assessment: A practical handbook.* New
York: Pergamon Press.

Hersen, M., & Barlow, D.H. (1976a). *Single-case experimental designs: Strategies for studying behavior
change.* New York: Pergamon Press.

Hersen, M., & Barlow, D.H. (1976b). *Single-case experimental designs: Strategies for studying behavior
change.* New York: Pergamon Press.

Hersen, M., & Bellack, A.S. (Eds.) (1976). *Behavioral
assessment: A practical handbook* (1st ed.). New
York: Pergamon Press.

Hersen, M., & Bellack, A.S. (1981). *Behavioral assessment: A practical handbook* (2nd ed.). New York:
Pergamon Press.

Hersen, M., & Turner, S.M. (1984). DSM-III and behav-
ior therapy. In S.M. Turner & M. Hersen (Eds.),
Adult psychopathology: A behavioral perspective.
New York: Wiley.

Hines, F.R., & Williams, R.B. (1975). Dimensional
diagnosis and the medical students' grasp of psychiatry. *Archives of General Psychiatry, 32,* 525–528.

Holtzman, W.H. (1958). *The Holtzman inkblot technique.* New York: Psychological Corporation.

Honigfeld, G., & Klett, C. (1965). The Nurse's Observation Scale for Inpatient Evaluation (NOSIE): A new
scale for measuring improvement in schizophrenia.
Journal of Clinical Psychology, 21, 65–71.

Jensen, A.R. (1983, August). Nature of the white-black
differences on various psychometric tests. Invited address, American Psychological Association Convention, Anaheim, CA.

Kanfer, F.H., & Grimm, L.G. (1977). Behavior analysis:
Selecting target behaviors in the interview. *Behavior
Modification, 1,* 7–28.

Kanfer, F.H., & Saslow, G. (1969). Behavioral diagnosis.

In C.M. Franks (Ed.), *Behavior therapy: Appraisal and status*. New York: McGraw-Hill.

Katz, R.C., & Woolley, F.R. (1975). Improving patients' records through problem orientation. *Behavior Therapy*, 6, 119–124.

Kazdin, A.E. (1983). Psychiatric diagnosis, dimensions of dysfunction, and child behavior therapy. *Behavior Therapy*, 14, 73–99.

Klonoff, H., & Cox, B. (1975). A problem-oriented system approach to analysis of treatment outcome. *American Journal of Psychiatry*, 132, 841–846.

Lazarus, A.A. (1973). Multimodal behavior therapy: Treating the 'basic id.' *Journal of Nervous and Mental Disease*, 156, 404–411.

Lezak, M. (1976). *Neuropsychological Assessment*. New York: Oxford University Press.

Longabaugh, R., Fowler, D.R., Stout, R., & Kriebel, G. (1983). Validation of a problem-focused nomenclature. *Archives of General Psychiatry*, 40, 453–461.

Machover, K. (1949). *Personality projection in the drawing of the human figure: A method of personality investigation*. Springfield, IL: Charles Thomas.

Marks, P.A., Seeman, W., & Haller, D.L. (1974). *The actuarial use of the MMPI with adolescents and adults*. Baltimore: Williams & Wilkins.

McFie, J. (1975). *Assessment of organic intellectual impairment*. London: Academic Press.

McLean, P.D., & Miles, J.E. (1974). Evaluation and the problem-oriented record in psychiatry. *Archives of General Psychiatry*, 31, 622–625.

Meehl, P.E. (1954). *Clinical vs. statistical prediction*. Minneapolis, MN: University of Minnesota Press.

Menninger, K.A. (1952). *A manual for psychiatric case study*. New York: Grune & Stratton.

Murray, H.A. (1938). *Explorations in personality*. New York: Oxford University Press.

Nathan, P.E. (1981). Symptomatic diagnosis and behavioral assessment: A synthesis. In D.H. Barlow (Ed.), *Behavioral assessment of adult disorders*. New York: Guilford.

Nathan, P.E., Zare, N.C., Simpson, H.F., & Ardberg, M.M. (1969). A systems analytic model of diagnosis: I. The diagnostic validity of abnormal psychomotor behavior. *Journal of Clinical Psychology*, 25, 3–9.

Nelson, R.O. (1980). The use of intelligence tests within behavioral assessment. *Behavioral Assessment*, 2, 417–423.

Nelson, R.O., & Hayes, S.C. (1979). Some current dimensions on behavioral assessment. *Behavioral Assessment*, 1, 1–16.

Overall, J.E., & Gorham, J.R. (1962). The brief psychiatric rating scale. *Psychological Reports*, 10, 799–812.

Rapaport, D. (1945). *Diagnostic psychological testing*. Chicago: Year Book Publications.

Raskin, A. (1982). Assessment of psychopathology by the nurse or psychiatric aide. In E.I. Burdock, A. Sudilovsky, & S. Gershon (Eds.), *The behavior of psychiatric patients: Quantitative techniques for evaluation*. New York: Marcel Dekker.

Reitan, R.M., & Davison, L.A. (1974). *Clinical neuropsychology: Current status and applications*. Washington, DC: V.H. Winston and Sons.

Robins, S.L., Helzer, J., Croughan, N.A., & Ratcliff, K. (1981). National Institute of Mental Health Diagnostic Interview Schedule. *Archives of General Psychiatry*, 38, 381–389.

Rohde, A.R. (1957). *The sentence completion method*. New York: Ronald Press.

Rosen, A.J., Sussman, S., Mueser, K.T., Lyons, J.S., & Davis, J.M. (1981). Behavioral assessment of psychiatric inpatients and normal controls across different environmental contexts. *Journal of Behavioral Assessment*, 3, 25–36.

Sandifer, M.G., Jr., Pettus, C., & Quade, D. (1964). A study of psychiatric diagnosis. *Journal of Nervous and Mental Disease*, 139, 350–356.

Scales, E.J., & Johnson, M.S. (1975). A psychiatric POMR for use by a multidisciplinary team. *Hospital and Community Psychiatry*, 26, 371–373.

Shneidman, E.S. (1952). *Make a picture test*. New York: The Psychological Corporation.

Spitzer, R.L., & Endicott, J. (1977). *Schedule for affective disorders and schizophrenia*. Technical Report. New York: New York State Psychiatric Institute, Biometrics Research Department.

Spitzer, R.L., & Williams, J.B.W. (1983). *Instruction manual for the structured clinical interview for DSM-III (SCID)*. New York: New York State Psychiatric Institute, Biometrics Research Department.

Spitzer, R.L., Endicott, J., & Robins, E. (1977). *Research Diagnostic Criteria (RDC) for a selected group of functional disorders*. Bethesda, MD: National Institute of Mental Health.

Swensen, C.H. (1957). Empirical evaluations of human figure drawings, 1957–1966. *Psychological Bulletin*, 54, 431–466.

Swensen, C.H. (1968). Empirical evaluations of human figure drawings. *Psychological Bulletin*, 20, 20–44.

Szondi, L. (1952). *Experimental diagnostics of drives*. New York: Grune & Stratton.

Taylor, C.B. (1983). DSM-III and behavioral assessment. *Behavioral Assessment*, 5, 5–14.

VanLennep, D.J. (1951). The four-picture test. In H.H. Anderson & G.L. Anderson (Eds.), *An introduction to projective techniques*. New York: Prentice-Hall.

Wechsler, D. (1944). *The measurement of adult intelligence*. Baltimore, MD: Williams & Wilkins.

Weed, L.L. (1964). Medical records, patient care, and medical education. *Irish Journal of Medical Sciences*, 6, 271–282.

Weed, L.L. (1968). Medical records that guide and teach. *New England Journal of Medicine*, 278, 593–600.

Weed, L.L. (1969). *Medical records, medical education, and patient care*. Cleveland, OH: Case Western Reserve University Press.

White, D.K., Turner, L.B., & Turkat, I.D. (1983). The etiology of behavior: Survey data on behavior therapists' contributions. *The Behavior Therapist*, 6, 59–60.

Wolpe, J. (1977). Inadequate behavior analysis: The Achilles heel of outcome research in behavior therapy. *Journal of Behavior Therapy and Experimental Psychiatry*, 8, 1–3.

Zubin, J. (1967). Classification of the behavior disorders. *Annual Review of Psychology*, 18, 373–406. Palo Alto, CA: Annual Reviews Inc.

Zubin, J. (in press). Inkblots do not a test make. *Contemporary Psychology*.

PART II
PSYCHOMETRIC FOUNDATIONS

2 TEST CONSTRUCTION

Charles J. Golden
Robert F. Sawicki
Michael D. Franzen

INTRODUCTION

Recent years have witnessed a proliferation of psychological assessment instruments. Many of these instruments assess single constructs such as androgyny (Bem, 1974, 1977), assertion (Galassi, Delo, Galassi, & Bastien, 1974), and depression (Carroll, Fielding, & Blashki, 1973). Other recent tests focus on multiple traits, including the Personality Inventory for Children (Lachar & Gdowski, 1979), the Millon Personality Inventory (Millon, 1982), and the Luria-Nebraska Neuropsychological Battery (Golden, Hammeke, & Purisch, 1980).

Due to space limitations, it is not possible to review all of the work done on test development by persons like Anastasi (1982) or Fiske (1978) within this chapter. Rather, the intent is to present an overview of the major steps in test construction, with special attention to the practical considerations inherent in scale development and validation in order to provide an appreciation of the issues underlying this process and encourage test-oriented research in the future.

There are at least three approaches to scale construction (Wiggins, 1973). The analytic approach relies most heavily on theory to determine the selection of items, procedures, and criteria for assessing individuals. Under this approach, items are chosen on the basis of whether they appear to tap an aspect of the construct under consideration. For example, if the theory specifies that an important aspect is the age at which a person was toilet trained, then a question regarding that information would be included in the scale.

Under the empirical approach, the first step in scale construction is to select an operational index of the construct to be measured. For example, in devising the Minnesota Multiphasic Personality Inventory (MMPI), the authors of the test used psychiatric diagnosis as the operational index. The second step was to select items that were assumed to be associated with the index. With the MMPI, the authors asked clinicians to generate items that corresponded to the psychiatric diagnoses. Next, the method of contrasted groups was used to see which items discriminated among the diagnostic groups. It is clear that under this approach, items are chosen on the basis of empirically demonstrated relationships with the criterion, and theory plays less of a role than under the analytic approach.

A third strategy is the rational approach or, as Jackson (1975) has labeled it, the sequential system approach. The sequential system model tries to combine the features of the analytic and the empirical approaches in a logical sequence as well as evaluating the psychometric properties of the resultant scales. It operates under the guidance of four principles, which are: (a) the importance of psychological theory, (b) the necessity for suppressing variance due to response style, (c) the balance of scale homogeneity with generalizability, and (d) the evaluation of convergent and discriminant validity. Items are originally generated on the basis of a coherent theory but are retained on the basis of their psychometric properties and empirical relationships. Because of its flexibility and applicability, the sequential system model is the method most often used today in scale construction and is the approach that provides a broad outline for the discussion in this chapter. Because the authors are most familiar with neuropsychology, many of the examples are drawn from that field. However, the discussion is broad enough to be applicable to other areas in psychology for which scale construction is an issue.

INITIAL ITEM SELECTION

The first step in the development of any test is to determine what domain the test responses will represent. A thorough understanding of what the test is expected to measure will guide both initial validation research and later clinical interpretation of individual results. Such theoretical understanding of what a given test is expected to produce also guides the development of an initial item pool.

Since the initial item pool is selected to maximize data gathering along some trait or skill dimension, it is useful for persons who are designing their first test to construct a Table of Specifications (Hopkins & Antes, 1978) in order to increase their chances of identifying an item pool that will represent their domain of interest. Initially many more items are selected than actually necessary. This set of items is then paired down by the validation process.

The Table of Specifications can be described as a two-dimensional matrix where one dimension represents the skills or traits of interest and the other the behaviors representative of these characteristics. This blueprint can be used to determine both the number of items that will be selected to represent each aspect (behavior) of the domain of interest and the type of items that will be used. Thus a comprehensive test battery may include diverse and seemingly unrelated items. A limited purpose test may include only very specific and highly similar items. Table 2.1 provides specifications for the Luria-Nebraska Motor Scale. This table has been greatly simplified for descriptive purposes. In actual practice the functions could be further subdivided into much smaller skill areas (e.g., Motor Integration, Oral) and topic areas could be weighted by the theoretical importance of a given subarea (e.g., 30% of the items would be selected to represent motor organization).

TABLE 2.1. SPECIFICATIONS.

	Task	
Function	Simple	Complex
Motor Organization	Items 1–4 28–31	Items 21–27 32–33
Tactile-Motor Integration	Items 5–6	Items 7–8
Visual-Spatial-Motor Integration	Items 9–18	Items 36–47
Verbal-Motor Integration	Items 19–20	Items 48–51

Items are most often chosen by face validity. In the best of cases, items are derived from a comprehensive theory that dictates the types of items that may be necessary for a given test. In other instances, item selection may be based on "professional nomination," the result of suggestions by experts, or simply by sampling many items used in other tests or clinical practice. In general, since some items will probably be dropped subsequent to validation, it is better at this stage to be overinclusive in the selection of items. It is recommended that the original item pool include from two to four times the number that one wishes to include in the final version of the test. Overall limitations on the number of items in the initial pool will occur as a factor of practical issues: tests that will require individual administration (i.e., IQ tests) will probably start out with a smaller pool than those that permit group administration (i.e., personality inventories).

ITEM FORMATS

Items may either be open-ended or restricted in terms of response options. Restricted items are defined here as forced choice (e.g., true/false) or multiple choice items. Such items are more popular with group administered tests. Open-ended items allow more projective responses from patients; however, by necessity, they must be individually administered and scored because of the infinite variety of answers that must be evaluated by an examiner. Open-ended item construction requires careful selection due to the amount of interpretation that will be required of an examiner to accurately score such items. These items are less likely to meet the requirements for standardization as they are discussed below.

Item content or presentation is not limited by the type of response format chosen. For example, inkblots may be used in tests that are open ended. However, we could design an inkblot test that was multiple choice: Is the above inkblot [a] a. bat; b. person; c. two persons; d. dying swan. Whether such a test would measure the same thing as the more open-ended format is, of course, a question of construct validity that must be empirically explored. The item format influences the amount of information gathered from a given item. Open-ended/projective items are more useful when the clinician wishes to observe and analyze the process a patient uses to arrive at a response, while forced choice and multiple choice items are more concerned with the resulting pattern of responses than the process. The interpretive meaning of such a pattern is determined by empirically derived correlates.

Items may also be classified as objective or projective. Objective items include not only the forced choice and multiple choice items but also items that allow more flexible responses, for which there are consensually determined correct answers. An example of the latter is the question, "What does the word 'summer' mean?" Projective items, on the other hand, are deliberately vague and ambiguous. There is a wide range of correct responses to which an interpretive system must be applied in order to derive meaningful scoring. Although some writers would exclude such ambiguous material from the arena of standardized tests, the present authors see no reason to do this as long as the set of items meets the general criteria for a standardized test.

Limitations to Item Formats

In deciding the item format to use within a test, one must be cognizant of the limitations of each format type. Such limits must be weighed against the amount of useful information that a particular format will generate. Though multiple choice items can be scored quickly, provide greater interrater reliability, and sample a larger content area, they are open to interpretive error due to guessing and random response sets. Such tests also take longer to construct, since both test items and distractors must be designed. In the initial stages of test construction, such items may also be misplaced on a scale, since the researcher must intuitively determine the level of difficulty of each item before it is seen by a patient (Hopkins & Antes, 1978). Similar criticisms may be applied to the true/false format. In addition, the forced choice format is greatly affected by the wording used within items. Poorly stated items undermine a test's clinical usefulness.

Although the open-ended/projective items may be constructed more quickly, do not permit guessing, and allow the clinician to observe the problem-solving process, they require that examiners have extensive training in a scoring system so that responses may be validly interpreted. In addition, scoring takes much longer and "styles" of scoring may limit the overall reliability of the open-ended test.

Standardization: Administration

At this point in the test construction process, there are two major requirements for standardization: (a) standard administration and (b) standard scoring. An item must lend itself to both of these processes in order to be acceptable at this stage of development. Forced choice and multiple choice items meet such criteria without difficulty. The patient is read or reads the item and chooses a response alternative or states his answer. If additional material is used (e.g., pictures), these are identical for all patients. Such structure facilitates group applications for such items.

Open-ended items can (but do not need to) present more difficulties for standard administration. Standardization is achieved by having the examiner state the test instructions in a standard form and as much as possible say "root" demands in a standard manner. Again, whenever possible, each patient handles the same set of ancillary test materials. Problems arise with open-ended items on two occasions: (a) when an examiner attempts to elicit further information within an item procedure rather than first getting a scoreable response, then goes back to test the limits of a response; and

(b) when the patient produces an entirely novel response that does not fit into any established scoring criteria. Open-ended questions are also more open to questioning by a patient, thus offering the possibility of disrupting the administration procedure.

The first difficulty usually arises when an examiner does not completely understand the intent of an item. Such a problem raises the possibility that the item itself may contain unintended ambiguity. Thus an individual examiner's interpretation of the item's intent may break standard administration and invalidate the item.

This problem can be handled in one of several ways. The most common approach has been to demand strict adherence to rigid administration rules regardless of outside concerns. Examiners are instructed to adopt testing the limits procedures after eliciting a scoreable response in order to gain sufficient additional information that is needed to avoid interpretive difficulties.

A second more complex approach is to allow more flexible examination procedures within a standard administration format. For example, the administration of an item requiring a motor response (e.g., finger tapping) may begin with the standard verbal demand. If the patient does not comprehend the task requirements, the examiner may follow up with an alternative verbal explanation, followed by an actual demonstration until the patient understands what is necessary to make a scoreable response to the item. Again, the issue is one of being very clear on what the intent of an item is and offering assistance only to the degree that it does not invalidate the item. By writing such procedures into the standardized administration instructions, one can offer both flexibility and standardization. For this to be functional, more detailed training of examiners is necessary to insure that not only the item procedure, but also the item intent is comprehended by the clinician.

In writing such procedures, the item author must be personally aware of the intent of an item in order to maintain scoring and interpretive integrity. For example, a demonstration could not be allowed when testing a patient's ability to follow spoken instructions, but is quite appropriate in the previous finger tapping example. Similarly, written instructions could be used as an additional procedure for an item measuring verbal comprehension, but not for an item requiring auditory analysis.

In all cases, item materials must be identical. Small differences in legibility, color, shape, size, or other dimensions can create wide, artifactual variations in response to items. In cases where identical materials cannot be easily or reliably employed (for whatever reason), research must identify the effect of such differences on subject responses. Such study is intended to identify the salient aspects of stimuli in order to make subsequent interpretation of patient data more meaningful. For example, it may not matter which type of tape recorder is used to present auditory stimuli for an item, but the quality of reproduction across tape recorders may create unintended differences in the overall results of a set of items measuring subtle tonal discrimination. Thus quality control becomes an important issue not only for individual items but also for any ancillary test materials employed.

Standardization Scaling

A number of scaling methods may be used with items, depending on the domain of interest that the test is intended to measure. Scaling methods can roughly be characterized into three types: nominal, ordinal, or interval scales. Ratio scales have not been applied to psychological data.

Nominal scaling reflects regrouping responses into arbitrarily defined categories, which are only meaningful in the context of the measure within which they were created. Such categories are not assumed to have characteristics of counting numbers. It is usually the frequency of responses within a given category that provides the focus of interest for the clinician. This method of scaling is most often used when scoring represents an analysis of the process used to achieve an answer rather than the tabulation of the answer alone. The scoring system of the Rorschach Inkblot Test (Exner, 1974) is an example of such a scaling system. Responses may be regrouped under such category headings as "Form," "Location," "Shading," and so forth. Some neuropsychological tests may count the number of responses that may be classified as "perseveration," "neglect," or "impulsiveness."

Ordinal scaling reflects a ranking of responses along some underlying dimension (e.g., adequacy of performance). Thus an item may be scored as "0" (normal), "1" (borderline), "2" (mild impairment), "3" (moderate impairment), and "4" (severe impairment). Ordinal scaling does not assume that the distance between numbers is equal, only that the ranking is meaningful. Thus, the change in severity from 0 (normal) to 1 (borderline) is not assumed to have similar magnitude as the change in severity from 3 (moderate impairment) to 4 (severe impairment). Since there is generally a lack of empirical support for quantifiable parallel increases between psychometric data and behavioral changes, most psychological data could be classified as ordinal in nature.

Interval scaling is also ordered, but the distances between data points are assumed to be equal. The distances between points are meaningful; that is, the difference between "1" and "3" is twice as large as the difference between "1" and "2." The zero point is determined arbitrarily and does not necessarily indicate the absence of the quality measured. Psychophysiological measures serve as the best example of such scaling. Though one would be hard pressed to identify assessment instruments that meet such a scaling criteria, most psychological data is treated as though it were on an interval scale.

Gaito (1970) defends the assumptions that indicate that a set of scores may take on the characteristics of more than one type of scaling. He suggests that scaling descriptions are guidelines and that rigid adherence only promotes the wasting of data. In an example he states,

> the same data may be considered to have the properties of two or more scales, depending on the context in which it is considered. For example, if we look at the response of one subject (S) to a single item, the properties of the data are those of a nominal scale, i.e., right or wrong. However, if we concentrate on the total score for one S or the total scores for a group of S's, we have at least an ordinal scale. (p. 65)

Gaito emphasizes that it is not the property of a given scale which has overriding importance but the degree to which items produce data that are normally distributed in a large sample of subjects. This matter is an important point for the use of parametric tests to describe the reliability and validity of a set of items that have undergone a scaling transformation. It may be that few of the assumptions underlying parametric tests need be met with any great accuracy, although this point is debated by some (e.g., Hays, 1973).

Item Analysis:
Administration Difficulties

After the initial items have been designed and written, it is best to administer them to several normal individuals to see how they "work." This can be a valuable step, saving much time later, as one will find that some of the items simply do not perform as expected. In some cases, administration as envisioned will be demonstrated to be impossible on a practical level. This may be because subjects cannot comprehend the instructions, the administration is too difficult for an examiner without three arms, or other related possibilities.

Different examiners may be unable to agree on scoring. For example, in the development of the Luria-Nebraska, we initially had an item, "Show me how to frown." While it appeared simple on the surface, we were unable to come up with scoring criteria from which to get reliable data. Items may require more time than expected. Subjects may balk at an item's content or fail to comprehend an item's demand, no matter how it is presented.

In all of these instances, items may be revised or eliminated prior to starting a full validation project. Many of these difficulties are much less frequent with group administered tests, such as personality inventories.

ITEM ANALYSIS:
ITEM EFFICIENCY

After these initial steps have been completed, the test may be administered to a sample of interest. This step should include a minimum of two to three times the number of subjects as test items. If the test is aimed at several different groups, testing with a sample from each group will be necessary. In administering the items, it is important to ensure that the conditions of testing, as well as the items, are standardized. Lighting conditions, ambient noise, distractions, and other environmental conditions should be closely controlled. Even a factor such as room temperature can severely interfere with the interpretability of initial test results if it is not closely observed.

Items should be administered in the same order to all subjects. Examiners must be thoroughly trained to ensure that the test is administered identically to all subjects. Subjects selected for initial pilot studies of the new item set should be cooperative and strongly encouraged to provide their most valid, honest, and accurate performance. An attempt must also be made to select an initial subject pool that is representative of the population to whom the test will later be applied.

After this step has been completed, several analyses may be used to further evaluate items. The *Item Difficulty Index* results from a simple analysis, which demonstrates the relative efficiency of items in groups that do and do not possess the characteristic of interest. In its simplest form, the Item Difficulty Index represents the percentage of a given group that fails an item. If one were testing a given ability that was assumed to be randomly distributed within a population and using a sample randomly drawn from that population, the expected item difficulty for any given item would be .50. As the item difficulty level moves toward 1.0, a given item is too difficult, since at 1.0 no one is passing the item. As the item difficulty approaches 0.0, a given item is too easy, since hardly anyone is missing the item. Items that are too easy or difficult are useless in a test, since they offer no discriminations among subjects. Understanding what is communicated by item difficulty in a psychological test is a little more complex.

When analyzing items from a psychological instrument, it is useful to compute difficulty indices for both the sample of interest and the comparative or control sample. Before performing the computations, one must understand that passing or failing an item must be redefined as responding in the scoreable direction or responding otherwise. Thus, if one has designed a set of true/false items that are expected to identify depression, the scoreable direction is the way in which a depressed person would endorse an item. Therefore, if one has designed a perfect set of items, one expects that difficulties for the depressed group approach 1.00, while difficulties for the comparison (nondepressed) group would tend toward 0.0, suggesting that the items discriminate between the two groups. The total hypothetical sample (both depressed and not depressed) of difficulty indices would approach .50 given the within-group disparities.

On neuropsychological tests where items also involve some ability dimensions, one expects that item difficulty in a heterogeneous sample of brain impaired will be at .50 or greater, while unimpaired controls ought to have difficulty indices of .30 or less. The latter may be expected in a heterogeneous group of unimpaired normals due to the

biological variance for performance measures that is assumed in the general population. Thus, one may see that item difficulty is computed by dividing the number of persons who responded in the scoreable direction by the total number of persons who responded to the item. The formula (Hopkins & Antes, 1978, p.187) below would be applicable to an item that can be scored correct/incorrect. By the nature of the test it is the incorrect response that serves to discriminate among subjects.

$$\text{Item Difficulty} = \frac{\text{Number of subjects who failed the item}}{\text{Number of subjects who responded to item}}$$

Since the Item Difficulty Index is severely affected by the characteristics of the sample, the initial subject pool must be carefully screened for underlying characteristics that may bias the findings. Thus, deriving such an index from an impaired sample that has a great proportion of Alzheimer's patients will produce a set of results that are an artifact of the sample rather than descriptive of item efficiency in a generalizable sense. Similarly, using a sample of normals with below-average cognitive abilities will also create incorrect impressions about item difficulty.

In an appropriate sample those items with difficulties below .2 and above .8 must be closely examined before inclusion in the final test. Again, in an appropriate, heterogeneous sample, item difficulty ought to approach .5 for maximum discrimination on the variable of interest. In order to include a broad base of items, item difficulties should be gathered from samples who contain greater and lesser amounts of the variable of interest. Thus, one would intentionally test very bright and less bright people as separate groups if one were creating a test of cognitive efficiency in order to select items that would discriminate accurately along the full spectrum of cognitive abilities.

In examining the item difficulties for neuropsychological tests, one expects that in a heterogeneous sample of brain impaired item difficulties will approximate .5. One may use such knowledge to observe item difficulties in more homogeneous samples of brain impaired persons in order to get a sense of the functions that are impaired within such a homogeneous group. Items that showed difficulty indices above the .7 to .8 range would indicate a localized impairment, which hopefully would be consistent with the known impairment of the homogeneous group. Such findings could then be used to support the content validity (which will be discussed later in the chapter) of sets of items.

The *Discrimination Index* is a method of differentiating persons high on a given variable from those low on such a characteristic. Thus, if one assumes that a high overall score on the motor scale of the Luria-Nebraska indicates greater impairment in the higher cortical functions associated with motor movements, one would select two sets of subjects from the sample: those having the highest one third of the scores on the Motor Scale and those having the lowest one third on the Motor Scale and compare item efficiency in these two groups. The formula for the discrimination index (Hopkins & Antes, 1978, p.189) is

$$\text{Discrimination Index} = \frac{\text{Number in the Upper Group} - \text{Number in the Lower Group}}{\text{Number of Subjects in Either Group}}$$

When a greater number of subjects in the upper group respond in the scoreable direction than the number of subjects in the lower group, the discrimination index is positive. On the other hand, when a greater number of subjects in the lower group respond in the scoreable direction the discrimination index is negative, and one may assume that there is either something wrong with the item or the sample on whom it is being tested. According to Hopkins and Antes (1978) the discrimination index may take on values from -1.0 to $+1.0$; values above .40 suggest effective items, while values between $+.20$ and $+.39$ are considered satisfactory. It must be remembered that items with negative discrimination indices are discriminating in the wrong direction and ought to be reconsidered.

An alternative way to compare high and low scoring groups is to compare a Phi-coefficient. This coefficient is based on a correlation between group membership (high score and low score) and item score (pass, fail). Like all correlation coefficients it may vary between -1.0 and $+1.0$, with higher scores indicating greater discrimination. High negative scores indicate substantial discrimination but in the wrong direction. This may suggest a scoring or criterion problem. Tables for calculating this coefficient may be found in Jurgensen (1947).

The *Validity Index* is a correlation between a score on a given item and some criterion variable. For example, one may dummy code a criterion variable as 1 = unimpaired and 2 = impaired and correlate each item response with such a variable. In this case items correlating positively would be related to impairment, while items correlated negatively would be related to performance by the unimpaired group. If the test is intended to describe impairment, negatively correlated items will need to be reconsidered. It is up to the researcher to determine the level at which a validity coefficient is acceptable. Because it is a correlation coefficient, it can be squared in order to determine the approximate shared variance between the criterion variable and any given item.

A final method used by test developers to observe item efficiency is to calculate a point biserial correlation between an item and the overall test score in order to discern the degree to which an item represents what the test measures as a whole. Since the item contributes to the general test score, the test score must be recalculated without the given item before the computation is performed. This avoids artificially inflating the item-test relationship.

Items should be positively correlated with the overall test performance. The exact size of the ideal correlation again varies with the intent of the test. In a test measuring a broad skill or personality category, correlations may be in the .4 to .6 range; in a test that purports to measure a single, highly specific skill, correlations should be substantially higher. In the actual selection of items for the final form, intercorrelations among items must also be considered in the manner discussed later in this chapter.

Within multiple choice tests, analyses may also be performed on the distractors from which the subject must select the correct alternative. One may compute a discrimination index for each distractor. In general, alternatives that are not endorsed are useless, and alternatives that are endorsed to high degrees by subjects who do not contain the characteristic of interest also need to be reevaluated. Obviously such indices will again vary with the characteristics of the subject pool and the overall item difficulty.

A much more complex model of item analysis has been suggested by various theorists based on latent trait models (Anastasi, 1982; Baker, 1977; Weiss & Davison, 1981; Wright & Stone, 1979). These models assume nothing more than a mathematical existence for the characteristic being measured. Based on theoretical models that differ in underlying assumptions, these models can be used to establish item characteristic curves that represent a comparison of item difficulty against the expected scores of the hypothesized trait (usually estimated by the total test score). From these curves, several parameters of item difficulty may be established. In particular, the one parameter logistic model (Rasch model) holds promise for future developments (Rasch, 1966). A more detailed discussion of such methods is not within the scope of this chapter.

Further item analyses may be performed by observing scale characteristics. This discussion will be included within the context of the broader discussion of scale development.

SCALE DEVELOPMENT

A major difference among tests relates to the number of subscales present within a given test. Item scores may be assembled in a variety of ways, each of which has examples in the literature and in clinical and research applications. More recent tests (e.g., Millon Personality Inventory, Luria-Nebraska Neuropsychological Battery) as well as modifications over the years of tests such as the MMPI illustrate a growing recognition that a test can recombine items that were initially validated and created by different methods.

The most intuitive method of scale construction is simple face validity. The most basic case of this method is the single scale that is assumed to describe a single dimension. Items are chosen because they are assumed to measure this dimension, and such items usually vary only in difficulty levels. In some cases, there is the assumption that items may be ranked according to difficulty within the scale, so that missing a simpler item implies that more difficult items will also be failed. An example of such a test is the Bender-Gestalt Test (Bender, 1938). Each item is assumed to be a measure of a basic visuo-integrative skill that is also related to visual-motor integration. While items vary in complexity (difficulty), they are assumed to all measure the same ability. Thus, items appear to be arranged in order of difficulty.

A face valid depression scale could be put together by picking items that represent the apparent symptoms of depression (e.g., "I feel sad"; "My appetite has decreased"). In this method, the scale may be based simply on the impressions of the test developer, other experts, or it may reflect an underlying theory of what "depression" is assumed to be. In general, scales that have a strong theoretical background are preferred, since this allows the application of more sophisticated validation techniques.

In summing items to represent scales, all items must be represented on the same scaling system. This may necessitate transforming some items within a test so that they are all similarly scaled, since an item that is only scored "right/wrong" cannot be meaningfully added to another item that represents the number of correct responses within a given time limit. In addition to the type of scaling already discussed, linear transformations of data may also be performed in order to make individual item results more comparable. One may use z scores or, if one wishes to avoid negative values, t scores.

Further, frequencies within nominal categories may be summed to form scales drawn from responses to all items. Thus, on the Rorschach the *Pure Form* scale represents the total number of occurrences of unmodified form responses across all responses. Similarly, in neuropsychology, one could identify a *Perseveration* scale. Although the initial data are nominal, the summing process creates at least ordinal data (Gaito, 1970). In order to make further comparisons among subjects, these raw sums can then be transformed into some form of standard score (e.g., t score).

In addition to the face validity approach to scale formation, scales may also be identified on the basis of empirical properties of the items. These scales are usually based on three basic methodologies: (a) a set of items that discriminate maximally between two groups, (b) a set of items that show high correlations with an external representation of the variable of interest, and (c) a set of items that group together empirically as the result of a factor analytic procedure.

The first methodology may be illustrated by the construction of the original *Depression* scale of the MMPI. This scale was formed by comparing the responses of a group of psychiatrically diagnosed depressed patients with the responses derived from a control group. Items selected for the scale were those that maximally discriminated the two groups. Another example would be a screening test for brain damage, which could be put together from a set of items that are observed to maximally separate the brain impaired from unimpaired persons.

In the second case, items are selected on the basis of their correlation with an outside criteria. Thus, a depression scale may be formed by correlating item performance with psychiatric ratings of depressed persons on a scale from 1 to 7. If one were more biologically inclined, correlations could be calculated between the results of the dexamethasone suppression test and a set of items assumed to measure depression. This would link the diagnosis of depression to a specific biological marker rather than clinical impression alone. A test of brain damage could be developed by correlating items with ventricular size as derived from a cranial computed tomograph.

The validity of the scales developed by these first two methods is dependent on the adequacy of the group or the external criteria selected. This, however, is not always the case. The MMPI is a perfect example of a test that has been criticized for its method of norm group definition but has been found to have enormous clinical value as the result of later empirical study. However, in such cases the empirically based method of interpretation may not resemble the original procedures intended by the test makers.

In the third method, scales are factor analytically derived based on the intercorrelations among items within an item pool. Items that load on the same factor are assumed to relate to an underlying trait that can be represented by a factor score. By orthogonally rotating the initial solution and employing some criterion factor loading, sets of items that load on given factors can be identified as a group of independent scales.

An additional factor analytic method that may be used to create a scale includes the use of marker variables, that is, variables that are known to be representative of a given trait. With this method, a depression scale may be constructed from a general pool of items by factor analyzing these items along with a set of variables known to be associated with depression. Items that share factors with the marker variables can then be included in the depression scale.

There are several limitations to the factor analytic procedures that must be considered in using such a methodology. First, one must thoroughly understand the theory that guided the initial item selections or constructions, since the resulting factors can only be interpreted accurately within the context of a theoretical base. Secondly, each factor solution and rotational method carries with it a set of theoretical assumptions that guides its meaningful application. It is up to the test designer to determine which analysis will create the least distortion in the original data while producing interpretable results. Thus, in choosing a rotational method one must understand, for instance, that the computational method in a Varimax rotation conserves variance down columns and thus

creates a large first factor, partially as a consequence of the computational procedure.

Thirdly, an exploratory (initial) factor analytic solution may be unstable across groups. Therefore, it is important to replicate factor analytically derived dimensions across groups in order to feel some assurance that one is observing a stable (reliable) structure; that is, that items are not simply going together as an artifact of the study at hand.

A fourth limitation to the factor analytic method results from the sample employed. Since dimensions are formed based on how items (variables) covary, the presence of subgroups in the sample that show both great within-group similarity on a set of items and great between-group differences on the same set of items offer the possibility of identifying dimensions that reflect the a priori group differences. This is a problem if it is unintended by the investigator. It can be a benefit if within-group characteristics are being used as marker variables.

Underlying characteristics that may bias responses may also create artificial factor dimensions. Thus, factors may actually reflect such variables as scoring approach, age, education, socioeconomic status, cultural, or gender differences.

Finally, the results of a factor analysis are influenced by the items available for the analysis. Thus, underrepresentation of certain skills or traits in the item pool will prevent such variables from emerging as meaningful factors, even if such skills are important to the domain of the test. The best way to avoid such difficulties is to start with the Table of Specifications, which was described earlier in this chapter, as a blueprint for item construction.

Scales may, of course, be created by a combination of any of these methods. For example, original items may be chosen by screening based on face validity, then confirmed by correlational analysis. The resultant items may then be factor analyzed in an attempt to validate assumptions about the structure of the test. This would be an example of Jackson's (1975) sequential model, which was referred to earlier.

The latter process may also be used to create new scales from the existing pool of items within a test. For example, the original items on the Luria-Nebraska were selected based on face validity and validated by item-scale correlations. Localization scales were derived from comparisons among groups with known characteristics (localized brain injury), and factor scales were identified from the test item pool.

After initial creation of scales, further item analysis can be performed. For example, items within a scale that are redundant (highly intercorrelated) may be eliminated. Other items may be eliminated due to their overall lack of relationship with the total score of the scale. For scales validated against outside criteria, items showing the least relationship with these criteria may be removed from the scale. Scale factors analytically derived may be shortened by determining the fewest number of items that maximize prediction of the characteristic of interest.

The final decisions regarding scale length must result from several considerations: (a) theoretical concerns, which are an attempt to insure that the domain of interest is being adequately sampled; (b) practical concerns (e.g., time for administration); (c) procedural concerns, that is, the elimination of items that create excessive administrative difficulty while yielding limited clinical information; (d) psychometric concerns or the need to maintain adequate levels of reliability and validity. Though we are speaking about making some final decisions about an instrument at this point, it is optimally useful to enter the next phase of study with several versions of a scale (differing usually only in length) to see which is the most useful for the intended purpose of the test.

Reliability

Once a scale has been established, attention can be directed toward the analysis of the psychometric properties of the scale itself. As has been previously suggested, additional item analyses may be performed during this phase, but this topic will not be further addressed in the following sections. Within the following sections, the topic areas will focus on reliability, validity, and methods of norming the test battery.

Kerlinger (1973) suggests several synonyms for reliability. They are dependability, stability, consistency, predictability, or accuracy. He describes reliability as the rating of the precision of a given instrument. Theoretically, the number, which we observe as the reliability estimate of a given test, represents the degree to which our constructed test overlaps a perfect measure of the characteristic of interest. Psychometrically, reliability is the squared correlation between the observed scores and the true scores for the trait of interest (Allen & Yen, 1979). The true score is a theoretical concept that can only be inferred and not directly measured. Each of the computational methods to estimate reliability are in fact an estimate of this relationship between the perfect measure of a given characteristic and our test.

There are several computational forms of reliability that are used depending on the characteristic that a test purports to measure, the type of items, and the needs of the test user.

Test-Retest Reliability

The most obvious type of reliability deals with the *stability* of test scores over time. In this method, scores from an initial administration are correlated with scores on the same instrument after some interval. To use this method of describing the reliability of a test, one must start with the assumption that the characteristic measured by the test has some temporal stability. Thus, the test-retest method would be a poor estimate for an instrument used to assess state anxiety or one designed to assess degree of acute impairment after a head injury. No test, even of a stable trait, should be expected to demonstrate perfect test-retest reliability, as there are many factors that influence test scores other than what the test purports to measure. These include: (a) fatigue, which may create differential concentration and motivation levels between two administrations; (b) differential environmental conditions, such as temperature, outside noise, ambient distractions, scheduling demands, unexpected personal events between sessions; (c) administration errors on the part of the examiner. Test-retest reliability will also be affected by the sample. If homogeneous samples showing either very high or very low scores on the initial administration are used for the second administration, the extremity of their initial scores will capitalize on chance fluctuation and will in all likelihood underestimate the stability of the test.

In interpreting a test-retest coefficient the following limitations must be taken into account. The experience of the first administration may affect the subject's performance during the second administration. Such carry-over effects can work to either underestimate or overestimate an instrument's stability (Allen & Yen, 1979). The length of time between tests creates differential effects depending on the characteristic being measured. Allen and Yen (1979) indicate that short intervals create effects due to memory, practice, or mood; longer intervals create effects due to the possibility of acquiring new information and changes in

mood. In summary, test-retest estimates of reliability are most appropriate for tests involving
abilities rather than achievement or for personality traits that are assumed to be stable.

Alternate-Form Reliability

This method is similar to test-retest stability except another form of the test is administered at the
second session. Thus, this coefficient represents
both temporal stability as well as the degree of
redundancy across forms. One must remember
that the maximum alternate-form reliability will
be limited by the test-retest reliability.

Adequate alternate-form reliability suggests
that the items on the two forms are both samples
from the same population of items that represents
a hypothesized trait or skill. Low alternate-form
reliabilities suggest that the two test forms are not
measuring the same thing. If the tests sample
from the same item population but different components of that population, the correlation may
also be small. As an example, let us hypothesize
alternate-form scales that sample from the universe of motor skills. If one scale is weighted heavily with finger dexterity tasks and the other is
weighted with hand strength tasks, the two scales
may exhibit small correlations.

Alternate-form reliability has many of the same
limitations as test-retest reliability. Thus, one may
expect this computational type to show effects
from both carry-over and length of interval between sessions. These latter factors may be most
evident in a test that requires a specific cognitive
style for problem solving or demands a cognitive
set that is applicable to both forms.

Split-Half Reliability

In split-half reliability, a type of alternate-form
reliability is produced by dividing a single scale
into two halves. This computational method estimates the degree of consistency across items.
Though it does not measure temporal stability, it
offers the advantage of a single administration.
This method assumes that all of the items contribute equally to the measurement of a central construct.

The major problem with this method rests on
the issue of how to split the items. In general, the
most convenient method is to correlate odd numbered items with even numbered items (odd-even
split). Alternatively, one may correlate the first
half of the test items with the latter half; however,
this method is inadequate with speeded tests,

where the subject may not reach the second half,
or with tests that arrange their items by degree of
difficulty, where the latter part of the test is much
more difficult than the first part. Halves may also
be created by random selection, without replace-
ment, but this is a cumbersome and usually unnecessary procedure.

Since this method uses only one half of the
items that are seen in the other reliability measures, split-half reliabilities may be lower than
other reliability estimates. The Spearman-Brown
formula may be used to estimate the correlation if
the number of items have not been reduced. The
estimated correlation is equal to:

$$\frac{2r}{(1 + r)}$$

where r represents the correlation of the two
halves.

The more general form of the Spearman-
Brown formula can be used to estimate the effects
on reliability by increasing or decreasing the number of items for a scale. The general formula is:

$$\frac{n\,r}{1 + (n - 1)\,r}$$

where n is the ratio of the number of items in each
form. Thus, if the number of items started at 60
and $r = .5$ and one is interested in the effect on
reliability of increasing the number of items to
150, n would equal 150/60 or 2.5, and the estimated increased reliability would be .71. Such
calculations allow one to quickly estimate the effects on scale reliability from either adding or
removing items before going to the work of actually constructing the items.

Internal Consistency Reliability

Although split-half reliability is a measure of internal consistency, it only looks at one possible
division of items instead of all possible splits.
Other formulas have been developed to make
more conservative estimates of internal consistency reliability. These are the Kuder-Richardson
20 formula (KR20) and coefficient alpha (Cronbach, 1951; Ebel, 1965; Kaiser & Michael, 1975;
Kuder & Richardson, 1937).

The KR20 formula is generally intended for
tests with items that have only two possible alternatives (e.g., true/false, right/wrong), while
coefficient alpha is usually applied to test items
that have multiple possible answers. The results of

these techniques represent an average of all possible split-half reliabilities formed by all possible combinations of items. Formulas for these coefficients may be found in the above references.

Coefficient alpha has a number of additional properties that are useful to note for the purposes of test construction. Alpha is a low estimate of the reliability of a test, which is a less than perfect estimate of the true score for the characteristic of interest; it is the upper estimate of the variance accounted for by the first factor, when the test is factor analyzed (Allen & Yen, 1979). It is this latter characteristic of alpha that allows the degree of homogeneity among test items to be inferred. Obviously, since the first factor accounts for a greater amount of variance (larger alpha reliability), the test may be described more unidimensionally. This is also one of the limits of the alpha reliability estimate. It will tend to underestimate the reliability of a heterogeneous test.

It should be emphasized, however, that there is no particular virtue in raising or lowering the results of these calculations. In a case where the domain of interest is multidimensional, a heterogeneous scale may be more useful. Perfectly homogeneous sets of items do not exist, since multiple skills go into the performance of any item. Often, an extremely homogeneous scale will fail to correlate well with external criterion variables. Usually, there is a need to compromise between a desire to make the scale as internally consistent as possible and demands that the test be useful in the real world.

Interscorer Reliability

Another estimate of a test's reliability may be derived by the use of multiple examiners to score the same protocol of responses. In most tests, except for the simplest, it is useful to analyze the effect on the test created by a variety of scorers. This is especially important for standardized tests as discussed here, since we are assuming that administration and scoring will provide a consistent base across clinicians for interpretive purposes. This becomes a crucial issue for projective tests of personality and open-ended tests, both of which require the examiner to perform subjective analyses of behavior.

Interscorer reliability can be determined from either (a) obtaining protocols and having them scored by two different investigators, (b) having two examiners observe and score the performance of the same patient at the same time, or (c) having two scorers independently evaluate data from the same patient. In the latter case, a better evaluation of the effects of different administration techniques is achieved, but a poorer measure of scoring errors occurs because of complications by test-retest effects. The first two methods do not estimate the effects of different administrators at all, since the test is only given a single time.

In summary, all of the above methods of evaluating reliability assume a univariate structure underlying the test; however, many scales are multidimensional. For example, Galassi et al.'s (1974) assertion scale can be broken down into expression of positive affect, expression of negative affect, and asking one's needs to be met. If one wishes to observe the internal consistency reliability of such a test, Bentler's (1975) procedure, which is applicable to these multidimensional situations, may be applied.

Analyzing Variance

Anastasi (1982) has observed that these different estimates of reliability can be used to parcel out test variance among subjects, which is true variance (due to the characteristic of interest) from that attributable to error variance (effects unrelated to the characteristic of interest). She identifies the following techniques as measuring specific types of error variance: (a) test-retest—variance due to time interval; (b) alternate form, immediate administration—variance due to content; (c) alternate form, delayed administration—variance due to both time and content; (d) split-half—variance due to content sampling; (e) KR20 and alpha—variance due to content sampling and heterogeneity; (f) interscorer—variance due to examiner and administration style.

Since the difference between the square of a reliability coefficient and 1.0 represents the percentage of variance we can attribute to a specific factor, we can calculate the total amount of explained and error variance from this information if we assume that the test under consideration is perfectly reliable. For example, if the test-retest reliability is .9, we can calculate that $1.0 - (.9)^2$ or $1.0 - .81$ or an estimated 19% of the variance is due to time. If in the same test, the KR20 is .8, we can calculate that item content and heterogeneity account for $1.0 - (.8)^2$ or 36% of the total variance. Finally, if the interscorer reliability is .95, we can estimate that the examiner effect is responsible for 9.75% of the variance. If these percentages are summed, the total amount of variance attributable to error factors is 64.75%, which leaves, theoretically, 35.25% as true variance.

Further, since true variance can be translated into a theoretical reliability for this scale, the correlation would be the square root of .3525 or just less than .6. Since most test designers find a test with a reliability in the .7 to .8 range to be adequate, it may be inferred that the amount of error variance in most tests is between 30% and 50%. However, one must note the previously described method of estimating error contributions to a test may inflate the error estimate, since components of that error effect may overlap between estimation methods (i.e., both alternate form and test-retest are affected by time interval).

Limits of Correlational Estimates

Since all measures of reliability are correlational in nature, all are affected by the way variance is distributed across both items and subjects. First, as the sample being tested becomes more homogeneous, the correlation between measures will decrease to the restricted range of variance available in one or both measures. Second, tests for which speed is a factor (only subsets of items are completed due to the time limitations of the test and the subject's abilities) make calculation of inter-item and internal consistency measures impossible, without altering the testing procedures. Anastasi (1982) suggests procedures such as correlating item performance during one time period (the first 10 minutes) with performance in another time period (the last 10 minutes) as a way to get around such difficulties.

Correlational estimates will also differ within ability levels. For example, the Luria-Nebraska correlates .84 with the WAIS IQ in a sample whose average IQ was under 115 but correlates less than .2 in a sample with IQs greater than 120. Such factors suggest the need to observe the scales' performance in relation to traits which it is not intended to measure. The multitrait multimethod approach to validity is one way to respond to such issues and will be discussed in the next section.

Validity

The issue of validity answers the questions "Does the test measure what it was intended to mea-

sure?" and "Does the test produce information that will be useful to clinicians?" The majority of research with a test usually focuses on validity issues. Consequently, this is also the area of investigation that breeds the most controversy. The major types of validity of concern to the researcher are content validity, criterion related validity, and construct validity. Each of these will be discussed separately.

Content Validity

Content validation starts as the initial items are selected for a test. It is easiest to demonstrate when the test has been built from a well-defined theoretical orientation, and the designer has started from a Table of Specifications in order to adequately sample a representative group of items.

Subsequent analysis of content validity may differ markedly from the original validation. Subsequent investigators may assume a different underlying theory or support a different set of representative items. When items or scales are shown to have limited content validity, it is usually a result of either incomplete understanding of the underlying theory, lack of a theory, or a tendency to overgeneralize in item construction. Thus, for example, one may assume that a person capable of doing short-term memory tasks is also capable of doing tasks requiring long-term storage: an assumption that is not accurate. Selection of items that only demonstrate long-term storage will not be effective in determining short-term memory impairment.

Content validity becomes more of an issue for tests of achievement or ability and less a concern for tests of personality, where high content validity may limit the overall usefulness of the test. It is also useful for tests of cognitive skills that require an assessment of a broad range of skills in a given area.

Content validity is commonly confused with a form of validity called "face validity." Face validity does not deal with what a test actually measures but rather with what a scale appears to measure based on the reading of various items. The researcher will often find that what an item appears to measure on the surface will differ considerably from what the scale measures in actual practice. What an item actually measures in a test will depend not only on the structure of the item, but the conditions under which it is administered and scored. Changes in timing, instruction, and scoring procedures can cause relationships with external correlates to vary considerably. Thus, face validity is essentially a limited concept that may not reflect intended content.

Despite this fact, face validity does play a role in test construction. While it is not important to the professional, it is through face validity that the subject receives an impression of what the test is measuring. If a test appears too easy, too hard, inappropriate to what the patient wants, or unnecessarily intrusive, it may affect the patient's test-taking attitude (e.g., level of cooperation, honesty, etc.). These factors should also be taken into account in order to insure the widest usefulness for the test.

Criterion Based Validity

Criterion validity is extremely important and used widely throughout the construction of psychological tests. This form of validity deals with the ability of test scores to predict behavior, either as represented by other test scores, observable behaviors, or other accomplishments such as grade point averages.

Criterion validity can be subdivided into two types: concurrent and predictive. The difference between these forms of criterion validity lies primarily in the temporal relationship between the test and the external criterion. Concurrent validity involves prediction to an alternative method of measuring the same characteristic of interest, while predictive validity attempts to show a relationship with future behavior. For example, concurrent validity would assume a relationship between a new test and an existing test if both are assumed to be sensitive to a dementing process. On the other hand, a design involving predictive validity would attempt to classify future dements based on their performance on the new instrument. The accuracy of such a classification over time would serve as the measure of predictive validity. Since designs involving concurrent validity are generally easier to operationalize due to the absence of the temporal constraint, concurrent procedures are occasionally substituted, though the intent is clearly predictive. Thus, we may assess anxious students already referred to a college counseling center to validate a test with a group of high anxiety students. Patterns identified during such a study could then be used to predict which freshman students are likely to develop anxiety disorders during their college experience. Care must be taken in such cases, since the assumed predictive relationship is not confirmed by the current data and awaits the passage of time.

The existence of concurrent relationships between criterion variables and the results of psychological tests is one of the main advantages of employing psychological tests, since they usually are less expensive and take considerably less time to perform. Using a neuropsychological example, one may note that the presence of brain damage can be determined reasonably well by collecting an incisive history, a CT scan, EEG, PET scan, NMR, and regional cerebral blood flow measures, along with other appropriate biochemical tests; however, such a work up costs thousands of dollars. Thus, the existence of concurrent relationships between the results of a neuropsychological battery and the results of such broad based physiological measures allow the possibility of saving both time and money. Further predictive relationships between neuropsychological findings and changes in function after brain injury provide information in addition to the information delivered by the physiologically based tests. This is not to suggest that a neuropsychological battery should be rotely substituted for the extensive physical workup. Rather, it is suggestive of the complementary nature of the two forms of evaluation and an indication of the ideal relationship between any new form of assessment and existent instruments and procedures.

Tests should be validated against as many criteria as there are behaviors that may reasonably be predicted from the data. Generally such research will identify the limits of a test; that is, test scores will be better predictors for some events and worse for others. Such a pattern of findings helps to identify the appropriate test for a given need. Both clinical users and research users must recognize that no test is appropriate in all circumstances or for all purposes, and it is the purpose of assessment research to clarify those limits for each test.

Both predictive and concurrent validities are accepted by deciding the appropriate level of validity coefficient or correlation between a test score and some criterion variable. The appropriate acceptance level depends on the intended use of the test. For example, if one wishes to predict group membership, a classification analysis, or a similar technique that determines placement, accuracy based on test scores would be appropriate.

This is a noncorrelational method of validation. Whatever technique is used, the research must take into account the limitations and strengths of the statistic that will be employed.

Construct Validity

Construct validity is the most newly recognized type of validity (see Cronbach & Meehl, 1955). This approach is much more complex than the other forms of validity that we have discussed, requiring an accumulation of data over a long period of time. Construct validity involves studying test scores in their relationship not only to variables that the test is intended to assess, but also to variables that should have no relationship to the domain underlying the instrument. Thus, one builds a nomothetic net or inferential definition of the characteristics that a test is measuring. Hypotheses may be generated in a wide variety of ways depending on the characteristic of interest.

For example, when cognitive skills are studied, theories can be used to predict developmental changes that are expected in a trait over time. Such changes are then sought in test scores given at different age levels. This research can obviously be extended over the total life span and is not only limited to children.

A second approach includes predictions to other tests that are assumed to measure the same underlying trait as well as those measures that describe unrelated traits. Thus, we may predict that a specific intellectual skill should have a moderate correlation with a measure of general IQ, little or no correlation with a measure of hypochondriasis, and a strong correlation to another test measuring the same intellectual skill. It should be clear that in examining such interrelationships the efficacy of the research depends on the accuracy of the original hypothesis, which in turn is related to the investigator's comprehension of the trait under study. Researchers and consumers must be careful not to confuse a researcher's misunderstanding of either the intention of an instrument or the underlying theory with the inefficiency of the instrument itself.

In a major paper, Campbell and Fiske (1959) expanded these notions into an analytic model that includes the concepts of discriminant and convergent validity. Discriminant validity includes those tests that should show little or no relationship to the test at hand, while convergent validity represents concurrent relationships with the test at hand. Based on this model, they proposed the use of a multitrait/miltimethod design. In such a design, the trait under study is measured in a number of alternative ways, which includes the test that is being evaluated. At the same time measures of assumed unrelated traits are also included. The pattern of intercorrelation among the various measures creates a multitrait/multimethod matrix. The validity of a test is supported if it shows moderate to high relationships with instruments assumed to measure a similar characteristic, while demonstrating low to zero correlations with instruments measuring unrelated characteristics.

Although the Campbell and Fiske (1959) article represents an important consideration in the evaluation of a psychological test, their suggested methodology can be improved. Jackson (1969) has raised criticisms of the methodology and has suggested an alternative evaluation model. Most of Jackson's (1969) criticisms center around the fact that Campbell and Fiske's (1959) methodology compares individual criterion correlations and does not examine the overall structure. Pattern correlations between traits may be influenced by the method of variance engendered in measuring the traits under consideration.

Jackson (1969) instead recommends a factor analysis of the monomethod matrix. In such an analysis, the matrix is first orthogonalized and submitted to a principle components analysis, followed by a varimax rotation. The expected number of factors is set equal to the number of traits under consideration. Although Jackson's analysis helps meet certain shortcomings of the earlier methodology, it is also open to criticism. Because Jackson's procedure capitalizes on the discrepancy between the characteristics of interest, it is not useful for conceptually related traits. Because it uses a monomethod matrix, it cannot be used to examine the influence of different methods. Therefore, these two methods of validational analysis (i.e., Campbell & Fiske's and Jackson's) may be seen as being complementary to each other, and it is advisable to use both in the complete analysis of an assessment instrument.

A further development in the evaluation of multitrait-multimethod matrices involves the use of the structural equations approach. Kallenberg and Kluegel (1975) describe three advantages of this method. The structural equations approach provides a mechanism for describing the correlation between trait and method factors. It provides a mechanism for describing the relationships of both trait and method factors under consideration. Finally, in order to use the structural equations method, one must first specify one's assumptions regarding the construct under consideration.

Another way to study construct validity is through factor analysis. One may postulate a factorial structure for a specific instrument given one's assumptions about both the trait that is being measured and the theory from which it was derived. A confirmatory factor analysis is then performed to test the hypothesis. For example, in our own work with the Luria-Nebraska, predictions were made from Luria's theory of brain functioning. Such predictions were operationalized in terms of item interrelationships, and the factoring process is used to test such hypotheses (see Golden et al., 1982, for an example).

In the case of tests in which a limited number of scores or a single score is generated, marker variables with meanings that are more completely understood may be included in the analysis. Factorial relationships with such marker variables can then be used to determine the meaning of the new test scores. In such analyses and all factor analytic procedures, it is useful to perform a series of factor analyses in order to determine if the factor structure and the factorial relationships are stable across time and across groups.

Normative Data

Once the items of a test have been established, normative data can be obtained. However, before turning to this topic several comments are in order. First, although the above test construction process has been laid out in a linear manner by necessity, the actual process is much more dynamic and integrated. Since no test is a perfect measure of what it is trying to assess (behavior), the process of test refinement may be an endless one. Validity data may lead one back to earlier stages of the design process, necessitating revision of the instrument. Since perfection is not likely attainable, the constructor must work with the test until validity and reliability are suitable for the intended purpose of the instrument. Suitable endpoints will differ in relation to the intended use of the measure.

Moreover, even after a test is completed, additional work may be done in terms of providing alternate or improved versions of the test. One of the unfortunate drawbacks of this area has been the tendency for tests to stagnate even after research has shown defects that could be corrected. This inertia is usually explained as the need for users to have an unchanging instrument, the unwillingness of users to change administration methods, or the difficulty involved in renorming or revalidating a new version of a test. Even though the practical problems of such work are appreciated by the authors, this general attitude undermines the effectiveness of the field by permitting errors to be endlessly repeated. Moreover, it leads many consumers to the erroneous conclusion that a given technique is perfect because it has been around a long time without change. The science of test construction is better served by an attitude that the design of any instrument is an on-going process, which demands continuous reevaluation in the context of both validational research and feedback from consumers.

After the test has reached an acceptable initial form, normative data may be established. In some cases, this may be done as an integral part of the previously mentioned validation investigations or in a separate phase. Such a decision usually depends on the constraints that the test designer faces as well as the initial results of validation efforts. Several approaches may be taken to form normative data.

Norms will differ depending on the scaling scheme used for a scale or for individual items, a topic which has been discussed earlier. As indicated, a given scaling approach is dependent on the type of information desired and the inferences that will be drawn from the data. Similarly, the eventual scoring system employed, whether percentiles, t scores, z scores, or the like, will depend on many of the same factors. Of greater importance to this chapter is the issue of relativity of norms.

Norms for a given test may differ considerably depending on the characteristics of the standardization sample that was used. In addition, the future sample to which the instrument is applied may differ considerably from the group on whom it was normed, even though both may be from the same general population. This presents serious problems for the test designer as well as the test user.

Although attempts are made to gather representative samples whose characteristics will be appropriate to a wide variety of subjects, this is essentially a futile task, since any limited sample cannot hope to adequately represent a broad population like "the American student," for example, or even more restricted groups like "all ten-year-olds." Individuals within such groups are simply too diverse. A large number of factors will affect individual scores: motivation, environment, culture, age, developmental level, language, training, educational quality, personal experience, gender, and attitude to name a few. Although such factors may average out across a large group, they grossly affect the interpretation of an individual protocol. Thus, even if a sample of 3,000 subjects were to include the same percentage of American Indians as exists in the population as a whole, to argue that the mean scores of such a sample are as representative of an individual American Indian's performance as the modal subject's performance is of questionable validity. The degree to which such an assumption is accurate may only be determined by norming the test within subgroups that exist within the majority population. The investigator should keep well in mind that no single set of norms can be used in all circumstances, and that norms must take into account both individual and group factors in order to be meaningful.

Such an understanding results in a greater emphasis on the use of local or specific norms aimed at individual groups. The degree to which these groups must be precisely described is determined to a great extent by the trait or skill that is being measured. For example, if we wish to look at the population of college educated individuals, fewer persons are necessary in the sample and less discrimination in subject selection is needed if the task to be measured is reading the word "cat," a skill for which there will be limited within-group variation in such a population. On the other hand, a complex skill requiring the comprehension of nuclear engineering will be strongly affected by individual coursework and in turn will affect the norms that are derived. Care must be taken in situations where different cultures or language backgrounds will limit exposure to the domain that a test is intended to assess. Thus, in selecting samples in order to create norms, the factors that will vitiate the characteristic being measured must be considered.

Local or specific group norms may be established in two ways. First, norms may be defined in reference to a given subgroup. Thus, on an IQ test, one may establish that Group A has a mean score of 92 and a standard deviation of 18, rather than the more general mean of 100 and a standard deviation of 15. For a member of such a group, we would consequently define a score of 65

as within two standard deviations of normal (92 ± 36), while we would not have done so using the more general norm (i.e., 100). Alternately, we could equate an IQ of 92 in our group with an IQ of 100, using appropriate tables to redefine every other score within our group in a similar manner. This latter method has the advantage of allowing the same interpretive statements to be applied to members of the subgroup; however, it loses the relative information conveyed by the difference between the scores of our group and the more general norm group.

An example of this may be seen in tests of memory. If we were to put together special norms for individuals with IQs below 70, we could redefine what would be a "normal" score for such a group. But this would obscure the fact that a person with such an IQ may have poor memory functions. The latter issue becomes important if we are attempting to make recommendations for treatment or rehabilitation of an individual. Use of the same norms but different interpretations, which take into account vitiating factors, allows greater flexibility to deal with such issues.

For example, although standard scores are used across all scales on the Luria-Nebraska, interpretations regarding the absence or presence of brain impairment are modified based on the presence or absence of certain demographic factors. Thus, a score of 70 on the *Reading* scale generally suggests poor reading in English but does not indicate impaired performance in an individual who has never been formally educated. The same score for a college graduate with a degree in English Literature would indicate impaired performance. Such a system based on a common scoring scheme has the advantage of allowing one to simultaneously correct for multiple extraneous factors without the need to create a multitude of tables in order to anticipate every novel subject characteristic.

In such a system, the reference group serves only to anchor the norms and need not be representative of any specific population. Interpretation is not based on any assumption regarding such a norm group or its representativeness. Rather, interpretations are derived from a sample of interest; that is, a group that is high on the characteristic being described by the instrument. Such an interpretive reference group should not have any unusual characteristics that would mitigate against accurate comprehension of resulting protocols. For example, if the interpretive reference group were individuals with an average IQ of 12, too many groups will score several standard deviations from the reference norms, creating interpretive difficulties due to the exaggerated differences between individuals.

Another advantage of such a system is the ease with which other investigators may develop local or specific group norms, which may be communicated to other researchers in simple and understandable terms. This also permits one to develop alternate test forms with scores that can be related to the original reference group, which further insures comparability of scoring across forms.

The use of such locally derived subgroup norms in relation to a fixed reference group produces a situation in which one is never done collecting normative data. Future investigators may develop norms for their own samples of interest, which may be quite divergent from the original reference sample. They may also investigate the effects of variables such as age, education, anxiety, and so on in order to further refine the limits of interpretation.

A related issue is the use of a national anchor group to insure comparability of scores across tests (rather than within a single test form only). Such an anchor group insures comparability by defining scores on an alternative measure in terms of the scores of the original test. Scores on the new test are assumed to be equal to the scores achieved on the earlier test.

SUMMARY

As the reader can see, test construction is ideally a set of interrelated steps ranging from theoretical description of a measure, to item development and selection, to psychometric investigation, to normative studies. This is an on-going process that must continue beyond the initial development of the test as items, scores, and normative data are further refined in order to increase the overall usefulness of an instrument across a wide variety of needs and people. Such work is characterized by the recognition that the ideal test does not exist and can only be approximated. And each setting, need, and group may have its own variation on such an approximation. Ideal development of tests must include research that insures the appropriateness of a given test to given samples and clinical issues, as well as empirical feedback that points the direction in which each test must evolve in order to provide maximum clinical utility.

REFERENCES

Allen, M.J., & Yen, W.M. (1979). *Introduction to measurement theory.* Monterey, CA: Brooks/Cole.

Anastasi, A. (1982). *Psychological testing.* New York: Macmillan.

Baker, F.B. (1977). Advances in item analysis. *Review of Educational Research, 47,* 151–178.

Bem, S.L. (1974). The measurement of psychological androgyny. *Journal of Consulting and Clinical Psychology, 42,* 155–162.

Bem, S.L. (1977). On the utility of alternative procedures for assessing psychological androgyny. *Journal of Consulting and Clinical Psychology, 45,* 196–205.

Bender, L. (1938). A visual motor gestalt test and its clinical use. *American Orthopsychiatric Association, Research Monographs,* No. 3.

Bentler, P.M. (1975). A lower bound method for the dimension free measurement of internal consistency. *Social Science Research, 60,* 1–9.

Campbell, D.T., & Fiske, D.W. (1959). Convergent and discriminant validation by the multitrait-multimethod matrix. *Psychological Bulletin, 56,* 81–105.

Carroll, B.J., Fielding, J.M., & Blashki, T.G. (1973). Depression rating scales: A critical review. *Archives of General Psychiatry, 28,* 361–366.

Cronbach, L.J. (1951). Coefficient alpha and the internal structure of tests. *Psychometrika, 16,* 297–334.

Cronbach, L.J., & Meehl, P.E. (1955). Construct validity in psychological tests. *Psychological Bulletin, 52,* 281–302.

Ebel, R.L. (1965). *Measuring educational achievement.* Englewood Cliffs, NJ: Prentice-Hall.

Fiske, D.W. (1978). *Strategies for personality research.* San Francisco: Jossey-Bass.

Gaito, J. (1970). Scale classification and statistics. In E.F. Heermann & L.A. Braskamp (Eds.), *Readings in statistics for the behavioral sciences.* Englewood Cliffs, NJ: Prentice-Hall.

Galassi, J.P., Delo, J.S., Galassi, M.D., & Bastien, S. (1974). The college self-expression scale: A measure of assertiveness. *Behavior Therapy, 5,* 165–171.

Golden, C.J., Hammeke, T.A., & Purisch, A.D. (1980). *The Luria-Nebraska Neuropsychological Battery manual.* Los Angeles, CA: Western Psychological Services.

Golden, C.J., Hammeke, T.A., Purisch, A.D., Berg, R.A., Moses Jr., J.A., Newlin, D.B., Wilkening, G.N., & Puente, A.E. (1982). *Item interpretation of the Luria-Nebraska Neuropsychological Battery.* Lincoln, NE: University of Nebraska Press.

Hays, W.L. (1973). *Statistics for the social sciences.* New York: Holt, Rinehart, & Winston.

Hopkins, C.D., & Antes, R.L. (1978). *Classroom measurement and evaluation.* Itasca, IL: F.E. Peacock Publishers, 1978.

Jackson, D.N. (1969). Multimethod factor analysis in the evaluation of convergent and discriminant validity. *Psychological Bulletin, 72,* 30–49.

Jackson, D.N. (1970). A sequential system for personality scale development. In C.D. Spielberger (Ed.), *Current topics in clinical and community psychology.* New York: Academic Press.

Jurgensen, C.E. (1947). Table for determining phi coefficients. *Psychometrika*, **12**, 17–29.

Kaiser, H.F., & Michael, W.B. (1975). Domain validity and generalizability. *Educational and Psychological Measurement*, **35**, 31–35.

Kallenberg, A.L., & Kluegel, J.R. (1975). Analysis of the multitrait multimethod matrix: Some limitations and an alternative. *Journal of Applied Psychology*, **60**, 1–9.

Kerlinger, F.N. (1973). *Foundations of behavioral research*. New York: Holt, Rinehart, & Winston.

Kuder, G.F., & Richardson, M.W. (1937). The theory of estimation of test reliability. *Psychometrika*, **2**, 151–160.

Lachar, D.L., & Gdowski, C.L. (1979). *Actuarial assessment of child and adolescent personality: An interpretive guide for the Personality Inventory for Children profile*. Los Angeles, CA: Western Psychological Services.

Millon, T. (1982). *Millon Clinical Multiaxial Inventory manual*. Minneapolis, MN: National Computer Systems.

Rasch, G. (1966). An individualistic approach to item analysis. In P.F. Lazarsfeld & N.W. Henry (Eds.), *Readings in mathematical social sciences*. Cambridge, MA: MIT Press.

Weiss, D.J., & Davison, M.L. (1981). Test theory and methods. *Annual Review of Psychology*, **32**, 629–658.

Wiggins, J.S. (1973). *Personality and prediction: Principles of personality assessment*, Reading, MA: Addison-Wesley.

Wright, B.D., & Stone, M.H. (1979). *Best test design: Rasch measurement*. Chicago: Mesa Press.

3 SCALING TECHNIQUES

Mark D. Reckase

INTRODUCTION

When assessment instruments are administered, the goal is to gather information about the characteristics of the individual being tested. The characteristics may be directly observable, such as height, weight, or hair color, and the assessment instrument may be merely a form that is used to record the results of the observations. A more complex situation exists when the characteristic is not directly observable or when the required observations are much too extensive to be practical. In those cases, the information obtained from the assessment instrument is used to infer the characteristics of the person. Examples of these kinds of characteristics include intelligence, introversion, and anxiety. The vast majority of psychological assessment instruments describe characteristics that fall into the latter category.

In addition to merely gathering information about an individual's characteristics, there is usually interest in determining the amount of each characteristic that a person has. This implies that the recording scheme used must quantify observations in some way. The resulting numerical scores not only give an indication of the level of each characteristic, but also allow comparisons to be made between persons and give a convenient procedure for summarizing observations.

The numerical scores also lend themselves to further analyses that may help discover relationships that exist among different characteristics of a person. That is, the numerical values are used to infer relationships among the underlying causative variables (hypothetical constructs) that explain a person's behavior.

The quantification of observations was a necessary first step before many of the areas of science were able to develop. It is hard to imagine the fields of physics and chemistry without the presence of quantitative information. Psychology has followed the same trend. As both theory and practice have developed, advances have been facilitated by the quantification of the observations of psychological traits. The early work of Galton (1870) stressed the quantification of psychophysical observations, and since that time the trend has been to develop numerical descriptions of an individual's characteristics.

The process that is used to assign numbers to observations is the topic of this chapter. This process is called *scaling*. If scaling is successful, the numerical score that is obtained from an assessment instrument can be used to accurately infer the characteristics of a person. In a very basic psychological sense, scaling can be defined as the

38

assignment of psychological meaning to a set of numbers.

The purpose of this chapter is to present some basic information about psychologically derived numerical scales and their use. The chapter is organized around two major topics: (a) the theory behind scale formation, and (b) the relation of that theory to the formation of several psychological scaling procedures. However, the goal of the chapter is to do more than present a catalogue of scaling procedures. Rather, a basic philosophical orientation will be presented that can be used to develop new scales for the assessment of psychological traits. Much practical information will be presented, but it will always be related to the basic philosophy of scale formation.

SCALING THEORY

The basic concept in the theory of scale formation is that of a property (see Rozeboom, 1966, for a more abstract development of the concepts presented here). A property can be thought of in at least two different ways. It is more commonly used to denote a characteristic, trait, or quality of an entity. Bananas are yellow; yellow is a property of bananas. Human beings are mammals; being a mammal is a property of human beings. This usage of the term *property* is sufficient for conversational use, but it is not precise enough for use in scaling theory. For the purposes of this chapter, a *property* will be defined by a set of entities. Any set of entities defines a property, but some sets are more interesting than others. For example, the set of dogs defines the property "dog." If an entity belongs to that set, it is a dog. We can determine if an entity is a dog by checking if it is a member of the set (see Figure 3.1). A less interesting property, x, might be made up of some random selection of entities. Each entity has the property that it is a member of x. The generality of the set definition of a property is useful from a theoretical perspective, but it still does not make property x interesting from a psychological perspective.

When used in a psychological context, the sets of entities (usually people) that define properties are more restricted in their scope than the "dog" example given above. Most psychological characteristics exist at various levels. Therefore, psychological properties are usually defined by sets of people having the same level of the trait of interest. For example, a set of people that all have

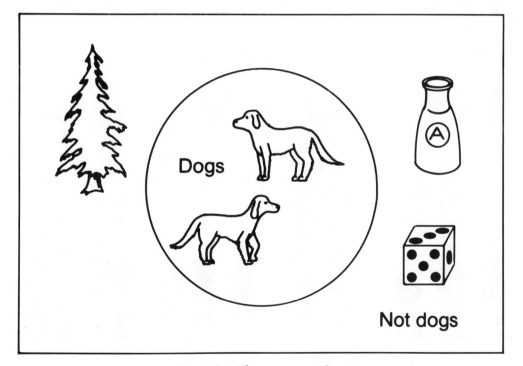

Figure 3.1. The property—"dogs."

the same amount of test anxiety defines the property of that level of test anxiety. Another set of people defines another, different level of test anxiety. A different set of people is hypothesized to exist for each different level of test anxiety, and each of these defines a property. Thus, when a person is said to have a high anxiety level, that means the person belongs to the set of people that have been labeled as highly anxious. All of the people in that set have the property of having a high level of anxiety.

Defining a Property

The actual process that is required to define a property is that of determining equivalence. All persons who have a property are equivalent on the trait of interest and are different from those persons who do not have the property. If a procedure can be developed to determine whether two individuals are equivalent on the trait of interest (in a practical sense), then the first step toward scale formation has been taken.

An example of the formation of the set of people that form properties can easily be given if height is used as the trait of interest. Imagine a room full of people of varying heights. It would not be a difficult task to sort the people into groups of individuals that have approximately the

same height. Each of the groups would define a property that could be labeled as a particular height.

Definition of a Natural Variable

A further step toward the formation of a scale can be demonstrated using the height example given above. If the room full of people contained the total population of people of interest as far as the trait "height" is concerned, the sets of people of equal height contain all of the possible properties related to the concept height. This situation is depicted in Figure 3.2. Further, each person belongs to only one set, and every person belongs to a set, even if that person is standing alone because no one else is of the same height. Sets containing one person are perfectly legitimate. Thus, each person has a height-property and no person has more than one.

The collection of sets that define the properties called levels of height together define a concept called a natural variable. A *natural variable* is a collection of properties in which every entity is included in a property and no entity is in more than one property. The variable is called "natural" because it exists in the real world and does not have anything to do with abstract symbols such as numbers.

Figure 3.2. The natural variable "height."

All of the variables that are commonly dealt with in psychology are assumed to be natural variables. When the variable "intelligence" is used, it is assumed that at any moment in time numerous groups could be formed, each of which contain persons that are equivalent in their level of intelligence. All persons are assumed to have some level of intelligence, and no person is assumed to have more than one level of intelligence at a given time. This set of conditions holds for any psychological trait for which a scale can be formed.

Of course, the procedure for forming a natural variable described above is impractical in reality. The example was given only to illustrate the concept of a variable that is commonly used in psychology. It is merely a collection of sets of individuals that are equal on the trait of interest. In order for the concept of variable to be of use, some means must be determined to identify the particular set to which a person belongs without going through the sorting process. The general procedure that will be proposed is to assign an abstract label to each property set and then to develop a set of rules for determining the label that goes with each person.

Definition of a Scaled Variable

Up to this point, rather cumbersome language has been used to describe a property and a natural variable. This description can be simplified considerably if abstract symbols are used instead of the actual individuals. Suppose, in the height example given above, that each person in the room had been randomly assigned a number between 1 and 10. The individuals could then be grouped according to the number that had been assigned to them to form a collection of sets. If each person were given one number, and no person received more than one number, this collection of sets forms a variable that can be called "The number assigned to each person." This variable does not have any connection to an underlying trait. It is strictly an abstract variable. This type of variable will be labled a *scaled variable* (see Figure 3.3).

An infinite number of scaled variables are possible. Any arbitrary set of numbers can be assigned to a set of individuals, and if the properties of a variable are maintained (i.e., each person gets one number and no person gets more than one), then the result is a scaled variable. If the scaled variable is related to a natural variable, a very powerful result is obtained.

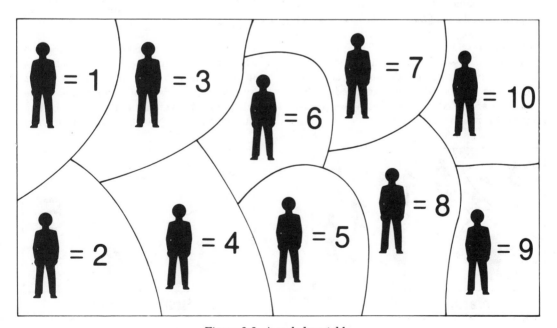

Figure 3.3. A scaled variable.

Definition of a Scaling

If each person having the same height property is assigned the same number, then the grouping of sets that defines the natural variable height is exactly the same as the grouping of sets that defines the scaled variable. If this relationship between the variables occurs, the result is called a *scaling* or a *nominal scaling* of the variable height. The relationship between a natural variable and a scaled variable for a nominal scaling is shown in Figure 3.4.

The scaling of a variable is very powerful. The individuals no longer have to be present to tell if they are equal in height. The numbers assigned to them need only be compared. If two persons have been assigned the same number, they are equal in height. If they have been assigned different numbers, they are different in height.

It should be clear that the critical part of scaling a variable is the procedure for assigning the numbers. If the numbers are accurately assigned to the properties of the trait of interest, a perfect scaling results, and all of the information present in the natural variable is present in the scaled variable. For most natural variables of interest to a psychologist, it is not possible to assign numbers so that every member of a property set gets the same number because of errors in the assignment process. In most cases, the scaling would be considered successful if most persons in a property were assigned the same number. To the extent that the correct assignment is made, the numerical assignment is said to be *reliable*. The greater the frequency of persons assigned the wrong numbers, the more unreliable is the numerical assignment. The numerical values assigned to the properties are called *measurements* when the assignment is reasonably reliable.

Scale Types

When using the results of the scaling of a psychological variable, more information is usually desired than merely indicating whether a person does or does not have a property. Information about the magnitude of the level of the trait is also desired. In order for this information to be obtained, it must first be possible to order the properties of the natural variable. For the height example given above, the procedure for doing the ordering is quite obvious. Persons with the various height properties can be compared and ranked according to height. If the numbers assigned to the property sets have the same order as the properties in the natural variable, the scaling that results will contain information about the ordering and is called an *ordinal scale*.

Still more information can be included in the scaling of the variable if an assumption can be made about the properties in the natural variable. If it can be assumed that when the ordered properties of a natural variable differ by an equal amount, the numerical values in the corresponding scaled variable also differ by an equal amount, the resulting scaling is called an *interval scale*. That is, if numbers are assigned in such a way that when the distances between sets of numerical values are equal the psychological differences in the elements of the corresponding properties of the natural variable are also equal, then an interval scaling is the result.

The measurement of temperature using the Celsius scale is a common example of measurement of the interval scale level. When Anders Celsius developed this scale he assigned 0 to the freezing point of water and 100 to the boiling point of water and divided the temperature range

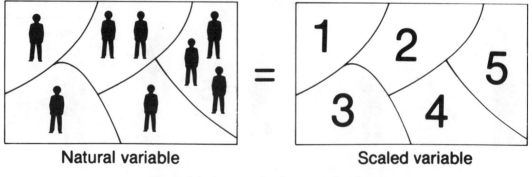

Natural variable　　　　　**Scaled variable**

Figure 3.4. An example of a nominal scaling.

in between into 100 units. This numerical rule defined the scaled variable now labeled Celsius temperature. The equal units on the Celsius scale correspond to the increase in the temperature of 1 cubic centimeter of water brought about by the application of 1 calorie of heat. The physical sets of objects of equal temperature define the properties in the natural variable. Thus, for this temperature scale, equal differences in the natural variable correspond to equal numerical differences on the Celsius scale. Therefore, the Celsius temperature scale is an interval scale.

The classification of scales as ordinal or interval takes on importance because psychometric theorists (e.g., Stevens, 1959) have pointed out that many common statistical procedures (e.g., the mean, standard deviation, etc.) require interval scale measurements for proper application. These procedures use the difference between scores to compute the descriptive statistics. Since the distance between scores is not clearly defined for ordinal scales, the meaning of the statistics for these scales is questionable.

The opposing point of view is that most psychological scales give a reasonably close approximation to interval scales, and therefore the interval based statistics can be applied. Labovitz (1970) performed a study that supported this point of view. He demonstrated that only if the size of the scale intervals varied by great amounts were the statistics adversely affected. Adams, Fagot, and Robinson (1965) also argued that it is the interpretations of the natural variable that are important. If the scaled variable and the statistics applied to it yield useful information about the natural variable (e.g., the scaled variable is found to correlate with other variables of interest), the level of measurement is not considered a concern. The majority of psychologists now consider that most scales give a reasonable approximation of an interval scale unless severe distortions in the scale properties are noted.

One other type of scale has been included in the typology of scales developed by Stevens (1959). In this type of scale, one of the property sets is defined by the group of individuals that has absolutely none of the variables of interest. This property defines the true zero point of the scale. In addition to the existence of the property defining the true zero point, the natural variable must also meet all the requirements for an interval scale. That is, equal differences in the numbers assigned to the properties must correspond to equal psy-

chological differences in the properties. Of course, the entities in the true zero property must be assigned the number zero.

If all of these conditions are met, the resulting scaling is called a *ratio scale*. Ratio scales are relatively rare when psychological traits are scaled because of the difficulty in defining the zero point. While objects approaching zero height are relatively easy to find (e.g., very thin paper), persons approaching zero intelligence are hard to imagine. Even if an object such as a rock is defined as having zero intelligence, the equal steps of intelligence required to get the interval properties of the scale are difficult to determine. For example, is the difference in intelligence between a dog and a rock the same as the difference between a person and a dog? At some point in the future we may be able to develop psychological scales with ratio scale properties, but currently the best that can be expected are interval scales.

Definition of Validity

Up to this point, various scale types have been defined, and the reliability of a numerical assignment has been defined as the proportion of overlap between the numerically scaled variable and the natural variable. In some cases, a scaled variable can be formed that has properties that do not conform at all to the properties of the natural variable in question. In these cases, there is more of a problem than occasionally misclassifying a person—the sets clearly do not match. This case is illustrated in Figure 3.5. When the sets do not match, the scaling does not result in a *valid* measure of the natural variable. The scaled variable does not give useful information about an entity's membership in the properties of the natural variable. Obviously, the most important task in forming a scale is insuring that a valid scale is the result. The next section of this chapter deals with the techniques that are available for forming scales and checking their validity.

TECHNIQUES FOR SCALE FORMATION

The purpose of psychological scaling techniques is to assign numbers to individuals in such a way that a scaling is the result. That is, a rule must be developed for assigning the numbers in such a way that most of the persons in the same property set of the natural variable are assigned the same

Properties in the Natural Variable

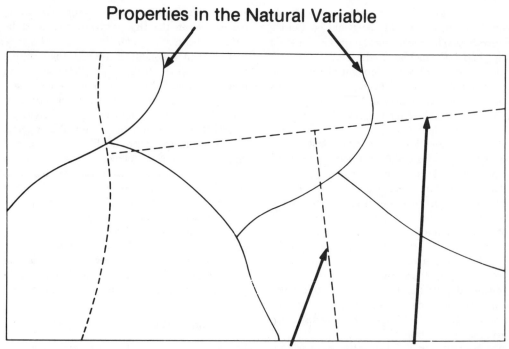

Properties in the Scaled Variable

Figure 3.5. Example of an invalid scaling.

number. Many different techniques have been developed for this purpose. All of the techniques define a scaled variable through numerical assignment and conceptually define a natural variable. A sampling of procedures will now be presented that vary substantially in the way in which a scaling is performed.

Guttman's Scalogram Approach

According to Guttman's scalogram approach to the formation of a scale, the properties in a natural variable can be ordered in such a way that individuals in a higher level property include all of the characteristics of those in lower level properties plus at least one more. That is, if the properties in a natural variable are labeled in increasing order starting with a_1 to a_n, then those individuals in property a_i have all of the characteristics of the persons in properties a_1 to a_{i-1} plus at least one more. The task involved in scale formation is to find a series of behaviors such that all those persons who exhibit a particular set of behaviors belong to the same property, and those in the next higher property exhibit at least one additional behavior.

The classic example of a Guttman scale is the measure of fear developed for use with soldiers in World War II (Stouffer, 1950). For that scale, those who did not experience "violent pounding of the heart" formed the lowest property set, while those who did formed the next higher property in the natural variable. If a sinking feeling in the stomach as well as a violent pounding of the heart were reported, the person belonged in the next higher property. If, in addition to the other two characteristics, trembling all over were reported, the person belonged in the next higher property level on the natural variable "fear" (see Figure 3.6). In all, 10 fear properties were defined in this way.

The scaled variable corresponding to the natural variable was formed by simply counting up the number of characteristics that were present. If no characteristics were present, the person was assigned a score of 0. If only violent pounding of the heart were present, a score of 1 was assigned. If both violent pounding of the heart and being sick to the stomach were reported, a score of 2 was assigned. Because of the cumulative nature of this type of natural variable, the case where a person

Property Characteristics

None	Violent pounding of heart	Violent pounding Sick to stomach	Violent pounding Sick Trembling all over

Figure 3.6. Characteristics of the properties of the natural variable "fear."

is sick to the stomach but does not have a pounding heart occurs infrequently. Therefore, the meaning of a score of one is unambiguous.

The scaled variable is formed by grouping together all of the individuals who have been assigned the same score into a property set. If all of the individuals with the same score have the same level of the trait (belong to the same property of the natural variable), a scaling results. Usually this scaling is of at least the ordinal level because of the cumulative nature of the Guttman procedure. If the added characteristics that distinguish the different levels of the properties indicate an equal amount of change in the trait level from a psychological point of view, an interval scale is formed.

The relationship between the properties in the natural variable and the presence of characteristics is usually shown by a two-way table. Across the top of the table are listed the characteristics of the individuals that are used to classify them into the properties. Down the side of the table are listed the properties. In the body of the table, a 1 is placed at the intersection of a property and a characteristic if all persons in the property have the characteristic. An example of such a table is presented in Figure 3.7. If all persons in a property do not have the characteristic, a 0 is placed in the table. If a Guttman scale is present, the 1s in the table form a triangular pattern when the properties and characteristics are arranged by order of magnitude.

Characteristics

Properties		A	B	C	D	E
	5	1	1	1	1	1
	4	0	1	1	1	1
	3	0	0	1	1	1
	2	0	0	0	1	1
	1	0	0	0	0	1
	0	0	0	0	0	0

Figure 3.7. Representation of a perfect Guttman scale.

In reality, we do not know the composition of the properties of the natural variable and must substitute the properties of the scaled variable for the rows of the table. In this case, the perfect triangular form may not be present. To the extent that the relationship between the scaled variable and the characteristics cannot be put into the triangular form, a scaling has not taken place. There are two possible reasons why a proper scaling might not be accomplished. First, the trait for which the measure is being developed may not easily be put into the hierarchical form required by the Guttman procedure. For example, holding liberal political beliefs does not mean that a person also holds all the beliefs of a person of conservative bent, even though the properties in the natural variable defined by political beliefs can generally be ordered along a continuum. The second reason a scaling may not be possible is that the properties of the scaled variable do not match the properties of the natural variable because of errors in the assignment of the numerical values. A person may not report a characteristic when it is really present, an observer may miss an important activity, or a record may be inaccurately kept.

In order to judge whether the scaled variable matches the natural variable sufficiently closely, Guttman (1950) has suggested a statistic called the coefficient of reproducibility. This coefficient is simply the proportion of ones and zeros in the "person × characteristic" table that are in the appropriate place. If a one or zero is not in the appropriate place, the perfect triangular form will not be possible. The number of inappropriately placed zeros and ones is given by the number of ones below the diagonal and the number of zeros above the diagonal. In the table given below (Figure 3.8), the number of inappropriately placed zeros and ones is 3 out of a total of 30 entries. The number of appropriate values is then $30 - 3 = 27$. The coefficient of reproducibility is given by $27/30 = .90$. Guttman felt that the coefficient of reproducibility should be at least .90 for the scaling to be considered reasonable.

Since Guttman's early work, procedures for determining the quality of a Guttman scale have become much more elaborate (See McIver & Carmines, 1981; White & Saltz, 1957, for example). However, these procedures are all conceptually related to the coefficient of reproducibility. They all check to determine whether the properties of the scaled variable have the cumulative relationship with the observed characteristics.

All of the ideas presented concerning the Guttman Scalogram analysis can be used to determine whether this approach should be used to form a scale. The first step in this process is to evaluate the properties of the natural variable in question to determine if they have the necessary cumulative relationship. If they do not, the Guttman procedure should not be used. One of the other methods given later in this chapter may be appropriate. If the cumulative relationship exists among the properties, the next step is to determine the characteristics that distinguish the properties of the natural variable. For example, a particular type of self-destructive behavior may distinguish one type of psychological disorder from another. This behavior can then be used as an item to assign the score needed to form the scaled variable. Usually a number of different behaviors are tentatively selected, and only those that can be used to form the triangular pattern of responses shown above are used to form the scale. It is usually difficult to find more than five or six behaviors that have the required cumulative relationship.

Once the behaviors have been selected and data have been collected on the presence or absence of the behavior for a new group of individuals, a variant of the reproducibility coefficient is computed to determine if a reasonable Guttman scale has been obtained. If this coefficient is sufficiently high, the scaling is accepted.

Thurstone's Method of Equal-Appearing Intervals

Guttman's method of scale formation is fairly limited in its application because of the requirement of cumulative properties in the natural variable.

Characteristics

1	0	1	1	1
0	1	1	1	1
Persons 0	0	1	1	1
0	0	1	0	1
0	0	0	1	0
0	0	0	0	1

Figure 3.8. An imperfect Guttman scale.

As was mentioned previously, many natural variables do not have the cumulative property. Yet, the properties in the natural variable are distinguishable. In order to identify the persons belonging to each property, Thurstone (1927) developed a model of the interaction between a person and statements describing possible attitudes toward an object. Based on the theory presented there, Thurstone's model indicates that a person who is a member of a particular property set will endorse some attitude statements and not others. Persons in a different property set will endorse a different, although possibly overlapping, set of alternatives. Those persons who endorse similar sets of statements are hypothesized to belong to the same property.

By merely sorting persons into categories on the basis of the responses to a set of attitude statements, a variable can be defined, but this variable does not contain any information about the level of an attitude toward an object. All that is obtained is groups of individuals, each of which is composed of persons with similar attitudes. In order to add the information about the relative level of attitude into the scaling, Thurstone suggests that the attitude statements themselves first be scaled.

The scaling of the attitude statements is performed in a very straightforward manner. A set of 11 properties is hypothesized for the natural variable of interest. These properties range from sets of statements that are very unfavorable to the object of interest to those that are very favorable. The sixth property is assumed to contain those statements that are neutral. The 11 properties can be arranged in order from very unfavorable through neutral to very favorable. This set of properties is the scaled variable for the attitude staements.

In order to determine which statements belong in each of the property sets, a number of judges (Thurstone used 300) are asked to sort the statements (usually over 100) into the appropriate sets (see Figure 3.9). The judges were instructed to perform this sorting on the basis of the favorableness or unfavorableness of the statements, not on the statements' level of agreement with the judges' position. If the statements differed solely on their degree of favorableness, and if the judges were totally consistent in their judgments, it would be expected that a statement would be put into the same property set by each judge. In reality, variations in the classifications are found, which Thurstone called discriminal dispersion. In other words, the placement of the statements into the property sets is not perfectly reliable.

Since there usually is variation in the placement of the statements, a procedure is needed for forming a scaled variable using the statements. The procedure suggested by Thurstone first assigns the numbers 1 to 11 to the properties. When a statement is sorted into one of the properties by a judge, the corresponding number is assigned to the statement. After all of the judges classify all of the statements, the median and quartile deviation are computed using the numbers assigned to each statement.

If the quartile deviation for a statement is large, the statement is ambiguous in some sense, as indicated by the fact that the judges could not agree on the property set into which the statement should be placed. For a statement with a low quartile deviation, the median value is used as the scale value for the statement. The numbers that are assigned in this way are used to form the scaled variable for the statements. Two statements that have been assigned the same number are assumed to fall into the same property set. The

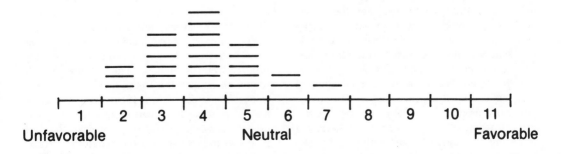

Figure 3.9. Judgments for a statement with a scale value of about 4.

statements and their associated scale values are used to produce the instrument that is used to assign numerical values to individuals and thereby form the scaled variable for people.

Recall that individuals who endorse roughly the same sets of statements are assumed to come from the same property on the natural variable. If the mean scale value for these statements were computed, each person in the same property set would obtain the same mean scale value. Thus, Thurstone decided to form the scaled variable on people by assigning each person the mean scale value of the statements that they endorsed. In order to have a sufficient range of statements for all the persons who are being measured, Thurstone suggested producing the measuring instrument by selecting 2 statements from each of the 11 property sets. This results in an attitude measuring device consisting of 22 statements. To use it, a person is asked to simply check the statements that they agree with. Their score is the average scale value for the statements endorsed.

Of course, there is some error in the procedure resulting from the fact that persons can agree with different sets of statements and obtain approximately the same score. To the extent that this occurs, the scaled variable does not match the natural variable and the results of the scaling are unreliable.

The level of scaling of the scores obtained from the Thurstone equal-appearing interval procedure depends on the quality of the judgments made concerning the attitude statements. Clearly, a person who endorses favorable statements has a more positive attitude toward the topic in question than one who endorses less favorable statements. Therefore, the procedure results in at least an ordinal scale. Whether an interval scale is achieved or not depends on whether the 11 properties of the natural variable used to classify the attitude statements are equally spaced. Thurstone and Chave (1929) contended that the judges would subjectively make adjacent properties equally distant when they classified the items. To the extent that this conjecture is true, the scaling procedure results in an interval scale.

At this point, an example of the application of the Thurstone equal-appearing interval technique may prove useful in clarifying the steps in this procedure. Suppose it were desirable to develop a measuring instrument for determining attitudes toward nuclear power. The first step in the process would be to write over 100 statements that

varied in their degree of favorableness toward nuclear power. These should be statements of opinion, not fact. For example, the statement, "Nuclear power will vastly improve the quality of life," is a favorable statement. "The use of nuclear power will destroy this country" is a negative staement. After these statements have been produced, several hundred individuals should be asked to rate the statements on their favorableness toward nuclear power using the 11-point scale. Next, the median and quartile deviation of each statement are computed. Those statements with large quartile deviations are dropped and, from the statements remaining, two statements are selected from each of the 11 categories. For this purpose, the median for the statement is used as a scale value. The resulting 22 statements comprise the attitude measuring device for nuclear power.

To use the measuring instrument that has been developed, individuals are asked to check the statements to which they agree. Each person's attitude score is the average of the scale values for the statements that they have checked.

Item Response Theory

Within the last 10 years, a new approach to the formation of scales of measurement has become popular. This approach, called item response theory or IRT (Lord, 1980), has been applied mostly for aptitude and achievement measurement, but it can also be used for other types of psychological assessment problems. As with the Guttman and the Thurstone procedures, this scaling procedure assumes that the properties in the natural variable can be arranged along a continuum based on the magnitude of the trait possessed by the persons in each property set. If a test item is administered to the persons in one of these properties, this model assumes that all of the persons will have the same probability of responding correctly, but that they may not all give the same response to the item because of errors in measurement.

For example, suppose the item "Define democracy" is given to all of the persons in a particular property set. Because of errors in the persons' responses, ambiguities in the question, problems in deciding if the answer is correct or incorrect, and so on, some of the persons miss the item, and others answer it correctly. However, the IRT model assumes that all persons in that property set have the same probability of answering the item correctly. Persons in a different property set will have a different probability of a correct response. If the probability of a correct response for a person to an item is known, then the person can be classified into the appropriate property of the natural variable.

One of the basic assumptions that is usually made for IRT models is that if the properties are ordered according to the probability of correct response to an item, they are also ordered according to increasing ability on the natural variable. That is, the probability of a correct response is assumed to have a monotonically increasing relationship to the ability of interest. Thus, if persons can be placed into the properties on the basis of the probability of correct response, at least an ordinal scale results.

If the natural variable has properties that are evenly spaced, the relationship between the ability properties and the probability of a correct response for persons in a property is assumed to have a particular form. The mathematical forms commonly used for this purpose are the one-parameter logistic model (Rasch, 1960), the two-parameter logistic model (Birnbaum, 1968), the three-parameter logistic model (Lord, 1980), and the normal ogive model (Lord, 1952). The usual practice is to assume one of these forms for all of the items in the measuring instrument to be produced. Figure 3.10 presents an example of the

relationship typically found between the properties of a natural variable and the probability of a correct response.

As with the two other procedures described earlier, the purpose of this procedure is to determine to which property in the natural variable a person belongs. If the probability of correct responses for a person to a single item could be observed, the determination of the appropriate property could be accomplished with one item. Of course, when a person is administered an item, a discrete score is obtained (usually a 0 or a 1)— no probability is observed. Therefore, a person cannot be classified into a property using one item if IRT methods are used. Instead, an instrument composed of many items is administered, and a person is classified into the property that has the highest probability of giving the observed responses to the set of items.

For example, suppose two items are administered to the person in two different property sets. Suppose further that the probability of a correct response for the two items for persons in the two properties are given in Figure 3.11. If a person were administered the two items and answered the first incorrectly and the second correctly, that set of responses would have a probability of $(1 - .1) \times .6 = .54$ for those in property A but a probability of $(1 - .7) \times .9 = .27$ for those in

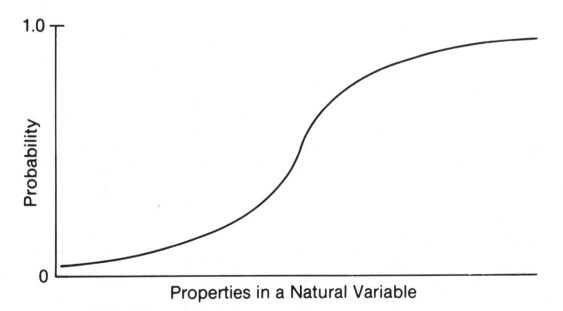

Figure 3.10. Typical relationship between the properties of a natural variable and a correct response.

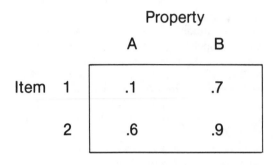

Figure 3.11. The probability of a correct response to two items for persons in different properties.

property B. Since the probability of the responses was higher for property A, the examinee would be placed in property A. This principle of classification is called maximum likelihood ability estimation.

In practice, the properties of the scaled variables are indexed by numerical values, and the probability of a correct response to each item is determined by a mathematical formula. For example, the formula for the two-parameter logistic latent trait model is given by:

$$P(x_{ij} = 1) = \frac{e^{a_i(\theta_j - b_i)}}{1 + e^{a_i(\theta_j - b_i)}},$$

where $P(x_{ij} = 1)$ is the probability of a correct response for person j on item i, e is the constant 2.718. . ., θ_j is the ability of person j, and a_i and b_i are the item parameters that control the shape of the mathematical function. The estimate of θ_j indicates the property on the scaled variable to which the person belongs.

The values of a_i and b_i for an item are determined in much the same way as the scale values in Thurstone's equal appearing interval procedure. A set of test items are administered to a large number of individuals and values of a_i and b_i are computed from the responses. The values of b_i are related to the proportion responding correctly to the item, and the values of a_i are related to the correlation of the item score with the values of the scaled variable. These values are determined from a scaling of the item along two dimensions, while the ability estimates are a scaling of the people taking the items. The process of determining the

values of a_i and b_i for a set of items is called *item calibration*.

Using item response theory for the process of scaling is conceptually more complicated than for the Guttman or Thurstone procedures because of the complicated mathematics involved. However, in practice the procedures are simpler because computer programs are available to perform all of the analyses. For example, suppose we want to measure a personality characteristic by administering a series of items with instructions to check those that apply to the examinee. If this scale is to be developed using item response theory, the items would first be administered to a large number of individuals who vary on the trait of interest. These data are analyzed using one of the available calibration programs to determine the item parameters. The calibration program is selected depending on which of the item response theory models is assumed. If the items are assumed to vary only in difficulty, the one-parameter logistic model is appropriate, and a program like BICAL (Wright, Mead, & Bell, 1979) can be used to obtain the item parameters. If the items are assumed to also vary in their discriminating power, the two-parameter logistic model is appropriate, and the BILOG program can be used for calibration. Finally, if there is a non-zero base rate for positive responses to the items, the three-parameter logistic model is appropriate, and the LOGIST (Wingersky, Barton, & Lord, 1982) program can be used for item calibration. Of course, new programs are constantly being produced for these methods, and the literature should be checked for the most current versions for a particular model before performing the item calibration.

After the items are calibrated, the items for the measuring instrument are selected. A procedure similar to Thurstone's can be used if the population to be measured ranges widely on the trait of interest. The items may also be selected on the discriminating power if high precision is required. Many of the computer programs also give a measure of fit between the models and the data. These fit measures may also be used to select items to insure that the model being used is appropriate.

Once the items for the instrument are selected, an estimation program or a conversion table can be used to obtain an estimate of the level of the trait for each person. In general, as with the Guttman and Thurstone procedures, those persons with similar patterns of responses will get a similar trait estimate. These trait estimates form the scaled variable for the trait in question. As with any of the other procedures, this scaled variable must be checked to determine whether it matches the natural variable and therefore yields a reliable and valid measure.

Likert Scaling Technique

Another commonly used procedure for forming attitude measuring instruments was developed by Likert (1932). This procedure also begins by assuming a natural variable with properties that can be ordered according to the magnitude of the trait possessed by the persons in each property set. The form of the item used by the Likert procedure is a statement concerning the concept in question, followed by five answer choices ranging from strongly agree to strongly disagree. It is assumed that the five answer choices divide the natural variable into five classes that are ordered with respect to the attitude toward the concept.

If only one item is used in the measuring instrument, the five categories would be numbered from 1 (strongly disagree) to 5 (strongly agree) and each person is assigned the score corresponding to the response selected. If the statement being rated has a negative connotation, the scoring is reversed. The score assignment forms the scaled variable for this procedure.

In reality, more than one item is usually used with the Likert procedure. Each of these items is assumed to divide up the natural variable in a similar, but not exactly the same, way. Thus, for two items the natural variable may be divided up as shown in Figure 3.12. In this figure, the boundaries between the sets of properties are not exactly aligned. Therefore, it is possible for one person to respond with strongly agree responses to two items, while another person may respond with strongly agree and agree. The latter person has a

slightly lower trait level than the former. To indicate this fact on the scaled variable, the scores on the two items are simply summed. The first person receives a score of 10 on the scaled variable while the second receives a 9.

As more items are added to the instrument, the score for each person is obtained by simply summing the numbers assigned to each response category. Because the division of the natural variables into five categories is seldom exactly the same, each additional item brings about a greater subdivision of the natural variable. If 20 items were used in an instrument, the natural variable could be divided up into as many as $(5-1)20+1 = 81$ categories. Each of these would be assigned a score which is the sum of the item scores. The persons with the same score would constitute properties in the scaled variable. To the extent that the properties in the scaled variable match those of the natural variable, a reliable and valid scaling is the result.

Although for the 20-item example given above each score is assumed to result from only one pattern of responses (one region on the natural variable), in reality there are many ways to get the same score. A total of $5^{20} = 9.5 \times 10^{13}$ patterns of response are possible. To the extent that other than the 81 mentioned above are present, the underlying model does not hold. These response patterns are usually attributed to errors of measurement and result in a mismatch between the scaled score and natural variable reducing the reliability of the results of the scaling. The Likert procedure tends to be robust to the violations, however, and items that result in many inappropriate responses are usually removed at a pretesting phase in instrument construction. This is done by correlating the score for each item with the total score on the instrument and dropping those that have a low correlation.

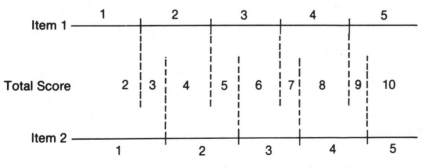

Figure 3.12. Score categories for a two-item Likert scale.

The level of scaling obtained from the Likert procedure is rather difficult to determine. The scale is clearly at least ordinal. Those persons from the higher level properties in the natural variable are expected to get higher scores than those persons from lower properties. Whether an interval scale is obtained depends on a strong assumption. In order to achieve an interval scale, the properties on the scaled variable have to correspond to differences in the trait on the natural variable. Since it seems unlikely that the categories formed by the misalignment of the five response categories will all be equal, the interval scale assumption seems unlikely. However, as the number of items on the instrument is increased, each property of the scaled variable gets fairly small, and the differences in category size may be unimportant. Practical applications of the Likert procedure seem to show that the level of scaling for this method is not an important issue. That is, treating the scores as if they were on an interval scale does not seem to cause serious harm.

An example of the construction of an attitude scale using the Likert procedure should clarify all of the issues discussed. As with the Thurstone procedure, the first step in producing a Likert-scaled attitude instrument is to write more statements about the concept of interest than are expected to be used. In this case, about twice as many statements as are to be used should be enough. These should be statements of opinion, not fact, and both positive and negative statements should be included in approximately equal numbers. The five response categories (strongly agree, agree, neither agree nor disagree, disagree, strongly disagree) are then appended to each statement. For positive statements the categories are scored 5, 4, 3, 2, and 1, and for negative statements they are scored 1, 2, 3, 4, and 5.

For example, if a measure of body image were desired, one item might be:

I have a well proportioned body.
  (a) strongly disagree
  (b) disagree
  (c) neither agree nor disagree
  (d) agree
  (e) strongly agree.

A negatively phrased item might be:

I am noticeably overweight.
  (a) strongly disagree
  (b) disagree
  (c) neither agree nor disagree
  (d) agree
  (e) strongly agree.

For the first item (a) would be scored as 1, (b) as 2, (c) as 3, (d) as 4, and (e) as 5. For the second item, the scoring would be reversed: (a) 5, (b) 4, (c) 3, (d) 2, (e) 1.

The attitude items are next tried out on a sample of approximately 100 individuals who represent the population of interest. For each statement, the correlation is computed between the score on the statement and the sum of the scores on all of the statements. If the correlation is negative, the phrasing for the statement has probably been misclassified as to whether it is positive or negative. If it has not been misclassified, the statement should be deleted from the instrument as being ambiguous. Statements with low correlations (less than .3) are also dropped from consideration because the correlation indicates that these statements are not forming a scaled variable that is consistent with the other items. From the items that meet the above criteria, 10 to 20 are selected with about equal numbers that are positively and negatively phrased. Both positively and negatively phrased items are needed to reduce response bias. The items selected constitute the measuring device.

THE REQUIREMENTS FOR SCALE FORMATION

In the formation of measurement devices presented, there is a common starting point for all the techniques. In all cases, a natural variable is hypothesized to exist. Without this initial step, the concept of instrument validity is meaningless because the focus of the instrument is unknown. Once the natural variable has been defined, the scale construction task becomes one of devising a method for determining which persons belong in each of the property sets of the natural variable. Conceptually this could be done by developing a detailed description of the persons in each property set and then observing each individual until he/she could be accurately classified into a property. This is essentially the procedure that is used for some infant intelligence scales.

The more common procedure is to develop a series of items and use these items to obtain a highly structured sample of behavior (i.e., item responses). Those persons who exhibit similar behavior are assigned the same numerical score and are assumed to belong to the same property of the natural variable. For the Guttman procedure, behaviors that are cumulative in nature are used, and the numerical assignment rule is based on a count of the number of behaviors present. For the Thurstone procedure, the behavior is the endorsement of an attitude statement, and the numerical assignment rule is based on the average scale value of the items endorsed. The IRT approach is very similar to Thurstone's procedure in that the items are first scaled, and the results are used to determine the estimate of the trait level for a person. For Likert's procedure, the behavior used in the scaling is the rating of attitude statements, and the numerical assignment is based on the sum of the ratings.

Note that for all the procedures some sort of prescreening of items is required. The Thurstone and IRT procedures require a scaling of items and some measure of fit to the underlying model. The Guttman and Likert procedures also use a measure of fit: the reproducibility coefficient in the former case and the item total score correlation in the latter. The presence of these procedures for evaluating the quality of the items in the measuring instruments reflects the fact that merely assigning numbers to persons does not result in the meaningful measurement of a trait. The numbers must be assigned in a way that is consistent with the natural variable. The procedures described for each of the methods provide a check on the consistency. Even when the scales produced by these methods are shown to be internally consistent, this fact does not insure that measurements obtained from the instruments are valid. The measures must still be shown to interact with other variables in the way suggested by the natural variable. If this is not the case, a good measure has been developed of some unknown quality.

REFERENCES

Adams, E.W., Fagot, R., & Robinson, R.E. (1965). A theory of appropriate statistics. *Psychometrika*, 30, 99–127.

Birnbaum, A. (1968). Some latent trait models and their use in inferring an examinee's ability. In F.M. Lord, & M.R. Novick, (Eds.), *Statistical theories of mental test scores*. Reading, MA: Addison-Wesley.

Galton, F. (1870). *Hereditary genius: An inquiry into its laws and consequences*. London: D. Appleton.

Guttman, L.I. (1950). The basis for scalogram analysis. In S.A. Stouffer, L. Guttman, E.A. Sushman, P.W. Lagarsfeld, S.A. Star, & J.A. Clausen (Eds.), *Studies in social psychology–World War II, Volume IV*. Princeton, NJ: Princeton University Press.

Labovitz, S. (1970). The assignment of numbers to rank order categories. *American Sociological Review*, 35, 515–524.

Likert, R. (1932). A technique for the measurement of attitudes. *Archives of Psychology*, 140, 44–53.

Lord, F.M. (1980). *Applications of item response theory to practical testing problems*. Hillsdale, NJ: Lawrence Erlbaum Associates.

Lord, F.M. (1952). A theory of test scores. *Psychometric Monograph*, 7.

McIver, J.P. & Carmines, E.G. (1981). *Unidimensional scaling*. Beverly Hills, CA: Sage Publications.

Rasch, G. (1960). *Probabilistic models for some intelligence and attainment tests*. Copenhagen: Danish Institute for Educational Research.

Rozeboom, W.W. (1966). Scaling theory and its nature of measurement. *Synthese*, 16, 170–233.

Stevens, S.S. (1959). Measurement. In C.W. Churchsman (Ed.), *Measurement: Definitions and theories*. New York: Wiley.

Stouffer, S.A. (1950). An overview of the contributions to scaling and scale theory. In S.A. Stouffer, L. Guttman, E.A. Sushman, P.W. Layersfeld, S.A. Star, & J.A. Clausen (Eds.), *Studies in social psychology–World War II, Volume IV*. Princeton, NJ: Princeton University Press.

Thurstone, L.L. (1927). Psychophysical analysis. *American Journal of Psychology*, 38, 368–389.

Thurstone, L.L. & Chave, E.J. (1929). *The measurement of attitude*. Chicago: University of Chicago Press.

White, B.W. & Saltz, E. (1957). Measurement of reproducibility. *Psychological Bulletin*, 54, 81–99.

Wingersky, M.S., Barton, M.A., & Lord, F.M. (1982, February). *LOGIST user's guide*. Princeton, NJ: Educational Testing Service.

Wright, B.D., Mead, R.J. & Bell, S.R. (1979). *BICAL: Calibrating items with the Rasch model* (Research Memorandum No. 23B). Chicago: University of Chicago, Department of Education, Statistical Laboratory.

PART III
ASSESSMENT OF INTELLIGENCE

4 INTELLECTUAL ASSESSMENT OF CHILDREN

Irla Lee Zimmerman
James M. Woo-Sam

INTRODUCTION

Individual intellectual assessment can be defined as the process by which a trained professional collects information about an individual that allows for the identification of skills or disabilities that enhance or interfere with the subject's functioning in his/her environment. The intellectual assessment of children was the original and for years the primary occupation of most psychologists. Historically, such a role could be dated from the construction of the first Binet-Simon Scale at the turn of the century (Binet & Simon, 1905). This instrument was the first to demonstrate that intellectual skills were measurable.

The practical implications were quickly realized in America, where, as in France, the test (translated and modified by various authors) was used to identify children who could profit in a regular classroom setting from those who had special educational requirements. The most successful modification was the Stanford Binet developed by Terman and his associates in 1908. This scale is still in use today, the latest revision known as the Stanford Binet LM (Terman & Merrill, 1973).

Once the basic idea was discovered that intellectual skills could be measured by tasks involving the use of mentation, other scales were soon developed, the most successful of this later group being the Wechsler series.

It is apparent that testing has thrived. Public Law 94-142, recently enacted by Congress, insures that testing will continue to be in demand, as schools adhere to the basic premise that education must be tailored to the individual intellectual needs of the child. Today as many as 16,000 psychologists working in schools find the intellectual assessment of children their primary occupation (Reschly, 1981), while thousands more are employed in universities, clinics, hospitals, or private practice devoted to the study and/or service of children.

Assessment typically occurs in a medical, school, or preschool setting and is initiated by a parent or teacher concerned about the child's functioning. In a medical setting, assessment may explore the effects of a physical handicap or trauma such as brain damage (Eiser, 1981). Clinics often need to study children with emotional problems to determine how their disturbance impinges on their cognitive abilities or the extent to which they might profit from specific kinds of intervention such as medication or play therapy (Stanton, Wilson, & Brumback, 1981). Assessment may also be used to determine possible risk factors of importance for children where early intervention is deemed necessary (Harder, Kokes, Fisher, Cole, & Perkins, 1982; Ziger & Tricket, 1978). Or concern might be based on a desire to seek the proper setting for the child, such as early school entry, grade acceleration, or a program for the gifted and talented (Fell & Fell, 1982). The most common referral is because of difficulties in learning that would require specific teaching procedures, tutoring, retention, or special class placement (Salvia & Ysseldyke, 1978).

Even though children are typically referred for intellectual assessment because of problems, one of the most encouraging results of administering a test of intelligence is the discovery of skills and strengths that had never been discovered in the home or classroom. In fact, intelligence test results can far surpass the observations, hunches, or impressions with which they may be replaced. As an example, in a recent study, Hartsough, Elias, and Wheeler (1977) reported that none of the children whose teachers nominated them as possibly retarded or gifted was subsequently found to be eligible for these programs. In other words, intelligence testing is called upon in a variety of settings to meet the varied needs of children.

At the same time that tests of intelligence are in the most widespread use, criticisms of them have reached a peak, as witnessed by litigations in several federal and state courts and the ban on such tests in California (Reschly, 1980). The history of this movement can be traced to the period when tests of intelligence were introduced. Their pragmatic nature appealed to the American public during the early years of the century. The mental age concept was instantly accepted, and the (ratio) IQ became a catchword in America, gaining acceptance as a "scientific" label that many believed immutable.

Inherent in this trend was the tendency to confuse *intelligence*, the kind of behavior the tests were intended to assess, with the scores (IQs) obtained from such tests, a step leading to "the illusion of objectivity" (Ryan, 1972). Meanwhile, a growing interest in eugenics, or the influences that improve hereditary qualities of a race, led some to turn to IQ tests as offering "scientific" evidence for the intellectual inferiority of some groups. Even Terman became a eugenic Frankenstein, falling under the spell of his monster. Noting the lower scores of "Indians, Mexicans, and Negros" on the first Stanford Binet, he mused that "the whole question of racial differences will have to be taken up anew. . . . [They] constitute a grave problem because of their prolific breeding" (1916, p. 6). To some, at least, the intelligence test had

moved from representing an assessment of a child's educational potential at a particular point in time to representing innate fixed biological limitations not only of individuals, but of particular ethnic and racial groups (Blank, 1982). The issue of genetic, racial, and ethnic differences was to be challenged, as psychologists pointed out the cultural and socioeconomic factors confounding such simplistic theorizing. As early as 1914, Stern had noted that intellectual tests differentiated between children of different socioeconomic status, quite apart from race (Stern, 1914). Eells (1951) speculated that minority children were unfairly judged on the basis of test items requiring cultural experiences different from their own.

By the time of the Civil Rights movement, the use of intelligence tests began to be attacked by those concerned with the fairness of their use with low socioeconomic and ethnic minority persons. Serious attempts to construct tests that were "culture free" or "fair" failed to meet this goal (Samuda, 1975). As Marquart and Bailey (1955) pointed out at the time, it is difficult to select items that will be equally familiar to individuals of all areas and all social groups. Even if this goal were to be met, the validity of such tests would still be in question (Noll, 1960). This, indeed, became the issue. The culture fair movement led to a reevaluation of tests of intelligence in terms of their goals. Returning to the original focus of Binet, tests were seen as of value to the extent to which they aided in the assessment of potential learning ability and the prediction of school success. However, critics saw intelligence tests as classifying children as mildly retarded and noted the extent to which minority children were apparently overrepresented in special classes. As the courts were called in to resolve this dilemma, law suits in California and Illinois utilized the same testimony to arrive at diametrically opposed conclusions, disavowing or affirming the use of intelligence tests. Meanwhile, Congress attempted to answer such stalemates by demanding "nondiscriminatory assessment" (Oakland, 1977). The irony of the situation, as Bersoff (1980) points out in his review of the Larry P. case, is that the court decision in California has condemned intelligence tests while implying that such tests will have to be relied on in the future.

To resolve this problem, those who are concerned with the welfare and education of children must look for ways in which intelligence tests can be properly selected and constructively used to achieve the goals mandated for testing. In the following pages, we review the current status of intellectual assessment of children, focusing on the process involved, including the contribution of the examiner, examinee, and the testing situation. The chapter concludes with a review of the major tests in use for individual assessment and an analysis of their adequacy to meet the requirements of nondiscriminatory assessment.

THE ASSESSMENT PROCEDURE

In evaluating the intellectual functioning of children there are four major sources of variables which impact upon the process. These relate to those governed by (a) the examiner, (b) the examinee, (c) the conditions during testing, and (d) the instruments used. We shall consider these in turn.

Examiner Variables

It goes without saying that the examiner must be trained and skillful to obtain the most meaningful results from an intelligence test. This fact has long been recognized, as can be noted in this statement by Stern (1914):

> It must be understood that tests of intelligence are not easy to conduct. Their administration demands extended practice, psychological training, and a critical mind. Thus, for instance, the average teacher, whose work has been with the wholly different methods of pedagogical questioning and examining, is very apt to apply psychological tests in those forms in which their value would be positively illusory. If, accordingly, the use of tests for practical purposes shall attain any large currency, the training of a specially psychologically drilled personnel will become a necessity. School psychologists would then take their place side by side with the school physician. (pp. 11–12)

But skill is not the only important variable. Unlike measurement in the physical sciences where personality factors play a minimal role, the interaction between examiner and examinee can be crucial, and therefore the examiner's personality as it contributes to or influences the interaction

must be considered. Binet himself warned against the subtle effects the examiner may have on test behavior (Bersoff, 1973). Understanding the contribution of the examiner is critical in a situation where the examiner becomes, in part, the testing instrument. In an attempt to refine the examination process, Schafer (1954) described a number of styles noted in the personality of examiners. Such examiner aspects as dependency, hostility, and masochism must inevitably influence the perception of the task as seen by the child or the results as interpreted by the examiner. Recognition of these factors as they impinge upon the child's responses and reactions to the examination permit the interpretation of test results in a way that transcends whatever the derived scores may be. Inherent in this approach is the need for awareness of the ways different examiners interact with children and what role this plays in eliciting a response from the child. As Glasser and Zimmerman (1967) point out, a rather motherly, easygoing woman examiner would be quick to note that she is reacted to as an ogre by a particular child, while a practical, no-nonsense male examiner would be concerned about the self-control of a youngster who sat on the edge of the desk, whistled loudly, and accused the examiner of tricking him. In both instances, the examiners would be judging behaviors in terms of their congruence with that usually seen in their examining sessions. Such a process permits the examiner to obtain information about the examinee far beyond that gained in test scores alone, and such information used predictively can outstrip that based on test scores alone (Zimmerman, Bernstein, & Eiduson, 1983).

Easier to explore, if not control, are examiner aspects that are associated with such variables as vulnerability to positive and negative halo effects. A series of studies have explored the influence of such variables. For example, if an examinee is perceived as "bright," will the examiner be apt to give more credit for equivocal responses than if he/she is perceived as "dull?" Sattler, Hillex, and Neher (1970) found such a halo effect, while Saunders and Vitro (1971) did not. When the WISC-R was used, no halo effects were seen in scoring, whether the responses were in a hypothetical protocol attributed to a bright or dull subject (Goetz, 1978), or in the actual examination of children of average intelligence who were placed in the experimental conditions randomly

(Sneed, 1976). It is perhaps a tribute to the objectivity of the instrument used (typically the WISC-R) that examiner experience, sex, or personality styles did not seem to effect scoring accuracy (Grossman, 1978; Sattler, 1973).

Examinee

Just as the role of the examiner influences the test situation, the role of the examinee is equally important. The child approaching the test situation brings with him/her a set of attitudes, developed through and reflecting such aspects as individual problem-solving activities, emotions, and perceptions (Gibson, 1978). Certain of these limit success on a standard test. For example, children rated as impulsive rather than reflective tend to score lower on intelligence tests (Brannigan & Ash, 1977). Highly anxious children characteristically perform at a lower level than do low anxious children (Carrubba, 1976). On the other hand, children whose IQ scores increased during the periods between 3 and 12 years of age were found to be self-assured and competitive, while those showing losses in IQ were seen as passive and dependent (Sontag, Baker, & Nelson, 1958).

Test Conditions

Under ideal conditions, the test situation should be standardized. It should be possible to specify (and duplicate) what is being tested and the conditions of testing. This insures repeatability of results, a model that clearly fits the physical sciences. In psychological testing, the objective is less easily defined or achieved. However, awareness of the different factors that may influence test results allows the examiner to consider their importance and make allowance for them. The following aspects are among those that should be considered.

Race and Sex of Examiner

Whether children should be tested by an examiner of their own race has been debated for years, but present research seems extensive enough to have resolved the problem. Hanley (1978), for example, used an equal number of black and white male and female examiners (19 in all) to test 120 black and white first graders. Results indicated no IQ differences attributable to examiner's race or

sex. In a detailed review, Graziano, Varca, and Levy (1982) concluded that race of examiner effects were minimal and did not affect the validity of intelligence tests.

Language

Current requirements for assessment, according to regulations issued by the Office of Education, are that children must be tested in their native language. Whether the effects of language will influence test results can be equivocal. Even the question of what language to use is far from resolved. Zimmerman, Steiner, and Pond (1974) found that preschool children referred as Spanish speaking were often equally (or more) fluent in English, or, in a number of cases, were seriously lagging in both languages.

Morales (1977) found bilingual children obtained lower WISC-R scores when tested by Spanish-speaking rather than English-speaking examiners. Guzman (1977) administered the Spanish WISC and the WISC-R to a sample of normal (nonreferred) bilingual Mexican-American children. The mean WISC-R FIQ surpassed the mean of all other measures. Clearly, language primacy must be determined before testing, and bilingualism does not justify rejecting standard intelligence tests.

Rapport

A series of studies have attempted to explore variables associated with rapport by artificially altering test conditions. For example, examiners were instructed to be particularly "friendly" (Feldman & Sullivan, 1971), or cold, remote, and aloof (Silverstein, Mohan, Franken, & Rhone, 1964), or even deliberately discouraging of the child during his performance (Witmer, Bornstein, & Dunham, 1971). All such studies turned out to be equivocal, especially since they were not based on "standard" test administration. An atmosphere of warmth and encouragement is considered basic to any examination, as can be seen in the manuals of such tests as the Binet and WISC-R.

Motivation

Motivation is often questioned in the case of disadvantaged children who are administered tests of intelligence. External incentives have been assumed by some to be necessary in order to obtain a maximum response from such children. Attempts to optimize test performance by using positive verbal comments significantly improved selected WISC subtest scores of an educationally mentally retarded population (Saigh & Payne, 1976), but the same effect was not found for a similar sample given the WISC-R (Tufana, 1975). In a further study, the effects of token and verbal praise seemed significant for measures calling for concentration (arithmetic) but not for tests requiring reasoning (Saigh & Payne, 1979). Kieffer and Goh (1981) believe that differences might be related to the relevance of the incentive to the child. A further study of the effects of race of examiner and type of reinforcer suggested an interaction effect for black children. Tangible rewards resulted in significantly higher scores, regardless of the race of the examiner. However, culturally relevant social reinforcement was meaningful only when received from a black examiner (Terrell, Terrell, & Taylor, 1980).

Enhancing Test Conditions

The setting in which testing occurs should be one that best allows the child to demonstrate his/her capabilities. A number of investigators have explored the effects of the familiarity of the child with the setting, the examiner, or the tasks involved. Corey (1970) compared preschool children tested in the familiarity of their nursery school or in a private office and found no significant difference in WPPSI results. Whether prior exposure to the examiner would increase a child's performance was explored by Tyson (1968), who did not find any such effect. Kinnie (1970), however, found that familiarizing the child with the examiner seemed to be associated with higher scores (on performance tests only) than did mere practice in test taking. Finally, portraying the test as a "game" in order to reduce the child's anxiety did not enhance performance, according to Orfanos (1979).

The Instrument

The most skillful examiner working under idealized conditions will not obtain desired results without proper instrumentation. Without the electronic microscope, there is no way to visually examine cellular activity. Without a computer there is no way to work rapid calculations of large amounts of data. In the measurement of the intellectual skills of children, the adequacy of the testing instrument is explored in terms of the standardization, reliability, and validity.

Standardization

In the measurement of intelligence, the performance of the subject is compared to a certain reference group. This reference group is known as the standardization sample or the normative group, and its scores will be employed as a standard against which scores of later examinees will be compared. The standardization sample must be chosen to be a large and very representative sample of the children to be assessed. This means that to be appropriate for most children, it should include adequate portions of children of varied ages, racial, ethnic, and socioeconomic backgrounds, as well as geographic locations.

Reliability

Adequate standardization is not enough. A test must give consistent scores when it is used to evaluate the same person under variable examining conditions. If a test is not reliable, it is not useful because scores could fluctuate haphazardly. This sort of consistency is usually expressed in terms of a reliability coefficient: .80 or higher is generally acceptable. The coefficient of reliability can be obtained under the following three conditions: (a) test-retest, or the stability of results over time; (b) use of alternative forms; or (c) internal consistency (split-half reliability). This latter form is similar to an alternative form, except that the same test is divided into two equivalent halves, which are then compared.

Validity

The third desirable test characteristic is perhaps the most critical—the accuracy with which a test measures what it is supposed to measure. The key phrase is "what it is supposed to measure." This can be defined in terms of validity, which consists of three types: content, construct, and criterion.

Content validity determines whether the test items are relevant and representative of what is purported to be assessed by the instrument. In a test of intelligence the items must measure some mental function. Content is frequently challenged by laymen, who assume that they can recognize invalid content by simple inspection. In the case of Larry P., California District Judge Peckham found the items unacceptable. In sharp contrast, in Illinois, Judge Grady of the Federal District Court concluded that the same items were largely unbiased. A more objective approach in assessing content validity is to determine whether the items selectively differentiate children from various socioeconomic and ethnic groups (Sandoval, Zimmerman, & Woo-Sam, 1983).

Construct validity determines whether or not the items relate to the theoretical constructs that the test purports to measure. Construct validity for children's tests of intelligence may involve such aspects as age differentiation, since clear-cut increases in ability occur with increasing age. According to Anastasi (1982), construct validity may also be inferred by the association of one test with another already accepted as measuring the construct in question. In recent years, factor analysis has been accepted as a tool that can arrive at some approximation of construct validity.

Criterion validity relates to the relationship between the test in question and some type of criterion or outcome. For example, if intelligence is predictive of school achievement, then a particular test of intelligence should correlate with grades or tests of academic achievement. Two forms of criteria-related validity exist: concurrent validity, which tells how well scores relate to some current criterion, such as another test given at the same time, and predictive validity, which tells of the correlation between test scores and some relevant criterion assessed in the future.

In summary, the assessment of children's intelligence is a complicated process involving the interlacing contributions of the examiner, examinee, situation, and the instrument itself. Recognition of this should lead to a consideration of all these factors when interpreting or reviewing test results.

In the next section the more prominent tests of children's intelligence will be reviewed. These include the Stanford Binet, the Wechsler Intelligence Scale for Children—Revised, the Wechsler Preschool and Primary Scale of Intelligence, the McCarthy Scales of Children's Abilities, and the Kaufman Assessment Battery for children. In each case, a brief history is presented, the test is described, and the strengths and weaknesses assessed.

THE STANFORD BINET

The Binet is generally credited as the first test of intelligence. It was introduced in 1905 to select children in French schools who were unable to profit from regular classroom instruction. Alfred Binet and his collaborators had remarkable insight into the principles of individual differences, which they had studied experimentally. Binet had moved away from previous work on sensory motor factors and began the study of complex and higher mental processes. His observations of his own children led him to the development of specific tests of individual differences, such as the study of attention in apparently bright and dull children. From this background, he accepted the challenge of Paris school officials to produce the first practical mental test.

The Binet was developed without any explicit theoretical foundation about the nature of intelligence that might have aided in the development or selection of items. Instead, Binet used a pragmatic approach to devise items that measured general mental development. As Binet and Simon (1916) explained,

> It seems to us that in the intelligence there is a fundamental faculty. . . . This faculty is judgment, otherwise called good sense, practical sense, initiative, the faculty of adapting oneself to circumstances. To judge well, to comprehend well, to reason well, these are the essential activities of the intelligence. (p. 24)

The Binet Simon Scale was enthusiastically adopted in the United States, particularly for the evaluation of the mentally retarded. However, it was the work of L.M. Terman who produced the Stanford Revision of the Binet Scale in 1916 (Terman, 1916) that made the Binet an American phenomenon. This version not only allowed for the screening of the "dull," but extended the application of Binet's method to normal and "gifted" children. As noted by Tuddingham (1962),

> The success of the Stanford Binet was a triumph of pragmatism for it demonstrated the feasibility of mental measurement. . . . Equally important, it led to a public acceptance of testing which had important consequences. (p. 414)

The first Binet scale utilized the principle that mental development could be expressed in terms of the average capacities of children at various ages. This, the so-called mental age (MA), was to characterize all Binet scales.

By the time Terman introduced the Stanford revision, the notion of the intelligence quotient, or IQ, was added. This represented the ratio of the child's mental age to his/her chronological age, multiplied by 100 to avoid decimals. This was a critical concept for the future of intelligence tests. The mental age was clearly applicable to the period in which the test was given and had no implication for future functioning. A child of 6 with a mental age of 3 could be described for that year, but several years later, how was his functioning to be labeled? The ratio IQ provided an instant answer: At 8, that child would have a mental age of 4, continuing the ratio 3/6 to 4/8, IQ 50. The ratio IQ tended to reify the idea of IQ in the public's mind. Retesting would not be required, since future functioning could be determined by using the ratio. Children once identified as retarded could be placed in special programs without concern for such problems as age-related errors in measurement or inadequate norms. With continued experience and research, a more realistic understanding of intelligence tests developed, paralleling successive changes in the Binet itself.

The Stanford Binet was revised in 1937, 1960, and 1973. Like the earlier versions, the Binet is intended to assess the child's global or general intelligence, expressed in a single IQ score. Since the 1960 revision, the ratio IQ has been replaced with a deviation IQ, in which the individual is compared with children of the same age in the standardization sample.

Description

The current Stanford Binet is an individual test of intelligence taking 30 to 60 minutes to administer and suitable for children as young as 2. It covers ages 2 through 18, and consists of a total of 142 tests arranged by age levels made up of tests passed by normal children. From ages 2 through 5, when developmental changes are most rapid, there are six tests plus one alternative at each half-year interval. Above age 5, intervals are spaced one year apart. (Table 4.1 presents tests for the 4½, 5, and 6 year intervals.) The tests can be classified or sorted into those requiring such skills as language, manipulation, memory, arithmetic, reasoning, evaluation, cognition, and problem solving. These sortings are arbitrary, based on the

TABLE 4.1. STANFORD BINET LM.

Year 4–6
1. Aesthetic comparison (selects "prettier" of pairs of pictures)
2. Opposite analogies I (finishes analogies, i.e., "brother is a boy, sister is a—")
3. Pictorial similarities and differences (identifies "different" object in array)
4. Materials (identifies what an object is made of, i.e., house)
5. Three commissions (follows three instructions in the proper order)
6. Comprehension III (answers common sense questions, i.e., what do we do with our eyes?)
A. Pictorial identification (points to correct picture after being told of use)

Year 5
1. Picture completion: man (adds two or more missing parts to an incomplete drawing)
2. Paper folding: triangle (folds paper in imitation)
3. Definitions (defines words such as ball)
4. Copying a square (copies a square)
5. Pictorial similarities and differences II (identifies pairs or pictures as same or different)
6. Patience: rectangles (combines 2 triangular pieces to compose a rectangle)
A. Knot (ties a knot like examiner's)

Year 6
1. Vocabulary (identifies such words as named, i.e., orange)
2. Differences (defines the difference between two objects, i.e., bird & dog)
3. Mutilated pictures (Names missing part of a picture)
4. Number concepts (counts out blocks)
5. Opposite analogies II
6. Maze tracing (traces shorter path to objective)
A. Response to pictures, Level II (describes action in a picture)

judgment of various authorities (Lutey, 1977; Meeker, 1969; Sattler, 1965; Valett, 1964), and in spite of their often engaging rationales, none of the classifications have been supported by factor analytic studies (Wikoff, 1971).

The Binet, restandardized in 1972, kept the test materials and format the same as in the last revision (1960), while the mental ages obtained "remain exactly the same as those that have always been in use for the 1960 Revision, and these, in turn, are essentially the same as those use in the 1937 Revision" (Terman & Merrill, 1973, p. 360). The mental ages on the Binet range from 2 years to 22 years 11 months, and a mental age is still calculated by adding months for each test passed. Since no changes were introduced in the mental age, the increase in level of performance of children, especially at the preschool levels (Garfinkel & Thorndike, 1976) have changed the traditional relationship between mental age, chronological age, and IQ. As the manual explains, a child of 5 would need to achieve a MA of 5–6 to be considered average (i.e., IQ 100). The confusion likely to arise when Binet MAs are reported led Salvia, Ysseldyke, and Lee (1975) to suggest that a corrected "test age" be utilized, in which a child's performance can again be equated with that of an average child performing at the same level, although Christian, Sutton, and Koller (1981), after comparing results with Wechsler test ages, questioned the validity of such a correction.

Standardization

The renorming of the Binet, according to the authors (Terman & Merrill, 1973), took advantage of the large-scale norming enterprise for the Cognitive Abilities Test. The Binet was standardized by measuring children believed to represent the spectrum of intellectual ability as assessed on the Verbal Battery of the Cognitive Abilities Test, "because this was believed to be the one that would correspond most closely in content and correlate most highly with the Binet" (Terman & Merrill, 1973, p. 356). The normative testing with the Cognitive Abilities Test had covered ages 8 through 17. Children to be given the Binet were selected from those previously given the Cognitive Abilities Test, and at other ages, their siblings. Subjects consisted of 2,351 children, averaging 112 per age level, from a low of 43 at age 2-0 to a high of 150 at age 7-0. Subjects were "stratified so that the distribution of standard age scores of the group-tested siblings corresponded to the national distribution of group-tested standard age scores" (Terman & Merrill, 1973, p. 357). In the communities in which Binet testing was carried out (California, Colorado, Connecticut, Indiana, Texas, and Utah), the authors noted that there were substantial fractions of black and Spanish-surnamed children, but the exact percentages included in the standardization were not determined. The sample was not stratified on other variables such as socioeconomic status, ethnic group (as noted), or sex.

Reliability

Reliability of the 1973 Binet is not discussed in the manual, nor have reliability studies been reported in the following years (Waddell, 1980). However,

the unchanging content of the Binet allows some reliance to be placed on earlier comparison studies, such as forms L versus M of the 1937 versions. Terman and Merrill (1953) reported reliabilities ranging from .90 to .98, differing by age and ability level. Although the Binet format does not readily lend itself to split-half reliability, Silverstein (1969) utilized a sophisticated form of this procedure for a sample of institutionalized mentally retarded subjects and reported a reliability coefficient of .95. Unfortunately, such findings tell little of the reliability of the Binet for today's children.

Validity

The fact that many tests in the Binet have a long history—some dating directly from the 1905 version—means that the content validity of this scale is generally accepted.

Where once the Binet was the standard by which intelligence as a construct or trait was compared, its validity is now assessed against its stepchildren, especially the Wechsler scales. These findings, cited in the criterion section below, continue to confirm the construct validity of the Binet. Factor analytic studies confirm the presence of a general factor, consistent with the global IQ. However, other factors varied from age to age, limiting their interpretation (Garfinkel, 1976; Wikoff, 1971).

The criterion validity of the 1973 Binet, while not presented in the manual, has been determined by correlating it with other measures of intellectual functioning. The present authors summarized comparisons of the Binet with normal and referred subjects. For five samples of normal children, the Binet correlated from .69 to .82 (average .75) with the WISC-R FIQ. For four samples of referred children consisting mainly of suspected mentally retarded and learning disabled youngsters, the correlation was even higher, ranging from .81 to .85 (average .84). Since the Binet is considered a "verbal" scale, a comparison of the Binet with the Verbal and Performance Scales of the WISC-R indicated the expected increase in correlation with the former over the latter. Correlations with other major tests of ability are at the same level (see the following sections). The predictive validity of the Binet is generally inferred from concurrent testing with a measure such as the Wide Range Achievement Test. Correlations between the two measures confirm that the Binet is useful in predicting achievement, with median correlations about .55 (Sattler, 1982).

General Evaluation

The latest version of the Binet can rest on its laurels as a measure of ability that has survived for 80 years. Over the years, as there was no generally accepted definition of intelligence, it became popular to say that intelligence was what an intelligence test measures, and few would argue that the Binet was the test referred to. The wide range of ages and abilities tapped is one of its strengths. At the lower levels, children as young as 2, or extremely retarded school children, will achieve some success and be adequately evaluated. At the other end of the spectrum, bright children can be administered challenging tests because of the extended coverage through the adult level. The rapid alternation of tests of widely varying content assures the interest of children and tends to minimize the frustration of successively more difficult items of the same type given in sequence.

However, the Binet has certain limitations, some reflecting long-term problems, others aspects of the new standardization. As noted, the standardization is not as broad and detailed as those of other current tests and may not meet the standards set by the American Psychological Association and today's legal requirements (Salvia & Ysseldyke, 1978). Specifically, no systematic provision was made for minority representation, varied parental occupational levels, or broad geographic representation. The use of mental ages derived from the Binet is no longer appropriate because of changes in the abilities of children, which have altered the meaning of the standard ages.

The specific format of the Binet, with an all-or-none scoring of items, has the advantage of simplifying and objectifying administration and scoring. However, it also results in the loss of potentially useful material that would have been incorporated into a point scale. The shifting of material from test to test also extends and complicates administration. Also, the mixture of tests placed pragmatically on the basis of their differentiating between age levels results in a constant shift in test content from age to age (Gallagher & Moss, 1963). Below age 6, over half the tests are nonverbal. At school age, when verbal items predominate, the Binet can be a markedly different instrument, inappropriate for children with speech or language problems. In other words, measuring "giftedness" on the Binet can penalize the highly verbal preschool child, who might perform significantly better by age 8 when content has changed. Equally, a younger child who might be identified as "gifted" at one age level may not qualify at another. The changes in mental abilities measured at different ages can mean that an almost entirely different test may be administered when retesting is required. In reporting results, the yearly shift in item content makes a qualitative summary of abilities essential, but this would be largely dependent upon the age level covered and the examiner's interpretation of item meaning. Attempts to profile the child's performance in any standard form, such as Meeker's Structure of Intellect analysis, have not proved to be consistent or meaningful (Michelberg, 1982).

Although the Binet is almost synonymous with measures of "giftedness" or eligibility for special programs, the ceiling is insufficient for bright adolescents (Kennedy, Moon, Nelson, Lindner, & Turner, 1961). Finally, the focus of the Binet (after year 5) on verbal skills (seen clearly in the current norming which used a verbal scale for selection of subjects) does not allow for measurement of the abilities of more physically oriented or language impaired children.

In summary, the Binet remains the one test of children's intelligence that covers the total age spectrum from 2 through 18. It is most useful in evaluating children below 6 and those at either extreme of the ability continuum. Since the Stanford Binet has been used for years as the standard against which other tests have been gauged, most of the major tests of individual intelligence can be viewed as revisions or variations of it. In view of the extensive research results available and its long-term acceptance as the prototype of intelligence tests, the Binet is assured a permanent place in the evaluation of children. Nevertheless, examiners should be aware of problems with standardization and mental age that can limit its use.

WECHSLER INTELLIGENCE SCALE FOR CHILDREN— REVISED (WISC-R)

Two movements characterized the period after the introduction of the 1916 Stanford Binet: its increasing use to measure adult intelligence and numerous attempts to develop profiles from the Binet that would reflect a subject's skills or deficits. As Wechsler (1944) was to note, "The concept of mental age, fundamental as it is to the definition of juvenile intelligence, may be grossly misleading when applied to the definition of adult mental capacity" (p. 18). Citing this as the most basic reason why tests such as the Sanford Binet were unsuitable for measuring adult intelligence, Wechsler introduced the Wechsler Bellevue I (1939). Later a parallel form, the Wechsler Bellevue II, was introduced (Wechsler, 1944).

So successful was the Wechsler Bellevue that Wechsler soon found it desirable to extend the same adult-type items to children. Revising the little used Wechsler Bellevue II, he introduced the Wechsler Intelligence Scale for Children (WISC) in 1949. As in the adult form, the concept of mental age was replaced with the deviation IQ. The popularity of the WISC was unparalleled. Twenty-five years later, the revision known as the WISC-R was published in 1974. Changes reflected research findings and strengthened the reliability and validity of the scale. The basal age was increased from 5 to 6 years, and the ceiling raised from 15-11 to 16-11. Over one-fourth of the items were changed to make the contents more representative of current values. Enthusiastic reviews noted this as a "revision that really is!" (Krichev, 1975).

Like all of the Wechsler Scales, the WISC-R was designed to measure a concept of intelligence defined as "the aggregate or global capacity of the individual to act purposefully, to think rationally, and deal effectively with his environment" (Wechsler, 1944, p. 3). This broad definition included not only cognitive skills but also "such traits as persistence, zest, impulse control, and goal awareness—traits which, for the most part, are independent of any particular ability" (Wechsler, 1974, p. 6). For this reason, these traits are called "nonintellective" factors of intelligence. Their inclusion in the definition of intelligence broadened the concept considerably and led to far more sophisticated understanding of intellectual functioning.

Description

Twelve subtests make up the scale, although in normal use only ten are administered. The tests are grouped into two major divisions called Verbal and Performance Scales (Table 4.2).

The subtests in the Verbal Scale are:

- *Information*—a list of 30 questions arranged in order of increasing difficulty, which sample a broad range of knowledge. Although the content is general, this subtest is considered to be related to school achievement, and deficiencies here may reflect learning problems.
- *Similarities*—a list of 17 paired concepts, again of increasing difficulty, in which the child must delineate the common elements of each pair. Even though the task is abstract in nature, it is one of the best measures of general intelligence.

TABLE 4.2. WECHSLER INTELLIGENCE SCALE FOR CHILDREN—REVISED.

Verbal subtests
  Information
  Similarities
  Arithmetic
  Vocabulary
  Comprehension
  (Digit Span—alternative)

Performance subtests
  Picture Completion
  Picture Arrangement
  Block Design
  Object Assembly
  Coding
  (Mazes—alternative)

- *Arithmetic*—18 orally presented problems, which must be solved mentally, involving basic arithmetical manipulations of increasing difficulty. This is the most school oriented subtest in the scale.
- *Vocabulary*—a list of 38 words, which must be defined, presented in order of increasing difficulty and of varying degrees of familiarity and abstractness. Language impairment can impact on this subtest, which is otherwise one of the best measures of intellectual functioning.
- *Comprehension*—17 questions designed to tap the child's familiarity with prevailing social mores and values, listed in order of increasing difficulty. A "street wise" child would presumably find this subtest easier than an overprotected youngster.
- *Digit Span*—groups of numbers that the child is required to repeat after oral presentation. The first section consists of number groups increasing from 3 through 9 to be repeated in the

sequence presented (forward). The second section consists of number groups increasing from 2 through 8, to be repeated backward. This subtest, which occurs in almost every test of children's intelligence, is not normally administered, serving as an alternative for a "spoiled" subtest or as an additional measure for tapping behavior, which appears to relate to school success.

The subtests of the Performance Scale are:

- *Picture Completion*—26 sketches of objects from everyday life in which some important element is missing, presented in order of increasing difficulty. The child must identify the missing element. The task allows evaluation of visual acuity in a practical sense.
- *Picture Arrangement*—12 series of illustrations, comic-strip fashion, tending to make social commentary and presented in order of increasing difficulty. The child is required to place each picture in the correct sequence.
- *Block Design*—one-inch cubes of solid white or red on 4 sides or half-red, half-white diagonally on 2 others are used to construct 11 designs from copies, these of increasing difficulties. This is a visual motor task, which proves to be an excellent measure of general intelligence.
- *Object Assembly*—4 cut-up puzzles, consisting of a manikin, horse, face, and car, to be assembled by the child within a time limit. This task is a simple and familiar visual motor task that is a weak measure of general intelligence but of value in assessing children of limited ability and experience.
- *Coding*—a two-part substitution task. Part A, for children under 8, requires the child to match simple geometric shapes by inserting the appropriate lines and circles. Part B, for children 8 years of age and older, requires the child to match numbers by inserting geometric symbols. Random placement of designs and numbers requires the child to maintain attention. This is the only regular subtest requiring pencil usage, and it appears to be related to learning problems.
- *Mazes*—a series of nine mazes of increasing complexity which the child must navigate by drawing a line out. This is an optional test that is not usually administered, but it is recommended for use with younger children (Kaufman, 1979).

Standardization

The WISC-R was standardized on 2,200 children ages 6½ through 16½ in 11 yearly age groups, with 100 boys and 100 girls included at each age level. Every effort was made to represent the 1970 U.S. Census in terms of race, geographic regions, occupation of head of household, and urban-rural residence. Minorities included blacks, Mexican-Americans, American Indians, and Orientals in approximately the same proportion as they were represented in the 1970 Census. The adequacy of this normative sample, especially in regard to minority representation, has been considered by Oakland (1977), Reschly (1978), and Sandoval (1982), all of whom were able to compare the Wechsler norms with large samples of normal minority children with equivalent findings.

Reliability

According to the manual (Wechsler, 1974), split-half reliability coefficients for each of the 11 age groups, each subtest, and the verbal, performance, and full scale IQ meet requirements for reliability. Average subtest reliability ranged from .70 for Object Assembly to .86 for Vocabulary. Average reliability for the Verbal, Performance, and Full Scale were respectively .94, .90, and .96. Comparable results have been obtained when the test was administered to referred children (Smith & Rogers, 1978).

Stability was established by retesting a group of 303 children from six age groups in the standardization sample after a 1-month interval (Wechsler, 1974). Coefficients of .95 for the Full Scale, .93 for the Verbal Scale, and .90 for the Performance Scale indicated a very stable test. Stability for referred children was equally impressive (Smith & Rogers, 1978; Vance, Blixt, Ellis, & DeBell, 1981).

Validity

Arguing for the validity of the adult scale, Wechsler (1958) noted that each of the subtests chosen fitted the definition of intelligence; that similar tasks have been successfully used in previously developed scales of intelligence; and that such scales have been demonstrated to be of value in clinical experience. An identical set of arguments can be applied to the WISC-R.

The construct validity of the WISC-R has been supported through an examination of age differentiation. Reynolds (1980) found the relationship between age and performance on the WISC-R to be consistent across race, sex, and age. Further support of the construct validity of the WISC-R can be discerned from the many factor analytic studies now available. The robust verbal comprehension and perceptual organization factors found for each age group in the standardization sample (Kaufman, 1975), blacks and whites (Gutkin & Reynolds, 1981; Reschly, 1978), Mexican-Americans and American Indians (Reschly, 1978), and a wide variety of referred children (Blaha & Vance, 1979; Swerdlik & Schweitzer, 1978), serve to support the construct validity of the Verbal and Performance Scales.

The concurrent validity of the WISC-R is the most frequently reported, both in the manual and in subsequent publications. The present authors have summarized a variety of studies that compare the WISC-R to other measures of ability (Zimmerman & Woo-Sam, 1982). For the Binet, correlations averaged .75 for samples of normal children and .84 for referred samples. Correlations with the McCarthy were somewhat lower: for normal children these averaged .71, close to that for referred samples (.69).

Numerous studies have compared the WISC-R to tests of achievement. These are usually considered as aspects of predictive validity. Results range from a low of − .31 to a high of .76, with the median correlation in the high 50s. Like the WISC before it, the WISC-R is clearly related to scores on academic achievement tests, both for normal and referred children. A review of studies comparing grades with WISC-R results is equally encouraging.

General Evaluation

Among tests of children's intelligence, the WISC-R represents the most widely used instrument for school age children, a position not likely to be challenged in the immediate future.

The Verbal and Performance format is an important characteristic, making the scale of particular value in assessing children who may show specific strengths or limitations in one aspect or the other. For example, the WISC-R may be administered to physically limited individuals such as the blind, deaf, or orthopedically handicapped, for whom only a part of the test is applicable. Typically, the Performance Scale can be administered to the deaf child (Hirshoren, Hurley, & Kavale, 1979; Sullivan, 1979), while the verbal scale is appropriate for the blind or cerebral palsied (Sattler, 1982; Tillman, 1973). However, for children whose impairment is suspected but not clearly determined, administration of both scales may give an estimate of the degree of limitation involved.

A particular advantage of the WISC-R is the availability of 12 subtests (10 standard and 2 alternatives), so that a broad range of tasks may be evaluated. The wide samples of behavior and though processes present at every age level are in contrast to the Binet, where progressively greater emphasis is placed on abstract verbal tasks by 8 years and beyond. The grouping of items into subtests also assures that each child will be measured on similar materials, and differences can be determined from one area to the next. The serial format also assures that the child need not be given item after item beyond his ability, but will return to a new subtest before feelings of frustration build up. Equally, the WISC-R can be given in a more standard time interval (slightly over an hour), since a set number of subtests are administered. The use of subtests allows for the calculation of an IQ on the basis of only a portion of the total test ("short forms"), an important time saver, permitting a meaningful interpretation of results when testing must be interrupted before completion. When as many as five subtests are given, the correlation with the full IQ will be in the .90s (Silverstein, 1975).

The analysis of the WISC-R in a wide variety of current studies of normal and referred children confirms the representative nature of the standardization sample. Other studies confirm the validity of the WISC-R for black and Chicano children; these include factor analytic studies (Gutkin & Reynold, 1981; Kaufman, 1975; Reschly, 1978) and examination of item bias, such as studies by Sandoval, Zimmerman, and Woo-Sam (1983) and Ross-Reynolds and Reschly (1983). Various studies show the reliability and validity of the WISC-R to be at least comparable to the Binet and surpassing the older scale in many areas.

The WISC-R format has led to considerable analysis of patterns and recombinations of subtests, including scores based upon factor analytic findings or armchair groupings, such as Meeker's Structure of Intellect analysis (1975) or the Bannatyne classifications (Bannatyne, 1974). The search for clear diagnostic patterns has been uniformly disappointing. Even if "average" differences are detected for groups such as the learning disabled, the identification of the individual child has repeatedly proved to be impossible (Kaufman, 1981).

However, the nature of the response, rather than the numerical outcome, can give a qualitative picture of personality that is frequently predictive of adjustment. Discriminating signs can be determined from the child's reaction to the test situation, such as brashness, impulsivity, and the flooding of emotional material at presumably innocuous questions (Zimmerman, Bernstein, & Eiduson, 1983).

In all, the WISC-R has a firm place in the assessment of children. If there is any problem with the test, it is the endless possibility for reworking and reanalyzing the subtests, which may lead an intrigued examiner to overlook the rich fund of information to be gained from the child's total response to the test.

WECHSLER PRESCHOOL AND PRIMARY SCALE OF INTELLIGENCE (WPPSI)

The success of the WISC after its introduction in 1949 led to requests for a downward revision suitable for younger children. By the 1960s, when programs for preschool children such as Head Start were in full swing, Wechsler presented the Wechsler Preschool and Primary Scale of Intelligence (WPPSI) (Wechsler, 1967). Representing a new scale (rather than merely a downward extension of the WISC), it was specifically designed for children ages 4 through 6½. Paralleling its older sibling, the WPPSI consisted of a battery of verbal and performance subtests. Wechsler (1967) specifically noted, however, that the Verbal and Performance scales and their subtests were so grouped "not because the author believes they represent different kinds of intelligence, but because the dichotomy has proved diagnostically useful," while the subtests, far from being reified into kinds of intelligence, serve to "alert the examiner to the manner or degree to which a subject's assets and liabilities may influence his overall functioning" (p. 2).

Description

The WPPSI consists of 11 subtests that are analogous to those in the WISC-R (Table 4.3). Five of the subtests making up the regular verbal scale (Information, Vocabulary, Arithmetic, Similarities, and Comprehension) actually overlap the WISC-R in content. However, memory for digits (Digit Span) was replaced with a measure of meaningful content (Sentences), which proved to be a more consistent measure of memory for younger children. Of the five performance tests, only one (Picture Completion) overlaps to any extent with the regularly administered WISC-R subtests. Mazes, an alternative test on the WISC-R, is part of the regular scale, while Block Design is simplified by the use of two- rather than three-dimensional blocks. Animal Houses replaces Coding, requiring placement of pegs instead of fine pencil control, while copying Geometric Designs proves to be more suitable for younger children than the omitted Object Assembly.

Standardization

The WPPSI was standardized by using 1,200 children at six age levels with selection controlled for sex, ethnicity, father's occupation, geographic region, and rural or urban residence, based on the 1960 U.S. Census.

Reliability

The split-half reliabilities reported in the WPPSI manual ranged from .91 to .96 for the three scale IQs. Average subtest reliabilities were similar to those reported for the WISC-R, ranging from .77 for Animal Houses to .87 for Mazes. Equally adequate estimates of reliability have been confirmed for a variety of referred children (Woo-Sam & Zimmerman, 1973). Test stability was established by retesting normal 5-year-olds, with encouraging results (.86 VIQ, .88 PIQ, .91 FIQ) (Wechsler, 1967). These results were also confirmed for low socioeconomic black children retested after one year (.89 FIQ) (Croake, Keller, & Catlin, 1973).

Validity

The content validity of the WPPSI would appear similar to those cited for all the Wechsler scales, as noted in the previous section. The construct validity of the WPPSI can be seen in age differentiation

TABLE 4.3. WECHSLER PRESCHOOL AND PRIMARY SCALE OF INTELLIGENCE (WPPSI).

Verbal subtests
  Information
  Vocabulary
  Arithmetic
  Similarities
  Comprehension
  Sentences

Performance subtests
  Animal Houses
  Picture Completion
  Mazes
  Geometric Designs
  Block Design

and measures of internal consistency, as noted in the manual. Furthermore, factor analysis of the standardization sample confirmed two principal factors, Verbal and Performance, which support the division of the WPPSI into the usual Wechsler format (Carlson & Reynolds, 1980), thus providing further construct validity for the scale. The same factor structure has been reported for a variety of racial and cultural groups (Sattler, 1982; Woo-Sam & Zimmerman, 1973), confirming its value for minority children.

Concurrent validity of the WPPSI is based on numerous studies comparing it with the Binet, WISC-R, McCarthy, and other ability measures. When the WPPSI was compared to the WISC-R for three samples of normal children, the average correlation was .77 (Zimmerman & Woo-Sam, 1982), this often covering a long period between tests. The WPPSI correlated with the Binet in a series of mainly counterbalanced studies averaging .80 (Woo-Sam & Zimmerman, 1973). The predictive validity of the WPPSI was summarized by White and Jacobs (1979), who reported a range of correlations from .36 to .63 (median .41) for a variety of achievement measures. These correlations are not as substantial as those reported for the Binet or WISC-R, and further analysis is called for. Since most samples involve achievement at Grade 1, longitudinal follow-up is required.

General Evaluation

The WPPSI shares the same theoretical and methodological approaches to the assessment of mental ability as does the WISC-R and has many of the advantages of the latter. In terms of validity, the WPPSI is measuring something similar to the Binet, and to about the same degree as the WISC-R. The WPPSI was the first major test of children's intelligence to have been standardized on a representative sample in terms of ethnic composition. Its reliability and validity are excellent. The variety of tasks and the verbal and performance format are useful for understanding the variability of functioning so typical of children. The content is interesting and entertaining for the young child, and if testing needs to be curtailed for any reason, the portion of the scale administered can still provide a meaningful measure of ability (Silverstein, 1970).

The limitations of the WPPSI include item composition. Certain subtests proved to be less "linear" than desired, measuring better for older than younger children. The omission of three subtests used in the WISC-R did not totally solve the problem, and the scale has insufficient "easy" items to differentiate abilities of the very young and the moderately to severely retarded. The manual suggests that the test may be too difficult for 4-year-olds with IQs below 75. This problem can be seen on a subtest such as Similarities, where some children are unable to grasp the nature of the task. Also, the serial format, in spite of its many advantages, can mean that a young child is literally bombarded with what to him/her are monotonously similar questions, as compared to the continual item changes of the Binet.

In all, however, the WPPSI is a useful member of the Wechsler series and can be an important addition to the measurement of preschool children.

McCARTHY SCALES OF CHILDREN'S ABILITIES (MCSCA)

Even though the introduction of the WPPSI in 1967 had been considered a welcome addition to the early intellectual assessment of children, problems still arose as clinics and special education programs received increasing numbers of preschool children for evaluation. The Binet had long been considered limited because of the single global score produced. The WPPSI had a limited age range (4–6) and proved to be inadequate for the assessment of younger low functioning children. The need to evaluate children as young as 2 led McCarthy (1972) to develop an instrument suitable for preschool and primary children age 2½–8½, the McCarthy Scales of Children's Abilities.

Description

The McCarthy Scales are composed of 18 separate tests (Table 4.4), which are grouped into six scales. The first three scales (Verbal, Perceptual Performance, and Quantitative) make up the General Cognitive Index (GCI). The Verbal Scale explores language comprehension and use and the child's ability to express him/herself verbally, allowing for assessment of the maturity of the child's verbal concepts. Verbal tests range from memory for words to opposite analogies. The Perceptual Performance Scale involves nonverbal tasks that tap reasoning, including drawing and conceptual grouping. The Quantitative Scale measures the child's facility with numbers and quantitative words. In addition to these three

TABLE 4.4. McCARTHY SCALES OF CHILDREN'S ABILITIES.

Verbal Scale
  Pictorial Memory
  Word Knowledge
  Verbal Memory I (words & sentences)
  Verbal Memory II (story)
  Verbal fluency
  Opposite analogies

Performance Scale
  Block building
  Puzzle solving
  Tapping sequence
  Right-left orientation
  Draw-a-Design
  Draw-a-Child
  Conceptual groupings

Quantitative Scale
  Number questions
  Numerical Memory I (digits forward)
  Numerical Memory II (digits backward)
  Counting and sorting

Memory Scale
  (3 verbal, 1 performance, 2 quantitative tests from
   the above)

Motor Scale

General Cognition
  (verbal, performance, and quantitative subtests
   summed)

scales which make up the General Cognitive Index, three tests embedded in the above scales are summed separately as a measure of short-term memory involving verbal, performance, and quantitative skills. Further, for children age 2½–5, the Motor Scale assessed coordination in a variety of gross and fine motor tasks.

Each of the six scales is presented as a standard score. Five of these use a mean of 50 and a standard deviation of 10. This format apparently seeks to minimize any tendency to label children with various "IQs." Only the General Cognitive Scale uses the typical mean of 100 and standard deviation of 16, labeled the GCI. The term IQ is specifically avoided "because of the many misinterpretations of that concept and the unfortunate connotations that have become associated with it" (McCarthy, 1972, p. 5).

Standardization

The standardization of the McCarthy Scales was based on a nationwide sample of 1,032 children, stratified according to the 1970 Census on major variables including age, sex, ethnicity, geographic region, and father's occupation. While listing by father's occupation (also characteristic of the WPPSI) is somewhat archaic in view of the number of single parent households, the standardization is otherwise unexcelled for this age level.

Reliability

The reliability of the McCarthy Scales is determined both from estimates of internal consistency (split-half reliability) and from stability coefficients based on the standardization sample, and reported in the manual (McCarthy, 1972). Split-half reliability averaged .93 for the GCI, while a measure of stability reached .90. Adequate stability over longer time periods was confirmed by Davis and Slettedahl (1976) at .85. Further studies such as Valencia (1983) confirm stability for Mexican-American, English-speaking children but report lower stability for Spanish-speaking youngsters.

Validity

As with other measures of children's ability, content validity of the McCarthy must be based on the often familiar items embedded in the various scales. Construct validity, based on a factor analytic approach, appears to confirm the meaningfulness of the various scales (Kaufman, 1975) and appears confirmed for both black and white children (Kaufman & DiCuio, 1975).

The concurrent validity of the McCarthy as reported in the manual ranged from .71 for the WPPSI to .81 for the Binet. However, a series of studies is now available comparing normal children given the WISC-R and MCSCA in counterbalanced order. The median correlation of the FIQ and the GCI was .82. For a variety of samples of referred children, the median correlation was .68. The predictive validity of the McCarthy appears to be equivalent to that of the Binet and WPPSI in terms of its correlation with achievement measures (Naglieri, 1980).

General Evaluation

This "inviting and interesting test" (Hynd, Quackenbush, Kramer, Conner, & Weed, 1980) offers the most valid method of assessing development of children as young as 2½. It provides both a summary score, the GCI, which has the same parameters as the IQ on conventional intelligence tests, and a diagnostic profile of abilities tapping verbal, performance, qualitative, memory, and motor skills. An analysis of the first ten years of use (Kaufman, 1982) indicates that the McCarthy has lived up to expectations and holds considerable promise as a nondiscriminatory assessment tool.

However, the McCarthy is limited to some extent. The age range from 2½–8½, while ideal for preschoolers, limits retesting for school age children. Also, both ceiling and floor are curtailed, reducing use for both severely retarded and gifted youngsters.

Nevertheless, the McCarthy Scales are considered promising tools for younger children.

KAUFMAN ASSESSMENT BATTERY FOR CHILDREN (K-ABC)

As has been pointed out in preceding sections, individual tests of intelligence have developed over the last 80 years in a pragmatic framework, based on a trial-and-error approach, seeking tasks that "work," as indicated by their predictive abilities. The results are seen in the relatively unchanging omnibus format of the Binet. The

Wechsler and McCarthy Scales appeared to answer some concerns: Specifically, both authors used a verbal and performance format, composed of a variety of tests or subtests. Even though many users have assumed a theoretical rationale behind such a format, Wechsler himself (1967) specifically denied this.

The latest addition to the field of intellectual assessment of children is the Kaufman Assessment Battery for Children (K-ABC) (Kaufman & Kaufman, 1983). The intelligence scales, according to the authors, are derived from theories of mental processing developed and studied by cognitive psychologists and neuropsychologists. The focus is on the differential functions of the left and right hemispheres of the brain. The battery is suitable for children 2½–12½ years of age.

Description

The K-ABC utilizes two scales: The Sequential Processing Scale involves the solution of problems presented in a serial or temporal order, while the Simultaneous Scale requires the integration and synthesis of problem materials. In an innovative move, a third section specifically separates the assessment of knowledge and skills that should be acquired in the cultural and school environment.

TABLE 4.5. KAUFMAN ASSESSMENT BATTERY FOR CHILDREN.

Sequential Processing
  Hand movements
  Number recall
  Word Order

Simultaneous Processing
  Magic window (preschool)
  Face recognition (preschool)
  Gestalt closure
  Triangles
  Matrix analogies
  Spatial memory
  Photo scenes

Achievement
  Expressive vocabulary (preschool)
  Faces and places
  Arithmetic
  Riddles
  Reading/decoding
  Reading/understanding

Global scales
  Sequential processing
  Simultaneous processing
  Mental processing composite
  Achievement

It is this separation of fact-oriented or skill-related items from the measures of intelligence as mental processing or problem-solving stimuli that the Kaufmans hope will provide fair or universal stimuli and answer the constant criticism that intelligence tests are biased in favor of the white middle-class child. By the same token, measures of both "intelligence" and "acquired knowledge" in the same test allow the computation of ability-achievement discrepancies from a common normative base.

Standardization

The K-ABC was standardized on 2,000 children stratified on variables of sex, ethnic group (white, black, Hispanic, other), geographic region, and community size, based on the 1980 U.S. Census Bureau data. Rather than parental occupation, the education of the parent was used, coupled with the child's educational placement. An additional sample of black and white children was added to develop supplementary sociocultural norms.

Reliability

For the four Global Scales, average split-half reliability coefficients ranged from .86 to .97. Reliability of the subtests tended to be in the .80s.

Validity

The construct validity of the K-ABC is based on the results of factor analysis presented in the manual and supports the existence of the two mental processes of Simultaneous and Sequential Processing. The concurrent validity of the K-ABC when compared with such accepted measures of intelligence as the Binet, WISC-R, and McCarthy, ranged from .60 to .79. Still to be reported are details of predictive validity.

General Evaluation

As a test that has not yet reached the general public, the promise of the K-ABC awaits its field applications. However, it appears to have a great deal to offer. Specifically, the internal measure of achievement and the detailed standardization answer many criticism of older scales. Only further studies will determine the contribution of the K-ABC.

SUMMARY

In the years since the introduction of the Binet, the intellectual assessment of children has reflected the increasing technical sophistication of measuring instruments. The standardization of major tests is now automatically based on representative samples of the children for whom the tests are intended. Composers of such tests are cognizant of the need for determining the reliability and stability of test scores. Validity studies to determine the predictive value of intelligence tests add to our understanding of the construct of intelligence.

A recurring criticism is that all major measures of intelligence are variations of the original Binet, even using unchanged items dating back to the beginning of the century. Such a charge cannot be denied. However, the burden of proof must be whether such items continue to be valid estimates of ability. Despite a changing culture, children continue to develop in the same way.

The future of testing would seem to involve an increasing validation of current measures. Still to be explored are the contributions of neuropsychology, such as direct measures of brain functioning, the contributions of left versus right brain, or sequential versus simultaneous problem solving, the latter now assessed by the new K-ABC. Intelligence tests will continue to be challenged, and the current emphasis on education for all will continue to mandate their use. The combined results of these two trends can only increase the contribution of intellectual assessment for the welfare of children.

REFERENCES

Anastasi, A. (1982). *Psychological testing*. New York: Macmillan.

Bannatyne, A. (1974). Diagnosis: a note on recategorization of the WISC scaled scores. *Journal of Learning Disabilities, 7,* 272–274.

Bersoff, D.N. (1973). Silk purses into sows' ears: The decline of psychological testing and a suggestion for its redemption. *American Psychologist, 28,* 892–899.

Bersoff, D.N. (1980). P. vs Riles: Legal perspective. *School Psychology Review, 9,* 112–122.

Binet, A., & Simon, T. (1905). Methodes nouvelles pour le diagnostic du niveau intellectuel des anormaux. *L'Année Psychologique, 11,* 191–244.

Binet, A., & Simon, T. (1916). *The development of intelligence in children.* Translated by E.S. Kite. Baltimore: Williams & Wilkins.

Blaha, J., & Vance, H. (1979). The hierarchical factor structure of the WISC-R for learning disabled children. *Learning Disabilities Quarterly. 2,* 71–75.

Blank, M. (1982). Intelligence testing. In C.B. Kopp & J.B. Krakow, (Eds.), *The child: Development in a social context.* Reading, MA: Addison-Wesley.

Brannigan, G.C., & Ash, T. (1977). Cognitive tempo and WISC-R performance. *Journal of Clinical Psychology, 33,* 212.

Brooks, C.R. (1977). WISC, WISC-R, Stanford Binet LM, WRAT relationships and trends among childrens ages 6 to 10 referred for psychological evaluation. *Psychology in the Schools, 14,* 30–33.

Carlson, L.C., & Reynolds, C.R. (1980, September). *Specific variance of the WPPSI subtests at six age levels.* Paper presented at the meeting of the American Psychological Association Convention, Montreal.

Carrubba, M.J. (1976). The effect of two timing procedures, level of test anxiety, and their interaction on performance on the WISC-R. *Dissertation Abstracts International, 37,* 2070A.

Christian, B.T., Sutton, G.W., & Koller, J.R. (1981). A comparison of obtained and adjusted mental age scores on the Stanford Binet. *Psychology in the Schools, 18,* 420–421.

Corey, M.T. (1970, September). The WPPSI as a schools admissions tool for young children. In R.S. Morrow (Chair), *Diagnostic and educational application of the WPPSI.* Symposium presented at the American Psychological Association Convention, Miami.

Croake, J.W., Keller, J.F., & Catlin, N. (1973). WPPSI, Rutgers, Goodenough, Goodenough-Harris IQs for lower socioeconomic black preschool children. *Psychology, 10,* 58–65.

Davis, E.E., & Slettedahl, R.W. (1976). Stability of the McCarthy Scales over a one year period. *Journal of Clinical Psychology, 32,* 798–800.

Eells, K., Davis, A., Havighurst, R.J., Herrick, V.E., & Tyler, R.W. (1951). *Intelligence and cultural differences.* Chicago: University of Chicago Press.

Eiser, C. (1981). Psychological sequalae of brain tumors in childhood: a retrospective study. *British Journal of Clinical Psychology, 20,* 35–38.

Feldman, S.E., & Sullivan, D.S. (1971). Factors mediating the effects of enhanced rapport on children's performance. *Journal of Consulting and Clinical Psychology, 36,* 302.

Fell, L., & Fell, S.S. (1982). Effectiveness of WISC-R short forms in screening gifted children. *Psychological Reports, 51,* 1019–1020.

Gallagher, J.J., & Moss, J.W. (1963). New concepts of intelligence and their effect on exceptional children. *Exceptional Children, 30,* 1–5.

Garfinkel, R.S. (1976). A comparison of item responses of 2 preschool samples on the SBIS. (Doctoral dissertation, Columbia University Teachers College), *Dissertation Abstracts International, 36,* 3002B.

Garfinkel, R., & Thorndike, R.L. (1976). Binet item difficulty then and now. *Child Development, 47,* 959–965.

Gibson, J.T. (1978). *Growing: A study of children.* Reading, MA: Addison-Wesley.

Glasser, A.G., & Zimmerman, I.L. (1967). *The clinical interpretation of the WISC.* New York: Grune & Stratton.

Goetz, T.M. (1978). Sex differences in scoring the WISC-R. (Doctoral dissertation, Indiana University), *Dissertation Abstracts International, 38,* 5409A.

Graziano, W.G., Varca, P.E., & Levy, J.C. (1982). Race of examiner effects and the validity of intelligence tests. *Review of Educational Research, 52,* 469–498.

Grossman, F.D. (1978). The effect of an examinee's reported academic achievement and/or physical condition on examiner's scoring of the WISC-R verbal IQ. (Doctoral dissertation, University of Iowa), *Dissertation Abstracts International, 38,* 4091A.

Gutkin, J.B., & Reynolds, C.R. (1981). Factorial similarity of the WISC-R for white and black children from the standardization sample. *Journal of Educational Psychology, 73,* 227–231.

Guzman, M.D.C. (1977). A comparative study of the WISC-R, the Spanish WISC, PPVT, English version, PPVT, Spanish version, and the CMMS on Mexican American children. *Dissertation Abstracts International, 37,* 7–8A.

Hanley, J.H. (1978). A comparative study of the sensitivity of the WISC and WISC-R to examiner and subject variables. (Doctoral dissertation, St. Louis University), *Dissertation Abstracts International, 39,* 1480B.

Harder, D., Kokes, R.F., Fisher, L., Cole, R.E., & Perkins, P. (1982). IV Parent psychopathology and child functioning among sons at risk for psychological disorders. In A.L. Baldwin, R.E. Cole, C.P. Baldwin (Eds.), Parent psychology, family interaction, and the competence of the child in school. *Monograph of the Society of Research in Child Development, 47,* 1–90.

Hartsough, C.S., Elias, P., & Wheeler, P. (1977). The validation of a nonintellectual assessment procedure for the early screening of gifted and EMR pupils (ETS PR-77-15). Princeton, NJ: Educational Testing Service.

Hirshorn, A., Hurley, O.L., & Kavale, K. (1979). Psychometric characteristics of the WISC-R performance scale with deaf children. *Journal of Speech and Hearing Disorders, 44,* 73–79.

Hynd, G.W., Quackenbush, R., Kramer, R., Connor, R., & Weed, W. (1980). Concurrent validity of the McCarthy Scales of Children's Abilities with native American primary grade children. *Measurement and Evaluation in Guidance, 13,* 29–34.

Kaufman, A.S. (1975a). Factor analysis of the WISC-R at 11 age levels between 6½ and 16½. *Journals of Consulting and Clinical Psychology, 43,* 135–147.

Kaufman, A.S. (1975b). Factor structure of the McCarthy Scale at 5 age levels between 2½ and 8½. *Educational and Psychological Measurement, 35,* 641–656.

Kaufman, A.S. (1979). *Intelligent testing with the WISC-R.* New York: Wiley Interscience.

Kaufman, A.S. (1981). The WISC-R and learning disabilities assessment: State of the art. *Journal of Learning Disability, 14,* 520–526.

Kaufman, A.S. (1982). An integrated review of almost a decade of research on the McCarthy Scales. In T.R. Kratochwill (Ed.), *Advances in school psychology, Vol. II.* Hillsdale, NJ: Erlbaum.

Kaufman, A.S., & DiCuio, R.F. (1975). Separate factor analysis of the McCarthy Scales for groups of black and white children. *Journal of School Psychology, 13,* 10–18.

Kaufman, A.S., & Kaufman, N.L. (1983). *K-ABC: Kaufman Assessment Battery for Children*. Circle Pines, MN: American Guidance Service.

Kennedy, W.A., Moon, H., Nelson, W., Lindner, R., & Turner, J. (1961). The ceiling of the new Stanford Binet. *Journal of Clinical Psychology, 17*, 284–286.

Kieffer, D.A., & Goh, D.S. (1981). The effects of individually contracted incentives of intellectual test performances of middle- and low-SES children. *Journal of Clinical Psychology, 37*, 175–179.

Kinnie, E.J. (1970). *The influence of nonintellective factors on the IQ scores of middle- and lower-class children*. Doctoral dissertation, Purdue University. (University Microfilms, No. 71-9414)

Krichev, A. (1975). Test review: A revision that really is—the WISC-R. *Psychology in the Schools, 12*, 126–128.

Lutey, C.L. (1967). *Individual intellectual testing: A manual*. Greeley, CO: Author.

Marquart, D.I., & Bailey, L.L. (1955). An evaluation of the culture-free test of intelligence. *Journal of Genetic Psychology, 86*, 353–358.

McCarthy, D. (1972). *Manual for the McCarthy Scale of Children's Abilities*. New York: Psychological Corporation.

Meeker, M.N. (1975). *Structure of intellect analysis of the WISC-R test*. El Segundo: SOI Institute.

Meeker, M.N. (1969). *The structure of intellect*. Columbus, OH: Merrill.

Michelberg, J.A. (1982). Equivalence of WISC-R and Stanford Binet SOI profiles for elementary school children. (Doctoral dissertation, University of Texas at Austin), *Dissertation Abstracts International, 43*, 733A.

Morales, E.S. (1977). Examiner effects on the testing of Mexican-American bilingual children in the early elementary grades. (Doctoral dissertation, Texas Tech University), *Dissertation Abstracts International, 38*, 685A.

Naglieri, J.A. (1980). McCarthy and WISC-R correlations with WRAT achievement scores. *Perceptual and Motor Skills, 51*, 392–394.

Noll, V.H. (1960). Relation of scores on Davis-Eells games to socio-economic status, intelligence test results, and school achievement. *Educational and Psychological Measurement, 20*, 119–129.

Oakland, T. (Ed.). (1977). *Psychological and educational assessment of minority children*. New York: Brunner/Mazel.

Orfanos, S.D. (1979). Effects of "game" versus "test" portrayal on performance of a complex cognitive task. *Measurement and Evaluation in Guidance, 12*, 121–124.

Public Law No. 94-142. The education for all handicapped children act of 1975. 89 stat. 773.

Reschly, D.J. (1978). WISC-R factor structures among Anglos, Blacks, Chicanos, and Native American Papagos. *Journal of Consulting and Clinical Psychology, 46*, 417–422.

Reschly, D.J. (1980). Psychological evidence in the Larry P. opinion: A case of right problem—wrong solution? *School Psychology Review, 9*, 123–135.

Reschly, D.J. (1981). Psychological testing in educational classification and placement. *American Psychologist, 36*, 1094–1102.

Reynolds, C.R. (1980). Differential construct validity of intelligence as popularly measured: Correlations of age with raw scores on the WISC-R for blacks, whites, males, and females. *Intelligence, 4*, 371–379.

Reynolds, C.R., Bossard, M.D., & Gutkin, T.B. (1980, April). *A regression analysis of test bias on the Stanford Binet Intelligence Scale*. Paper presented at the American Educational Research Association Convention, Boston.

Ross-Reynolds, J.R., & Reschly, D.J. (1983). An investigation of item bias on the WISC-R in four sociocultural groups. *Journal of Consulting and Clinical Psychology, 51*, 144–146.

Ryan, J. (1972). IQ, the illusion of objectivity. In K. Richardson & D. Spears (Eds.), *Race and intelligence*. Baltimore: Penguin.

Saigh, P.A., & Payne, D.A. (1976). The influence of examiner verbal comments on WISC performances of EMR students. *Journal of School Psychology, 14*, 342–345.

Saigh, P.A., & Payne, D.A. (1979). The effect of type of reinforcer and reinforcement schedule on performances of EMR students on four selected subtests of the WISC-R. *Psychology in the Schools, 16*, 106–110.

Salvia, J., & Ysseldyke, J.E. (1978). *Assessment in special and remedial education*. Boston: Houghton Mifflin.

Salvia, J., Ysseldyke, J.E., & Lee, M. (1975). 1972 Revision of the Stanford Binet: A farewell to the mental age. *Psychology in the Schools. 12*, 421–422.

Samuda, R.J. (1975). *Psychological testing of American minorities: Issues and consequences*. New York: Harper & Row.

Sandoval, J. (1982). The WISC-R factorial validity for minority groups and Spearman's hypotheses. *Journal of School Psychology, 20*, 198–204.

Sandoval, J., Zimmerman, I.L., & Woo-Sam, J.M. (1983). Cultural differences on WISC-R verbal items. *Journal of School Psychology, 21*, 49–55.

Sattler, J.M. (1965). Analysis of functions of the 1960 Stanford Binet Intelligence Scale Form LM. *Journal of Clinical Psychology, 21*, 173–179.

Sattler, J.M. (1973). Examiners' scoring style, accuracy, ability, and personality scores. *Journal of Clinical Psychology, 29*, 38–39.

Sattler, J.M. (1982). *Assessment of children's intelligence and special abilities* (2nd ed.). Boston: Allyn and Bacon.

Sattler, J.M., Hillex, W.A., & Neher, L.A. (1970). Halo effect in examiner scoring of intelligence test responses. *Journal of Consulting and Clinical Psychology, 34*, 172–176.

Saunders, B.T., & Vitro, F.T. (1971). Examiner expectancy and bias as a function of the referral processes in cognitive assessment. *Psychology in the Schools, 8*, 168–171.

Schafer, R. (1954). *Psychoanalytic interpretation in Rorschach testing*. New York: Grune & Stratton.

Silverstein, A.B. (1969). The internal consistency of the Stanford Binet. *American Journal of Mental Deficiency, 73*, 753–754.

Silverstein, A.B. (1970). Reappraisal of the validity of the WAIS, WISC, and WPPSI short forms. *Journal of Consulting and Clinical Psychology, 34*, 12–14.

Silverstein, A.B. (1975). Validity of WISC-R short forms. *Journal of Clinical Psychology, 31*, 696–697.

Silverstein, A.B., Mohan, P.J., Franken, R.E., & Rhone, D.E. (1964). Test anxiety and intellectual performance in mentally retarded school children. *Child Development*, 35, 1137–1146.

Smith, M.D., & Rogers, C.M. (1978). Reliability of standardized assessment instruments when used with learning disabled children. *Learning Disabilities Quarterly*, 1, 23–31.

Sneed, G.A. (1976). An investigation of examiner bias, teacher referral reports, and socioeconomic status with the WISC-R. (Doctoral dissertation, University of Toledo), *Dissertation Abstracts International*, 36, 4367A.

Sontag, L.W., Baker, C.T., & Nelson, V.L. (1958). Mental growth and personality development, a longitudinal study. *Monographs of the Society for Research in Child Development*, 23 (2, whole No. 68).

Stanton, R.D., Wilson, H., & Brumback, R.A. (1981). Cognitive improvement associated with tricyclic antidepressant treatment of childhood major depressive illness. *Perceptual and Motor Skills*, 53, 219–234.

Stern, W. (1914). *The psychological methods of testing intelligence*. Baltimore: Warwick & York.

Sullivan, P.M. (1979). Psychological assessment of hearing impaired children. *School Psychology Digest*, 8, 271–290.

Swerdlik, M.E., & Schweitzer, J.A. (1978). A comparison of factor structure of the WISC and WISC-R. *Psychology in the Schools*, 15, 166–172.

Terman, L.M. (1916). *The measurement of intelligence*. Boston: Houghton Mifflin.

Terman, L.M., & Merrill, M.A. (1973). *Stanford Binet Intelligence Scale, 1972 Norms Edition*. Boston: Houghton Mifflin.

Terman, L.M., & Merrill, M.A. (1953). Tests of intelligence B. 1937 Stanford Binet Scales. In A. Weiden (Ed.), *Contributions toward medical psychology* (Vol. 2). New York: Ronald Press.

Terrell, F., Terrell, S.L., & Taylor, S. (1980). Effects of race on examiner, examinee, and type of reinforcement on the intelligence test performance of lower class black children. *Psychology in the Schools*, 17, 270–272.

Tillman, M.H. (1973). Intelligence scales for the blind: A review with implications for research. *Journal of School Psychology*, 11, 80–87.

Tuddingham, R.D. (1962). The nature and measurement of intelligence. In L.J. Postman, (Ed.), *Psychology in the making*. New York: Knopf.

Tufana, L.G. (1976). The effect of effort and performance reinforcement on WISC-R IQ scores of black and white EMR boys. (Doctoral dissertation, University of Georgia), *Dissertation Abstracts International*, 36, 5961–5962.

Tyson, M.H. (1968). *The effect of prior contact with the examiner on the Wechsler Intelligence Scale for Children scores of third grade children*. Doctoral dissertation, University of Houston. (University Microfilms, No. 69-784)

Valencia, R.R. (1983). Stability of the McCarthy Scale of Children's Ability over a one year period for Mexican American children. *Psychology in the Schools*, 20, 29–34.

Valett, R.E. (1964). A clinical profile for the Stanford Binet. *Journal of School Psychology*, 2, 49–54.

Vance, H.B., Blixt, S., Ellis, R., & DeBell, S. (1981). Stability of the WISC-R for a sample of exceptional children. *Journal of Clinical Psychology*, 37, 397–399.

Waddell, D.D. (1980). The Stanford Binet: An evaluation of the technical data available since the 1972 restandardization. *Journal of School Psychology*, 18, 203–209.

Wechsler, D. (1939). *Manual, Wechsler Bellevue I*. New York: Psychological Corp.

Wechsler, D. (1944). *The measurement of adult intelligence*, Baltimore: Williams & Wilkins.

Wechsler, D. (1958). *The measurement and appraisal of adult intelligence* (4th ed.). New York: Psychological Corp.

Wechsler, D. (1967). *Manual for the WPPSI*, New York: Psychological Corp.

Wechsler, D. (1974). *Manual for the WISC-R*. New York: Psychological Corp.

White, D.R., & Jacobs, E. (1979). The prediction of first grade reading achievement from WPPSI scores of preschool children. *Psychology in the Schools*, 16, 189–192.

Wikoff, R.L. (1971). Subscale classification schemata for the Stanford Binet Form LM. *Journal of School Psychology*, 9, 329–337.

Witmer, J.M., Bornstein, A.V., & Dunham, R.M. (1971). The effects of verbal approval and disapproval upon the performance of third and fourth grade children on four subtests of the WISC. *Journal of School Psychology*, 9, 347–356.

Woo-Sam, J.M., & Zimmerman, I.L. (1973). Research with the WPPSI, the first five years. *School Psychology Monograph*, 1, 25–50.

Zigler, E., & Tricket, P.K. (1978). IQ, social competence, and evaluation of early childhood intervention programs. *American Psychologist*, 33, 789–798.

Zimmerman, I.L., Bernstein, M., & Eiduson, B.T. (1983, April). *Early precursors of school success*. Paper presented at the Western Psychological Association Convention, San Francisco.

Zimmerman, I.L., Steiner, V.G., & Pond, R.L. (1974). Language status of preschool Mexican American children—Is there a case against early bilingual education? *Perceptual and Motor Skills*, 38, 227–230.

Zimmerman, I.L., & Woo-Sam, J.M. (1972). Research with the WISC, 1960–1970. *Psychology in the Schools*, 9, 232–271 Special Monograph Supplement.

Zimmerman, I.L., & Woo-Sam, J.M. (1982, April). *Concurrent validity of the WISC-R*. Paper presented at the Western Psychological Association Convention, Sacramento.

5 INTELLECTUAL ASSESSMENT OF ADULTS

James E. Lindemann
Joseph D. Matarazzo

INTRODUCTION

Since the dawn of civilization, men and women have subjectively assessed or tested their abilities (intelligence) against others. Survival itself is a test, as are most "games." Raw measures of physical superiority soon became measures of individual difference; "Omar is the best tentmaker; Anna the best keeper of goats."

As tests moved from unstandardized *in situ* observation of performance to more objective samples of traits, (e.g., "quickness of mind") or specific achievements as in ancient Greece (Doyle, 1974), China (DuBois, 1970), or the Ottoman Empire (Inalcik, 1973), they were closely associated with selection for ability to learn. Therefore, it should be no surprise that the first modern attempt to construct an intelligence scale was related to school placement, and that age (and closely associated grade placement) became the criteria against which Binet and Simon validated their 1905 test. Small wonder that today it is conventional wisdom that intelligence tests are better predictors of academic achievement than of anything else.

If this were a chapter on children's intelligence tests, this introduction could be concluded. But it is not. It is a chapter on adult intelligence tests, and the fact is that tests of intelligence, developed against age and school placement criteria, *because they are available*, have been used for a multitude of purposes, including applications in *adult* selection, guidance, and differential diagnosis. Therefore, this chapter will describe commonly used adult intelligence tests, especially the Wechsler Adult Intelligence Scale (WAIS) and Wechsler Adult Intelligence Scale—Revised (WAIS-R), today's most frequently used adult tests. The chapter's emphasis will be on applications to adults: individual evaluation and career counseling; psychodiagnosis including assessment of mental retardation and functional impairment of cognitive ability; neuropsychological evaluation; and measurement of intelligence as a genetic marker.

HISTORY AND DEVELOPMENT

The scholarly roots of the study of intelligence lie in the discussions of early philosophers who did little to operationalize its definition, let alone to consider its measurement. Galton (1869) wrote about ability, general and specific, but limited attempts at measurement to psychophysical methods. William James (1890) was interested in the nature and attributes of intelligence without reference to measurement. In the years that followed, psychologists have generated many definitions of intelligence without consensual agreement, reflecting the inferential nature of the concept. We measure what people have learned or how they perform, and from that we infer intelligence.

It was Alfred Binet who first began to systematically identify items of achievement and performance that would reflect intellectual development. Like any good pragmatist, he eventually seized upon a criterion that, although crude, was readily available and objective: the grade placement of school children. From the rudimentary scale developed by Binet and Theophile Simon in 1905 came the Binet-Simon scales of 1908 and 1911, each of which incorporated the concept of *mental age*. In 1912 William Stern suggested that mental age could be divided by chronological age, thus bringing into existence the concept of IQ—*intelligence quotient*. The conciseness and implied accuracy of that numerical statement has surely done more to bring about the use and misuse of intelligence tests than any other single factor. The development of age scale tests of intelligence suitable for assessment of the *individual* was carried forward in 1916 by Terman and in 1937 and 1960 by Terman and Merrill (1973). Wechsler (1939, 1944, 1955, 1974, 1981) dropped the mental age and introduced the deviation quotient for determining the IQ. He deliberately set out to incorporate different *ways* of measuring individual intelligence within one scale. From this tributary centered around tests for individual administration has come today's large-scale industry involving the assessment of individuals, which constitutes a major component of today's institution-based as well as fee-for-service clinical psychology. Concurrently, the measurement of intelligence with application to large groups was given impetus during World War I, when Robert Yerkes and others (1921) developed two group tests, the Army Alpha (for literates) and the Army Beta (for the non-English speaking). From this second development has flowed a whole movement of group ability testing applied to industrial and military selection as well as to vocational and educational planning for individuals.

THEORETICAL UNDERPINNINGS

While Binet in Paris was pragmatically constructing a test of "intelligence," Spearman (1904) was striving to understand its nature and to define it (in London). His correlational studies led him to the conclusion that intelligence is a unitary factor, which became known as g or *general intelligence*, with secondary *specific* or *s* components. In New York City, Thorndike and his colleagues (Thorndike, Lay, & Dean, 1909) interpreted their data quite differently, finding only minimal correlations among various measures of ability. This position was advanced by Thurstone and Thurstone (1941) who developed measures of *primary mental abilities*. Theirs was essentially a multiple (specific) factor theory of intelligence, although their measures could be analyzed in ways that suggested the influence of a general factor. The conflict between proponents of general and multiple factor theories of intelligence, although their measures could be analyzed in ways that suggested the influence of a general factor. The conflict between proponents of general and multiple factor theories of intelligence, with analysis and reanalysis, interpretation and reinterpretation, often of the same data, continues after 75 years. Happily, a great deal of *pragmatically* useful information has been accrued that psychologists can apply in their professional activity while simultaneously accumulating further data for the scientific quest.

Significant positions on the contemporary stage of intelligence theorizing are occupied by Guilford, Cattell, and their respective colleagues. Guilford has advanced a tridimensional model of the structure of intelligence (Guilford & Hoepfner, 1971), derived from factor analysis. Intelligence is conceptualized by means of a three-dimensional cube, which includes *contents* (four variables), *operations* (five variables) and *products* (six variables). The result is a theoretical model of 120 different kinds of "abilities," for some of which measures have yet to be devised. In contrast to this multiple-variable theory, Cattell (1971) postulates only two major dimensions of intelligence: *fluid* intelligence (Gf), which is an ability to perceive relationships based on the individual's unique physiological structures and processes and *crystallized* intelligence (Gc), which is a product of original fluid ability plus the effects of cultural and educational experiences. Cattell's theory has been elaborated and advanced by

Horn (1980) especially in the study of adult development, with a major focus on the postulated decline of fluid intelligence during the "vital years of adulthood" from ages 20 to 60.

Some researchers recently (e.g., Sattler, 1982) have made the interpretive assumption that the Performance Scale tests of the WAIS-R may be viewed as measures of fluid intelligence and the Verbal Scale tests as measures of crystallized intelligence. Whether that assumption will be substantiated is a matter for further investigation.

On the forefront of some exciting new approaches to the conceptualization of intelligence is a group of modern theorist-psychologists whose backgrounds are in research in cognition, computers, artificial intelligence, and information processing. Their approach to theory-building in intelligence involves study of the strategies employed in learning new material, rather than in psychological assessment or psychometrics. On the surface these developments bear no linear relationship to those of Binet or the succession of theorists from Spearman through Guilford and Cattell. The interested reader will find the writing of leaders in this newest development such as Detterman, Glaser and Hunt in the pages of *Intelligence: A Multidisciplinary Journal* and in books by these and other authors (e.g., Detterman & Sternberg, 1982). Although it is early to speculate, the findings of these modern researchers in the field of intelligence may prove to be related and compatible with the views of Spearman and earlier theorists.

We shall now turn to a discussion of tests available for the assessment of adult intelligence.

ADULT INTELLIGENCE TESTS DESCRIBED

Wechsler's Scales

The composition of Wechsler's scales directly reflects David Wechsler's (1944) definition of intelligence as ". . . the aggregate or global capacity of the individual to act purposefully, to think rationally, and to deal effectively with his environment" (p. 3). Impelled by his conviction that intelligence should include the ability to handle practical situations as well as to reason in abstract terms, Wechsler proceeded to select a group of tests that up to now, at least, have effectively withstood the test of time as well as the analysis of

theoreticians, psychometricians, and factor analysts. The 11 tests that comprised the original Wechsler-Bellevue Scale (Wechsler, 1939, 1944) were retained, with revision, in the Wechsler Adult Intelligence Scale (1955) and, with further revision, in the Wechsler Adult Intelligence Scale—Revised (1981). Six tests comprise the Verbal Scale: Information, Digit Span, Vocabulary, Arithmetic, Comprehension, and Similarities. The remaining five comprise the Performance Scale: Picture Completion, Picture Arrangement, Block Design, Object Assembly, and Digit Symbol. In the WAIS, all six Verbal tests were administered consecutively, followed by the five Performance tests. In the WAIS-R they are systematically alternated on the assumption that varying the task will help to maintain the subject's interest.

The WAIS tests, which do not appear to differ substantively from those of the WAIS-R with regard to item content or overall interpretation have been described by Wechsler (1939, 1955). Additionally, Matarazzo (1972) and Zimmerman and Woo-Sam (1973) provide extensive coverage of the interpretation and relevant research findings on the WAIS and its subtests. The following sections will include an abbreviated description of each WAIS-R subtest, the factors it is presumed to measure, the revisions that were made from WAIS to WAIS-R, and the correlation of the WAIS-R test with Full Scale, Verbal Scale, and Performance Scale scores for the combined nine age groups included in the WAIS-R standardization. The reader should note that such correlations differ from one age level to another, and reference should be made to the WAIS-R manual (Wechsler, 1981) for precise application at a specific age level. This is especially recommended when the WAIS-R is used as an aid in decision making involving assessment under any of the currently extant federal guidelines that require an assessment of individual intelligence.

WAIS-R Verbal Tests

Information

The WAIS-R Information test includes 29 questions that sample the subject's range of general information and are related to intellectual alertness, motivation, and retention of information. Eight WAIS items were replaced because they were technically unsuitable or unfair to some sub-groups. Some new questions reflect a concern for cultural balance in item selection, for example, "Who was Louis Armstrong?" and "What was Marie Curie famous for?" Correlation with the WAIS-R Full Scale Score is .76, Verbal Score .79, and Performance Score .62, each corrected for "contamination," (i.e., the effect of being part of the total score with which it was correlated).

Digit Span

The Digit Span test measures memory for series of digits, forwards and backwards, increasing in difficulty up to seven digits and is related to auditory recall, attention, and freedom from dis-tractibility. The content of WAIS and WAIS-R is identical. WAIS-R administration (and scoring) is changed to include administration of two se-ries of digits at each level of difficulty. Correla-tion (corrected for contamination) with the WAIS-R Full Scale Score is .58, Verbal Score .57, and Performance Score .50.

Vocabulary

The Vocabulary test includes 35 words to be defined and tests understanding of words. This test is considered to be an excellent measure of general intelligence and is commonly believed to be influenced by education and cultural oppor-tunities. Seven words have been eliminated from the WAIS and two added. Correlation (corrected for contamination) with the WAIS-R Full Scale Score is .81, Verbal Score .85, and Performance Score .65.

Arithmetic

The Arithmetic test includes 14 orally presented, timed, arithmetic "story" problems and is be-lieved to measure arithmetic reasoning, ability to comprehend verbal instructions, concentration, and freedom from distractibility. Performance on this test is believed to be influenced by education. One WAIS item was eliminated, one added, and bonus point scoring was modified. Correlation (corrected for contamination) with the WAIS-R Full Scale Score is .72, Verbal Score is .70, and Performance Score is .62.

Comprehension

This test consists of 16 questions about aspects of everyday living and social situations and is some-times called a test of common sense. It requires

evaluation of past experience, application of judg-ment to practical situations, and ability to verbal-ize. Two items were eliminated from the earlier WAIS and four added. Some new items include: "What are some reasons why many foods need to be cooked?" and "Why is a free press important in a democracy?" Correlation (corrected for con-tamination) with the WAIS-R Full Scale is .74, Verbal Score .76, and Performance Score .61.

Similarities

In this test the subject is asked to abstract and report what is alike about 14 paired items. This requires perception of essential features, associa-tive thinking, and conceptual judgment. One WAIS item has been modified, two eliminated, and three new items added, e.g., "In what way are a button and a zipper alike?" Correlation (corrected for contamination) with the WAIS-R Full Scale is .75, Verbal Score .74, and Perfor-mance Score .64.

WAIS-R Performance Tests

Picture Completion

This test includes 20 pictures in which some im-portant feature is missing. It requires ability to recognize familiar objects and to differentiate es-sential from nonessential details. Six items from the WAIS were dropped, and five new ones added. Correlation (corrected for contamination) with the WAIS-R Full Scale is .67, Verbal Score .61 and Performance Score .65.

Picture Arrangement

The Picture Arrangement test consists of 10 sets or series of pictures that the subject is required to put in the proper sequence to tell a story, as in cartoon strips. This involves the ability to size up and comprehend a total primarily social situation, which may be influenced by social-cultural back-ground. Two WAIS items were eliminated and four new ones added. Time bonuses have been eliminated on the WAIS-R, and administration is discontinued after four consecutive failures. Cor-relation (corrected for contamination) with the WAIS-R Full Scale is .61, Verbal Score .57, and Performance Score .56.

Block Design

This test includes nine designs to be constructed from red and white blocks following patterns pre-sented on cards. It measures form perception, problem solving, visual-motor integration, and speed of performance. One item was eliminated from the WAIS, and rules of scoring were revised to allow greater additional credit for quick accurate completion. Correlation (corrected for contamination) with the WAIS-R Full Scale is .68, Verbal Score .61, and Performance Score .70.

Object Assembly

The Object Assembly test consists of four simple jigsaw puzzles with large pieces to be assembled into a *Manikin*, a *Profile*, a *Hand* and an *Elephant*. It measures visual analysis, ability to synthesize parts into wholes, and assembly skill. The *Manikin* figure from the WAIS was modified. Correlation (corrected for contamination) with the WAIS-R Full Scale is .57, Verbal Score .49, and Performance Score .62.

Digit Symbol

This test requires the subject to mark, in a series of squares, symbols presented in association with the numbers 1 through 9. It measures speed and accuracy, ability to learn an unfamiliar task, and visual-motor dexterity. The number of sample items was slightly reduced and the number of performance items slightly increased in the WAIS-R. Correlation (corrected for contamination) with the WAIS-R Full Scale is .57, Verbal Score .54, and Performance Score .52.

Stanford-Binet

One might question the inclusion of the Stanford-Binet (S-B) in a chapter on adult intelligence tests. There was, of course, a time (1911–1939) before the Wechsler Scales existed when the S-B was *the* individual intelligence test for children and adults alike. It will be given brief mention here, primarily because there are instances when the S-B remains the instrument of choice (or necessity) for adults. Examples include: (a) those situations in which the WAIS-R has been recently administered and an alternate test is desired; and (b) more importantly, when measuring the intelligence of a severely retarded adult, where an IQ lower than 45 (lowest possible on the WAIS-R) is anticipated.

The Stanford-Binet Intelligence Scale, Form L-M (Terman & Merrill, 1973) is a direct descendant of the scale devised by Binet and Simon (1905, 1908, 1911; see Kite, 1916 translation). It was revised by Terman in 1916 and by Terman and Merrill in 1937, prior to the currently used third revision of 1960. It is an age scale, and a major criterion for the selection of tests or items for inclusion from the first scale to the present was that they show an increase in percent passing at successive age levels (Terman & Merrill, 1973). Items chosen because success increases with age have limited usefulness for continuous point scales, not only because of their limited range, but also because increasing their complexity alters the type of ability measured by the tests. Although not all of the items at the Adult and Superior Adult levels are of this type, this point of emphasis in the construction of the S-B, the heavy orientation toward verbal abilities, especially at higher levels, along with the fact that the 1972 norms numbered just 86 in the 18 and older age group, suggests that adult applications of the Stanford-Binet might judiciously be restricted to those mentioned in the preceding paragraph. In such usage of the Stanford-Binet one should also take into consideration the consistency with which WAIS IQ scores have been found to exceed S-B scores, as described by Zimmerman and Woo-Sam (1973).

For a more extended discussion of the Stanford-Binet as a child intelligence test the reader is referred to Zimmerman and Woo-Sam's chapter in the present volume.

Other Adult Intelligence Tests

The Eighth Mental Measurements Yearbook (Buros, 1978) lists 11 individual intelligence tests that extend to *all* or *part* of the adult years. These include the WAIS (Wechsler, 1955) and the Naylor-Harwood Adult Intelligence Scale (Naylor & Harwood, 1972), which is an Australian adaptation of the WAIS.

Several others are primarily associated with children, including the WISC-R (Wechsler, 1974), which extends only to age 16, and the Kaufman Development Scale (Kaufman, 1974), which is primarily intended for use from birth to age 9 but is suggested for mentally retarded subjects of all ages. The Hiskey-Nebraska Test of Learning Aptitude (Hiskey, 1966) is an age scale intended for use with deaf or hearing impaired subjects aged 3 through 17 years. The Stanford-Binet (Terman & Merrill, 1973) is described in the preceding section.

Buros also lists several picture vocabulary tests that primarily measure verbal comprehension. These include the Peabody Picture Vocabulary Test (Dunn, 1965), the Full Range Picture Vocabulary (Ammons & Ammons, 1948), and the Quick Test (Ammons & Ammons, 1962).

The tenth and eleventh of these tests are The Porteus Maze Test (Porteus, 1965), a nonlanguage test of mental ability that involves finding the path through a series of mazes; and the Detroit Tests of Learning Aptitude (Baker & Leland, 1967), an extensive battery of tests with a very limited standardization population.

SELECTED RESEARCH FINDINGS

Research on the structure and applications of the Wechsler-Bellevue Intelligence Scale, Wechsler Adult Intelligence Scale, and Stanford-Binet has been voluminous and has been summarized many times (e.g., see Matarazzo, 1972). Our review of research findings, for the most part, will be restricted to studies with the more recently published Wechsler Adult Intelligence Scale—Revised, which in utilization is rapidly replacing its predecessor, the WAIS. At the time of this writing, the WAIS-R has been available for 2 years, and the flood of research papers based on its standardization data has already caused the editor of a major journal (Garfield, 1982) to caution against repetition. It can comfortably be predicted that the volume of studies of the WAIS-R will equal or better that of its predecessors.

The norms of the WAIS-R (Wechsler, 1981) are based on a group of 1,880 adults, ranging in age from 16 years to 74 years 11 months. This sample was stratified on the basis of age (nine groups), sex, race (white, nonwhite), geographic region (Northeast, North Central, South, West), occupation (six groups), education (five levels) and urban-rural residence, following 1970 census reports. The scaled scores for each of the 11 tests in the scale were derived for each age group from the scores of the 500 standardization subjects in the 20- to 34-year age groups. As in the WAIS, these *scaled scores* were converted to a mean of 10 and a standard deviation of 3, allowing for comparison of the score of any subject with the 20–34 reference group. This is in contrast to IQ scores, which, are directly comparable from one age group to another, although derived in relation to each subject's own age group. Thus, as in the WAIS, IQs were derived so that the mean IQ for each of the nine age groups is 100, with a standard deviation of 15.

The reliability of the WAIS-R has been computed by split-half and test-retest methods as well as computation of the standard error of measurement. Split-half reliability was computed for nine of the subtests across all nine age groups. Test-retest reliability of two subtests (Digit Span and Digit Symbol) was calculated from repeated testing of four age groups. The average reliability coefficients of the six Verbal tests range from .83 (Digit Span) to .96 (Vocabulary). The average reliability coefficients of the five Performance tests range from .68 (Object Assembly) to .87 (Block Design). The average reliability coefficients, as derived from all nine age groups of the standardization population, are .97 for Verbal IQ, .93 for Performance IQ, and .97 for Full Scale IQ.

Test-retest reliability (stability) was examined by administration of the WAIS-R twice (within 2 to 7 weeks intervening) to 71 subjects aged 25 to 34 and 48 subjects aged 45 to 54. The test-retest reliability coefficients for Verbal IQ, Performance IQ, and Full Scale IQ ranged from .89 to .97.

The standard errors of measurement (SE_{ms}) for the 11 WAIS-R tests ranged from .61 scaled score points on Vocabulary to 1.54 scaled score points on Object Assembly. Average SE_{ms} of the Verbal, Performance, and Full Scale IQs were 2.74, 4.14, and 2.53 IQ points, respectively.

The WAIS-R manual (Wechsler, 1981) offers little in the way of original validity data, pointing instead to the continuity of its structure with its predecessors, the WAIS and Wechsler-Bellevue. Each of the earlier scales included the same 11 tests with similar and often identical content. These scales were originally validated on the basis of correlations with other tests of intelligence, ratings by experienced clinicians, and studies of groups of known intellectual level, among many other criteria (Matarazzo, 1972). The 1981 WAIS-R manual does provide a comparison of the WAIS and WAIS-R as administered to 72 adults, ages 35–44. Correlations of WAIS and WAIS-R scores of the 11 tests ranged from .50 (Picture Arrangement) to .91 (Vocabulary). Correlation of the WAIS and WAIS-R Scales were Verbal IQ .91, Performance IQ .79, and Full Scale IQ .88.

For the population mentioned in the preceding paragraph (ages 35–44) the WAIS Verbal, Performance, and Full Scale IQ scores were approximately 7, 8, and 8 points higher, respectively, than their WAIS-R counterparts. Unfortunately, this tendency for WAIS scores to be higher may not be the full extent of the problem in comparing WAIS and WAIS-R scores. On the WAIS-R, unlike its predecessors, the standard deviations of the sums of scaled scores varied among the nine age groups of the standardization population, and some of the differences between standard deviations reached significance. Since these differences were adjusted in constructing IQ tables, the practical implication for any single WAIS-R IQ is insignificant. It may be significant, however, in comparing WAIS and WAIS-R scores at various age and intelligence levels, especially when the same individual is examined and then re-examined on the same scale years later, when he or she is older and will be compared with the norms of another group. Until such differences are further explored, the clinician should consider making such comparisons by use of the scaled score equivalents of raw scores at the appropriate age levels, as found in the WAIS and WAIS-R manuals. At the very least, the clinician should be aware of this statistical problem whenever dealing with a client at or near an IQ value mandated by law in quasi-judicial examinations.

The research literature is replete with factor analytic studies of the structure of the WAIS and other Wechsler scales. Most of these have been consistent with and interpreted from the viewpoint of either the paradigm suggested by Vernon (1950), which includes a general (*g*) factor and two major group factors, verbal-educational (*v:ed*), and spatial-perceptual (*k:m*), or the paradigm suggested by Cohen (1957), which elicited three factors (Verbal Comprehension, Perceptual Organization, and Memory or Freedom from Distractibility). These have been reviewed in detail by Matarazzo (1972). Many of these studies are being duplicated with the WAIS-R. Blaha and Wallbrown (1982) have applied an hierarchical factor solution to the subtest intercorrelation data for the nine age groups included in the WAIS-R standardization sample, concluding that the general intelligence factor accounts for 47% of the total subtest variance, the verbal educational factor 6%, and the spatial-perceptual factor 5%. Silverstein (1982a) applied a two-factor solution to the same data and found Cohen's two highly stable factors, Verbal Comprehension and Perceptual Organization. Silverstein noted Cohen's third factor (Freedom from Distractibility) in the three youngest age groups of the WAIS-R standardization sample. Blaha and Wallbrown as well as Silverstein interpreted their findings as supportive of Wechsler's development of separate Verbal and Performance Scales with their respective IQs.

Much of the recently published, early research utilizing the WAIS-R standardization sample data is addressed to the problem of making valid comparisons among the subtests and scales. Thus, Naglieri (1982), utilizing the standard errors of measurement given in the WAIS-R manual, has computed the intervals needed for the 85%, 90%, 95% and 99% levels of confidence in statistically based, psychometric comparisons of the Verbal, Performance, and Full Scale IQ scores. Naglieri recommends that confidence intervals be routinely stated in order to address the psychometric properties of the test.

Silverstein (1982b) discusses the statistical problems in making multiple comparisons of subtest scores and presents a solution based on the standard error for comparing a subject's score on each of the Verbal or Performance subtests with the average Verbal or Performance subtest score or the overall average. The differences required for significance at the .05 and .01 levels in comparing WAIS-R subtest scores are presented in Table 5.1. Silverstein presents similar data for the WAIS, WISC, WISC-R, and WPPSI, and the reader is referred to the original article for that information.

The practitioner will be especially interested in Silverstein's discussion of PIQ-VIQ differences. He reminds us that some differences are due to the *unreliability* of these measures; namely, the error one expects in one *single* measure of a variable such as VIQ-PIQ difference when one obtains the measure only once, in contrast to the repeated measurement of that variable on the same individual. He then contrasts the statistical "unreliability" of a single score with its "abnormality"; that is, its unusualness due to the fact that such a magnitude of difference was found to occur so infrequently in the standardization sample that one may regard it as abnormal or deviant. Matarazzo (1972) and Matarazzo, Carmody and Jacobs (1980) have added that any VIQ-PIQ difference of 15 points, or a difference between 3–5 scaled-score points between two subtests, is potentially clinically important and worthy of further analysis and study (e.g., in relation to the person's medical, occupational, cultural, and personal history).

As to the effect of age on intellectual performance, Matarazzo (1972) and many others have pointed out a likely flaw in early studies of aging and intelligence: The conclusion that intelligence declined gradually with age, beginning at about age 28. These early studies, based on cross-sectional samples at various ages, failed to take into account the differences in educational level in the various generations represented. Horn (1980) and

TABLE 5.1. DIFFERENCES REQUIRED FOR SIGNIFICANCE
WHEN COMPARING EACH WAIS-R SUBTEST SCORE
WITH AN AVERAGE SUBTEST SCORE.

Subtest	Verbal average .05	.01	Performance average .05	.01	Overall average .05	.01
Information	2.4	2.8	—	—	2.6	3.1
Digit Span	2.9	3.5	—	—	3.4	3.9
Vocabulary	1.8	2.1	—	—	1.9	2.2
Arithmetic	2.8	3.3	—	—	3.1	3.7
Comprehension	2.9	3.4	—	—	3.3	3.8
Similarities	3.0	3.5	—	—	3.4	4.0
Picture Completion	—	—	3.0	3.5	3.4	4.0
Picture Arrangement	—	—	3.2	3.9	3.8	4.4
Block Design	—	—	2.5	3.0	2.8	3.2
Object Assembly	—	—	3.5	4.2	4.1	4.8
Digit Symbol	—	—	3.0	3.6	3.5	4.0

Note. Adapted with permission from "Pattern analysis as simultaneous statistical inference" by A.B. Silverstein, 1982, *Journal of Consulting and Clinical Psychology*, 50, 237.

others have refocused the study of aging and intelligence by reference to the concept of fluid and crystallized intelligence, postulating that crystallized intelligence may actually *increase* with age, while fluid intelligence may be expected to decline. Additionally, working on the assumption mentioned earlier in this chapter, that the WAIS-R Verbal tests may be equated with crystallized intelligence and the Performance tests with fluid intelligence, Sattler (1982) has examined the scaled-score points assigned to identical raw scores at various age levels. Table 5.2 presents the additional scaled-score points given at each age level for a score which in the Reference Group (age 25–34) would be assigned a scaled score of 10. As can be seen, a raw score on a Performance test that would be assigned a scaled score of 10 for a subject aged 25–34 would receive a scaled score of 14 to 16 for a subject in his or her seventies. A similar comparison with Verbal tests would yield

TABLE 5.2. ADDITIONAL SCALED-SCORE POINTS BY AGE
AWARDED TO WAIS-R SUBTESTS WHEN THE (25–34 YEAR OLD)
REFERENCE GROUP RECEIVES A SCALED SCORE OF 10.

Test	Age group 35–44	45–54	55–64	65–69	70–74
Verbal Scale					
Information	0	0	0	0	1
Digit Span	0	0	1	1	1
Vocabulary	−1	0	0	0	1
Arithmetic	0	0	1	1	1
Comprehension	0	0	0	1	1
Similarities	1	1	1	2	3
Performance Scale					
Picture Completion	1	1	2	2	4
Picture Arrangement	1	1	2	4	5
Block Design	1	1	2	3	4
Object Assembly	0	1	2	4	4
Digit Symbol	1	2	3	5	6

Note. "Age effects on Wechsler Adult Intelligence Scale—Revised Tests," by J.M. Sattler, 1982, *Journal of Consulting and Clinical Psychology*, 50, 786. Reprinted with permission.

much smaller differences with the 70-year old receiving scaled scores from 11 to 13. Sattler concludes that fluid intelligence shows a much more severe decrement with age than does crystallized intelligence.

CLINICAL APPLICATIONS OF INDIVIDUAL ADULT INTELLIGENCE TESTS

This section will describe the following uses of adult intelligence tests: as part of an assessment battery in individual evaluation and career counseling; in psychodiagnosis, such as evaluation for possible mental retardation; in examination for indices of emotional or psychotic processes as seen in thought disorders accompanying serious psychiatric illness; in neuropsychological evaluation; and in determining the overall intellectual level and more discrete dimensions of cognitive processes in individuals identified as being at risk for genetic disorders.

The generation of an IQ score is an important and useful product yielded by the standardized individual intelligence evaluation. The clinical usefulness of the IQ score is rivaled, however, by the rich observational material that becomes available to the skilled clinician while interacting with the client/patient during this structured cognitive task. Goals of this section will be to present guidelines within which these qualitative observations can be systematized, as well as to comment on some uses that appear to have received minimal attention in the literature of individual intelligence testing; namely their applications in career counseling as well as in the investigation of genetic disorders. Illustrative case histories will be included.

Individual Evaluation and Career Counseling

The literature in the field of vocational evaluation and career counseling makes regular reference to the individual intelligence test, usually endorsing its use as an instrument to predict the client's potential for reaching a certain educational or occupational level. The capacity of intelligence tests to predict one's educational attainment has been long established. Indeed, at lower age levels intelligence test scores and school grade place-

ments have a chicken–egg relationship. This is not surprising, since many of the items included in the first tests of intelligence were chosen because they successfully differentiated students at increasingly higher grade (and age) levels. Furthermore, the relationship between intelligence test scores and occupational level has been documented in many studies (e.g., the one reported by Harrell & Harrell, 1945, which related the Army General Classification Test to 64 civilian occupations). A review of that literature may be found in Matarazzo (1972). Herman (1982) points out that the standardization data of the WAIS-R show a moderately strong relationship between mean IQ and occupational level, with a spread of 22 points between the average IQs of subjects in occupational groups 1 and 5 (the highest and lowest categories of employed persons that were included).

The literature of vocational psychology usually makes a gesture toward individual intelligence tests as they relate to educational and occupational levels and then refers the reader to multiple aptitude or special aptitude tests. Thus, Cronbach (1960) recommended tests of specialized aptitude for vocational guidance, and Super and Crites (1962) suggested that the use of intelligence test scores be limited to total or verbal scores as a rough index of the educational or occupational level that the person may *actuarially* be expected to attain. Although the authors of textbooks on vocational psychology typically are sophisticated psychologists, there is rarely mention in such textbooks of the potential contribution of qualitative observations, obtained from client–examiner interaction, to the process of vocational evaluation and career counseling. Tyler seems to adopt a slightly different stance. Commenting on the search in the 1930s for prototypical evidence that different occupations were characterized by their own occupational ability profiles, Tyler wrote (1978): "What proved discouraging, however, was that success in the occupation did not seem related to whether or not one possessed the proper profile and that a wide variety of profiles existed within any occupation" (p. 95). Although seeing possible utility in some general aptitude battery profiles, Tyler mentions a number of other interesting possibilities in measuring human ability. For instance, she suggests that psychologists might consider assessing *directions* of development (e.g., what *kinds* of competency) in addition to *levels* of intelligence. She also observes that: "It requires a certain level of the ability intelligence tests measure to *enter* one of the more prestigious occupations, but once one gets in, how successful one is depends on factors other than intelligence" (1978, p. 80). For example, published frequency distributions of the IQ levels of a sample of young U.S. physicians as well as a sample of faculty members at the University of Cambridge reveal a range in IQ from 111 to 150 in each sample (Matarazzo, 1972). Tyler (1978) has also emphasized cognitive and conceptual styles (e.g., analytic-descriptive, reflective-impulsive) as important dimensions of individual difference that need assessment.

Despite these problems, it is our opinion that the individual adult intelligence test contributes more to effective career counseling than appears to be recognized in the literature, and that its contribution could be potentially greater, given recognition of this fact and increased systematic investigation of vocational applications. The authors are aware, from their own practices and their service as consultants to agencies which utilize vocational psychological evaluations, that the use of individual intelligence tests as part of such evaluations is almost universal. That this should be the case is not surprising, in view of the findings of Brown and McGuire (1976) and Lubin, Wallis and Paine (1971), which reported the WAIS to be the third and second most frequently used psychological test, respectively, at the time of their studies. More recently Reynolds (1979) reported that psychologists ranked the WAIS second in psychometric quality (after the WISC) among the 10 most used tests. It is clear that psychologists both respect and rely heavily upon the individual adult intelligence test as one of the main tools in their assessment batteries, and it is the authors' observation that this extends to vocational psychological assessment.

The psychological assessment used to evaluate potential for employment typically includes observations about the client's approach, demeanor, cognitive style, response to challenge and failure, and other relevant characteristics manifested during the test session. Such an assessment also includes arrival at an estimate of the client's potential for success at various levels of educational or occupational attainment, as these latter are predicted by the total IQ score, as well as inferences about more specific abilities such as verbal, spatial, and (with appropriate qualification)

numerical ability. In some instances, such vocational evaluations may include tests of special aptitudes (e.g., verbal reasoning, numerical reasoning, clerical aptitude, manual dexterity).

The use of the standardized test situation as a controlled setting to observe variability of behavioral response is hardly a new idea. Psychologists have done it regularly. Garner (1966) cites Terman's 1924 comparison of the standardized test administration to the controlled experiment. What remains to be done even today is to systematize and study the relevant variables of such observations, so that they may be subjected to verification and refinement. As an example, Table 5.3 includes some descriptors of cognitive style that are used by one of the authors (JEL) to help systematize the observation (and later reporting) of client behavior in the testing situation, as well as for teaching such observation procedures to psychology interns.

From this brief treatment of the subject, it no doubt is clear to the reader that there is a need for a greater rapprochement between those psychologists who regularly use individual intelligence tests and those who study occupations. Such a marriage would facilitate developing a pool of

TABLE 5.3. DESCRIPTORS OF COGNITIVE STYLE.

1. *Persistence.* Keeps trying? Gives up easily? Declines to attempt difficult items? Puzzles and works at difficult or failed items—even becomes obsessed and keeps going back to them?
2. *Anxiety.* General anxiety about being tested? Reacts to failure with anxiety, flustering, blocking? Becomes anxious or blocks about a specific set of items, e.g., arithmetic?
3. *Reaction to failure.* Won't attempt when unsure of an item? Gets flustered and upset at failure? Gives arbitrary answers just to "satisfy" the situation?
4. *Approach.* Methodical or systematic? Block design—trial and error, analytic-insightful, a combination of both? Reasoned or impulsive responses? Comprehensive or fragmented associations? Whole to part, or part to whole?
5. *Concentration.* On simple material, e.g., digit span? On complex material, e.g., difficult arithmetic questions, block designs, comprehension or picture arrangement?
6. *Pace.* Fast or slow? Erratic?
7. *Verbal expression.* Articulate, well spoken? Awkward, imprecise?
8. *Attitude.* Casual or serious about the whole thing? Competitive?
9. *Reaction to authority.* Ability to conform to the demands of the task as presented by the examiner?

empirical findings on the utility of intelligence test subscales for measuring abilities relevant to occupational success, *insofar as success can be predicted from such cognitive measures*.

The following brief case histories were chosen to highlight some of the ways an intelligence test provides useful information in career planning. All names used are pseudonyms and information that might identify the subjects has been withheld or modified.

Case History—
A Restless Young Man

Kenny is an 18-year-old with bright red hair, the youngest son in a blue-collar family. He has hemophilia (moderate), and he and his family have been followed by a psychologist-consultant for many years in a hemophilia treatment center. His mother was fondly indulgent and "too good-natured" to set firm limits. Kenny, who was bright and verbal, learned to be "cute" and mildly exploit the effects of his hemophilia, which were frequently genuinely painful. He was mischievous and hyperactive. His school attendance was more irregular than the disease necessitated. Nevertheless, he learned fairly well and always passed because of his superior intelligence. He saw school as a chore and did not develop effective study habits. There was no academic tradition in the family, and even though his parents thought he should "do better," there was no pressure to perform at the superior level of which he was capable.

When seen for a formal test evaluation at age 16 years, 6 months, Kenny appeared as a grown-up version of the mischievous, hyperactive child he had been in the past. He now tended to be a clown and to act out verbally rather than physically. He was earning a B average in high school and enjoyed his classes in health, shop, and English literature. He disliked biology and science. He expressed a great deal of uncertainty about vocational direction, but did think he might like to be a nurse or a teacher.

The results of psychological evaluation are summarized in Table 5.4. Despite his verbal gifts, during testing Kenny was tense and unsure, although also alert, quick, and persistent. He verbalized a good deal, but despite what appeared to be superior intelligence, he had difficulty being precise, for example, in giving exact definitions. As may be seen, Kenny is intellectually very able, with Verbal Scale and Full Scale IQs of 127 and 120 respectively and Performance Scale IQ of 108. Although the VIQ-PIQ difference of 19 points is large, the fact that Kenny had received thorough and comprehensive diagnostic and treatment services from a variety of specialists all of his life with no hint of neurologic deficit, along with the fact

TABLE 5.4. PSYCHOLOGICAL ASSESSMENT FINDINGS IN A RESTLESS YOUNG MAN.

WAIS		Strong-Campbell Interest Inventory
VIQ	127	*Highest Theme Scores*—Realistic, Social, Enterprising, Conventional
PIQ	108	
FSIQ	120	
		Highest Basic Interest Scales—Adventure, Military Activities, Medical Service, Athletics, Sales
Information	12	
Comprehension	13	
Arithmetic	14	
Similarities	16	*Highest Occupational Scale Scores*—Navy Officer, Police Officer, Business Education Teacher, Purchasing Agent, Realtor, Funeral Director, Credit Manager, Buyer, Chamber of Commerce Executive, Recreation Leader
Digit Span	16	
Vocabulary	11	
Digit Symbol	8	
Picture Completion	11	
Block Design	13	*Academic Orientation Scale*—43
Picture Arrangement	13	
Object Assembly	10	*Introversion-Extroversion Scale*—34

Self-Description Inventory
Highest Scores—Adventurous
Imaginative
Outgoing
Forceful

that the Digit Symbol test contributed to his lowered Performance IQ and he did well both qualitatively and quantitatively on the spatial-motor aspects of Block Design, all led to the conclusion that this VIQ-PIQ differential was likely a product of his superior verbal ability rather than a reflection of neurologic impairment.

On the Strong-Campbell Interest Inventory Kenny answered "Dislike" to only 3 of the 325 items, resulting in an elevated profile. High scores on Adventure, Athletics, and Sales suggested a preference for action and variety. Many scores (including Introversion-Extroversion) suggested a preference for being close to people, either in a business (sales) or a helping (medical service) relationship. Scores on many of the physical science occupations were low.

Combining Kenny's restless, outgoing, gregarious orientation with his high verbal ability, indifference toward academics, and dislike of science suggested, considering both training and job requirements, that there might be other occupations that he would be more suited for, rather than his stated potential choices of nursing or teaching. These latter early choices reflected, to a large extent, his schooling and those "success" occupations to which he had been exposed as he obtained frequently needed medical care (nursing). In the 18 months following evaluation, Kenny was seen for continued counseling on three occasions, using the findings as background information in career discussion. He was introduced by the psychologist to the idea of business administration (sales) and responded at first with skepticism. After a period of exploration and thought he began to regard this goal more positively and at his most recent visit (at age 18) was investigating post-secondary-school education resources with the aid of his vocational rehabilitation counselor. Kenny is dubious about commitment to a 4-year college program, primarily because of the time commitment rather than the financial requirements. He proposes to seek a 2-year community college course that offers him the option of transfer credit should he choose to continue.

Kenny's case illustrates the confluence of interests (seeking action, variety, and people orientation), cognitive functioning (bright, verbal, imprecise), and personality traits (adventurous, outgoing, forceful) in arriving at an intelligent career choice. Not the least of the variables that contributed to the counsel offered by the psychologist-consultant was the restless, quick, imprecise,

highly verbal cognitive style that Kenny displayed in the individual test setting.

Now let us turn to the case of a midcareer vocational choice in a person without obvious physical or psychological handicaps.

Case History—Middle-age Malaise

Mr. Hurst is 42 and self-referred for career planning assistance. He has held a secure, well-paying job as an accountant for a small firm for 4 years and is "bored." He is a tall, heavy-set, and talkative man with a resonant voice, who appeared for each appointment in casual dress. His opening social conversation was relaxed and friendly. However, as the interview progressed to more personal levels, he became increasingly guarded and almost obsessive in seeking the "right words" to describe his thoughts.

He related that his parents had been strict and that he found his father "difficult," so had avoided him when he could. He did well in grade and high school without trying very hard. He worked for awhile in the family carpeting business and enjoyed himself when he looked at a job well done. For several years he went to community college and "fooled around." He worked for a time as a policeman. Upon returning to college he discovered accounting and remained on the dean's list thereafter. After college graduation he held a government job for 7 years, leaving it when his marriage failed. He took a trip around the world, returned and tried selling real estate, then settled into his present accountant's job. He does his job effectively and enjoys his standard of living. He has a stable relationship with a woman to whom he is engaged. He says his job is not challenging and that he would like to work with his hands in a field like architecture or engineering.

The results of Mr. Hurst's psychological evaluation are summarized in Table 5.5. During the WAIS-R administration the need to be precise previously observed on interview was even more exaggerated, and it became evident that Mr. Hurst's preciseness stemmed from the fear of making a mistake. His final verbal productions were good, but he frequently showed obsessive indecision in formulating verbal descriptions. In dealing with numbers, he was rapid and accurate. When confronting the complexities of the more difficult Block Design and Object Assembly items, he became highly anxious and aware of being timed but nevertheless was able to maintain sufficient

TABLE 5.5. PSYCHOLOGICAL ASSESSMENT FINDINGS IN A CASE OF MIDDLE-AGE MALAISE.

WAIS-R		Strong-Campbell Interest Inventory
VIQ	126	*Highest Theme Scores*—Realistic,
PIQ	117	Investigative, Artistic
FSIQ	126	
		Highest Basic Interest Scales—Agriculture,
Information	14	Nature, Mechanical Activities, Science,
Digit Span	16	Medical Science, Medical Service,
Vocabulary	12	Music/Dramatics, Art, Domestic Arts
Arithmetic	14	
Comprehension	14	*Highest Occupational Scale*
Similarities	13	*Scores*—Optometrist, Engineer, Radiologic
		Technician, Veterinarian, Computer
Picture Completion	10	Programmer, Math-Science Teacher, Architect,
Picture Arrangement	15	Musician, Photographer, Physical Sciences,
Block Design	14	Health Fields
Object Assembly	9	
Digit Symbol	10	*Academic Comfort Scale*—53
		Introversion-Extroversion Scale—57

Edwards Personal Preference Schedule
High Needs: Endurance, Heterosexuality, Succorance
Low Needs: Deference, Autonomy, Abasement, Affiliation, Dominance

organization to be reasonably effective. Throughout it was evident that he was most comfortable working with highly structured tasks where the "rules" were clear, as in numerical operations. He could not make precise formulations of ambiguous problems and became anxious when he met complexity. The latter qualities were most evident on the WAIS-R when he was dealing with spatial relations and assembly materials.

The Strong-Campbell Interest Inventory results shown in Table 5.5 suggested interests that are technical-creative, indicating a wish to work with tangibles in a creative way. Interest in the visual arts was strong. He displayed a desire *not* to work closely with people or to have supervisory responsibility. The Edwards Personal Preference Schedule suggested avoidance of highly independent or dominant roles and an orientation toward achievement through persistence.

It appeared to the psychologist that Mr. Hurst's aspiration to creativity (as expressed on the interest test) was at odds with his insecurity in the face of ambiguity and consequent difficulty in making judgments and decisions. Interestingly, this need for structure and certainty seemed to prevail only in his employment setting or when he perceived a decision as "serious." He was able to be casual in ordinary social interaction and to enjoy changes in his life situation.

Based on his history and the test findings in Table 5.5, Mr. Hurst was counseled to satisfy his need for change through a move to a new job setting (but not occupation) and to seek creative expression through avocational pursuits. Face-to-face observation of his cognitive style aided significantly in arriving at this recommendation, and Mr. Hurst was able to recognize the validity of this observation in the course of counseling.

At this writing, just a few months after Mr. Hurst was seen, he is seeking a change to an accounting position in a company whose products and procedures are markedly different from those of the employer with whom he is presently affiliated.

Psychodiagnosis

Mental Retardation

The individual intelligence test, compassionately and intelligently used, can be extremely useful in the overall assessment of mental retardation and in determination of the areas of strength around which the retarded person may be helped to build a more fulfilling life. Such a test possesses a degree of structure and objectivity that ordinarily

TABLE 5.6. AAMD CLASSIFICATION OF MENTAL RETARDATION.

| | | I.Q. Range | |
Classification	Range in Standard Deviation Units	Stanford-Binet S.D. 16	WAIS-R S.D. 15
Mild	−2.01 to −3.00	52–67	55–69
Moderate	−3.01 to −4.00	36–51	40–54
Severe	−4.01 to −5.00	20–35	25–39
Profound	Below −5.00	0–19	0–24

exceeds opinions based on nonsystematic observation. Along with an index of measured intelligence, the requirement of a complementing measure of adaptive behavior for the diagnosis of mental retardation adds a valuable dimension and helps in detecting those cases where the true strengths of the individual may not be adequately measured by the intelligence test alone. Certainly the results of the test need to be evaluated in terms of the cultural background of the individual and the conditions of its administration. Litigation during the past decade provides evidence that there have been misapplications of intelligence tests and misinterpretations of their results. In the experience of the authors, errors of this type have rarely been attributed to psychologists who are fully trained and qualified in the utilization of standardized individual tests.

The most common use of intelligence tests to assess possible mental retardation is for school placement, and this typically involves the administration of a test designed for use with children. Subsequently, adult intelligence tests are used to monitor the functioning of the retarded adult over time; to document the existence of retardation where the person may be eligible for benefits either in his/her own right or as a "dependent child"; to assist in determining competence (or incompetence) to handle funds; to assist in determining employability (or unemployability); and to identify assets for use in vocational planning.

Where a formal determination of mental retardation is mandated by law or semijudicial requirements, standards for classification have been established by the American Association on Mental Deficiency (Grossman, 1973). These specify *mild* mental retardation as falling between two and three standard deviations below the mean of the test being utilized, *moderate* between three

and four standard deviations below the mean, *severe* between four and five standard deviations below the mean, and *profound* below five standard deviations below the mean. The IQ ranges for these classifications using the WAIS-R and Stanford-Binet are found in Table 5.6. A case history follows.

Case History—
Retarded Identical Twins

Linda and Rhonda Robertson are the 35-year-old daughters of a disabled laborer and his wife. They were referred for psychological evaluation to determine if they could be considered "dependent children" for purposes of compensation.

Linda promptly and proudly announced that the sisters are "mirror," in that she is left-handed and Rhonda is right-handed. They are extremely similar in appearance, each short, overweight, with a round, red face. Each talked rapidly and was easily excited. They differed slightly in that Linda would become argumentatively defensive when threatened by difficult material, and Rhonda would sigh anxiously and act put-upon.

The sisters grew up in a rural area, and their mother stated that there was no special education in their little school. They had difficulty with their lessons from the earliest grades, were frequently teased, and left school at the seventh grade. Later they spent a few years in the state institution for the retarded, but the girls didn't like being away from their folks and were allowed to return home. In recent years they have been enrolled in sheltered workshops, but (they rationalized) "Mom needed us worser at home." At home they help with housework and the dishes. During the psychological assessment each named the other as her best friend. They differed in their attitudes toward boys: Linda was indifferent, and

TABLE 5.7. PSYCHOLOGICAL ASSESSMENT FINDINGS OF LINDA AND RHONDA—IDENTICAL TWINS.

WAIS-R			Vineland Social Maturity Scale		
	Linda	Rhonda		Linda	Rhonda
VIQ	67	61	Total Score	78	75.5
PIQ	72	71	Age Equivalent	10.3	9.5
FSIQ	68	63	Social Quotient	41	38
Information	5	4			
Digit Span	2	1			
Vocabulary	4	3			
Arithmetic	2	2			
Comprehension	5	3			
Similarities	5	3			
Picture Completion	5	5			
Picture Arrangement	4	4			
Block Design	5	4			
Object Assembly	4	3			
Digit Symbol	3	4			

Rhonda showed disdain. They both like to watch television.

The results of the psychological assessment of Linda and Rhonda are summarized in Table 5.7. They displayed their individualized characteristics in the test situation, Linda responding defensively to difficulty and Rhonda with ineffective, random trial and error methods. Each had a low frustration tolerance and thus occasionally had to be "nursed" through one or another part of the evaluation. Each could, however, be directed to task, and the measures obtained appeared to be representative.

Despite some differences, there was much more similarity than difference in the twins' overall WAIS-R response pattern. As is seen in Table 5.7, Linda scored somewhat higher, with better verbal reasoning skills and was generally more assertive. Linda showed some ability to approach performance tasks systematically, while Rhonda proceeded strictly on random trial and error for much of the test. The most striking similarity in their responses came on the Comprehension question "Why are child labor laws needed?" Linda— "some kidnapping and stuff." Rhonda—"kidnapping, picking up people's kids." They were examined in succession, without contact in the interim, and thus had no opportunity to compare notes. When the second one had been evaluated, the first was waiting outside the office door. Without a signal, each moved beside the other,

the left arm of one, and the right arm of the other shot around the partner's waist, and they made off in stride down the corridor, chattering like very close but much younger best friends.

In addition to the WAIS-R, the Vineland Social Maturity Scale was administered with the mother serving as informant. Again, as summarized in Table 5.7, the sisters' capacities were parallel. Thus, although they take care of their own dressing and hygiene needs and are relatively good at self-help and household chores, their communication, socialization, recreation and self-responsibility skills are very limited. The result is that each achieved a Social Quotient (41 and 38 respectively) some 25–27 points below her own Intelligence Quotient.

The diagnosis of mild mental retardation was thus made on the basis of combined intelligence and behavior measures: (i.e., 68 and 41 for Linda and 63 and 38 for Rhonda; scores in the lower 1% of the adult population). In view of the twins' demonstrated inability to function independently out of the family setting and the results of this more standardized appraisal, they were eligible to be viewed under existing legislation as dependent "children." Even though they were not seen as having the potential for competitive employment, some contact out of the home, such as in an activity center, was recommended in order for them to develop better social skills and flexibility, which will be helpful to them in making the transition to another sheltered living setting at the time when it is no longer possible for them to live with their parents.

Functional Cognitive Impairment

The interrelationship and inseparability of personality characteristics, cognitive styles, and personal preferences in individual functioning is a commonly accepted idea, notwithstanding the prevalence of standardized psychological tests whose scores are interpreted as representing measures of independent "traits." The experienced clinical psychologist relates findings about various

aspects of the person in ways that reflect this functional unity, and rightly so. Our earlier discussion of cognitive style, the listing of "descriptors" in Table 5.3, and interpretation of elements relevant to career directions in individuals each reflected this. Just as "normal" characteristics will, to some degree, influence all aspects of behavior, it is recognized that characteristics considered to be deviant or pathological will also manifest themselves in one or another dimension of a person's behavior. In general, the more influence those characteristics such as neuroticism, sociopathy, depression, or psychosis exert on a person's intellectual functioning, the greater will be

TABLE 5.8. EXCERPTS FROM HUNT-ARNHOFF STANDARDIZED SCALES FOR DISORGANIZATION IN SCHIZOPHRENIC THINKING.

Scale Point*	Response	Mean	SD
Vocabulary Scale			
1	Gamble—To take a chance, a risk	1.00	0.00
	Seclude—To go away and be alone, to seclude oneself	1.50	0.63
2	Gown—Garment you wear for lounging	1.75	0.93
	Shrewd—Careful in a sneaky, clever way	2.19	0.75
3	Join—Has to do with organization	2.62	0.96
	Peculiarity—Action one doesn't usually engage in	3.00	1.15
4	Espionage—Crooked, not truthful	4.12	1.09
	Seclude—To put somewhere in the dark	3.81	1.11
5	Juggler—Acts in front of a person, respects himself as a juggler	5.00	0.82
	Espionage—A type of sinful devilment	5.44	0.89
6	Nail—Metal I guess, let's say a metal which is made scientifically for purpose of good and bad use	5.75	0.93
	Diamond—A piece of glass made from roses	6.44	0.63
7	Cushion—To sleep on a pillow of God's sheep	6.75	0.45
	Fable—Trade good sheep to hide in the beginning	6.81	0.40
Comprehension Scale			
1	Envelope—Deposit it in the mail box	1.06	0.25
2	Land in the city—Because they got more accommodations in the city than in the country	2.00	0.96
3	Envelope—Pass it by or mail it	2.87	0.81
	Theatre—Turn in an alarm so that everyone wouldn't get burned up	3.00	0.82
4	Marriage—Proof and identification so you wouldn't get someone else's wife	3.00	0.82
5	Laws—It is reasonable for a group of people to come to some agreement and acceptance of a common good and to aid what has proven to be the best for the many; that is, they are made to prevent illegal activities	4.87	0.96
6	Marriage—For ownership you might say and to take care of each other according to health	5.87	0.96
7	Forest—I'm not good at telling directions. Just walk uphill and when you get to the top it is easier going down	6.31	0.71
	Marriage—For scientific purposes and for the identification of siblings, siblings of the association of the parents		

*Disorganization rated from none (1) to maximum (7).

Note. Adapted from Hunt, W.A., & Arnhoff, F.N. (1955). "Some standardized scales for disorganization in schizophrenic thinking." *Journal of Consulting Psychology,* **19,** 171–174.

the degree of pathology seen. Hunt and his associates studied various aspects of disorganizaton in thinking, and Hunt and Arnhoff (1955) published what have become widely used scales of disorganization in thinking based on vocabulary items from the Binet and Wechsler-Bellevue Scales and comprehension items from the Wechsler-Bellevue. They used ratings by skilled clinicians to develop their final pedagogically useful list of scaled gradations of schizophrenic thought disorganization. Excerpts from these scales are included in Table 5.8. As one moves down from a scaled test item reply of 1 (normal) to items scored as 7, note how each successive item mirrors more and more psychopathology.

Psychopathology may be reflected in many aspects of cognitive functioning, including those tapped by performance tests. The patient may approach the block design task in a compulsive or ritualistic fashion. Examiner-solicited associations to picture arrangement cards may be bizarre. However, pathology appears to be more frequently observed in respect to verbal tasks, although research on this topic is lacking. In addition to the work of Hunt and Arnhoff (1955), Zimmerman and Woo-Sam (1973) provide examples of clinical interpretations of responses to comprehension items on the WAIS. These include responses that may indicate phobia ("germs kill you"), self-reference ("I never see a train"), literalness ("but I don't pay taxes"), passive dependence ("wait until found") or negativism ("not true!"). Matarazzo (1972) lists some unusual modes of response to vocabulary items in those who have thinking disturbances. These include: (a) overelaboration—giving irrelevant details; (b) overinclusion—mentioning attributes that are shared by many objects, e.g., "has cells"; (c) ellipsis—omitting words necessary to the meaning of a phrase; (d) self-reference—incorporating personalized elements; and (e) bizarreness—idiosyncratic associations or juxtaposition of disconnected ideas. An illustrative case history follows.

Case History—An Avoidant Personality with Depression and Dependency

Bill Smithers, 22 years old, was referred for an evaluation of the level of his emotional stability and to determine his intellectual potential. He was a "late" child, the youngest of elderly but successful parents. His father was a businessman

and his mother an artist-homemaker. In his youth he was diagnosed as maladroit and suffering from being a member of "a high-expectation family." He completed high school with difficulty and subsequently took a few community college courses. He held two jobs briefly: one was temporary and obtained for him by his aunt; one he left in order to go on vacation. He has no car as he has been unable to pass the driver's test. He stays home and occasionally plays tennis or volleyball.

During the opening interview Bill was soft spoken and mild. He was inconsistent and frequently did not understand the intent of questions until they were made very explicit. He was reluctant to make judgments or generalizations about any aspects of his life.

The results of the psychological evaluation are summarized in Table 5.9. On the WAIS-R Bill was inconsistent and erratic. He failed simple items and passed more difficult ones, thus displaying intratest "scatter." His reasoning was generally good as long as he had only a limited number of concepts to deal with. He did well on similarities and basic arithmetic functions but poorly on complex arithmetic problems. He clutched the pencil like an ice-pick and consequently was slow and made primitive productions. He was anxious, with poor tolerance for stress of any kind, and desperate to please. When he could not answer immediately his pace became frantic, he paid little attention to detail, and in verbal responses he would confabulate answers to "please" the examiner. Some unusual verbal responses were: *Sanctuary*—"a place safe" [sic]; *Evasive*—"afraid of somebody, trying to get away from"; *Fortitude*—"a strong attitude"; *Deaf people*—"they can't sound it out" Q. "they can if they look at paper and see how it is divided into syllables."

Bill's medical history, his older mother, the 8-point (almost 3 standard deviation) intertest "scatter" between his scores on the Comprehension and the Similarities subtests, and his difficulty in word finding and organizing verbal concepts, collectively suggested the presence of a neurological impairment that was interfering with his verbal expression and verbal organization. It is possible that the academic and social difficulties stemming from this postulated dysfunction may well have been the stimulus early in his life for family overprotection as well as rejection and sometimes ridicule from peers. At the present time Bill's passivity, dependence, ineptness, depression, and withdrawal represent greater impediments than

TABLE 5.9. PSYCHOLOGICAL ASSESSMENT
FINDINGS IN AN AVOIDANT PERSONALITY
WITH DEPRESSION AND DEPENDENCY.

WAIS-R		16PF Test
VIQ	91	*High Score Descriptions*—Astute (not
PIQ	89	forthright), Outgoing, Tender-minded,
FSIQ	89	Apprehensive, Self-sufficient
Information	8	*Low Score Descriptions*—Sober, Expedient,
Digit Span	8	Shy, Undisciplined self-conflict, Less intelligent
Vocabulary	10	
Arithmetic	9	Trailmaking
Comprehension	4	Part A 10 credits
Similarities	12	Part B 6 credits
		Part C 16 credits
Picture Completion	10	All scores in range of control subjects
Picture Arrangement	8	
Block Design	9	
Object Assembly	11	
Digit Symbol	7	

Peabody Individual Achievement Test

	Grade equivalents
Mathematics	12.9
Reading Recognition	9.4
Reading Comprehension	12.8
Spelling	12.9

Bender
Primitive, but not suggestive of perceptual impairment

Rotter Incomplete Sentences Blank
Perplexed. Directionless. Self-blame—feels immobilized. People puzzling.
Independence seen as threatening. Suppressed anger toward parent.

this possible underlying organic impairment. Bill is being provided supportive therapy to help him make the transition from the family home into a sheltered residential setting and to help him find work where options are clear, changes from routine are minimized, and time is available to absorb new instructions.

Neuropsychological Evaluation

Large-scale systematic attempts to use intelligence tests to measure cognitive impairment due to organic brain dysfunction followed the publication of the Wechsler-Bellevue Scales. Wechsler identified the subtests on which he believed functioning would be impaired by organic brain damage and suggested a deterioration index that was the ratio of such "don't-hold" to "hold" subtests. That this index was not satisfactorily validated may have been related as much to the unreliability of neurological and neurosurgical diagnoses as it was to the neuropsychological instrument.

Neuropsychological assessment was carried forward by Ralph Reitan, who built upon the earlier work of Ward Halstead as well as Wechsler. Reitan validated neuropsychological measures against groups of patients who were carefully diagnosed as having left hemisphere, right hemisphere, or diffuse brain lesions. He helped develop what later was called the Halstead-Reitan Battery of Neuropsychological Tests (Reitan & Davison, 1974), of which the Wechsler scales are a part.

A history of some of the most relevant research pertinent to the use of the Wechsler scales in neuropsychological assessment has been published by Matarazzo (1972). For our purpose, it is sufficient to point out that much of the research on brain-behavior relationships suggests that the WAIS and WAIS-R are highly sensitive to some aspects of organic dysfunction of the brain that are useful in differential diagnosis. For example, the evidence is accumulating that a large difference between the Verbal IQ and Performance IQ should be a signal to search for medical, personal history, and other extra-test evidence of organic brain dysfunction. Accumulating research findings suggest that a VIQ versus PIQ deficit in Verbal IQ may be related to left hemisphere dysfunction, whereas a deficit in Performance IQ may be related to right hemisphere dysfunction. A current review of this growing literature is available in Bornstein and Matarazzo (1982). That review indicates that recent studies suggest that these discrepancies between Verbal and Performance IQ appear more often in males than in females.

The research in neuropsychological assessment with intelligence tests and other instruments is burgeoning and is too voluminous for inclusion in this overview chapter on measures of adult intelligence. However, the interested reader will find more detailed discussion of this important topic in the section of this book devoted to neuropsychological assessment.

Measurement of Intelligence as a Genetic Marker

Even though the relative role of inheritance in individual intelligence has been a matter of bitter debate, the relationship between intellectual impairment and certain inherited genetic disorders (e.g., Down's Syndrome) has been generally accepted. Early studies of the relationship between intelligence and specific genetic disorder frequently utilized measures of intelligence that varied from the standardized individual test to casual observation based on interview. As genetic research became more sophisticated, the need for reliable and more finely discriminating measures became apparent.

Jackson (1981) has summarized the psychological findings in four major genetic disorders: phenylketonuria (PKU), Turner's Syndrome, Klinefelter's Syndrome, and Huntington's Disease. Because of the development of a simple and cost-effective screening method, it has become possible to identify individuals with phenylketonuria within a few days of birth and, with proper dietary measures, to avoid the brain damage that results in mental retardation in untreated PKU. Intellectual evaluation involves examination of siblings as well as the identified patient, and continued monitoring of these individuals as dietary controls is changed over time.

Turner's Syndrome is found in females who lack one of the two X sex chromosomes (XO instead of XX). A consistent pattern of intellectual deficit has been found, in that such patients typically score lower on performance (spatial) abilities while not differing from siblings or controls in verbal abilities. Such patients may also have difficulty carrying out arithmetic functions. The case history following this section provides a representative example of cognitive functioning in Turner's Syndrome. Recently, Rovet and Netley (1982) have begun to examine more closely the earlier recognized impairment of spatial abilities in Turner's Syndrome, with results suggesting that speed of response on rotational tasks (where transformation of spatially presented information is required) is primarily responsible for the deficit in Performance IQ.

Klinefelter's Syndrome involves males with an extra X chromosome (XXY instead of XY). Here the intelligence test findings are the obverse of those in Turner's Syndrome, with those affected typically having an impaired Verbal IQ, while their Performance IQ is unaffected relative to controls and siblings. Robinson, Lubs, Nielsen and Sorensen (1979) also describe delayed speech development, delayed emotional development, and school maladjustment in patients with Klinefelter's Syndrome.

Huntington's Disease usually has its onset between ages 35 and 45 and eventually results in gross intellectual deficit. The normal-appearing individual whose parent is affected is "at risk," with a 50:50 chance of having inherited the disease. Retrospective studies show that those members of the "at risk" group who later develop the disease show IQ values that are lower than controls, but psychological measures in general have not been satisfactory for such predictive purposes. Josiassen, Curry, Roemer, DeBease, and Mancall (1982) report a consistent pattern in recently diagnosed Huntington's patients (in comparison with those "at risk"), with impairment in Arithmetic, Digit Span, Digit Symbol, and Picture Arrangement subtests.

The relationship between intelligence theory and measurement and genetic research is not necessarily a unidirectional one. Even though intelligence test results have demonstrated value in helping to identify genetic syndromes, continuing genetic research may well produce significant contributions to our understanding of intelligence, especially the thorny problem of the relationship between heredity and intelligence. A case history follows.

*Case History—A Young Lady
with Turner's Syndrome*

Tanya Metsgy was referred for consultation at age 17, when she was a senior in high school. She was a tiny girl, alert and spontaneous on interview. Although she was bright and had a good sense of humor, she had experienced a great deal of teasing from fellow students because of her diminutive size. She had a comfortable but mildly dependent relationship with her parents.

Tanya listed her physical problems as poor finger dexterity, trouble standing for prolonged periods, and the problems attendant to being short. Her grades were average, although she had to struggle to pass a general math course. The formal results of her psychological evaluation are summarized in Table 5.10.

Tanya's pattern of intellectual functioning as seen on the WAIS appears to be classic for Turner's Syndrome. Vocabulary and verbal reasoning are superior. She had moderate difficulty with visual-spatial relationships (see her low scores on the five Performance subtests), relying on trial-and-error methods to solve space relations problems. In addition, limitations in arithmetic ability were observed on the WAIS as well as on the Peabody Individual Achievement Test (PIAT).

The test results (which included a Verbal IQ of 118) were interpreted as suggesting that Tanya should be able to function with average expenditure of effort in a 4-year college of average academic standards, although she might have difficulty with math requirements. She had expressed interest in nursing or teaching. She was encouraged toward teaching because of the relatively difficult physical demands and math requirements in nursing and because her interest test profile was more compatible with teaching.

Six years after the evaluation shown in Table 5.10 it was learned that Tanya was in her last quarter of work toward a B.A. in history. College had been difficult, and she had dropped out for several brief periods. She had changed her major from education because she could not successfully complete the required math. She is living independently and expresses satisfaction with her social adjustment. Her plans are to seek a position in the occupational world commensurate with her B.A. degree, and her chances for success appear to be relatively good.

FUTURE DIRECTIONS

Future directions for exploration of the nature of intelligence, its measurement, and its application

TABLE 5.10. PSYCHOLOGICAL ASSESSMENT FINDINGS
IN A YOUNG LADY WITH TURNER'S SYNDROME.

WAIS		Strong-Campbell Interest Inventory
VIQ	118	*Highest Theme Score*—Social
PIQ	99	*Highest Basic Interest Scales*—Medical
FSIQ	110	Service, Social Service
Information	14	*Highest Occupational Scale*
Comprehension	15	*Scores*—Elementary Teacher, Director of
Arithmetic	7	Christian Education
Similarities	13	
Digit Span	9	*Academic Orientation Scale*—99
Vocabulary	15	*Introversion-Extroversion Scale*—46
Digit Symbol	8	
Picture Completion	9	
Block Design	9	
Picture Arrangement	10	
Object Assembly	8	

Peabody Individual Achievement Test

	Grade equivalents
Mathematics	5.7
Reading Recognition	12.9 +
Reading Comprehension	12.9 +
Spelling	12.9 +

may be conceptualized in terms of two major forces: those that may bring us closer to understanding the physiological correlates of intelligence and those directed toward its most effective application.

Research in genetics, neuropsychology, and developmental psychology may be expected to enlighten us further on the physiological correlates: how "intelligent" characteristics are inherited and the patterns in which they are inherited; how these characteristics are represented in neuroanatomical and neurophysiological functioning; and how intelligent behaviors unfold in the biological and social developmental process. Hopefully such research will allow us to develop strategies and tests for assessing intelligent behavior and intellectual abilities beyond those that have been intuitively included in intelligence tests to date. Such future research also may well provide us with the capacity to measure intellectual potential more directly, for example, at a physiological or even anatomical level. Assuming the future existence of such measures, however, one might note that as long as the goal of measurement is the use of intelligence in environments where motivation and personal style impinge on its application, measures of *intelligent behavior* as well as *intellectual capacity* will be required.

Research using computer models and concepts of "artificial intelligence" may contribute to our knowledge of the most effective way to apply one's intelligence. The direction of these efforts is to study strategies of learning and the procedures involved in information processing. In addition to developing an understanding of the strategies and procedures, they may also help to expand the mechanical limits of intellectual processing, thus reducing some of the "reality" limitations to learning and creative analysis.

SUMMARY

This chapter traces the development of the intelligence test from the rudimentary age scale of Binet and Simon to the publication of the Wechsler Adult Intelligence Scale—Revised. The historical conflict between proponents of general and multiple specific factor theories of intelligence is reviewed, noting the development of pragmatically useful knowledge and instruments, despite the continuing debate. The more recent concepts of *fluid* and *crystallized* intelligence are described, as

is their relationship to studies of the factor analytic structure of intelligence tests.

A number of intelligence tests intended for adult populations are listed and briefly annotated. Major attention is then focused on the WAIS-R, which is discussed in relation to its predecessor, the Wechsler Adult Intelligence Scale. Recently published findings regarding the reliability, validity, and factor analytic structure of the WAIS-R are reviewed, and some differences in statistical properties between the WAIS and WAIS-R are noted.

Applications of adult intelligence tests are described, including their use in individual evaluation for career counseling; evaluation of mental retardation or thought disorders; neuropsychological assessment; and evaluation of individuals at risk for genetic disorders. Illustrative case histories are included.

The chapter concludes by noting two major directions for the future: exploration of physiological correlates of intelligence and development of more effective methods for the application of human intelligence. These are related to ongoing research in genetics, neuropsychology, developmental psychology, and concepts of "artificial intelligence."

REFERENCES

Ammons, R., & Ammons, C. (1962). *The Quick Test.* Missoula, MT: Psychological Test Specialists.

Ammons, R., & Ammons, S. (1948). *Full-Range Picture Vocabulary Test.* Missoula, MT: Psychological Test Specialists.

Baker, H., & Leland, B. (1967). *Detroit Tests of Learning Aptitude.* Indianapolis: Bobbs-Merrill.

Binet, A., & Simon, T. (1905). Application des methodes nouvelles au diagnostic du niveau intellectual chez des enfants normaux et anormaux d'hospice et d'ecole primaire. *L'Année Psychologique, 11,* 245–336.

Binet, A., & Simon, T. (1908). Le development de l'intelligence chez les enfants. *L'Année Psychologique, 14,* 1–94.

Binet, A., & Simon, T. (1916). *The development of intelligence in children (The Binet-Simon Scale).* E.S. Kite (Trans.). Baltimore: Williams & Wilkins.

Blaha, J., & Wallbrown, F.H. (1982). Hierarchical factor structure of the Wechsler Adult Intelligence Scale—Revised. *Journal of Consulting & Clinical Psychology, 50,* 652–660.

Bornstein, R.A., & Matarazzo, J.D. (1982). Wechsler VIQ versus PIQ differences in cerebral dysfunction: A literature review with emphasis on sex differences. *Journal of Clinical Neuropsychology, 4,* 319–334.

Brown, W.R., & McGuire, J.M. (1976). Current psychological assessment practices. *Professional Psychology, 7,* 475–484.

Buros, O.K. (1978). *The eighth mental measurements yearbook*. Highland Park, NJ: The Gryphon Press.

Cattell, R.B. (1971). *Abilities: Their structure, growth and action*. Boston: Houghton Mifflin.

Cohen, J. (1957). The factorial structure of the WAIS between early adulthood and old age. *Journal of Consulting Psychology*, 21, 283–290.

Cronbach, L.J. (1960). *Essentials of psychological testing* (2nd ed.). New York: Harper & Row.

Detterman, D.K., & Sternberg, R.J. (1982). (Eds.). *How can and how much can intelligence be increased*. Norwood, NJ: Ablex.

Doyle, K.O., Jr. (1974). Theory and practice of ability testing in ancient Greece. *Journal of the History of the Behavioral Sciences*, 10, 202–212.

Dubois, P.H. (1970). *A history of psychological testing*. Boston: Allyn and Bacon.

Dunn, L. (1965). *Peabody Picture Vocabulary Test*. Circle Pines, MN: American Guidance Service.

Galton, F. (1869). *Hereditary genius: An inquiry into its laws and consequences*. London: MacMillan.

Garfield, S. (1982). Editor's note. *Journal of Consulting and Clinical Psychology*, 50, 652.

Garner, A.M. (1966). Intelligence testing and clinical practice. In I.A. Berg & L.A. Pennington (Eds.), *An Introduction to clinical psychology*. New York: Ronald Press.

Grossman, H.J. (1973). *Manual on terminology and classification in mental deficiency*. Washington DC: American Association on Mental Deficiency.

Guilford, J.P., & Hoepfner, R. (1971). *The analysis of intelligence*. New York: McGraw-Hill.

Harrell, T.W., & Harrell, M.S. (1945). Army general classification test scores for civilian occupations. *Educational and Psychological Measurement*. 5, 229–239.

Herman, D.O. (1982). Demographic factors in performance on WAIS-R. In D. Herman (Chair), *Wais-R factor structures and patterns of performance in various groups*. Symposium presented at the ninetieth annual convention of the American Psychological Association, Washington DC.

Hiskey, M. (1966). *Hiskey-Nebraska Test of Learning Aptitude*. Lincoln, NE: Hiskey.

Horn, J.L. (1980). Concepts of intellect in relation to learning and adult development. *Intelligence*, 4, 285–317.

Hunt, W.A., & Arnhoff, F.N. (1955). Some standardized scales for disorganization in schizophrenic thinking. *Journal of Consulting Psychology*, 19, 171–174.

Inalcik, K.H. (1973). *The Ottoman empire*. New York: Praeger.

Jackson, R.H. (1981). Other genetic disorders. In J.E. Lindemann (Ed.), *Psychological and behavioral aspects of physical disability*. New York: Plenum.

James, W. (1890). *The principles of psychology*. New York: Dover.

Josiassen, R.C., Curry, L., Roemer, R.A., DeBease, C., & Mancall, E.L. (1982). Patterns of intellectual deficit in Huntington's Disease. *Journal of Clinical Neuropsychology*, 4, 173–183.

Kaufman, H. (1974). *Kaufman Developmental Scale*. Chicago: Stoelting Co.

Kite, E.S. (1916). Translation of A. Binet and T. Simon. *The Development of intelligence in children*. Baltimore: Williams & Wilkins.

Lubin, B., Wallis, R.R., & Paine, C. (1971). Patterns of psychological test usage in the United States: 1935–1969. *Professional Psychology*, 2, 70–74.

Matarazzo, J.D. (1972). *Wechsler's measurement and appraisal of adult intelligence* (5th ed.). Baltimore: Williams & Wilkins.

Matarazzo, J.D., Carmody, T.P., & Jacobs, L.D. (1980). Test-retest reliability and stability of the WAIS: A literature review with implications for clinical practice. *Journal of Clinical Neuropsychology*, 2, 89–105.

Naglieri, J.A. (1982). Two types of tables for use with the WAIS-R. *Journal of Consulting and Clinical Psychology*, 50, 319–321.

Naylor, G., & Harwood, E. (1972). *Naylor-Harwood adult intelligence scale*. Hawthorne, Victoria, Australia: Australian Council for Educational Research.

Porteus, S. (1965). *Porteus maze test*. Palo Alto: Pacific Books.

Reitan, R.M., & Davison, L.A. (1974). (Eds.). *Clinical neuropsychology: Current status and applications*. Washington, DC: Winston.

Reynolds, W.M. (1979). Psychological tests: Clinical usage versus psychometric quality. *Professional Psychology*, 3, 324–329.

Robinson, A., Lubs, H.A., Nielsen, J., & Sorensen, K. (1979). Summary of clinical finding: Profiles of children with 47,XXY, 47,XXX and 47,XYY karyotypes. *Birth defects: Original article series*, 15, 261–266.

Rovet, J., & Netley, C. (1982). Processing deficits in Turner's Syndrome. *Developmental Psychology*, 18, 77–94.

Sattler, J.M. (1982). Age effects on Wechsler Adult Intelligence Scale—Revised tests. *Journal of Consulting and Clinical Psychology*, 50, 785–786.

Silverstein, A.B. (1982a). Factor structure of the Wechsler Adult Intelligence Scale—Revised. *Journal of Consulting and Clinical Psychology*, 50, 661–664.

Silverstein, A.B. (1982b). Pattern analysis as simultaneous statistical inference. *Journal of Consulting and Clinical Psychology*, 50, 234–240.

Spearman, C. (1904). "General intelligence," objectively determined and measured. *American Journal of Psychology*, 15, 201–293.

Stern, W.L. (1912). "Uberdie psychologischen Methoden der Intelligenzprufung. *Ber. V. Kongress Exp. Psychol.*, 16, 1–160. American translation by G.W. Whipple. *The psychological methods of testing intelligence*. Educational Psychology Monographs, No.13. Baltimore: Warwick & York, 1914.

Super, D.E., & Crites, J.O. (1962). *Appraising vocational fitness by means of psychological tests* (rev. ed.). New York: Harper & Row.

Terman, L.M. (1924). The mental test as a psychological method. *Psychological Review*, 31, 93–117.

Terman, L., & Merrill, M. (1973). *Stanford-Binet Intelligence Scale*. Boston: Houghton Mifflin.

Thorndike, E.L., Lay, W., & Dean, P.R. (1909). The relation of accuracy in sensory discrimination to general intelligence. *American Journal of Psychology*, 20, 364–369.

Thurstone, L.L., & Thurstone, T.G. (1941). Factorial studies of intelligence. *Psychometric Monographs, No. 2.* Chicago: University of Chicago Press.

Tyler, L.E. (1978). *Individuality.* San Francisco: Jossey-Bass.

Vernon, P.E. (1950). *The structure of human abilities.* New York: Wiley.

Wechsler, D. *The measurement of adult intelligence.* Baltimore: Williams & Wilkins. 1939, 1944.

Wechsler, D. (1955). *Manual for the Wechsler Adult Intelligence Scale.* New York: The Psychological Corporation.

Wechsler, D. (1974). *Wechsler Intelligence Scale for Children—Revised.* New York: The Psychological Corporation.

Wechsler, D. (1981). *Wechsler Adult Intelligence Scale—Revised.* New York: The Psychological Corporation.

Yerkes, R.M. (Ed.). (1921). Psychological examining in the U.S. Army. *Memoirs of the National Academy of Sciences, 15,* Washington, DC: GPO.

Zimmerman, I.L., & Woo-Sam, J.M. (1973). *Clinical interpretation of the Wechsler Adult Intelligence Scale.* New York and London: Grune & Stratton.

6 GROUP INTELLIGENCE TESTS

Julia R. Vane
Robert W. Motta

INTRODUCTION

The aim of group intelligence tests is the measurement of the current intellectual status of individuals taking the test. Group intelligence tests have a long history and have been administered under different names in one form or another for many centuries. Lin Chuan-ting (1980) indicates that research has shown that the Chinese were using some form of mental testing for appointment to the Imperial Court as early as the third century. At that time the belief was that the speed of speaking and writing could be used as an index of intelligence. By the seventh and eighth centuries sentence completion items were widely used in the Imperial examination, and various methods of paired antithetical phrases were used, similar to the opposite analogies found in present day individual and group intelligence tests. A seven-piece puzzle also was developed as a nonverbal intelligence test, comparable in nature to the differentiation of shapes and forms that appears today on many group tests of nonverbal intelligence. Even then concern was expressed about the predictive value of the test results and the interpretation of achievement in terms of group reference.

Today, group intelligence tests are used in many different ways. There are tests that will permit differentiation of individuals at the kindergarten,

elementary, high school, college, and professional school level. In addition, there are tests for a great variety of employment opportunities. Because group testing is used so extensively, it plays an important part in the lives of many people. For this reason, testing and the use made of test results usually have been a subject of considerable interest to the public and professionals.

HISTORICAL PERSPECTIVE

The impetus for the widespread use of group intelligence tests in the United States began with entrance of this country into World War I in 1917. At that time, the American Psychological Association, whose president was Robert Yerkes, offered its services to the United States Army. The Army was interested in a rapid means of sorting and classifying recruits for different levels of training. Psychologists, such as Terman, Yerkes, Otis, and others, developed what came to be known as the Army Alpha Intelligence Test, which was designed for literate recruits, and the Army Beta Intelligence Test designed for illiterate recruits. Testing was carried out in 35 camps, and 1,726,966 men were tested.

The experience with these tests was considered so successful that at the end of the war psychologists urged expansion into civilian testing. Within a short period of time various versions of the Army Alpha and similar group tests had been given in many hundreds of schools. At this stage, group intelligence testing was acclaimed as an educational aid that helped to identify the abilities of students more accurately than traditional methods of teacher evaluation and marks. It also was seen as a means of discovering talented individuals and as a way of opening doors for the talented poor. There was concern as well for identifying bright children who were forced to maintain an average pace in the classroom and the dull children who were forced to work at a level beyond their ability. This orientation won general acceptance in educational circles, and group intelligence testing became part of the general school routine, with classes of children being tested on a regular basis, often once a year or once every several years. In addition, use of such tests was extended as a means to select candidates for college and professional school admission and to screen applicants for employment.

The growth was so rapid that by 1923 Pintner published a book, *Intelligence Testing*, in which he was able to list 37 group intelligence tests, among which were five nonlanguage and six nonverbal tests. The nonlanguage tests were entirely pictorial in nature; the directions were given in pantomine and by samples demonstrated by the examiner. The nonverbal tests were pictorial in content and did not require a knowledge of reading or writing on the part of the test takers. At this time it was assumed that intelligence was a recognizable, inherent attribute that could be assessed through the use of intelligence tests, although not measurable in the same sense as physical attributes such as height or weight. Also, the level of tested intelligence was thought to be stable over the individual's life span.

Despite this general acceptance, controversy was touched off by the incautious conclusions drawn by professionals and especially articles in the popular press. The data collected through the use of testing on army recruits were extensive and as such formed the basis for a large number of articles. The conclusions drawn from the data were often less than scientific and, to some minds, highly inflammatory. There were suggestions that the level of mental maturity among the men in the army was about 12 to 13 years, and that certain ethnic groups who did well on the tests, particularly those with English and Scotch backgrounds, were superior to those who did poorly, namely individuals from southern and eastern European countries. Little account was taken of the language, cultural, and environmental differences experienced by these groups.

Cronbach (1975) and Haney (1981) give good descriptions of the controversy that erupted in the early twenties, with Walter Lippman (1922a, 1922b, 1923) leading a press attack on the concept of IQ testing with articles such as "The Mental Age of Americans," "Tests of Hereditary Intelligence," and "Rich and Poor, Girls and Boys." Rebuttals were undertaken by Freeman (1922), Terman (1922a, 1922b), Brigham (1923), and Yerkes (1923).

It would be a mistake to believe that the controversy was limited to professionals on one side and the public and press on the other. Many professionals did not hold with the position that intelligence tests measured innate potential, and a series of studies followed that indicated that environmental influences play a part in affecting tested intelligence. In 1923 the work of Gordon, with canal boat and gypsy children in England, showed that the IQ levels of these children were depressed, and the level of depression appeared related to the amount of schooling they received, which was usually very little. Five years later, studies by Freeman, Holzinger, and Mitchell (1928) as well as those of Burks (1928) showed that when orphans were placed in good foster homes there was an improvement in the tested intelligence.

Following this flare-up of interest by the public in the 1920s, professionals continued to debate the relative influence of nature and nurture on tested intelligence, but the public showed little interest. Despite the fact that more than twice as many men were tested for military assignments in World War II than had been tested in the first World War, little attention was paid to this in the popular press.

In 1958, following the launching of Sputnik by the Russians, group intelligence and aptitude tests were encouraged by the passage of the National Defense Education Act, which provided funds to the states to: "establish and maintain a program for testing aptitudes and abilities of students, and . . . to identify students with outstanding aptitudes and abilities" (Goslin, 1963, p. 71). The development of automated optical test scoring equipment by Lindquist and others at the Measurement Research Center in 1955 facilitated the expansion of large-scale testing programs. In this same year, the National Merit Scholarship Corporation was established to identify high school students of exceptional ability. With such a proliferation of testing, a number of critical articles appeared challenging the "tyranny of testing," as Hoffman (1962) phrased it. After another short quiet period, a significant upturn of public interest occurred in the late 1970s, which has continued to this day.

Although concern about intelligence testing in the United States has been linked to the egalitarian belief espoused by many that "all men are created equal," similar concerns can be found in articles published in many other countries. As an example, half a century ago Lommatzsch (1929) discussed a study done at a school in Dresden in which group intelligence tests were found to predict school performance no better than previous school grades. Lommatzsch questioned the value of the tests and noted, "The Saxon Philological Society is now undertaking a number of investigations for the further elaboration of the problem" (p. 346).

Cronbach (1975), in his article that chronicled the cycles of public acceptance and rejection of intelligence testing in the United States, indicated that the potential is always there for heightened public interest in professional findings that impinge upon the lives of the public, but that the form this interest will take usually is dependent upon the mood of the times. A good example of a challenging idea regarding testing that appeared at the wrong time was the work of Eels, Davis, Havighurst, Herricks, and Tyler (1951), who developed a "culture fair" test to identify bright children from the lower class, whom other tests and the educational system failed to locate. This is something that would have been highly interesting in the 1970s and 1980s, but it elicited little interest among the press, public, or educators at that time. In contrast, when Rosenthal and Jacobsen (1968) presented their point of view that teacher expectations strongly influence how well children from the lower class, whom other tests and the educational system failed to locate. This is audience. Despite the fact that Rosenthal's data were weak and most of the conclusions have not been substantiated, this point of view is still widely accepted in educational and popular circles, perhaps because this is a notion that many individuals find attractive at this time. The extent of acceptance is indicated by the fact that many educators and psychologists speak of "the Rosen-

thal effect" as though it were an established fact.

In viewing the present controversy regarding testing, Cronbach (1975) suggests that it is just another example of one of the cycles that he mentions. Linn (1982) points out, however, that the present attacks are different. In the earlier cycles, the attacks were limited to professional journals and the popular press, in which the debates took place. The most recent attacks, which began in 1970, have gone beyond the earlier ones and today are being debated in the national and state legislatures, and the outcome has been more serious than before in terms of curtailment of the use of both individual and group testing.

MAJOR OBJECTIONS TO INTELLIGENCE TESTING

The fact that standardized testing in general, and intelligence testing in particular, have engaged the interest of the public and the press for so many years is perhaps a reflection of the power the results of testing are perceived to exert over society, from early school entry to later opportunities for employment and promotion. This concern is exemplified by the titles of some of the articles and books published in the last 20 years. Such titles as *They Shall Not Pass* (Black, 1962), *The Brain Watchers* (Gross, 1962), "Born Dumb" (*Newsweek*, 1969), *How Racists Use Science to Degrade Black People* (Rowan, 1970), *The Stranglehold of the IQ* (Fine, 1975), *The War on Testing: David, Goliath and Gallup* (Lerner, 1980), *Soul Searching in the Testing Establishment* (Fiske, 1981) and *The Reign of ETS: The Corporation that Makes up Minds* (Nairn, 1980) give a flavor of the information purveyed to the public.

Attacks upon group intelligence testing by the public and professionals usually fall into three categories. There are criticisms of the way in which tests are used, there are criticisms of the conclusions drawn from the results of testing and the theories underlying these conclusions, and there are criticisms of the tests themselves.

CRITICISMS OF USE OF TESTS AND TESTING

Criticism of some of the ways in which tests are used or misused has been well founded. Misuses often cited have included classification of bilingual and foreign born students as retarded on the basis of tests given in English, group tests administered and interpreted by poorly trained personnel, and employment tests given that have little relation to the jobs for which they are supposed to be assessing the applicants. Those who criticize often suggest that misuse of testing is so widespread that there should be a ban on all testing, and in particular intelligence tests. Their major complaint is that such tests discriminate against minorities, especially blacks, Hispanics, native Americans, and individuals from low socioeconomic backgrounds. These groups cite examples such as the fact that in California in 1970, the enrollment in special classes for the mildly retarded was about 25% black, whereas the total black population of students was only about 10%. There is also a recent analysis in New Jersey revealing that black and Hispanic students comprised 18% and 7%, respectively, of the total student body but constituted 43% and 14%, respectively, of the enrollment in classes for the mildly retarded (Reschly, 1981). As the result of the activity and court suits brought by various groups of such critics, there is now a moratorium on IQ testing in the schools in California, Minneapolis, New York City, and Philadelphia. However, when methods other than IQ testing were used to evaluate California children for special class placement, the same percentage of minority children was found to be in need of special class placement as had been determined when IQ testing was used. The proportion of these children dropped only after a rigid quota system was imposed by the courts on placement of minorities in these classes.

As may be noted from the last example, banning testing is a nonsolution because the alternatives suggested, namely teacher evaluation, past grades, achievement tests, assessment of motivation, and cultural background have a greater potential for arriving at biased decisions than do the tests they are meant to replace. Although past performance and grades have been shown to be fairly good predictors of future performance, intelligence tests benefit those individuals who may have considerable ability as demonstrated by the tests but are handicapped by poor past performance and/or a dismal academic record. Even Gordon and Terrell (1981), who strongly criticize the misuse of standardized tests state, "To argue that standardized testing should be done away with or radically changed simply because ethnic minorities and disadvantaged groups do not earn as high scores as do middle class whites is an untenable position" (p. 1170). The authors do suggest, however, that the use of standardized tests be greatly reduced because they do not believe these tests serve a useful purpose. They propose the development of alternate devices and procedures that would be "process sensitive instruments designed to elicit data descriptive of the functional and conditional aspects of learner behavior" (p. 1170).

It would be naive to suppose, however, that if the ideal tests were developed that would do all the things that Gordon and Terrell and other critics suggest, these tests would be above criticism. As Hargadon (1981) states

> As a subject that invites debate and controversy, tests and their uses must rank with religion, politics and sex. Tests, at least in part, are designed to do a dirty job: they help us make discriminating judgments about ourselves, about others, about levels of accomplishment and achievement, about degrees of effectiveness. They are no less controversial when they perform their tasks well than when they perform them poorly. Indeed, it can be argued that the better the test, the more controversial its use becomes." (p. 1113)

CRITICISM OF CONCLUSIONS BASED UPON RESULTS OF INTELLIGENCE TESTING

The conclusions drawn from the results of large-scale intelligence testing usually arouse the greatest passion because they often suggest that one group of citizens is inferior to another based upon the inheritance of intelligence. In the past decade professionals and the public have become sensitive to these theoretical positions through the controversy generated by articles by Jensen (1969), Herrnstein (1971), and others, which suggested that aspects of general intelligence may be inherited and may be present to a greater or lesser degree in some ethnic groups. As was noted earlier, this theoretical position was strongly advanced in the 1920s, and although it created a furor at that time it eventually died down without the far-reaching effects it has had today.

It is possible to make use of group intelligence testing without embracing such positions with respect to them. As Carroll and Horn (1981) state,

"While questions about the heritability of human abilities are probably worthwhile scientific issues they are irrelevant to consideration about the use of tests in placement and selection" (p. 1013). In other words, one can use tests to select and differentiate without necessarily subscribing to any particular position with respect to the heritability of intelligence or to the extent to which it is a single characteristic, a multiple characteristic, or modifiable by the environment. As the above authors continue:

> Present theories about human abilities do not provide a sound basis for the assertion that a particular IQ score represents a hereditary defect, but the theories do provide a reasonable basis for the probabilistic statement that individuals obtaining a particular IQ score are not likely to do a good job in an occupation where the abilities represented in the IQ test have been shown to be related to good performance in that occupation. (p. 1017)

CRITICISMS OF
THE TESTS THEMSELVES

Criticisms of the actual tests are usually oriented to the fact that they do not predict adequately what they are designed to predict, tend to favor groups who are sophisticated test takers, are subject to improvement with coaching or repetition, emphasize unimportant aspects at the expense of aspects crucial for success in school or employment, and have not been standardized adequately on certain populations.

Any evaluation of the criticism of group intelligence tests requires some understanding of how the tests are constructed and the underlying theory relating to the test construction. Most of the widely used standardized group intelligence tests are developed and distributed by professional testing agencies that use accepted procedures prescribed for designing an effective test. It is true that testing is big business as the critics maintain, but to meet the requirements of the standards set by the court, legislators, and professional agencies, it is necessary to have a large staff of highly trained experts. The American Psychological Association, the American Education Research Association, and the National Council on Measurement in Education have jointly established and published their own set of standards for good testing practice (1974). A revision of these standards is now in progress. These standards require that large-scale research be carried out with respect to test reliability and validity, and that the tests be normed on large samples representative of the population for which the tests are to be used. In addition, a test manual, as well as technical supplements, must be provided to permit the qualified user to make a sound judgment regarding the use and interpretation of test scores. Anyone ordering sample tests will be supplied with this information, although technical manuals must be requested as they do not usually come with the specimen sets.

Criticisms that intelligence tests do not predict adequately what they have been designed to predict or have not been standardized adequately on certain populations are attacks upon the validity of the tests. As has been established in earlier articles, a test's validity is the extent to which scientifically valuable or practically useful inferences can be drawn from the scores. There are, as we know, four types of validity: content, criterion, current, and construct.

Content validity, also known as face validity, is most relevant to achievement tests, job knowledge tests, and work sample tests. A test has content validity when the items in the test appear, on the face of it, to be relevant to the performance it is designed to measure. For example, on a test of mechanical knowledge, not mechanical aptitude, the items would have to represent a broad area of mechanical information. This type of validity is not a crucial aspect of group intelligence tests, although intelligence tests are sometimes attacked because some of the items do not seem to be related to the critic's ideas of what should be on an intelligence test.

Criterion validity, also known as correlational or predictive validity, is measured by the ability of the test scores to predict performance in some criterion external to the test itself. For example, an elementary school intelligence test would be said to have good criterion validity if the test scores correlated highly with achievement scores or grades in school, because students who score high on an intelligence test are expected to achieve well in school and those who score on the low end are not expected to achieve well. Critics attack the criterion validity of group intelligence tests when they give examples of individuals who did poorly on tests, but turned out to be successful in college, professional school, or in later life. No one who supports testing disagrees that the tests do not predict perfectly, but they make the point that on the whole tests predict better than other measures. If the correlation between the intelligence test score and the criterion measure were perfect, namely 1.00, human beings would be perfectly predictable in the area tested. Correlations between intelligence and achievement tests tend to range between .50 and .80, with the lower correlations usually relating to younger children. These correlations take into account not only errors due to misclassification as the result of poor test construction, but also errors that occur because of poor motivation, poor testing conditions, and a number of other factors that enter into test taking. Test publishers, as well as those who do research in this area, have offered extensive evidence of test validity based on large scale studies of representative samples of the population. On the other hand, critics of test validity usually base their attacks on isolated examples of individuals who have been misclassified. It is the rare critic who produces actual data to show that any other method of prediction is superior to intelligence tests in the area for which they are designed.

An example of a study used to determine criterion validity is one in which 5,000 elementary school pupils in Milwaukee were given an intelligence test in the fourth grade, and the results were compared with the results of an achievement test given in the sixth grade. The correlation between the two was .75 (Crano, Kenny, & Campbell, 1972). Another study by the same authors showed that the correlation between the results of the Lorge-Thorndike Intelligence Scale given in the fourth grade and the Iowa Tests of Basic Skills, an achievement test, given in the sixth grade was .73 for a sample of 3,900 suburban children and .61 for a sample of 1,500 inner city children. Although in both of the above samples the correlation was between two different types of tests, it is difficult to find studies of elementary school or high school students that attempt to predict in other areas, since whether children are achieving in terms of their potential is of major interest to the schools.

Concurrent validity is the correlation of a previously unvalidated test with an already validated test. This is rarely the only method used to validate a published test. If this should be so, the user should exercise caution when using it, until further data are supplied.

Construct validity is most important from the standpoint of science, just as criterion validity is most important in terms of practical use of the tests. Construct validity is used to determine if the test predicts behavior in specific situations that would be deduced from a theory. For example, if a theory of intelligence involved the idea that ability to deal effectively with abstractions was the measure of intelligence, then an intelligence test should be a better predictor of performance in work involving abstract reasoning than work involving interaction with people. As has been indicated, one need not subscribe to any particular theory to use an intelligence test, but if general conclusions are to be drawn from the results, the user should be aware of the theory espoused by the test designer.

The construction of most group intelligence tests tends to reflect the theoretical belief that individuals possess an underlying general ability factor, called "g," which can partially account for the differences in competence among them. All intelligence tests, if they are good, will differentiate among people in terms of ability to succeed in educational, professional, and employment areas of life. Efforts at improving our understanding and measurement of intelligence may come from laboratory studies of the cognitive processes that are sampled by the various tests of intelligence. Guilford (1959), Hunt (1978), and Pellegrino and Glaser (1980), among others, have attempted to describe the task requirements that distinguish different abilities by applying theories and methods of laboratory research to cognitive processes. Despite these efforts there are no clear-cut signs at the present time to indicate how to design the "best" measure of intelligence.

The large number of group intelligence tests available, although they bear certain similarities in content and format, use different items to tap a wide variety of cognitive functions. These items when combined into a single test score are purported to assess intelligence, mental ability, or cognition. Actually, the fact that all good group intelligence tests correlate highly with one another suggests that even though there are differences among them, the "g" factor may be tapped in a number of different ways. It is possible that so many separate subabilities comprise overall intellectual ability that no one test can sample all of them, and the different tests may assess different aspects of "g" or general intelligence. Even tests with quite different titles, such as the Scholastic Aptitude Test, the Medical College Admission Test, the Law School Aptitude Test, and the Graduate Record Examination are almost as highly correlated with one another as are equivalent forms of the same test. For example, Fricke (1975) reported a correlation of .80 between the Scholastic Aptitude Test scores taken by 1,400 students for college admission and the scores obtained on the Graduate Record Examination 4 years later.

When test content is considered, it becomes apparent that the range of items that can be employed in constructing group intelligence tests is large. One form of test item is the vocabulary word, which is usually presented as follows:

generous means/charitable/openhanded/loving/careful.

Vocabulary items frequently are the subject of criticism because they are said to measure an individual's education and background. This is true to some extent, but these items show the highest correlation with other different type items that have been found to be good measures of general intelligence. Acquisition of vocabulary is not just a matter of learning and memory but requires discrimination, generalization, and education. During childhood and life nearly everyone hears more different words than ever become part of one's vocabulary. Some people, however, acquire much larger vocabularies than others, and this is true even among siblings of the same family. Vocabulary items can be presented in pictorial form as well and can be used with children and nonreaders, and sometimes appear on group intelligence tests in the lower grades.

Items to tap an individual's range of general information may also be used on group intelligence tests and are open to the same criticism as vocabulary items. They correlate highly with other noninformational measures of intelligence because an individual's range of knowledge is a good indication of ability. These items provide the most problems with respect to cultural differences because it is hard to determine what range of information an individual from a different culture might be expected to know. For this reason vocabulary items and general information items do not appear as frequently on many group intelligence tests today as they once did.

The most common items on group intelligence tests are those classified as requiring reasoning ability. These may be problems presented in verbal form, numerical form, or pictorial form. For example, an analogies item in verbal form would be:

WOOD is to TREE as PAPER is to:
  LAKE   IRON   PEN   MILL   PULP.
Analogies in a figural format would be:

Other types of verbal reasoning items include similarities, in which the question might be:
  SMART means the same as:
  LIVELY HAPPY AGREEABLE CLEVER.
Another type of item called oddities, or odd man out as the British title it, is as follows:
  Underline the word that does not belong with the others:
  BOOK PENCIL PEN PAD WRITING
Logical reasoning is another type of item that is popular. An example of this is:
  Mary is shorter than Ellen
  Joan is taller than Mary
  Who is shortest?
Items that depend upon reasonable inferences and judgment based upon the information given are called inferential conclusions. These items are similar in form to items of reading comprehension, except that when used in intelligence tests, the level of vocabulary and reading difficulty is kept simple so that items are not dependent upon vocabulary or reading per se. An example of this kind of item, reported by Jensen (1980, p. 151) and taken from Womer (1970) is as follows:

In a particular meadow there are a great many rabbits that eat the grass. There are also many hawks that eat the rabbits. Last year a disease broke out among the rabbits and most of them died. Which one of the following things most probably occurred?
  a) The grass died and the hawk population decreased.
  b) The grass died and the hawk population increased.
  c) The grass grew taller and the hawk population decreased.

d) The grass grew taller and the hawk population increased.

e) Neither the grass nor the hawks were affected by the death of the rabbits.

In a random sample of the U.S. adult population, 52 percent chose the correct answer, which was "c."

Other test items involve numbers such as those shown below:

Numerical reasoning:

Tom is twice as old as Jim, who is four years old. How old will Tom be when Jim is 15 years old?

Number series:

Write the number that will complete the following series:

3   8   13   18   23   _____

As may be seen, most of these items fall into the category of multiple choice items. Critics decry their use on the grounds that such items tap only surface knowledge. Multiple choice items can be good or bad depending upon the amount of time put into developing them. The amount of knowledge or reasoning required depends upon the level of the item itself. As may be seen from the item quoted from Womer, a high level of reasoning is involved. Another sample is given by Glaser and Bond (1981). They contrast two multiple choice questions, both requiring similar knowledge but the first item requires only knowledge, the second knowledge and reasoning.

1) The mean of a set of values is:
   a. the lowest value
   b. the average value
   c. the middle value
   d. the most frequent value

2) The correlation of SAT-verbal or SAT math among all test takers is about .5. For a group of applicants admitted to Harvard, the correlation is probably
   a. greater than .5
   b. about .5
   c. less than .5
   d. Anything—no basis for guess

For the second question the student would have to reason that since Harvard is highly selective, the group admitted would have relatively homogeneous test scores, so the correlation will be lower than that of the national group.

There are a large number of other types of verbal and nonverbal test items, all of which have been shown to make a contribution to "g." Jensen (1980) has an exhaustive list of these. When tests must be administered to large groups as most group intelligence tests are, issues such as ease of administration and ease of scoring become important factors, and these influence the selection of items.

One of the more popular group intelligence tests that is intended to provide a measure of "g," the general intellective ability factor, is the Otis-Lennon Mental Ability Test (OLMAT). The OLMAT is an outgrowth of the original Army Alpha Examiniation which was used in classifying World War I recruits. The current test reflects many characteristics of the earlier version but is more refined with regard to psychometric properties. The kindergarten level form of this test taps areas such as following directions, quantitative reasoning, and comprehension of verbal concepts. Here we can see something of an intuitive arrangement of areas of reasoning that are contributors to and reflect the operation of "g." Scales applicable up to the third grade level would include more difficult items in these categories but also involve reasoning by analogy items. At higher grade levels, various types of verbal and nonverbal items sample a wide range of mental processes, all believed to reflect and contribute to the general intellective ability factor. Items are hand or machine scored and the final score is a normalized standard score, called a deviation IQ, which has a mean of 100 and a standard deviation of 16. Although an IQ is derived, the authors of the test appear to take a tentative stand regarding the issue of whether the test is, in fact, a measure of intelligence. At one point the test is called a measure of general mental ability, yet, at a later point, the reader is informed that the tests do not measure native endowment. Despite the issue of whether group intelligence tests do measure intelligence, virtually all of these measures report statistically significant reliability and validity figures. The OLMAT, for example, yields reliability coefficients from about .84 to .90, with the variation a function of the particular age and grade level being assessed. The OLMAT, like most of the group intelligence tests in wide use, is based upon a large standardization sample. The OLMAT reports a standardization sample of 200,000 children in kindergarten through high school in 117 school districts throughout the country. Validity coefficients of .73 and .78 with the individual Wechsler Scales are reported.

The Lorge-Thorndike Intelligence Test is another popular group administered scale that is applicable to grades 3–12. This test is clearly stated to be a measure of "abstract intelligence," and like the OLMAT, contains both verbal and nonverbal items. The verbal battery is made up of five subtests, which include vocabulary, verbal classification, sentence completion, arithmetic reasoning, and verbal analogies. The nonverbal battery contains subtests of pictorial classification, pictorial analogies, and numerical relationships.

The current edition, called the Multi-Level Edition, has more representative norms than the earlier Separate Level Edition. Validity estimates are readily established, as the Lorge-Thorndike was normed upon the same samples used for the Iowa Test of Basic Skills, a group administered test for grades 3–8 and the Tests of Academic Progress for grades 9–12. Correlations with school performance are typical of the various group tests, and in one case are reported to be .87 with reading and .76 with math. Moderate but significant correlations are found between the Lorge-Thorndike and the WISC and Stanford Binet and range from .54 to .77. The conglomerate of different types of verbal and nonverbal items, again appears to represent an attempt to assess "g" by utilizing some arrangement of tests that correlate with each other and which therefore are assumed to share a common global or general intellective process.

The Test of Cognitive Skills (TCS) is an academic abilities test that evolved from the Short Form Test of Academic Aptitude, known as the SFTAA. The latter test is an outgrowth of the Short Form of the California Test of Mental Maturity. The California Test, which was published in 1957, has a wide application and has primary, elementary, and secondary levels and a level for adults. On the primary level, test items are entirely nonverbal, with successive levels employing increasingly more complex verbal and numerical material. The California Test includes items called inferences and are of the type:

A is shorter than B

B is shorter than C

Who is the shortest, A, B, or C?

Also included are number series, like the OLMAT; and numerical quantity, which are items requiring the student to solve arithmetic problems. Finally, there are verbal concepts, in which the student is required to select from four choices the word that is synonymous with the key word. IQs can be obtained from verbal, nonverbal, and total scores.

The Short Form Test of Academic Aptitude (SFTAA), which was published in 1970 and evolved from the Short Form of the California Test of Mental Maturity (1963), is designed specifically for use in grades 1.5–12. The developers of the SFTAA claim that a number of items on the California Test were ambiguous, unreliable, and not sound predictors of academic performance. Thus, items were dropped and replaced by more robust and reliable ones, resulting in an 85-item test, as compared to the SF-CMMT's 100, which sampled areas of vocabulary, analogies, sequences, and memory. Resulting scores yield MAs, IQs, percentiles, and stanines.

The recently developed Test of Cognitive Skills (1981) is the latest step in the series and retains many of the features of the earlier tests. The Test of Cognitive Skills (TCS) is applicable to grades 2 through 12. The test's developers claim that this is a major revision of the SFTAA, yet two of the four major areas of the TCS, namely sequences and analogies, remain the same as the SFTAA in structure and rationale. The SFTAA vocabulary test has been replaced by a verbal reasoning test on the TCS. Some of the verbal reasoning items involve inferring relationships among ostensibly unrelated words, identifying essential aspects of objects or concepts, and drawing logical conclusions from information given in a short passage. This modification appears to have been done in order to make comparisons between the TCS and achievement batteries commonly given in schools. Although the SFTAA and TCS both contain a memory test, the two subtests do differ. On the former test, a story is read at the beginning of the test period. Recall items require not only the ability to recall facts and ideas, stated or implied, but also to make inferences and recall the logical flow of the story. On the TCS, the memory test is designed to provide a measure of memory that is not dependent on reasoning or reading comprehension skills. At upper levels of the TCS, 20 obscure words and their definitions are presented to the students. At some later point students are required to associate the definition with the appropriate word after having been presented with a set of obscure words.

In terms of testing for college entrance, one test dominates the field, and this is the College Entrance Examination Board's Scholastic Aptitude Test, better known as the SAT. This test is given by the College Board to all high school students throughout the nation who wish to take it. The results are then sent to the colleges the student wishes to enter. Most selective colleges require SAT scores, but in many colleges the scores are only one of the factors used in admitting students. Most colleges, however, do have minimum cut-off scores.

The SAT is a paper-and-pencil test comprised of 150 multiple choice items involving five choices each. There is a verbal section involving reading comprehension, antonyms, verbal analogies, and sentence completion. The mathematics section consists of numerical and quantitative reasoning items, but does not tap formal mathematical knowledge per se. The SAT would undoubtedly load very heavily on the "g" factor in any factor analytic study that included other mental ability tests. The verbal section has been found to correlate higher with grade point average in college than the mathematics score.

The validity of the SAT scores in predicting scores of minority group students has frequently been challenged. In a study by Stanley and Porter (1967), students in three black coeducational 4-year state colleges were compared with students in 15 predominantly white state colleges in Georgia. Correlations of the combined scores with freshman grade point averages were .72 for white females, .63 for black females, and .60 for both white and black males, suggesting that the prediction for white females is better than for the other three groups. A number of studies have shown that high school grade point averages predict college grade point averages better than the SAT for whites, but the reverse is true for blacks (Cleary, 1968; McKelpin, 1965; Munday, 1965; Peterson, 1968).

In the area of employment, tests have been used in making such decisions in the United States for over 70 years. Although there are many content validated job knowledge tests and job sample tests, such as typing tests, the mostly commonly used have been measures of cognitive skills, called either aptitude or ability tests. According to Schmidt and Hunter (1981), who have done a meta analysis of a larger number of studies in the field of employment testing, the results show that

professionally developed cognitive ability tests are valid predictors of performance on the job and in training for all jobs in all settings. . . . [and that] cognitive ability tests

are equally valid for minority and majority applicants and are fair to minority applicants in that they do not underestimate the expected job performance of minority groups. (p. 1128)

The authors offer considerable evidence of the money saved by the use of group tests of general ability. They report that about 10 years ago one large company responded to pressure from the government and dropped all tests of job aptitude. Like many large companies, this one had a policy of promoting from within. After about 6 to 7 years, the company found that a large percentage of the people they had hired were not promotable, so that the problem was transferred from the hiring level to the promotional level. Schmidt, Hunter, and Pearlman (1981) reported the results of a study of 370,000 clerical workers showing that the validity of seven cognitive abilities was essentially constant across five different clerical job families. All seven abilities were highly valid in all five job families. The article by Schmidt and Hunter contains a great deal of information about the value and validity of employment testing and should be read by all interested in this area.

One of the group intelligence tests designed for use in employment selection is the Wonderlic Personnel Test. The author intentionally uses the term *personnel* rather than intelligence to reduce the anxiety of those who must take the test. Despite this, the test manual clearly indicates that the intended use of the instrument is to assess mental ability so that a suitable match can be made between the applicant's ability and the ability level demanded for a particular job area. One of the advantages, from a personnel screening standpoint, is that the test is administered in only 12 minutes. There are 50 questions, which examinees usually do not finish, that require them to reason in terms of words, numbers, symbols, and to think using ideas. The test has 14 different forms and has been standardized in business situations, using large numbers of people and test sites. Minimum scores are reported for professions, ranging from custodian to administrators and executives. The score reported is the number correct instead of an IQ, thus reducing some of the controversial issues evoked by the latter term. Norms are available based upon sex, age, race and educational level.

A sampling of items includes the following: Assume the first two statements are true.

Is the final statement
(1) true,   (2) false,   (3) not certain
Harry is the same age as John.
John is younger than Tom.
Harry is older than Tom _____ .

It is of interest to note that this item is quite similar to one that might be found in the Inference section of the Short Form of the California Mental Maturity Scale, despite the fact that the two tests were designed for different purposes.

Other types of items that are similar to those found on the Wonderlic are the following:

How many square inches are there on a panel that measures 1 foot by 2 feet?

Are the meanings of the following sentences (1) similar, (2) contradictory or (3) neither

_____ .

Still water runs deep. You can't tell a book by its cover.

A question that readily comes to mind is how valid can an instrument be if it claims to do in 12 minutes what other, more established measures do in an hour or more. In a recent study by Dodrill (1981), the Wonderlic was given to a varied group of 120 adults along with the WAIS and other measures. Correlations between these two tests ran from .91 to .93. Dodrill concluded that when groups of normal individuals are considered, the average error is about 1 IQ point. When persons are considered individually, the Wonderlic yields IQ scores within 10 points of the WAIS 90 % of the time. This high degree of similarity is attained even with scorers who are not professionally trained. Drawbacks of the Wonderlic are that reading skill is required to take the test, speed is required (and therefore anyone with a deficit that would affect psychomotor speed would be handicapped), and the test does not break down intelligence into verbal and nonverbal measures and may not be as diagnostically useful as longer tests. These disadvantages appear to be greatly outweighed by the obvious benefits of a reliable and valid group measure of intelligence that is so easily administered and scored.

Not only are group intelligence tests used for educational and employment purposes, but as might be expected, the Armed Forces employs a test of general ability for use in selecting and classifying men in the services. This is the Armed Forces Qualification Test, a 100-item multiple choice group test. The results classify men into five categories: Category I includes men with scores of 80–100; II, 74–88; III, 53–73; IV, 25–52; and V, 1–24. Those falling in category V are rejected.

A study by Grunzke, Guinn, and Stauffer (1970) comparing men in category IV inducted into the Air Force with men in the top three categories showed that the category IV men were less likely to complete basic training, had more unsuitable discharges, and were less likely to attain the required levels of skill needed on the job. Correlation between test scores and job training grades was about .50, but this dropped to about .30 for ratings of performance on the job. It was also found that men scoring low on the test had a greater tendency to become disciplinary cases.

Another type of group intelligence test is represented by the Cattell Culture Fair Intelligence Tests. There are other tests that aim to be culture fair, culture free, or culture reduced; as mentioned previously, Davis and Eels developed a test in this area in 1951, but it never gained popularity. Cattell (1940) listed a group of highly universal concepts that would span most cultures and provide a common basis for developing reasoning questions. Among them were common objects: human body and its parts, footprints, trees (except for Eskimos), four-legged animals, earth, sky, clouds, sun, moon, stars, lightning, fire, smoke, water, parents, and children. In addition he proposed using common processes such as breathing, choking, coughing, sneezing, eating, drinking, sleeping, and so on. Despite this original interest by Cattell in common objects and processes, the items in the Cattell Tests are entirely content free and are composed of abstract figural items forming sets of problems in series progression, classification, matrices, and discovering common properties. An example that is similar to the items appearing on the Cattell Culture Fair Test is shown below.

The tests are in paper-and-pencil format and have time limits for each subtest. Scale 1 is intended for children 4 to 8 years and retarded

adults. It has eight subtests, each with a time limit varying from 2 to 4 minutes. There are lengthy instructions for each subtest, and although the test time is only 22 minutes, the total time is 60 minutes. Scale 2 is for ages 8 to 13 and average adults, and Scale 3 for high school, college, and superior adults. The subject's total working time is only 12½ minutes, but the total time is about 30 minutes. Criticisms of this test are strong with respect to the lengthy instructions, which cause children to lose attention and become bored. One other problem is that bright adults with learning disability deficits, particularly left-right and reversal difficulties, obtain low scores on this test.

Unfortunately, despite the aims of Cattell and others, the Culture Fair Tests have not functioned the way it was hoped they would. Spuck and Stout (1969) gave the Cattell Culture Fair Test, the California Test of Mental Maturity, and the SCAT-V and SCAT-Q to a group of 32 low socioeconomic Mexican American freshmen admitted to college. All correlations between these tests and the FPA were nonsignificant.

A number of other studies have been done with Cattell's tests with mixed results. It has been shown that there are moderate correlations from .20 to .50 with scholastic achievement, and predictive validities have been fairly impressive for certain groups and criteria. Correlations with other intelligence tests are mostly in the .50 to .70 range, which suggests that the test is measuring the "g" factor. The tests have been tried on many culturally different groups outside the United States, with comparable scores even across quite dissimilar groups, (e.g., children in the United States, France, England, Hong Kong, and Taiwan). The tests show somewhat lower correlations with socioeconomic status than culture loaded or verbal tests. Also, some bilingual immigrant groups score higher on these tests than on conventional IQ tests. However, the Cattell test does not necessarily reduce the magnitude of racial differences found with other tests or yield higher scores, on the average, with native-born culturally disadvantaged groups, particularly blacks.

At the other end of the continuum are those tests designed to reflect a unique knowledge of a given culture. An example of this type of scale is the BITCH Culture Specific Test by Williams (1972). The acronym stands for Black Intelligence Test of Cultural Homogeneity. What the author of this test set out to demonstrate is that one's performance on a test can be affected by prior cultural experience. The test contains a vocabulary that reflects black slang; as might be expected, blacks score significantly better than whites. The test's value is probably that it sensitizes us to the extent to which one's performance can vary due to prior knowledge, but its major drawback is that it does not correlate with known measures of intelligence (Matarazzo & Weins, 1977). This latter finding can, of course, be countered by the notion that one would not expect to find a correlation between popular standardized intelligence tests that are considered by some to be culturally biased in terms of the dominant culture and one that is biased in favor of a minority group.

The fact remains that standardized intelligence tests, in general, predict the ability of individuals to succeed in the dominant culture better than the use of other instruments. It would be desirable to have a test that would be able to locate potentially promising children and adults from minority cultures.

The controversy regarding whether or not group intelligence tests in use today predict the ability of individuals from minority cultures to succeed in early education, college, professional schools, and later life is too large an area to treat in this chapter. Articles in the special issue of the *American Psychologist* (1981) on testing address many aspects of this problem, as does Jensen's 1980 book *Bias in Mental Testing*, the article "Critical factors in testing Hispanic Americans" by Padilla (1979), the article by Gordon (1977), "Diverse human populations and problems in education program evaluation via achievement testing," and the article by Garcia, "The futility of a comparative IQ research." All of these writings contain extensive references and supporting data. There can be no doubt that it is in the best interest of all concerned citizens that tests affecting the lives of so many be designed and used so that they provide a fair evaluation of all our citizens. Professionals, educators, and the public have an obligation to look at research findings on both sides of the question, not only the side to which they have an emotional attachment.

A review of some of the changes made in response to the criticisms leveled at group intelligence testing gives some perspective of a field in the process of change. As may be seen, some of the changes have resulted in improvements; others have not had such a favorable outcome.

LEGISLATED CHANGES

As mentioned previously, there are court ordered moratoriums on group intelligence testing in California and other large cities of the nation. In California there is additionally a court mandate that no more than a certain percentage of minority children may be placed in special classes for the retarded. As of March 1983, the courts in Chicago were being asked by a group of parents to ban an assessment battery in use in Chicago schools to re-evaluate children who were in classes for the retarded (Cordes, 1983). The school system, as part of its court approved desegregation plan and in an attempt to meet the objections of the critics, had adopted a ban on standardized intelligence tests and made a commitment to reassess all children classified as mildly mentally retarded, using other methods. To do so they developed a battery including psychometric tests, assessment of adaptation, clinical techniques, behavioral observations, consultations, and team discussions. No cut-off scores on any measures were used. Although the critics originally had objected to the use of standardized intelligence tests, at this juncture they are bringing suit because the present battery has not been standardized or validated, and there are no cut-off scores. It is apparent that it is easy to legislate changes, but the changes do not always improve the situation, even in the eyes of the critics.

Another legislated change took place in New York in 1980. This was the passage of the "truth-in-testing" law, aimed at giving the consumer more knowledge regarding the product being utilized. This law requires that questions and answers that determine an examinee's score on college and professional school admission tests, many of which are group intelligence tests although they are not always labeled as such, be disclosed within 30 days of release of test scores. As soon as this law went into effect, the Association of American Medical Colleges brought suit against the state of New York on the grounds that there are a limited number of high quality questions that can be designed for a test such as the Medical College Admissions Test. Within a month, a federal judge ordered a preliminary injunction exempting this test from the New York law until the legal merits of the case could be considered in court. To date this has not been decided. Also, as a reaction to this law, Psychological Corporation, publishers of the Miller

Analogies Test, stopped administering it in New York state. The Educational Testing Service reduced the number of times certain Graduate Record Examinations were scheduled to be given and eliminated giving certain sections of this examination entirely in New York. Students who wish to take some of these examinations must go to neighboring states to do so. The actions of these companies were based on their claim that they cannot continue to make up new, reliable questions, which they would have to do if test questions and answers were made public on a regular basis. The difficulty of developing highly discriminating effective test items was highlighted in a number of well-publicized cases from the "truth-in-testing" law. The newspapers and those opposed to testing enjoyed the fact that a school boy in Florida was able to demonstrate that his answer on one question on the Scholastic Aptitude Test was the correct one, although it was not the answer designated as correct by the publishers of the test, the Educational Testing Service. "Youth outwits merit exam, raising 240,000 scores," stated the *New York Times* of March 17, 1980. As Haney (1981) reports, there were several other incidents of this type involving an SAT mathematics question, two faulty items on the Graduate Record examination, and another on a Law School Admissions Test. Clearly, incidents of this kind are bound to make those who develop and review the test questions very careful, but it is questionable how relevant errors of this sort are with respect to the large issues involved.

CHANGES MADE BY TEST DEVELOPERS AND PUBLISHERS

One of the criticisms directed at the tests themselves was that some groups have more experience and are better prepared to take tests than others and that test scores improve as the result of this better preparation and with practice. These criticisms are based on research that has shown that short orientation and practice sessions can be effective in equalizing test sophistication (Millman, Bishop, & Ebel, 1965), and that significant mean gains have been shown when alternate forms of the same test have been administered over time within a range of one day to several years (Angoff, 1970; Droege, 1966).

To answer this criticism the large test companies, such as Psychological Corporation, Educational Testing Service, the College Board, as well as the United States Employment Service, have prepared booklets on how to take tests. In addition, the United States Employment Service has a more extensive orientation for use with educationally disadvantaged applicants (U.S. Department of Labor, 1968, 1970, 1971).

In order to assess the impact of a new booklet, *Taking the SAT*, that it prepared (Alderman & Powers, 1980), the College Board sent a pre-publication copy to a sample of 1,000 high school juniors who had registered for the SAT. This group also received a copy of an earlier booklet, *About the SAT*. A control group of 1,000 comparable registrants received only the earlier booklet. The new booklet contained detailed analyses of different item types included on the SAT along with suggestions for answering the items. In addition, there was a complete form of the SAT and a scoring key that the student could take under standard testing conditions. After the actual administration of the SAT, both groups were sent questionnaires. The results showed that nearly all respondents in the experimental sample reported some use of the booklet, but only 38% had read the entire booklet. Only 36% reported having tried to answer all of the questions, and 23% had answered none. Significantly, more experimental than control subjects believed that their test performance had been helped by the material they had received, but their actual scores showed no difference between the groups. It would appear that the original material was as effective as the more extensive material in terms of outcome. But in view of the fact that studies have shown that test-retest with alternate forms improves scores, the results might have been different if 100% of the experimental group had taken the sample test.

The criticism that test scores improve as the result of coaching is not new and has been the subject of considerable research. Anastasi (1981) covers many of these studies, some of which were done in England over a long period and others in the United States. The British studies were concerned with examinations given there to all 11-year-old school children as a means of assigning them to different types of advanced education. In general, these studies showed that the extent of improvement depended on the ability and earlier educational experiences of the examinees, the nature of the tests, and type of coaching. Children with poor educational backgrounds benefited most from special coaching, and the closer the similarity between test content and coaching material, the greater the improvement in test scores.

At the present time there are a large number of coaching courses offered in the United States for those preparing to take the College Entrance examinations as well as professional examinations in areas such as law and psychology. Studies conducted by the College Board on the effects of coaching courses on subsequent scores showed that the usual short high school coaching programs yielded average gains of approximately 10 points in SAT verbal scores and approximately 15 points in SAT mathematical scores. More intensive and longer commercial programs showed gains as high as 20 points on the verbal scores and 30 on the mathematics scores.

Most of the gains achieved through coaching are short lived because knowledge obtained through intensive drill does not translate into increased ability to do well on the criterion measure, which is usually college or professional school performance. It takes a long time to accumulate the relevant knowledge that is part of what many psychologists consider intelligence and that contributes to a person's readiness to learn more advanced material. When coaching improves test performance without adding to the individual's permanent store of knowledge, it reduces test validity, and the test becomes a poorer measure of the broad abilities it was designed to assess. Well-constructed tests employ items shown to be least susceptible to drill and short-term coaching, so that the tests may continue to be an accurate means of ascertaining whether the individual has acquired the skills and knowledge necessary for success in the criterion.

One of the problems in meeting the criticisms made of group intelligence tests is the difficulty of finding satisfactory substitutes for them. As was seen in the Chicago schools, the new evaluation techniques found no more favor with the critics than did the original tests. Another example of this was reported in the *New York Times* on March 10, 1983. The story by Treaster is headlined "New Police Test is Called Unfair," and goes on to report that "scores of New York City police sergeants are charging that a new Police Department examination that was designed to overcome racial and sexual biases was unfair to them. Four lawsuits have been filed." According to the article, the new test was designed to overcome the objections of the courts that previous police examinations, which had consisted entirely of multiple choice questions and was similar to a group intelligence test, was discriminatory. The new test was somewhat of a departure from the usual pencil-and-paper tests. In the first part the candidates were given a basket of papers that the department said was typical of what a lieutenant would find when he reported for work at a precinct station, and they were asked to respond to the problems raised in the papers by indicating answers to 47 multiple choice questions. The second part consisted of 75 multiple-choice questions about police procedures and regulations. In the third part the candidates were asked to assume the role of a lieutenant and conduct a 30-minute meeting with a person playing the role of a police sergeant who, the candidate was told, had been experiencing some job performance problems. This part was videotaped and graded at the headquarters of the company that had designed the test. This new test showed that the pass rate was 30% for white males, 29% for women, 23% for Hispanics, and 20% for blacks. Previous tests had shown almost no women, Hispanics, or blacks passing. As may be seen, innovative methods of testing can be developed to meet the criticisms leveled at group intelligence tests, but besides being expensive to construct and administer, they need to be validated by on-the-job performance and are clearly not beyond challenges.

SUMMARY

A review of the literature suggests that it is unlikely that testing will disappear despite the attacks and actions in the legislatures and courts. In highly developed countries such as our own and in emerging cultures there is a continuing demand for some means of evaluation and selection to aid in personal decisions in educational and employment areas. Articles from other cultures indicate they are struggling with the same problems concerning group intelligence tests as we are. For example, Watkins and Astilla (1980) report on a follow-up of 1,149 freshmen at a major Filipino University. This showed that the College entrance examination, the Otis Lennon Mental Abilities Test, and high school grade point average were only moderately successful predictors of college performance. When they looked at nonintellective factors, however, such as socioeconomic status, scholastic expectations, family constellation, and results of the California Personality Inventory, they found these of no value as predictors.

Another attempt to find predictors for success in completing the West African School Certificate

Examination was reported by O'bemesta (1980) in the *West African Journal of Educational and Vocational Measurement*. One group of secondary school students was given a preliminary test in Yoruba, and a control group was given it in English. Five years later their progress was checked, and it was found that both tests showed moderate correlations with success on the Certificate examination, but that the tests given in Yoruba predicted no better than the tests given in English.

It is clear that tests will continue to be a part of modern life. In view of this, it is hoped that users of group intelligence tests will bear in mind the social context within which the tests are to be used, the professional manner in which they should be used, and the adequacy of their construction. The public and professional controversies that have been reviewed have been valuable in highlighting some of the problems associated with testing. It is hoped that these controversies will serve as an impetus for psychologists to look at testing in new and creative ways and work to develop tests that will serve the public good.

REFERENCES

Alderman, D.L., & Powers, D.E. (1980). The effects of special preparation on SAT verbal scores. *American Educational Research Journal*, 17, 239–253.

American Psychological Association, American Educational Research Association, & National Council on Measurement in Education. (1974). Standards for educational and psychological tests. Washington, DC: Author.

Anastasi, A. (1981). Coaching, test sophistication, and developing abilities. *American Psychologist*, 36, 1086–1093.

Angoff, W.H. (Ed.) (1971). *The College Board admissions testing program: A technical report on research and development activities relating to the Scholastic Aptitude test and achievement tests*. New York: College Entrance Examination Board.

Black, H. (1962). *They shall not pass*. New York: Random House.

Born dumb? (1969). *Newsweek*, 73, 84.

Brigham, C.C. (1923). A study of American intelligence. Princeton, NJ: Princeton University Press.

Burks, B.S. (1928). The relative influences of nature and nurture upon mental development. *27th Yearbook of National Society for the Study of Education*, I, 219–316.

California Short-Form Test of Mental Maturity (1963). Monterey, CA: CTB/McGraw-Hill.

Carroll, J.B., & Horn, J.L. (1981). On the scientific basis of ability testing. *American Psychologist*, 36, 1012–1020.

Cattell Culture Fair Intelligence Tests. (1973). Champaign, IL: Institute for Personality and Ability Testing.

Cattell, R.B. (1940). A culture free intelligence test, Part I. *Journal of Educational Psychology,* 31, 161–179.

Cleary, T.A. (1968). Test bias: Prediction of grades of negro and white students in integrated colleges. *Journal of Educational Measurement,* 5, 115–124.

Cleary, T.A., Humphreys, L.G., Kendrick, S.A., & Wesman, A. (1924). Eduational uses of tests with disadvantaged students. *American Psychologist,* 30, 15–41.

Cordes, C. (1983). Chicago school reassesment renews debate on role of tests. *APA Monitor,* 14, 14–15.

Crano, W.D., Kenny, D.A., & Campbell, D.T. (1972). Does intelligence cause achievement? A cross lagged panel analysis. *Journal of Educational Psychology,* 63, 258–275.

Cronbach, L. (1975). Five decades of public controversy over mental testing. *American Psychologist,* 3, 1–14.

Dodrill, C.B. (1981). An economical method for the evaluation of general intelligence in adults. *Journal of Consulting and Clinical Psychology,* 49, 668–673.

Droege, R.C. (1966). Effects of practice on aptitude scores. *Journal of Applied Psychology,* 50, 306–310.

Eels, K., Davis, A., Havighurst, R.J., Herricks, V.E., & Tyler, R. (1951). *Intelligence and cultural differences.* Chicago: University of Chicago Press.

Fine, B. (1975). *The stranglehold of the I.Q.* New York: Doubleday.

Fiske, E. (1981, April 28). Soul searching in the testing establishment. *New York Times.*

Freeman, F.N. (1922). A referendum of psychologists. *Century Illustrated Magazine,* 107, 237–245.

Freeman, F.N., Holzinger, K.J., & Mitchell, B.C. (1928). The influence of environment on the intelligence of school achievement and conduct of foster children. *27th Yearbook of the National Society for the Study of Education,* I, 103–217.

Fricke, B.G. (1975). *Report to the Faculty: Grading; Testing, Standards, and All That.* Ann Arbor: Evaluation and Examiniations Office, University of Michigan.

Garcia, J. (1975). The futility of a comparative IQ research. In N.A. Buchwald & M.A. Brazier (Eds.), *Brain mechanisms in mental retardation.* New York: Academic Press.

Glaser, R. & Bond, L. (1981). Testing: Concepts, policy, practice and research. *Amerian Psychologist,* 36, 997–1000.

Gordon, E.W. (1977). Diverse human populations and problems in educational program evaluation via achievement testing. In J.J. Wargo & D.R. Green (Eds.), *Achievement testing of disadvantaged and minority students for educational program evaluation.* New York: CTB/McGraw-Hill.

Gordon, E.W., & Terrell, M.D. (1981). The changed social context of testing. *American Psychologist,* 36, 1167–1171.

Goslin, D. (1963). *The search for ability.* New York: Russell Sage.

Gross, M. (1962). *The brain watchers.* New York: Random House.

Grunzke, N., Guinn, N., & Stauffer, G. (1970). Comparative performance of low-ability airmen (Technical Report 74). Lackland AFB, TX: Air Force Human Resources Laboratory.

Guilford, J.P. (1959). Three faces of intellect. *American Psychologist,* 14, 469–479.

Haney, W. (1981). Validity, vaudeville and values. *American Psychologist,* 36, 1021–1034.

Hargadon, F. (1981). Test and college admissions. *American Psychologist,* 36, 1112–1119.

Herrnstein, R. (1971, September). I.Q. *Atlantic Monthly,* 43–64.

Hoffman, B. (1962). *The tyranny of testing.* New York: Collier.

Hunt, E. (1978). Mechanics of verbal ability. *Psychological Review,* 85, 109–130.

Jensen, A.R. (1969). How much can we boost IQ and scholastic achievement? *Harvard Educational Review,* 39, 1–123.

Jensen, A.R. (1980). *Bias in mental testing.* New York: The Free Press.

Lerner, B. (1980). The war on testing: David, Goliath and Gallup. *Public Interest,* 60, 119–147.

Lin Chuan-ting. (1980). A sketch on the methods of mental testing in ancient China. *Acta Psychologica Sinica,* 12, 75–80.

Linn, R.L. (1982). Admissions testing on trial. *American Psychologist,* 37, 279–291.

Lippman, W. (1922a). The mental age of Americans. *New Republic,* 32, 213–215.

Lippman, W. (1922b). Tests of hereditary intelligence. *New Republic,* 32, 328–330.

Lippman, W. (1923). Rich and poor, girls and boys. *New Republic,* 34, 295–296.

Lommatzsch, H. (1929). Sur frage der intelligenzprufungen. *Hohere Schule i Sachsen,* 7, 345–347.

Lorge, I., Thorndike, R.L., & Hagen, E. (1964). *The Lorge-Thorndike Intelligence Tests.* Boston: Houghton Mifflin.

Matarazzo, J.D., & Wiens, A.N. (1977). Black Intelligence test of Cultural Homogeniety and Wechsler Adult Intelligence Scale scores of black and white police applicants. *Journal of Applied Psychology,* 62, 57–63.

McKelpin, J.C. (1965). Some implications of the intellectual characteristics of freshmen entering a liberal arts college. *Journal of Educational Measurement,* 2, 161–166.

Millman, J., Bishop, C.H., & Ebel, R. (1965). An analysis of test-wiseness. *Educational and Psychological Measurement,* 25, 707–726.

Munday, L. (1965). Predicting college grades in predominantly Negro colleges. *Journal of Educational Measurement,* 2, 157–160.

Nairn, A. (1980). *The reign of ETS: The corporation that makes up minds.* Washington: Nader.

O'Bemesta, J.O. (1980). A verbal intelligence test in the mother tongue as a predictor of success in the School Certificat Examination. *West African Journal of Educational and Vocational Measurement,* 5, 7–12.

Otis, A.S., & Lennon, R.T. (1968). *Otis-Lennon Mental Ability Test: Manual for Administration.* New York: Harcourt-Brace Jovanovich.

Padilla, A.M. (1979). Critical factors in the testing of Hispanic Americans. In R.W. Tyler & S.H. White (Eds.), *Testing, teaching and learning: Report of a conference on testing.* Washington, DC: National Institute of Education.

Pellegrino, J.W., & Glaser, R. (1980). Components of inductive reasoning. In R.E. Snow, P.A. Federico, & W.E. Montague (Eds.), *Aptitude, learning and instruction. Vol. 1.* Hillside, NJ: Erlbaum.

Peterson, R.E. (1968). Predictive validity of a brief test of academic aptitude. *Educational and Psychological Measurement, 28,* 441–444.

Pintner, R. (1923). *Intelligence Testing.* New York: Holt, Rinehart & Winston.

Reschly, D.J. (1981). Psychological testing in educational classification and placement. *American Psychologist, 36,* 1094–1102.

Rosenthal, R., & Jacobsen, L. (1968). Pygmalion in the classroom. New York: Holt, Rinehart, & Winston.

Rowan, C.T. (1970). How racists use "science" to degrade black people. *Ebony, 25,* 31–40.

Schmidt, F.L., & Hunter, J.E. (1981). Employment testing: Old theories and new research findings. *American Psychologist, 36,* 1128–1137.

Schmidt, F.L., Hunter, J.E., & Pearlman, K. (1981). Task differences and validity of aptitude tests in selection: A red herring. *Journal of Applied Psychology, 66,* 166, 185.

Short Form Test of Academic Aptitude. Monterey, CA: CTB/McGraw-Hill.

Spuck, W., & Stout, R. Predicting college success among minority youth. An analysis in highly selected colleges. Preprint copy, June 1969. (reported in Cleary (1975).

Stanley, J.C., & Porter, A.C. (1967). Correlation of Scholastic Aptitude Test scores with college grades for Negroes versus whites. *Journal of Educational Measurement, 4,* 199–218.

Test of Cognitive Skills. Monterey, CA: CTB/McGraw-Hill.

Terman, L.M. (1922a). The great conspiracy. *New Republic, 33,* 116–120.

Terman, L.M. (1922b). The psychological determinist: Or democracy and the IQ. *Journal of Educational Research, 6,* 57–62.

Treaster, J.B. (1983, March 20). New police test called unfair. *New York Times,* 24.

U.S. Department of Labor, Employment and Training Administration. (1968). Pretesting orientation exercises. (Manual: Test Booklet). Washington, DC: U.S. Government Printing Office.

U.S. Department of Labor, Employment and Training Administration. (1970). Pretesting orientation on the purposes of testing. (Manual: Illustrations). Washington, DC: U.S. Government Printing Office.

U.S. Department of Labor, Employment and Testing Administration. (1971). Doing your best on aptitude tests. Washington, DC: U.S. Government Printing Office.

Watkins, D., & Astilla, E. (1980). Intellective and non-intellective predictors of academic achievement at a Filipino university. *Educational and Psychological Measurement, 40,* 245–249.

Williams, R.L. (1972). The BITCH Test (Black Intelligence Test of Cultural Homoegeneity). St. Louis: Black Studies Program, Washington University.

Womer, F.B. (1970). National assessment says. *Measurement in Education,* 1–8.

Wonderlic, E.F. (1978). Wonderlic Personnel Test Manual. Northfield, IL: E.F. Wonderlic & Associates.

Yerkes, R.M. (1923). Testing the human mind. *Atlantic Monthly, 131,* 358–370.

Youth outwits merit exam, raising 240,000 scores. (1980, March 17). *New York Times.*

PART IV

ACHIEVEMENT, APTITUDE, AND INTEREST

7 ACHIEVEMENT TESTS

Lynn H. Fox
Barbara Zirkin

INTRODUCTION

Standardized achievement tests are so widely used and generally so well developed in comparison with other types of tests that their value is rarely questioned. Indeed, standardized achievement tests represent a multimillion dollar industry. The primary use of such tests by educational institutions is for instructional and administrative purposes, such as program evaluation or student selection and placement. Such instruments are also useful for counseling and guidance, research, and are sometimes employed by business and industry for assessment of the job-related skills of employees or prospective employees. For the purposes of this chapter, achievement tests are defined as instruments designed to measure the extent to which a person has acquired certain information or mastered certain skills, usually as a result of specific instruction (Stanley & Hopkins, 1972). There are two major categories: broad-based survey batteries and tests of specific content or skill domains. Within this second group, distinctions are sometimes made between tests that are called *diagnostic* and those termed *prognostic*.

The fact that achievement tests are used for such a wide variety of purposes is a reflection of their close relationship to measures of aptitude. How are achievement tests different from apti-tude or intelligence measures? Anastasi (1982) has suggested that the aptitude-achievement distinction is one of a degree of specificity about the past learning experiences that are to be assessed. If the test purports to measure the learning of content in a narrow curricular domain, such as a high school course in French or algebra, it is considered a measure of achievement. If a test measures skills and processes of problem solving that can be tied closely to in-grade curricular goals, it is an achievement measure. If a test contains measures of behaviors less clearly tied to specific instructional content and reflects the more cumulative effects of living, it is considered to be a measure of aptitude. Such a distinction is often difficult to make. When achievement tests are used to predict future behavior, such as learning at the next level of instruction, they are being used like an aptitude measure. If the same test were used for other purposes, such as diagnosing areas for instructional remediation or curriculum evaluation, it would be viewed as an achievement measure. Thus, a particular test that is classified as an achievement measure in terms of item content may or may not function as an achievement measure, depending upon the purpose of the testing and the interpretations that are to be made from the results.

To understand standardized achievement tests, one must appreciate the following:

1. The history of the development of standardized achievement tests and their relationship to nonstandardized achievement measures;
2. The types and characteristics of standardized achievement tests;
3. The technical strengths and weaknesses of achievement tests, including the proper uses and some limitations;
4. The current social and technological changes that are likely to impact on the development and uses of these instruments in the future.

HISTORICAL FOUNDATIONS

The development of standardized tests has evolved from a complex interaction of theoretical and technical developments. Although the beginnings of standardized testing can be traced as far back as 2200 BC, when the Chinese were reported to have developed rigorous Civil Service Examinations, the foundation for modern day achievement testing in the schools was laid in 1845 when Horace Mann criticized the use of oral examinations and argued for the superiority of written examinations. In his arguments he outlined the concepts of reliability, validity, and usability that are now the cornerstones of today's measurement theories (Stanley & Hopkins, 1972).

The earliest reported use of an objective achievement test was in 1864 when the Rev. George Fisher constructed an objective measure of handwriting. The concept of grade norms was later introduced by Joseph M. Rice in 1897 in his work with the development of standardized spelling tests. In 1904, E. L. Thorndike published the first textbook on educational measurement, thus formalizing the educational testing movement by relating statistical procedures to psychometric theory.

The use of subtests, standardized instructions with strict time limits, organization of items by difficulty, and weighted scores were brought together in one test by Stone in 1908 (DuBois, 1970). The first formal achievement battery, however, was the Stanford Achievement Test developed in 1923 by Lewis Terman, Truman Kelley, and G.M. Ruch. Wide-scale use of such measures escalated greatly after the development of machine scoreable tests around 1935. Indeed, by 1940, there were purportedly over 2,600 achievement tests (Cook, 1950).

Standardized tests seemed firmly entrenched in American educational practice in the era following World War II. Although optical scanning developed by Lindquist in 1955 and the founding of the Educational Testing Service in 1947 influenced theory and practice in many subtle ways, the basic nature of achievement testing has not changed dramatically for several decades. Predictions for the 1980s, however, suggest that some radical changes may occur due to the increasing interest in the use of mastery tests, concerns over test bias and misuses of testing, and the growing use of computer technology within the schools and homes of today's students.

It is important to note that while teacher constructed tests of achievement may resemble standardized measures in their use of objective item formats such as multiple-choice questions, there are certain important differences between the two types of tests. While standardized tests involve a yearly or semiannual systematic sampling of large numbers of students, teacher-made tests generally are developed for small classes. Teacher-made tests usually are designed to cover small units of work, while standardized examinations are designed to include a wide span of content thought to be common across most classrooms at the same grade level. The teacher tests reflect specific instructions more directly and frequently and can be used to monitor students' progress more closely. Standardized tests, however, are subject to closer psychometric scrutiny, and their interpretation and use differs significantly from that of teacher-made instruments. Because standardized tests provide comparisons of skill development and content learning against a national standard of learning, their greatest value may be in administrative uses for program evaluation. Both tests are necessary, since they have different but complementary purposes.

TYPES OF TESTS

Achievement tests can be divided into two basic categories: general survey batteries and special content tests. All standardized achievement tests are, in reality, criterion referenced measures. For most of these tests, especially survey batteries, the criterion is the mean performance of a large representative sample of school children and schools, and thus they are considered norm referenced tests (NRT). A few standardized tests are an alternative criterion and should be referred to as mastery tests. Although any standardized achievement test could be developed as a mastery test rather than a norm referenced measure, most efforts to develop mastery tests have focused on tests for special content domains rather than on the large survey batteries.

General Survey Batteries

General survey batteries are usually designed to test basic skills in most major academic subject areas. Although available at all levels, kindergarten, college and beyond, survey batteries are most

TABLE 7.1. SAMPLE TEST ITEMS.
Typical sample test items used in achievement tests of different types.

General Survey Battery

DIRECTIONS

This test will show how well you do mathematics problems. Use scratch paper to work the problems. Fill in the space that goes with the answer you choose. If the correct answer is not given, fill in the space that goes with *"None of the above."*

Do Sample Item M and mark your answer.

SAMPLE ITEM M

Jack has 1 orange. Susan has 2 oranges. How many oranges do they have altogether?

f   1
g   2
h   3
j   4
k   *None of the above*

Note. From California Achievement Tests. Reproduced by permission of the publisher, CTB/McGraw-Hill, 2500 Garden Road, Monterey, California 93940. Copyright ©1977 by McGraw-Hill, Inc. All rights reserved. Printed in the U.S.A.

Special Content Tests

GENERAL MATHEMATICS:

Choose the *one* best answer for each of the following mathematics problems. Use a separate sheet of paper to do any necessary figuring. Do not make any marks in this test booklet.

Sample
$8 + 9 - 3 =$
A. 14
B. 17
C. 20
D. 86
E. 92

WORLD HISTORY:

Choose the *one* best answer to each of the following questions concerning world history. Mark the corresponding letter on your answer sheet. Do not make any marks in this test booklet.

Sample

America was discovered in 1492 by

A. Clara Barton.
B. Christopher Columbus.
C. King George III.
D. Catherine de Médicis.

Note. Reproduced by permission of American Testronics, P.O. Box 2270, Iowa City, Iowa 52244.

Criterion-Referenced/Diagnostic

READING:

Sample:

Find the word *cold*.

○ sold   ○ roll

○ call   ● cold

Sample:

The man was *exhausted* from working so hard.

This sentence gives you the idea that **exhausted** means—

pretty   alone   tired
○   ○   ●

Sample:

Which picture shows a box?

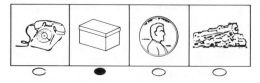

Note. Reproduced by permission. Copyright ©1975, 1974, by Harcourt Brace Jovanovich, Inc. All rights reserved.

often used in the elementary school grades. Most survey batteries contain subtests in spelling, vocabulary, reading comprehension, language usage, arithmetic computation, and arithmetic concepts. Some batteries also contain study skills, reference skills, or a combination of these as additional subtests. Scores are generally reported for all subtests as well as the composite totals. These scores may be reported in a variety of ways. Grade equivalents or percentiles are typical, but more recently stanines or normal curve equivalents (NCE) are being used. Survey battery publishers generally provide detailed information regarding test norms and development procedures, various characteristics of the norming sample, and lists of objectives as well as technical data enabling the user to better understand each battery as completely as possible. Separate norms are usually provided by test level or grade. In the ideal situation, norms are reported by geographic region, school system type and size, racial and ethnic groups, and sex. Some samples of survey batteries commonly used at the elementary school level are the Iowa Tests of Basic Skills, the Stanford Achievement Tests, and California Achievement Test.

Special Content Tests

Standardized tests intended to measure achievement in specific interest areas constitute the second broad category. These tests also cover virtually all grade levels from kindergarten through graduate and professional school and many diversified academic and professional content areas from basic arithmetic to the Graduate Record Achievement Tests of the College Board (see Table 7.2). Some specialized vocational assessment examinations are available as well. This test type becomes of increasing importance in the senior high school years and beyond as the curriculum differentiates considerably and the need for assessment of specific learning is indicated. Such tests must obviously be chosen for their close content validity to the specific instructional objectives of the curriculum.

These tests have a variety of uses. At the junior and senior high school level these assessment materials can be used as year-end examinations or as examinations at the end of a prescribed course of study. An example of this usage of achievement tests can be found in the Comprehensive Assess-

ment Program tests such as Algebra I or World History. Other achievement tests of this type are used at the college level. The College Level Examination Program (CLEP) exams are often given to assess knowledge in a specific college course and can be used to assess the comparability of such courses at different colleges or for a more standardized assessment of college courses across instructors. Sometimes such a test can also be used to assess "life-learning" of adult students in an attempt to grant college level credit for experience. Yet another example of content achievement test use is seen in the College Advanced Placement Examinations. These standardized test results of specific high-level content material are used by many colleges to make placement decisions about high school students entering their institutions. The credit granting institutions may decide to award a number of credits based upon the results of the tests and the match of the test content with their own course content requirements.

Criterion Referenced Measures

The criterion referenced test (CRT) is designed so that an individual's performance can be compared to a specified behavioral criterion established for the specific test. The question answered here is: "How did the student do?" This is in comparison to the norm referenced test (NRT), which is designed so that an individual's performance is measured in reference to the mean of a norm group taking the same test measure. Both types of assessments are keyed to a set of objectives, and both are assumed to have content validity. Most norm referenced measures are based on an overview of some broad content domain in contrast to the CRT, which samples a more specified or constricted content domain.

The major principal use of CRT measures has been in the development of mastery learning tests. These tests are designed to indicate whether an individual has or has not attained master of a specific content area, and the level of mastery that must be reached is generally assigned by the test interpreter (Brown, 1976). The content of mastery assessment measures is usually designed to test acquisition of a rather small domain of content or skills. An example of a test for mastery might be mathematics addition skills or the ability to add only two or three digit numbers. These

TABLE 7.2. LIST OF REPRESENTATIVE TESTS.*

GENERAL ACHIEVEMENT BATTERIES

Test	*Publisher*
Boehm Test of Basic Concepts (1971)	Psychological Corporation
California Achievement Tests (1977)	CTB/McGraw-Hill
Comprehensive Tests of Basic Skills (1982)	CTB/McGraw-Hill
Iowa Tests of Basic Skills	Riverside Publishing Company
Primary (1978)	
Multilevel (1978)	
Iowa Tests of Educational Development	SRA
Metropolitan Achievement Tests	Psychological Corporation
(Survey Battery)	
Peabody Individual Achievement Test	American Guidance Service
Sequential Tests of Educational Problems	Addison-Wesley
(STEP)	
Stanford Achievement Test	Psychological Corporation
Stanford Test of Academic Skills	Psychological Corporation
(TASK)	
Test of Achievement and Proficiency	Riverside Publishing Company
(TAP) (1981)	
Wide Range Achievement Test-Revised Edition	Jastak

SPECIFIC ACHIEVEMENT TESTS

ACT Proficiency Examination Program	
Advanced Placement Tests	ETS
College Board Achievement Tests	ETS
College Level Examination Program	ETS
(CLEP)	
Cooperative Achievement Tests	Addison-Wesley
English, Reading, Literature, Mathematics, Sciences,	
Social Studies	
Comprehensive Achievement Series 7-12	Scott Foresman
Comprehensive Assessment Program	Scott Foresman
High School Subjects Tests	
Metropolitan Achievement Tests	
Reading Instructional; Language Instructional;	
Mathematics Instructional	

PROGNOSTIC TESTS

Circus	Addison-Wesley
General Educational Development	American Council on Education
Metropolitan Readiness Tests	Psychological Corporation
Orleans Hanna Algebra Prognosis Test	Psychological Corporation
Tests of Basic Experiences (1979)	
(TABE)	

DIAGNOSTIC TESTS

Comprehensive Achievement Series 4-6	
Diagnostic Mathematics Inventory	CTB/McGraw-Hill
Diagnostic Reading Scales	CTB/McGraw-Hill
Prescriptive Reading Inventory	CTB/McGraw-Hill
Skills Monitoring System-Reading	Psychological Corporation
Stanford Diagnostic	Psychological Corporation
Reading; Mathematics	

*Tests representative of those discussed in the text. The names of the publishers have been included should the reader wish to obtain further information about these or any other tests.

tests are most often useful for assessment of learning within a particular school, grade level, or the individual classroom. One example of a broad based survey battery that is being used as a criterion referenced measure is the National Assessment of Educational Progress (NEAP) (Mehrens & Lehmann, 1978).

Diagnostic Measures

Although survey batteries or specific content tests can be used to diagnose areas of strengths and weaknesses for a class or group, they are not designed for detailed analyses of areas for remediation for individuals. In the areas of reading and mathematics, several tests have been developed to provide this in-depth assessment for individuals. Such measures differ from the typical survey test in several ways. Diagnostic tests provide more items of a similar type or on the same concept or skill than do survey tests. They are designed for use with students who are performing below average for their grade level or who are suspected to have a learning problem. They are not normed on large general samples of students the way survey tests are normed. Grade equivalents or percentile ranks are irrelevant. Emphasis is upon identifying errors that students make and the smallest components of skills that can reasonably be measured, such as word recognition, rate of reading, word attack skills, and so forth. Indeed, some of these tests do not use a multiple choice format but rather have students supply answers to better enable the teacher to identify the errors the child is making.

Even though diagnostic tests may lack some of the technical precision of survey batteries, they can be valuable clinical tools when used by persons who have the appropriate training in the subject area and diagnostic methods such as a school psychologist. These tests alone are not sufficient to fully describe a student's abilities or problems. They do not explain etiology or causes of the errors, nor examine other possible relevant learner characteristics such as problems in vision, hearing, or emotional factors.

Readiness and Prognostic Measures

A number of tests have been designed to assess students' readiness for instruction. At the elementary school level there are tests of reading readi-

ness or broader measures, such as the CIRCUS in which readiness for school is assessed. At the secondary level the tests are often called prognostic or aptitude tests, such as the Orleans Hanna Algebra Prognosis Test or the Modern Language Aptitude Test. Although these measures are really specialized aptitude measures, they are generally included in discussions of achievement testing because the test items are, in many instances, more typical of achievement than aptitude tests. For example, the reading readiness measures are assessing presumably learned language skills. These skills are expected, however, to have been learned in a nonacademic or informal rather than formal instructional program. Determining whether or not a child recognizes letters of the alphabet seems to be more of an achievement than aptitude measure. Although these measures may be used for prediction and/or decisions about program placement, they are also sometimes used for diagnostic purposes, especially in the early elementary years. Thus, a child who is not judged as ready for reading instruction might be given a prescription for readiness activities based on the test analysis. These measures, then, are the hybrids of achievement and aptitude meassurement.

TECHNICAL CHARACTERISTICS

The value of any test can only be judged in relation to its use in a specific situation with a particular population. Three principles of measurement that describe the general parameters for evaluation of standardized norm-referenced tests are reliability, validity, and usability. The discussion of usability is restricted to the interpretation of scores and norms.

Reliability

Most standardized achievement tests report high reliability estimates. Some thought needs to be given to how these estimates are derived. For example, a test-retest reliability over an interval of several months may be confounded by real learning that occurs related to the content domain for some but not all the children. One's knowledge of social studies or ability to compute two-digit multiplication problems should perhaps be easier to define (and thus to measure reliability) than constructs of abilities or traits such as creativity or self-concept. Yet, achievement by its very nature is not static, and thus the measurement of stability of achievement in most instances is inappropriate as an estimate of reliability per se.

Measures of internal consistency are considered appropriate for tests or subtests that assess a homogeneous domain of content or skills. The Kuder-Richardson formula 20 (KR-20) is commonly reported. The KR-20 estimate is less easy to interpret or is less meaningful in the cases of composite scores on batteries that include a wide variety of skills and content.

Since most major achievement series have two forms at most grade levels, it is possible to compute and report the reliability coefficient of an equivalent form. Indeed, equivalent forms given a few days apart may provide the most conservative and useful estimate of the consistency of the test.

In evaluating a test, consideration should also be given to the heterogeneity of the population and the speededness of the test. Reliability estimates will be spuriously high for samples that include several grade levels, and measures of internal consistency will be inflated if many students fail to complete the test.

Thus, estimates of both equivalence and internal consistence for homogeneous tests or subtests should ideally be reported by grade level, along with evidence that shows that the test was completed by the majority of students in the study. Since many test users may have difficulty interpreting reliability coefficients, test manuals should report and explain the standard error of measurement, and student scores should be reported as percentile bands.

Although caution is always advised for interpreting individual scores, the high reliability estimates for standardized achievement measures lead to great confidence in comparisons of group mean scores. Thus, such tests can be excellent tools for program evaluation. Issues of student growth after a year of instruction, trend analysis of scores before and after curricular changes and achievement levels predicted from aptitude compared with actual achievement levels can all be addressed.

Validity

Content validity is the critical issue in determining the proper uses and interpretation of achievement test results. In the development of major tests, many experts are consulted to determine the domain of content and skills to be included in the test for each level as well as the accuracy or preciseness of the wording of the items. The content validity for a specific child, class, school, or school system, however, must be determined also by a systematic comparison of the similarity of the test objectives to the curricular content of the specific instructional program. In the ideal situation, these skill/content specifications for items are presented in the manual, and computer printouts by item and objective for each student, class, and school are available. In such a situation the use of the school data for individual diagnosis, instructional planning, and curricular evaluation is greatly enhanced.

When tests of achievement are used to make decisions about student placement for instruction or selection of applicants for college or jobs, some analysis of predictive or criterion-related validity is necessary. Past achievement is often as good or a better predictor of future achievement than some aptitude measures. Indeed, Bracht and Hopkins (1972) found fairly high correlations among composite test scores on achievement tests for students from grades 3 to 11 and high correlations from grades 7 to 11. Correlations from grades 1 or 2 to later grade levels were somewhat lower.

Then, validity for the purpose and population for which the tests are to be used should be carefully researched. Such local validation is not always easy to provide but is highly desirable.

Construct validity is rarely discussed in cases of achievement tests. There are, however, some issues surrounding assessment of achievement that could be clarified by more analysis of the discriminant and convergent validity of different achievement measures. For example, items that attempt to assess problem solving in mathematics should not be confounded by the readability of the word problems. The measurement of problemsolving should be independent of the measurement of reading ability. Thus, a child with limited reading skills should not perform more poorly on an arithmetic problem presented in a written multiple-choice format than he or she would have performed on the problem had it been presented.

Since the development of achievement batteries is a long and expensive process, a major concern is the timeliness or relevance of the test items in terms of evolving curricular guidelines. This is more of a problem in areas such as science than in the measurement of basic reading skills or processes. Changes in scientific theories reported in textbooks and discussions of current events in the classroom may not be reflected in achievement tests until several years later. On the other hand, efforts to switch to metric measurements may be occurring in tests more quickly than in the classroom. While such problems cannot be totally eliminated, there may be a reduction in time-lag problems as testing moves in the direction of computerized sequencing and other techniques. In the meantime, the best control lies in the informed analysis of test item content and program curriculum in each situation by the user.

Usability

There are a variety of standard scores that can be used to report test results. Most widely used for achievement tests are percentile ranks, stanines, and grade equivalents. Even though it is believed that these are more easily understood by students, parents, and teachers than other standard scores, such as t or z scores, there are still some problems of misinterpretation, especially regarding grade-equivalent scores. For example, a sixth grader who scores three standard deviations above the mean of sixth graders on a reading test may receive a score of reading grade level 9.0. This does not mean that the student actually reads as well as the average ninth grader, since the actual mean score for ninth graders is for a form of the test used for ninth rather than sixth graders. How the sixth-grade student reads in comparison with ninth graders can only be accurately determined by testing the student on the ninth-grade form of the test. A similar problem of interpretation exists if the student scores well below grade level.

Reporting student scores as a percentile band that uses the standard error of measurement of the test to construct a confidence interval around the student's score may be the most appropriate report form. The interpretation of a child's score, however, should always be accompanied by some discussion of the content of the test domain and its relationship to the student's academic program. A student might score rather poorly on a measure of mathematics that included geometry and number theory items because his or her school curriculum had not yet introduced those topics. Some major test publishers provide individual student reports with detailed item analysis as well as class or school summaries. This is extremely desirable.

Another consideration in score interpretation is the normative sample or reference group upon which the test norms were determined. An important question is whether or not any relevant characteristics of the reference group are different from those students being tested by a specific school. Most major test publishers attempt to create a normative sample that is representative of the pool of potential users. Thus, they typically try to balance the reference group on such factors as sex, geographic region, size of school and school system, community setting, and sometimes school type or racial composition. Some, but not all, provide subgroup norms for special populations such as large city school systems. Those systems that intend to use test data for program evaluation should ideally develop their own local norms.

An example of the importance of understanding the characteristics of the reference group can be illustrated by reference to the norms reported for eighth graders versus ninth graders on a test of Algebra I. Generally, one expects ninth graders to score higher than eighth graders, but the mean score for eighth graders on Algebra I is higher than the mean for ninth graders. A student with a raw score of 25, for example, receives a slightly higher percentile rank when compared to ninth graders. Why? Typically, the only students who are encouraged to take Algebra in the eighth grade are those judged as mathematically able on the basis of grades and achievement test scores in grade 7. Thus, on the average, the mathematically less able students take Algebra in grade 9.

ISSUES AND THE FUTURE

In response to shifting educational concerns and technological advances, the nature of achievement tests may change in the near future. Prominent among educational concerns are test "bias" with special or minority populations and a mastery learning model of achievement testing for decision making about certification or for individualization of instruction. While the model of adaptive testing relates to these aforementioned concerns, its implementation awaits widespread availability of computers for testing.

Test Bias

The concept of bias in tests and testing is an issue that has received increasing attention from test developers and users. Although many of the criticisms have centered on aptitude and intelligence tests, specialists in educational measurement, as well as those more intimately involved in test result decisions, have become concerned about bias in achievement tests as well.

An achievement test is thought to be biased if it does not measure the same thing for different groups of equal ability. This limited definition of bias can similarly be applied to specific individual test items as well. The question remains as to what it is each specific test or subtest is designed to measure (Cole, 1978). A distinction must be made between two basic bias types: bias centered within the test itself and bias attributed to administrative and educational use (Shephard, 1982).

The scores children receive on these tests are important determiners of their individual futures. Therefore, the dual nature of potential bias—from the test itself or its use—necessitates two separate approaches to determining test fairness. For example, if a vocabulary test was composed of a sizable number of rural reference words, and the children taking the test were low SES, inner city youths, then the bias would seem to lie within the test itself and the test development procedures for this instrument. However, if a particular group of urban youth score low on this particular portion of the test, and the school system makes a decision to place this particular group in remedial or special programs of some type, then the bias might lie within the educational interpretation of the assessment measure. This latter example would be considered "unfair use" of the test. Thus, while some contend that "an a priori assumption that an achievement test is essentially unbiased seems much more reasonable than the assumption it is biased" (Ebel, 1975, p. 21), others contend equally vociferously that all tests should be developed with a constant eye on the problem of bias.

Bias studies are all related to validity issues; the basic concerns center around the content and construct validities of the test measurement. Content bias is considered to be the most important of the above types. Ebel (1975) maintains that there can be no bias within the context of content validity, since the content is valid for some subgroup of individuals and that this compilation of groups creates an unbiased total test—balanced for perhaps biased items for each specific group. It is this content domain of the test that is most often labeled as culturally or socioeconomically biased, since it is assumed the test is composed of objec-

tives not germain to all groups tested. As a result, the problem of content validation and potential test bias arises from the use of the results and the movement from interpreting the scores to mean that a pupil "did perform" on a certain objective to interpreting the scores to mean that a student "has not learned" (Cole, 1978). Thus, construct validity is assumed from the test interpretation, rather than having such validity psychometrically established before such interpretation occurs; that is, interpretations are not always limited to a reference to the specific content domain of a test but to some more basic concept or construct. If the item content when scrutinized was judged to be measuring the intended construct or content in spite of unusual group differences, it was assumed to be fair. When the scrutiny of item content suggested that an untested or irrelevant construct or concept was being measured, then the item might be considered biased (Cole, 1978).

Predictive validity is established by showing a relationship between the test and some criterion measure. In reference to an achievement test, such a criterion is difficult to establish, and, indeed, many test publishers have not been able to produce longitudinal studies of their testing instruments. The bias here is detected in the use of achievement tests for placement into specific classes and/or programs without specific documentation of the predictive validity of the test.

Statistical documentation of bias can be obtained through several different psychometric devices: transformed item difficulty, (Angoff & Ford, 1973; Cardall & Coffman, 1964), item discrimination (Green, 1975; Green & Draper, 1972), chi-square method (Schueneman, 1979), and item characteristic curve (Lord, 1977; Wright, 1977). Comparisons of these methods and a detailed discussion can be found in Ironson (1979) and Burrill (1982). The issue of bias in achievement testing continues to be important to the educational and business communities that use them. With the elaborate methodology that exists for detailing such bias, test publishers are beginning to more widely publish the data collected regarding potential test bias. Achievement test publishers began their efforts to control and eliminate test bias with the specification of the content domain sample and are continuing through diligent attention to norming groups and tryout procedures. Reviews at each step are carried out to guard against as much cultural, SES, sex, and racial bias as possible.

Computers in Educational Testing

Computers are already playing a large role in educational assessment. They are now used to score tests, analyze group results, and provide group and individual psychometric data. This allows for greater use of test results for counseling, administrative, and instructional purposes. The possible expansion of computer use into the area of more individualized testing within the school setting is an exciting trend for the future. The typical sequential or adaptive testing model involves a two-step process. The examinee takes a short test on the computer, which may contain test items along a wide difficulty range. The individual's performance on the short test form indicates the level at which the student is to begin a longer and more detailed testing, sometimes viewed schematically as a pyramid paradigm. The examinee then begins a series of questions. If he/she answers the first correctly, the computer then chooses a more difficult second question. If the testee answers incorrectly, an easier test item is chosen. This process continues in similar fashion until a specified total of items have been answered for this test portion (Anastasi, 1982; Mehrens & Lehmans, 1978). The examinee's score is based not only on the correct answers, but the level of difficulty of the items. The computer can then assess all aspects of the student's performance and report that information quickly and accurately to the teacher and others for administrative and instructional purposes. This expanded use of computers will greatly reduce teacher preparation and scoring time, increase the efficiency of testing, and provide reporting procedures that are immediately useful.

Mastery Testing

The growing use of mastery testing previously discussed has raised several concerns regarding the use and limitations of the model. One of the most basic issues revolves around the setting of the "mastery" criterion score. Two important questions are raised: (a) how many items are needed to provide reliable assessment and (b) what proportion of items must be correct to establish mastery (Brown, 1976). Usually, such decisions are reached in a logical but judgmental fashion, depending upon test use and the decisions to be made. Assuming that the mastery testing/teach-ing/testing paradigm could go on indefinitely until the individual achieves "mastery," the question arises as to whether mastery after several trials is equivalent to mastery on the first trial. Several authors make note that a determination of mastery under certain conditions may be problematical, and the true assessment of subject matter learning may be more a function of time-on-task conditions and not real learning in a more classical sense. Arguments for and against mastery learning models are concerned with many non-psychometric issues, such as instructional methodology, aptitude or ability to learn, and "perseverance" or motivation of the student (Carroll, 1971). Additionally, concern with mastery testing must also begin to address the issue of the type or quality of instruction that takes place during the testing/teaching/testing sequence. Anastasi proposes that a three-way distinction should be made: mastery, non-mastery and some intermediate or "review" category.

The increased use of computers in testing may help eliminate some of the psychometric and judgmental problems. Item difficulty ranges and mastery scores would become established in a more standardized manner and, thus, comparisons of individual scores would have greater reliability.

SUMMARY

Predictions for the continued widespread use of standardized achievement tests depend upon how valuable such measures are, particularly norm-referenced achievement surveys. Although these tests can be used for a variety of purposes, ranging from vocational counseling to instructional feedback of classroom teachers, their greatest use is probably best described as administrative. In the hands of local and state educational agencies, these measures serve as a national standard for judging the adequacy of curriculum and specific instructional programs.

Although the true control of public educational institutions lies at the state and local rather than national level, one cannot ignore the desirability for some agreement on curricular content and instructional objectives among the various levels and across state lines. Nationally standardized testing programs help to promote greater uniformity in the content domain of many courses at the high school level. For example, if a school system evaluates students on a nationally standardized test of Spanish or Algebra I or biology after a year's instruction and finds that they perform as a group relatively poorly compared with the national norms, this may prompt a review of the curriculum and objectives of these courses.

National achievement test programs such as the Advanced Placement examinations or College Entrance Examination Board achievement tests developed by the Educational Testing Service can be extremely valuable to colleges in at least two ways. First, they provide one standard for evaluating students' preparation for college level work in the admissions and placement processes. Second, they can be used as a guide in curriculum development at the college level. Some colleges even award college credit to gifted students who can demonstrate their mastery of content at a college level on such tests. This saves the student time and money. Such admission testing programs are also useful for evaluating objectives of secondary programs. Indeed, for the past 10 years the College Board has been working on a project to strengthen the academic quality of secondary education.

Despite the overall technical excellence of most standardized achievement tests, they are not without critics. Some critics of norm-referenced standardized tests object to the use of the normal distribution curve as a standard. Questions are raised as to the interpretation of mean scores for a school that falls in the lower stanines. Should that school be judged as "poor?" Perhaps the students have actually mastered a great deal of material and skills and are simply not functioning like students in the average and above average ranked schools because they are less able as a group. Critics of standardized tests are often concerned about the invidious comparisons among subgroups in society and presumably would be more comfortable with the mastery test model. But most criticisms of standardized tests are actually directed toward misuses, misinterpretations of test results, and the ensuing social consequences. While such concerns are valid, they do not negate the need for some uniform standards of educational outcomes.

Advocates for standardized testing programs are likely to make the following analogy: "You don't shoot the messenger because he or she brings bad news, just as you shouldn't throw out the tests because you don't like the results." The arguments for development of standardized measures put forth by Horace Mann in 1845 still seem valid to many educators today. Teacher-made tests for small groups of students are likely to be less reliable and thus less valid for making decisions about individuals or groups than carefully developed standardized tests. Should judgments about educational placement or programs for individuals or groups be made on the basis of possibly unreliable impressions of teachers, based on unspecified standards of acceptable performance, such as, Mary doesn't read very well, or Johnny is doing poorly in arithmetic, or Betty is incapable of college level work? Is it not better to evaluate a student's achievement against objective criteria for his/her peer group in relation to other independent assessments of aptitude?

Clearly, standardized tests are not perfect and can be misused and misunderstood. Yet they are currently the best instruments educators have available for assessing the quality of curriculum and instruction and for individualizing and improving instructional programs for each child. Continued research and work on the development of mastery tests and adaptive testing models are likely to lead to new tests that retain the technical excellence of their predecessors but are better able to satisfy the wide variety of demands of critics and advocates alike.

REFERENCES

Anastasi, A. (1982), *Psychological testing*. New York: Macmillan.

Angoff, W.H., & Ford, S.F. (1973), Item-race interaction on a test of scholastic aptitude. *Journal of Educational Measurement*, 10, 95–105.

Bracht, G.H., & Hopkins, K.D. (1972). Stability of educational achievement. In G.H. Bracht, K.D. Hopkins, & J.C. Stanley (Eds.), *Perspectives in educational and psychological measurement*. Englewood Cliffs, NJ: Prentice-Hall.

Brown, F.G. (1976). *Principles of educational and psychological testing*. New York: Holt, Rinehart, & Winston.

Burrill, L.E. (1982). Comparative studies of item bias methods. In R.A. Berk (Ed.), *Handbook of methods for detecting test bias*. Baltimore, MD: The Johns Hopkins University Press.

Cardell, C., & Coffman, W.E. (1964, November). A method for comparing the performance of different groups on the items in a test (Colelge Entrance Examination Board Research and Development Report 64–5, No. 9, ETS Research Bulletin 64–61). Princeton, NJ: Educational Testing Service.

Carroll, J.B. (1971). The problems of measurement related to the concept of learning for mastery. In J.H. Block (Ed.), *Mastery learning*. New York: Holt, Rinehart, & Winston.

Cole, N.S. (1978, March). *Approaches to examining bias in achievement test items*. Paper presented at the annual meeting of the American Personnel and Guidance Association, Washington, DC.

Cook, W.W. (1950). Achievement tests. In W.S. Monroe (Ed.), *Encyclopedia of Educational Research* (rev. ed.). New York: Macmillan.

Dawis, R.V., Pinto, P.R., Weitzel, W., & Nezzer, M. (1974). Describing organizations as reinforcer systems: A new use for job satisfaction and employee attitude surveys. *Journal of Vocational Behavior, 4,* 55–66.

DuBois, P.H. (1970); *A history of psychological testing*. Boston: Allyn & Bacon.

Ebel, R.L. (1975, March). *Constructing unbiased achievement tests*. Paper delivered at the NIE Conference on Test Bias, Annapolis, MD.

Green, D.R. (1975). What does it mean to say a test is biased? *Education and Urban Society,* 8, 33–52.

Green, D.R., & Draper, J.F. (1972, September). *Exploratory studies of bias in achievement tests*. Paper presented at the annual meeting of the American Psychological Association, Honolulu.

Ironson, G.H., & Subkoviak, M.A. (1979). A comparison of several methods of assessing item bias. *Journal of Educational Measurement,* 16, 209–225.

Lord, F.M. (1977). Practical applications of item characteristic curve theory. Preliminary report. Princeton, NJ: Educational Testing Service.

Lord, F.M., & Novick, M.R. (1968). *Statistical theories of mental test scores*. Reading, MA: Addison-Wesley.

Mayfield, E.C. (1964). The selection interview: A reevaluation of published research. *Personnel Psychology,* 17, 239–260.

McFillen, J.M. (1978). Supervisory power as an influence in supervisor-subordinate relations. *Academy of Management Journal,* 21, 419–433.

Mehrens, W.A., & Lehmann, I.J. (1978). *Measurement evaluation in education and psychology.* New York: Holt, Rinehart, & Winston.

Mehrens, W.A., & Lehmann, I.J. (1978). *Standardized tests in education*. New York: Holt, Rinehart, & Winston.

Schmidt, F.L., Greenthal, A.L., Hunter, J.E., Berner, J.G., & Seaton, F.W. (1977). Job sample vs. paper-and-pencil trades and technical tests: Adverse impact and examinee attitudes. *Personnel Psychology,* 30, 187–197.

Schueneman, J.D. (1979). A method of assessing bias in test items. *Journal of Educational Measurement,* 16, 143–152.

Shepard, L.A. (1982). Definitions of bias. In R.A. Berk (Ed.), *Handbook of methods for detecting item bias*. Baltimore, MD: The Johns Hopkins University Press.

Stanley, J.C., & Hopkins, K.D. (1972). *Educational and psychological measurement*. Englewood Cliffs, NJ: Prentice-Hall.

Stogdill, R.M. (1965). *Job satisfaction and job expectations manual*. Ohio State University, Columbus, OH.

Stone, E.F. (1976). The moderating effect of work-related values on the job scope-job satisfaction relationship. *Organizational Behavior and Human Performance,* 15, 147–167.

Wright, B.D. (1977). Solving measurement problems with the Rasch model. *Journal of Educational Measurement,* 14, 97–116.

8 APTITUDE TESTS

Daniel J. Reschly

INTRODUCTION

Psychological and educational tests are used extensively in educational settings for a variety of purposes. This chapter will emphasize the use of aptitude tests in making decisions about student classification and placement.

The use of aptitude tests for these purposes has become increasingly controversial in recent years. The controversies involve fundamental questions about the *utility* of such tests for all student populations (i.e., do the tests combined with other information improve decisions?) and the *fairness* of these tests to minority students (i.e., do such tests unfairly penalize minority students and thereby reduce their opportunities?).

The analysis of these issues will require discussion of certain basic features of tests, test uses (and misuses), and empirical research with tests. There is fairly broad consensus on how certain groups perform on various tests and the effects of using tests as part of the decision-making process with these groups. What is unclear, however, is whether we *should* use tests as part of important decisions and whether we *ought* to provide various compensations for lower scoring groups. The "should" and "ought" questions, involving deep philosophical issues, reflect concerns about test use as an instrument of social policy. Efforts to

resolve these questions, especially by legislation and the courts, will also be discussed in this chapter. First, the nature of classification/placement decisions needs to be explored.

Classification/Placement Decisions

In public school settings, classification/placement involves two related decisions. The first is whether the individual is eligible to be classified as handicapped. (In some states, students may also be classified as gifted.) If characteristics of more than one handicap are present, a primary handicapping condition must also be specified in most instances. If classified, then the kind of program, usually within special education, must be selected so the individual is provided with an "appropriate education."

Placements in special education may vary from 2 to 3 hours per week to full-time. The amount of time spent within special education usually is directly related to the severity of the handicap, which, in turn, is often related to the amount of interaction with normal peers. Full-time programs often are self-contained classrooms where one teacher is responsible for nearly all of the instruction for as few as 4 or 5 students to as many as 15 or so. It is important to see special education placements as a continuum from "less restrictive environments," such as individual or small group tutoring for as little as 2 or 3 hours per week, to more restrictive, self-contained classrooms. In addition to less contact with normal peers and regular educational activities, the more restrictive programs usually reflect less emphasis on intellectual/academic skills and more emphasis on functional (practical) academic skills and broadly conceived social competencies.

Classification/placement is potentially a very significant event in the lives of children. The decision to classify/place may be critical to the development of compensatory mechanisms that enhance the handicapped person's opportunities to lead a normal life. Many examples could be cited. Tutoring that enables an otherwise bright high school student with a learning disability to develop basic reading skills is likely to markedly increase social and vocational opportunities. Speech therapy, which is effective in overcoming stuttering, physical therapy for persons with cerebral palsy, mobility training for the blind, social skills development for withdrawn or aggressive students, and many other very beneficial special education services become available only *if* the individual is classified and placed. To be denied these services because the student was not or could not be classified as handicapped might very well significantly limit opportunities for an "appropriate education." Court decisions and legislation at the state and federal level guarantee the rights of handicapped students to an appropriate education at public expense.

There is another side to classification/placement decisions. Placement can involve, for example, a public school curriculum that is so different that pursuit of a college education would be very difficult, if not impossible. Furthermore, classification/placement can expose the individual to the stigma associated with being "named" mildly (educable) mentally retarded or emotionally disturbed. These, too, are significant consequences. Improper classification and misplacement through human error, inaccurate assessment information, or misapplication of eligibility criteria might cause very serious harm to the individual. To call a potential Einstein retarded or to attach that name to someone of more modest intellect (like D.J. Reschly) would indeed be most unfortunate.

In view of the potentially enormous consequences of classification/placement decisions, it is not surprising that carefully constructed safeguards have been developed. These safeguards are designed to ensure that classification/placement decisions in educational settings are proper; that those truly handicapped persons *do* receive the special education services they need; and that classification/placement does not occur with students who are *not* truly handicapped. The safeguards, now firmly entrenched through court opinions and legislation, have vast implications for psychoeducational assessment of students (Reschly, 1983). A summary of these principles and the implications for assessment are provided in Table 8.1.

Aptitude testing is almost always a significant part of the process whereby classification/placement decisions are made about students. The nature of aptitudes and the devices used to assess aptitudes are an integral part of classification/placement decisions. Results of aptitude assessment, especially if done poorly, may put a person into an improper classification/placement or deny a needed classification/placement. In view of the consequences of these decisions, it is not surprising that aptitude testing has been scrutinized carefully in recent years.

THE APTITUDE-INTELLIGENCE-ACHIEVEMENT DISTINCTION

Aptitude, achievement, and intelligence tests are not easily distinguishable. The traditional distinction was that achievement tests reflected the effects of learning, whereas aptitude and intelligence reflected the individual's potential for success. In this traditional view, both aptitude and intelligence were seen as relatively enduring traits of the individual, not easily modified by experience or special training. In some instances both aptitude and intelligence tests results were regarded as indications of innate capacity.

These traditional meanings of aptitude, achievement, and intelligence tests are rejected in all of the leading measurement texts (e.g., Anastasi, 1976; Brown, 1983). Anastasi pointed out that these tests were recognized as being essentially the same as early as 1927. Still, the idea that these tests are very different persists, especially in introductory psychology or educational psychology texts.

TABLE 8.1. LEGAL PRINCIPLES AND EDUCATION OF THE HANDICAPPED: IMPLICATIONS FOR ASSESSMENT.

Principle	Effects	Implications for Assessment
Right to Education	—More students classified as handicapped. —New populations of handicapped students entered the public schools.	—Greatly increased need for individual psychoeducational assessment. —Need for specialized skills in assessment of low incident and more severely handicapped.
Least Restrictive Environment	—Handicapped students served in as normal an environment as possible, including regular classrooms with support services or part-time special education.	—More emphasis on assessment in the natural environment through observation, etc., and the development and evaluation of interventions in the natural environment.
Individualized Educational Program	—Development of detailed plans to guide interventions with learning or behavior problems. —Annual reviews of effects of interventions.	—More emphasis on descriptions of specific educational needs and problem behaviors. —More emphasis on use of assessment information to design interventions and to monitor progress.
Due Process PARC v. Pa (1972)	—Formal procedures to ensure fairness through informed consent, access to records, appeal, and hearing.	—Greater scrutiny of the entire decision-making process, including psychoeducational assessment. —More emphasis on open communication with parents concerning instruments, results, and recommendations based on assessment data.
Protection in Evaluation Procedures	—Numerous guidelines concerning the preplacement and reevaluation of handicapped students: multifactored assessment, multidisciplinary team, valid procedures, appropriate in terms of handicap, primary language, nondiscrimination, etc.	—More emphasis on adaptive behavior, sociocultural status, and primary language, and less emphasis on global measures such as IQ. —More emphasis on determination of specific educational need, and less emphasis on underlying dynamics. —Assessment tailored to nature of child. —Assessment conducted by a team of professionals.

Current measurement texts stress certain commonalities among aptitude, achievement, and intelligence tests. All are tests of what now is characterized as "developed abilities," indicating that all of these tests reflect the effects of experience or, simply, learning. They also are characterized as being "maximum performance" tests, meaning that the examinees are encouraged to exhibit their very best efforts or to do as well as possible. This is in contrast to "typical performance" measures, such as interest inventories and personality tests, on which examinees are encouraged to respond according to their *usual* thoughts, feelings, or actions.

Perhaps the single most persuasive bit of evidence on the commonalities among these types of tests is that the same type of test item or even the exact same test battery may be used as a measure of achievement or aptitude at different times with different examinees. This apparently was the case with the Iowa Tests of Educational Development (ITED), which according to Mercer (1979a) was widely used as an achievement test battery with high school students and as an aptitude test in the National Merit Scholarship competition. When the same test is used as an achievement measure in one instance and as an aptitude test in another, it clearly is impossible to argue that the differences among achievement and aptitude reside in characteristics of the test content, format, or process. A final example to illustrate this point is the often mentioned but, as far as I know, never reported or researched activity of placing the items from aptitude and achievement tests on cards, mixing up the cards, and then attempting to sort the items according to whether they reflect aptitude or achievement content, format, or process. Presumably, it would be difficult if not impossible to exceed chance in the assignment of items.

If not test type, then what is/are the difference(s) among aptitude, achievement, and intelligence? Snow (1980) argued that each was an important and useful psychological construct that facilitated the development of theory, research, and practice. The most important differences among them have to do with how they are used and with assumptions about *antecedent experiences* (Anastasi, 1980; Brown, 1983).

The achievement construct and associated tests are attempts to measure learning that occurred in a specific circumscribed situation. Achievement has a past and present reference (Brown, 1983). In contrast, aptitude has a future reference. The aptitude construct involves general and incidental learning experiences that are related to how persons perform in future learning or training situations (Anastasi, 1976; Brown, 1983). As a construct, aptitude is used quite broadly, especially in the theory and research on aptitude by treatment interactions (ATI) (Cronbach & Snow, 1977; Snow, 1980). Here, aptitude is virtually any psychological characteristic of the person that *predicts* differences among people in later learning or training situations. Included in this very broad conception of aptitude are general ability, specific cognitive skills and prior achievement, all cognitive or thinking/knowledge characteristics, and personality/affective characteristics such as anxiety and achievement motivation.

Obviously, the situation can be very confusing. Conspicuous by its absence in the above discussion is the construct of intelligence, perhaps the most controversial of the aptitude, achievement, intelligence trilogy. Intelligence, sometimes used synonymously with ability, is usually seen as somewhere between achievement and aptitude on the continuum of test use and antecedent experiences. Intelligence is often described as having a present reference, reflecting very broad and general learning experiences. Moreover, intelligence as a form of test is often used in diagnostic work with individuals, which, as Anastasi (1976, 1980) demonstrates, is essentially the same as prediction.

It now appears we have gone nearly full circle! However, there are trends today in test development that, if followed consistently in the future,

will reduce much of this confusion. First, intelligence is rarely used in the names of newly developed tests, which for all intents and purposes are similar in content and intended use to traditional intelligence tests. The use of the term *IQ* to signify a kind of score also is used less frequently in the newer tests. The trend away from intelligence and IQ is particularly strong with group administered tests designed for school age children (Lennon, 1980). These tests increasingly use names such as school ability, cognitive ability, and scholastic aptitude. Newly developed individual intelligence tests reflect a similar trend (e.g., Kaufman & Kaufman, 1983; McCarthy, 1972). Interestingly, at least part of the acceptance of these newer tests depends on whether they are highly similar to traditional intelligence tests. This was quite apparent in Kaufman and Kaufman's (1977) contention that the General Cognitive Index on the McCarthy Scale of Children's Ability was essentially equivalent in meaning to an IQ score from well-accepted, older intelligence tests such as the Stanford-Binet Intelligence Test or the Wechsler Intelligence Scale for Children.

General Aptitude or Intelligence

In at least one major segment of the testing profession today the terms *general aptitude* and *intelligence* are nearly synonymous. The tests used in public education with school age groups to *diagnose* learning problems and *predict* likely level of academic performance are increasingly called general aptitude, scholastic aptitude, or school ability tests. These tests are *not* different in any significant respect from traditional general intelligence tests. The change in name does imply a change in the interpretation of results from these tests, a topic discussed later. Moreover, certain older individual tests such as the Wechsler Intelligence Scale for Children-Revised (WISC-R) and the Stanford-Binet (SB) still use scores called IQs and retain intelligence in their names. However, in at least one instance to date, the publisher of the WISC-R, The Psychological Corporation, permitted a seemingly radical change in the name and interpretation of the conventional WISC-R IQ scores. In the System of Multicultural Pluralistic Assessment (SOMPA) (Mercer, 1979a), the WISC-R IQ score was renamed the School Functioning Level (SFL). Thus, the trend away from intelligence and IQ is even apparent with the traditional tests.

Tests of general aptitude or intelligence used in public education settings have the following general characteristics: (a) heterogeneous item types and formats (usually within the same test); (b) complex cognitive operations are required (as opposed to simple recognition or memory); (c) an emphasis on power rather than speed; and (d) a general factor is apparent, sometimes augmented by less robust but stable group factors. The WISC-R is a prime example of this kind of test. The WISC-R typically is used to diagnose or predict, which are, as noted earlier, believed to be very similar activities. Clearly, the WISC-R is a test of developed abilities, as are all aptitude, achievement, and intelligence tests. The antecedent experiences reflected in the WISC-R are not defined at all precisely and might be characterized generally as ". . . growing up in America in the twentieth century" (Anastasi, 1980, p. 7). As an aside, that characterization might be broadened even further to something like, "any twentieth century literate, technological society," since translated versions of the WISC-R are used widely and successfully in Europe and Japan. After a brief section on specific aptitude tests, the discussion of uses of general aptitude tests will continue.

Specific Aptitudes or Tests of Psychological Processes

Tests of specific aptitudes, or what are sometimes called the psychological processes related to learning, are also used in the public schools as part of classification/placement and/or program planning/intervention decisions. These specific aptitude tests, in contrast to general scholastic aptitude or intelligence tests, usually have fairly homogeneous items that are intended to assess rather specific, discrete (presumably independent) abilities. Numerous underlying learning processes have been postulated, and even more tests attempting to measure these functions have been developed. Some examples of these special aptitudes are visual-motor memory, auditory discrimination, visual closure, auditory sequential memory, etc.

The special aptitude tests have been used for three kinds of decisions in the public schools. First, criteria for classifying students as handicapped sometimes require demonstration of deficits in one or more of these special aptitudes or

processes. This is most likely to be the case with the area of learning disabilities, although the definitive trend in that field is toward less emphasis on process variables or specific aptitudes. A second use is to establish objectives for remedial interventions. In this instance, the process deficit in, say, auditory closure becomes the educational objective. A wide variety of materials and activities have been designed to develop these processing skills. The final and most frequent current use is to choose a teaching method or strategy based upon apparent strengths in particular processes or "modalities." The most frequent strategy choice is between sight/whole word versus phonic approaches to teaching reading. Presumably, students with strengths in the visual-motor modality and a weakness in the auditory-vocal modality would do best if a sight/whole word method was used. Conversely, phonic methods would be expected to be most beneficial for students with auditory-vocal strengths and visual-motor weaknesses. These predictions are almost identical to our earlier description of an aptitude by treatment interaction (ATI), that is, a psychological characteristic of the learner that predicts different reactions to treatment conditions.

Specific aptitude or psychological process assessment and teaching have not fared at all well in the research conducted over the past 10 years or so. Although various methodological difficulties certainly do exist in this research, the nearly inescapable conclusions are that: (a) Most of the special aptitude or process measures have poor psychometric characteristics, e.g., low reliability and doubtful validity (Salvia & Ysseldyke, 1981); (b) there is little evidence that the processes can be successfully taught, and even less evidence that improvements in these processes lead to better performance in relevant academic subjects (see Hammill & Larsen, 1974, 1978; and Newcomer, Larsen, & Hammill, 1975; for another perspective on this literature, see Lund, Foster, & McCall-Perez, 1978; Minskoff, 1975); and (c) there is virtually no evidence for aptitude by treatment interactions using these process measures and currently available teaching strategies (Ysseldyke & Mirkin, 1982). For these reasons, along with the development of other criteria for classifying children as learning disabled, there has been a steady decline in the use of process measures in public school settings. However, the recent expansion of neuropsychological concepts to explain some learning disorders among school age children (Hynd & Obrzut, 1981), which in many respects is a revival of process concepts using different terminology and another set of theoretical constructs, will ensure that specific aptitude tests will continue to be used at least on a limited basis. Specific aptitude tests are not used as widely nor have they been as central to educational classification/placement and program planning/intervention decisions as general aptitude or intelligence tests.

USES OF GENERAL APTITUDE TESTS

General aptitude tests or what earlier were called tests of intelligence are used for a variety of purposes in educational settings. A number of group and individually administered tests are available from the major test publishers.

Group Tests

Group tests are probably used less frequently than previously. The results of group tests are hardly ever used as a significant part of classification/placement decisions with handicapped students but may be a key part of identification of gifted students.

Group tests of academic aptitude may be given to students two to three times during their public school careers. In contrast, group administered achievement tests are given far more often, usually annually or every other year. It is my impression that the use of group aptitude tests has declined significantly in recent years due to the criticisms of their utility, concerns about labeling effects, and as a result of pressure from minority representatives. In some areas group scholastic aptitude or intelligence tests are banned. Group tests generally have these characteristics: (a) use of a pencil-and-paper format where the examinee reads the items and selects responses, usually on a machine scorable answer sheet; (b) use of time limits, although the time limits are generally established so that nearly all examinees can complete the test; and (c) multiple-choice format where a best or correct answer is selected from a limited number of options. Group scholastic aptitude tests are typically used to establish general expectations for level of academic achievement and as part of the initial stages of identifying students as intellectually gifted. These general

screening functions of group aptitude tests are emphasized as opposed to diagnostic or classification/placement decisions.

A definite trend in recent years is the shift from titles or terminology involving mental ability or intelligence to newer terminology that has fewer connotations of innate ability. Two examples are the change of the Lorge-Thorndike Intelligence Test to the Cognitive Ability Test and the change of the Otis-Lennon Mental Ability Test to the Otis-Lennon School Ability Test. The changes in terminology appear to be efforts to delimit interpretations of scores and to restrict inferences to the school setting (Lennon, 1980).

Group aptitude tests are very efficient means of collecting information that has very high reliability and validity, at least for groups. The result of group intelligence tests would undoubtedly be useful to persons doing individual psychoeducational assessments of students suspected of being handicapped. For example, it is highly unlikely that a student who scores in the average range or above on a group administered test would obtain a significantly lower score on an individually administered test. An average or above score for a youngster who is referred would then obviate the need for administering the individual intelligence test, an activity that is very time consuming and expensive. However, it should be emphasized that students who obtain low scores on group ability tests should be administered an individually administered test before inferences are made about scholastic aptitude. It is necessary to use the individual test before such inferences are made because the student may have been penalized on the group test due to reading difficulties, inability to work efficiently, as well as a variety of other reasons. It should be noted that these interpretations have the effect of giving the individual the benefit of doubt. To put it another way, we accept at face value evidence indicating the individual has average or above average scholastic aptitude, but we regard low scores on group tests with considerable skepticism, requiring confirmation from individually administered tests and a variety of other information as well.

Group adminimistered scholastic aptitude tests are used widely with young adults. These tests are typically administered prior to college entrance, where they frequently are called scholastic aptitude tests. More advanced and sophisticated versions of these kinds of tests are administered as

part of the process whereby individuals are selected for entrance to professional schools, law,
dentistry, medicine, or to graduate programs in a
variety of areas. These scholastic aptitude tests are
generally regarded as being fair to minority students when precise statistical criteria are used to
assess fairness, a topic discussed further later in
this chapter (Flaugher, 1978).

Individual Tests

Individual tests are administered only under special conditions. The vast majority of students in
the public school setting are never administered
an individual test of intelligence, and, as noted
above, some places do not use group tests of intelligence. Individually administered tests of intelligence typically involve: (a) subtests that are
presented orally by the examiner to a single examinee, (b) questions typically are administered
one at a time without a great deal of emphasis on
speed of response, and (c) the individual usually
has the opportunity to construct his/her response
rather than being required to select a response
from a limited number of options. Most individually administered tests must be administered by
someone who has, at a minimum, a masters degree in a relevant area, most often psychology or
school psychology.

Individual scholastic aptitude tests, such as the
WISC-R, the Stanford-Binet, McCarthy's Scale of
Children's Ability, and in all likelihood in the
future, the new Kaufman Assessment Battery for
Children (K-ABC), are typically given in public
school settings by school psychologists. There are
approximately 15,000 school psychologists working in the public schools in the United States. The
major responsibility of these professionals is to
conduct psychoeducational assessments with students who are referred, most often by teachers,
due to learning and/or adjustment problems in
the classroom. It should be noted that school psychologists provide a variety of services in the
public schools, but the most frequent is psychoeducational assessment.

A complex, not very well understood process is
involved in classification/placement decisions
(Bickel, 1982). Psychoeducational assessment is an
important component. However, other steps, such
as failure in the regular classroom, insufficiency of
regular education remedial services, referral, and
screening, are also very important.

Individual tests are most often crucial in classification decisions with the *mildly* handicapped.

Mildly handicapped students most often involve
classifications of learning disability, educable or
mild mental retardation, and emotional/behavior
disorders. These handicaps account for a large
percentage of the public school age population of
handicapped students. These handicaps typically
are mild in degree, meaning that: (a) The learning or adjustment problem is not so severe to
render the individual incapable of being involved
with regular classroom instruction; (b) the handicapping condition usually is not visible, that is,
individuals do not display physical, sensory or
motor disabilities that are easily recognized; and
(c) these handicapping conditions usually are
identified first in a school setting, and the individual so identified may be regarded as normal in
other settings and at preschool or adult ages.

The criteria for classification in the mildly handicapping categories usually require underlying
intellectual/aptitude dimensions that often can
only be examined through the use of standardized
tests. This is particularly true with mild or educable mental retardation where intelligence or scholastic aptitude is fundamental to the classification
criteria. Intelligence or scholastic aptitude tests
are also used in almost all classification decisions
involving children with learning disabilities (LD).
The emphasis on intelligence with LD classification has increased in recent years as a result of
dissatisfaction with the process variables discussed
earlier and the corresponding greater emphasis on
"severe discrepancy" (Federal Register, 1977a). In
LD classification, the severe discrepancy almost
always means examining the difference between
an individual intelligence test and a measure of
educational achievement in certain areas, such as
reading or mathematics. If this discrepancy is
large enough to be regarded as "severe," which is
a difficult judgment fraught with possible measurement artifacts and logical inconsistencies
(Cole, 1978; Salvia & Ysseldyke, 1981), the student may be classified as LD. Recall the earlier
discussion of the overlap in the constructs and the
tests of achievement and aptitude (intelligence).
Depending on the nature of the test and the assumptions about preceding experiences, the
search for the severe discrepancy may involve
comparing measures of the same attribute. In this
instance, by no means entirely unrealistic, it is
hard to know what any difference among the
measures might mean. Despite these and many
other problems in LD classification/placement,
the number and percent of students classified as
LD continues to expand. At the present time,

efforts to develop more stringent criteria for LD classification are underway in most states (Sontag, 1983), usually involving more stringent criteria for the size of the discrepancy that can be regarded as "severe."

Individual scholastic aptitude tests are less important in classification of emotional disturbance/behavior disorders, but surveys of school assessment indicate that such tests are almost always used with these students. Individual scholastic aptitude tests also are given quite frequently to students who have more visible handicaps, such as sensory or physical deficits like hearing impairment or cerebral palsy. In these areas, though, intelligence tests are not used as part of the basic classification process, which, more often than not, is accomplished by medical specialists. Here, the individual test results are used to estimate likely levels of academic performance as well as to rule out the possibility of the associated handicap of mental retardation (Gerken, 1979). Intelligence test use with these populations of handicapped persons (the more severely handicapped) is not particularly controversial because there is no significant overrepresentation in these handicapping areas by race, social status, or gender. Use of individual tests with the mildly handicapped has become increasingly controversial in recent years because of concern about fairness to specific sociocultural groups.

APTITUDE TESTING AND MINORITY STUDENTS

The use of intelligence (general aptitude) tests as part of the process of educational classification/placement has been severely castigated by a number of minority educators and psychologists. Jones and Wilderson (1976) suggested that poor assessment practices and use of biased tests were part of an overall pattern of institutional racism. These very serious charges have also been made by a number of other educators and psychologists.

Williams (1970) commented, "Ability testing is being utilized to dehumanize, damage, and destroy black children and youth through improperly labeling and classifying them" (p. 5). Samuda (1975) stated that: "The implications and consequences of testing for minority group individuals are real, drastic, and pervasive in their effects at all stages in the lives of minority individuals" (p. 69). Finally, the following remarks by Hilliard mention the major topics of this section: overrepresentation, litigation, test bias, and concepts of fairness:

> At any point when a certain cultural group is overrepresented in a particular category of special education, the special educator should spare no effort to review the system of assessment for cultural bias. . . . It is a shame and a disgrace that the courts and the legislature are left to overrule the bad practices which are so widespread among us. (1980, p. 587)

Overrepresentation

Disproportionate representation occurs whenever an identifiable group has significantly greater or fewer members in a particular classification than would be expected from their actual numbers or percentages in the general population. Some kinds of over- or underrepresentation are well known and widely accepted, for example, more males have problems in learning to read. Other forms of disproportionate classification are viewed with skepticism, and overrepresentation of black students in the educational classification/placement of educable mentally retarded (EMR) has provoked a considerable controversy that is far from resolved. The facts accepted by all participants in this dispute are that black (as well as other minority and economically disadvantaged) students are overrepresented in EMR special education programs. Moreover, the EMR classification/placement process almost always involves the administration of individual intelligence tests, and specific IQ cut-off scores are almost always used to determine eligibility. Beyond these areas of agreement, there are intense and sometimes even bitter arguments over the meaning, causes, and remedies for overrepresentation. Before analyzing these arguments, the overrepresentation data need a closer look.

When the famous *Larry P.* case was originally filed in 1971, the major defendant, the San Francisco Public Schools, had substantial overrepresentation of black students in EMR programs. Black students constituted 28% of the total student population, but 66% of the EMR student population. Later the *Larry P.* defendants were expanded to all school districts in California, where 10% of the student population was black, but 25% of the EMR enrollment was black (*Larry P. v. Riles*, 1979; Meyers, MacMillan, & Yoshida,

1978; Reschly, 1980a). Similar data were reported by Mercer (1973) for the Riverside Public Schools and by Manni, Winikur, and Keller (1980). These data are analyzed in Table 8.2. But before looking at those analyses, the reader is encouraged to estimate the actual percentage of black students in EMR programs in California from the previously given percentages (10% and 25%). The result in Table 8.2 is usually suprising to most persons.

As indicated in Table 8.2, the overrepresentation in EMR programs involves a very small percentage of minority students. This same trend apparently holds for the entire nation, according to a recent report in which Federal Office for Civil Rights (OCR) survey data were cited (Heller, Holtzman, & Messick, 1982). The OCR survey, which I suspect may exaggerate the amount of overrepresentation, concluded that the percentages of black and white students in EMR programs were 3.46 and 1.07, respectively. These results are similar to data in Table 8.2 for three localities from the 1960s and 1970s. In all instances, the percent of black students in EMR programs was three to four times the percent of white students. However, these percentages have often been misinterpreted and exaggerated. The percent of EMR enrollment (e.g., 25% black) compared to the percent of total enrollment (e.g., 10% black) has been distorted by some who imply that large percentages, perhaps even 25%, of all black students are labeled retarded. This obviously is not the case. However, the overrepresentation is real, and legal action concerning EMR overrepresentation may have profound influences on aptitude assessment and educational classification/placement.

TABLE 8.2. ANALYSIS OF OVERREPRESENTATION DATA.

Riverside, CA Public Schools[1] — 1960s

Group	Percent of Total Population	Percent of EMR Enrollment	Number in Total Population	Number in EMR Classes	Percent of Each Group in EMR classes
White	82	53	20,500	133	0.6
Hispanic	9.5	32	2,375	80	3.4
Black	7	12	1,750	30	1.7

State of California, 1968–69 and 1976–77[2]

Group	Percent of Total Population	Percent of EMR Enrollment		Percent of Each Group in EMR classes	
		68–69	76–77	68–69	76–77
White	72	43	—	0.8	0.4
Black	10	25.5	25.4	3.2	1.1
Hispanic	15	29	—	2.6	1.3

State of New Jersey, 1979–80[3]

	White	Black	Hispanic
Percent of Total Enrollment	73	18	7
Percent of Total EMR Enrollment	43	43	13
Percent of Total Handicapped Enrollment	71	21	7
VS			
Percent of Group in EMR	0.5	1.9	1.4
Percent of Group in TMR	0.2	0.4	0.3
Percent of Group in ED	0.8	2.3	0.7
Percent of Group in LD	2.8	2.3	1.4
Percent of Group in Handicapped	10.4	12.5	10.1

[1]Based on data reported by Mercer (1973) and personal communication from Mercer in 1979 indicating that the total enrollment in the Riverside Public Schools in the mid-1960s was about 25,000 students, of which about 1% were in special classes for the mildly retarded.
[2]Based upon estimates derived from data reported in Larry P. (1979), Yoshida et al. (1976), and personal communication with the California State Department of Education in 1979.
[3]Data from Table 1, p. 10 of Manni et al., 1980.

Litigation and Legislation

Over the last 15 years or so there has been a recognizable cycle of litigation-legislation-litigation (Bersoff, 1982a). The overall effects of a number of court cases and legislation have been to establish a set of principles that attempt to guarantee certain rights, establish procedural safeguards, and ensure appropriate assessment procedures. These principles and their implications for assessment practices were presented earlier in Table 8.1. In this section the specific legal influences on aptitude testing will be discussed.

Overrepresentation of minorities in EMR programs has provoked suspicion of continued segregation by race in several cases filed in federal district courts. Segregation by race in public educational settings was, of course, ruled unconstitutional in the famous *Brown* decision in 1954. The *Brown* decision usually is cited as the seminal event in judicial scrutiny of the assessment procedures used in educational classification/placement (Bersoff, 1979, 1981, 1982a). The *Brown* decision has been refined and extended by numerous succeeding cases and legislation. The courts now often view practices that have a disproportionate impact on minorities with special scrutiny. At times, this special scrutiny has meant that the burden of proof is shifted to defendants rather than residing with the plaintiffs because the courts are concerned about removing all vestiges of segregation in education. This very complicated legal issue, which continues to evolve as cases are decided through the district courts, the appellate courts, and the U.S. Supreme Court, is parallel in many ways to the competing concepts of fairness to be discussed in a later section. However, the crucial issue is whether discriminatory intent is required or whether the far less stringent criterion of disproportionate impact on minorities is sufficient to establish constitutionally impermissible discrimination. The courts to date have vacillated on this question, mirroring the rather ambivalent views of the entire society on the most appropriate and equitable methods to remove all vestiges of discrimination. But, as we shall see, burden of proof is extremely important in aptitude testing cases, since it is virtually impossible to unequivocally prove either that tests are biased or that tests are fair with the available research.

The major classification/placement court cases have been class action suits pressed by minority plaintiffs alleging discrimination in EMR classification/placement. The overrepresentation data, covered earlier, were used in plaintiffs' arguments that the defendant school districts and state departments of education were using practices that reestablished or preserved segregation by race. In all of the court cases to 1983 the classification of concern was EMR and the objectionable placement was the self-contained special class. Overrepresentation in other classifications or in other placements has not to date provoked the same sort of litigation for reasons to be discussed later.

Pre-1975 Litigation

Class action court cases on behalf of black, Hispanic, and native American students (e.g., Diana, 1970; Guadalupe, 1972) in the early 1970s either were decided in favor of minority plaintiffs or settled by consent decrees agreeable to plaintiffs (Reschly, 1979). Fairness of intelligence tests was the central issue, and little or no attention was devoted to other aspects of the referral-placement process. The cases settled prior to 1975 generally involved a variety of poor and sometimes unethical practices in addition to the test fairness issue (MacMillan, 1977; Reschly, 1979). For example, some bilingual students were classified as mentally retarded and placed in special education programs on the basis of *verbal* IQ scales that unfairly penalized them for lack of familiarity with English. In other instances, defendant school districts did not even contest plaintiffs' allegations that short-form intelligence scales and even group-administered verbal scales were used by poorly trained personnel as the basis for classification of bilingual students. In addition, parents were at least occasionally not even informed, let alone accorded rights of consent, when their children were referred, evaluated, and placed in a special education program.

The plaintiffs described deplorable conditions in the special education programs. These included little academic emphasis, poor facilities, inadequately trained teachers, and in one instance, actual exploitation of students to perform menial labor on the school campus (MacMillan, 1977). For obvious reasons, defendants in the early cases (school districts and state departments of education) had little choice other than to acknowledge plaintiff complaints and agree to various reforms establishing due process, informed consent, and other protections for parents and children (MacMillan, 1977; Reschly, 1979).

These early cases also established several requirements concerning assessment practices. Classification decisions were to be based on a broad variety of information, including adaptive behavior outside of school, not just IQ test scores. The child's primary language was to be determined, and assessment devices were to be administered in this language. For bilingual students, more emphasis was to be placed on nonverbal or performance measures. This was particularly relevant for Hispanic and Native American Indian students.

These reforms were entirely consistent with the best practice standards and had the effect of eliminating some very poor practices that were probably *not* typical of assessment practices at that time, but which did, nevertheless, exist in some places.

Legislation

State and federal legislation in the mid-1970s incorporated many of the key reforms from the early placement bias cases (Prasse, 1979). The Federal Education for All Handicapped Children Act of 1975, Public Law 94-142, and the accompanying rules and regulations (Federal Register, 1977b) was the most important and most widely applicable legislative act. The Protection in Evaluation Procedures Provision section of the 94-142 rules and regulations had enormous implications for assessment (see Table 8.3). Many of these requirements have unequivocal language, "must. . .," but no definitions of key concepts, nor criteria for evaluating assessment practices. For example, no criteria for determining discrimination are provided nor are there suggestions for the level and kind of validity evidence that might be needed. Is overrepresentation evidence of discrimination? Are nonbiased tests required, or is an equal placement rate sufficient? How valid? Is a correlation of .5 with a relevant criterion sufficient? How specific must the validity evidence be? This latter concern may be a particularly difficult problem due to the very sparse research based on test use with handicapped persons (Sherman & Robinson, 1982). In view of these rather sweeping generalizations, further litigation to define the meaning of these legislative requirements was a near certain outcome. That has indeed been the case in the late 1970s to date.

TABLE 8.3. PROTECTION IN EVALUATION PROCEDURES OF PL 94-142.

a. Nondiscriminative "Testing and evaluation materials and procedures used for the purposes of evaluation and placement of handicapped children must be selected and administered so as not to be racially or culturally discriminatory."
b. "Full and individual evaluation of the child's educational needs."
c. Use of ". . . child's native language or other mode of communication, unless it is clearly not feasible to do so."
d. Tests and other evaluation devices ". . . have been validated for the specific purpose for which they are used . . ."
e. Administered by trained personnel.
f. ". . . assess specific areas of educational needs and not merely . . . a single general intelligence quotient."
g. *No* single procedure used as sole criterion for classification or placement.
h. Multidisciplinary team.
i. Multifactored assessment required in preplacement evaluation.
j. Reevaluation of classification and placement at least every three years.

Note. Quoted statements are from *Federal Register*, 1977b, pp. 42496–42497.

Litigation 1975–1983

Two potentially landmark classification/placement cases are at various stages in the Federal Courts at the time this was written (*Larry P.* v. *Riles*; *PASE* v. *Hannon*). These cases involve identical issues: overrepresentation of black students in EMR programs and allegations that IQ tests such as the WISC-R are biased against black students. The briefs by plaintiffs in both cases cited previous court cases and the nondiscrimination requirement in the PL 94-142 Rules and Regulations. Neither case involves allegations of unethical practices. Both were heard in court trials and decided by federal district court judges on their merits. Similar testimony involving some of the same expert witnesses, several of whom were prominent psychologists, appeared in both cases. However, there was nothing at all similar in the judges' opinions.

In *Larry P.*, California Federal District Court Judge Peckham determined that intelligence tests were biased against black students, and EMR special classes reflected impermissible segregation.

His opinion in 1979 relied on constitutional protections, civil rights laws, and PL 94-142. His remedy was to ban the use of IQ tests, "Defendants are enjoined from utilizing, permitting the use of, or approving the use of any standardized intelligence tests, . . . for the identification of black EMR children or their placement into EMR classes" (Larry P. Opinion, p. 104). The defendants were also ordered to ". . . eliminate disproportionate placement of black children in California's EMR classes" (p. 105).

In sharp contrast, Illinois Federal District Court Judge Grady concluded in 1980 that conventional IQ tests were largely unbiased, and that the small amount of bias that did exist would not result in improper classification/placement of minority students. Judge Grady upheld both the use of IQ tests in the Chicago Public Schools and the overrepresentation of black students in EMR programs in that school district.

Both Larry P. and PASE cases have been appealed. Figures close to the cases speculate that the sides are committed to pursuit of the cases to the Supreme Court. It is worthwhile noting at this point, after Bersoff (1982b), that the Supreme Court is not supreme because it is best, but because it is last. Although we can only speculate on the legal outcome of these cases, which is very hard to predict, we can analyze the reasoning and the empirical basis for the decisions.

Careful analyses of the reasoning in Larry P. and PASE reveals serious flaws in both (Bersoff, 1982b; Reschly, 1980a). Judge Peckham's analysis in Larry P. was regarded by Bersoff (1982b) as reflecting "unfortunate infirmities" (p. 88), and as "scanty and faulty" with regard to the pivotal issue of test bias. Peckham concluded, contrary to considerable evidence to be discussed in a later section, that the WISC-R and similar tests have a large number of biased items and that such tests are more valid for white than black students. For unknown reasons, Peckham chose to ignore, or perhaps he misunderstood, the substantial body of knowledge on test bias that leads to just the opposite conclusions. Moreover, in Peckham's view, IQ tests were the most important determinant of EMR classification/placement. By banning the tests Peckham apparently thought the use of overrepresentation would be eliminated.

Judge Grady, in sharp contrast, regarded the IQ test as only one part of a complex and cautious process whereby students may be classified and placed in EMR programs. Grady pointed to the numerous procedural safeguards, the wide variety of information that is considered, and the multidisciplinary team as adequate protections against improper classification and placement decisions. The most controversial aspect of Grady's opinion was the conclusion that the WISC, Stanford-Binet, and WISC-R were largely unbiased. Although probably correct, that conclusion was an entirely fortuitous outcome of a notoriously unreliable method of examining a test for unbiased items. Grady noted the contradictory testimony from expert witnesses, which he concluded left only his personal judgment as a basis for reaching a decision. Grady examined all of the items on the three intelligence tests, thought about their content, estimated the probable effects of cultural differences, and then decided whether or not they were biased against urban black children. Using this method of analysis, Grady found only eight biased items on the three tests. However, judgment, even expert judgment, of item bias is virtually worthless (Sandoval & Mille, 1980). For this and other reasons, Bersoff (1982b) regarded Judge Grady's opinion as "embarrassingly devoid of intellectual integrity" (p. 88); and as "unintelligent," "naive," and "devoid of empirical content" (p. 90).

We now have the spectacle of contradictory and unsophisticated court opinions on whether general aptitude tests are biased. Neither decision is sound. Both fail to reflect the subtle and equivocal findings of the test bias research. Perhaps this unsatisfactory outcome is inherent, at least in part, in the judicial mechanism for resolving social science issues. The tendency is toward definitive, unequivocal opinions, but the social science research is almost always conditional and equivocal (Reschly, 1979). However, the conclusions on test biases are not the major problem with these cases. In all of the placement bias litigation there have been numerous implicit issues and assumptions that were potentially more important than the intractable problem of test bias. For unknown reasons, all parties to this litigation—plaintiffs, defendants, and judges—have generally ignored these implicit factors.

Implicit Issues and Assumptions

That more than IQ tests and overrepresentation were involved in plaintiffs' motives is apparent from the Larry P. opinion and analyses of other educational classification/placement data. The

Larry P. opinion reflected plaintiffs' assertions that : (a) IQ tests were biased; (b) IQ and achievement tests "autocorrelated," i.e., they were the same; and (c) "The customary uses of achievement tests are not questioned by plaintiff, even though black children also tend not to do well on these tests" (*Larry P.* Opinion, p. 120). That reasoning makes little sense unless factors other than IQ tests were of concern. Furthermore, economically disadvantaged, minority students are overrepresented in a variety of educational programs including Head Start, Chapter I (formerly Title I), and Follow Through. This overrepresentation is well known, but apparently, acceptable. An additional incongruity is the substantially larger per pupil expenditure in EMR than in regular education programs. The implicit issues and assumptions, discussed briefly here, provide an explanation for these seemingly inconsistent trends in plaintiffs' positions (Reschly, 1981a).

Nature-Nurture

The debate over the relative effects of heredity and environment in determining intelligence predates the development of measures of intelligence. This very old debate has not been resolved and is not likely to be resolved in the foreseeable future. The controversy was increased dramatically in the 1970s with the extension of the hereditarian view to explain differences between racial groups (Jensen, 1969). Since the debate over the source or cause of observed group differences in measured intelligence cannot be resolved with presently available data (Loehlin, Lindzey, & Spuhler, 1975), minority critics have attempted to force a kind of resolution through the courts. Indirectly, the real defendants in the court cases were the advocates of hereditarian explanations of race differences in measured intelligence, e.g., Arthur Jensen and William Shockley. Their views were a major component in the motivation of plaintiffs to press these cases. A comprehensive ban on IQ tests would accomplish little in resolving the debate and would not address the educational problems exhibited by minority students currently classified as EMR. Finally, an IQ test ban, if not accompanied by rigid quotas, might very well result in increasing rather than decreasing overrepresentation!

Meaning of IQ Test Results

A number of myths regarding the meaning of intelligence test results have been around for several decades. Of particular concern are the beliefs that IQ test results are predetermined by genetic factors, that intelligence is unitary and is measured directly by IQ tests, and that IQ test results are fixed. The available evidence clearly refutes these myths (Hunt, 1961), and the vast majority of professional psychologists do not harbor such misconceptions. Kaufman (1979) provided an excellent discussion of the underlying assumptions and the meaning of intellectual assessment. His views are probably typical of most professional psychologists. However, many consumers of IQ test results such as teachers, parents, and the lay public generally hold these misconceptions. A significant portion of the testimony in the litigation was devoted to disproving these myths, which hardly any psychologists believe anyway. However, some judges apparently have been surprised that IQ tests do not measure innate potential, which, in turn, has contributed to judicial skepticism about the fairness and usefulness of such tests (Bersoff, 1982a).

Role of Tests

In several court cases and much of the placement bias literature it was implicitly assumed that IQ tests were the primary if not the sole basis for the classification of students as mildly retarded (Larry P. opinion, 1979; Mercer, 1973). The role of standardized tests in the classification process has been exaggerated. From reading this literature one might reach the totally erroneous conclusion that classified and placed students were performing well until a psychologist came along and ensnared unsuspecting children in a pernicious psychometric net. However, the single most important determinant of classification is the academic failure in the regular classroom leading to referral. It is only in this context that individual IQ tests are given and classification even considered. Research conducted with randomly selected samples of students reveals that some children who would meet eligibility requirements are never referred, hence classification and placement (and IQ testing) are never considered (Reschly & Jipson, 1976). Disproportionate numbers of minority (as well as economically disadvantaged and male) students are referred due to academic or behavioral problems. Although research on the entire process is somewhat meager, the available data suggest that IQ tests either have a neutral effect on overall disproportionality, or, perhaps, actually reduce the degree of overrepresentation that would exist from teacher referral alone (Reschly, 1979). Overall, IQ test *use* protects many students in all racial, social status, and gender groups from erroneous and inappropriate classification.

Labeling Effects

Implicit in the litigation was the assumption that classification as Educable Mentally Retarded was potentially stigmatizing and humiliating with probable permanent effects. The controversy over labeling is far from resolved. The available empirical evidence does not support the self-fulfilling prophecy notion, and direct effects of labels on the behavior of children or adults have been difficult to document (MacMillan, Jones, & Aloia, 1974). The dilemmas associated with classification have been prominent in the exceptional child literature for the past decade. The dilemma was described well by Gallagher (1972), who acknowledged the inevitability of classification but suggested that the crucial factor was whether the benefits of services provided as a result of the label were sufficient to justify the possible risks of the label.

Meaning of Mild Mental Retardation

The reasoning of the *Larry P.* decision was that the plaintiffs were not "truly retarded" despite the low IQs, low academic achievement, and teacher referral. The effort to identify "true" mental retardation appears to be related to confusion of mild with more severe levels of mental retardation. The criteria for "true" mental retardation are apparently believed to require comprehensive incompetence, permanence, and evidence of biological anomaly (Mercer, 1973, 1979a). In contrast, the American Association on Mental Deficiency (AAMD) classification system does not specify etiology or prognosis (Grossman, 1983). In addition, different domains of adaptive behavior are emphasized depending on the age of the individual. There was little doubt that the plaintiffs in the placement litigation had serious academic problems. The question was whether they were "truly" retarded or merely performed within the retarded range due to biases in the IQ tests. Confusion over the meaning of mild mental retardation and questions concerning the criteria for adaptive behavior were key issues in the cases.

Effectiveness of EMR Special Classes

The special education program usually provided in the past for students classified as mildly retarded was the self-contained special class. Self-contained special classes often involve a large degree of separation from the regular school program and curriculum and less contact with "normal" students. The recent emphasis on "mainstreaming" suggests reduced use of special classes with the mildly retarded, a trend fostered in part by court opinions viewing overrepresentation of minorities in special classes as constituting unlawful segregation of students by race. Although the research problem is extremely complex, precious little empirical support exists for these classes at the elementary and junior high school grade levels. Any benefits that do exist appear to be in the areas of social and personal adjustment, not academic achievement. The doubts about special classes were accepted as fact by the *Larry P.* court. In the *Larry P.* opinion, special classes were characterized at least 27 times as "dead-end," "inferior," and so on. If these programs were as poor as alleged, then no student, regardless of race or social class, should have been placed in them. However, the negative characterization of special classes may be overdrawn. The efficacy of special classes at the high school level involving work-study experience is supported by evidence, and the common-sense experiences of many educators suggest that self-contained special classes are a desirable and beneficial alternative for some students. Without doubt, the most difficult problem in this litigation was justifying the placement. Proper classification followed by poor treatment is quite justifiably viewed negatively. Recent trends toward more emphasis on regular education alternatives before referral and greater use of part-time special education placements for EMR students may alleviate some of the concern about the effectiveness of special classes.

Meaning of Bias

Many definitions of bias in tests have been proposed in the psychological and educational measurement literature (see Reynolds, 1982). Rather narrow and simplistic criteria have been used by plaintiffs. The definitions of bias used by the courts have been overrepresentation percentages and the rather simplistic notion of mean differences. On the basis of these criteria, all current measures of achievement and ability would be regarded as biased. However, other criteria for bias such as item content, predictive validity, and construct validity have been studied with minority samples using conventional tests. Current tests typically are not biased according to these criteria.

Research on Test Bias

In many quarters, standardized tests are simply assumed to be biased. The concepts of bias used in the litigation and literature on placement bias have been rather narrow and nontechnical. Mean differences between cultural groups often are cited as indicating bias by those who assume that a fair test of "potential" would yield identical distributions and means for all cultural groups. This assumption was explicit in the *Larry P.* opinion and mentioned in several other court opinions (Bersoff, 1982a).

The argument about mean differences usually proceeds to assertions that environments differ with respect to opportunities for learning whatever is required on the test (which is certainly true), to considerations of degree of cultural loading of test items, and to protracted and heated debates concerning the causes of mean differences. Content bias, based on citing one or several items, usually is suggested as the cause of the mean differences. The famous "fight" item on the Wechsler Comprehension Subtest is perhaps the most frequently cited example of content or item bias. This item requires children to specify what they would do if a child "much smaller than yourself" initiated a fight. The keyed answers, to avoid the fight, are judged *subjectively* to be unfair to minority students. Subjective judgments of this kind have appeared frequently in the literature.

The deficiencies of subjective judgments of item bias were well illustrated in recent work by Jon Sandoval with the WISC-R, the most widely used individual intelligence test. Interjudge agreement among minority persons concerning which items were biased was very low (Sandoval & Mille, 1980), and most important, application of empirical criteria yielded little or no evidence of item bias on commonly used tests (Ross-Reynolds & Reschly, 1983; Sandoval, 1979).

A wide variety of other criteria for assessing bias in tests has appeared in the measurement literature (Cole, 1981; Flaugher, 1978). Research applying these criteria to various IQ and achievement tests has flourished in recent years. Conventional tests are nearly always found to be largely unbiased on the basis of the technical criteria—for example, internal psychometric properties, factor structure, item content, atmosphere effects, and predictive validity (Cleary, Humphreys, Kendrick, & Wesman, 1975; Jensen, 1980; Reschly, 1982). In the measurement literature, conventional tests are usually defended on the basis of predictive validity and other technical criteria, and improper or unwise *test use* is implicated as causing any bias that may exist (Cleary et al., 1975; Widgor & Garner, 1982).

Concepts of Fairness

Many of the professional and scholarly analyses of aptitude testing with minority students have emphasized fairly narrow criteria, particularly predictive validity. The Cleary et al. (1975) report is typical of the professional-scholarly responses to minority critics of standardized testing. Conventional standardized tests function in about the same way with minority students. Reliability is about the same. Validity coefficients and regression systems are nearly identical. Factor structure is nearly constant across various groups. According to these criteria, conventional standardized tests are fair, and any bias or discrimination from testing is due either to misuse or the general, pervasive bias or discrimination in the entire society. But the tests per se are not blamed in these accounts.

Minority critics of tests usually concede most, if not all, of these points. However, their concern is with the sociopolitical effects of test results and the impact of testing on the lives of individual children. Their concerns, stated more bluntly, are whether tests contribute more to the problem or solution of racism and whether they enhance or limit opportunities for individual students who have minority status. The reactions of Jackson (1975) and Bernal (1975) to the Cleary et al. (1975) report are typical of the views of many psychologists who have minority status. They were concerned with the broad social consequences of test use, not merely whether tests predicted equally well for different groups. Jackson and Bernal were particularly critical of the use of tests to perpetuate negative racial and ethnic stereotypes. Media accounts in recent years of mean differences among groups are especially destructive according to minority psychologists, who claim, perhaps with good reason, that such accounts have been used to justify lower governmental expenditures on compensatory education programs. Although Herrnstein (1982) strongly disputed claims of media bias on minority IQ test results, the fact remains that test results from different groups are often confused and distorted in the media.

The overall impact of standardized tests on the rate and level of minority group progress is very difficult to assess. Certainly, high test performance has been a key to expanded opportunities for many individuals with minority status. These high test scores prove, at a minimum, that there are exceptions to negative stereotypes about racial or ethnic group abilities. This is important, but insufficient. Test results have also been used to establish the case for greater expenditure of monies on educational programs for minority students. Here it seems that test use would be regarded as positive if the educational programs are worthwhile. As was noted with the EMR special classes, the expenditure of more money does not guarantee that educational programs will be perceived as worthwhile or more effective. However, most compensatory education programs *are* very popular with minority critics of testing, and test results are a major part of the case that is made for the need for these programs.

In a real sense, the issue continues to be a matter of test use. Test use is perceived as positive if more monies and, presumably, better opportunities are the outcomes. However, if test use leads to decisions that greater percentages of minority individuals failed to meet certain criteria, as in minimum competency testing for high school diplomas (*Debra P.* v. *Turlington*, 1979) or lower admission rates to professional schools (law, medicine, and dentistry), then test use often is criticized by minority spokespersons as an instrument that perpetuates discrimination. These rather ambivalent attitudes toward testing are related to different notions of fairness and to different ethical positions.

In recent years two rather different notions of fairness have emerged from a variety of institutions and disciplines. These notions, called here equal treatment versus equal outcomes, have different underlying philosophical and ethical assumptions (Hunter & Schmidt, 1976). These differences lead to sharp contrasts in how tests are used and how various decisions are made (Lerner, 1981).

Equal Treatment

Equal treatment means to use exactly the same selection procedures and criteria regardless of the race, social class, sex, or ethnicity, of the individual. Other contemporary names for equal treatment are "color blind" or "nonsexist." The ethical and philosophical position of qualified individualism (Hunter & Schmidt, 1976) is consistent with the equal treatment notion of fairness. To discriminate is to treat persons differently on the basis of race, sex, or some other demographic variable.

The use of tests for selection, classification, and placement is usually endorsed by equal treatment advocates. Tests are seen as objective, color-blind devices that can eliminate the discrimination, conscious or unconscious, that is likely in more subjective methods such as supervisor ratings, recommendations, and personal interviews (Cleary et al., 1975). A useful and fair test has the characteristics of equal validity and equal prediction regardless of group membership (Cleary, 1968). The same test score is related to the same level of performance on some criterion, regardless of group membership. Group differences in means on the test used as a predictor, such as an individual intelligence test, are permissible *if* approximately the same group differences are found on the criterion, for example, grades or teacher ratings.

This is generally the case with current aptitude tests with a variety of criteria, groups, and tests (Reschly & Sabers, 1979). There are group mean differences on *both* the predictor and the criterion. Validity is virtually the same, and prediction is, likewise, nearly identical regardless of group membership.

Applying the equal treatment approach to educational classification/placement with minority students would involve careful examination of referral, screening, preplacement evaluation, and placement decisions. If minority students are treated in essentially the same way at all steps in this classification/placement process, and the tests and other evaluation procedures are equally valid, the entire process would be regarded as unbiased and fair from the equal treatment notion of fairness. The problem with the equal treatment is that there are group differences at all stages in the classification/placement process leading to un-equal outcomes. The equal treatment notion of fairness, for which there is broad support in the general public (Lerner, 1981), leads inevitably to minority overrepresentation in EMR classification and disproportionate selection, classification, and placement at all educational levels, from kindergarten through post-BA graduate and professional schools.

Equal treatment is a rather slow method of eliminating group differences in career patterns, income, and educational levels. Existing group differences, for example, black versus white income levels, are changed so slowly that several decades, perhaps several generations, would be needed before the disparities are eliminated. Impatience with the effects of equal treatment have led to the development of another notion of fairness, equal outcomes.

Equal Outcomes

The equal outcomes notion of fairness is very straightforward: Selection, classification, and placement percentages should match the group percentages in the general population. If 10% of the population is black, then 10% of any group—EMR, gifted, law school admissions, etc.—should also be black. Substantial variations from these percentages are regarded as discriminatory. The equal outcomes notion of fairness is consistent with the ethical position of quotas (Hunter & Schmidt, 1976). Fairness means that all groups should have an equal, proportional share of whatever rewards are available.

Advocates of equal outcomes have quite different positions on the use of tests. Williams (1974) claimed that aptitude tests and the usual criteria share the same biases, producing a spurious relationship between a biased predictor and a biased criterion. In this view, most standardized tests were regarded as largely useless. The development of pluralistic norms for conventional tests (Mercer, 1979) is another method of producing equal outcomes. Here, the assumed biases in a conventional test (the WISC-R) are corrected through a complex procedure that results in adding substantial numbers of points to the conventional WISC-R IQ scores of most minority students. This procedure eliminates mean differences, and, if followed precisely, disproportionate classification/placement is reduced (Reschly, 1981b). Another method of test use with the equal

outcomes criterion of fairness is the differential weighting of the aptitude test scores of minority students. Complex methods of establishing the weights have been described (Novick & Petersen, 1976), but the essential idea is the same; test results are treated differently depending on whether the examinee is minority or majority.

The vast philosophical differences and the very important practical implications of equal treatment and equal outcomes need to be emphasized. In one, to treat differently is to discriminate. In the other, to *not* treat differently, at least to the point of establishing proportional outcomes, is to discriminate. Advocates of equal outcomes argue that racism has existed for so long and is so pervasive and deeply rooted that extraordinary measures must be invoked. Therefore, a period, perhaps several decades, of reverse discrimination (or "positive" discrimination) is necessary and just. Lerner (1981) was very critical of the equal outcomes criterion. She viewed the reverse discrimination that must be followed to produce equal outcomes as particularly unwise from legal, social, and economic perspectives. According to Lerner (1981), classification and placement on some basis other than merit creates mismatches that require further compromise of standards, accommodations, and remedial programming, all of which are disastrous. Finally, equal outcomes and reverse discrimination may very well retard the progress of equal opportunity because the general public is opposed to these measures, which have the further dubious effect of ". . . cast[ing] a shadow over the accomplishment of the very large number of black scholars and workers who scorned special preferences and earned their rewards in exactly the same way that their white counterparts did" (p. 9).

As noted in the early portion of this chapter, test use is often a central issue in controversies about how best to achieve equity and fairness. There is little remaining doubt about how various minorities perform on tests. The effects of different methods of using tests also are well known. The critical questions having to do with how tests "ought" or "should" be used cannot be resolved by academic or professional psychologists. Psychologists can present options and estimate the probable effects of different policies on classification/placement decisions. But the policies as such must be determined as part of the broad sociopolitical process involving all citizens and their political representatives.

FUTURE DIRECTIONS

Aptitude testing continues to be an important part of educational classification/placement decisions despite severe criticism from some minority scholars and intense legal scrutiny. Standardized testing generally and aptitude testing specifically have been carefully and critically examined over the past ten years. The usual result continues to be (a) endorsement of the purposes of aptitude testing; (b) recognition of the value of information from current tests; (c) prohibitions against the use of aptitude test results as the sole or primary basis for important decisions; (d) implicit conclusions that tests usually are used wisely and fairly; and (e) attribution of problems in testing to misuse of tests, not the tests per se. These conclusions certainly were prominent in three of the most important recent reviews of standardized testing (Cleary et al., 1975; Heller, Holtzman, & Messick, 1982; Wigdor & Garner, 1982). Three conclusions from the National Academy of Sciences (NAS) Committee on Ability Testing Report are especially pertinent to the future uses of aptitude tests in educational classification and placement.

> Test scores play a central, often a determinative, role in special education placement. Used appropriately, they can help to identify pupils who should be studied individually to determine in what educational setting they will prosper.
>
> An unbiased count of the children who are expected to have severe difficulty with instruction at the regular pace would surely find a greater proportion of poor children, including minority children, in that category. Radical social change would have to take place to alter that prediction significantly.
>
> Skepticism about the value of tests in identifying children in need of special education has probably been carried too far; people making those decisions should, whenever practicable, have before them a report on a number of professionally administered tests, in part to counteract the stereotypes and misperceptions that contaminate judgmental information. (Wigdor & Garner, 1982, pp. 176, 179)

Clearly, as indicated in the NAS Panel Report, one of the most important current trends is re-newed acceptance of standardized testing. Whatever movement there was to sharply restrict or even ban tests appears to be far less prominent today than 5 to 15 years ago. Part of this change is a matter of pendulum phenomena—the cycle of action and reaction that so often occurs. Beyond that, I believe the greater acceptance of standardized testing today is, at least in part, a result of research indicating that tests do function in about the same way regardless of sociocultural group. These essential findings were not available in the early years of what became a movement to restrict or ban tests. In that era there was serious question about the technical characteristics of conventional tests when used with minority students (Deutsch, Fishman, Kogan, North, & Whitman, 1964). Minority students were sometimes not included in standardization samples. There was little or no research examining technical characteristics such as reliability, validity, and factor structure with different groups. As noted in an earlier section, findings of recent research indicate the technical characteristics of conventional tests are nearly constant for the major sociocultural groups in the United States.

There are a number of current trends that hold promise for improving the technology and the use of aptitude assessment. The trends in test use generally involve more conservative interpretations of results, lower levels of inference, and greater emphasis on treatment utility (Reschly, 1980b). The trends in instrument development seem, in some instances, to be in the opposite direction! Experimental or newly published aptitude tests have been designed to assess problem-solving style, neuropsychological preferences, learning acquisition rate, and so on.

Interpretation and Use

There are several subtle modifications in how aptitude test information is used. In some instances names for tests or scores are changed; in other cases the interpretation is changed. The effect of these changes is to protect the individual from gross misuse or misunderstanding of test results.

Lower Level of Inference

Level of inference refers to the relationship between the behavior observed and the interpretation of that behavior. Recall the "fight" item from the WISC-R and assume a child misses that and similar items. An uncomplicated description of the behavior would use a low level of inference, such as, "Items requiring descriptions of appropriate behavior in dealing with other children were missed." A medium level of inference would be reflected in a statement that describes the intellectual process or cognitive operation, such as, "Items requiring social judgment were missed." A high level of inference would be reflected in efforts to identify underlying dynamics, "Poor ego control and underdeveloped superego functions were revealed in the inability to describe appropriate courses of action in dealings with peers."

There is an unfortunate tradition in professional psychology, far weaker today than before, of highly inferential, speculative (sometimes called "clinical"), interpretations of test responses. Some of the older, but still popular, clinical methods texts often emphasized highly inferential interpretations (Rapaport, Gill, & Schafer, 1968). The deeply dynamic and global assertions about motives and emotions that are generated from "clinical" interpretations of aptitude test performance are sometimes attributed to a mysterious process of clinical insight. Unfortunately, there is hardly ever any way to empirically examine these assertions.

For a variety of reasons, highly inferential, dynamic interpretations are far less common today, but they are far from extinct. The trend toward lower levels of inference is part of a more behavioral-empirical emphasis generally in applied psychology. Furthermore, the greater accountability imposed on professionals, generally, as well as the increased legal scrutiny of psychologists' work (Ziskin, 1975), also have the effect of moving professionals toward less inferential and more data-based interpretations.

Behavioral Assessment

Although behavioral assessment has not replaced assessment of cognitive traits, an event anticipated by some, behavioral approaches have influenced interpretation and use of aptitude test results. Behavioral analysis of cognitive operations has been suggested as a means of linking aptitude assessment with eduational interventions (Bergan, 1977). Behavioral methods are increasingly seen as a part of comprehensive assessment for classification/placement decisions (Alessi, 1980). In many instances aptitude testing is done to determine classification, but behavioral assessment is used to determine placement, intervention goals, and treatment strategies. Finally, Nelson's (1980)

conceptualization of the use of intelligence tests within a behavioral assessment framework is, in my view, likely to become a classic paper in the aptitude assessment literature. Nelson demonstrated the use of low inference, behavioral interpretations of test performance that will be useful in decision making. Moreover, she provided cogent explanations, using behavioral concepts, for why IQ tests predict certain behaviors. Although aptitude testing is hardly a behavioral assessment method, recent developments in behavioral assessment have improved the interpretation and application of aptitude test results.

Empirical Foundations

A development related to lower levels of inference is the increasing availability and use of empirical studies as the basis for interpretation and use of aptitude test results. There is far more relevant research today, and professional psychologists are far more likely to use what is available due to changes in graduate programs and increased emphasis on continuing education. Numerous examples of changes in interpretation and use due to empirical findings could be cited. A few will be discussed here.

Some of the most important empirical findings in recent years are the base rates for subtest differences on commonly used tests such as the WISC-R (Kaufman, 1976, 1979). Base rates refer to the naturally occurring rate of some phenomenon in the general population. The essential conclusion in the base rates research is that scatter is normal; IQ scale differences (Verbal IQ versus Performance IQ) are common; and flat profiles are very unusual. This is the opposite of the implicit assumptions in the traditional clinical literature, where scatter (i.e., differences in subtest scores) was seen as indicative of cognitive or emotional difficulties. If most persons have a high degree of scatter, then it is impossible for scatter to be a unique, diagnostically significant feature of any syndrome that occurs rarely. Base rates, usually determined from studies of standardization samples, must be known before assertions are made about the clinical significance of aptitude test profiles. Due to the base rate research, the general trend now is toward far less use of personality, emotional, or motivational interpretations of aptitude test profiles.

The use of names other than IQ for scores from aptitude tests and alternates to the term *intelligence* is based in part on empirical findings. The primary validity evidence for general aptitude or intelligence tests is prediction of success in academic settings. Academic success is related (imperfectly) to a number of other very important criteria such as income level, occupational attainment, and so on (Matarazzo, 1972). Nevertheless, academic success is not all that is important. As noted earlier, most recently developed or restandardized tests have dropped the term intelligence in favor of terms like School Ability, Academic Aptitude, Cognitive Abilities, and School Functioning Level. These changes are consistent with empirical findings and are part of the general trend toward more circumscribed, cautious interpretations of results.

Treatment Utility

Treatment utility (Heller, Holtzman, & Messick, 1982) or an outcomes criterion (Reschly, 1979) are efforts to emphasize the broad effects of test use for individuals and groups. Essential questions are how test use influenced opportunities for the individual and whether test results were useful in developing interventions or treatments. Here, it is very important to recognize the limitations of general aptitude tests. General aptitude tests are useful in identifying persons who are far below or far above average on the kinds of cognitive operations required in academic settings. Persons who are far below or far above average often need and benefit from alternative educational programs. Aptitude tests have treatment utility for this very general, but important, kind of decision. General aptitude tests are not very useful in identifying specific educational objectives or strategies.

The trend toward greater emphasis on treatment utility, especially as a means to address the problem of bias against minority students, implies continued but limited use of aptitude tests. Use of aptitude tests, along with other information, for general classification/placement decisions has been endorsed recently by the National Academy of Science reports (Heller, Holtzman, & Messick, 1982; Wigdor & Garner, 1982). This endorsement was, however, conditional on the delivery of more effective interventions as a result of classification/placement decisions. In recent discussions of test use, the absence of bias according to statistical criteria was seen as a prerequisite to fair use and treatment utility. Absence of statistical bias is important, but not sufficient. Treatment utility must be regarded as the predominant criterion (Reschly, 1979).

Instrument Development

There has been an upsurge in the initial development and restandardization of individually administered general aptitude or intelligence tests over the past 15 years. These activities represent substantial expenditures by test publishing companies, who apparently are fairly optimistic about the future of intelligence assessment. This optimism has probably been fostered by the increased need for individual psychoeducational assessment brought about by legal requirements concerning education of the handicapped (see earlier discussion and Table 8.1) as well as other trends just noted. Many more well-developed instruments are available today, and a number of innovative approaches to intellectual assessment have appeared in recent years. Some of these innovative approaches are discussed in this section.

Pluralistic Norms

The System of Multicultural Pluralistic Assessment (SOMPA) (Mercer, 1979a) includes several assessment innovations, one of which is the development of pluralistic norms. These pluralistic norms are generated by a statistical procedure that guarantees the elimination of group mean differences. According to the simplistic notion of test bias as mean differences, the pluralistic norms produce a fair, unbiased test. Application of the pluralistic norms also reduces, but does not necessarily eliminate, disproportionate classification (Reschly, 1981b).

Mercer developed pluralistic norms as an alternate method of interpreting the WISC-R. The principle underlying pluralistic norms is that children should only be compared to other children who are similar to them in race or ethnicity, socioeconomic status, and family characteristics. These factors are known to be related (imperfectly) to intelligence test performance. Children from more "favorable" circumstances are assumed to have better opportunities to learn what is required on the WISC-R, while children from less "favorable" circumstances have fewer opportunities. Mercer contends, at least implicitly, that inferences about "intelligence" or "intellectual ability" should be restricted to instances where opportunities are similar.

In SOMPA two scores for each of the WISC-R scales are developed. The conventional WISC-R Verbal, Performance, and Full Scale scores are renamed as School Functioning Level (SFL) rather than IQ. The WISC-R scale scores reflecting the pluralistic norms are called Estimated Learning Potential (ELP). These ELP scores are derived in a complex process that, simplified here, involves determining: (a) the child's sociocultural status (roughly, a combination of socioeconomic status and ethnic/racial group); (b) how the child performed in comparison to other children with similar ethnic-racial and socioeconomic characteristics; and (c) the statistical transformation of this comparison to a distribution with a mean of 100 and a standard deviation of 15. The practical effect is to add from 0 to 29 points (average of about 13) to the conventional WISC-R scores of black and Hispanic students (Mercer, 1979a; Reschly, 1982). These adjusted scores are claimed by Mercer to be a more accurate reflection of the child's ability or learning potential.

Sharp debate has been stimulated by the publication of SOMPA (Brown, 1979; Goodman, 1979; Mercer, 1979b; Oakland, 1980). Mercer's claims for the ELP construct are unsubstantiated to date, and the kinds of studies required to provide evidence acceptable to Mercer concerning the validity of ELP scores are very difficult to conduct. There is one current effort (Taylor, 1983) to develop an appropriate study, acceptable to advocates and critics, of the validity of ELP.

The concept of ELP, especially if not taken too literally, is quite useful in reducing misunderstanding of conventional WISC-R scores. Use of ELP reminds test users that IQ scores do reflect environmental influences, and environments *do* vary. However, it is unlikely that ELP will be useful for prediction of academic performance or for educational classification/placement decisions. Use of the SOMPA ELP for those purposes clearly is premature at present.

Direct Assessment of Learning

The direct assessment of learning through a test-teach-test approach has attracted a great deal of attention recently. The current leader in this area is Reuven Feuerstein, an Israeli scholar who has written extensively on a method of assessment and teaching that is called *structural cognitive modifiability* (SCM) (Feuerstein, Haywood, Rand, & Hoffman, 1982; Feuerstein, Rand, & Hoffman, 1979). The purpose of SCM is nothing less than to determine the potential for modification of basic cognitive structures, i.e., the information processing strategies and problem-solving operations used by the individual. Haywood (1982), probably the leading expert on the Learning Potential Assessment Device (LPAD) in the United States, sees this approach as particularly useful for economically disadvantaged children.

LPAD uses a variety of test items to assess SCM, most of which involve nonverbal or performance kinds of items. These tasks would generally be regarded as less culturally loaded than conventional intelligence test tasks, especially in comparison to verbal or language oriented items. Most are similar to the crystallized general ability tasks described by Cattell (1963). Assessment with LPAD is a loosely structured, interactive process where the examiner develops and tests hypotheses about the child's cognitive structures. The LPAD is not standardized in the fashion of conventional tests such as the WISC-R, where the examiner's role is restricted to certain kinds of interactions with the child. In other words, general encouragement of effort is usually permitted, but precise, contingent feedback about item responses is not. Haywood (1983) recommends extensive training in the LPAD of 80 hours or so for professionals who already have training and experience in individual psychoeducational assessment. Obviously, the LPAD is a very complex procedure.

The LPAD is not designed for classification/placement purposes according to Haywood. There are no LPAD norms. The purpose of LPAD is to determine which cognitive operations are deficient, to estimate the likelihood the child can master those operations, and then to design and carry out the modification plan. However, LPAD interpretations often make inferences such as, "performed very well for his age," "capable of doing acceptable school work at a level at least on a par with his age peers," and so on (Haywood, 1983). These statements are, indeed, informal classification/placement recommendations that are roughly parallel to more formal recommendations involving EMR or other exceptional child classification and placement decisions. It is unlikely that classification/placement implications can be avoided completely with LPAD or any other technique that involves the general cognitive development of the individual. However, the major purpose of LPAD, modifiability of cognitive structures, is potentially of vast significance to the construct of aptitude and the development of educational programs. The theory and techniques associated with LPAD are far more oriented to treatment validity than any other aptitude theory and technique we have encountered.

Simultaneous-Sequential Processing

A trend in recent years has been greater emphasis on the underlying cognitive processes related to aptitude test performance and problem solving in other contexts. This trend is perhaps most apparent in the Kaufman Assessment Battery for Children (K-ABC) (Kaufman & Kaufman, 1983). The K-ABC was designed around the construct of simultaneous-sequential processing described by Luria (1966) and Das, Kirby, and Jarman (1979). Sequential problem solving involves correct arrangement of stimuli in sequential or serial order. In contrast, simultaneous problem solving involves spatial or analogic tasks on which the child must integrate and synthesize the information simultaneously. These two basic problem-solving strategies have been identified in several independent lines of research but with different constructs and varying descriptions of underlying processes (Kamphaus, Kaufman, & Kaufman, 1983).

The K-ABC reflects several exemplary practices. The clear delineation of theoretical underpinnings enhances research as well as clinical practice with the K-ABC. The large number of studies conducted with the K-ABC prior to publication, by the authors and others with the assistance of the authors, is nearly unprecedented. These studies provide a solid basis for use of the K-ABC for various types of decisions and with various populations.

The K-ABC movement (and that word is chosen deliberately; I hope it doesn't become a cult) is not without blemishes. Although there is much to admire about the entire K-ABC project, reflecting very favorably on the authors as well as the publisher, American Guidance Service (AGS), there, too, is much about which to be concerned. There are the claims of lack of bias with minorities, without specification of purpose of assessment or criteria for bias. The authors, distinguished scholars with solid research credentials, know the literature on bias intimately and, most important, know better than to make sweeping claims about lack of bias. The mean differences criterion for bias was used implicitly by the authors. This criterion is very limited. Other criteria for bias should have been examined or the claims concerning lack

of bias, made in many places from a news conference at the 1982 Washington D.C. Convention of the American Psychological Association to AGS promotional literature, should have been carefully limited to the criteria used.

Cautious use of the K-ABC in classification/ placement decisions is probably justified in view of the research conducted thus far. Whether different decisions result, especially regarding EMR overrepresentation of minorities, remains to be seen. Research on classification/placement effects will undoubtedly be published soon.

Inferences about neurological organization, particularly right hemisphere-left hemisphere interpretations, are almost inevitable despite the author's disclaimers. The simultaneous-sequential processing notion parallels the right brain-left brain distinction emphasized recently, both in psychology and the popular press. This dichotomy and the associated implicit assumptions about neurological organization are probably naive simplifications of actual neurological organization and processing (Hardyck & Haapanen, 1979). The K-ABC will almost undoubtedly be misused in hemispheric inferences about children, an outcome about which the authors also are concerned.

The Kaufmans also have made rather specific assertions about the educational implications of the K-ABC Sequential-Simultaneous Scales. Specific educational methods are believed to be uniquely beneficial if matched to the child's processing strength. This notion is virtually identical to the Aptitude-by-Treatment interaction assumption underlying the use of tests of specific aptitudes discussed earlier in this chapter (see also Ysseldyke & Mirkin, 1982). Apparently, research on these questions is being conducted by the Kaufmans and others, which, again, deserves commendation.

SUMMARY

Aptitude testing for the purposes of educational classification/placement is alive and well today, even flourishing. The naive reader may sense a bit of surprise (and cynicism) in that conclusion, which is a reaction to the projected imminent demise of aptitude or intelligence assessment that was so popular in the late 1960s and 1970s. Aptitude testing has changed in subtle but important ways. The criticism from minority professionals and the legal scrutiny in the courts, though often misdirected, in my view, has prompted subtle changes in interpretation, gradual reform of procedures, and vigorous pursuit of better tests and sounder testing practices. These very positive changes virtually guarantee continued use of general aptitude or intelligence tests in educational classification/placement decisions.

Much remains to be accomplished. The presently available research on validity of aptitude tests needs to be expanded to include more groups of participants and a wider variety of criteria. The issue of treatment utility needs to be addressed in many more studies. The greatest need is for data on program effects with students varying in general aptitude. A variety of program alternatives need to be examined with students now classified as EMR.

These program alternatives should be developed around the results of longitudinal studies, especially of the early adjustment of EMR and borderline ability groups. These studies should significantly augment our knowledge base and technological resources concerning general scholastic aptitude or intelligence. In anticipating those developments, we are building on a solid research base and a rich tradition of using tests to enhance opportunities for individuals.

REFERENCES

Anastasi, A. (1976). *Psychological testing* (4th ed.). New York: Macmillan.

Anastasi, A. (1980). Abilities and the measurement of achievement. In W.B. Schrader (Ed.), *Measuring achievement: Progress over a decade. New directions for testing and measurement*. San Francisco: Jossey-Bass.

Alessi, G.J. (1980). Behavioral observation for the school psychologist: Responsive-discrepancy model. *School Psychology Review*, 9, 31–45.

Bergan, J. (1977). *Behavioral consultation*. Columbus, OH: Merrill.

Bernal, E. (1975). A response to "Educational uses of tests with disadvantaged subjects." *American Psychologist*, 30, 93–95.

Bersoff, D. (1979). Regarding psychologists testily: Legal regulation of psychological assessment in the public schools. *Maryland Law Review*, 39, 27–120.

Bersoff, D.N. (1981). Testing and the law. *American Psychologist*, 36, 1047–1056.

Bersoff, D.N. (1982a). The legal regulation of school psychology. In C.R. Reynolds & T.B. Gutkin (Eds.), *The handbook of school psychology*. New York: John Wiley.

Bersoff, D. (1982b). Larry P. and PASE: Judicial report cards of the validity of individual intelligence tests. In T. Kratochwill (Ed.), *Advances in school psychology* (Vol. II). Hillsdale, NJ: Erlbaum.

Bickel, W.E. (1982). Classifying mentally retarded students: A review of placement practices in special education. In K.A. Heller, W.H. Holtzman, & S. Messick (Eds.), *Placing children in special education: A strategy for equity*. Washington, DC: National Academy Press.

Brown, F.G. (1979). The algebra works—but what does it mean? *School Psychology Digest*, 8, 213–218.

Brown, F.G. (1983). *Principles of educational and psychological testing* (3rd ed.). New York: Holt, Rinehart, & Winston.

Cattell, R.B. (1963). Theory of fluid and crystallized intelligence: A critical experiment. *Journal of Educational Psychology*, 54, 1–22.

Cleary, T.A. (1968). Test bias: Prediction of grades of Negro and White students in integrated colleges. *Journal of Educational Measurement*, 5, 115–124.

Cleary, T., Humphreys, L.G., Kendrick, S.A., & Wesman, A. (1975). Educational uses of tests with disadvantaged students. *American Psychologist*, 30, 15–41.

Cole, N.S. (1981). Bias in testing. *American Psychologist*, 36, 1067–1077.

Coles, G.S. (1978). The learning disabilities test battery: Empirical and social issues. *Howard Educational Review*, 48, 313–340.

Cronbach, L.J., & Snow, R.E. (1977). *Aptitudes and instructional methods*. New York: Wiley (Halstead Press).

Das, J.P., Kirby, J., & Jarman, R.F. (1979). *Simultaneous and successive cognitive processing*. New York: Academic Press.

Debra P. v. Turlington. Case No. 78-892-Civ-T-C(M.D.Fla.1979)

Deutsch, M., Fishman, J., Kogan, I., North, R., & Whitman, M. (1964). Guidelines for testing minority group children. *Journal of Social Issues*, 20, 129–145.

Diana v. State Board of Education, C-70 37RFP, District Court Northern California (February, 1970).

Federal Register. Procedures for Evaluating Specific Learning Disabilities. Author, December 29, 1977, p. 65082–65085. (a)

Federal Register. Regulations implementing Education for All Handicapped Children Act of 1975 (Public Law 94-142). Author, August 23, 1977, p. 42474–42518. (b)

Feuerstein, R., Haywood, H., Rand, Y., & Hoffman, M. (1982). *Examiners manuals for the Learning Potential Assessment Device* (rev. ed.). Jerusalem: Hadassah-WIZO-Canada Research Institute.

Feuerstein, R., Rand, Y., & Hoffman, M. (1979). *The dynamic assessment of retarded performers: The Learning Potential Assessment Device: Theory, instruments, and techniques*. Baltimore: University Park Press.

Flaugher, R. (1978). The many definitions of test bias. *American Psychologist*, 33, 671–679.

Gallagher, J. (1972). The special education contract for mildly handicapped children. *Exceptional Children*, 38, 527–535.

Gerken, K.C. (1979). Assessment of high-risk and preschoolers and children and adolescents with low-incident handicapping conditions. In G.D. Phye & D.J. Reschly (Eds.), *School psychology: Perspectives and issues*. New York: Academic Press.

Goodman, J. (1979). Is tissue the issue? A critique of SOMPA's models and tests. *School Psychology Digest*, **8**, 47–62.

Grossman, H.J. (Ed.). (1983). *Classification in mental retardation*. Washington, DC: American Association on Mental Deficiency.

Guadalupe v. *Tempe Elementary School District*, 71-435, District Court for Arizona, January, 1972.

Hammill, D., & Larsen, S. (1974). The effectiveness of psycholinguistic training. *Exceptional Children*, **41**, 5–14.

Hammill, D., & Larsen, S. (1978). The effectiveness of psycholinguistic training: A reaffirmation of position. *Exceptional Children*, **44**, 402–414.

Hardyck, C., & Haapanen, R. (1979). Education both halves of the brain: Educational breakthrough or neuromythology? *Journal of School Psychology*, **17**, 219–230.

Haywood, H.C. (1982). Compensatory education. *Peabody Journal of Education*, **59**, 272–300.

Haywood, H.C. (1983). *Dynamic assessment: The Learning Potential Assessment Device (LPAD)*. Unpublished manuscript, Vanderbilt University, Nashville.

Heller, K., Holtzman, W., & Messick, S. (Eds.). (1982). *Placing children in special education: A strategy for equity*. Washington, DC: National Academy Press.

Herrnstein, R.J. (1982, August). IQ testing and the media. *Atlantic Monthly*, 68–74.

Hilliard, A. (1980). Cultural diversity and special education. *Exceptional Children*, **46**, 584–588.

Hunt, J. (1961). *Intelligence and experience*. New York: Ronald Press.

Hunter, J., & Schmidt, F. (1976). Critical analysis of the statistical and ethical implications of various definitions of test bias. *Psychological Bulletin*, **83**, 1053–1071.

Hynd, G., & Obrzut, J. (1981). *Neuropsychological assessment of the school-age child: Issues and procedures*. New York: Grune & Stratton.

Jackson, G. (1975). On the report of the ad hoc committee on educational uses of tests with disadvantaged students. *American Psychologist*, **30**, 88–92.

Jensen, A.R. (1969). How much can we boost IQ and scholastic achievement? *Harvard Educational Review*, **39**, 1–123.

Jensen, A.R. (1980). *Bias in mental testing*. New York: The Free Press.

Kamphaus, R., & Kaufman, N. (1982, August). *A cross-validation study of sequential-simultaneous processing at ages 2½–12½ using the Kaufman Assessment Battery for Children (K-ABC)*. Paper presented at the Annual Convention of the American Psychological Association, Washington, DC.

Kaufman, A. (1976). A new approach to interpretation of test scatter on the WISC-R. *Journal of Learning Disabilities*, **9**, 160–168.

Kaufman, A. (1979). *Intelligent testing with the WISC-R*. New York: Wiley.

Kaufman, A., & Kaufman, N. (1977). *Clinical evaluation of young children with the McCarthy Scales*. New York: Grune & Stratton.

Kaufman, A., & Kaufman, N. (1983). *Kaufman Assessment Battery for Children (K-ABC)*. Circle Pines, MN: American Guidance Service.

Larry P. v. *Riles* 495 F. Supp. 926 (N. D. Cal 1979).

Lennon, R. (1980). The anatomy of a scholastic aptitude test. *NCME Measurement in Education*, **11**, 1–8.

Lerner, B. (1981). Equal opportunity versus equal results: Monsters, rightful causes, and perverse effects. In W.G. Schrader (Ed.), *Admissions testing and the public interest: New directions for testing and measurement* (Number 9). San Francisco: Jossey-Bass.

Loehlin, J., Lindzey, G., & Spuhler, J. (1975). *Race differences in intelligence*. San Francisco: Freeman.

Lund, K., Foster, G., & McCall-Perez, F. (1978). The effectiveness of psycholinguistic training: A reevaluation. *Exceptional Children*, **44**, 310–321.

Luria, A.R. (1966). *Human brain and psychological processes*. New York: Harper & Row.

MacMillan, D. (1977). *Mental retardation in school and society*. Boston: Little, Brown, & Co.

MacMillan, D., Jones, R., & Aloia, G. (1974). The mentally retarded label: A theoretical analysis and review of research. *American Journal of Mental Deficiency*, **79**, 241–261.

Manni, J., Winikur, O., & Keller, M. (1980). *A report on minority group representation in special education programs in the state of New Jersey*. Trenton, NJ: State Department of Education.

Matarazzo, D. (1972). *Wechsler's measurement and appraisal of adult intelligence* (5th and enlarged ed.). Baltimore: Williams & Wilkins.

McCarthy, D. (1972). *Manual for the McCarthy Scales of Children's Abilities*. New York: Psychological Corporation.

Mercer, J. (1973). *Labeling the mentally retarded*. Berkeley, CA: University of California Press.

Mercer, J. (1979a). *System of Multicultural Pluralistic Assessment Technical Manual*. New York: Psychological Corporation.

Mercer, J. (1979b). In defense of racially and culturally nondiscriminatory assessment. *School Psychology Digest*, **8**, 89–115.

Meyers, C., MacMillan, D., & Yoshida, R. (1978). Validity of psychologists identification of EMR students in the perspective of the California decertification experience. *Journal of School Psychology*, **16**, 3–15.

Minskoff, E. (1975). Research on psycholinguistic training: Critique and guidelines. *Exceptional Children*, **42**, 136–144.

Nelson, R. (1980). The use of intelligence tests within behavioral assessment. *Behavioral Assessment*, **2**, 417–423.

Newcomer, R., Larsen, S., & Hammill, D. (1975). A response to Minskoff. *Exceptional Children*, **42**, 144–148.

Novick, M., & Petersen, N. (1976). Toward equalizing educational and employment opportunity. *Journal of Educational Measurement*, **13**, 77–88.

Oakland, T. (1980). An evaluation of the ABIC pluralistic norms, and estimated learning potential. *Journal of School Psychology*, **18**, 3–11.

PASE (Parents in Action on Special Education) v. *Joseph P. Hannon*. U.S. District Court, Northern District of Illinois, Eastern Division, No. 74 (3586), July, 1980.

Prasse, D. (1979). Federal legislation and school psychology: Impact and implication. *Professional Psychology*, **9**, 592–601.

Rapaport, D., Gill, M., & Schafer, R. (1968). *Diagnostic*

psychological testing (rev. ed. by R. Holt). New York: International Universities Press.

Reschly, D. (1979). Nonbiased assessment. In G. Phye & D. Reschly (Eds.), *School psychology: Perspectives and issues*. New York: Academic Press.

Reschly, D. (1980a). Psychological evidence in the *Larry P.* Opinion: A case of right problem—wrong solution. *School Psychology Review*, 9, 123–135.

Reschly, D. (1980b). School psychologists and assessment in the future. *Professional Psychology*, 11, 841–848.

Reschly, D. (1981a). Psychological testing in educational classification and placement. *American Psychologist*, 36, 1094–1102.

Reschly, D. (1981b). Evaluation of the effects of SOMPA measures on classification of students as mildly mentally retarded. *American Journal of Mental Deficiency*, 86, 16–20.

Reschly, D. (1982). Assessing mild mental retardation: The influence of adaptive behavior, sociocultural status and prospects for nonbiased assessment. In C. Reynolds & T. Gutkin (Eds.), *The handbook of school psychology*. New York: Wiley Interscience.

Reschly, D. (1983). Legal issues in psychoeducational assessment. In G. Hynd (Ed.), *The school psychologist: Contemporary perspectives*. Syracuse, NY: Syracuse University Press.

Reschly, D.J., & Jipson, F.J. (1976). Ethnicity, geographic locale, age, sex, and urban-rural residence as variables in the prevalence of mild retardation. *American Journal of Mental Deficiency*, 81, 154–161.

Reschly, D., & Sabers, D. (1979). Analysis of test bias in four groups with the regression definition. *Journal of Educational Measurement*, 16, 1–9.

Ross-Reynolds, J., & Reschly, D. (1983). An investigation of item bias on the WISC-R with four sociocultural groups. *Journal of Consulting and Clinical Psychology*, 51, 144–146.

Reynolds, C.R. (1982). The problem of bias in psychological assessment. In C.R. Reynolds & T.B. Gutkin (Eds.), *The Handbook of School Psychology*. New York: Wiley.

Salvia, J., & Ysseldyke, J. (1981). *Assessment in special and remedial education* (2nd ed.). Boston: Houghton Mifflin.

Samuda, R.J. (1975). *Psychological testing of American minorities: Issues and consequences*. New York: Dodd, Mead.

Sandoval, J. (1979). The WISC-R and internal evidence of test bias with minority groups. *Journal of Consulting and Clinical Psychology*, 47, 919–927.

Sandoval, J., & Mille, M. (1980). Accuracy of judgments of WISC-R item difficulty for minority groups. *Journal of Consulting and Clinical Psychology*, 48, 249–253.

Sherman, S.W., & Robinson, N.M. (1982). *Ability testing of handicapped people: Dilemma for government, science, and the public*. Washington, DC: National Academy Press.

Snow, R.E. (1980). Aptitude and achievement. In W.B. Schrader (Ed.), *Measuring achivement: Progress over a decade. New directions for testing and measurement*. San Francisco: Jossey-Bass.

Sontag, E. (1983, May 16). Address at the Fourth National Institute on Legal Problems of Educating the Handicapped, San Francisco.

Taylor, R. (1983). *Florida Norms for SOMPA* (Project Report, Title 6B Grant). Tallahassee: Florida State Department of Education.

Wigdor, A.K., & Garner, W.R. (Eds.). (1982). *Ability testing: Uses, consequences, and controversies*. Washington, DC: National Academy Press.

Williams, R. (1970). Danger: Testing and dehumanizing the black child. *Clinical Child Psychology Newsletter*, 9, 5–6.

Williams, R. (1974). The problem of match and mismatch in testing black children. In L. Miller (Ed.), *The testing of black students: A symposium*. Englewood Cliffs, NJ: Prentice-Hall.

Yoshida, R., MacMillan, D., & Myers, C. (1976). The decertification of minority group EMR students in California: Student achievement and adjustment. In R. Jones (Ed.), *Mainstreaming and the minority child*. Reston, VA: Council for Exceptional Children.

Ysseldyke, J.E., & Mirkin, P.K. (1982). The use of assessment information to plan instructional interventions: A review of the research. In C.R. Reynolds & T.B. Gutkin (Eds.), *The handbook of school psychology*. New York: Wiley.

Ziskin, J. (1975). *Coping with psychiatric and psychological testimony*. Beverly Hills, CA: Law and Psychology Press.

9 INTEREST INVENTORIES

Jo-Ida C. Hansen

INTRODUCTION

The importance of interests in job selection was first recognized by educators in the 1900s and shortly thereafter by industry. Early theorists in the field, such as Parsons (1909), hypothesized that occupational adjustment was enhanced if an individual's characteristics and interests matched the requirements of the occupation. As E.K. Strong, Jr. pointed out in *Vocational Interests of Men and Women* (1943), interests provide additional information, not available from analyses of abilities or aptitudes, for making career decisions. Consideration of interests, along with abilities, values, and other personality characteristics, provides a thorough evaluation of an individual that is superior to considering any trait in isolation.

HISTORY OF INTEREST INVENTORIES

The earliest method for assessing interests was *estimation*, accomplished by asking individuals to indicate how they felt about various activities. To improve the accuracy of their estimation, people were encouraged to *try out* activities before making their estimates. However, try-out techniques for evaluating interests were time consuming and

costly, which led to the development of interest *checklists* and *rating scales* (Kitson, 1925; Miner, 1922) and, eventually, to *interest inventories* that used statistical procedures for summarizing an individual's responses to a series of items representing various activities and occupations.

The Earliest Item Pool

Construction of interest inventories is based on several assumptions:

1. a person can give informed responses of degree of interest (e.g., like, indifferent, dislike) to familiar activities and occupations;
2. unfamliar activities have the same factor structure as do familiar activities;
3. therefore, familiar activities and occupations can be used as items in interest inventories to identify unfamiliar occupational interests.

The first item pool of interest activities was accumulated by a seminar taught by Clarence S. Yoakum at Carnegie Institute of Technology in 1919. The 1,000-item pool was developed using a *rational sampling approach* designed to represent

157

the entire domain of interests. Over the years, statistical analyses were performed to determine the worth of each item, and numerous inventories used that original item pool as the foundation for their development [e.g., Occupational Interest Inventory (Freyd, 1923); Interest Report Blank (Cowdery, 1926); General Interest Survey (Kornhauser, 1927); Vocational Interest Blank (Strong, 1927); Purdue Interest Report (Remmers, 1929); Interest Analysis Blank (Hubbard, 1930); Minnesota Interest Inventory (Paterson, Elliott, Anderson, Toops, & Heidbreder, 1930)].

Characteristics of Good Items

Interest inventory items should be evaluated periodically, since societal changes can make items obsolete as well as create the need for new items. Several qualities that contribute to the excellence of items, and ultimately to the excellence of an interest inventory, can be used to assess the value of each item.

First, items should differentiate among groups, since the purpose of interest inventories is to distinguish people with similar interests from those with dissimilar interests. Figure 9.1 presents the mean "Like" response percentage to the Strong-Campbell Interest Inventory item *Planning a large party* for 137 occupational samples. The occupations are spread over a wide range, from a low of 15% (meaning that few people in the sample answered "Like" to the item) to a high of 81% (meaning that the vast majority in the sample responded "Like").

Second, samples with similar interests should have similar item response rates, and clusters of groups with high or low response rates should make sense. In Figure 9.1, for example, the samples of restaurant managers, public relations directors, home economics teachers and recreation leaders had a high "Like" response rate of 78–81%. Physicists, farmers, and foresters, however, had low "Like" response rates to the same item. Those clusters of high and low response rate samples are intuitively satisfying and illustrate the item's content validity; one expects restaurant managers, for example, to enjoy planning parties. Even the high response rate for the funeral directors makes sense; they do spend the majority of their time making arrangements (e.g., ordering flowers, reserving a hall, arranging transportation, coordinating activities) that are similar in job task to making arrangements for a party.

Third, items should be sex-fair; no item should suggest that any occupation or activity is more appropriate for one sex than the other. In addition to sex-fair items, all interpretive and instructional materials for interest inventories also should be sex-fair.

Fourth, items should be culture-fair. Inventories can be adapted more easily to other cultures for use with ethnic minorities or for international use if the items are easy to translate. Also, unambiguous items are more likely to have the same meaning for everyone taking the inventory regardless of cultural or occupational orientation.

Fifth, items should be kept current. The key to the inventory item pool is familiarity. The face validity, as well as content validity, of an interest inventory is affected if the item pool contains obsolete items that are unfamiliar to the respondents. On the other hand, as new technologies develop, new items should be generated to insure that the entire domain of interests is represented in the item pool.

Sixth, items should be easy to read. All materials that accompany interest inventories (e.g., instructions, profile, interpretive information) and the item pool itself should be easy to read to make the inventory useful for a wide educational range of the population and for exploration at young ages.

Theories of Vocational Interest

The earliest interest inventories were developed using the atheoretical, empirical method of contrast groups that is based on an assumption that people with similar interests can be clustered together and at the same time be differentiated from groups with dissimilar interests. The inventory that best illustrates this technique is the Strong Vocational Interest Blank (SVIB), now called the Strong-Campbell Interest Inventory (SCII) (Campbell & Hansen, 1981), first published by E.K. Strong, Jr. in 1927.

Later, results from empirical investigations of interests were used to develop hypotheses about the structure of interests. Theorists Anne Roe (1956) and John Holland (1959), for example, used the factor analysis of Guilford and his colleagues (Guilford, Christensen, Bond, & Sutton, 1954), who found seven interest factors: (a) mechanical, (b) scientific, (c) social welfare, (d) aesthetic expression, (e) clerical, (f) business, and (g) outdoor work.

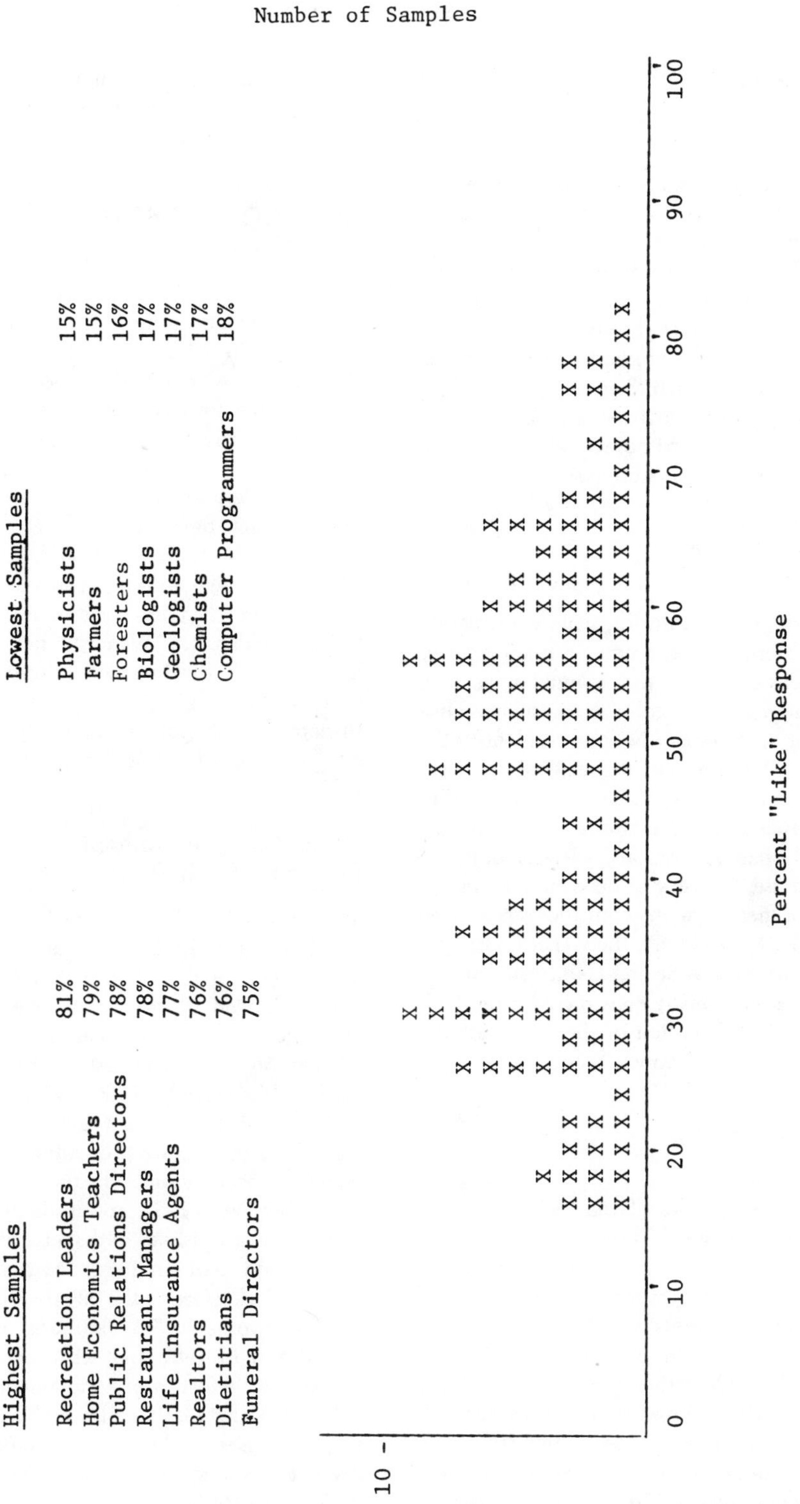

Figure 9.1. Percent "Like" responses to the SCII-SVIC item *Planning a large party* for 137 occupational samples.

CONSTRUCTION OF INTEREST INVENTORY SCALES

Most interest inventories feature either *homogeneous* or *heterogeneous* scales; the Minnesota Vocational Interest Inventory (MVII) (Clark, 1961) and the SVIB-SCII are two instruments that combine heterogeneous Occupational Scales and homogeneous Basic Interest Scales. Heterogeneous scales are more valid for predictive uses of interest inventories (e.g., predicting future job entry or college major), but homogeneous scales are more useful for providing parsimonious descriptions of the structure of a sample's interests.

Homogeneous Scale Development

Items may be selected during scale construction based on internal consistency or homogeneous scaling. Items chosen in this manner have high intercorrelations. Empirical methods such as cluster or factor analyses can be used to identify the related items. For example, the scales of the Vocational Interest Inventory (VII) (Lunneborg, 1976) were constructed using factor analysis. Or the scales may be based on rational selection of items; this method uses a theory to determine items appropriate for measuring the construct represented by each scale. For example, the General Occupational Themes of the Strong-Campbell Interest Inventory were rationally constructed using Holland's theoretical definition of the six vocational types to guide item selection.

Heterogeneous Scale Development

The Occupational Scales of the SVIB-SCII and the Kuder Occupational Interest Survey Form-DD (KOIS-DD) (Kuder, 1966) are composed of items with low intercorrelations and, therefore, are called heterogeneous scales. Heterogeneous scales are atheoretical; the choice of items is based on empirical results rather than an underlying theory. The SVIB-SCII uses the empirical method of contrast groups to select items; this technique compares the item response rates of occupational criterion groups and contrast groups, representing the interests of people in general, to identify items that significantly differentiate the two samples. The KOIS-DD uses a different empirical method

that compares an individual's item response pattern directly to the item response patterns of criterion samples that represent the interests of various occupations and college majors.

CURRENT INTEREST INVENTORIES

The most frequently used of all interest inventories is the Strong-Campbell Interest Inventory, the most recent revision of the Strong Vocational Interest Blank. Other widely used inventories include various forms of the Kuder, the Vocational Preference Inventory, and the Self-Directed Search (Engen, Lamb, & Prediger, 1982; Zytowski & Warman, 1982). Less often used instruments, which have more restricted applications than the SCII, Kuder, VPI, and SDS in terms of appropriate age and appropriate exploration goals, include the Ohio Vocational Interest Survey (OVIS) (D'Costa, Winefordner, Odgers, & Koons, 1969), the Vocational Interest Inventory (VII) (Lunneborg, 1976), the Career Assessment Inventory (CAI) (Johansson, 1975), and the Jackson Vocational Interest Survey (JVIS) (Jackson, 1977).

Strong-Campbell Interest Inventory (SVIB-SCII)

The Strong-Campbell Interest Inventory (Campbell & Hansen, 1981) is the latest version of the Strong Vocational Interest Blank. The SVIB-SCII has the longest history of all inventories; it has been under continuous research, revision, and use for over 50 years. The first version of the SVIB-SCII, published in 1927 (Strong), used the empirical method of contrast groups to construct Occupational Scales representing the interests of men in 10 occupations. The first form for women was published in 1933, and until 1974 the instrument was published with separate forms for women and men. In 1974, the two forms were combined by selecting the 325 best items from the previous women's (TW398) and men's (T399) forms, and in 1981 another revision was completed in an effort to provide matched-sex Occupational Scales (e.g., male- and female-normed Forester Scales, male- and female-normed Flight Attendant Scales, male- and female-normed Personnel Director Scales).

The item booklet for the SVIB-SCII includes 325 items, divided into seven sections: Part 1, Occupational Titles; Part 2, School Subjects; Part

3, Work-related Activities; Part 4, Spare-time Activities; Part 5, Types of People; Part 6, Forced-choice Preference Between Two Activities; Part 7, Self-Description Characteristics. The item format requires respondents to indicate the degree of their interest in each item by responding "Like," "Indifferent," or "Dislike," for example:

Actor/Actress	Ⓛ I D	
Watching an open-heart operation	Ⓛ I D	
Sports pages in the newspaper	Ⓛ I D	
Outspoken people with new ideas	L I Ⓓ	

The SVIB-SCII profile includes 3 sets of scales: 6 General Occupational Themes, 23 Basic Interest Scales, and 162 Occupational Scales that represent professional and nonprofessional occupations (e.g., farmers, geographers, photographers, social workers, buyers, credit managers).

Occupational Scales

The Occupational Scales of the SVIB-SCII are a classic example of test construction using the empirical method of contrast groups. The first step in the procedure is to determine the base rate of popularity of each item with contrast samples called Women-in-General (WIG) for female-normed Occupational Scales and Men-in-General (MIG) for male-normed scales. This step is necessary because items vary in popularity. For example, only 30% of WIG say "Like" to the item *Expressing judgments publicly, regardless of what others say,* but 58% of WIG say "Like" to the item *Skiing.* To ignore this variance would result in extremely popular items appearing on most of the scales and unpopular items appearing on very few scales. The WIG and MIG are each composed of 300 subjects selected from a wide variety of occupations.

The next step is to collect a national sample of 200 to 300 females and 200 to 300 males from a specific occupation to serve as criterion samples. Subjects included in the criterion sample are at least 25 years old, have been in the occupation at least 3 years, and are satisfied with their jobs.

The response rate percentage of the criterion sample to each item is compared to the response rate percentage of the appropriate-sex contrast sample (i.e., WIG or MIG) to identify items that differentiate the two samples. Usually 50 to 70 items are identified as the interests ("Likes") or the aversions ("Dislikes") of each occupational criterion sample.

The raw scores for an individual scored on the Occupational Scales are converted to standard scores based on the Occupational criterion sample, with mean set equal to 50 and standard deviation of 10. As shown in Figure 9.2, the scores indicate how similar the respondent's interests are to those of the criterion group for each scale.

Every effort has been made to provide matched-sex Occupational Scales on the SVIB-SCII profile. As Figure 9.2 shows, only 8 of the 85 occupations (162 Scales) are represented by just one scale (e.g., f Dental Assistant, f Dental Hygienist, f Home Economics Teacher, f Secretary, m Vocational Agriculture Teacher, m Skilled Crafts, m Investment Fund Manager, and m Agribusiness Manager). The Occupational Scales are ordered on the profile according to their Holland Code, beginning with occupations whose primary codes are Realistic and continuing with Investigative occupations, then Artistic, Social, Enterprising, and Conventional occupations.

Separate-sex Occupational Scales continue to be developed because interests of men and women are too dissimilar to provide valid combined-sex scales. E.K. Strong, Jr. (1943) attempted combined-sex construction without success, and more recent attempts have been equally disappointing (Campbell & Hansen, 1981; Hansen, 1976; Kuder, 1977; Webber & Harmon, 1978). Until the interests of women and men converge, separate-sex Occupational Scales provide the most valid results and the greatest breadth of interest exploration for both sexes.

General Occupational Themes

The General Occupational Themes (GOT) are a merger of Strong's empiricism with Holland's theory of vocational types. The six homogeneous Themes each contain 20 items selected to represent Holland's definition of each type—Realistic, Investigative, Artistic, Social, Enterprising, and Conventional. The GOT correlate highly (.72 to .79) with same-named Vocational Preference Inventory scales (Hansen, 1983); correlations between the GOT indicate that the hexagonal order that Holland proposes to describe the relationship between his types (adjacent types have more in common than to diametrically opposed types) also describes the relationship between the SVIB-SCII Themes (Campbell & Hansen, 1981).

Figure 9.3 illustrates the score information provided on the GOT portion of the SVIB-SCII

Code	Scale	Sex Norm	Std. Score	Very Dis.	Dissim.	Mod. Dis.	Mid-Range	Mod. Sim.	Similar	Very Sim.	Code	Scale		Code	Scale
RC	Air Force Off'r	f	52						*		I	Geographer		SE	YMCA Director
RC	Air Force Off'r	m	31								I	Mathematician		SE	School Administ
RC	Army Officer	f	48						*		I	Mathematician		SE	School Administ
RC	Army Officer	m	28								IA	College Prof.		SCE	Guid. Counselor
RC	Navy Officer	m	38								IA	College Prof.		SEC	Guid. Counselor
R	Navy Officer	f	55							*	IA	Sociologist		SEC	Social Sci. Tchr.
RE	Police Officer	f	41					*			IA	Sociologist		SEC	Social Sci. Tchr.
RE	Police Officer	m	26								IAS	Psychologist		EA	Flight Attend't.
RCE	Voc. Agric. Tchr.	m	-2								IAS	Psychologist		EA	Flight Attend't.
RC	Farmer	f	21	12	2?	27	39	45	54	60	AIR	Architect		EA	Beautician
R	Farmer	m	24								AIR	Architect		E	Beautician
R	Forester	m	36								AI	Lawyer		E	Dept. Store Mgr
R	Skilled Crafts	m	22								AI	Lawyer		E	Dept. Store Mgr.
R	Rad.Tech.(x-ray)	f	35				*				AE	Public Rel. Dir.		E	Realtor
RI	Rad.Tech.(x-ray)	m	29								AE	Public Rel. Dir.		E	Realtor
RI	Forester	f	58							*	AE	AdvertisingExec		E	Life Ins. Agent
RI	Engineer	f	53						*		AE	AdvertisingExec		E	Life Ins. Agent
RI	Engineer	m	38								AE	Int. Decorator		E	Elect. Publ. Off
RI	Veterinarian	m	39	12	21	27	39	45	54	60	AE	Int. Decorator		E	Elect. Publ. Off
RIC	Lic. Pract. Nurse	f	12	*							A	Musician		E	Public Administ
RAS	Occup.Therapist	f	52						*		A	Musician		EI	Invest.FundMgr
RAS	Occup.Therapist	m	40								A	Comm'l. Artist		EI	Marketing Exec.
IR	Veterinarian	f	54							*	A	Comm'l. Artist		EI	Marketing Exec.
IR	Chemist	f	57							*	A	Fine Artist		E	Personnel Dir.
IR	Chemist	m	53								A	Fine Artist		E	Personnel Dir.
IR	Physicist	f	52					*			A	Art Teacher		E	Ch. of Comm. Ex.
IR	Physicist	m	45								A	Art Teacher		E	Restaurant Mgr.
IR	Geologist	f	57	12	21	27	39	45	54	*60	A	Photographer		EC	Restaurant Mgr.
IR	Geologist	m	52								A	Photographer		EC	Ch. of Comm. Ex.
IR	Med. Technol.	f	51					*			A	Librarian		EC	Buyer
IR	Med. Technol.	m	34								A	Librarian		EC	Buyer
IR	Dental Hygienist	f	39				*				A	For. Lang. Tchr		EC	Purchas'g Agent
IR	Dentist	f	61							*	A	For. Lang. Tchr		EC	Purchas'g Agen
IR	Dentist	m	50								A	Reporter		ERC	Agribus. Mgr.
IR	Optometrist	f	62							*	A	Reporter		ES	Home Econ. Tc
IR	Optometrist	m	57								A	English Teac		ECS	Nurs. Home Adm
IR	Phys. Therapist	f	56	12	21	27	39	45	54	*60	AS	English Teac		EC	Nurs. Home Adm
IR	Phys. Therapist	m	33								SA	Speech Patho		EC	Dietitian
IR	Physician	f	61							*	SA	Speech Pathol.		ECR	Dietitian
IR	Physician	m	49								SA	Social Worker		CER	Exec. Housek'p'r
IRS	Regist. Nurse	m	26								SA	Social Worker		CER	Exec. Housek'p'p
IRS	Math-Sci. Tchr.	m	37								SA	Minister		CES	Bus. Ed. Teache
IRC	Math-Sci. Tchr.	f	30				*				SIE	Minister		CES	Bus. Ed. Teachi
IRC	Systems Analyst	f	53							*	SI	Regist. Nurse		CE	Banker
IRC	Systems Analyst	m	39								S	Lic. Pract. Nurse		CE	Banker
IRC	Computer Progr.	f	59	12	21	27	39	45	54	60	S	Special Ed. Tchr		CE	Credit Manager
IRC	Computer Progr.	m	45								S	Special Ed. Tchr		CE	Credit Manager
IRE	Chiropractor	f	39				*				S	Elem. Teacher		CE	IRS Agent
IRE	Chiropractor	m	31								S	Elem. Teacher		CE	IRS Agent
IE	Pharmacist	m	31								SR	Phys. Ed. Tchr.		CA	Public Adminis
I	Pharmacist	f	58							*	SR	Phys. Ed. Tchr.		C	Accountant
I	Biologist	f	61							*	SRE	Recreat. Leader		C	Accountant
I	Biologist	m	51								SRE	Recreat. Leade		C	Secretary
I	Geographer	f	67								SE	YWCA Direct		C	Dental Assist

Figure 9.2. Portion of the SVIB-SCII Profile showing scores on the Occupational Scales.

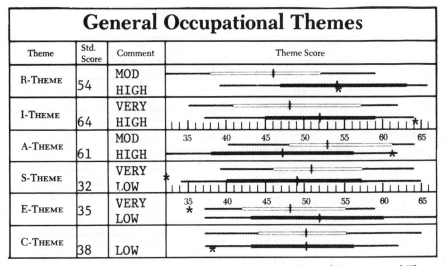

Figure 9.3. Portion of the SVIB-SCII Profile showing scores on six General Occupational Themes. Open and closed bars represent the distribution of scores for 300 Women-in-General and 300 Men-in-General, respectively.

profile. The standard scores are based on a General Reference Sample composed of 300 women and 300 men with mean set equal to 50 and standard deviation of 10. In addition to standard scores, interpretive comments based on distributions for the respondent's own sex are presented, and shaded and open interpretive bars provide a visual representation of the distribution of Men- and Women-in-General, respectively.

The integration of Holland's theory with Strong's empiricism provides the organizational framework for the current SVIB-SCII. The Occupational Scales (Figure 9.2) are coded with one to three Holland types based on the criterion sample's highest scores on the General Occupational Themes. The codes, in turn, are used to order the Occupational Scales on the profile. The Basic Interest Scales (BIS) also are clustered according to Holland types by identifying the GOT with which each BIS has its highest correlation.

Basic Interest Scales

The 23 Basic Interest Scales (BIS) were constructed using the statistical technique of cluster analysis to identify highly correlated items (Campbell, Borgen, Eastes, Johansson, & Peterson, 1968). The BIS were developed to focus on the measurement of only one interest factor per scale and, consequently, are easier to interpret than the heterogeneous Occupational Scales that incorporate several interest factors as well as likes and aversions in each scale.

The BIS scale names, as indicated in Figure 9.4, describe the homogeneous item content and the interest trait measured by each scale. Like the GOT, standard scores based on a combined-sex General Reference Sample and interpretive comments and bars based on Women- and Men-in-General are presented on the profile.

Reliability and Validity

The test-retest reliability of the scales of the SVIB-SCII is substantial over short and long intervals. Median reliabilities over 2-week, 30-day, and 3-year periods for the General Occupational Themes were .91, .86, and .81; for the Basic Interest Scales were .91, .88, and .82; and for the Occupational Scales were .91, .89, and .87 (Campbell & Hansen, 1981).

Concurrent validity data for the GOT and BIS, which by their homogeneous scaling nature are more useful for description of interests rather than for prediction, include mean scores for hundreds of occupational samples on each scale. Generally, the scales distribute occupations over 2–2½ standard deviations, and the patterns of high and low scoring occupations indicate that scores on these scales are related to pursued occupations (Campbell & Hansen, 1981).

Basic Interest Scales

Th.	Scale	Std. Score	Comment	Scale Score
R-THEME	AGRICULTURE	43	AVE	
	NATURE	58	MOD HIGH	
	ADVENTURE	57	HIGH	
	MILITARY ACTIVITIES	55	HIGH	
	MECHANICAL ACTIVITIES	58	HIGH	
I-THEME	SCIENCE	58	MOD HIGH	
	MATHEMATICS	61	HIGH	
	MEDICAL SCIENCE	63	HIGH	
	MEDICAL SERVICE	40	MOD LOW	
A-THEME	MUSIC/ DRAMATICS	63	MOD HIGH	
	ART	55	AVE	
	WRITING	56	AVE	
S-THEME	TEACHING	40	MOD LOW	
	SOCIAL SERVICE	37	VERY LOW	
	ATHLETICS	55	MOD HIGH	
	DOMESTIC ARTS	41	LOW	
	RELIGIOUS ACTIVITIES	33	VERY LOW	
E-THEME	PUBLIC SPEAKING	43	AVE	
	LAW/ POLITICS	46	AVE	
	MERCHANDISING	39	MOD LOW	
	SALES	37	VERY LOW	
	BUSINESS MANAGEMENT	37	LOW	
C-TH	OFFICE PRACTICES	36	LOW	

Figure 9.4. Portion of the SVIB-SCII Profile showing scores on 23 Basic Interest Scales. Open and closed bars represent the distribution of scores for 300 Women-in-General and 300 Men-in-General, respectively.

Concurrent validity for the Occupational Scales is determined by identifying the power of each scale to discriminate between the criterion samples and the appropriate sex-in-general sample. The median overlap between scores of the criterion and contrast samples is 34%, representing about 2 standard deviations of separation between the samples.

Because interest inventories are used to make long-term decisions, predictive validity is important. The SVIB-SCII has a long history of predictive validity studies, and the finding is that high scores on the Occupational Scales are related to occupations eventually entered; generally, between one half and three fourths of the subjects in predictive validity studies enter occupations predictable from their earlier scores (Campbell, 1966; Dolliver, Irvin & Bigley, 1972; Harmon, 1969; Spokane, 1979). A recent study assessed the usefulness of the SVIB-SCII for predicting college majors and found hit rates similar to those reported for occupational entry (Hansen & Swanson, 1983).

Kuder's Interest Inventories

The Personal Preference Record—Form A was published in 1939 by G. Frederick Kuder and included seven almost independent homogeneous scales. Kuder added two more homogeneous scales in 1943 (Form B) and another homogeneous scale in 1948 (Form C). The Kuder Occupational Interest Survey-DD (KOIS-DD) was published in 1966.

Kuder Preference Record— Vocational

The Kuder Preference Record—Vocational (Form C) is composed of homogeneous scales that measure interest in 10 broad areas: Outdoor, Mechanical, Computational, Scientific, Persuasive, Artistic, Literary, Musical, Social Service, and Clerical. Kuder originally grouped related items on the basis of content validity; later he used item analyses to determine groups of items (scales) with high internal consistency.

The item booklet contains 168 forced-choice triads reported to be at the ninth grade reading level. The respondent compares each of the three activities with the other two and ranks them as most preferred (M) and least preferred (L). For example:

	M		L
a. Take special notice of people when you are traveling	O	a	O
b. Take special notice of the scenery when you are traveling	●	b	O
c. Take special notice of the crops when you are traveling	O	c	●
d. Read lessons to a blind student	O	d	●
e. Keep a record of traffic past a certain point	●	e	O
f. Interview people in a survey of public opinion	O	f	O

The Kuder Preference Record may be hand scored or machine scored; both techniques produce raw scores that are entered on the profile sheet shown in Figure 9.5. The respondent's raw scores are compared with percentile distributions of either norm groups of boys or girls in grades 9 through 12 or of men or women.

The Kuder General Interest Survey—Form E is designed for use with grades 6 to 12. It uses easier vocabulary than does Form C but measures the same 10 areas of interest.

Kuder Occupational Interest Survey—Form DD

The KOIS-DD is composed of 100 triads of work-related activities similar to those of the Kuder—Form C already described. The profile includes 126 Occupational Scales and 48 College Major Scales that, like the SVIB-SCII, compare the respondent's interests to those of people in criterion samples. Unlike the SVIB-SCII, the KOIS-DD does not use the empirical method of contrast groups for scale construction. Instead, the individual's responses are compared directly to those of the criterion samples, and scores are reported as Lambda coefficients, which do not allow comparison of scores across different persons' profiles as can be done with standard scores. Thus, a respondent's KOIS-DD scores derive meaning only from the rank each scale occupies among all of the scales.

This form of the Kuder must be machine scored; the respondent receives the profile illustrated in Figure 9.6. The 126 Occupational Scales represent 27 occupations (54 Scales) that were developed using both male and female criterion samples, 52 that are based on male criterion samples only, and 20 based on female criterion samples only. The 48 College Major scales represent 12 majors (24 Scales) that are based on female and

0 44	1 38	2 31	3 26	4 62	5 17	6 12	7 7	8 45	9 58
OUTDOOR	MECHANICAL	COMPUTATIONAL	SCIENTIFIC	PERSUASIVE	ARTISTIC	LITERARY	MUSICAL	SOCIAL SERVICE	CLERICAL

Figure 9.5. Profile for the Kuder Preference Record-Vocational showing scores on 10 homogeneous scales. Percentiles are based on boys or girls in grades 9 through 12.

OCCUPATIONAL SCALES	NORMS		OCCUPATIONAL SCALES (CONTINUED)	COLLEGE MAJOR SCALES
	M	F		
CHEMIST	.51*		>COUNSELOR,HI SC	PHYSICAL SCIENCE
>COMPUTR PROGRAMR	.51*		ELEM SCHL TCHR	>MATHEMATICS
MATHEMATICIAN	.50*		>INSURANCE AGEN	ENGINEERING,CHE?
STATISTICIAN	.50*		>PHYS THERAPIST	AGRICULTURE
>COMPUTR PROGRAMR		.49*	>BANKER	
METEOROLOGIST	.49*		>PHYS THERAPIST	>BIOLOGICAL SCI
ENGINEER		.47*	BLDG CONTRACTC	ENGINEERING,ELEC
ENG,MINING/METAL	.47*		PODIATRIST	FORESTRY
PLANT NURSRY WKR	.47*		NUTRITIONIST	ENGINEERNG,CIVIL
PSYCHOLOGY PROF	.47*		OSTEOPATH	ENGINEERING,MECH
ENGINEER, CIVIL	.45*		>X-RAY TECHNICI,	ANIMAL HUSBANDRY
ENGINEER, ELEC	.45*		DIETITIAN, ADM:	>MATHEMATICS
>SCIENCE TCHR, HS	.44		>LIBRARIAN	BUS ACCT AND FIN
ENG,HEAT/AIR CON	.43		>PSYCH, CLINICAL	
ENGINEER, MECH	.43		PERSONNEL MANAGI	ECONOMICS
FORESTER	.43		PLUMBING CONTRA'	>MUSIC & MUSIC E(
>ACCT,CERT PUBLIC		.42	>BOOKSTOR MANAGE	LAW-GRAD SCHOOL
>ACCT,CERT PUBLIC	.42		>INTERIOR DECORA	>BIOLOGICAL SCI
>MATH TCHR,HI SCH	.42		POSTAL CLERK	>FOREIGN LANGUAGE
PSYCH,INDUSTRIAL	.42		>AUDIOL/SP PATHC	PREMED/PHAR/DENT
SOC WORKR,SCHOOL		.41	>NURSE	MILITARY CADET
>BOOKSTOR MANAGER	.41		SUPERVSR,INDUS1	BUS MANAGEMENT
OPTOMETRIST	.41		DEAN OF WOMEN	
>SCIENCE TCHR, HS		.40	>INTERIOR DECORA	AIR FORCE CADET
COUNTY AGRI AGT	.40		SECRETARY	BUS & MARKETING
>FLORIST	.40		POLICE OFFICER	>HISTORY
>JOURNALIST	.40		>SOCIAL CASEWORKI	>POLITICAL SCI
>LAWYER	.40		>SOC WORKER,PSYC	>PSYCHOLOGY
PEDIATRICIAN	.40		>INSURANCE AGENT	ARCHITECTURE
PSYCHOLOGIST		.39	>X-RAY TECHNICI/	>ELEMENTARY EDUC
ENGINEER, INDUS	.39		PHARMACEUT SAL!	>ENGLISH
>LIBRARIAN	.39		>FLORIST	
TRAVEL AGENT	.39		AUTO SALESPERS	BUS ED & COMMERC
>ARCHITECT	.38		BRICKLAYER	>MUSIC & MUSIC ED
>BANKER	.38		ELECTRICIAN	>PHYSICAL EDUC
>FILM/TV PROD/DIR	.38		>SOC WORKER,GRC	>SOCIOLOGY
PHARMACIST	.38		WELDER	HEALTH PROFES
>VETERINARIAN	.38		BANK CLERK	>POLITICAL SCI
>PHYSICIAN		.37	>BOOKKEEPER	>PSYCHOLOGY
>DENTIST	.37		>COUNSELOR,HI SCI	>FOREIGN LANGUAGE
RADIO STATON MGR	.37		HOME DEMONST AG'	
SCHOOL SUPT	.37		>SOC WORKER,PSYC	>PHYSICAL EDUC
>DENTIST		.36	>VETERINARIAN	>HISTORY
BUYER	.36		MACHINIST	>ART AND ART EDUC
PHOTOGRAPHER	.36		PLUMBER	HOME ECON EDUC
REAL ESTATE AGT	.36		OCCUPA THERAPI	DRAMA
>ARCHITECT		.35	>SOCIAL CASEWOF	>ENGLISH
>JOURNALIST		.35	>SOC WORKER,GRO	SOCIAL SCI, GENL
CLOTHIER, RETAIL	.35		SOC WORKER,MED	>ELEMENTARY EDUC
>PHYSICIAN	.35		AUTO MECHANIC	
>PSYCH, CLINICAL	.35		OFFICE CLERK	NURSING
>FILM/TV PROD/DIR		.34	STENOGRAPHER	>ART AND ART EDUC
>LAWYER		.34	YMCA SECRETARY	>SOCIOLOGY
>MATH TCHR,HI SCH		.34	DENTAL ASSISTAN	TCHG CATH SISTEF

Figure 9.6. Portion of the KOIS-DD Profile showing scores on Occupational and College Major Scales. > indicates sex-matched scales; * identifies the top Lambda coefficients.

male criterion samples, 17 based on male samples only, and 7 on female samples.

Reliability and Validity

An inventory, such as the KOIS-DD, which provides rank-ordered results intended to discriminate interests within the respondent rather than to discriminate among people, has special requirements for analyses of reliability. Test-retest reliability can be assessed only in terms of how consistent the order of scores is for each subject from one testing to the next. Kuder and Diamond (1979) reported individual 2-week test-retest reliabilities computed for high school and college age students; the median reliability for all cases was .90.

A large predictive validity study for the KOIS-DD (Zytowski, 1976) involved over 800 women and men who were located 12 to 19 years after taking the Kuder. Fifty-one percent were employed in an occupation predicted by their scores on the KOIS-DD.

Holland's Interest Inventories

The emergence of John Holland's theory of careers (Holland, 1959, 1966) began with development of the Vocational Preference Inventory (VPI) (Holland, 1958). Based on interest data collected with the VPI as well as data from other interest, personality, and values inventories and from structure analyses of interests, Holland formulated his theory of vocational life and personality. According to Holland, people can be divided into six types or some combination of six types: Realistic, Artistic, Investigative, Social, Enterprising, and Conventional. Holland indicates that the types can be organized in the shape of a hexagon in the R-I-A-S-E-C order; the types adjacent to one another on the hexagon (e.g., Realistic-Investigative or Enterprising-Conventional) are more related than types that are diametrically opposed to one another (e.g., Realistic-Social or Artistic-Conventional). Attempts to verify Holland's hexagonal representation of the world of work show in general that the structure of interests approximates the theoretical organization proposed by Holland (Campbell & Hansen, 1981; Cole & Hanson, 1971; Edwards & Whitney, 1972; Prediger, 1982).

Holland's theory has led to development of inventories and sets of scales to measure his six types, for example, his own Self-Directed Search

(Holland, 1971), the ACT Interest Inventory (Lamb & Prediger, 1981), the System for Career Decision-making (Harrington & O'Shea, 1976), and the General Occupational Themes of the SVIB-SCII (Campbell & Holland, 1972; Hansen & Johansson, 1972).

Vocational Preference Inventory

Development of the Vocational Preference Inventory (VPI) was based on a series of theoretical and empirical reports. Holland surveyed personality, vocational choice, and vocational interest literature; identified interest-personality factors; and hypothesized how they related to one another. Then, he used 160 occupational titles to develop an item pool that represented the interest factors or types, for example:

Criminologist	(Yes)	No
Restaurant Worker	Yes	(No)
Photoengraver	Yes	(No)
Wild Animal Trainer	(Yes)	No

The current version of the VPI (Holland, 1978) has seven homogeneous scales, constructed in a series of rational-empirical steps that measure Control (self-control), plus the six types hypothesized in Holland's theory: Realistic, Investigative, Artistic, Social, Enterprising, and Conventional. Other VPI scales developed using empirical methods of scale construction include: Acquiescence, measuring willingness to say "yes" to items; Status, indicating interest in occupational status; Masculinity, measuring masculinity-femininity; and Infrequency, assessing the tendency to answer items in an atypical direction.

The VPI is hand scored; raw scores are plotted on the profile shown in Figure 9.7. Even though Holland is a strong proponent of the use of raw scores for predicting occupational membership, the profile is calibrated to provide standard scores based on either 378 female or 354 male college students and employed adults to provide comparisons across scales.

Self-Directed Search

The Self-Directed Search, similar to the VPI, was developed to measure Holland's six types. It may be self-administered, self-scored, and to a limited degree, self-interpreted. The 228-item assessment booklet includes four sections: Activities the respondent would like to do; Competencies; Occupations; and Self-Estimates:

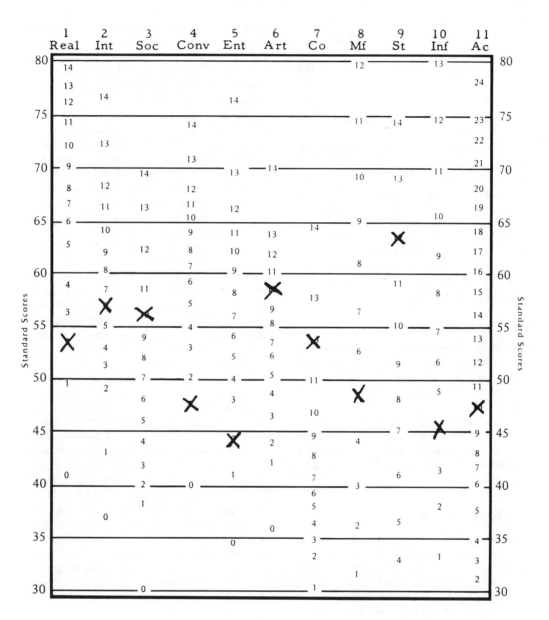

Figure 9.7. Profile for the Vocational Preference Inventory. Standard scores are based on 378 female college students and employed adults.

		L	D
(Act)	Fix electrical things	■	☐
(Comp)	I understand how a vacuum tube works	Y ☐	N ■
(Occ)	Poet	Y ☐	N ■

		High						Low
(S-E)	Teaching Ability	7	6	5	④	3	2	1

The reading level of the SDS is estimated at the seventh- or eighth-grade level; a Form Easy (E), which has only 203 items, is rated at the fourth-grade level. As illustrated in Figure 9.8, the most important feature of the SDS profile is the summary codes. The three highest raw scores represent the respondent's primary, secondary, and tertiary code assignments. Holland (1979) suggests flexibility in using the three summary codes for occupational exploration, since the codes are approximate, not precise.

Reliability and Validity

The median test-retest reliability coefficient for the seven VPI scales over a 2-week interval is .72; over the same period the median reliability coefficient for the six SDS scales is .82 (Holland, 1978, 1979).

Studies of the predictive validity of the VPI and SDS for choice of occupation and college major over 1-, 2-, and 3-year intervals, ranges from 35 to 66% accuracy (Holland, 1962, 1979; Holland & Lutz, 1968).

Other Interest Inventories

Several other interest inventories have been developed more recently than the Strong, Kuder, or Holland inventories. They are not as frequently used as the previously described inventories, represent a variety of scale construction techniques, and are appropriate for only a restricted range of the population.

Jackson Vocational Interest Survey

The Jackson Vocational Interest Survey (JVIS) (Jackson, 1977), appropriate for high school and college students, is composed of 289 forced-choice items describing occupational activities. The 34 homogeneous scales that measure *work roles* and *work styles* each contain 17 items estimated to be at the seventh-grade reading level. The work role

scales include 5 that characterize specific occupations (e.g., Engineering, Elementary Education) and 21 that represent a cluster of jobs (e.g., Creative Arts, Social Science). The eight work style scales measure preferences for environments that require certain behaviors (e.g., Dominant Leadership, Accountability). The JVIS profile also includes 10 General Occupational Themes measuring broad patterns of interests that reflect the respondent's *orientation toward work* rather than interests (e.g., Logical, Enterprising).

Development of the 34 homogeneous Basic Interest Scales relied on the theory-based technique of scale construction. The process began with identification of the interests to be measured from previous research in vocational psychology. Then 3,000 items were written to represent the interest constructs. Finally, the item pool was submitted to a series of factor analyses to identify the 289 items that had high correlations with factor scores on their own scales and low correlations with other JVIS scales. The 10 General Occupational Themes later were constructed by factor analyzing the 34 Basic scales.

Norms for the Basic scales are based on a combined-sex sample of 500 female and 500 male high school and college students. One problem with the use of a combined-sex normative sample for standardization is the large male-female differences on several scales. Interpretation of scores on scales exhibiting large sex differences (e.g., males score 4.34 raw score points higher than do females on Engineering; females score 3.71 raw score points higher on Elementary Education than do males) will result in comparatively fewer people from one sex or the other scoring high. The profile scores for the themes are based on the same combined-sex sample as those for the basic scales; however, the scores are reported as percentiles rather than standard scores.

Vocational Interest Inventory

The Vocational Interest Inventory (VII) (Lunneborg, 1976, 1981), designed for use with young people, is similar to the JVIS on several dimensions. First, the interests to be measured were selected based on theoretical considerations. The eight homogeneous scales of the VII were developed to represent the eight groups described in Roe's theory of occupational classifications: Service, Business Contact, Organization, Technical,

HOW TO ORGANIZE YOUR ANSWERS

Start on page 4. Count how many times you said L for "Like." Record the number of Ls or Ys for each group of Activities, Competencies, or Occupations on the lines below.

Activities (pp. 4-5)

4	6	5	6	7	0
R	I	A	S	E	C

Competencies (pp. 6-7)

7	8	1	10	5	6
R	I	A	S	E	C

Occupations (p. 8)

2	6	10	1	2	0
R	I	A	S	E	C

Self Estimates (p. 9)
(What number did
you circle?)

6	7	1	6	1	4
R	I	A	S	E	C

6	6	4	4	4	4
R	I	A	S	E	C

Total Scores
(Add the five R scores,
the five I scores, the
five A scores, etc.)

25	33	21	27	19	14
R	I	A	S	E	C

The letters with the three highest numbers indicate your summary code. Write your summary code below. (If two scores are the same or tied, put both letters in the same box.)

SUMMARY CODE

I	S	R
Highest	2nd	3rd

Figure 9.8. Profile for the Self-Directed Search.

Outdoor, Science, General Culture, and Arts and Entertainment. Second, the scales were constructed using a series of factor analyses that reduced the initial item pool to the final 112 forced-choice items. The eight scales each contain 28 response choices that have high correlations with factor scores on their own scales and low correlations with other VII scales. Third, the scales were normed on a combined-sex sample of students. According to the author (Lunneborg, 1981), only two scales were unaffected by sex; thus, the VII has the same potential problem of sex bias as does the JVIS.

Ohio Vocational Interest Survey

The Ohio Vocational Interest Survey (OVIS) (D'Costa, Winefordner, Odgers, & Koons, 1969, 1970) also was developed for use with young people, especially those in grades 8 through 12. The 24 homogeneous OVIS interest scales were developed based on the data-people-things model of the *Dictionary of Occupational Titles* (1965). The scales (e.g., Machine Worker, Crafts, Customer Service, Nursing) were rationally derived; in other words, persons familiar with definitions of the 24 scales to be developed were asked to assign items to, in their estimation, the appropriate scale or scales. After initial rational clustering of related items, a series of factor analyses were employed to refine the item pool, resulting in 280 items that correlated more highly with their own scales than with any other scale. Each scale is comprised of 11 items; the profile reports raw scores as well as percentile ranks based on normative samples composed of subjects of the respondent's own grade level and sex.

Career Assessment Inventory

The Career Assessment Inventory (CAI) (Johansson, 1975; Johansson & Johansson, 1978), developed for use with individuals considering immediate career entry, community college education, a 4-year degree, or vocational-technical training, was modeled after the SVIB-SCII. The CAI test booklet includes 305 items and the profile, like the SVIB-SCII, reports 3 sets of scales: 6 homogeneous General Themes, 22 homogeneous Basic Interest Areas, and 89 heterogeneous Occupational Scales representing 69 occupations (e.g., electrician, computer programmer, author/writer, chiropractor, personnel director, accountant). The CAI also uses Holland's theory to organize the Basic Interest Areas and Occupational Scales on the profile, clustering together those that represent each of Holland's six types.

The General Themes and Basic Areas are normed on a combined-sex reference sample composed of subjects drawn from 36 of the criterion samples. However, in addition to the standard scores based on a combined-sex sample, the CAI profile presents bars for each scale representing the range of scores for females and males in the reference sample. These additional data help to circumvent the problem of sex differences on some of the homogeneous scales. The Occupational Scales are standardized on the criterion sample used for scale construction. Like the SVIB-SCII, the CAI provides separate-sex Occupational Scales; unlike the SVIB-SCII, the CAI includes a large number of occupations that are represented with scales for only one sex (21 occupations with male- and female-normed scales; 29 male-normed only; 18 female-normed only).

STABILITY OF INTERESTS

The degree to which interests are stable is important to the predictive power of inventories. If interests are fickle and unstable, interest inventory scores will not explain any of the prediction variance.

Stability of interests was one of the earliest concerns of researchers in interest measurement (Strong, 1943). Cross-sectional and longitudinal methods have been used in a plethora of studies to document that interests are stable even at relatively young ages of 15 or 16 years. By age 20, the stability of interests is obvious even over test-retest intervals of 5 to 10 years, and by age 25, interests are very stable (Johansson & Campbell, 1971).

During the long history of the SVIB-SCII, over 30 occupations have been tested at least three times: in the 1930s, 1960s, and 1970s/80s. Analyses of these data have shown that interests of randomly sampled occupational groups are stable. Figure 9.9, a profile of interests for chemists collected in the 1930s, 1960s, and 1970s, illustrates the typical finding for all the occupations:

1. the configuration of the interests of an occupation stays the same over long periods of time, and
2. even when interests change to some small extent, the relative importance of various interests stays the same (Hansen, 1981, 1982).

General Occupational Themes

Theme	30's	60's	70's	
R-THEME	55	53	55	
I-THEME	59	61	62	
A-THEME	45	49	49	
S-THEME	44	47	44	
E-THEME	44	46	44	
C-THEME	49	46	48	

Basic Interest Scales

Scale				
NATURE	49	49	51	
ADVENTURE	49	52	50	
MECHANICAL ACTIVITIES	59	58	59	
SCIENCE	63	64	63	
MATHEMATICS	58	59	60	
MEDICAL SERVICE	53	53	54	
MUSIC/ DRAMATICS	46	51	50	
ART	45	47	47	
WRITING	45	48	49	
TEACHING	47	52	49	
SOCIAL SERVICE	42	44	42	
ATHLETICS	49	47	45	
PUBLIC SPEAKING	46	52	50	
LAW/ POLITICS	46	50	50	
MERCHANDISING	44	43	44	
SALES	45	45	45	
BUSINESS MANAGEMENT	45	46	46	
OFFICE PRACTICES	46	44	46	

Figure 9.9. Mean interest profile for male Chemists tested in the 1930s (●————●), the 1960s (x————x), and the 1970s (○————○).

USE OF INTEREST INVENTORIES

Interest inventories are used to efficiently assess interests by a variety of institutions including high school and college advising offices, social service agencies, employment agencies, consulting firms, corporations, and community organizations such as the YWCA.

Career Exploration

The major use of assessed interests, usually reported as interest inventory scores, is in career counseling that leads to decisions such as choosing a major, selecting an occupation, making a midcareer change, or preparing for retirement. First, counselors use the interest inventory profiles to develop hypotheses about clients that may be discussed, confirmed, or discarded during career exploration. Then, the interest scores and profile provide a framework for interest exploration and a mechanism for helping the client to integrate her or his past history with current interests.

The inventory results serve as a starting point for evaluating interests, as an efficient method for objectively identifying interests, and as a structure for the counseling process. Inventory results help some counselees to increase the number of options they are considering; some use the results to begin to narrow the range of possible choices. Others only want to confirm educational or vocational decisions that they already have made.

Selection and Placement

Interest inventories also are used to assess interests during employment selection and placement evaluations. Among qualified candidates, interest inventories help to identify those most likely to complete the training program and stay in the profession (Berdie & Campbell, 1968; Reeves & Booth, 1979). Even after initial selection, interest inventories may be used to help an employee find the right job within the company (Dunnette & Kirchner, 1965).

Research

Researchers use measures of interests (e.g., checklists, self-estimates, rating scales, interest inventories) to operationalize interest traits, investigate the origin and development of interests, explore changes or stability in society, and understand the relationship between interests and other psychological variables such as abilities, satisfaction, success, and personality. Studies assessing the structure of interests and also the interests of various occupational groups provide information for understanding the organization of the world of work and the relationships among occupations.

Most interest inventories are constructed to measure vocational interests. Recent research, however, indicates that instruments such as the SVIB-SCII measure not only vocational interests but also leisure interests (Cairo, 1979). Holland (1973) has proposed that instruments measuring his six personality types also can identify a respondent's preferences for environments and types of people as well as job activities.

FUTURE DIRECTIONS

The frequency of test use in counseling has not changed appreciably in the last 25 years; however, the use of interest inventories has increased while the use of other tests (e.g., ability, aptitude, achievement) has decreased (Zytowski & Warman, 1982). A wide variety of new interpretive materials, career guidance packages, and interactive computerized systems for inventory interpretation and career exploration are available. Thus far, evaluations of the use of interest inventories indicate that various modes and mediums of presentation are equally effective (Johnson, Korn, & Dunn, 1975; Maola & Kane, 1976; Miller & Cochran, 1979; Rubinstein, 1978; Smith & Evans, 1973). The trend in the future, with decreasing budgets and personnel in educational institutions, will be toward even greater use of computers for interest inventory administration and interpretation and for integration into computerized career counseling modules.

Techniques for developing reliable and valid interest inventories are available now, and the construction methods have reached a plateau of excellence in reliability and validity. Therefore, publishers can direct their efforts toward an increased emphasis on interpretation and counselor competency. Test manuals traditionally were written to provide data required by the APA Technical Standards on Testing; now, interpretive manuals are prepared in addition to technical manuals to help the professional maximize the usefulness of inventory results (Hansen, 1984; Holland, 1971; Zytowski, 1981).

As the use of interest inventories expands to new populations, research must also move in that direction to aid in understanding the characteristics of the populations as well as the best methods for implementing interest inventories with them. The cross-cultural use of interest inventories also is increasing the demand for valid translations of inventories and for data on the predictive accuracy of inventories normed on U.S. populations for non-English-speaking respondents.

SUMMARY

Interest inventories will be used in the future as in the past to operationalize the trait of interests in research. Attempts to answer old questions, such as the interaction of interests and personality, success, values, satisfaction, and ability will persevere.

Holland's theory undoubtedly will continue to evoke research in the field. Studies designed to understand educational and vocational drop-outs and changers, to analyze job satisfaction, to understand the development of interests, and to predict job or academic success will draw on Holland's theoretical constructs for independent variables and on interest inventories to identify interests.

The exploration of vocational interests has always been a popular topic in counseling psychology; the increased use of inventories and career guidance programs indicates that interest inventories will continue to be an important component in psychological research.

REFERENCES

Berdie, R.F., & Campbell, D.P. (1968). Measurement of interest. In D.K. Whitla (Ed.), *Handbook of measurement and assessment in behavioral sciences*. Reading, MA: Addison-Wesley.

Cairo, P.C. (1979). The validity of the Holland and Basic Interest Scales of the Strong Vocational Interest Blank: Leisure activities versus occupational membership as criteria. *Journal of Vocational Behavior*, 15, 68–77.

Campbell, D.P. (1966). Occupations ten years later of high school seniors with high scores on the SVIB life insurance salesman scale. *Journal of Applied Psychology*, 50, 369–372.

Campbell, D.P., Borgen, F.H., Eastes, S.H., Johansson, C.B., & Peterson, R.A. (1968). A set of basic interest scales for the Strong Vocational Interest Blank for Men. *Journal of Applied Psychology Monograph*, 52, 1–54.

Campbell, D.P., & Hansen, J.C. (1981). *Manual for the SVIB-SCII* (3rd ed.). Palo Alto, CA: Stanford University Press.

Campbell, D.P., & Holland, J.L. (1972). Applying Holland's theory to Strong's data. *Journal of Vocational Behavior*, 2, 353–376.

Clark, K.E. (1956). *Manual for use of the Navy Vocational Interest Inventory*. Minneapolis: University of Minnesota Press.

Cole, N.S., & Hanson, G. (1971). *An analysis of the structure of vocational interests* (ACT Research Report No. 40). Iowa City: American College Testing Program.

Cowdery, K.M. (1926). Measurement of professional attitudes: Differences between lawyers, physicians, and engineers. *Journal of Personnel Research*, 5, 131–141.

D'Costa, A.G., Winefordner, D.W., Odgers, J.G., & Koons, P.B., Jr. (1969). *Ohio Vocational Interest Survey*. New York: Harcourt, Brace and World.

D'Costa, A.G., Winefordner, D.W., Odgers, J.G., & Koons, P.B., Jr. (1970). *Ohio Vocational Interest Survey Manual for Interpreting*. New York: Harcourt Brace Jovanovich.

Dolliver, R.H., Irvin, J.A., & Bigley, S.E. (1972). Twelve-year follow-up of the Strong Vocational Interest Blank. *Journal of Counseling Psychology*, 19, 212–217.

Dunnette, M.D., & Kirchner, W.K. (1965). *Psychology applied to industry*. New York: Appleton-Century-Crofts.

Edwards, K.J., & Whitney, D.R. (1972). A structural analysis of Holland's personality types using factor and configural analysis. *Journal of Counseling Psychology*, 19, 136–145.

Engen, H.B., Lamb, R.R., & Prediger, D.J. (1982). Are secondary schools still using standardized tests? *Personnel and Guidance Journal*, 60, January, 287–290.

Freyd, M. (1922–1923). The measurement of interests in vocational selection. *Journal of Personnel Research*, 1, 319–328.

Guilford, J.P., Christensen, P.R., Bond, N.A., Jr., & Sutton, M.A. (1954). A factor analysis study of human interests. *Psychological Monographs*, Whole No. 375, 68, 1–38.

Hansen, J.C. (1976). Exploring new directions for Strong-Campbell Interest Inventory occupational scale construction. *Journal of Vocational Behavior*. 9, 147–160.

Hansen, J.C. (1981, August). *Changing interests: Myth or reality?* Paper presented at the meeting of the American Psychological Association, Los Angeles.

Hansen, J.C. (1982, July). *The effect of history on the vocational interests of women*. Paper presented at the meeting of the International Congress of Applied Psychology, Edinburgh, Scotland.

Hansen, J.C. (1983). *Correlation between VPI and SCII scores*. Unpublished manuscript. Center for Interest Measurement Research, University of Minnesota.

Hansen, J.C. (1984). *Counselor's interpretive guide to the SVIB-SCII*. Palo Alto, CA: Stanford University Press.

Hansen, J.C., & Johansson, C.B. (1972). The applications of Holland's vocational model to the Strong

Vocational Interest Blank for Women. *Journal of Vocational Behavior*, 2, 479–493.

Hansen, J.C., & Swanson, J.L. (1983). Stability of interests and the predictive and concurrent validity of the 1981 Strong-Campbell Interest Inventory. *Journal of Consulting Psychology*, 30, 194–201.

Harmon, L.W. (1969). The predictive power over 10 years of measured social service and scientific interests among college women. *Journal of Applied Psychology*, 53, 193–198.

Harrington, T.F., & O'Shea, A.J. (1976). *Manual for the Harrington/O'Shea Systems for Career Decision-making*. Needham, MA: Career Planning Associates.

Holland, J.L. (1958). A personality inventory employing occupational titles. *Journal of Applied Psychology*, 42, 336–342.

Holland, J.L. (1959). A theory of vocational choice. *Journal of Counseling Psychology*, 6, 35–45.

Holland, J.L. (1962). Some explorations of a theory of vocational choice: I. One- and two-year longitudinal studies. *Psychological Monographs*, 76, 26.

Holland, J.L. (1966). *The psychology of vocational choice*. Waltham, MA: Blaisdell.

Holland, J.L. (1971). *The counselor's guide to the Self-Directed Search*. Palo Alto, CA: Consulting Psychologists Press.

Holland, J.L. (1973). *Making vocational choices: A theory of careers*. Englewood Cliffs, NJ: Prentice-Hall.

Holland, J.L. (1978). *Manual for the Vocational Preference Inventory* (3rd ed.). Palo Alto, CA: Consulting Psychologists Press.

Holland, J.L. (1979). *The Self-Directed Search Professional Manual*. Palo Alto, CA: Consulting Psychologists Press.

Holland, J.L., & Lutz, S.W. (1968). Predicting a student's vocational choice. *Personnel and Guidance Journal*, 46, 428–436.

Hubbard, R.M. (1930). Interest Analysis Blank. In D.G. Paterson, R.M. Elliott, L.D. Anderson, H.A. Toops, & E. Heidbrider (Eds.), *Minnesota Mechanical Ability Tests*. Minneapolis: University of Minnesota Press.

Jackson, D.N. (1977). *Jackson Vocational Interest Survey Manual*. London, Ontario: Research Psychologists Press.

Johansson, C.B. (1975). *Manual for the Career Assessment Inventory*. Minneapolis: National Computer Systems.

Johansson, C.B., & Campbell, D.P. (1971). Stability of the Strong Vocational Interest Blank for Men. *Journal of Applied Psychology*, 55, 24–26.

Johansson, C.B., & Johansson, J.C. (1978). *Manual Supplement for the Career Assessment Inventory*. Minneapolis: National Computer Systems.

Johnson, W.F., Korn, T.A., & Dunn, D.J. (1975). Comparing three methods of presenting occupational information. *Vocational Guidance Quarterly*, 24, September, 62–65.

Kitson, H.D. (1925). *The psychology of vocational adjustment*. Philadelphia: Lippincott.

Kornhauser, A.W. (1927). Results from a quantitative questionnaire of likes and dislikes used with a group of college freshmen. *Journal of Applied Psychology*, 11, 85–94.

Kuder, G.F. (1939). *Kuder Preference Record-Form A*. Chicago: University of Chicago Bookstore.

Kuder, G.F. (1943). *Vocational Preference Record-Form B*. Chicago: Science Research Associates.

Kuder, G.F. (1948). *Kuder Preference Record-Form C (Vocational)*. Chicago: Science Research Associate.

Kuder, G.F. (1966). *General Manual: Occupational Interest Survey Form-DD*. Chicago: Science Research Associates.

Kuder, G.F. (1977). *Activity interests and occupational choice*. Chicago: Science Research Associates.

Kuder, G.F., & Diamond, E.E. (1979). *Kuder-DD Occupational Interest Survey General Manual* (2nd ed.). Chicago: Science Research Associates.

Lamb, R.R., & Prediger, D.J. (1981). *Technical Report for the unisex edition of the ACT Interest Inventory*. Iowa City: American College Testing Program.

Lunneborg, P.W. (1976). *Manual for the Vocational Interest Survey*. Seattle: University of Washington, Educational Assessment Center.

Lunneborg, P.W. (1981). *Vocational Interest Inventory Manual*. Los Angeles: Western Psychological Services.

Maola, J., & Kane, G. (1976). Comparison of computer-based versus counselor-based occupational information systems with disadvantaged vocational students. *Journal of Counseling Psychology*, 23, 163–165.

Miller, M.J., & Cochran, J.R. (1979). Evaluating the use of technology in reporting SCII results to students. *Measurement and Evaluation in Guidance*, 12, 166–173.

Miner, J.B. (1922). An aid to the analysis of vocational interests. *Journal of Educational Research*, 5, 311–323.

Parsons, F. (1909). *Choosing a vocation*. Boston: Houghton Mifflin.

Paterson, D.G., Elliott, R.M., Anderson, L.D., Toops, H.A., & Heidbreder, E. (Eds.). (1930). *Minnesota Mechanical Abilities Test*. Minneapolis: University of Minnesota Press.

Prediger, D.J. (1982). Dimensions underlying Holland's hexagon: Missing link between interests and occupations? *Journal of Vocational Behavior*, 21, 259–287.

Reeves, D.J., & Booth, R.F. (1979). Expressed versus inventoried interests as predictors of paramedical effectiveness. *Journal of Vocational Behavior*, 15, 155–163.

Remmers, H.H. (1929). The measurement of interest differences between students of engineering and agriculture. *Journal of Applied Psychology*, 13, 105–119.

Roe, A. (1956). *The psychology of occupations*. New York: Wiley.

Rubinstein, M.R. (1978). Integrative interpretation of vocational inventory results. *Journal of Consulting Psychology*, 25, 306–309.

Smith, R.D., & Evans, J. (1973). Comparison of experimental group and individual counseling facilitators of vocational development. *Journal of Counseling Psychology*, 20, 202–208.

Spokane, A.R. (1979). Occupational preferences and the validity of the Strong-Campbell Interest Inventory for college women and men. *Journal of Counseling Psychology*, 26, 312–318.

Strong, E.K., Jr. (1927). *Vocational Interest Blank*. Palo Alto: CA: Stanford University Press.

Strong, E.K., Jr. (1943). *Vocational interests of men and women*. Palo Alto, CA: Stanford University Press.

U.S. Department of Labor, Bureau of Employment Security. (1965). *Dictionary of Occupational Titles, Third Edition*. Washington, DC: U.S. Government Printing Office.

Webber, P.L., & Harmon, L.W. (1978). The reliability and concurrent validity of three types of occupational scales for two occupational groups. In C.K. Tittle & D.G. Zytowski (Eds.), *Sex-fair Interest Measurement: Research and Implications*. Washington, DC: National Institute of Education.

Zytowski, D.G. (1976). Predictive validity of the Kuder Occupational Interest Survey: A 12- to 19-year follow-up. *Journal of Counseling Psychology, 3*, 221–233.

Zytowski, D.G. (1981). *Counseling with the Kuder Occupational Interest Survey*. Chicago: Science Research Associates.

Zytowski, D.G., & Warman, R.E. (1982). The changing use of tests in counseling. *Measurement and Evaluation in Guidance, 15*, 147–152.

PART V
NEURO-PSYCHOLOGICAL ASSESSMENT

10 COMPREHENSIVE NEUROPSYCHOLOGICAL ASSESSMENT BATTERIES

Gerald Goldstein

INTRODUCTION

This chapter is the first of three covering the area of neuropsychological assessment. It will therefore provide a general introduction to the field of neuropsychological assessment and deal specifically with the extensive standard test batteries used with adults. Neuropsychological assessment is a relatively new term that has essentially replaced the older terms "testing for brain damage" or "testing for organicity." Lezak (1983) indicates that these procedures are used for three purposes: diagnosis, provision of information important for patient care, and research. A significant component of the patient care function is rehabilitation planning and monitoring (Golden, 1978; Goldstein & Ruthven, 1983). The focus of neuropsychological assessment has traditionally been on the brain damaged patient, but there have been major extensions of the field to psychiatric disorders (Gruzelier & Flor-Henry, 1979), functioning of normal individuals (Kimura & Durnford, 1974) and normal aging (Goldstein & Shelly, 1975; Reed & Reitan, 1963).

Perhaps the best definition of a neuropsychological test has been offered by Ralph Reitan, who describes it as a test that is sensitive to the condition of the brain. If performance on a test changes with a change in brain function, then the test is a neuropsychological test. However, it should be pointed out that comprehensive neuropsychological test batteries should not only contain neuropsychological tests. They should also contain some tests that are generally insensitive to brain dysfunction, primarily because such tests are often useful for providing a baseline against which extent of impairment associated with acquired brain damage can be measured. Most neuropsychological assessment methods are formal tests, but some work has been done with rating scales and self-report measures. Neuropsychological assessment is rarely conducted through a structured interview procedure or systematic behavioral observation outside of a test situation.

A comprehensive neuropsychological test battery is ideally a procedure that assesses all of the major functional areas generally affected by structural brain damage. We use the term ideally because none of the standard, commonly available procedures entirely achieves full comprehensiveness. Some observers have described the comprehensive procedures as screening batteries, because feasibility and time constraints generally require a sacrifice of detailed investigations of specific areas in order to achieve comprehensiveness. In Dr. Hamsher's chapter, we will learn more about what a clinical neuropsychologist does when asked to explore a particular area in detail rather than do a comprehensive evaluation. While the term *screening* may be justifiable in certain respects, the extensive standard batteries in common use should not be grouped with the brief, paper-and-pencil screening tests used in many clinical and industrial settings. That is, they do not simply screen for presence or absence of brain damage, but also evaluate a number of functional areas that may be affected by brain damage. Since brain damage most radically affects cognitive processes, most neuropsychological tests assess various areas of cognition, but perception and motor skills are also frequently evaluated. Thus, neuropsychological tests are generally thought of as assessment instruments for a variety of cognitive, perceptual, and motor skills. That is not to say that brain damage does not affect other aspects of the personality, but traditionally the standard neuropsychological tests do not typically assess these other areas. Perhaps the most important reason for this preference is that the cognitive tests have proven to be the most diagnostic ones. While personality changes may occur with a wide variety of psychiatric, general medical, and neurological conditions, cognitive changes appear to occur most dramatically in individuals with structural brain damage.

Numerous attempts have been made to classify the functional areas typically affected by brain damage, but the scheme proposed in what follows is a reasonably representative one. Perhaps the most ubiquitous change is general intellectual impairment. Following brain damage, the patient is not as bright as he or she was before. Problems are solved less effectively, goal-directed behavior becomes less well organized, and there is impairment of a number of specific skills such as solving arithmetic problems or interpreting proverbs. Numerous attempts have been made to epitomize this generalized loss, perhaps the most successful one being Goldstein and Scheerer's (1941) concept of impairment of the abstract attitude. The abstract attitude is essentially a phenomenological concept having to do with the way in which the individual perceives the world. Some consequences of its impairment involve failure to form concepts or to generalize from individual events, failure to plan ahead ideationally, and inability to

transcend the immediate stimulus situation. While the loss is a general one involving many aspects of the individual's life, it is best observed in a testing setting where the patient is presented with a novel situation in which some problem must be solved. Typically these tests involve abstraction or concept formation, and the patient is asked to sort or categorize in some way. The Goldstein-Scheerer tests (1941), perhaps the first neuropsychological battery, consist largely of sorting tests, but also provide the patient with other types of novel problem-solving tasks.

Probably the next most common manifestation of structural brain damage is impairment of memory. Sometimes memory impairment is associated with general intellectual impairment, sometimes it exists independently, and sometimes it is seen as an early sign of a progressive illness that eventually impairs a number of abilities other than memory. In most but not all cases, recent memory is more impaired than remote memory. That is, the patient may recall his or her early life in great detail, but may be unable to recall what happened during the previous day. Often, so-called primary memory is also relatively well preserved. That is, the patient may be able to immediately repeat back what was just presented to him, such as a few words or a series of digits, but will not retain new information over a more extended period of time, particularly after intervening events have occurred. In recent years, our capacity to examine memory has benefited from a great deal of research involving the various amnesic syndromes (e.g., Butters & Cermak, 1980; Squire, Slater, & Chace, 1975; Warrington & Weiskrantz, 1982), and we have become quite aware that not all brain damaged patients experience the same kind of memory disorder (Butters, 1983). It generally requires a detailed assessment to specifically identify the various types of memory disorder, and the comprehensive batteries we will be discussing here generally can only detect the presence of a memory disorder and provide an index of its severity.

Loss of speed in performing skilled activities is an extremely common symptom of brain damage. Generally, this loss is described in terms of impaired psychomotor speed or perceptual-motor coordination. While its basis is sometimes reduction of pure motor speed, in many instances pure speed is preserved in the presence of substantial impairment on tasks involving speed of some mental operation or coordination of skilled movement with perceptual input. Thus, the patient may do well on a simple motor task such as finger tapping, but poorly on a task in which movement must be coordinated with visual input, such as a cancellation or substitution task. Tasks of this latter type are commonly performed slowly and laboriously by many kinds of brain damaged patients. Aside from slowness, there may be other disturbances of purposive movement that go under the general heading of apraxia. Apraxia may be manifested as simple clumsiness or awkwardness, an inability to carry out goal directed movement sequences as would be involved in such functional activities as dressing, or as an inability to use movement ideationally as in producing gestures or performing pretended movements. While apraxia in one of its pure forms is a relatively rare condition, impairment of psychomotor speed is quite common and seen in a variety of conditions.

A set of abilities that bridge movement and perception may be evaluated by tasks in which the patient must produce some form of construction or copy a figure from a model. Among the first tests used to test brain damaged patients was the Bender-Gestalt (Bender, 1938), a procedure in which the patient must copy a series of figures devised by Wertheimer (1923) to study perception of visual gestalten. It was found that many patients had difficulty copying these figures, although they apparently perceived them normally. These difficulties manifested themselves in reasonably characteristic ways, including various forms of distortion, rotation of the figure, simplification, or primitivation and perseveration. The copying task has continued to be used by neuropsychologists, either in the form of the Bender-Gestalt or a variety of other procedures. Variations of the copying task procedure have involved having the patient draw the figure from memory (Benton, 1963; Rey, 1941), from a verbal command, e.g., "Draw a Circle" (Luria, 1973), or copy a figure that is embedded in an interfering background pattern (Canter, 1970). Related to the copying task is the constructional task, in which the patient must produce a three-dimensional construction from a model. The most popular test for this purpose is the Kohs Blocks or Block Design subtest of the Wechsler Scales (Wechsler, 1955). While in the timed versions of these procedures the patient may simply fail the task by virtue of running out of time, at least some brain damaged patients

make errors on these procedures comparable to what is seen on the copying tasks. With regard to block design type tasks, the errors might involve breaking the contour of the model or incorrectly reproducing the internal structure of the pattern (Kaplan, 1979). Thus, a constructional deficit may not be primarily associated with reduction in psychomotor speed, but rather with the inability to build configurations in three-dimensional space. Often, this ability is referred to as visual-spatial skill.

Visual-spatial skills also form a bridge with visual perception. When one attempts to analyze the basis for a patient's difficulty with a constructional task, the task demands may be broken down into movement, visual, and integrative components. Often, the patient has no remarkable impairment of purposive, skilled movement and can recognize the figure. If it is nameable, the patient can tell you what it is or if it is not, it can be correctly identified on a recognition task. However, the figure cannot be accurately copied.

While the difficulty may be with the integration between the visual percept and the movement, it has also been found that patients with constructional difficulties, and indeed patients with brain damage in general, frequently have difficulties with complex visual perception. For example, they do poorly at embedded figures tasks (Teuber, Battersby, & Bender, 1951) or at tasks in which a figure is made difficult to recognize through displaying it in some unusual manner, such as overlapping it with other figures (Golden, 1981) or presenting it in some incomplete or ambiguous form (Mooney, 1957). Some brain damaged patients also have difficulty when the visual task is made increasingly complex through adding elements in the visual field. Thus, the patient may identify a single element, but not two. When two stimuli are presented simultaneously, the characteristic error is that the patient reports only seeing one. The phenomenon is known as extinction (Bender, 1952) or neglect (Heilman, 1979).

Many brain damaged patients also have deficits in the areas of auditory and tactile perception. Sometimes, the auditory impairment is such that the patient can hear, but sounds cannot be recognized or interpreted. The general condition is known as agnosia and can actually occur in the visual, auditory, or tactile modalities. Agnosia has been defined as "perception without meaning," implying the intactness of the primary sense modality but loss of the ability to comprehend the incoming information. Auditory agnosia is a relatively rare condition, but there are many disturbances of auditory perception that are commonly seen among brain damaged patients. Auditory neglect can exist and is comparable to visual neglect; sounds to either ear may be perceived normally, but when a sound is presented to each ear simultaneously, only one of them may be perceived. There are a number of auditory verbal problems that we will get to when we discuss language. Auditory attentional deficits are common and may be identified by presenting complex auditory stimuli, such as rhythmic patterns, which the patient must recognize or reproduce immediately after presentation. A variety of normal and abnormal phenomena may be demonstrated using a procedure called dichotic listening (Kimura, 1961). It involves presenting two different auditory stimuli simultaneously to each ear. The subject wears earphones, and the stimuli are presented using stereophonic tape. Higher level tactile deficits generally involve a disability with regard to identifying symbols or objects by touch. Tactile neglect may be demonstrated by touching the patient over a series of trials with single and double stimuli, and tactile recognition deficits may be assessed by asking the patient to name objects placed in his or her hand or to identify numbers or letters written on the surface of the skin. It is particularly difficult to separate primary sensory functions from higher cognitive processes in the tactile modality, and many neuropsychologists perform rather detailed sensory examinations of the hands, involving such matters as light touch thresholds, two-point discrimination, point localization, and the ability to distinguish between sharp and dull tactile stimuli (Semmes, Weinstein, Ghent, & Teuber, 1960).

The neuropsychological assessment of speech and language has in some respects become a separate discipline involving neuropsychologists, neurologists, and speech and language pathologists. There is an extensive interdisciplinary literature in the area (Albert, Goodglass, Helm, Rubens, & Alexander, 1981), and several journals that deal almost exclusively with the relationships between impaired or normal brain function and language (e.g., *Brain and Language*). Aphasia is the general term used to denote impairment of language abilities as a result of structural brain damage, but not all brain damaged patients with communicative difficulties have aphasia. While aphasia is a general term covering numerous subcategories, it is now rather specifically defined as an impairment of communicative ability associated with focal damage to the hemisphere of the brain that is dominant for language—the left hemisphere in most people. Aphasia is generally produced as a result of disorders that have a sudden onset, notably stroke and head trauma, but may sometimes be seen in cases of other localized diseases such as brain tumors and focal infections. Stroke is probably the most common cause of aphasia.

Historically, there have been numerous attempts to categorize the subtypes of aphasia (Goodglass, 1983), but in functional terms, the aphasias involve a rather dramatic impairment of the capacity to speak, to understand the speech of others, to find the names for common objects, to read (alexia), write (agraphia), calculate (acalculia), or to use or comprehend gestures. However, a clinically useful assessment of these functional disorders must go into their specific characteristics. For example, when we say the patient has lost the ability to speak, we may mean that he or she has become mute or can only produce a few utterances in a halting, labored way. On the other hand, we may mean that the patient can produce words fluently, but the words and sentences being uttered make no sense. When it is said that the patient does not understand language, that may mean that spoken but not written language is understood, or it may mean that all modalities of comprehension are impaired. Thus, there are several aphasic syndromes, and it is the specific syndrome that generally must be identified in order to provide some correlation with the underlying localization of the brain damage and to make rational treatment plans. We may note that the standard comprehensive neuropsychological test batteries do not include extensive aphasia examinations. There are several such examinations available, such as the Boston Diagnostic Aphasia Examination (Goodglass & Kaplan, 1972) and the Western Aphasia Battery (Kertesz, 1979). Even though they may be used in conjunction with a neuropsychological assessment battery, they are rather lengthy procedures in themselves and require special expertise to administer and interpret.

For various reasons, it is often useful to assess attention as part of the neuropsychological examination. Sometimes, an attention deficit is a cardinal symptom of the disorder, but even if it isn't, the patient's level of attention may influence performance on tests of essentially all of the functional areas we have been discussing. A discussion of attention may be aided by invoking a distinction between "wide aperture" and "narrow aperture" attention (Kinsbourne, 1980). Wide aperture attention has to do with the individual's capacity to attend to an array of stimuli at the same time. Attention may be so narrowly focused that the total picture is not appreciated. Tests for neglect may in fact be assessing wide aperture attention. Narrow aperture attention has to do with the capacity to sustain attention to small details. Thus, it can be assessed by vigilance tasks or tests like the Picture Completion subtest of the Wechsler scales. Brain damaged patients may manifest attentional deficits of either type. They may fail to attend to a portion of their perceptual environment, or they may be unable to maintain sufficient concentration to successfully complete tasks requiring sustained occupation with details. Individuals with attentional deficits are often described as distractable or impulsive, and in fact, many brain damaged patients may be accurately characterized by those terms. Thus, the assessment of presence and degree of attention deficit is often a highly clinically relevant activity.

In summary, neuropsychological assessment typically involves the functional areas of: general intellectual capacity; memory; speed and accuracy of psychomotor activity; visual-spatial skills; visual, auditory, and tactile perception; language; and attention. Thus, a comprehensive neuropsychological assessment may be defined as a procedure that at least surveys all of these areas. In practical terms, a survey is all that is feasible if the intent of the assessment is to evaluate all areas. It is obviously generally not feasible to do an in-depth assessment of each of these areas in every patient, nor is it usually necessary to do so.

SPECIAL PROBLEMS IN THE CONSTRUCTION AND STANDARDIZATION OF NEUROPSYCHOLOGICAL TEST BATTERIES

It will be assumed here that neuropsychological tests share the same standardization requirements as all psychological tests. That is, there is the need for appropriate quantification, norms, and related test construction considerations, as well as the need to deal with issues related to validity and

reliability. However, there are some special considerations regarding neuropsychological tests, and we will turn our attention to them here.

Practical Concerns in Test Construction

Neuropsychological test batteries must of necessity be administered to brain damaged patients, many of whom may have severe physical disability, cognitive impairment, or a combination of the two. Thus, stimulus and response characteristics of the tests themselves, as well as the stimulus characteristics of the test instructions, become exceedingly important considerations. Neuropsychological test material should, in general, be constructed with salient stimuli that the patient can readily see or hear and understand. Material to be read should not require high levels of literacy, nor should grammatical structures be unduly complex. With regard to test instructions, the potential for multimodal instruction giving should ideally be available. If the patient cannot see or read, it should be possible to say the instructions, without jeopardizing one's opportunity to use established test norms. The opportunity should be available to repeat and paraphrase instructions until it is clear that they are understood. It is of crucial importance in neuropsychological assessment that the examiner achieve maximum assurance that a test was failed because the patient could not perform the task being assessed, not because the test instructions were not understood. This consideration is of particular importance for the aphasic patient, who may have a profound impairment of language comprehension. With regard to response parameters, efforts should be made to assure that the test response modality is within the patient's repertoire.

In neuropsychological assessment, it is often not failure to perform some specific task that is diagnostic, but failure to perform some component of a series of tasks in the presence of intact function in other areas. As an example, failure to read a passage is not specifically diagnostic, since the inability to read may be associated with a variety of cognitive, perceptual, and learning difficulties. However, failure to be able to transfer a grapheme or a written symbol to a phoneme or sound in the presence of other manifestations of literacy could be quite diagnostic. Individuals with this type of deficit may be able to "sight-read" or recognize words as perceptual patterns, but when asked to read multisyllabic, unfamiliar words, they are unable to break the word down into phonemes and sound it out. In perhaps its most elegant form, neuropsychological assessment can produce what is called a double dissociation (Teuber, 1959); a task consistently failed by patients with a particular type of brain disorder accompanied by a corresponding task that is consistently passed, and the reverse in the case of patients with some other form of brain disorder. Ideally, then, neuropsychological assessment aims at detailed as possible specification of what functional deficits exist in a manner that allows for mapping of these deficits onto known systems in the brain. There are several methods of achieving this goal, and not all neuropsychologists agree with regard to the most productive route. In general, some prefer to examine patients in what may be described as a linear manner, with a series of interlocking tasks involving component abilities, while others prefer using more complex tasks in the form of standard, extensive batteries and interpretation through examination of performance configurations. The linear approach is best exemplified in the work of A. R. Luria and various collaborators (Luria, 1973), while the configural approach is seen in the work of Ward Halstead (Halstead, 1947), Ralph Reitan (Reitan & Davison, 1974) and their many collaborators. In either case, however, the aim of the assessment is largely that of determining the pattern of the patient's preserved and impaired functions and inferring from this pattern what the nature might be of the disturbed brain function. The difficulty with using complex tasks to achieve that end is that such tasks are really only of neuropsychological interest if they can be analyzed by one of the two methods described here.

Issues Related to Validity and Reliability

Neuropsychological assessment has the advantage of being in an area where the potential for development of highly sophisticated validation criteria has been very much realized in recent years and will surely achieve even fuller realization in the near future. We will begin our discussion with this consideration, and so we will first be occupied with the matters of concurrent and predictive validity. A major review of validation studies was accomplished by Klove (1974) and updated by Boll (1981). These reviews essentially only cov-

ered the Wechsler scales and the Halstead-Reitan Battery, but there are several reviews of the work with the Luria-Nebraska Neuropsychological Battery as well (e.g., Golden, 1981). We will not deal with the content of those reviews at this point, but rather focus on the methodological problems involved in establishing concurrent or predictive validity of neuropsychological tests. With regard to concurrent validity, the criterion used in most cases is the objective identification of some central nervous system lesion arrived at independently of the neuropsychological test results. Therefore, validation is generally provided by neurologists or neurosurgeons. Identification of lesions of the brain is particularly problematic because, unlike many organs of the body, the brain cannot usually be visualized directly in the living individual. The major exceptions occur when the patient undergoes brain surgery or receives the rarely used procedure of brain biopsy. In the absence of these procedures, validation is dependent upon autopsy data or the various brain imaging techniques. Autopsy data are not always entirely usable for validation purposes, in that numerous changes may have taken place in the patient's brain between time of testing and time of examination of the brain. Of the various imaging techniques, the CT scan is currently the most fruitful one. Cooperation among neuroradiologists, neurologists, and neuropsychologists has already led to the accomplishment of several important studies correlating quantitative CT scan data with neuropsychological test results (Hill & Mikhael, 1979). Beyond the CT scan, however, we can see the beginnings of even more sensitive indicators, including measures of cerebral metabolism such as the PET scan (Positron Emission Tomography), the Xenon enhanced CT scan, and the advanced imaging techniques that may develop from the new method of nuclear magnetic resonance (NMR). These exciting new developments in brain imaging and observation of brain function will surely provide increasingly definitive criteria for neuropsychological hypotheses and assessment methods.

Within neuropsychological assessment, there appears to have been a progression regarding the relationship between level of inference and criterion. Early studies in the field as well as in the development of new assessment batteries generally addressed themselves to the matter of simple presence or absence of structural brain damage. Thus, the first question raised had to do with the accuracy with which an assessment procedure could discriminate between brain damaged and nonbrain damaged patients, as independently classified by the criterion procedure. In the early studies, the criterion utilized was generally clinical diagnosis, perhaps supported in some cases by neurosurgical data or some laboratory procedure such as a skull X-ray or an EEG. It soon became apparent, however, that many neuropsychological tests were performed at abnormal levels, not only by brain damaged patients, but by patients with several of the functional psychiatric disorders. Since many neuropsychologists worked in neuropsychiatric rather than general medical settings, this matter became particularly problematic. Great efforts were then made to find tests that could discriminate between brain damaged and psychiatric patients or, as sometimes put, between "functional" and "organic" conditions. There have been several reviews of this research, (Goldstein, 1978; Heaton, Baade, & Johnson, 1978; Heaton & Crowley, 1981; Malec, 1978), all of which were critical of the early work in this field in light of current knowledge about several of the functional psychiatric disorders. The chronic schizophrenic patient was particularly problematic, since such patients often performed on neuropsychological tests in a manner indistinguishable from the performance of patients with generalized structural brain damage. By now, this whole issue has been largely reformulated in terms of looking at the neuropsychological aspects of many of the functional psychiatric disorders (e.g., Gruzelier & Flor-Henry, 1979; Henn & Nasrallah, 1982), largely under the influence of the newer biological approaches to psychopathology.

Neuropsychologists working in neurological and neurosurgical settings were becoming increasingly interested in validating their procedures against more refined criteria, notably in the direction of localization of brain function. The question was no longer only whether a lesion was present or absent, but if present, whether or not the tests could predict its location. Major basic research regarding this matter was conducted by H. L. Teuber and various collaborators over a span of many years (Teuber, 1959). This group had access to a large number of veterans who had sustained open head injuries during World War II and the Korean conflict. Because the extent and site of their injuries were exceptionally well documented by neurosurgical and radiological data,

and the lesions were reasonably well localized, these individuals were used productively in a long series of studies in which attempts were made to relate both site of lesion and concomitant neurological defects to performance on an extensive series of neuropsychological procedures ranging from measures of basic sensory functions (Semmes, Weinstein, Ghent, & Teuber, 1960) to complex cognitive skills (Teuber & Weinstein, 1954). Similar work with brain wounded individuals was accomplished by Freda Newcombe and collaborators at Oxford (Newcombe, 1969). These groups tended to concentrate on the major lobes of the brain (frontal, temporal, parietal, and occipital), and would, for example, do contrasts between the performances of patients with frontal and occipital lesions on some particular test or test series (e.g., Teuber, 1964). In another setting, but at about the same time as the Teuber group was beginning its work, Ward Halstead and collaborators conducted a large-scale neuropsychologically oriented study of frontal lobe function (Halstead, 1947). Ralph M. Reitan, who was Halstead's student, adopted several of his procedures, supplemented them, and developed a battery of tests that were extensively utilized in localization studies. Reitan's early work in the localization area was concerned with differences between the two cerebral hemispheres more than with regional localization (Reitan, 1955). The now well-known Wechsler-Bellevue studies of brain lesion lateralization (see review in Reitan, 1966) represented some of the beginnings of this work. The extensive work of Roger Sperry and various collaborators (Sperry, Gazzaniga, & Bogen, 1969) with patients who had undergone cerebral commisurotomy also contributed greatly to validation of neuropsychological tests with regard to the matter of differences between the two hemispheres; particularly the functional asymmetries or cognitive differences. Since the discoveries regarding the major roles of subcortical structures in the mediation of various behaviors (Albert, 1978), neuropsychologists have also been studying the relationships between test performance and lesions in such structures and structure complexes as the limbic system (Scoville & Milner, 1957) and the basal ganglia (Butters, 1983).

The search for validity criteria has become increasingly precise with recent advances in the neurosciences as well as increasing opportunities to collect test data from various patient groups. One major conceptualization largely attributable to Reitan and his coworkers is that localization does not always operate independently with regard to determination of behavioral change, but interacts with type of lesion or the specific process that produced the brain damage. The first reports regarding this matter related to differences in performance between patients with recently acquired lateralized brain damage and those who sustained lateralized brain damage at some time in the remote past (Fitzhugh, Fitzhugh, & Reitan, 1961, 1962). Patients with acute lesions were found to perform differently on tests than patients with chronic lesions. It soon became apparent, through an extremely large number of studies (cf. Filskov & Boll, 1981), that there are many forms of type-locus interaction, and that level and pattern of performance on neuropsychological tests may vary greatly with the particular nature of the brain disorder. This development paralleled such advances in the neurosciences as the discovery of neurotransmitters and the relationship between neurochemical abnormalities and a number of the neurological disorders that historically had been of unknown etiology. We therefore have the beginnings of the development of certain neurochemical validating criteria (Davis, 1983). Indeed, during the process of writing this chapter, the gene responsible for Huntington's disease was discovered. In general, the concurrent validity studies have been quite satisfactory, and many neuropsychological test procedures have been shown to be accurate indicators of many parameters of brain dysfunction. A persistent problem in the past has been the possible tendency of neuropsychological tests to be more sensitive than the criterion measures. In fact, a study by Filskov and Goldstein (1974) demonstrated that neuropsychological tests may predict diagnosis more accurately than many of the individual neurodiagnostic procedures commonly used in assessment of neurological and neurosurgical patients (e.g., skull X-ray). It would appear that with the advent of the CT scan and the even more advanced brain imaging procedures this problem will be diminishing. A related problem involves the establishment of the most accurate and reliable external criterion. We have always taken the position (Goldstein & Shelly, 1982; Russell, Neuringer, & Goldstein, 1970) that no one method can be superior in all cases, and that the best criterion is generally the final medical opinion based on a comprehensive but pertinent evaluation, excluding, or course, behavioral data. In

some cases, for example, the CT scan may be relatively noncontributory, but there may be definitive laboratory findings based on examination of blood or cerebral spinal fluid. In some cases (e.g., Huntington's disease) the family history may be the most crucial part of the evaluation. It is not being maintained here that the best criterion is a doctor's opinion, but rather that no one method can stand out as superior in all cases when dealing with a variety of disorders. The diagnosis is often best established through the integration by an informed individual of data coming from a number of sources. A final problem to be mentioned here is that objective criteria do not yet exist for a number of neurological disorders, but even this problem appears to be undergoing a rapid stage of solution. Most notable in this regard is the *in vivo* differential diagnosis of the degenerative diseases of old age, such as Alzheimer's disease. There is also no objective laboratory marker for multiple sclerosis, and diagnosis of that disorder continues to be made on a clinical basis. Only advances in the neurosciences will lead to ultimate solutions to problems of this type.

In clinical neuropsychology, predictive validity has mainly to do with course of illness. Will the patient get worse, stay the same, or deteriorate? Generally, the best way to answer questions of this type is through longitudinal studies, but very few such studies have actually been done. Even in the area of normal aging, in which many longitudinal studies have been accomplished, there really have been no extensive neuropsychologically oriented longitudinal studies. There is, however, some literature on recovery from stroke, much of which is attributable to the work of Meier and collaborators (Meier, 1974). Levin, Benton, and Grossman (1982) provide a discussion of recovery from closed head injury. Of course, it is generally not possible to do a full neuropsychological assessment immediately following closed head injury, and so prognostic instruments used at that time must be relatively simple ones. In this regard, a procedure known as the Glasgow Coma Scale (Teasdale & Jennett, 1974) has well-established predictive validity. Perhaps one of the most extensive efforts directed toward establishment of the predictive validity of neuropsychological tests was accomplished by Paul Satz and various collaborators, involving the prediction of reading achievement in grade school based on neuropsychological assessments accomplished during kindergarten (Fletcher & Satz, 1980; Satz, Taylor, Friel, &

Fletcher, 1978). At the other end of the age spectrum, there are currently several ongoing longitudinal studies contrasting normal elderly individuals with dementia patients (Danziger, 1983; Wilson & Kaszniak, 1983). However, we do not yet know from these studies and other ongoing longitudinal investigations what the best prognostic instruments are for predicting the course of dementia or for determining whether or not an elderly individual suspected of having dementia will deteriorate or not.

An important aspect of predictive validity has to do with prediction of treatment and rehabilitation outcome. Ben-Yishay, Gerstman, Diller, and Haas (1970) were able to show that a battery of neuropsychological tests could successfully predict length of time in rehabilitation and functional outcome in patients with left hemiplegia. There have been several studies (reviewed by Parsons & Farr, 1981) concerned with predicting outcome of alcoholism treatment on the basis of neuropsychological test performance. The results of these studies are mixed, but in general it would appear that test performance during the early stages of treatment may bear some relationship to outcome as evaluated by follow-up. Before leaving this area, it should be mentioned that there are several not fully documented but apparently reasonable clinical principles related to prediction of treatment outcome. In general, patients with relatively well-circumscribed deficits and perhaps underlying structural lesions, tend to do better in treatment than do patients with more global deficits. There are some data that suggest that early intervention for aphasic adults, perhaps within 2 months postonset, is more effective than treatment initiated later (Wertz, 1983). Ben-Yishay, Diller, Gerstman, and Gordon (1970) have suggested that initial level of competence on a task to be trained is related to ability to profit from cues utilized in the training procedure.

In general, studies of predictive validity in neuropsychological assessment have not been as extensive as studies involving concurrent validity. However, the data available suggest that neuropsychological tests can predict degree of recovery or deterioration to some extent and have some capacity to predict treatment outcome. Since many neurological disorders change over time, getting better or worse, and the treatment of neurological disorders is becoming an increasingly active field (Reisberg, Ferris, & Gershon, 1980), it is often important to have some foreknowledge of

what will happen to the patient in the future in a specific rather than general way and to determine whether or not the patient is a good candidate for some form of treatment. The extent to which neuropsychological assessment can provide this prognostic information will surely be associated with the degree of its acceptance in clinical settings.

Studies of the construct validity of neuropsychological tests represent a great amount of the corpus of basic clinical neuropsychological research. Neuropsychology abounds with constructs: short-term memory, attention, visual-spatial skills, psychomotor speed, motor engrams, and cell-assemblies. Tests are commonly characterized by the construct they purport to measure; Test A is a test of long-term memory; Test B is a test of attention; Test C is a test of abstraction ability; Test D is a measure of biological intelligence, etc. Sometimes we fail to recognize constructs as such because they are so well established, but concepts like memory, intelligence, and attention are in fact theoretical entities used to describe certain classes of observable behaviors. Within neuropsychology, the process of construct validation generally begins with an attempt to find a measure that evaluates some concept. Let us begin with a simple example, say the desire to develop a test for memory. Memory, as a neuropsychological construct, would involve a brain-behavior relationship. That is, neuropsychologists are concerned with how the brain mediates memory and with how impaired brain function affects memory. There are memory tests available, notably the Wechsler Memory Scale (Wechsler & Stone, 1945), but without experimental studies, that scale would only have face validity; that is, it appears to be a test of memory on the basis of the nature of the test items. However, if we ask the related questions, "Does the patient who does well on the scale have a normal memory?" and "Does the patient who does poorly on the scale have an abnormal memory?" we would have to know more about the test in regard to how well it assesses memory as a construct. Reasonable alternative hypotheses might be that the scale measures intelligence, educational level, or attention, or that these influences confound the test such that impairment of memory *per se* cannot be unequivocally identified.

The problem may be approached in numerous ways. A factor analytic strategy may be used in which subtests of the Wechsler Memory Scale are placed into a factor analysis along with educational level and tests of intelligence and attention. It may be found that the memory scale subtests load on their own factor or on factors that receive high loadings from the intelligence and attention tests or from educational level. Another approach may involve giving the test to patients with amnesia and to nonamnesic brain damaged patients. A more sophisticated study may involve administering the Wechsler Memory Scale to these subjects along with other tests. Studies of these types may reveal some of the following hypothetical findings. The Wechsler Memory Scale is highly correlated with IQ, and so it is not possible to tell whether it measures the construct memory specifically or intellectual ability. Some patients cannot repeat stories read to them because they are aphasic and cannot produce words, not because of poor memories. Therefore, interpretation of the measure as an indicator of memory ability cannot be made unequivocally in certain populations. Certain amnesic patients do exceedingly poorly on certain components of the Wechsler Memory Scale, but well on other components. Such a finding would suggest that memory, as a neuropsychological construct, requires further refinement, since there appears to be a dissociation in patients known to have profound loss of memory between certain memory skills that are intact and others that are severely impaired. Still another approach, suggested by Cronbach (1960), is correlation with practical criteria. Individuals given the Wechsler Memory Scale could be asked to perform a number of tasks all of which involve practical memory in some way, and the obtained data could be analyzed in terms of what parts of the scale predict success or failure at the various tasks.

It is particularly important to note that, at least in recent years, the construct validation of neuropsychological tests has involved a multidisciplinary effort with colleagues in cognitive psychology, the experimental psychology of memory and learning (utilizing both human studies and animal models), linguistics, and sensory and perceptual processes. For example, aphasia testing has been profoundly influenced by basic research in psycholinguistics (Blumstein, 1981), while memory testing has been correspondingly influenced by recent developments in information theory and the experimental psychology of memory and learning (Butters & Cermak, 1980). These experimental foundations have aided significantly in the interpretation of clinical tests, and indeed, many new clinical tests are actually derived from laboratory procedures.

While neuropsychological tests should ideally have reliability levels commensurate with other areas of psychometrics, there are some relatively unique problems. These problems are particularly acute when the test-retest method is used to determine the reliability coefficients. The basic problem is that this method really assumes the stability of the subject over testing occasions. When reliability coefficients are established through the retesting of adults over a relatively brief time period that assumption is a reasonable one, but it is not as reasonable in samples of brain damaged patients who may be rapidly deteriorating or recovering. Indeed, it is generally thought to be an asset when a test reflects the appropriate changes. Another difficulty with the test-retest method is that many neuropsychological tests are not really repeatable because of substantial practice effects. The split-half method is seldom applicable, since most neuropsychological tests do not consist of lengthy lists of items, readily allowing for odd-even or other split-half comparisons. In the light of these difficulties, the admittedly small number of reliability studies done with the standard neuropsychological tests batteries have yielded perhaps surprisingly good results. Boll (1981) has recently reviewed reliability studies done with the Halstead-Reitan Battery, while the test manual (Golden, Hammeke, & Purisch, 1980) reports reliability data for the Luria-Nebraska Battery. The details of these matters will be discussed later in our reviews of these two procedures. In any event, it seems safe to say that most neuropsychological test developers have not been greatly preoccupied with the reliabilities of their procedures, but those who have studied the matter appear to have provided sufficient data to permit the conclusion that the standard, commonly used procedures are at least not so unreliable as to impair the validities of those procedures.

AN INTRODUCTION TO THE COMPREHENSIVE BATTERIES

The number of generally available comprehensive standard neuropsychological test batteries for adults is not entirely clear. *The Handbook of Clinical Neuropsychology* (Filskov & Boll, 1981) only contains chapters on two batteries: the Halstead-Reitan and Luria-Nebraska. Lezak (1983) lists the Halstead-Reitan, the Smith Neuropsychological Battery, and two versions of batteries derived from Luria's work; one by Christensen (1975a, 1975b, 1975c) and Golden, Hammeke, and Purisch's Luria-Nebraska (originally South Dakota) Battery (1980). Jones and Butters (1983) reviewed the Halstead-Reitan, Luria-Nebraska, and Michigan batteries. In this chapter, we will only consider the Halstead-Reitan and Luria-Nebraska procedures. The Michigan Battery (Smith, 1975) will not be reviewed, primarily because it consists largely of a series of standardized tests, all of which have their own validity and reliability literature. This literature is thoroughly reviewed by Lezak (1983).

The Halstead-Reitan Battery

History

The history of this procedure and its founders has recently been reviewed by Reed (1983). He traces the beginnings of the battery to the special laboratory established by Halstead in 1935 for the study of neurosurgical patients. The first major report on the findings of this laboratory appeared in a book called *Brain and Intelligence: A Quantitative Study of the Frontal Lobes* (Halstead, 1947), the title of which suggests that the original intent of Halstead's tests was describing frontal lobe function. In this book, Halstead proposed his theory of "Biological Intelligence" and presented what was probably the first factor analysis done with neuropsychological test data. Perhaps more significantly, however, the book contains descriptions of many of the tests now contained in the Halstead-Reitan battery. As Reed (1983) suggests, the theory of "Biological Intelligence" never was widely accepted among neuropsychologists, and the factor analysis had its mathematical problems. But several of the tests that went into that analysis survived, and many of them are commonly used at present. In historical perspective, Halstead's major contributions to neuropsychological assessment, in addition to his very useful tests, include the concept of the neuropsychological laboratory in which objective tests are administered in standard fashions and quantitatively scored, and the concept of the impairment index, a global rating of severity of impairment and probability of the presence of structural brain damage.

Ralph M. Reitan was a student of Halstead at Chicago and was strongly influenced by Halstead's theories and methods. Reitan adopted the methods in the form of the various test procedures and with them established a laboratory at the University of Indiana. He supplemented these tests with a number of additional procedures in order to obtain greater comprehensiveness and initiated a clinical research program that is ongoing. The program began with a cross-validation of the battery and went on into numerous areas, including validation of new tests added to the battery (e.g., the Trail Making test), lateralization and localization of function, aging, and neuropsychological aspects of a wide variety of disorders such as alcoholism, hypertension, disorders of children, and mental retardation. Theoretical matters were also considered. Some of the major contributions included the concept of type-locus interaction (Reitan, 1966), the analysis of quantitative as opposed to qualitative deficits associated with brain dysfunction (Reitan, 1958, 1959), the concept of the brain-age quotient (Reitan, 1973), and the scheme for levels and types of inference in interpretation of neuropsychological test data (Reitan & Davison, 1974). In addition to the published research, Reitan and his collaborators developed a highly sophisticated method of blind clinical interpretation of the Halstead-Reitan Battery that continues to be taught at workshops conducted by Dr. Reitan and associates. The Halstead-Reitan Battery, as the procedure came to be known over the years, also has a history. It has been described as a "fixed battery," but that is not actually the case. Lezak (1976) says in reference to this development, "This set of tests has grown by accretion and revision and continues to be revised" (p. 440). Halstead's original battery, upon which the factor analyses were based, included the Carl Hollow Square test, the Dynamic Visual Field Test, the Henmon-Nelson tests of mental ability, a flicker fusion procedure, and the Time Sense test. None of these procedures are now widely used, although the Time Sense and Flicker Fusion tests were originally included in the battery used by Reitan. The tests that survived included the Category test, the Tactual Performance test, the Speech Perception test, and Finger Tapping. Halstead also used the Seashore Rhythm test, which is included in the current version of the battery, but was not included in the subbattery used by Halstead in his factor analyses. There have been numerous additions, including the various Wechsler Intelligence Scales, the Trail Making test, a subbattery of perceptual tests, the

Reitan Aphasia Screening test, the Klove Grooved Pegboard, and other tests that are used in some laboratories but not in others. Alternative methods have also been developed for computing the impairment index (Russell, Neuringer, & Goldstein, 1970).

Bringing this brief history into the present, the Halstead-Reitan Battery continues to be widely used as a clinical and research procedure. Numerous investigators utilize it in their research (e.g., Goldstein & Shelly, 1972; Vega & Parsons, 1967), and there have been several successful cross-validations done in settings other than Reitan's laboratory. In addition to the continuation of factor analytic work with the battery, several investigators have applied other forms of multivariate analysis to it in various research applications. Several investigations have been conducted relative to objectifying and even computerizing interpretation of the battery, the most well-known efforts probably being the Selz-Reitan rules for classification of brain function in older children (Selz & Reitan, 1979) and the Russell, Neuringer and Goldstein "Neuropsychological Keys" (Russell et al., 1970). The issue of reliability of the battery has recently been addressed, with reasonably successful results. Clinical interpretation of the battery continues to be taught at workshops and in numerous programs engaged in training of professional psychologists.

Structure and Content

Although there are several versions of the Halstead-Reitan Battery, the differences tend to be minor, and there appears to be a core set of procedures that essentially all versions of the battery contain. The battery must be administered in a laboratory containing a number of items of equipment and generally cannot be completely administered at bedside. Various estimates of length of administration are given, but it is probably best to plan on about 6 to 8 hours of patient time. Each test of the battery is independent and may be administered separately from the other tests. However, it is generally assumed that a certain number of the tests must be administered in order to compute an impairment index.

Scoring for the Halstead-Reitan varies with the particular test, such that individual scores may be expressed in time to completion, errors, number correct, or some form of derived score. For research purposes, these scores are generally converted to standard scores so that they may be profiled. Matthews (1981) routinely uses a T score profile in clinical practice, while Russell et al. (1970) rate all of the tests contributing to the impairment index on a 6-point scale, the data being displayed as a profile of the ratings. In their system the impairment index may be computed by calculating the proportion of tests performed in the brain damaged range according to published cut-off scores (Reitan, 1955) or by calculating the average of the ratings. This latter procedure provides a value called the Average Impairment Rating. Russell el al. (1970) have also provided quantitative scoring systems for the Reitan Aphasia Screening test and for the drawing of a Greek cross that is part of that test. However, some clinicians do not quantify those procedures, except in the form of counting the number of aphasic symptoms elicited. We will return to other aspects of the battery's structure after the following description of the component tests.

A. Halstead's Biological Intelligence Tests

1. The Halstead Category Test: This test is a concept identification procedure in which the subject must discover the concept or principle that governs various series of geometric forms, verbal, and numerical material. The apparatus for the test includes a display screen with four horizontally arranged numbered switches placed beneath it. The stimuli are on slides, and the examiner uses a control console to administer the procedure. The subject is asked to press the switch that the picture reminds him or her of, and is provided with additional instructions to the effect that the point of the test is to see how well he or she can learn the concept, idea, or principle that connects the pictures. If the correct switch is pressed, the subject hears a pleasant chime, while wrong answers are associated with a rasping buzzer. The conventionally used score is the total number of errors for the seven groups of stimuli that form the test.

2. The Halstead Tactual Performance Test: This procedure utilizes a version of the Seguin-Goddard Formboard, but it is done blindfolded. The subject's task is to place all of the 10 blocks into the board, using only the sense of touch. The task is repeated three times, once with the preferred hand, once with the nonpreferred

hand and once with both hands, following which the board is removed. After removing the blindfold, the subject is asked to draw a picture of the board, filling in all of the blocks he or she remembers in their proper locations on the board. Scores from this test include time to complete the task for each of the three trials, total time, number of blocks correctly drawn, and number of blocks correctly drawn in their proper locations on the board.

3. The Speech Perception Test: The subject is asked to listen to a series of 60 sounds, each of which consist of a double e digraph with varying prefixes and suffixes (e.g., geend). The test is given in a four alternative multiple choice format, the task being that of underlining on an answer sheet the sound heard. The score is number of errors.

4. The Seashore Rhythm Test: This test consists of 30 pairs of rhythmic patterns. The task is to judge whether the two members of each pair are the same as or different from each other and to record the response by writing an S or a D on an answer sheet. The score is either number correct or number of errors.

5. Finger Tapping: The subject is asked to tap his or her extended index finger on a typewriter key attached to a mechanical counter. Several series of 10-second trials are run, with both the right and left hand. The scores are average number of taps, generally over five trials, for the right and left hand.

B. *Tests Added to the Battery by Reitan*

1. The Wechsler Intelligence Scales: Some clinicians continue to use the Wechsler-Bellevue, some the WAIS, and some the WAIS-R. In any event, the test is given according to manual instructions and is not modified in any way.

2. The Trail Making Test: In Part A of this procedure the subject must connect in order a series of circled numbers randomly scattered over a sheet of 8½ × 11 paper. In part B, there are circled numbers and letters, and the subject's task involves alternating between numbers and letters in serial order (e.g., 1 to A to 2 to B, etc.). The score is time to completion expressed in seconds for each part.

3. The Reitan Aphasia Screening Test: This test serves two purposes in that it contains both copying and language related tasks. As an aphasia screening procedure, it provides a

brief survey of the major language functions: naming, repetition, spelling, reading, writing, calculation, narrative speech, and right-left orientation. The copying tasks involve having the subject copy a square, Greek cross, triangle, and key. The first three items must each be drawn in one continuous line. The language section may be scored by listing the number of aphasic symptoms or by using the Russell et al. quantitative system. The drawings are not formally scored or are rated through a matching to model system also provided by Russell et al.

4. Perceptual Disorders: These procedures actually constitute a subbattery and include tests of the subject's ability to recognize shapes and identify numbers written on the fingertips, as well as tests of finger discrimination and visual, auditory, and tactile neglect. Number of errors is the score for all of these procedures.

C. *Tests Added to the Battery by Others*

1. The Klove Grooved Pegboard Test: The subject must place pegs shaped like keys into a board containing recesses that are oriented in randomly varying directions. The test is administered twice, once with the right and once with the left hand. Scores are time to completion in seconds for each hand and errors for each hand, defined as number of pegs dropped during performance of the task.

2. The Klove Roughness Discrimination Test: The subject must order four blocks covered with varying grades of sandpaper presented behind a blind with regard to degree of roughness. Time and error scores are recorded for each hand.

3. Visual Field Examination: Russell et al., (1970) include a formal visual field examination utilizing a perimeter as part of their assessment procedure.

It should be noted that many clinicians, including Reitan and his collaborators, frequently administer a number of additional tests mainly for purposes of assessing personality and level of academic achievement. The MMPI is the major personality assessment method used, and achievement may be assessed with such procedures as the Wide Range Achievement Test (Jastak & Jastak, 1965) or the Peabody Individual Achievement Test (Dunn & Markwardt, 1970). Some clinicians have also adopted the procedure of adding the Wechsler Memory Scale to the battery, either in its original form (Wechsler & Stone, 1945) or the Russell modification (Russell, 1975a). Some form of lateral dominance examination is also generally administered, including tests for handedness, footedness, and eyedness.

Quantitative Structural
Considerations

Factor analysis is probably the clearest way of providing a quantitative description of the structure of a test battery. Many such analyses have been accomplished with the Halstead and Halstead-Reitan Battery, going back to Halstead's (1947) original work. Unfortunately, it is exceed-

ingly difficult to compare one factor analytic study with another, largely because the battery has not remained stable over the years. For example, Halstead's original factor analysis involved the Flicker Fusion and Dynamic Visual Field tests, procedures that are rarely if ever used in current versions of the battery. Similarly, more recent factor analytic studies (Newby, Hallenbeck, & Embretson, 1983; Swiercinsky, 1979) utilized the Wechsler Memory Scale and other procedures that Halstead did not use, nor do many users of the battery. We will therefore take the solution of using some of our own factor analytic work (Goldstein & Shelly, 1971, 1972) as illustrative of the results one might achieve using a

TABLE 10.1. TWO FACTOR ANALYSES OF THE HALSTEAD-REITAN BATTERY.

Test	Rotated Factor Loadings for Alcoholic Group					Rotated Factor Loadings for General Psychiatric Group			
	1	2	3	4	5	1	2	3	4
WAIS Information	.87	.14	− .05	− .04	.06	.81	.20	− .04	.00
WAIS Comprehension	.70	.08	.14	.09	.05	.72	.22	.03	.04
WAIS Similarities	.69	.11	.11	.19	.08	.73	.25	.07	.06
WAIS Vocabulary	.84	− .05	.19	− .02	.20	.88	.12	− .02	.04
WAIS Picture Completion	.68	.37	.30	.22	.02	.52	.56	.18	.14
Aphasia Screening	.51	− .12	.15	.25	.17	.68	.21	.27	.08
WAIS Block Design	.03	.50	.39	.30	.20	.40	.62	.30	.15
WAIS Object Assembly	.13	.82	.41	.05	.16	.29	.63	.27	.11
Perceptual Disorders	.19	.61	.33	.16	.27				
Finger Agnosia—R						.20	.15	.64	.14
Finger Agnosia—L						.14	.24	.66	.09
Finger Writing—R						.07	.32	.60	.17
Finger Writing—L						− .01	.31	.60	.10
Halstead Category	.09	.68	− .03	.10	.25	.38	.55	.34	.07
Trail Making	.04	.64	.44	.17	.18	.42	.51	.32	.11
Tactual Performance Test—Time	− .02	.55	.36	.40	.08	.10	.69	.27	.20
WAIS Digit Symbol	.19	.18	.67	.22	.15	.41	.53	.32	.29
WAIS Picture Arrangement	.33	.25	.52	.11	− .03	.44	.60	.21	.12
Speech Perception	.38	.21	.51	− .11	− .03	.59	.24	.34	.19
Finger Tapping—DH	.06	.14	.71	.15	− .10	.08	.16	.20	.92
Finger Tapping—NDH						.10	.22	.17	.62
Seashore Rhythm	.10	.17	.69	.12	.20	.41	.24	.27	.13
Tactual Performance Test—Memory	.33	.38	.12	.79	− .15	.24	.65	.20	.14
Tactual Performance Test—Location	.09	.14	.20	.61	.04	.21	.60	.16	.07
WAIS Arithmetic	.20	.33	− .02	.07	.63	.64	.30	.23	.02
WAIS Digit Span	.38	.13	.24	− .18	.50	.57	.20	.20	.14
% of Original Variance Explained	18.26	14.86	14.23	7.72	5.03	22.29	17.41	10.75	6.50

Note. Some of the scores have been reflected so that higher scores always indicate above average performance.

reasonably stripped down, core battery involving only Halstead's original tests that remain in common use, the WAIS and the other procedures added to the battery by Reitan. The first of the two analyses utilized a sample of 50 alcoholic inpatients, while the second utilized a sample of 619 neuropsychiatric inpatients with miscellaneous diagnoses. The rotated factor matrices, presented in Table 10.1, are similar in some respects and dissimilar in others.

In both cases, the WAIS verbal subtests in combination with the aphasia screening test form a grouping (Factor 1) that clearly taps language abilities. There is a second factor largely contributed to by the WAIS performance tests, the Category test, and the speed component of the Tactual Performance test. The Finger Tapping test shows a different pattern in the two studies. In the analysis involving only the alcoholic patients, it loads on a factor along with several other tests, including WAIS Digit Symbol and the Seashore Rhythm test. In the case of the larger, more miscellaneous sample, Finger Tapping essentially achieves simple structure, forming its own factor. Thus, what the two factor analyses have in common are a verbal and a complex problem-solving factor. In the case of the alcoholic sample, there are three other factors, one that we have described as involving perceptual and motor skills, one that receives salient loadings only from the memory and location components of the Tactual Performance Test, and one that receives loadings from the two WAIS numerical tests, Arithmetic and Digit Span. There was a total of only four factors extracted for the large miscellaneous sample: the language and problem-solving factors noted above, a factor that received substantial loadings only from the tactual functions perceptual tests, and a factor that only received high loadings from the Finger Tapping test. While the factor analyses probably differ from each other because of differences in the samples and the specifics of the variables included (which were not precisely the same), the two analyses taken together provide a reasonably good impression of the abilities tapped by the Halstead-Reitan. They can readily be described as verbal skills, complex problem-solving abilities, and various perceptual and motor skills. In some cases, a purely numerical ability factor may emerge as well as a factor representing the nonverbal memory abilities involved in the memory and location components of the Tactual Performance test. In general, using standard fac-

tor extraction termination procedures, in our case Kaiser's rule (Kaiser, 1960), the battery seems to be satisfactorily structured into four or five factors. It is interesting to note that the original Halstead analysis (1947), even with its different tests and different factoring methods, also generated four factors.

Theoretical Foundations

There are really two theoretical bases for the Halstead-Reitan Battery, one contained in *Brain and Intelligence* and related writings of Halstead, the other in numerous papers and chapters written by Reitan and various collaborators (e.g., Reitan, 1966). They are quite different from each other in many ways, and the difference may be partly accounted for by the fact that Halstead was not primarily a practicing clinician and was not particularly interested in developing his tests as psychometric instruments to be used in clinical assessment of patients. Indeed, he never published the tests. He was more interested in utilizing the tests to answer basic scientific questions in the area of brain-behavior relationships in general and frontal lobe function in particular. Reitan's program, on the other hand, can be conceptualized as an effort to demonstrate the usefulness and accuracy of Halstead's tests and related procedures in clinical assessment of brain damaged patients. It is probably fair to say that Halstead's theory of biological intelligence and its factor analytically based four components (the central integrative field, abstraction, power, and the directional factor), as well as his empirical findings concerning human frontal lobe function have not become major forces in modern clinical neuropsychology. However, they have had, in my view, a more subtle influence on the field.

Halstead was really the first to establish a human neuropsychology laboratory in which patients were administered objective tests, some of which were semiautomated, utilizing standard procedures and sets of instructions. His Chicago laboratory may have been the initial stimulus for the now common practice of trained technician administration of neuropsychological tests. Halstead was also the first to utilize sophisticated, multivariate statistics in the analysis of neuropsychological test data. Even though Reitan did not pursue that course to any great extent, other researchers with the Halstead-Reitan Battery have done so (e.g., Goldstein & Shelly, 1971, 1972).

Thus, though the specifics of Halstead's theoretical work have not become well known and widely applied, the concept of a standard neuropsychological battery administered under laboratory conditions and consisting of objective, quantifiable procedures has made a major impact on the field of clinical neuropsychology. The other, perhaps more philosophical contribution of Halstead was what might be described as his Darwinian approach to neuropsychology. He viewed his discriminating tests as measures of adaptive abilities, as skills that assured man's survival on the planet. Many neuropsychologists are now greatly concerned with the relevance of their test procedures to adaptation—the capacity to carry on functional activities of daily living and to live independently (Heaton & Pendleton, 1981). This general philosophy is somewhat different from the more traditional models emanating from behavioral neurology, in which there is a much greater emphasis on the more medical-pathological implications of behavioral test findings.

Reitan, while always sympathetic with Halstead's thinking, never developed a theoretical system in the form of a brain model or a general theory of the biological intelligence type. One could say that Reitan's great concern has always been with the empirical validity of test procedures. Such validity can only be established through the collection of large amounts of data obtained from patients with reasonably complete documentation of their medical/neurological conditions. Both presence and absence of brain damage had to be well documented, and if present, findings related to site and type of lesion had to be well established. He has described his work informally as one large experiment, necessitating maximal consistency in the procedures used, and to some extent, the methods of analyzing the data. Reitan and his various collaborators represent the group that was primarily responsible for introduction of the standard battery approach to clinical neuropsychology. It is clear from reviewing the Reitan groups' work that there is substantial emphasis on performing controlled studies with samples sufficiently large to allow for application of conventional statistical procedures. One also gets the impression of an ongoing program in which initial findings are qualified and refined through subsequent studies.

It would probably be fair to say that the major thrust of Reitan's research and writings has not been espousal of some particular theory of brain function, but rather an extended examination of the inferences that can be made from behavioral indices relative to the condition to the brain. There is a great emphasis on methods of drawing such inferences in the case of the individual patient. Thus, this group's work has always involved empirical research and clinical interpretation, with one feeding into the other. In this regard, there has been a formulation of inferential methods used in neuropsychology (Boll, 1981; Reitan, 1974) that provides a framework for clinical interpretation. Four methods are outlined: level of performance, pattern of performance, specific behavioral deficits (pathognomonic signs) and right-left comparisons. In other words, one examines for whether or not the patient's general level of adaptive function compares with that of normal individuals, whether there is some characteristic performance profile that suggests impairment even though the average score may be within normal limits, whether there are unequivocal individual signs of deficits, and whether there is a marked discrepancy in functioning between the two sides of the body.

In general then, Reitan's theoretical framework is basically empirical, objective, and data oriented. An extensive research program, by now of about 30 years' duration, has provided the information needed to make increasingly sophisticated inferences from neuropsychological tests. It thereby constitutes to a significant extent the basis for clinical interpretation. The part of the system that remains subjective is the interpretation itself, but in that regard, Reitan (1974) has made the following remark: "Additional statistical methods may be appropriate for this problem but, in any case, progress is urgently needed to replace the subjective decisionmaking processes in individual interpretation that presently are necessary" (p. 46).

Standardization Research

The Halstead-Reitan Battery, as a whole, meets rigorous validity requirements. Following Halstead's initial validation (1947) it was cross-validated by Reitan (1955) and in several other laboratories (Russell et al., 1970; Vega & Parsons, 1967). As indicated above, reviews of validity studies with the Halstead-Reitan Battery have been written by Klove (1974) and Boll (1981).

Validity, in this sense, means that all component tests of the battery that contribute to the impairment index discriminate at levels satisfactory for producing usable cut-off scores for distinguishing between brain damaged and nonbrain damaged patients. The major exceptions, the Time Sense and Flicker Fusion tests, have been dropped from the battery by most of its users. In general, the validation criteria for these studies consisted of neurosurgical and other definitive neurological data. It may be mentioned, however, that most of these studies were accomplished before the advent of the CT scan, and it would probably now be possible to do more sophisticated validity studies, perhaps through correlating extent of impairment with quantitative measures of brain damage (e.g., CT scan density measures). In addition to what was done with Halstead's tests, validity studies were accomplished with tests added to the battery such as the Wechsler scales, the Trail Making test and the Reitan Aphasia Screening test, with generally satisfactory results (Reitan, 1966).

By virtue of the level of inferences made by clinicians from Halstead-Reitan Battery data, validity studies must obviously go beyond the question of presence or absence of brain damage. The first issue raised related to discriminative validity between patients with left hemisphere and right hemisphere brain damage. Such measures as Finger Tapping, the Tactual Performance test, the perceptual disorders subbattery, and the Reitan Aphasia Screening test all were reported as having adequate discriminative validity in this regard. There have been very few studies, however, that go further and provide validity data related to more specific criteria such as localization and type of lesion. It would appear from one impressive study (Reitan, 1964) that valid inferences concerning prediction at this level must be made clinically, and one cannot call upon the standard univariate statistical procedures to make the necessary discriminations. This study provided the major impetus for Russell et al.'s (1970) neuropsychological key approach, which was in essence an attempt to objectify higher order inferences.

There is one general area in which the discriminative validity of the Halstead-Reitan Battery is not particularly robust. The battery does not have great capacity to discriminate between brain damaged patients and patients with functional psychiatric disorders; notably chronic schizophrenia. There is an extensive literature concerning this matter, but it should be said that some of the research contained in this literature has significant methodological flaws, leaving the findings ambiguous. It may also be pointed out that the constructors of the Halstead-Reitan did not have the intention of developing a procedure to discriminate between brain damaged and schizophrenic patients, and the assumption that it should be able to do so is somewhat gratuitous. Furthermore, Heaton and Crowley (1981) find that with the exception of the diagnosis of chronic schizophrenia, the Halstead-Reitan Battery does a reasonably good job of differential diagnosis. They provided the following conclusion:

> The bulk of the evidence . . . suggests that for most psychiatric patient groups there is little or no relationship between the degree of emotional disturbance and level of performance on neuropsychological tests. However, significant correlations of this type are sometimes found with schizophrenic groups. (p. 492)

This matter remains controversial and has become exceedingly complex, particularly since the discovery of cerebral atrophy in a substantial portion of the schizophrenic population and the development of hypotheses concerning left hemisphere dysfunction in schizophrenics (Flor-Henry & Yeudall, 1979). The point to be made here is that the user of the Halstead-Reitan Battery should exercise caution in interpretation when asked to use the battery in resolving questions related to differential diagnosis between brain damage and schizophrenia. Some writers have advised the addition of some measure of psychiatric disability, such as the MMPI, when doing such assessments (Russell, 1975b, 1977).

Even though there have been several studies of the predictive validity of neuropsychological tests with children (Fletcher & Satz, 1980; Rourke, 1983) and other studies with adults that did not utilize the full Halstead-Reitan Battery (Meier, 1974), I know of no major formal assessment of the predictive validity of the Halstead-Reitan Battery accomplished with adults. Within neuropsychology, predictive validity has two aspects: predicting everyday academic, vocational, and social functioning and predicting course of illness. With regard to the former matter, Heaton and Pendleton (1981) document the lack of predictive validity studies using extensive batteries of the

Halstead-Reitan type. However, they do report one study (Newman, Heaton, & Lehman, 1978) in which the Halstead-Reitan successfully predicted employment status on 6-month follow-up. With regard to prediction of course of illness, there appears to be a good deal of clinical expertise in this regard, but no major formal studies in which the battery's capacity to predict whether the patient will get better, worse, or stay the same are evaluated. This matter is of particular significance in such conditions as head injury and stroke, since outcome tends to be quite variable in these conditions. However, it is necessary to point out that administration of procedures of the Halstead-Reitan type is often infeasible during the early stages of these conditions. The changes that occur during those stages are often the most significant ones related to prognosis (e.g., length of time unconscious).

In general, there has not been a great deal of emphasis on studies involving the reliability of the Halstead-Reitan Battery, probably because of the nature of the tests themselves, particularly with regard to the practice effect problem, and because of the changing nature of those patients for whom the battery was developed. Those reliability studies that were done produced satisfactory results, particularly with regard to the reliability of the impairment index (Boll, 1981). The Category Test can have its reliability assessed through the split-half method. In a study accomplished by Shaw (1966), a .98 reliability coefficient was obtained.

Norms for the Halstead-Reitan are available in numerous places (Russell et al., 1970; Vega & Parsons, 1967), but since the battery was never published as a single procedure, there is no published manual that one can refer to for definitive information. There are no published age or education corrected norms, although several laboratories have accumulated local norms. A great deal is known about the influence of age and education on the various tests in the Halstead-Reitan Battery, but this information was never consolidated into tables of norms or through the formulation of equations for calculating appropriate corrections. Similarly, sex differences generally reported only appear on Finger Tapping, with women tapping slightly more slowly than men. It is somewhat unusual for a procedure in as widespread use as the Halstead-Reitan not to have a commercially published manual, but Dr. Reitan has prepared an unpublished manual containing detailed instructions concerning administration

and scoring of the tests, and Swiercinsky (1978) has published a manual covering much of the same material.

In summary, the validity of the Halstead-Reitan seems well established by literally hundreds of studies, including several major cross-validations. These studies have implications for the concurrent, predictive, and construct validity of the battery. Reliability has not received nearly as much attention, but it seems apparent that the battery is sufficiently reliable to not compromise its validity. There are no published age or education related norms, but the relevance of such norms to neuropsychological assessment, particularly with regard to age, is a controversial and unsettled matter. There is no commercially available manual for the battery, and so the usual kinds of information generally contained in a manual are not available to the test user in a single place. However, the relevant information is available in a number of separate sources.

Evaluation

The Halstead-Reitan Battery is without doubt the most widely used standard neuropsychological battery, at least in North America and perhaps throughout the world. Aside from its widespread clinical application, it is used in many multidisciplinary research programs as the procedure of choice for neuropsychological assessment. It therefore has taken on something of a definitive status and is viewed by many experts in the field as the state-of-the-art instrument for comprehensive neuropsychological assessment. Nevertheless, several criticisms of it have emerged over the years, and some of them will be reviewed here. Each major criticism will be itemized and discussed.

1. *The Halstead-Reitan Battery is too long and redundant.* The implication of this criticism is that pertinent, clinically relevant neuropsychological assessment can be accomplished in subsequently less time than the 6–8 hours generally required to administer the full Halstead-Reitan battery. Other batteries are, in fact, substantially briefer than the Halstead-Reitan. Aside from simply giving fewer or briefer tests, another means suggested of shortening neuropsychological assessment is through a targeted, individualized approach rather than through routine administration of a complete battery. The difficulty with this latter alternative is that such an approach can

generally only be conducted by an experienced clinician, and one sacrifices the clinician time and expense that can be saved through administration by trained technicians. The response to the criticism concerning length is generally that shortening of the battery correspondingly reduces its comprehensiveness, and one sacrifices examination of areas that may be of crucial significance in individual cases. Indeed, the battery approach was, in part, a reaction to the naiveté inherent in the use of single tests for "brain damage." The extent to which the clinician reverts to a single test approach may reflect the extent to which there is a return to the simplistic thinking of the past. In general, the argument is that to adequately cover what must be covered in a standard, comprehensive assessment the length of the procedure is a necessity. From the point of view of patient comfort and fatigue, the battery can be administered in several sessions over a period of days if necessary.

2. *The tests in the Halstead-Reitan Battery are insufficiently specific, both in regard to the functions they assess and the underlying cerebral correlates of those functions.* Most of the tests in the battery are quite complex, and it is often difficult to isolate the source of impairment within the context of a single test. Even as apparently simple a procedure as the Speech Perception test requires not only the ability to discriminate sounds, but to read, make the appropriate written response, and attend to the task. Therefore, failure on the test cannot unequivocally point to a specific difficulty with auditory discrimination. Difficulties of this type are even more pronounced in such highly complex procedures as the Category and Tactual Performance tests. This criticism eventuates in the conclusion that it is difficult to say anything meaningful about the patient's brain or about treatment because one cannot isolate the specific deficit. In Luria's (1973) terminology one cannot isolate the functional system that is involved, no less the link in that system that is impaired. Failure to do so makes it difficult if not impossible to identify the structures in the brain that are involved in the patient's impairment as well as to formulate a rehabilitation program, since one doesn't really know in sufficiently specific terms what the patient can and cannot do.

This criticism ideally requires a very detailed response, since it implies a substantially different approach to neuropsychological assessment from the one adopted by developers of the Halstead-

Reitan. Perhaps the response can be summarized in a few points. The Halstead-Reitan Battery is founded on empirical rather than on content validity. Inferences are drawn on the basis of pertinent research findings rather than on the basis of what the tests appear to be measuring. The fact that one cannot partial out the various factors involved in successful or impaired performance on the Category test, for example, does not detract from the significant empirical findings related to this test based on studies of various clinical populations. The use of highly specific items in order to identify a specific system or system link is a procedure that is closely tied to the syndrome approach of behavioral neurology. Developers of the Halstead-Reitan typically do not employ a syndrome approach for several reasons. First, it depends almost exclusively on the pathognomonic signs method of inference to the neglect of other inferential methods, and second, the tying together of specific deficits into a syndrome is felt to be more often in the brain of the examiner than of the patient. The lack of empirical validity of the so-called "Gerstmann Syndrome" is an example of this deficiency in this particular approach (Benton, 1961). Another major point is that the Halstead-Reitan Battery is a series of tests in which interpretation is based not on isolated consideration of each test taken one at a time, but on relationships among performances on all of the tests. Therefore, specific deficits can be isolated, in some cases at least, through intertest comparisons rather than through isolated examination of a single test. Returning to our example, the hypothesis that there is impairment on the Speech Perception test because of failure to read the items accurately can be evaluated through looking at the results of the aphasia screening or reading achievement test given. Finally, complex tests are likely to have more ecological validity than simple tests of isolated abilities. Thus, the Category test or Tactual Performance test results can tell the clinician more about real world functioning than can the simpler tests. Simple tests were developed in the context of neurological diagnosis, while the tests in the Halstead-Reitan Battery seem more oriented to assessing adaptive functioning in the environment.

3. *The Halstead-Reitan Battery is not sufficiently comprehensive, in that it completely neglects the area of memory.* The absence of formal memory testing in this battery has been noted by many observers and appears to be a valid criticism. On

the face of it, it would appear that the battery would be incapable of identifying and providing meaningful assessments of patients with pure amnesic syndromes (e.g., patients with Korsakoff's syndrome). The absence of formal memory testing as part of the Halstead-Reitan is something of a puzzlement; although memory is involved in many of the tests, it is difficult to isolate the memory component as a source of impairment. Such isolation is readily achieved through such standard, commonly available procedures as list or paired associate learning.

We know of no formal response to this criticism, but the point of view could be taken that pure amnesic syndromes are relatively rare, and the Halstead-Reitan Battery would probably not be the assessment method of choice for many of the rarely occurring specific syndromes. I would view this response as weak in view of the recently reported significance of memory defect in a number of disorders (Butters, 1983). Apparently, Halstead did not work with patients of those types, particularly patients with Alzheimer's and Huntington's disease, and so may have failed to note the significance of memory function in those disorders. However, this criticism is probably the one most easily resolved, since all that is required is addition of some formal memory testing to the battery. Many clinicians have already added all or parts of the Wechsler Memory Scale or similar procedures.

4. *The Halstead-Reitan Battery cannot discriminate between brain damaged and schizophrenic patients.* This matter has already been discussed, and most of the evidence (Heaton & Crowley, 1981) indicates that the performance of chronic schizophrenics on the Halstead-Reitan may be indistinguishable from that of the patient with generalized, structural brain damage. There are essentially two classes of response to this criticism. First, there is a disclaimer that the Halstead-Reitan was ever designed for this kind of differential diagnosis, and so it is not surprising that it fails when it is inappropriately used for that purpose. Second, and perhaps much more significant, is the finding that many schizophrenics have brain atrophy as assessed by CT scan, and tests of the Halstead-Reitan type can now be viewed as accurately identifying the behavioral correlates of that condition (Weinberger & Wyatt, 1982).

5. *Findings reported from Reitan's laboratory cannot be replicated in other settings.* Here we

have particular reference to the criticisms raised by Smith of Reitan's early Wechsler-Bellevue laterality studies. In a series of papers, Smith (1965, 1966a, 1966b) presented empirical and theoretical arguments against the reported finding that patients with left hemisphere lesions had lower verbal than performance IQs on the Wechsler-Bellevue, while the reverse was true for patients with right hemisphere brain damage. Smith was unable to replicate these findings in patients with lateralized brain damage that he had Wechsler-Bellevue data available on and also presented theoretical arguments against the diagnostic and conceptual significance of this finding. Klove (1974) analyzed the Smith versus Reitan findings in terms of possible age and neurological differences between the studies. Reviewing the research done to the time of writing, he also concluded that most of the research, with Smith as the only pronounced exception, essentially confirmed Reitan's original findings.

In summary, many criticisms have been raised of the Halstead-Reitan as a comprehensive, standard neuropsychological assessment system. While pertinent and reasonable responses have been made to most or all of these critiques, members of the profession have nevertheless sensed in recent years the desire to develop alternative procedures. Despite the pertinent replies to criticisms, there appear to be many clinicians who still feel that the Halstead-Reitan Battery *is* too long, *does* neglect memory, and in many cases *is* insufficiently specific. Some holders of these views adopted an individualized approach, while others sought alternative standard batteries.

The Luria-Nebraska Neuropsychological Battery

History

This procedure, previously known as the Luria-South Dakota Neuropsychological Battery or as A Standard Version of Luria's Neuropsychological Tests, was first reported on in 1978 (Golden, Hammeke, & Purich, 1978; Purisch, Golden, & Hammeke, 1978) in the form of two initial validity studies. One could provide a lengthy history of this procedure, going back to Luria's original writings, or a brief one only recording events that occurred since the time of preparation of the two publications cited above. We will take the latter alternative, for reasons that will become apparent. Prior to the past two decades, Luria was a shadowy figure to most English-speaking neuropsychologists. It was known that he was an excellent clinician who had developed his own methods for evaluating patients as well as his own theory, but the specific contents were unknown until translations of some of his major works appeared in the 1960s (e.g., Luria, 1966). However, when these works were read by English-speaking professionals, it became apparent that Luria did not have a standard battery of the Halstead-Reitan type and did not even appear to use standardized tests. Thus, while his formulations and case presentations were stimulating and innovative, nobody quite knew what to do with these materials in terms of practical clinical application. One alternative, of course, was to go to the Soviet Union and study with Luria, and, in fact, Anne-Lise Christensen did just that and reported what she had learned in a book called *Luria's Neuropsychological Investigation* (Christensen, 1975a). The book was accompanied by a manual and a kit containing test materials used by Luria and his coworkers (Christensen, 1975b, 1975c). Even though some of Luria's procedures previously appeared in English in the *Higher Cortical Functions* (1966) and *Traumatic Aphasia* (1970), they were never presented in a manner that encouraged direct administration of the test items to patients. Thus, the English-speaking public had in hand a manual and related materials that could be used to administer some of Luria's tests. These materials did not contain information relevant to standardization of these items. There was no scoring system, norms, data regarding validity and reliability, or review of research accomplished with the procedure as a standard battery. This work was taken on by a group of investigators under the leadership of Charles J. Golden and was initially reported on in the two 1978 papers cited above. Thus, in historical sequence, Luria adopted or developed these items over the course of many years, Christensen published them in English but without standardization data, and finally Golden and collaborators provided quantification and standardization. Since that time, Golden's group as well as other investigators have produced a massive amount of studies with what is now known as the Luria-Nebraska Neuropsychological Battery. The battery was published in 1980 by Western Psychological Services (Golden et al., 1980b) and is now extensively used in clinical and research publications.

Structure and Content

The Luria-Nebraska is an evolving procedure, and the details presented here will no doubt change over the years. However, the basic structure of the battery will probably remain essentially the same. The current version contains 269 items, each of which may be scored on a 2- or 3-point scale. A score of 0 indicates normal performance, and a score of 2 indicates clearly abnormal performance. Some items may receive a score of 1, indicating borderline performance. The items are organized into the categories provided in the Christensen kit (Christensen, 1975c), but while Christensen organized the items primarily to suggest how they were used by Luria, in the Luria-Nebraska version the organization is presented as a set of quantitative scales. The raw score for each scale is the sum of the 0, 1, and 2 item scores. Thus, the higher the score, the poorer the performance. Since the scales contain varying numbers of items, raw scale scores are converted to T scores with a mean of 50 and a standard deviation of 10. These T scores are displayed as a profile on a form prepared for that purpose. The scores for the individual items may be based on speed, accuracy, or quality of response. In some cases, two scores may be assigned to the same task, one for speed and the other for accuracy. These two scores are counted as individual items. For example, one of the items is a block counting task, with separate scores assigned for number of errors and time to completion of the task. In the case of time scores, blocks of seconds are associated with the 0, 1, and 2 scores. When quality of response is scored, the manual provides both rules for scoring, and, in the case of copying tasks, illustrations of figures representing 0, 1, and 2 scores.

The 269 items are divided into 11 content scales, each of which is individually administrable. In Table 10.2, we present the name of each content scale, a brief description of each scale and a sample item.

In addition to these 11 content scales, there are 3 derived scales that appear on the standard profile form; the Pathognomonic, Left Hemisphere, and Right Hemisphere scales. The Pathognomonic scale contains items from throughout the battery found to be particularly sensitive to presence or absence of brain damage. The Left and Right Hemisphere scales are derived

TABLE 10.2. THE LURIA-NEBRASKA MAJOR SCALES.

SCALE	DESCRIPTION AND SAMPLE ITEM
Motor	Contains items assessing a wide variety of motor skills ranging from simple movements to more complex tasks including pretended movements and movements associated with complex verbal instructions. Sample Item: If I knock hard, you knock gently; if I knock gently, then knock hard.
Rhythm	Contains measures of primarily nonverbal auditory perception such as pitch discrimination and appreciation of rhythmic patterns. Sample Item: Now you are going to hear two tones on a tape from this tape recorder. I want you to tell me whether the tones you hear are the same or different.
Tactile	This scale is basically a sensory examination and contains measures of light touch localization, two point discrimination, and tactile recognition. Sample Item: I am going to touch you with the eraser end of the pencil. Tell me where I am touching you. (touching fingers, palm and forearm of each upper extremity).
Vision	Contains items assessing basic visual perceptual skills as well as more complex visual-spatial tasks. Sample Item: I am now going to show you several pictures. Tell me what they are. (Subject is presented with cards containing photographs of common objects.)
Receptive Speech	Contains items ranging from perception of single sounds to comprehension of complex grammatical structures. Sample Item: Someone has just told you that "Arnie hit Tom." Who was the victim?
Expressive Speech	Contains items assessing ability to repeat sounds, words, and word groups, to name objects and to produce narrative speech. Sample Item: Please make up a speech for me about the conflict between generations.
Writing	Contains items assessing ability to analyze words into letters and to write under varying conditions. Sample Item: Please write: physiology; probabilistic
Reading	Contains items assessing ability to make letter to sound transformations and to read simple material. Sample Item: I am going to show you several cards. Read the word on each card.
Arithmetic	Contains items assessing knowledge of numbers, number concept and ability to perform simple calculations. Sample Item: Please solve these problems. You may also write them down if you like: (1) 3 + 4; (2) 6 + 7
Memory	A brief, formal memory examination including list learning, immediate memory, short-term memory with interference, and paired-associate learning. Sample Item: Now I am going to read you a short story. I want you to listen carefully because when I am finished I want you to repeat to me all that you can remember about the story.
Intellectual Processes	A brief intellectual assessment containing sequencing, problem solving, and abstraction items. Sample Item: What is meant by these expressions: (1) "iron hand?" (2) "green thumb?"

from the Motor and Tactile scale items that involve comparisons between the left and right sides of the body. They therefore reflect sensory-motor asymmetries between the two sides of the body.

Several other scales have been developed by Golden and various collaborators, all of which are based on different ways of scoring the same 269 items. These special scales include new (empirically derived) right and left hemisphere scales (McKay & Golden, 1979a), a series of localization scales (McKay & Golden, 1979b), a series of factor scales (McKay & Golden, 1981), and double discrimination scales (Golden, 1979). The new right and left hemisphere scales contain items from throughout the battery and are based upon actual comparisons among patients with right hemisphere, left hemisphere, and diffuse brain damage. The localization scales are also empirically derived (McKay & Golden, 1979b), being based on studies of patients with localized brain

TABLE 10.3. THE LURIA-NEBRASKA FACTOR SCALES.

CODE	FACTOR SCALES
M1	Kinesthetic-Based Movement
M2	Drawing Speed
M3	Fine Motor Speed
M4	Spatial-Based Movement
M5	Oral Motor Skills
Rh1	Rhythm and Pitch Perception
T1	Simple Tactile Sensation
T2	Stereognosis
V1	Visual Acuity and Naming
V2	Visual-Spatial Organization
Rc1	Phonemic Discrimination
Rc2	Relational Concepts
Rc3	Concept Recognition
Rc4	Verbal-Spatial Relationships
Rc5	Word Comprehension
Rc6	Logical Grammatical Relationships
E1	Simple Phonetic Reading
E2	Word Repetition
E3	Reading Polysyllabic Words
Rg1	Reading Complex Material
Rg2	Reading Simple Material
W1	Spelling
W2	Motor Writing Skill
A1	Arithmetic Calculations
A2	Number Reading
Me1	Verbal Memory
Me2	Visual and Complex Memory
I1	General Verbal Intelligence
I2	Complex Verbal Arithmetic
I3	Simple Verbal Arithmetic

lesions. There are frontal, sensory-motor, temporal, and parietooccipital scales for each hemisphere. The factor scales are based on extensive factor analytic studies of the battery involving factor analyses of each of the major content scales (e.g., Golden & Berg, 1983). The factor scales and associated codes are listed below. The code consists of an abbreviation for the major content scale followed by the number of the scale (e.g., M3 is the third factor scale derived from the Motor scale).

The new right and left hemisphere, localization, and factor scales may all be expressed in T scores with a mean of 50. The double discrimination scales are still in an experimental phase, but have been shown to be effective in diagnosis of multiple sclerosis (Golden, 1979). This method involves development of two scales, one of which patients with a particular diagnosis do worse on

than the general neurological population and the other containing items patients do better on. Classification to the specific group is made when scores are in the appropriate range on both scales.

The Luria-Nebraska procedure involves an age and education correction. It is accomplished through computation of a cut-off score for abnormal performance based on an equation that takes into consideration both age and education. The computed score is called the critical level and is equal to .214 (Age) + 1.47 (Education) + 68.8 (Constant). Typically, a horizontal line is drawn across the profile at the computed critical level point. The test user has the option of considering scores above 60 as abnormal or scores above the critical level, which may be higher or lower than 60, as abnormal.

As indicated above, extensive factor analytic studies have been accomplished, and the factor structure of each of the major scales has been identified. These analyses were based on item intercorrelations, rather than on correlations among the scales. It is important to note that most items on any particular scale correlate more highly with other items on that scale than they do with items on other scales (Golden, 1981). This finding lends credence to the view that the scales are at least somewhat homogeneous, and thus that the organization of the 269 items into those scales can be justified.

Theoretical Foundations

As in the case of the Halstead-Reitan Battery, one could present two theoretical bases for the Luria-Nebraska, one revolving around the name of Luria and the other around the Nebraska group, Golden and his collaborators. It is to be noted in this regard that Luria himself had nothing to do with the development of the Luria-Nebraska Battery, nor did any of his coworkers. The use of his name in the title of the battery is, in fact, somewhat controversial, and seems to have been essentially honorific in intent, recognizing his development of the items and the underlying theory for their application. Indeed, Luria died some time before publication of the battery but was involved in the preparation of the Christensen materials, which he endorsed. Furthermore, the method of testing employed by the Luria-Nebraska was not Luria's method, and the research done to establish the validity, reliability, and clinical relevance of the Luria-Nebraska was not the kind of research done by Luria and his collaborators. Therefore, our discussion of the theory underlying the Luria-Nebraska Battery will be based on the assumption that the only connecting link between Luria and that procedure is the set of Christensen items. In doing so, it becomes clear that the basic theory underlying the development of the Luria-Nebraska is based on a philosophy of science that stresses empirical validity, quantification, and application of established psychometric procedures. Indeed, as pointed out elsewhere (Goldstein, 1982), it is essentially the same epistemology that characterizes the work of the Reitan group.

The general course charted for establishment of quantitative, standard neuropsychological assessment batteries involves several steps: (a) determining whether the battery discriminates between brain damaged patients in general and normal controls; (b) determining whether it discriminates between patients with structural brain damage and conditions that may be confused with structural brain damage, notably various functional psychiatric disorders; (c) determination of whether the procedure has the capacity to lateralize and regionally localize brain damage; (d) determination of whether there are performance patterns specific to particular neurological disorders, such as alcoholic dementia or multiple sclerosis. In proceeding along this course, it is highly desirable to accomplish appropriate cross-validations and to determine reliability. This course was taken by Golden and his collaborators, in some cases with remarkable success. Since the relevant research was accomplished during recent years, it had the advantages of being able to benefit from the new brain imaging technology, notably the CT scan, and the application of high speed computer technologies, allowing for extensive use of powerful multivariate statistical methods. With regard to methods of clinical inference, the same methods suggested by Reitan—level of performance, pattern of performance, pathognomonic signs, and right-left comparisons—are the methods generally used with the Luria-Nebraska.

Adhering to our assumption that the Luria-Nebraska bears little resemblance to Luria's methods and theories, there seems little point in examining the theoretical basis for the substance of the Luria-Nebraska Battery. For example, it seems that there would be little point in examining the theory of language that underlies the Receptive Speech and Expressive Speech scales or the theory of memory that provides the basis for the

Memory scale. An attempt to produce such an analysis was made by Spiers (1981), who examined the content of the Luria-Nebraska scales and evaluated it with reference not so much to Luria's theories, but to current concepts in clinical neuropsychology in general. However, despite the thoroughness of the Spiers review, it seems to miss the essential point that the Luria-Nebraska is a procedure based primarily on studies of empirical validity. One can fault it on the quality of its empirical validity studies, but not on the basis that it utilizes such an approach. One can only disagree with the approach. It therefore appears that the Luria-Nebraska Battery does not constitute a means of using Luria's theory and methods in English-speaking countries, but rather is a standardized psychometric instrument with established validity for certain purposes and reliability. The choice of using items selected by Christensen (1975b) to illustrate Luria's testing methods was, in retrospect, probably less crucial than the research methods chosen to investigate the capabilities of this item set. Indeed, it is somewhat misleading to characterize these items as "Luria's tests," since many of them are standard items used by neuropsychologists and neurologists throughout the world. Surely, one cannot describe asking a patient to interpret proverbs or determine 2-point thresholds as being exclusively "Luria's tests." They are, in fact, venerable, widely used procedures.

Standardization Research

Fortunately, there is a published manual for the Luria-Nebraska (Golden et al., 1980) that describes the battery in detail and provides pertinent information relative to validity, reliability, and norms. There are also several review articles (e.g., Golden, 1981) that comprehensively describe the research done with the battery. Very briefly reviewing this material, satisfactory discriminative validity has been reported in studies directed toward differentiating miscellaneous brain damaged patients from normal control and from chronic schizophrenics. Cross-validations were generally successful, but Shelly and Goldstein (1983) could not fully replicate the studies involved with discriminating between brain damaged and schizophrenic patients. Discriminative validity studies involving lateralization and localization achieved satisfactory results, but the localization studies were based on small samples. Quantitative indices from the Luria-Nebraska were found to correlate significantly with CT scan quantitative indices in alcoholic (Golden, Graber, Blose, Berg, Coffman, & Block, 1981) and schizophrenic (Golden, Moses, Zelazowski, Graber, Zatz, Horvath, & Berger, 1980) samples. There have been several studies of specific neurological disorders including multiple sclerosis (Golden, 1979), alcoholism (Chmielewski & Golden, 1980), Huntington's disease (Moses, Golden, Berger, & Wisniewski, 1981) and learning disabled adults, (McCue, Shelly, Goldstein, & Katz-Garris, in press), all with satisfactory results in terms of discrimination.

The test manual reports reliability data. Test-retest reliabilities for the 13 major scales range from .78 to .96. The problem of interjudge reliability is generally not a major one for neuropsychological assessment, since most of the tests used are quite objective and have quantitative scoring systems. However, there could be a problem with the Luria-Nebraska, since the assignment of 0, 1, and 2 scores sometimes requires a judgment by the examiner. During the preliminary screening stage in the development of the battery, items in the original pool that did not attain satisfactory interjudge reliability were dropped. A 95% interrater agreement level was reported by the test constructors for the 282 items used in an early version of the battery developed after the dropping of those items. The manual contains means and standard deviations for each item based on samples of control, neurologically impaired, and schizophrenic subjects. An alternate form of the battery is in preparation. To the best of our knowledge, there have been no predictive validity studies. It is unclear whether or not there have been studies addressed to the issue of construct validity. Stambrook (1983) suggested that studies involved with item-scale consistency, factor analysis, and correlation with other instruments are construct validity studies, but it does not appear to us that they are directed toward validation of Luria's constructs. The attempt to apply Luria's constructs has not in fact involved the empirical testing of specific hypotheses derived from Luria's theory. Thus, we appear to have diagnostic or discriminative validity established by a large number of studies. There also seems to be content validity, since the items correlate most highly with the scale to which they are assigned, but the degree of construct validity remains unclear. For example, there have been no studies of Luria's important construct of the functional system or of his hypotheses concerning frontal lobe function as those involving the programming, regulation, and verification of activity (Luria, 1973).

Evaluation

It is well known that the Luria-Nebraska Battery, at this writing, is a controversial procedure, and several highly critical reviews of it have appeared in the literature. Adams (1980) criticized it primarily on methodological grounds, Spiers (1981) on the basis that it was greatly lacking in its capacity to provide a comprehensive neuropsychological assessment, Crosson and Warren (1982) because of its deficiencies with regard to assessment of aphasia and aphasic patients, and Stambrook (1983) on the basis of a number of methodological and theoretical considerations. Replies were written to several of these reviews (e.g., Golden, 1980), and a rather heated literature controversy eventuated. This literature was supplemented by several case studies (e.g., Delis & Kaplan, 1982) in which it was shown that the inferences that would be drawn from the Luria-Nebraska were incorrect with reference to documentation obtained for those cases.

These criticisms can be divided into general and specific ones. Basically, there are two general criticisms: (a) The Luria-Nebraska Battery does not reflect Luria's thinking in any sense, and his name should not be used in describing it; and (b) there are several relatively flagrant methodological difficulties involved in the standardization of the procedure. The major specific criticisms primarily involve the language related and memory scales. With regard to aphasia, there are essentially two points. First, there is no system provided, nor do the items provide sufficient data to classify the aphasias in terms of some contemporary system (e.g., Goodglass & Kaplan, 1972). Second, the battery is so language oriented that patients with aphasia may fail many of the non-language tasks because of failure to comprehend the test instructions or to make the appropriate verbal responses indicative of a correct answer. For example, on the Tactile scale, the patient must name objects placed in the hands. Patients with anomia or anomic aphasia will be unable to do that even though their tactile recognition skills may be perfectly normal. With regard to memory, the Memory scale is criticized because of its failure to provide a state-of-the-art comprehensive memory assessment (Russell, 1981). Golden has responded to this criticism through adding additional items involving delayed recall to the next version of the battery to appear.

In providing an evaluation of the Luria-Nebraska, one can only voice an opinion, as others have, since its existence has stimulated a polarization into "those for it" and "those against it." I would concur with Stambrook's view (1983), which essentially is that it is premature to make an evaluation, and that major research programs must be accomplished before an informed opinion can be reached. This research involves more definitive validation with a greatly expanded data base, an evaluation of the actual constructs on which the procedure is based, and assessment of its clinical usefulness relative to other established procedures such as the Halstead-Reitan or individual approaches. The following remark by Stambrook (1983) appears to reflect a highly reasoned approach to this issue. "The clinical utility of the LNNB does not depend upon either the publisher's and test developer's claims, or on conceptual and methodological critiques, but upon carefully planned and well-executed research" (p. 266). In this regard, one might note the discrepancy between the nearly half a century of work with Halstead's test and the barely 5 years at this writing of work with Luria-Nebraska. Various opinions have also been raised with regard to whether it is proper to utilize the Luria-Nebraska in clinical situations. My view of the matter would be that it may be so used as long as inferences made from it do not go beyond what can be based on the available research literature. In particular, the test consumer should not be led to believe that administration and interpretation of the Luria-Nebraska Battery provide an assessment of the type that would have been conducted by Luria and his coworkers, or that one is providing an application of Luria's method. The procedure is specifically not Luria's method at all, and the view that it provides valid measures of Luria's constructs and theories has not been verified. Even going beyond that point, attempts to verify some of Luria's hypotheses (e.g., Drewe, 1975; Goldberg & Tucker, 1979) have not always been completely sucessful. Therefore, clinical interpretations, even when they are based on Luria's actual method of investigation, may be inaccurate because of inaccuracies in the underlying theory.

SUMMARY AND CONCLUSIONS

In the first part of this chapter, general problems in the area of standardization of comprehensive neuropsychological test batteries were discussed, while the second part contained brief reviews of the two most used procedures, the Halstead-Reitan and the Luria-Nebraska. It was generally concluded that these batteries have their advantages and disadvantages. The Halstead-Reitan is well established and detailed but is lengthy, cumbersome, and neglects certain areas, notably memory. The Luria-Nebraska is also fairly comprehensive and briefer than the Halstead-Reitan but is currently quite controversial and is thought to have major deficiencies in standardization and rationale, at least by some observers. I have taken the view that all of these standard batteries are screening instruments, but not in the sense of screening for presence or absence of brain damage. Rather, they may be productively used to screen a number of functional areas such as memory, language, or visual-spatial skills, that may be affected by brain damage. With the development of the new imaging techniques in particular, it is important that the neuropsychologist not simply tell the referring agent what he or she already knows. The unique contribution of standard neuropsychological assessment is the ability to describe functioning in many crucial areas on a quantitative basis. The extent to which one procedure can perform this type of task more accurately and efficiently than other procedures will no doubt greatly influence the relative acceptability of these batteries by the profesional community.

REFERENCES

Adams, K.M. (1980). In search of Luria's battery: A false start. *Journal of Consulting and Clinical Psychology,* 48, 511–516.

Albert, M.L. (1978). Subcortical dementia. In R.D. Terry and K.L. Bick (Eds.), *Alzheimer's disease: Senile dementia and related disorders.* New York: Raven Press.

Albert, M.L., Goodglass, H., Helm, N.A., Rubens, A.B. & Alexander, M.P. (1981). *Clinical aspects of dysphasia.* New York: Springer-Verlag/Wein.

Ben-Yishay, Y., Diller, L., Gerstman, L., & Gordon, W. (1970). Relationship between initial competence and ability to profit from cues in brain-damaged individuals. *Journal of Abnormal Psychology,* 78, 248–259.

Ben-Yishay, Y., Gerstman, L., Diller, L., & Haas, A. (1970). Prediction of rehabilitation outcomes from psychometric parameters in left hemiplegics. *Journal of Consulting and Clinical Psychology,* 34, 436–441.

Bender, L. (1938). A visual motor gestalt test and its clinical use. American Orthopsychiatric Association, Research Monographs No. 3.

Bender, M.B. (1952). *Disorders in perception.* Springfield, IL: Charles C. Thomas.

Benton, A.L. (1961). The fiction of the Gerstmann Syndrome. *Journal of Neurology, Neurosurgery and Psychiatry,* 24, 176–181.

Benton, A.L. (1963). *The Revised Visual Retention Test.* New York: Psychological Corporation.

Blumstein, S.E. (1981). Neurolinguistic disorders: Language-brain relationships. In S.B. Filskov and T.J. Boll (Eds.), *Handbook of clinical neuropsychology.* New York: Wiley-Interscience.

Boll, T.J. (1981). The Halstead-Reitan neuropsychology battery. In S.B. Filskov & T.J. Boll (Eds.), *Handbook of clinical neuropsychology.* New York: Wiley-Interscience.

Butters, N. (1983, August). *Clinical aspects of memory disorders: Contributions from experimental studies of amnesia and dementia.* Presented at American Psychological Association, Division 40 Presidential Address, Anaheim, CA.

Butters, N., & Cermak, L.S. (1980). *Alcoholic Korsakoff's syndrome.* New York: Academic Press.

Canter, A. (1970). *The Canter Background Interference Procedure for the Bender-Gestalt Test: Manual for administrations, scoring and interpretation.* Iowa City, IA: Iowa Psychopathic Hospital.

Chmielewski, C., & Golden, C.J. (1980). Alcoholism and brain damage: An investigation using the Luria-Nebraska Neuropsychological Battery. *International Journal of Neuroscience,* 10, 99–105.

Christensen, A.L. (1975a). *Luria's neuropsychological investigation.* New York: Spectrum.

Christensen, A.L. (1975b). *Luria's neuropsychological investigation: Manual.* New York: Spectrum.

Christensen, A.L. (1975c). *Luria's neuropsychological investigation: Test cards.* New York: Spectrum.

Cronbach, L.J. (1960). *Essentials of psychological testing* (2nd ed.). New York: Harper & Brothers.

Crosson, B., & Warren, R.L. (1982). Use of the Luria-Nebraska Neuropsychological Battery in aphasia: A conceptual critique. *Journal of Consulting and Clinical Psychology,* 50, 22–31.

Danziger, W. (1983, October). *Longitudinal study of cognitive performance in healthy and mildly demented (SDAT) older adults.* Paper presented at conference on Clinical Memory Assessment of Older Adults, Wakefield, MA.

Davis, K. (1983, October). *Potential neurochemical and neuroendocrine validators of assessment instruments.* Paper presented at conference on Clinical Memory Assessment of Older Adults, Wakefield, MA.

Delis, D.C., & Kaplan, E. (1982). The assessment of aphasia with the Luria-Nebraska neuropsychological battery: A case critique. *Journal of Consulting and Clinical Psychology,* 50, 32–39.

Drewe, E.A. (1975). An experimental investigation of Luria's theory on the effects of frontal lobe lesions in man. *Neuropsychologia,* 13, 421–429.

Dunn, L.M., & Markwardt, F.C. (1970). *Peabody Individual Achievement Test Manual.* Circle Pines, MN: American Guidance Service.

Filskov, S.B., & Boll, T.J. (1981). *Handbook of clinical neuropsychology.* New York: Wiley-Interscience.

Filskov, S.B., & Goldstein, S.G. (1974). Diagnostic validity of the Halstead-Reitan neuropsychological battery. *Journal of Clinical and Consulting Psychology,* 42, 382–388.

Fitzhugh, K.B., Fitzhugh, L.C., & Reitan, R.M. (1961). Psychological deficits in relation to acuteness of brain dysfunction. *Journal of Consulting and Clinical Psychology,* 25, 61–66.

Fitzhugh, K.B., Fitzhugh, L.C., & Reitan, R.M. (1962). Wechsler-Bellevue comparisons in groups of 'chronic' and 'current' lateralized and diffuse brain lesions. *Journal of Consulting Psychology,* 26, 306–310.

Fletcher, J.M., & Satz, P. (1980). Developmental changes in the neuropsychological correlates of reading achievement: A six-year longitudinal followup. *Journal of Clinical Neuropsychology,* 2, 23–37.

Flor-Henry, P. & Yeudall, L.T. (1979). Neuropsychological investigation of schizophrenia and manic-depressive psychoses. In J. Gruzelier & P. Flor-Henry (Eds.), *Hemisphere asymmetries of function in psychopathology.* Amsterdam: Elsevier/North Holland.

Goldberg, E., & Tucker, D. (1979). Motor preseveration and long-term memory for visual forms. *Journal of Clinical Neuropsychology,* 1, 273–288.

Golden, C.J. (1978). *Diagnosis and rehabilitation in clinical neuropsychology.* Springfield, IL: C.C. Thomas.

Golden, C.J. (1979). Identification of specific neurological disorders using double discrimination scales derived from the standardized Luria neuropsychological battery. *International Journal of Neuroscience,* 10, 51–56.

Golden, C.J. (1980). In reply to Adams' 'In search of Luria's battery: A false start'. *Journal of Consulting and Clinical Psychology,* 48, 517–521.

Golden, C.J. (1981). A standardized version of Luria's neuropsychological tests: A quantitative and qualitative approach to neuropsychological evaluation. In S.B. Filskov & T.J. Boll (Eds.), *Handbook of clinical neuropsychology.* New York: Wiley-Interscience.

Golden, C.J., & Berg, R.A. (1983). Interpretation of the Luria-Nebraska Neuropsychological Battery by item intercorrelation: The memory scale. *Clinical Neuropsychology,* 5, 55–59.

Golden, C.J., Graber, B., Blose, I., Berg, R., Coffman, J., & Block, S. (1981). Difference in brain densities between chronic alcoholic and normal control patients. *Science,* 211, 508–510.

Golden, C.J., Hammeke, T. & Purisch, A. (1978). Diagnostic validity of the Luria neuropsychological battery. *Journal of Consulting and Clinical Psychology,* 46, 1258–1265.

Golden, C.J., Hammeke, T. & Purisch, A. (1980). *The Luria-Nebraska battery manual.* Los Angeles: Western Psychological Services.

Golden, C.J., Moses, J.A., Zelazowski, R., Graber, B., Zatz, L.M., Horvath, T.B., & Berger, P.A. (1980). Cerebral ventricular size and neuropsychological impairment in young chronic schizophrenics. *Archives of General Psychiatry,* 37, 619–623.

Goldstein, G. (1978). Cognitive and perceptual differences between schizophrenics and organics. *Schizophrenia Bulletin,* 4, 160–185.

Goldstein, G. (1982, March). Overview: *Clinical application of the Halstead-Reitan and Luria-Nebraska batteries.* Invited lecture, NE-REMC Conference, Northport, NY.

Goldstein, G., & Ruthven, L. (1983). *Rehabilitation of the brain damaged adult.* New York: Plenum.

Goldstein, K., & Scheerer, M. (1941). Abstract and concrete behavior: An experimental study with special tests. *Psychological Monographs*, 53, (Whole No. 239).

Goldstein, G., & Shelly, C. (1971). Field dependence and cognitive, perceptual and motor skills in alcoholics: A factor analytic study. *Quarterly Journal of Studies on alcohol*, 32, 29–40.

Goldstein, G., & Shelly, C. (1972). Statistical and normative studies of the Halstead Neuropsychological Test Battery relevant to a neuropsychiatric hospital setting. *Perceptual and Motor Skills*, 34, 603–620.

Goldstein, G., & Shelly, C.H. (1975). Similarities and differences between psychological deficit in aging and brain damage. *Journal of Gerontology*, 30, 448-455.

Goldstein, G., & Shelly, C. (1982). A further attempt to cross-validate the Russell, Neuringer and Goldstein neuropsychological keys. *Journal of Consulting and Clinical Psychology*, 50, 721–726.

Goodglass, H. (1983, August). Aphasiology in the United States. In G. Goldstein (Chair), *Symposium: History of Human Neuropsychology in the United States*. Ninety-first annual convention of the American Psychological Association, Anaheim, CA.

Goodglass, H., & Kaplan, E. (1972). *The assessment of aphasia and related disorders*. Philadelphia, PA: Lee & Febiger.

Gruzelier, J., & Flor-Henry, P. (1979). *Hemisphere asymmetries of function in psychopathology*. Amsterdam: Elsevier/North-Holland.

Halstead, W.C. (1947). *Brain and intelligence: A quantitative study of the frontal lobes*. Chicago: The University of Chicago Press.

Heaton, R., & Crowley, T. (1981). Effects of psychiatric disorders and their somatic treatment on neuropsychological test results. In S.B. Filskov & T.J. Boll (Eds.), *Handbook of clinical neuropsychology*. New York: Wiley-Interscience.

Heaton, R.K., & Pendleton, M.G. (1981). Use of neuropsychological tests to predict adult patients' everyday functioning. *Journal of Consulting and Clinical Psychology*, 49, 807–821.

Heaton, R.K., Baade, L.E., & Johnson, K.L. (1978). Neuropsychological test results associated with psychiatric disorders in adults. *Psychological Bulletin*, 85, 141–162.

Heilman, K.M. (1979). Neglect and related disorders. In K.M. Heilman and E. Valenstein (Eds.), *Clinical neuropsychology*. New York: Oxford University Press.

Henn, F.A., & Nasrallah, H.A. (1982). *Schizophrenia as a brain disease*. New York: Oxford University Press.

Hill, S.Y., & Mikhael, M. (1979) Computerized transaxial and tomographic and neuropsychological evaluation in chronic alcoholics and heroin abusers. *American Journal of Psychiatry*, 136, 598–602.

Jastak, J.F., & Jastak, S.P. (1965). *The Wide Range Achievement Test: Manual of instructions*. Wilmington, DE: Guidance Associates.

Jones, B.P., & Butters, N. (1983). Neuropsychological assessment. In M. Hersen, A. S. Bellack, and A.E. Kazdin (Eds.), *The clinical psychology handbook*. New York: Pergamon Press.

Kaiser, H.F. (1960). The application of electronic computers to factor analysis. *Educational and Psychological Measurement*, 20, 141–151.

Kaplan, E. (1979). Presidential Address. Presented at the International Neuropsychological Society, Noordwijkerhout, Holland.

Kertesz, A. (1979). *Aphasia and associated disorders: Taxonomy, localization and recovery*. New York: Grune & Stratton.

Kimura, D. (1961). Some effects of temporal lobe damage on auditory perception. *Canadian Journal of Psychology*, 15, 156–165.

Kimura, D., & Durnford, M. (1974). Normal studies on the function of the right hemisphere in vision. In S.J. Dimond & J.G. Beaumont (Eds.), *Hemisphere function in the human brain*. London: Elek Science.

Kinsbourne, M. (1980). Attentional dysfunctions and the elderly: Theoretical models and research perspectives. In L.W. Poon, J.L. Fozard, L.S. Cermak, D. Arenberg & L.W. Thompson (Eds.), *New directions in memory and aging*. Hillsdale, NJ: Erlbaum.

Klove, H. (1974). Validation studies in adult clinical neuropsychology. In R.M. Reitan & L.H. Davison (Eds.), *Clinical neuropsychology: Current status and applications*. Washington, DC: V.H. Winston & Sons.

Levin, H.S., Benton, A.L., & Grossman, R.G. (1982). *Neurobehavioral consequences of closed head injury*. New York: Oxford University Press.

Lezak, M. (1976). *Neuropsychological Assessment*. (1st ed.). New York: Oxford University Press.

Lezak, M. (1983). *Neuropsychological assessment*. (2nd ed.). New York: Oxford University Press.

Luria, A.R. (1966). *Higher cortical functions in man*. New York: Basic Books.

Luria, A.R. (1970). *Traumatic aphasia*. The Hague: Mouton and Co. Printers.

Luria, A.R. (1973). *The working brain*. New York: Basic Books.

Malec, J. (1978). Neuropsychological assessment of schizophrenia vs. brain damage: A review. *Journal of Nervous and Mental Disease*, 166, 507–516.

Matthews, C.G. (1981). Neuropsychology practice in a hospital setting. In S.B. Filskov & T.J. Boll (Eds.), *Handbook of clinical neuropsychology*. New York: Wiley-Interscience.

McCue, M., Shelly, C., Goldstein, G., & Katz-Garris, L. (in press). Neuropsychological aspects of learning disability in young adults. *Clinical Neuropsychology*.

McKay, S., & Golden, C.J. (1979a). Empirical derivation of neuropsychological scales for the lateralization of brain damage using the Luria-Nebraska Neuropsychological Battery. *Clinical Neuropsychology*, 1, 1–5.

McKay, S., & Golden, C.J. (1979b). Empirical derivation of experimental scales for localizing brain lesions using the Luria-Nebraska Neuropsychological Battery. *Clinical Neuropsychology*, 1, 19–23.

McKay, S.E., & Golden, C.J. (1981). The assessment of specific neuropsychological skills using scales derived from factor analysis of the Luria-Nebraska Neuropsychological Battery. *International Journal of Neuroscience*, 14, 189–204.

Meier, M.J. (1974). Some challenges for clinical neuropsychology. In R.M. Reitan & L.A. Davison (Eds.), *Clinical neuropsychology: Current status and applications.* Washington, DC: V.H. Winston and Sons.

Mooney, C.M. (1957). Age in the development of closure ability in children. *Canadian Journal of Psychology,* 2, 219–226.

Moses, J.A., Golden, C.J., Berger, P.A., & Wisniewski, A.M. (1981). Neuropsychological deficits in early, middle, and late stage Huntington's disease as measured by the Luria-Nebraska Neuropsychological Battery. *International Journal of Neuroscience,* 14, 95–100.

Newby, R.F., Hallenbeck, C.E., & Embretson (Whitely), S. (1983). Confirmatory factory analysis of four general neuropsychological models with a modified Halstead-Reitan battery. *Journal of Clinical Neuropsychology,* 5, 115–133.

Newcombe, F. (1969). *Missile wounds of the brain: A study of psychological deficits.* Oxford: The Clarendon Press.

Newman, O.S., Heaton, R.K., & Lehman, R.A.W. (1978). Neuropsychological and MMPI correlates of patients' future employment characteristics. *Perceptual and Motor Skills,* 46, 635–642.

Parsons, O.A., & Farr, S.P. (1981). The neuropsychology of alcohol and drug abuse. In S.B. Filskov & T.J. Boll (Eds.), *Handbook of clinical neuropsychology.* New York: Wiley-Interscience.

Purisch, A.D., Golden, C.J., & Hammeke, T.A. (1978). Discrimination of schizophrenic and brain-injured patients by a standardized version of Luria's neuropsychological tests. *Journal of Consulting and Clinical Psychology,* 46, 1266–1273.

Reed, J. (1983, August). The Chicago-Indianapolis Group. In G. Goldstein (Chair), *Symposium: History of human neuropsychology in the United States.* Nintey-first annual convention of the American Psychological Association, Anaheim, CA.

Reed, H.B.C., & Reitan, R.M. (1963). A comparison of the effects of the normal aging process with the effects of organic brain-damage on adaptive abilities. *Journal of Gerontology,* 18, 177–179.

Reisberg, B., Ferris, S.H., & Gershon, S. (1980). Pharmacotherapy of senile dementia. In J.O. Cole & J.E. Barrett (Eds.), *Psychopathology in the aged.* New York: Raven Press.

Reitan, R.M. (1955). An investigation of the validity of Halstead's measures of biological intelligence. *Archives of Neurology and Psychiatry,* 73, 28–35.

Reitan, R.M. (1958). Qualitative versus quantitative mental changes following brain damage. *The Journal of Psychology,* 46, 339–346.

Reitan, R.M. (1959). Correlations between the trail making test and the Wechsler-Bellevue scale. *Perceptual and Motor Skills,* 9, 127–130.

Reitan, R.M. (1964). Psychological deficits resulting from cerebral lesions in man. In J.M. Warren & K. Akert (Eds.), *The frontal granular cortex and behavior.* New York: McGraw-Hill.

Reitan, R.M. (1966). A research program on the psychological effects of brain lesions in human beings. In N.R. Ellis (Ed.), *International review of research in mental retardation.* New York: Academic Press.

Reitan, R.M. (1973, August). Behavioral manifestations of impaired brain functions in aging. In J.L. Fozard (Chair), *Similarities and differences of brain-behavior relationships in aging and cerebral pathology.* Symposium presented at the American Psychological Association, Montreal, Canada.

Reitan, R.M., & Davison, L.A. (1974). *Clinical neuropsychology: Current status and applications.* Washington, DC: V.H. Winston and Sons.

Rey, A. (1941). L'examinen psychologique dans les cas d'encephalopathie traumatique. *Archives de Psychologie,* 28, 286–340.

Rourke, B.P. (1983). Reading and spelling disabilities: A developmental neuropsychological perspective. In U. Kirk (Ed.), *Neuropsychology of language, reading and spelling.* New York: Academic Press.

Russell, E.W. (1975a). A multiple scoring method for the assessment of complex memory functions. *Journal of Consulting and Clinical Psychology,* 43, 800–809.

Russell, E.W. (1975b). Validation of a brain damage versus schizophrenia MMPI. *Journal of Clinical Psychology,* 31, 659–661.

Russell, E.W. (1977). MMPI profiles of brain damaged and schizophrenic subjects. *Journal of Clinical Psychology,* 33, 190–193.

Russell, E.W. (1981). The pathology and clinical examination of memory. In S. B. Filskov & T. J. Boll (Eds.), *Handbook of clinical neuropsychology.* New York: Wiley-Interscience.

Russell, E.W., Neuringer, C., & Goldstein, G. (1970). *Assessment of brain damage: A neuropsychological key approach.* New York: Wiley.

Satz, P., Taylor, H.G., Friel, J., & Fletcher, J. M. (1978). Some developments and predictive precursors of reading disability. In A. L. Benton & D. Pearl (Eds.), *Dyslexia: An appraisal of current knowledge.* New York: Oxford University Press.

Scoville, W.B., & Milner, B. (1957). Loss of recent memory after bilateral hippocampal lesions. *Journal of Neurology, Neurosurgery, and Psychiatry,* 20, 11–21.

Selz, M., & Reitan, R.M. (1979). Rules for neuropsychological diagnosis: Classification of brain function in older children. *Journal of Consulting and Clinical Psychology,* 47, 258–264.

Semmes, J., Weinstein, S., Ghent, L., & Teuber, H.-L. (1960). *Somatosensory changes after penetrating brain wounds in man.* Cambridge, MA: Harvard University.

Shaw, D. (1966). The reliability and validity of the Halstead Category Test. *Journal of Clinical Psychology,* 22, 176–180.

Shelly, C., & Goldstein, G. (1983). Discrimination of chronic schizophrenia and brain damage with the Luria-Nebraska battery: A partially successful replication. *Clinical Neuropsychology,* 5, 82–85.

Smith, A. (1965). Certain hypothesized hemispheric differences in language and visual functions in human adults. *Cortex,* 2, 109–126.

Smith, A. (1966a). Intellectual functions in patients with lateralized frontal tumors. *Journal of Neurology, Neurosurgery, and Psychiatry,* 29, 52–59.

Smith, A. (1966b). Verbal and nonverbal test performances of patients with 'acute' lateralized brain lesions (tumors). *Journal of Nervous and Mental Disease*, 141, 517–523.

Smith, A. (1975). Neuropsychological testing in neurological disorders. In W.J. Friedlander (Ed.), *Advances in neurology* (Vol. 7). New York: Raven Press.

Sperry, R.W., Gazzaniga, M.S., & Bogen, J.E. (1969). Interhemispheric relationships: The neocortical commisures; syndromes of hemisphere disconnection. In P.J. Vinkin & G.W. Bruyen (Eds.), *Handbook of clinical neurology*. Amsterdam: North Holland.

Spiers, P.A. (1981). Have they come to praise Luria or to bury him? The Luria-Nebraska battery controversy. *Journal of Consulting and Clinical Psychology*, 49, 331–341.

Squire, L.R., Slater, P.C., & Chace, P.M. (1975). Retrograde amnesia: Temporal gradient in very long term memory following electroconvulsive therapy. *Science*, 187, 77–79.

Stambrook, M. (1983). The Luria-Nebraska Neuropsychological Battery: A promise that may be partly fulfilled. *Journal of Clinical Neuropsychology*, 5, 247–269.

Swiercinsky, D. (1978). *Manual for the adult neuropsychological evaluation*. Springfield, IL: C.C. Thomas.

Swiercinsky, D.P. (1979). Factorial pattern description and comparison of functional abilities in neuropsychological assessment. *Perceptual and Motor Skills*, 48, 231–241.

Teasdale, G., & Jennett, B. (1974). Assessment of coma and impaired consciousness: A practical scale. *Lancet*, 2, 81–84.

Teuber, H.-L. (1959). Some alterations in behavior after cerebral lesions in man. In A.D. Bass (Ed.), *Evolution of nervous control from primitive organisms to man*. Washington, DC: American Association for Advancement of Science.

Teuber, H.-L. (1964). The riddle of frontal lobe function in man. In J.M. Warren & K. Akert (Eds.), *The frontal granular cortex and behavior*. New York: McGraw-Hill.

Teuber, H.-L., & Weinstein, S. (1954). Performance on a form-board task after penetrating brain injury. *Journal of Psychology*, 38, 177–190.

Teuber, H.-L., Battersby, W.S., & Bender, M.B. (1951). Performance of complex visual tasks after cerebral lesions. *The Journal of Nervous and Mental Disease*, 114, 413–429.

Vega, A., & Parsons, O. (1967). Cross-validation of the Halstead-Reitan tests for brain damage. *Journal of Consulting Psychology*, 31, 619–625.

Warrington, E.K., & Weiskrantz, L. (1982). Amnesia: A disconnection syndrome? *Neuropsychologia*, 20, 233–248.

Wechsler, D. (1955). *Wechsler adult intelligence scale*. New York: The Psychological Corporation.

Wechsler, D., & Stone, C. P. (1945). *Wechsler memory scale manual*. New York: The Psychological Corporation.

Weinberger, D.R., & Wyatt, R.J. (1982). Brain morphology in schizophrenia: In vivo studies. In F.A. Henn & H.A. Nasrallah (Eds.), *Schizophrenia as a brain disease*. New York: Oxford University Press.

Wertheimer, M. (1923). Studies in the theory of gestalt psychology. *Psychologische Forschung*, 4, 301–350.

Wertz, R.T. (1983). Language intervention context and setting for the aphasic adult: When? In J. Miller, D.E. Yoder, & R. Schiefelbusch (Eds.), *Contemporary issues in language intervention*. Rockville, MD: The American Speech-Language-Hearing Association.

Wilson, R., & Kaszniak, A. (1983, October). *Progressive memory decline in progressive idiopathic dementia.* Paper presented at Conference on Clinical Memory Assessment of Older Adults, Wakefield, MS.

11 NEUROPSYCHOLOGICAL ASSESSMENT OF CHILDREN

H. Gerry Taylor
Jack M. Fletcher
Paul Satz

INTRODUCTION

Methods for the psychometric evaluation of children date back to the development of intelligence tests at the turn of the century. Since that time, a multitude of testing procedures has been developed for the evaluation of intelligence, academic achievement, and more specific abilities in children (e.g., language and perceptual-motor skills). "Neuropsychological" procedures for children are among the more recent of these developments. These procedures have become increasingly popular and are currently being applied to children with a wide variety of disorders. Candidates for neuropsychological evaluation include children with (a) demonstrable neurological conditions including epilepsy, traumatic brain injury, cerebral palsy, brain tumors, and mental retardation; (b) medical problems such as leukemia and diabetes; (c) specific developmental disorders such as learning disabilities and hyperactivity; and (d) emotional disturbances. Unfortunately, there is little agreement on what distinguishes child neuropsychological approaches from other modes of clinical assessment. In some circles, any assessment that might be meaningfully administered to brain-injured children is regarded as neuropsychological. In

other quarters, what qualifies a test as neuropsychological is that it has demonstrated sensitivity to brain disease in adults.

Standardized measures of intelligence, achievement, and behavioral adjustment are not intrinsically neuropsychological methods. Similarly, merely applying procedures developed for adults with brain disease to children does not, ipso facto, assure that such procedures will be useful in the neuropsychological evaluation of children (Fletcher & Taylor, 1983). What most clearly sets a neuropsychological approach apart from other forms of childhood assessment is the manner in which the results are interpreted. The two specific convictions that justify a neuropsychological evaluation are (a) that brain-related factors are relevant to the disorder in question, and (b) that neuropsychological methods permit an assessment of these factors. A proper conceptualization of the specific purposes and offerings of child neuropsychological assessment requires that these convictions be carefully appraised.

The purpose of the present chapter is to first examine the assumptions underlying neuropsychological approaches to children. We will do so by reviewing the historical background for this

211

type of assessment, and by considering the logical grounds for inferring CNS status on the basis of neuropsychological methods. Interpreting an individual child's performance on any test, neuropsychological or otherwise, presents a number of problems. Rational interpretation of test results demands that the premises for making CNS inferences be clearly understood and that the clinician avoid logical fallacies that would lead to overinterpretation of data (Fletcher & Taylor, 1983). After we have considered the problem of making CNS inferences in child assessments, we will describe what we have termed a *functional* approach to the neuropsychological evaluation of children. This approach rests on a conceptualization of developmental neuropsychology that is in keeping with the current knowledge base. Within this approach, the lack of well-established brain-behavior relationships in children is openly acknowledged, and the importance of studying relationships between behavioral variables is stressed. Neuropsychological performances are interpreted in a multifactorial context that requires the integration of environmental, social, and developmental factors, and that resists direct inferences from behavior to brain. Following discussion of several advantages of the functional approach, we will describe how it is employed in the assessment process. Our contention is that the specialized nature of developmental neuropsychology accrues primarily from the interest in CNS contributions to behavior, but that methods for neuropsychological assessment of children may be drawn from the general community of psychological approaches to children. A brief review of the historical underpinnings of child neuropsychology helps set the stage for exposition of the functional approach to assessment.

ORIGINS OF NEUROPSYCHOLOGICAL APPROACHES TO CHILDREN

Child neuropsychology has its roots in a number of historical developments. These roots can be traced back to the concept of cerebral dysfunction in children, the development of ability tests, and the emergence of applied psychology as a professional discipline. Other historical influences include studies of the nature of intelligence and clinical investigations of the effects of brain injury

on adult behavior. Since the current status of child neuropsychology can be best characterized by tracing its roots, the present section provides a brief historical review.

Concept of Cerebral Dysfunction

Although frequently overlooked, the concept of cerebral dysfunction in children has likely had more impact on current conceptualizations of child neuropsychological assessment than any other single factor. The concept itself seems to have stemmed from dual observations of (a) relatively distinct deficits in behavior and cognition of children with brain disease, and (b) similar deficits in children without established neurological disorders. Together, these observations have been used to justify the inference of cerebral dysfunction in cases where certain behavioral deficits are present but where definitive neurological disorder cannot be verified. Cerebral dysfunction is thus based on the conviction that similar behavioral patterns represent similar etiologies, rather than on direct proof of abnormal brain status.

The conviction that certain child behaviors reflect brain abnormalities has a long history in psychology and medicine. As early as 1902, Still attributed certain instances of impulsive, acting-out behavior to subtle brain disorders. He acknowledged that, in some cases, such behavior was associated with general impairment of intellect or recognizable physical disease (e.g., head trauma, epilepsy, or CNS infections). But he also pointed out that these etiologies did not account for all cases. Noting that these latter cases occurred more frequently in males than in females and that they were associated with a higher than normal incidence of physical stigmata and stressful births, Still proposed a biological explanation. He referred to these latter instances as "morbid failure of the development of moral control" (Still, 1902, p. 1080).

A similar theme is echoed in a classic paper by Kahn and Cohen (1934). In reaction to the pronounced tendency at that time to provide psychoanalytic explanations for all childhood disorders, these authors argued that certain cases of impulsive, overactive, and unmanageable behavior be construed as "organic drivenness." Such behavior was frequently observed in children who no longer displayed pathognomic signs of brain damage, but who had histories of birth trauma, head injury, or encephalitis. Kahn and Cohen argued that the distinct pattern of behavior observed in these children, combined with their abnormal medical histories, implicated a brain-stem syndrome. In contrast with the then prevailing psychogenic explanations for many childhood disabilities, Kahn and Cohen felt that faulty interaction with the environment was an insufficient explanation for these behavior disorders.

The most direct point of origin for the concept of cerebral dysfunction is the work of Strauss and his associates (e.g., Strauss & Lehtinen, 1947). Based on work with mentally retarded children, Strauss applied the term "minimal brain injury" to children who displayed combinations of impulsivity, hyperactivity, perseverative response tendencies, perceptual disturbances, and poor abstract reasoning. The concept of minimal brain injury was later extended to all children with similar symptoms, regardless of general intelligence or neurological status, and especially to children with deficiencies in academic achievement (Laufer & Denhoff, 1957). Although the existence of a group of nonretarded children displaying these specific characteristics has never been demonstrated (cf. Baumeister & MacLean, 1979), Strauss's concept of the brain-injured child was highly influential. A federal task force formed to define problems within the category discussed by Strauss relied heavily on his conceptualization of minimal brain injury. Pointing out that actual injury to the brain could not be demonstrated in cases of so called minimal brain injury, the task force changed Strauss's term to "minimal brain dysfunction" and expanded on the categories included (Clements, 1966). For the most part, however, the task force preserved the notion that certain behavior problems represented abnormal brain status (cf. Satz & Fletcher, 1980; Taylor, in press b).

The popularity of the concept of minimal brain dysfunction stemmed in part from the support it offered for the then popular notion of a "biological gradient" (Ingalls & Gordon, 1947). According to this notion and to the related concept of a "continuum of reproductive casualty" (Pasamanick & Knoblock, 1960), if serious brain damage can result in death, physical disability, or clear mental retardation, then less serious degrees of damage are held responsible for less extreme forms of mental and behavioral impairment.

Learning and attentional problems would be included in this latter category. The basic premise of the continuum hypothesis—that is, there is an isomorphism between disorders of behavior and disorders of brain—has been widely criticized (Benton, 1973; Fletcher & Taylor, 1983; Rutter, 1982; Satz & Fletcher, 1980; Taylor, in press b). Nevertheless, the idea that functional (i.e., behavioral) signs can provide a basis for making CNS inferences about children—even when the relationship of those signs to the CNS is not documented—has had an insidious influence on neuropsychological approaches to children. Neuropsychologists evaluating children continue to make unverified inferences about the CNS solely on the basis of psychometric test results and behavioral observations despite the lack of any direct confirmation for these inferences.

Influence of Adult Neuropsychology

Early conceptualizations of brain function proposed by such figures as Lashley (1929) and Goldstein (1939) have also helped to lay the groundwork for contemporary approaches to child neuropsychological assessment. These and other researchers observed what they felt to be qualitatively distinct effects of brain injuries on adult behavior. They interpreted these effects as evidence that certain skills were more vulnerable to neurological insult than others. Halstead's tests for biological intelligence and the Halstead Neuropsychological Test Battery for Adults that followed represent early outgrowths of these observations (Reitan & Davison, 1974). More recent developments are summarized in contemporary volumes by Filskov and Boll (1981), Hecaen and Albert (1978), Heilman and Valenstein (1979), and Lezak (1976).

The assumption that certain skills represent more direct reflections of cerebral status than other skills has had a similar influence on child neuropsychological assessment. This influence is represented by (a) the continued search for measures differentially sensitive to CNS dysfunction in children, (b) the frequent use of competence-achievement discrepancies in diagnosing learning problems, and (c) the emphasis on models of adult brain function for interpreting psychometric test results. Possibly because of the difficulties in conducting brain-behavior studies in children (due in part to the low frequency of non-diffuse brain lesions in children), adult models of brain-behavior organization have sometimes been assumed prima facie to apply to children. At the least, adult models have served as a source of hypotheses concerning patterns of behavioral dysfunction in children.

Despite problems with the wholesale application of adult models to children (Dennis, 1983; Fletcher & Taylor, 1983; Satz & Fletcher, 1981), reliance on adult models has been useful in several respects. The application to children of modes of neuropsychological interpretation developed initially for adults is one example. Interpretive modes based on levels of performance, pathognomic signs, lateralization of deficits, and differential patterns of performance across multiple testing procedures have proved helpful in recognizing potential brain-related disorders in children (Rourke, 1975). As a further example, the emphasis of adult neuropsychology on various dissociations in memory, language, and motor skills observed in brain-damaged adults has brought about an expanded awareness of the organization and complexity of higher cognitive functions. The development of the Halstead-Reitan approach and other experimental and clinical approaches to neuropsychology (cf. Benton, Hamsher, Varney, & Spreen, 1983; Goodglass & Kaplan, 1972) has led to growing recognition of the diversity of effects of brain injury on behavior. Application of these approaches to children has yielded many important empirical discoveries. The value of neuropsychological tests for distinguishing subvarieties of learning disabilities is representative of these findings (Rourke, in press). In addition, concepts like cerebral dysfunction and organicity have successfully drawn attention to the role of biological factors in many childhood disorders (e.g., specific developmental disorders and attention deficit disorders). Although direct evidence for physiological abnormality is generally lacking in the case of specific developmental disorders, the conviction that some components of these disabilities are brain-related remains warranted (Taylor & Fletcher, 1983).

Implications for Child Neuropsychological Assessment

The above-noted historical factors have culminated in a variety of neuropsychological approaches to children. One of these approaches is to apply modified versions of adult-originated tests to children or to create tests that attempt to measure abilities analogous to those tapped by adult neuropsychological batteries. The Luria-Nebraska Children's Battery provides the most obvious example of this approach (Golden, 1981). The second general approach is to render neuropsychological interpretations of more traditional procedures for children (e.g., the WISC-R, ITPA), sometimes in conjunction with tests developed specifically for neuropsychological assessment (e.g., Wilson, in press). The practitioners of this second approach vary considerably in terms of tests used and the caution they apply in making CNS inferences. Many practitioners use test results largely for their diagnostic-prescriptive utility, with statements regarding brain status serving as explanations for the ability deficits observed. A third approach employs measures derived in part from research on cognitive development. As such, the third approach represents the greatest departure from adult-derived methods and from the influence of the concept of minimal brain dysfunction. Dennis (1980, 1983) illustrates this approach in her research on the effects of stroke and hemispherectomy on the organization of cognitive skills in children. The primary concern of this third approach is with the age-related organization of *children's* abilities.

Although each of these approaches is somewhat different, all of them emphasize the relationship of test results and behavioral observations to brain status. As discussed earlier, the major problem in defining child neuropsychological assessment in this manner is that few brain-behavior relationships have been established in children (Rutter, 1981). For the wide spectrum of potentially relevant clinical problems, brain status is a virtual unknown, and the study of brain-behavior associations thus unfeasible. By default, an exclusive emphasis on brain-behavior relationships leads either to vague and misleading concepts such as cerebral dysfunction or to an overreliance on methods and models of brain function derived from adult studies.

The way out of this dilemma is to recognize that neuropsychologists are just as interested in relationships among behavioral variables as they are in the relationships of brain to behavior (Benton, 1962). The concordance of verbal comprehension deficits and paraphasic speech in patients with left-hemisphere disease provides a vivid example of the importance of behavioral interrelationships in neuropsychological investigation. As the history of aphasiology shows, behavioral associations and dissociations of this sort typically precede hypotheses concerning underlying brain mechanisms (Benton, 1964). In a similar fashion, analyses of child behavior may well lead the way to discovery of brain-behavior relationships in children (Dennis, 1983; Fletcher & Taylor, 1983).

The foregoing characterization of neuropsychology has several implications for the assessment of children. First, the child neuropsychologist's domain is not restricted to making CNS inferences. An understanding of behavioral relationships is vitally important to the practice of child neuropsychology. As an example, investigation of language correlates of reading disability can be valuable in determining the type of reading disability and in recommending treatment, even when nothing is known about the CNS basis for either the language disorder or the reading disability. Second, the child neuropsychologist need not rely solely on adult models. While adult models can be heuristic, it is also possible to draw from knowledge on the development and organization of normal children's abilities. Awareness of how language skills and reading abilities interrelate in normal children, for example, may suggest novel approaches to the study of childhood reading disabilities. Third, the child neuropsychologist' must explicitly acknowledge the influence of social and environmental factors on the child's behavior and test performance. Since there is little empirical justification for assuming that most neuropsychological measures are "culture-fair," it would seem unwise to interpret test performances without references to social-cultural factors. Fourth, the child neuropsychologist must attempt to incorporate developmental considerations into the assessment process. Developmental analyses require the neuropsychologist to look carefully at the manner in which the disability is manifested at different ages and at age-related changes in the pattern of behavioral correlates of the disability. With improved knowledge of these correlates and of the social-environmental influences on the disabilities of interest, the neuropsychologist should be better able to evaluate the influence of biological factors per se.

In the next section, we will detail a *functional* approach to the neuropsychological assessment of children. As with attempts to develop "brain-sensitive" measures, this approach makes use of our limited knowledge regarding the influence of CNS abnormalities on child behavior. In addition, however, this approach encourages the selection of assessment instruments according to their value as measures of children's abilities and their sensitivity to problems known to be present in developmentally disabled groups. Although this functional approach emphasizes behavioral relationships, it assumes that the neuropsychologist has special training and interest in the contributions of CNS factors to behavior. The functional approach is presented not as an alternative to other neuropsychological approaches or to standard intellectual or psychoeducational assessment, but as an integration of existing procedures. The focus is on thorough study of children's abilities as a means by which to eventually delineate the role of biological factors.

FUNCTIONAL APPROACH TO CHILD NEUROPSYCHOLOGICAL ASSESSMENT

Neuropsychological assessment is commonly conceptualized as an evaluation of abilities thought to reflect CNS integrity. Attempts at differential diagnosis of emotional versus organic disorders frequently form the basis for these assessments. The emphasis of a functional approach is somewhat different. Following this approach, the primary goal of neuropsychological assessment is to evaluate developing cognitive and behavioral skills associated with the disability in question. In conducting neuropsychological assessment, no single set of measures is either necessary nor sufficient in every case. While it may be important to evaluate the same general areas of skill in most cases (e.g., language, attention, memory), different clinical problems require alternative methods. Developmental and psychosocial considerations vary from child to child and necessitate a flexible approach to assessment.

Basic Premises

The functional approach is best described in terms of four basic postulates. The following postulates comprise the working assumptions of child neuropsychological assessment and help to clarify its unique standing vis à vis other modes of child assessment.

1. Neuropsychological evaluation of a developmental disability consists of (a) a descriptive analysis of the presenting problems, i.e., the child's *manifest disability*; (b) assessment of a

limited set of basic skills or competencies intrinsic to the child (i.e., the child's *basic competencies*); (c) consideration of socio-cultural and motivational-attitudinal variables likely to be more extrinsically determined (i.e., *moderator variables*); and (d) evaluation of the relationship of different *biological indices* to the child's performance.

2. Although the manifest disability is a product of weaknesses in basic competencies, the impact of these weaknesses on the child's ability to learn and behave as expected is dependent to some extent on the above-noted extrinsic factors or moderator variables. These factors include the child's ability to compensate for his/her weaknesses, the attitudes of the child toward learning, and the stimulation and encouragement provided the child by the family and school.

3. Although covariation of basic skills within individuals is usually high, dissociations between skills are characteristic of many disabled children. Such contrasting levels of skill are related to either congenital neurological variation or to outright neurological disorder. The study of the child who exhibits variations in basic competencies is of value in refining our understanding of the nature of these competencies and how they are deployed in more complex activities.

4. The CNS influences the manifest disability via the limits it imposes on these basic competencies. However, because both the manifest disability and the basic competencies are affected by moderator variables, the CNS can only be considered one of several influences. (These postulates have been stated somewhat differently in previous publications [Fletcher & Taylor, 1983], representing our continued efforts to refine and clarify this approach to child neuropsychology.)

According to this schema, the functional model is comprised of four types of variables: The first represents the child's manifest disability; the second represents the behavioral and cognitive correlates of the disability (basic competencies); the third represents environmental, social, and motivational factors that determine how the child copes with his/her basic skill weaknesses (moderator variables); and the fourth represents the status of the CNS and other biological indices. The first type of variable (manifest disability) is exem-

plified by the actual behavior of the hyperactive child, the academic performance of the disabled learner, and the expressive language abilities of the child aphasic. The second variable type (basic competencies) is illustrated by the hyperactive child's performance on attentional tasks and by the perceptual, linguistic, and memory deficits of the disabled learner or child aphasic. Examples of the third type of variable (moderator variables) include cultural deprivation and inappropriate responses of the parent or teacher to a child's learning problem and the child's resultant poor self-esteem or low frustration tolerance. The fourth type of variable (biological indices) refers to the condition of the CNS that predisposes the child toward a given disability and its behavioral and cognitive correlates. The actual brain lesion of the child with acquired aphasia or the presumed genetic irregularity underlying a familial case of reading disability provide examples of this fourth type of variable.

Advantages

Emphasis on Distinct Types of Variables

A major virtue of partitioning variables into different categories is that it draws attention to the variety of behavioral variables that must be considered in evaluating childhood disabilities and to the possibility of dissociating different skills. Children referred for neuropsychological evaluations have diverse problems of academic achievement, attention, and social adaptation. Even in those children whose difficulties are specific to certain areas of academic progress, the exact problems range widely from child to child. Some children with reading disability, for example, are able to understand what they read but have difficulty in decoding single words (Johnson, 1980; Perfetti, 1980). Others show difficulties in both comprehension and single word decoding, or may fail to comprehend what they read despite the ability to read constituent words (Isakson & Miller, 1976). There are many factors underlying reading failure and, especially in poor readers, multiple ways in which reading can break down (Calfee, 1982; Doehring, Trites, Patel, & Fiedorowicz, 1981; Guthrie, 1973). The same principles apply to other areas of disability of interest to the neuropsychologist. A necessary first step in determining the factors contributing to children's problems is to examine the exact manner in which they fail to spell, do arithmetic calculations, attend to their schoolwork, or behave in accordance with social expectations.

Neuropsychological assessment of the basic competencies on which these more complex skills rest is equally important. In fact, the special expertise of the neuropsychologist is in discovering deficits in basic skills that potentially contribute to the manifest disability. Children with specific learning disorders as well as those having documented brain disorders may show any one of a number of basic skill deficits (Benton, 1975; Rourke, 1980; Rutter, 1981). Children with reading disabilities, for example, may manifest weaknesses in abstract reasoning, visual-motor coordination, language, or memory. Although there are no fixed patterns of deficit associated with these broader categories of learning disorders or brain damage in children, studies of subtypes of developmental disability are promising. Several recent investigations have found evidence for subtypes of reading disabled children based on patterns of neuropsychological test results (Doehring et al., 1981; Rourke, in press; Satz & Morris, 1981). The neuropsychological approach to assessment, with its traditional emphasis on a broad spectrum of tests (Rourke, 1980), has been one factor responsible for the success of these studies. Similar analyses of neuropsychological performance patterns are likely to contribute to improved understanding of other forms of developmental disabilities, including those associated with early brain injury, attention deficit disorders, and even some forms of social maladaptation. Differentiation of subtypes based on neuropsychological profiles may also shed light on the role of CNS factors in developmental disabilities. Bale (1981), for example, found that pre- and perinatal complications were related to later reading disabilities, but only among children with visual-motor deficiencies.

The neuropsychologist must also heed the influence of moderator variables on the manifest disability and on basic competencies. Factors such as the child's attitude toward learning, tolerance for frustration, and the ability of the family and school to help the child cope with inherent difficulties all have some bearing on how these weaknesses will be manifest. Psychosocial factors have clear effects on cognitive development in both normal and disabled children (Mussen, Conger, & Kagan, 1979; Sarmeroff & Chandler, 1975; Walsh & Greenough, 1976). Examples of how environmental considerations are important in the study of developmental disabilities are provided by Siegel (1981) and Werner (1980), who demonstrated that developmental outcome in infants who sustained pre- or perinatal trauma depended in part on socioeconomic variables and on characteristics of the home environment. Another example is the fact that favorable outcomes in disabled learners are most frequently reported for brighter children from good socio-cultural backgrounds (Schonhaut & Satz, 1983). In children who sustain brain injuries, premorbid adjustment also contributes to the risk of the child's having subsequent problems (Rutter, 1982); and it is likely that risk status for chronic developmental handicaps in children who have learning difficulties upon entering school is related to their social-adaptational abilities and temperaments (Birch, Thomas, & Chess, 1964). The way in which the child responds to a handicap is another important moderator variable. Learning problems in hyperactive children may be exaggerated by the frustration and low self-esteem experienced by these children (Cunningham & Barkley, 1978; Douglas, 1980). A final moderating influence is the context in which the child is observed or tested. Difficulties in learning or social behavior manifested by children with basic skill deficits often vary from setting to setting (e.g., Kalverboer, 1976; McMahon, 1981). Consideration of moderator variables is therefore essential, not only for determining the impact of basic skill deficits on the child's ability to learn and adapt, but also for evaluation of the adequacy of the assessment procedures themselves.

Incentive to Study Relationships among Types of Variables

A second advantage of the functional approach is that it encourages the study of relationships among the different types of variables. Within the functional framework, the manner in which moderator variables influence manifest disabilities is a relevant issue. Studies of those factors that render a child vulnerable to developmental handicaps are encouraged. The functional approach also stimulates interest in how basic competencies might influence certain personality or social-adaptational (i.e., moderator) variables. Associations between basic competencies and social behavior in disabled learners are supported by the recent findings of Richman and Lindgren (1981)

and Rourke and Fisk (1981). A third interbehav-
ioral relationship of interest within the functional
approach occurs among manifest disabilities and
basic competencies. Several studies suggest a correspondence between manifest characteristics of a
child's learning disability and patterns of basic
skill deficits. Rourke and Finlayson (1978) found
that children with greater deficiencies in
arithmetic relative to spelling and reading exhibited different patterns of neuropsychological performance than did children with the converse
pattern of academic achievement. Looking at the
ability to spell from dictation, Sweeney and
Rourke (1978) found that those children who
made phonetically inaccurate spelling errors
showed greater difficulties on a variety of language tasks compared to children whose spelling
errors, while equally frequent, were more
phonetically accurate. Research on subtypes of
reading disability documents the possibility of
similar mappings of neuropsychological patterns
onto specific forms of reading disturbance
(Doehring et al., 1981; Taylor, Fletcher, & Satz,
1982).

Torgesen (1979) referred to the study of how
basic competencies contribute to the manifest
form of a child's disability as the "task-centered"
approach to assessment. Meichenbaum (1976)
used the term "cognitive-functional" in reference
to a similar approach. In addition to guiding the
selection of basic competencies for investigation,
careful analysis of the manifest disability may
provide clues regarding subtypes of disability and
may thus help to establish differential treatments.
Once we are aware of the cognitive skills that
enter into performance on a given academic task,
we can investigate how performance might be
improved, either through direct teaching of the
component skill or through coaching of the child
to accomplish the task without reliance on that
particular skill (Pellegrino & Glaser, 1979). Although studies that have paired treatments with
aptitudes have proved generally unsuccessful,
"aptitudes and treatments have been rarely analyzed in terms of similar underlying performance
processes that could relate the two . . ." (Pellegrino & Glaser, 1979, p. 85). Neuropsychological
assessment of basic competencies has the potential
to provide the more detailed information about
learner characteristics that may be required for
appropriate matching of instruction or remediation to individual children.

Relationship with Other Areas of Psychological Investigation

A further advantage of an emphasis on the study
of behavioral variables is that it encourages us to
make use of knowledge within other areas of psychological inquiry. To better analyze the psychological "substrate" of a given disability, the
concepts, findings, and methods of some approaches to cognitive and developmental psychology deserve special consideration. Cognitive
psychologists are concerned with component
mental processes in ways that parallel the neuropsychologists' interest in basic competencies.
Common to both cognitive psychology and some
approaches to neuropsychology is the premise that
cognitive functions may be decomposed into a
relatively small set of distinct component processes (Kail & Bisanz, 1982). Information processing constructs may thus provide valuable clues to
the neuropsychologist regarding ways in which to
define basic competencies.

In a recent and seminal paper espousing an
information processing point of view, Hunt (1983)
recommended that component processes be analyzed along three dimensions. The first dimension
pertains to the individual's ability to engage in
basic mental operations, including the storage
and retrieval of information and the transformation and manipulation of information in working
memory. The second dimension includes the information processing strategies by which the basic
operations are engaged in solving problems. The
third dimension involves the way in which individuals represent or encode problems (e.g., verbally versus spatially). In an earlier paper, Hunt
(1980) included a fourth dimension, which he
referred to as attentional resources. The capacity
of an individual to solve a problem would thus
depend not only on elementary processes, strategies, and means by which to encode problems,
but also on the availability of attentional resources to carry out each of these other mental
operations.

Whereas information processing constructs
may be criticized for being too theoretical and
lacking in application, they provide a rich source
of hypotheses and paradigms of relevance to child
neuropsychological assessment. Information processing procedures for studying memory and en-
coding may be helpful in discovering basic skill
deficits that contribute to a given learning problem. In fact, individual differences in elementary

information processes may be more pronounced for groups of disabled children than has been the case for the adult samples typically studied by cognitive psychologists (Hunt, 1980). It may also be worthwhile to consider the child's repertoire of information processing strategies. For some time, both neuropsychologists and cognitive psychologists have emphasized the importance of distinguishing tasks that demand application of previously acquired information from tasks that require either new learning or active problem solving (Brown, 1975; Rourke, 1980; Shallice, 1981). Torgesen (1980) has shown that learning disabled children often fail to spontaneously apply problem-solving strategies that, when experimentally induced, can facilitate task performance. Thus, some children may have skills necessary to improve their learning, but not put these skills to proper use. A further information processing concept of relevance to assessment is that of attentional resources. Although poorly defined, attentional disturbances may be an important correlate of learning failure (Douglas, 1980; Dykman, Ackerman, Clements, & Peters, 1971). Attentional disorders may involve either an absolute inability to sustain attention or control impulses, or inefficient focusing or deployment of available attentional resources. According to information processing research, automatization of lower level skills is required if sufficient attentional resources are to be available for more complex tasks (Kail & Bisanz, 1982). In the case of a reading disabled child, reading fluency and comprehension may be hampered by general inattention to the material being read or by more specific failure to automatize lower level skills (e.g., decoding of individual words). In either case, attentional resources are unavailable for higher-level processing of text. Although cognitive psychology may not always offer convenient methods for measuring attention and other information processing concepts, consideration of these variables may lead to valuable insights regarding basic competencies.

Child neuropsychological assessment also has much to gain from potential relationships with certain approaches to developmental psychology, particularly those emphasizing behavioral change (Siegel, Bisanz, & Bisanz, 1983; Wohlwill, 1973). Investigations of child development document the fact that children's skills change with time. Assessment of basic skills requires appreciation of these

changes in order that a given child's performance might be compared with social-cultural expectations of the child or with the performances of other children with whom the child competes at school. Familiarity with child development may also aid the neuropsychologist in searching for factors contributing to a child's disability. Cognitive and learning abilities as well as social behavior are determined by different factors in younger children than they are in older children. Parent-child interactions, for example, may have a more primary influence on the child's attitude toward learning or toward other children early in life, whereas social encounters outside of the home may play a greater role at a later point in time. Similarly, the factors influencing a child's ability to handle the demands of a given academic task vary with age. Early in reading acquisition, knowledge of phonological relationships plays a primary role in determining a child's competence. At later ages, semantic and syntactic knowledge is a more critical determinant of reading skill (Gibson & Levin, 1975). The basic competencies most closely associated with reading skill also change as the child develops (Doehring, 1976; Fletcher, 1981). From the perspective of development, childhood disabilities can be viewed as disruptions of the processes by which children acquire skills. Deficits at one age may thus predict later problems, sometimes of a different sort. By virtue of its focus on behavior, the functional model is compatible with procedures for assessing developmental change (Siegel et al., 1983), as well as with existing methods for evaluating the specific nature of manifest problems, basic competencies, and moderator variables at any given age.

View of CNS Status as One of Several Influences on Behavior and Learning

A final advantage of the functional approach is that neurological status is viewed primarily as setting limits on behavioral traits, discouraging brain-behavior isomorphisms. CNS factors are represented as constraints on an individual child's ability to meet behavioral or cognitive demands and to adapt to expectations. At least two confounded factors interfere with direct relationships between brain and behavior in children. The first factor is the fact that adaptive behavior, by its very complexity, is always to some extent dependent on learning history and eliciting conditions.

The second confound, noted earlier, is that moderator variables must always be considered in evaluating a child's current performance on neuropsychological tests. Moderator variables would include social and cultural factors, the child's experience with and acceptance of the demands of formal testing, and the strategies by which the child compensates for any intrinsic weaknesses.

In promoting the functional model, we reject the notion that a child's neurological endowment is directly expressed in any given set of behavioral traits. Because behavioral functions are viewed as products of both nature and nurture (Birch, 1964; Weisfeld, 1982), the influence of the CNS can be ascertained only by evaluating the influence of both CNS and non-CNS factors. Rather than assuming that certain behavioral tests or observations directly mirror brain function, we maintain that some behaviors are more directly related to CNS status than are other behaviors. More precisely, we assume that the proportion of interchild variability in a given skill that might be accounted for by CNS factors is relatively greater for some skills than for other skills. As an example, the facility with which a child recites a novel story after its first presentation may be regarded as more subject to native endowment than the child's ability to recall a previously learned story. In the latter case, learning history may contribute substantially to the fact that the child can recall the story. Although the child's efficiency in learning a new story will reflect abilities and strategies that have been learned in part by virtue of past experience, the acquisition process is likely to be less subject to these factors than the mere recall of previously learned material. The contrast between behaviors that are primarily CNS-related and behaviors that are more environmentally determined has been drawn by others. Developmental psychologists have long emphasized the importance of both physiological maturation and environmental conditioning in accounting for developmental change (McCall, 1981; Spiker, 1966). Unraveling these two types of influences on behavior and on child development is a central task for the child neuropsychologist.

One way to establish that a given behavior is primarily CNS-related is to show that variations in skill level are independent of environmental conditions. Such independence from environmental influences may be suggested either by invariance in a particular skill across different environments or by variability in the skill despite similar

environments. Associations with biological "markers" may also serve to identify given skills as CNS-related. As an example, Wolff (1981) recommended that various aspects of cognitive development be studied in relation to indices of sexual maturity among adolescents. If given aspects of cognition are more closely linked to parameters of sexual maturity than are other aspects of cognition, there is reason to suspect that the former aspects are more biologically related. Indices of biological-relatedness in addition to sexual maturity might include a family history of problems similar to the child's problem, electrophysiological abnormalities, minor physical anomalies, and pre- and perinatal complications.

A third tactic for isolating biologically related behaviors is to study children who have sustained definitive brain disorders. While no skills are categorically immune from the effects of brain damage, studies of brain-injured children suggest that some abilities may be more susceptible to early CNS insults than other abilities (Levin, Ewing-Cobbs, & Benton, in press; Taylor, in press a). Application of the information processing constructs noted earlier may help to better delineate those skills that are most susceptible to specific types of brain disorder. It is doubtful, however, that any one skill will emerge as the most sensitive to brain damage in general. The complexities of the brain and of human behavior prevent one-to-one correspondences between performance and brain status. The functional model encourages us to seek out those behavioral traits that vary in relation to CNS status, but only by looking more systematically at all sources of behavioral variability among children.

THE ASSESSMENT PROCESS

The several advantages of a functional approach are of practical value in conducting neuropsychological assessments of children having various forms of developmental disability. Incorporation of a functional approach makes it possible to conduct these assessments in ways that avoid dependence on brain-behavior isomorphisms or on adult models. Following the functional model, the contribution of CNS factors of special interest to the neuropsychologist can be evaluated in ways that are congruent with current knowledge and that provide appropriate evaluation of the multiple factors influencing the child. In the present section, we will detail a method for carrying out child neuropsychological assessments that is based on the functional model.

In our experience, referral for child neuropsychological assessment most often stems from concern over a child's failure to meet expectations at school or at home. This failure may involve inability to make expected progress in reading, spelling, or arithmetic, or it may involve poor work habits or behavioral transgressions. Although neuropsychological asessment is conducted to explore possible intrinsic disabilities that might be contributing to the problem (i.e., the basic competencies mentioned above), the functional approach allows the examiner to investigate each child's problem from a broader perspective. In the majority of cases, it is essential that the examiner consider the exact form of the disability as well as a variety of moderator variables. Only by considering the manifest disability, correlative basic skill deficits, and interactive psychosocial variables will the neuropsychologist be able to provide the family and school with impressions regarding all contributing factors. Furthermore, recommendations for appropriate treatment will be possible only after all such factors have been taken into account.

If the child neuropsychologist's role is to extend beyond the identification of deficits in basic competencies alone and to include more comprehensive assessment of the multiple factors that may be contributing to the child's problem, neuropsychological assessment must encompass many of the strategies used in child clinical and psychoeducational assessments. This does not require the neuropsychologist to conduct complete psychoeducational workups or personality assessments, but it does require the ability to identify problems within these complementary domains and familiarity with their assessment methodologies. The child neuropsychologist is thus operating in a boundary zone among several disciplines. Depending on training and interest, neuropsychological assessment may be limited to a determination of basic skills. If so, close liaisons with professionals from the child clinical and psychoeducational fields are necessary to assure that all aspects of functioning are evaluated. Alternatively, the neuropsychologist may wish to fulfill these multiple roles independently. In either case, the child neuropsychologist needs to be aware of several areas of expertise. When problems extend into areas not included as part of the neuropsychologists' expertise, appropriate referrals must be made to other child specialists. As child neuropsychologists often work within medical centers where the children they see are frequently in need of medical care or monitoring, an appreciation for medical (especially neurological) disorders and their treatment must be developed. Here again, the neuropsychologist's effectiveness in understanding the factors that contribute to a child's problem and in recommending appropriate treatment rests heavily on the ability to work in concert with other professionals.

The functional approach provides a structure by which to assure that all important aspects of the child's functioning are considered in the assessment process. According to this approach, assessment consists of the following aspects: (a) analysis of the manifest disability (e.g., reading disability, attention deficit); (b) measurement of basic competencies; (c) consideration of moderator variables; (d) review of indices of either direct or potential biological significance (e.g., medical or neurological history, relevant laboratory data, family history); and (e) integration of these various factors in order to explain the child's problems and recommend appropriate treatment. Each of these components of the assessment process are considered in turn below.

Analysis of the Manifest Disability

Determination of the child's difficulties is an essential aspect of assessment. In many cases, the nature of the presenting difficulties is often obscure and significant problems or "hidden agendas" may escape initial attention. Careful and thorough review of the reason for the child's referral and all possible problems manifested by the child is therefore critical.

Information regarding referral issues can be obtained in at least three ways. The first way is to collect data on the child prior to assessment. These data may include parent and teacher questionnaires, school and medical records, and the results of previous evaluations. Our standard practice is to request from the parents a list of primary concerns, information regarding medical history and current medical status, and completed checklists regarding the child's behavior. Formalized checklists such as the Conner's Parent Questionnaire (Barkley, 1981) or the Child Behavior Checklist (Achenbach, 1979) have proved helpful in identifying problem behaviors or areas of mal-adjustment. Similar questionnaires can be requested of teachers, along with teacher impressions of the child's problems and of management and remedial strategies currently in use.

The second means of obtaining information regarding the child's disability is the parent interview. In this interview, parents are asked to describe the nature and history of their child's problems and to present their views concerning the origins of these problems. To ensure that all potential problem areas are brought to light, parents are routinely questioned about several areas of their child's functioning (peer interaction, attentional abilities, behavior at home). The Vineland Adaptive Behavior Scales (Sparrow, Balla, & Ciccetti, in press), a significant improvement in adaptive behavior scales, will soon be available. These age-normed scales will provide formal data regarding several aspects of the child's functioning in his environment (Communication, Daily Living Skills, Socialization, and Motor Skills). Ways in which the child and parents are coping with existing problems can also be explored during the interview, along with the child's strengths and adaptational abilities. By surveying the parents' understanding of the problem, their fears for the child, and the relationships they have with their child and his/her teachers, the neuropsychologist is in a better position to build rapport with the parents. Parents are the best advocates for their children, and the clinician's ability to communicate impressions and recommendations to parents forms the foundation for effective intervention.

The third way in which the clinician can learn about the child's disability is to directly test problem areas or observe the child under conditions where the disability is apparent. If the primary complaint is a reading disability, tests of reading skills are administered to ascertain the exact nature of the reading problem. The Wide Range Achievement Test (Jastak & Jastak, 1978) provides an effective survey of word recognition, spelling to dictation, and arithmetic calculation abilities. To supplement the Wide Range Achievement Test, other tests of academic achievement can be given, including the Woodcock Reading Mastery Tests (Woodcock, 1973), The Gilmore Oral Reading Test (Gilmore & Gilmore, 1968), and the Peabody Individual Achievement Test (Dunn & Markwardt, 1970). If the presenting problem is

an attentional deficit or hyperactivity, formal tests of vigilance such as the Children's Checking Test (Keogh & Margolis, 1976) may be administered. Informal observations as to how the child approaches tests of basic competencies (see below) also help to delineate the nature of the attentional or organizational deficits. An interview with the child and observations of the child's response to failure, work habits, and attitudes toward self and examiner may shed further light on the child's problems. Children with traumatic brain injury frequently manifest memory difficulties for several years following the accident. Formal evaluation with memory tests (e.g., Levin, Benton, & Grossman, 1982) is important for evaluating this part of the manifest disability, along with school and parent reports.

Testing Basic Competencies

One set or battery of test procedures is not appropriate for all children, and exising standardized neuropsychological procedures fail to tap all important areas of skill. Depending on a given child's problems, the neuropsychologist will selectively emphasize certain types of assessment. For example, evaluation of actual reading skills is more important for assessing disabled readers than for evaluating children with traumatic brain injuries, in whom memory testing may be more important. Furthermore, because neuropsychological assessment is constantly evolving, experimental procedures may provide useful supplements to more routine and well-standardized measures. These experimental procedures may be designed to explore abilities not tapped by the standard techniques, or they may be added to further decompose a deficit skill area (e.g., breaking a naming deficit down into vocabulary knowledge versus memory retrieval). Nevertheless, because it is usually necessary to survey the child's strengths as well as weaknesses and to explore a wide range of abilities, tests of basic competencies ordinarily encompass most of the following seven general categories: intelligence, language, visual-spatial and constructional skills, somatosensory and motor functions, attention, memory and learning, and problem solving and abstract reasoning. A description of each competency area is given below. Within each category, the rationale for testing is provided, limitations are considered, and some specific tests are mentioned. The list of test procedures is not meant to be inclusive, but rather is intended to give the reader a sampling of the kinds of tasks contained within the child neuropsychologist's test repertoire.

Intelligence

Standard intelligence tests, most notably the Wechsler Intelligence Scale for Children—Revised (WISC-R) (Wechsler, 1974), contribute to neuropsychological assessment in several ways. First and foremost, tests like the WISC-R tap a wide range of verbal and nonverbal skills. The child's performance on different subtests of the WISC-R may be helpful as a point of departure for exploring cognitive abilities. Comparisons between the child's performance on subtests requiring primarily verbal, visual-spatial, or attentional skills may be helpful in delineating processing deficits in these areas (Kaufman, 1979b; Sattler, 1982). Secondly, because IQ tests measure several abilities and are well standardized, these procedures can be used to estimate a child's general range of mental functions. WISC-R results are also useful as points of reference in describing samples of children for research purposes. Finally, in conjunction with assessments of adaptive behavior, standardized IQ test results are of value in supporting placement recommendations and in surveying areas in which the child's skills may be relatively intact.

The usefulness of traditional IQ tests justifies their inclusion in neuropsychological assessment (or attempts to secure results from previous administrations of these tests). Often, however, the utility of IQ tests is overrated. The limitations of IQ tests must be recognized if the results are to be interpreted appropriately. First, IQ testing cannot be viewed as a pure measure of learning "potential." Performance on IQ tests reflects past learning history as well as genetic endowment (Bortner & Birch, 1970; Estes, 1981; Liverant, 1960). Related to this issue is the problem of defining some disabilities (e.g., learning disabilities) in terms of discrepancies between IQ and academic achievement. The fact that the same basic deficiencies that determine academic problems may also affect IQ scores challenges the frequent practice of defining learning disabilities in terms of an IQ-achievement discrepancy (Doehring, 1978; Yule, 1978). Similarly, the statistical limitations of computing discrepancies between moderately correlated IQ and achievement tests have received too little attention (Yule, 1978).

Another shortcoming is that IQ tests do not survey all possible areas of competency. The WISC-R in particular fails to measure many aspects of social adaptation, nonverbal problem solving, and information processing skills (Guilford, 1967; Kaufman, 1979a). Illustrative of this fact is the finding that correlations between many neuropsychological performances and academic achievement remain robust, even when partial correlations are carried out to adjust for differences in IQ (Taylor et al., 1982), and that IQs do not relate strongly to adaptive behaviors in mildly retarded individuals (Brown & French, 1979). Furthermore, IQ tests were designed for pragmatic reasons—to predict learning or achievement outside of the test situation—rather than as measures of distinct processing skills (Hunt, 1980; Kaufman, 1979a). For this latter reason, it is difficult to draw conclusions regarding basic skills from performance on these tests. Individual IQ subtests often measure combinations of skills that provide few clues as to the nature of an individual's component mental abilities.

Finally, IQ test results have not always been found useful for determining the treatment or remedial approach that is most likely to be successful for a given child. For example, there is no reason to believe that educational strategies beneficial to children with substandard IQs are any different from those that would be recommended for children with average or above average IQs (Resnick, 1979). In sum, although the results of IQ tests can be useful in the neuropsychological assessment of children, these results may be of relatively limited value and must be interpreted with caution.

Language Abilities

The high frequency of linguistic deficiencies among children with learning problems and brain injuries justifies comprehensive assessment of language skills. Research in this area indicates a need to survey several component language functions. Learning disabilities have been associated with difficulties in language comprehension, naming and expressive speech, and phonology and sound sequencing (Fletcher, 1981). Tests that can be used to tap some of these specific linguistic abilities include the Peabody Picture Vocabulary Test (Dunn & Dunn, 1981), the Token Test for Children (DiSimoni, 1978), the Expressive One-Word Picture Vocabulary Test (Gardner, 1979),

Word Fluency (Gaddes & Crockett, 1975), and the Auditory Analysis Test (Rosner & Simon, 1971). Other standardized tests may be drawn from existing language batteries for children, including the Sequenced Inventory of Communication Development (Hedrick, Prather, & Tobin, 1975), the Illinois Test of Psycholinguistic Abilities (ITPA) (Kirk, McCarthy, & Kirk, 1968), and the Comprehensive Evaluation of Language Functions Diagnostic Battery (CELF) (Semel & Wiig, 1980). Specific aphasia batteries such as the Neurosensory Center Comprehensive Examination of Aphasia (Gaddes & Crockett, 1975) may be particularly useful in evaluating the brain-injured aphasic child.

As with measures of intelligence, language tests may be sensitive to more than one component skill deficit. For instance, tests of syntactic comprehension of spoken sentences often require the child to make distinctions based on word meaning, as well as grammar. If the child's semantic knowledge is limited, performance deficits should not be interpreted as evidence of a problem in the area of syntax per se (Fletcher, 1981). Other cognitive deficiencies may also interfere with a child's performance in language testing, such as when an attention deficit results in poor memory for digit sequences or sentences. Overall, however, available language measures are comprehensive, fairly well standardized, and many of them tap isolated language competencies. Since language measures can help to refine the nature of reading or other academic problems (Fletcher, 1981) and since academic instruction places heavy demands on verbal abilities, language testing deserves special priority in neuropsychological assessment. In the case of children with developmental language disorders or acquired aphasia, language assessment is important for defining the manifest disability and for exploring basic competencies.

Visual-spatial and Constructional Performance

Visual-spatial and constructional problems are associated with many forms of developmental disability. Deficits in these areas are measured by procedures that require active manipulation and graphic skills or by procedures that are relatively "motor free." Tests of the motor free variety generally involve the matching of visual stimuli. The Recognition-Discrimination Test (Satz & Fletcher, 1982) and the Line Orientation Test (Lindgren &

Benton, 1980) illustrate this type of task. Tests involving an active motor component include the Bender Gestalt (Koppitz, 1964), Benton's 3-D Block Construction Test (Benton et al., 1983), and the Beery Test of Visual-Motor Integration (Beery, 1982). Longitudinal research by Satz and Fletcher (1982) documented the importance of visual-spatial and constructional abilities in predicting reading failure. Similarly, Mattis, French, & Rapin (1975) and Rourke (1978) have found assessment of visual-motor skills helpful in isolating subtypes of learning disabilities. Assessment in this area is also important in cases of children with actual brain disorders. Soare and Raimondi (1977) found that children with myelomeningocele with accompanying hydrocephalus had relatively greater deficits on the Beery VMI than would be expected based on IQ, and Rutter (1981) observed a special proclivity for visual-perceptual deficits in head-injured children. The fact that WISC-R Performance IQ tends to be more affected than Verbal IQ by early brain injury is also consistent with the possibility that brain-damaged children may have special vulnerabilities in this area of function (Taylor, in press a).

As in the case of other tests of basic skills, a major shortcoming of visual-perceptual tasks is that they are likely to engage multiple competencies. Factor analytic research shows that measures of visual-spatial and constructional skill load on a common factor and that this factor is distinct from other (e.g., verbal) factors (Fletcher & Satz, 1980). Nevertheless, visual-spatial and construction performances may well require abilities not strictly spatial or constructional in nature (for example, processing of novel material or the ability to approach a task systematically and to properly allocate attentional resources). At this time, it is not clear whether the value of these tasks stems from their spatial and constructional components or from the fact that they tap mental abilities on which other (notably verbal) tasks place lesser demands.

Somatosensory and Motor Functions

Somatosensory and motor tests are among the more traditional of the neuropsychologist's tools, at least in the sense that these tasks represent extensions of the standard neurological examination. Somatosensory functions include finger localization, stereognosis, graphesthesia, and right-left orientation. Procedures to measure these functions have been developed by Benton and his colleagues (Benton et al., 1983) and by Reitan (Reitan & Davison, 1974). Useful tests of motor skills are contained in the Klove-Matthews Motor Steadiness Battery (Reitan & Davison, 1974), which consists of tests of resting and kinetic steadiness, fine motor manipulative dexterity (Grooved Pegboard Test), and repetitive foot and finger tapping. The Bruininks-Oseretsky Test of Motor Proficiency (Bruininks, 1978) provides a further collection of motor tests of potential utility in neuropsychological assessment. The tests of fine motor coordination, ocular-motor control, motor overflow, steadiness, and alternating movements that comprise assessments of "soft neurological status" may also be employed in evaluating motor functions (for a discussion of these signs, see Taylor & Fletcher, 1983). In common with somatosensory and motor tests is their potential for measuring lateralized deficits. These tests provide sensitive indices of sensory-motor impairment in children with neurological disorders. When administered at an early age, these tests are also of value in predicting later reading achievement (Fletcher & Satz, 1980; Rourke & Orr, 1977). The value of selected sensory-motor tests has been further evidenced by their inclusion in test batteries that differentiate among subtypes of disabled learners (Fisk & Rourke, 1979; Petrauskas & Rourke, 1979).

A major limitation of somatosensory and motor tests is that many children with developmental handicaps perform adequately on these tasks, especially in mid or later childhood (Fletcher, Taylor, Satz, & Morris, 1982). Although deficits on these tests may help parents and teachers to be aware of inherent skill limitations, results sometimes have little bearing on treatment, particularly for disabled learners. These results are most directly pertinent to neurologically handicapped children with clear motor and somatosensory impairments, including cases of cerebral palsy and hydrocephalus. For other children, sensory-motor tests probably deserve lesser emphasis than other portions of assessment, at least until the value of these tests in diagnosis and treatment is more clearly indicated. While the presence of somatosensory and motor deficits may help to establish the biological-relatedness of an attention deficit or a specific developmental disorder, a restricted set of such tests may be sufficient in evaluating many children.

Attentional Resources

Clinical impressions suggest that a child's ability to pay attention has pervasive influences on both the manifest disability and the child's performance on tests of basic competencies. Because attention deficits are manifested in many different forms and have multiple etiologies, careful interview of the child's ability to pay attention at home is essential. Questions regarding the child's impulsivity, ability to follow directions, concentration skills, and compliance with rules all deserve special consideration. In fact, diagnoses of attention deficit disorder rest primarily on the information obtained from parents and teachers, rather than from formal assessment data (Berkley, 1981). Nevertheless, direct observation is often helpful in documenting reports of attentional problems. In some cases, observation may suggest previously undetected attentional problems to be a primary basis for a child's learning or behavioral disorder. By observing how well children are able to sustain interest in tasks, plan responses, self correct, and avoid careless mistakes, the neuropsychologist develops subjective impressions as to the adequacy of a child's attentional resources relative to those of other children of similar age. More formal assessment of attentional capacities can be carried out by administering tests of sustained vigilance, such as the Children's Checking Task (Keough & Margolis, 1976), or by examining the Freedom from Distractibility index from the WISC-R (Kaufman, 1979b).

The major shortcoming of assessment in this area is the lack of clarity surrounding the concept of attention. The child's ability to pay attention and to allocate attentional resources effectively may be defined in terms of the capacity to resist distraction, to selectively attend to certain aspects of the stimulus array, to maintain vigilance, or to engage in goal directed behavior (for discussion of different definitions of attention, see Hale & Lewis, 1979). It is difficult to know which of these several aspects of attention might be most deserving of assessment. A further problem is distinguishing attentional deficits from lack of interest or ability. Pending further research, an attentional difficulty that falls short of the classification of attention deficit disorder (Barkley, 1981) can only be described as a potential contributor to a child's manifest disability and is of uncertain significance regarding treatment.

Memory and Learning Skills

Memory is another area of function that has pervasive influences on test performances but which defies unitary definition. The information processing concepts of sensory registration, working memory, long-term memory, and information transfer are useful in considering ways in which to decompose memory skills in child neuropsychological assessment. Adult neuropsychological studies support similar decompositions and argue for a distinction between verbal and nonverbal memory systems (cf. Shallice, 1979). Tests available for memory assessment in children include the Benton Visual Retention Test (Benton, 1974), and the Target Test (Rourke, 1980). Tests of the child's ability to remember information over longer periods of time or to remember information that exceeds immediate memory capacity converges with assessments of learning ability. Selective reminding procedures developed initially by Buschke (1974) and extended to neurological groups by Levin et al. (1982) exemplify this type of memory test. Fletcher (in press) found a verbal selective reminding test and a nonverbal analogue to this procedure helpful in differentiating types of learning problems. The advantages of selective reminding procedures include their provision of separate measures of storage and retrieval abilities and sensitivity to neurological impairment (Levin et al., 1982). Other measures of the ability to acquire new information have been found helpful in the assessment of children with mild mental deficiency (e.g., Budoff, 1964). More experimental measures of serial memory ability (see review by Torgesen, 1978) and of efficiency of memory retrieval (Denckla & Rudel, 1976) also deserve careful consideration.

As in the case of so many other areas of assessment, a child's difficulty on a memory task may be difficult to ascribe to a memory dysfunction per se. Tests of immediate memory and the ability to rapidly retrieve information from long-term storage may be confounded with the child's attentional abilities. The fact that the Digit Span subtest of the WISC-R loads on the Freedom from Distractibility factor (Kaufman, 1979b) supports this possibility. Performance on memory tasks is additionally determined by the child's ability to employ rehearsal and other problem-solving strategies (Torgesen, 1980). A more practical limitation is that, apart from tests of immediate memory, few memory procedures have adequate age-based norms. Assuming that learning at school and at home is determined to some extent by the efficiency with which a child is able to remember and acquire new information, tests in this area are likely to figure more prominently in the assessment process than they have in the past (Resnick, 1979).

Problem Solving and Abstract Reasoning

The final area of basic competency assessment to which the neuropsychologist must attend concerns the manner in which the child is able to make use of component skills in solving more complex problems. This area of ability, while not easily described in terms of a single mental operation, has been referred to by Brown (1975) as "metacognition." The construct of individual differences in information processing strategies (Hunt, 1983) refers to a similar function. These abilities involve the capacity of the child to apply what he/she knows to novel situations. The WISC-R Block Design subtest, the Halstead Category Test, and the Tactual Performance Test exemplify procedures that tap the child's problem-solving abilities (Rourke, 1980). Richman and Lindgren (1981) isolated a similar ability dimension, referred to as "abstract reasoning," that was helpful for contrasting subgroups of children with verbal deficiencies. According to these investigators, tests loading on this factor include the Similarities and Block Design subtests of the WISC-R, and the Picture Identification, Picture Association, and Block Patterns subtests of the Hiskey-Nebraska Test of Learning Aptitude (Hiskey, 1966). Rourke (1982) and Kaufman (1979a) also argue in favor of assessment of the child's ability to reason abstractly and to solve novel problems. The new Kaufman Assessment Battery for Children (K-ABC) (Kaufman & Kaufman, 1983) and the British Ability Scales for Children (Elliot, Murray, & Pearson, 1978) were designed in part to fill this void. Subtests from these two batteries may be helpful in assessing problem solving skills.

A major disadvantage of testing in this area is that a variety of component skills contribute to a child's ability to solve a novel problem. Inefficiency in problem solving may thus reflect component skill deficits rather than poor strategizing or mental disorganization. The potential influence of motivational factors on the child's willingness to acquire or apply higher order mental processes represents a further confounding influence (Douglas, 1980). Application to children of well circumscribed problem-solving tasks (e.g.,

Sternberg, 1977) along with attempts to decipher the impact of moderator variables on task performance may allow more refined assessment of problem-solving capacities in the future. Although presently available tests of problem-solving skills may be less than fully satisfactory, clinical experience suggests that both formal and informal evaluation of these capacities may greatly enhance the sensitivity of the assessment process to childhood disabilities.

Assessing the Influence of Moderator Variables

Assessment of the extent to which social and environmental variables contribute to the manifest disability can take several forms. Children with learning problems, for example, are often anxious, frustrated, and lacking in self-confidence. Repeated failure at school may partially contribute to the child's low self-esteem, but the family's reaction to the child's learning problem is also critical in determining how the child copes with that problem. Excessive pressure at home, a curriculum that does not take limitations in basic competencies into account or teasing from friends all potentially contribute to the child's poor performance or misbehavior. A careful interview with the family along with information from teachers or other professionals are helpful in assessing the influence of these social-environmental factors. It is often useful to investigate the concordance of parental opinions regarding the child's problems and management. Exploring family problems is also important (e.g., marital difficulties, financial problems, conflicts within the family or between the family and other persons or agencies in the community). Finally, administration of formal ratings of behavioral problems (e.g., the Child Behavior Checklist; Achenbach, 1979) is helpful in determining whether parent opinion regarding the child is suggestive of clearly deviant behavior. Complaints of attentional problems are frequent in families that are disorganized or characterized by inconsistent parenting (Barkley, 1981). While it may not always be possible to determine how a psychosocial disturbance relates to other manifest problems, awareness of behavioral disorders is essential in planning treatment and in evaluating the impact of basic skill deficits per se on the child's functioning. The clinician who takes a careful history regarding the initial presentation of problems and the response of others to these problems may pro-

vide significant insights regarding the origins of the child's difficulties.

In cases of traumatic injury, family disruptions may result from resentment concerning the accident, from fear of loss of the child, or from the process of adjustment to the child's needs or changed mental capacities. This type of stress can have a destabilizing effect on family systems, with changed roles and expectations of family members and difficulties in maintaining pre-existing family rules. Although hyperactivity may be a consequence of brain injury in some cases (Rutter, 1981), failure of family members to maintain expectations of the child and to enforce limits may contribute to this type of behavior. Observation of the child during testing and investigation of the pervasiveness of such problems outside of the home can shed light on environmental factors influencing the child's manifest problem.

In spite of the belief by some that neuropsychological procedures are less susceptible to cultural influences than other psychometric methods (Selz, 1981), there is little empirical justification for such an assumption. Lower scores on neuropsychological tests may reflect social and cultural deprivation or lack of interest or incentive to perform to the best of one's ability. For some children, performance levels may reflect the amount of effort required by the task rather than skill per se, and it may therefore be necessary to retest the child on another occasion or to interpret test performances with reservation. Attempts to assess moderating influences on test behavior is essential to ensure appropriate interpretation of test data and treatment.

Investigating Biological Indices

Given the difficulties of inferring neurological status from neuropsychological performance in children (Fletcher & Taylor, 1983), the child neuropsychologist is rarely in the position of "discovering" a brain disorder in a child for whom such a disorder was not previously suspected or even documented. At the same time, information regarding neurological and medical evaluations, family history of learning or behavioral problems, and other direct and indirect indications of the biological-relatedness of the child's problems should always be gathered as part of the assessment process. In the case of children with learning problems, mental retardation, attention deficit disorders, and other disabilities where we lack basic knowledge regarding etiology, neurological and medical examinations are frequently negative and noncontributory. For example, EEGs and CT scans are rarely abnormal in disabled learners and should be performed only if the neuropsychological evaluation or behavioral reports on the child suggest some pathognomic sign of neurological dysfunction. Here it is important for the neuropsychologist to recognize these pathognomic signs and to refer to a pediatric neurologist or other appropriate medical specialist when appropriate. Signs that would indicate referral include any seizure-like behavior or any rapid change in mentation that would suggest a behavioral regression. Physical symptoms such as headaches, dizziness, and vomiting may also provide the occasion for referral to a medical specialist. Awareness of the "red flags" indicating the need for medical consultation often arises from working relationships between neuropsychologists and physicians. For those neuropsychologists working outside of medical settings, this knowledge base requires attempts by the neuropsychologist to form consultative liaisons with physicians in the community.

Biological markers such as minor physical anomalies, developmental delays, pre- and perinatal complications, and family histories of similar problems help to establish the biological-relatedness of the child's problems. Comprehensive neuropsychological evaluation thus entails the collection of these data. In cases of brain disease and insult, the child's performance should be reviewed in light of the findings from neurological and radiological evaluation. The post-traumatic course following a head injury, for example, may help to explain the severity of a child's residual deficits. Considerable intracranial swelling induced by delays in treatment increases the probability of diffuse insult (Levin et al., 1982). Similarly, the presence of any focal injuries on CT scan (e.g., subdural hematoma) should also be related to the child's test performance. While most tumors in children are deep in the base of the brain, influences on cortical functions can occur through growth of the tumor or through direct pressure on other brain areas. In order that the neuropsychologist appreciate the possible implications of their findings, he/she must be aware of the interpretation of biological indices of CNS conditions. For child neuropsychologists who work with neurologically disordered groups, an awareness of the pathophysiology of these disorders and their course is essential. Knowledge of neurological disorders can often help in determining how best to monitor a patient and in planning rehabilitation. Without a base in neuropathology, the neuropsychologist will find it difficult to discover associations between brain and behavior.

Interpretation and Management

Once testing is completed and information on moderator variables and biological indices have been collected, the clinician must derive a formulation of the factors most likely contributing to the child's problems. At this point the clinician should pull together the information collected in order to (a) present a composite picture of the child's strengths and weaknesses to the family or other referral sources, (b) discuss the factors most likely contributing to the child's problems, and (c) communicate the child's needs to the parents in order to make treatment recommendations. In discussing and interpreting findings with families, we have found it helpful to first discuss our impression of the child's problems and to highlight strengths and weaknesses we have noted in assessing the child. We then mention moderator variables that may also be contributing to the child's problems. The purpose is to explain our impression of the origin of the child's problems. Discussion of biological indices may help to justify impressions of weaknesses in basic skills. While stressing to parents that skill deficits make children vulnerable to certain problems, we also emphasize the options available to the family and school for helping the child to cope with these deficits. Care is taken to answer the parents' presenting questions as directly and honestly as possible. As the question of how best to help the child cope with his/her problem almost universally arises following discussion of contributing factors, intervention recommendations are then discussed. Problems that might be anticipated in the future may also be shared in order to help parents realize the need for continued assistance and to foster early recognition of any problems that may arise. Such anticipations, however, are presented with the understanding that later development is difficult to predict and that the best way of helping the child is providing appropriate assistance with current problems. In cases where issues are complex and multifaceted, it may occasionally be necessary to assign a priority to some issues and to leave others for later visits. Throughout the family interview, feedback from the parents or child helps to establish how much and what type of information the family is ready to absorb. At the end of the interview, follow-up arrangements are made in cases where monitoring of the child's progress is necessary or where actual treatment by the neuropsychologist is initiated.

Following the interview, the neuropsychologist may need to make referrals to other specialists or to communicate directly with referral sources. A written report summarizing the neuropsychologist's impressions and recommendations is provided for both parents and referral sources. Recommendations are an important part of the written report. To be profitable for those working with the child, recommendations should include realistic suggestions as to the kinds of educational programs that are likely to benefit the child, appropriate rehabilitational procedures, and behavioral management strategies. In short, recommendations must reflect an awareness of available school programs and community resources and must address all aspects of the child's problem. Through contacts with teachers, counselors, and other professionals, as well as treatment that the neuropsychologist may provide through follow-up visits, the neuropsychological assessment becomes a basis for action on the child's behalf.

SUMMARY

In this chapter, we have stressed that the major difficulties with current conceptions of child neuropsychology stem from overemphasis on brain-behavior relationships as the major feature distinguishing neuropsychological assessment of children from other modes of evaluation. Whereas discovery of brain-behavior relationships in children is a laudable goal, a primary focus on these relationships has a number of unfortunate consequences. To begin with, this focus misrepresents the little that we know about brain-behavior relationships in children. Many children referred for neuropsychological assessments either have no demonstrable brain disease (as yet discovered) or they have neurological disorders for which the pathophysiology is ill-defined. Studies of the behavioral implications of discrete or well-delineated brain lesions in children are few and far between. As a result, there is no established body of brain-behavior correlations from which to draw in making strong inferences regarding brain status from neuropsychological test findings. In fact, the potential set of childhood brain-behavior laws may well emphasize biological

indices concerned with acute injury (e.g., severity of closed head injury), diffuseness of injury, or history of insult—as opposed to specific areas of dysfunction or damage.

A second and related problem is that the overemphasis on brain-behavior relationships encourages direct extrapolation of adult findings to children, often without empirical justification for this extension. Since children's abilities are structured differently than those of adults, there is every reason to believe that brain-behavior relationships will vary from those observed in adults. Moreover, we would expect these relationships to change with age. The third major limitation of the application of simplistic brain-behavior models to children is the subtle promotion of the idea that some behaviors, notably those assessed by neuropsychological tests, are free from social and environmental influences. While we would agree that some skills and behaviors may provide a better reflection of neurologic status than others, it seems reasonable to suppose that all human behavior is to some extent dependent on learning history and social-environmental conditions. In order to better evaluate the influences of CNS variables, it is imperative that these influences be considered within the assessment process (Fletcher & Taylor, 1983).

Our contention is that child neuropsychological assessment must place increasing emphasis on the study of the child's behavior and cognitive development if it is to be effective in helping children with their problems and to lead to discoveries of brain-behavior relationships. To support this contention, we have described a *functional* approach to child neuropsychological assessment. The functional approach does not minimize the importance of studies of brain-behavior relationships in children. Instead, this approach recognizes the need to evaluate behavior as a first step toward linking behavioral and developmental disorders to biological factors. Finer-grained analyses of the child's problems and their developmental and cognitive underpinnings will not only lead to more appropriate management of the child, but also to a better appreciation of indirect biological "markers," such as family history, minor physical anomalies, and pre- and perinatal complications. Improved techniques for behavioral and cognitive analyses of developmental disorders may also allow us to put advances in brain imaging and neurochemical techniques to better use. By continuing to refine the study of disorders that are likely to have some biological basis, by increasing our understanding of the cognitive disabilities associated with these disorders, and by exploring psychosocial influences, a functional approach may serve as a catalyst for these discoveries.

In pursuit of these objectives, the functional approach promotes an openness to other domains of psychological inquiry, including developmental, cognitive, clinical, and educational psychology. The methods and concepts of these domains are frequently useful for conducting comprehensive neuropsychological evaluations. Existing tests of academic achievement, for example, are well-standardized and can be quite helpful in delineating the nature of the several forms of learning disability. Published tests of language and other basic skills may also be incorporated into the assessment process, along with standardized ratings of adaptive behavior and emotional adjustment. The importance of employing tests that satisfy standard psychometric criteria for reliability and validity cannot be underestimated. This is especially the case in neuropsychology, where these considerations have often been overlooked (Reynolds, 1982). At the same time, however, the child neuropsychologist cannot afford to ignore more experimental procedures from the fields of cognitive psychology, developmental psychology, or adult neuropsychology. The Buschke (1974) "selective reminding" method for assessing memory functions provides an example of such a procedure. Although originally developed for use with adult and normal children, Levin et al. (1982) and Fletcher (in press) have found the selective reminding procedure sensitive in assessing children with histories of head injury, leukemia, and learning disabilities. The system for examining component cognitive skills provided by information processing models of human ability and development holds similar promise for child neuropsychological assessment. Because of the limited set of known brain-behavior relationships in children and the fact that many cases referred for child neuropsychological assessment do not involve actual brain disease, we do not believe that tests can or should be selected according to their ability to distinguish brain damaged children from normal children. Sensitivity to known brain disease in children or the ability to discriminate groups of the children with developmental disabilities from normal children may provide leads in the search for dimensions of behavior that are sensitive to CNS status. For the most part, however, tests need to be chosen in accordance with models of cognitive development, since the findings will always be relative to the child's level of development (Dennis, 1980). Reference to these models will encourage comprehensiveness and at the same time provide hints as to how to study, or in Shallice's (1979) term "fractionalize," component cognitive functions. Regardless of the exact procedures employed in child neuropsychological testing, the focus of assessment should be on the analysis of ability structures rather than on the test per se.

Paralleling this emphasis on abilities and on the multitude of factors influencing behavior, the functional approach has implications for the role of child neuropsychologists in assessing childhood problems. In our view, the role of a child neuropsychologist is not restricted to that of making inferences as to brain status from test performance, but rather includes careful examination of the nature of the developmental disability and of the factors contributing to that disability. The emphasis of the functional approach is on a broad assessment of factors potentially contributing to the manifest disability in order to provide a complete formulation of the child's problems. This formulation will include judgments as to the likelihood that biological factors are involved, but it will also entail consideration of all factors likely to have contributed to a given problem and suggestions as to how the problem be managed. Fulfillment of this more comprehensive role requires a broad range of assessment skills, an understanding of social and cultural influences on behavior, and an ability to generate effective treatment plans. The need for these general clinical skills does not detract from the uniqueness of the child neuropsychologist among other clinicians. Above and beyond this core clinical knowledge, the child neuropsychologist requires a working knowledge of the neurosciences and of behavior neurology, an understanding of psychological methods from nonclinical areas such as developmental and cognitive psychology, and an indepth appreciation for disorders assumed to have biological antecedents (i.e., those disorders typically referred to the child neuropsychologist). Although a potential specialty in its own right, clinical child neuropsychology occupies a boundary zone between multiple disciplines of which the cardinal feature is an appreciation for the complexities of child behavior and development.

REFERENCES

Achenbach, T.M. (1979). The Child Behavior Profile: An empirically based system for assessing children's behavioral problems and competencies. *International Journal of Mental Health*, 7, 24–42.

Ackerman, P.T., Dykman, R.A., & Peters, J.E. (1977). Learning-disabled boys as adolescents: Cognitive factors and achievement. *Journal of the American Academy of Child Psychiatry*, 16, 296–313.

Bale, P. (1981). Pre-natal factors and backwardness in reading. *Educational Research*, 23, 134–143.

Barkley, R.A. (1981). *Hyperactive children: A handbook for diagnosis and treatment*. New York: Guilford Press.

Baumeister, A., & MacLean, W. (1979). Brain damage and mental retardation. In N.R. Ellis (Ed.), *Handbook of mental deficiency, psychological theory and research* (2nd ed.). Hillsdale, NJ: Erlbaum.

Beery, K.E. (1982). *Revised administration, scoring and teaching manual for the Developmental Test of Visual-Motor Integration*. Cleveland: Modern Curriculum Press.

Benton, A.L. (1962). Behavioral indices of brain injury in school children. *Child Development*, 33, 199–208.

Benton, A.L. (1964). Contributions to aphasia before Broca. *Cortex*, 1, 314–327.

Benton, A.L. (1973). Minimal brain dysfunction from the neuropsychological point of view. In F.F. de la Cruz, B.H. Fox, & R.H. Roberts (Eds.), *Minimal brain dysfunction*. New York: New York Academy of Sciences.

Benton, A.L. (1974). *Revised Visual Retention Test: Clinical and experimental application* (4th ed.). New York: The Psychological Corporation.

Benton, A.L. (1975). Developmental dyslexia: Neurological aspects. In W.J. Friedlander (Ed.), *Advances in neurology*. New York: Raven Press.

Benton, A.L., Hamsher, K. de S., Varney, N.R., & Spreen, O. (1983). *Contributions of neuropsychological assessment: A clinical manual*. New York: Oxford University Press.

Birch, H.G. (1964). The problem of "brain damage" in children. In H.G. Birch (Ed.), *Brain damage in children: The biological and social aspects*. Baltimore: Williams & Wilkins.

Birch, H.G., Thomas, A., & Chess, S. (1964). Behavioral development in brain-damaged children: Three case studies. *Archives of General Psychiatry*, 11, 596–603.

Bortner, M., & Birch, H.G. (1970). Cognitive capacity and cognitive competence. *American Journal of Mental Deficiency*. 74, 735–744.

Brown, A.L. (1975). The development of memory, knowing, knowing about knowing, and knowing how to know. In H.W. Reese (Ed.), *Advances in child development and behavior* (Vol. 10). New York: Academic Press.

Brown, A.L., & French, L.A. (1979). The zone of potential development: Implications for intelligence testing in the year 2000. In R.J. Sternberg & D.K. Detterman (Eds.), *Human intelligence: Perspectives on its theory and measurement*. Norwood, NJ: Ablex.

Bruininks, R.H. (1978). *Bruininks-Oseretsky Test of Motor Proficiency, examiner's manual*. Circle Pines, MN: American Guidance Service.

Budoff, M. (1964). "Learning potential" as an assessment approach to the adolescent mentally retarded. *Journal of Consulting Psychology*, 28, 433–439.

Buschke, H. (1974). Components of verbal learning in children: Analysis by selective reminding. *Journal of Experimental Child Psychology*, 18, 488–496.

Calfee, R. (1982). Cognitive models of reading: Implications for assessment and treatment of reading disability. In R.N. Malatesha & P.G. Aaron (Eds.), *Reading disorders: Varieties and treatments*. New York: Academic Press.

Clements, S.F. (1966). *Minimal brain dysfunction in children — terminology and identification* (NINDB Monograph No. 3). Washington, DC: U.S. Public Health Service.

Cunningham, C.E., & Barkley, R.A. (1978). The role of academic failure in hyperactive behavior. *Journal of Learning Disabilities*, 11, 15–21.

Denckla, M.B., & Rudel, R. (1976). Rapid "automotized" naming (R.A.N.): Dyslexia differentiated from other learning disabilities. *Neuropsychologia*, 14, 471–479.

Dennis, M. (1980). Language acquisition in a single hemisphere: Semantic organization. In D. Caplan (Ed.), *Biological studies of mental processes*. Cambridge: MIT Press.

Dennis, M. (1983). The developmentally dyslexic brain and the written language skills of children with one hemisphere. In U. Kirk (Ed.), *Neuropsychology of language, reading and spelling*. New York: Academic Press.

DiSimoni, F.G. (1978). *The Token Test for Children*. Boston: Teaching Resources.

Doehring, D.G. (1976). Acquisition of rapid reading responses. *Monographs of the Society for Research in Child Development*, 41, 1–54.

Doehring, D.G. (1978). The tangled web of behavioral research on developmental dyslexia. In A.L. Benton & D. Pearl (Eds.), *Dyslexia: An appraisal of current knowledge*. New York: Oxford University Press.

Doehring, D.G., Trites, R.L., Patel, P.G., & Fiedorowicz, A.M. (1981). *Reading disabilities: The interaction of reading, language, and neuropsychological deficits*. New York: Academic Press.

Douglas, V.I. (1980). Higher mental processes in hyperactive children: Implications for training. In R.N. Knights & D.J. Bakker (Eds.), *Treatment of hyperactive and learning disordered children: Current research*. Baltimore: University Park Press.

Dunn, L.M., & Dunn, L.M. (1981). *Peabody Picture Vocabulary Test — Revised, manual for forms L and M*. Circle Pines, MN: American Guidance Service.

Dunn, L.M., & Markwardt, F.C. (1970). *Peabody Individual Achievement Test manual*. Circle Pines, MN: American Guidance Service.

Dykman, R.A., Ackerman, P.T., Clements, S.D., & Peters, J.E. (1971). Specific learning disabilities: An attentional deficit syndrome. In H.R. Myklebust (Ed.), *Progress in learning disabilities* (Vol. II). New York: Grune & Stratton.

Elliott, C., Murray, D.J., & Pearson, L.S. (1978). *The British Ability Scales*. Windsor, England: The NFER—Nelson Publishing Company.

Estes, W.K. (1981). Intelligence and learning. In M.P. Friedman, J.P. Das, & N. O'Connor (Eds.), *Intelligence and learning*. New York: Plenum.

Filskov, S.B., & Boll, T.J. (Eds.). (1981). *Handbook of clinical neuropsychology*. New York: Wiley.

Fisk, J.L., & Rourke, B.P. (1979). Identification of subtypes of learning disabled children at three age levels. A neuropsychological, multivariate approach. *Journal of Clinical Neuropsychology*, 1, 29–310.

Fletcher, J.M. (1981). Linguistic factors in reading acquisition: Evidence for developmental changes. In F. Pirozollo & M.C. Wittrock (Eds.), *Neuropsychological and cognitive processes in reading*. New York: Academic Press.

Fletcher, J.M. (in press). External validation of learning disability typologies. In B.P. Rourke (Ed.), *Learning disabilities: Advances in subtypal analysis*. New York: Guilford.

Fletcher, J.M., & Satz, P. (1980). Developmental changes in the neuropsychological correlates of reading achievement: A six-year longitudinal follow-up. *Journal of Clinical Neuropsychology*, 2, 23–37.

Fletcher, J.M., & Taylor, H.G. (1983). Neuropsychological approaches to children: Towards a developmental neuropsychology. *Journal of Clinical Neuropsychology*, 5.

Fletcher, J.M., Taylor, H.G., Satz, P., & Morris, R. (1982). Finger recognition skills and reading achievement: A developmental neuropsychological analysis. *Developmental Psychology*, 18, 124–132.

Gaddes, W.H., & Crockett, D.J. (1975). The Spreen-Benton aphasia tests—normative data as a measure of normal language development. *Brain and Language*, 2, 257–280.

Gardner, M.F. (1979). *Expressive One-Word Picture Vocabulary Test*. Novato, CA: Academic Therapy Publications.

Gibson, E.J., & Levin, H. (1975). *The psychology of reading*. Cambridge, MA: MIT Press.

Gilmore, J.V., & Gilmore, E.C. (1968). *Gilmore Oral Reading Test: Manual of directions*. New York: Harcourt Brace Jovanovich.

Golden, C.J. (1981). The Luria-Nebraska Children's Battery: Theory and formulation. In G.W. Hynd & J.E. Orbzut (Eds.), *Neuropsychological assessment and the school-age child: Issues and procedures*. New York: Grune & Stratton.

Goldstein, K. (1939). *The organism*. New York: American Book Co.

Goodglass, H., & Kaplan, E. (1972). *The assessment of aphasia and related disorders*. Philadelphia: Lea & Feibinger.

Guilford, J.P. (1967). *The nature of human intelligence*. New York: McGraw-Hill.

Guthrie, J.T. (1973). Models of reading and reading disability. *Journal of Educational Psychology*, 65, 9–18.

Hale, G.A., & Lewis, M. (Eds.). (1979). *Attention and cognitive development*. New York: Plenum.

Hecaen, H., & Albert, M.L. (1978). *Human neuropsychology*. New York: Wiley.

Hedrick, D.L., Prather, E.M., & Tobin, A.R. (1975). *Sequenced Inventory of Communication Development*. Seattle: University of Washington Press.

Heilman, K.M., & Valenstein, E. (1979). *Clinical neuropsychology*. New York: Oxford University Press.

Hiskey, M.S. (1966). *Hiskey-Nebraska Test of Learning Aptitude*. Lincoln, NE: Union College Press.

Hunt, E. (1980). Intelligence as an information-processing concept. *British Journal of Psychology*, 71, 449–474.

Hunt, E. (1983). On the nature of intelligence. *Science*, 219, 141–146.

Ingalls, T.H., & Gordon, J.E. (1947). Epidemiologic implications of developmental arrests. *American Journal of Medical Science*, 241, 322–328.

Isakson, R.L., & Miller, J.W. (1976). Sensitivity to syntactic and semantic cues in good and poor comprehenders. *Journal of Educational Psychology*, 68, 787–792.

Jastak, J.F., & Jastak, S.R. (1978). *The Wide Range Achievement Test: Manual of instructions* (1978 revised ed.). Wilmington, DE: Jastak Associates.

Johnson, D.J. (1980). Persistent auditory disorders in young dyslexic adults. *Bulletin of the Orton Society*, 30, 268–276.

Kahn, E., & Cohen, L.H. (1934). Organic drivenness: A brain stem syndrome and experience. *New England Journal of Medicine*, 210, 748–756.

Kail, R., & Bisanz, J. (1982). Information processing and cognitive development. In H.W. Reese (Ed.), *Advances in child development and behavior* (Vol. 17). New York: Academic Press.

Kalverboer, A.F. (1976). Neurobehavioral relationships in young children: Some concluding remarks on concepts and methods. In R.M. Knights & D.J. Bakker (Eds.), *The neuropsychology of learning disorders: Theoretical approaches*. Baltimore: University Park Press.

Kaufman, A.S. (1979a). Cerebral specialization and intelligence testing. *Journal of Research and Development in Education*, 12, 96–107.

Kaufman, A.S. (1979b). *Intelligent testing with the WISC-R*. Somerset, NJ: Wiley.

Kaufman, A.S., & Kaufman, N. (1983). *The Kaufman Assessment Battery for Children*. Circle Pines, MN: American Guidance Associates.

Keogh, B.K., & Margolis, J.S. (1976). A component analysis of attentional problems of educationally handicapped boys. *Journal of Abnormal Child Psychology*, 4, 349–359.

Kirk, S.A., McCarthy, J.J., & Kirk, W.D. (1968). *The Illinois Test of Psycholinguistic Abilities*. Urbana: University of Illinois Press.

Koppitz, E.M. (1964). *The Bender Gestalt Test for Young Children*. New York: Grune & Statton.

Lashley, K.S. (1929). *Brain mechanisms and intelligence*. Chicago: University of Chicago Press.

Laufer, M.W., & Denhoff, E. (1957). Hyperkinetic behavior syndrome in children. *Journal of Pediatrics*, 50, 463–474.

Levin, H.S., Benton, A.L., & Grossman, R.G. (1982). *Neurobehavioral consequences of closed head injury*. New York: Oxford University Press.

Levin, H.S., Eisenberg, H.M., Wigg, N.R., & Kobayashi, K. (1982). Memory and intellectual ability after head injury in children and adolescents. *Neurosurgery,* 11, 668–672.

Levin, H.S., Ewing-Cobbs, L., & Benton, A.L. (in press). Age and recovery from brain damage: A review of clinical studies. In S. Scheff (Ed.), *Aging and recovery of function.* Plenum.

Lezak, M.D. (1976). *Neuropsychological assessment.* New York: Oxford University Press.

Lindgren, S.D., & Benton, A.L. (1980). Developmental patterns of visuospatial judgment. *Journal of Pediatric Psychology,* 5, 217–225.

Liverant, S. (1960). Intelligence: A concept in need of re-examination. *Journal of Consulting Psychology,* 24, 101–110.

McCall, R.B. (1981). Nature-nurture and the two realms of development: A proposed integration with respect to mental development. *Child Development,* 52, 1–12.

McMahon, R.C. (1981). Biological factors in childhood hyperkinesis: A review of genetic and biochemical hypotheses. *Journal of Clinical Psychology,* 37, 12–21.

Mattis, S. (1981). Dyslexia syndromes in children: Toward the development of syndrome-specific treatment programs. In F.J. Pirozzolo & M.C. Wittrock (Eds.), *Neuropsychology and cognitive processes in reading.* New York: Academic Press.

Mattis, S., French, J.H., & Rapin, I. (1975). Dyslexia in children and young adults: Three independent neuropsychological syndromes. *Developmental Medicine and Child Neurology* 17, 150–163.

Meichenbaum, D. (1976). Cognitive-functional approach to cognitive factors as determinants of learning disabilities. In R.M. Knights & D.J. Bakker (Eds.), *The neuropsychology of learning disorders: Theoretical approaches.* Baltimore: University Park Press.

Musser, P.H., Conger, J.J., & Kagan, J. (1979). *Child development and personality.* New York: Harper & Row.

Pasamanick, B., & Knoblock, H. (1960). Brain damage and reproductive casualty. *American Journal of Orthopsychiatry,* 30, 298–305.

Pellegrino, J.W., & Glaser, R. (1979). Cognitive correlates and components in the analysis of individual differences. In R.J. Sternberg & D.K. Detterman (Eds.), *Human intelligence: Perspectives on its theory and measurement.* Norwood, NJ: Ablex.

Perfetti, C.A. (1980). Verbal coding efficiency, conceptually guided reading, and reading failure. *Bulletin of the Orton Society,* 30, 197–208.

Petrauskas, R.J., & Rourke, B.P. (1979). Identification of subtypes or retarded readers: A neuropsychological, multivariate approach. *Journal of Clinical Neuropsychology,* 1, 17–37.

Reitan, R.M., & Davison, L.A. (Eds.). (1974). *Clinical neuropsychology: Current status and applications.* New York: Wiley.

Resnick, L.B. (1979). The future of IQ testing in education. In R.J. Steinberg & D.K. Detterman (Eds.), *Human intelligence: Perspectives on its theory and measurement.* Norwood, NJ: Ablex.

Reynolds, C.R. (1982). The importance of norms and other traditional psychometric concepts to assessment in clinical neuropsychology. In R.N. Malatesha &

L.C. Hartlage (Eds.), *Neuropsychology and cognition* (Vol. II). The Hague: Martinus Nijhoff.

Richman, L.C., & Lindgren, S.D. (1981). Verbal medication deficits: Relation to behavior and achievement in chidlren. *Journal of Abnormal Psychology,* 90, 99–104.

Rosner, J., & Simon, D.P. (1971). The auditory analysis test: An initial report. *Journal of Learning Disabilities,* 4, 40–48.

Rourke, B.P. (1975). Brain-behavior relationships in children with learning disabilities. *American Psychologist,* 30, 911–920.

Rourke, B.P. (1978). Reading, spelling, arithmetic disabilities: A neuropsychological perspective. In H.R. Myklebust (Ed.), *Progress in learning disabilities.* New York: Grune & Stratton.

Rourke, B.P. (1980). Neuropsychological assessment of children with learning disabilities. In S.B. Filskov & T.J. Boll (Eds.), *Handbook of clinical neuropsychology.* New York: Wiley-Interscience.

Rourke, B.P. (Ed.). (in press). *Learning disabilities in children: Advances in subtypal analysis.* New York: Guilford.

Rourke, B.P., & Finlayson, M.A. (1978). Neuropsychological significance of variations in patterns of academic performance: Verbal and visual-spatial abilities. *Journal of Abnormal Psychology,* 84, 412–421.

Rourke, B.P., & Fisk, J.L. (1981). Socio-emotional disturbances of learning disabled children: The role of central processing deficits. *Bulletin of the Orton Society,* 31, 77–88.

Rourke, B.P., & Orr, R. (1977). Prediction of the reading and spelling performances of normal and retarded readers: A four-year follow-up. *Journal of Abnormal Child Psychology,* 5, 9–20.

Rourke, B.P. (1982). Central processing deficiencies in children: Toward a developmental neuropsychological model. *Journal of Clinical Neuropsychology,* 4, 1–18.

Rutter, M. (1981). Psychological sequelae of brain damage in children. *The American Journal of Psychiatry,* 138, 1533–1544.

Rutter, M. (1982). Syndromes attributed to "minimal brain dysfunction" in childhood. *American Journal of Psychiatry,* 139, 21–33.

Sameroff, A.J., & Chandler, M.J. (1975). Reproductive risk and the continuum of caretaking casualty. In F. Horowitz (Ed.), *Review of child development research* (Vol. 4). Chicago: University of Chicago Press.

Sattler, J.M. (1982). *Assessment of children's intelligence and special abilities* (2nd ed.). Boston: Allyn & Bacon.

Satz, P., & Fletcher, J.M. (1980). Minimal brain dysfunctions: An appraisal of research concepts and methods. In H.E. Rie & E.D. Rie (Eds.), *Handbook of minimal brain dysfunctions: A critical review.* New York: Wiley.

Satz, P., & Fletcher, J.M. (1981). Emergent trends in neuropsychology: An overview. *Journal of Consulting and Clinical Psychology,* 49, 851–865.

Satz, P., & Fletcher, J.M. (1982). *Manual for the Florida Kindergarten Screening Battery,* Odessa, FL: Psycholocial Assessment Resources.

Satz, P., & Morris, R. (1981). Learning disability subtypes: A review. In F.J. Pirozzolo & M.C. Wittrock
(Eds.), *Neuropsycholocial and cognitive processes in
reading.* New York: Academic Press.

Schonhaut, S., & Satz, P. (1983). Prognosis of the learn-
ing disabled child: A review of the follow-up studies.
In M. Rutter (Ed.), *Developmental Neuropsychiatry.*
New York: Guilford.

Selz, M. (1981). Halstead-Reitan neuropsychological test
batteries for children. In G.W. Hynd & J.E. Orbzut
(Eds.), *Neuropsychological assessment in the school-
age child.* New York: Grune & Stratton.

Semel, E.M., & Wiig, E.H. (1980). *CELF: Clinical
Evaluation of Language Functions: Diagnostic battery, examiner's manual.* Columbus, OH: Merrill.

Shallice, T. (1979). Case study approach in neuropsychological research. *Journal of Clinical Neuropsychology,* 1, 183–211.

Shallice, T. (1981). Neuropsychological impairment of
cognitive processes. *British Medical Bulletin,* 37,
187–192.

Siegel, A.W., Bisanz, J., & Bisanz, G.L. (1983). Developmental analysis: A strategy for the study of psychological change. In J. Meachum & D. Kuhn (Eds.),
Contributions to human development (Vol. 8). Basel:
Karger.

Siegel, L.S. (1981). Infant tests as predictors of cognitive
and language development at two years. *Child Development,* 52, 545–557.

Soare, P.L., & Raimondi, A.J. (1977). Intellectual and
perceptual-motor characteristics of treated myelomeningocele children. *American Journal of Diseases
of Children,* 131, 199–204.

Sparrow, S.S., Balla, D.A., & Ciccetti, D.V. (in press).
*Vineland Adaptive Behavior Scales: A revision of the
Vineland Social Maturity Scale.* Circle Pines, MN:
American Guidance Service

Spiker C.C. (1966). IV. The concept of development:
Relevant and irrelevant issues. *Monographs for the
Society for Research in Child Development* (Serial
107), 31, 40–54.

Sternberg, R. (1977). *Intelligence, information processing, and analogical reasoning.* Hillsdale, NJ:
Erlbaum.

Still, G.F. (1902). Some abnormal psychological conditions in children. *Lancet,* 1, 1077–1082.

Strauss, A.A., & Lehtinen, L.E. (1947). *Psychopathology and education of the brain-injured child.* New
York: Grune & Stratton.

Sweeney, J.E., & Rourke, B.P. (1978). Neuropsychological significance of phonetically accurate and phonetically inaccurate spelling errors in younger and older
retarded spellers. *Brain and Language,* 6, 212–225.

Taylor, H.G. (in press a). Early brain injury and cogni-
tive development. In C.R. Almli & S. Finger (Eds.),
The behavioral biology of early brain damage. New
York: Academic Press.

Taylor, H.G. (in press b). MBD in perspective. In R.
Tarter & G. Goldstein (Eds.), *The neuropsychology
of childhood.* Plenum.

Taylor, H.G., & Fletcher, J.M. (1983). Biological foun-
dations of "specific developmental disorders":
Methods, findings, and future directions. *Journal of
Child Clinical Psychology,* 12, 46–65.

Taylor, H.G., Fletcher, J.M., & Satz, P. (1982). Component processes in reading disabilities: Neuropsychological investigation of distinct reading subskill
deficits. In R.N. Malatesha & P.G. Aaron (Eds.),
Reading disorders: Varieties and treatments. New
York: Academic Press.

Torgesen, J.K. (1978). Performance of reading disabled
children on serial memory tasks: A review. *Reading
Research Quarterly,* 19, 57–87.

Torgesen, J.K. (1979). What shall we do with psychological processes? *Journal of Learning Disabilities,* 12,
16–23.

Torgesen, J.K. (1980). Conceptual and educational implications of the use of efficient task strategies by
learning disabled children. *Journal of Learning Disabilities,* 13, 19–26.

Walsh, R.N., & Greenough, W.T. (Eds.). (1976). *Environments as therapy for brain dysfunction.* New
York: Plenum.

Wechsler, D. (1974). *Manual for the Wechsler Intelligence Scale for Children—Revised.* New York: Psychological Corporation.

Weisfeld, G.E. (1982). The nature-nurture issue and the
integrating concept of function. In B.B. Wolman
(Ed.), *Handbook of developmental psychology.*
Englewood Cliffs, NJ: Prentice-Hall.

Werner, E.E. (1980). Environmental interaction in minimal brain dysfunctions. In H.C. Rie & H.D. Rie
(Eds.), *Handbook of minimal brain dysfunctions: A
critical review.* New York: Wiley.

Wilson, B. (in press). An approach to the neuropsychological assessment of preschool children with developmental deficits. In S. Filskov & T. Boll (Eds.),
Handbook of clinical neuropsychology (Vol. 2). New
York: Wiley.

Wohlwill, J.F. (1973). *Study of behavioral development.*
New York: Academic Press.

Wolff, P.H. (1981). Normal variations in human maturation. In K.J. Connolly & H.F.R. Prechtl (Eds.),
*Clinics in Developmental Medicine No. 77/78: Ma-
turation and development: Biological and psychological perspectives.* London: William Heinemann
Medical Books.

Woodcock, R.W. (1973). *Woodcock Reading Mastery
Tests manual.* Circle Pines, MN: American Guidance
Service.

Yule, W. (1978). Diagnosis: Developmental psychological assessment. In A.F. Kalverboer, H.M. van Praag,
& J. Mendlewicz (Eds.), *Advances in biological psychiatry: Vol. 1. Minimal brain dysfunction: Fact or
fiction?* Basel: S. Karger.

12 SPECIALIZED NEUROPSYCHOLOGICAL ASSESSMENT METHODS

Kerry deS. Hamsher

INTRODUCTION

In neuropsychological assessment there is a dichotomy of clinical approaches. On the one hand, there is the specialized approach in which the choice of tests is individualized for each patient and will depend upon such things as the referral question, the clinical history and interview, and the patient's presentation during the examination itself. Arthur Benton (1977b) has called this the "flexible approach," the idea being that it is better to fit the assessment to the patient rather than vice versa. On the other hand, there is the comprehensive battery approach, which defines a fixed set of neuropsychological tests to be administered to all patients. This approach has been described and reviewed in Chapter 11.

Traditionally, the major concerns of the neuropsychological testing movement have been the identification and localization of focal brain lesions. Indeed, in the history of clinical neuropsychology there has been a strong emphasis on studying the behavioral consequences of focal brain lesions, since the results bear on the issues of hemispheric cerebral dominance and intrahemispheric specialization of function (Benton, 1977a). However, the competition from other neurodiagnostic technologies, such as computerized tomography (CT scan), positron emission tomography (PET scan), and nuclear magnetic reasonance (NMR scan), is gaining the upper hand when it comes to localization. Their accuracy and efficiency for localizing focal lesions in many conditions already surpass the offerings of neuropsychological assessment.

Some may apprehensively wonder what the future holds for clinical neuropsychology vis-à-vis a rapidly evolving and spreading technology in neurological medicine that has an ever improving capability for the identification and localization of structural and physiological abnormalities (Costa, 1983). These advances represent another phase of a "bootstrap" operation. By adding new and more precise information to one side of the brain-behavior equation, we can learn more about the other side. Rather than replacing neuropsychology, these exciting technological developments are likely to enhance the neuropsychologist's diagnostic role, by more sharply defining disease states with greater sensitivity and accuracy than ever before. To remain a sound and fit science, neuropsychology must evolve with the changing technological environment.

The assurance of a future lies in the nature of the data neuropsychologists collect and analyze, namely, the highest levels of human behavior. For

235

example, we know that there is a body of evidence (Davies, 1983) that links depletion of acetylcholine (or more precisely its marker substance, choline acetyltransferase) with Alzheimer's disease and a depletion of cells in the basal nuclei of Meynert—also known as the nucleus basalis, ganglion of Meynert, and "substantia innominata" of Reichert (Lockard, 1977). Suppose the new technologies reveal that a patient has a reduction in acetylcholine metabolism. Does this mean the patient is demented? Of course not! Dementia is a behavioral diagnosis, Alzheimer's disease is a histological diagnosis, and a "low rate of acetylcholine metabolism" would be a neurophysiological diagnosis. To what extent a diagnosis from one nosological system implies some particular diagnosis in a different nosological system is an empirical question. We do know that there are many etiologies resulting in the behavioral state that we classify under the rubric of *dementia*. Alzheimer's disease, multi-infarct dementia, and the dementia that follows severe head trauma are three examples. In fact, in general, neurologic and neuropsychological deficits appear primarily determined by the locus of lesion rather than its etiology (e.g., stroke, tumor, infection, trauma). If an etiology happens to imply a particular locus, then it may also imply a particular neurobehavioral disorder. So the biology of the central nervous system (including its ontogeny, chemistry, physiology, and pathology) is but one side of the coin occupied by neuropsychology on its opposite face. The parallelism may not be perfect, but it is certainly substantial in this field.

On the behavioral side of the brain-behavior equation, neuropsychology can be thought of as the study of the functional output of the central nervous system. Thus, the product of clinical neuropsychological assessment is of direct relevance to patients, their family members, their employers, as well as those involved in the patient's medical management, nursing care, and rehabilitation. From an evolutionary standpoint, it is precisely the brain's capacity for the production of rational thought, communication, memory, learning, emotional responsiveness, and social integration that defines the essence of being human. Public acceptance of this fact may be assumed given the newer emphasis of defining death on the basis of the loss of brain function rather than on the loss of functioning of other vital organs such as

the heart and lungs. Hence, as long as society and the health care system are concerned with the issues of mental status, there shall be a role for neuropsychologists (Hamsher, 1983).

DESCRIPTION OF A SPECIALIZED APPROACH

The specialized or flexible approach to neuropsychological assessment is commonly used in the major neurological training centers in the United States, and it appears to be the dominant approach in western Europe, Great Britain, and the Commonwealth countries. Beaumont (1983) calls it the "individual-centred normative approach" (p. 281). It falls between two extremes anchored at one end by the informal and highly individualistic bedside assessment that emphasizes efficiency and practicality at the expense of standardization, sensitivity, and validity, such as that often taught to clinical neurologists. At the other end of the spectrum is the day-long fixed assessment battery where the patient is subjected to a far-reaching assortment of tests that may be, in part, either irrelevant to the patient's presenting complaint or redundant with information already established in the patient's medical record—if not internally redundant as well. Nevertheless, as we shall see, there are common themes in the flexible approach that are often repeated in case after case. So one could think of the flexible approach as starting out within the framework of a very extensive fixed battery, but then allowing the examiner to delete tests when it is felt that they are not needed for the questions at hand.

While it is not possible to cover all case contingencies in this chapter, we shall review an assessment approach for the major nonaphasic neurobehavioral disorders. There are many highly interesting disorders that have distinctive clinical presentations, are pertinent to the development of neuropsychological theory, and have specific neurological correlates, but for which we have no standardized assessment methods beyond those employed in the clinical description of the disorders. While practicing neuropsychologists should be alert to their possible presence, in this chapter no attempt will be made to address these rare neurobehavioral disorders. Included in this category are the following: the sensory agnosias (Rubens, 1979); Klüver-Bucy syndrome (Lilly,

Cummings, Benson, & Frankel, 1983); frontal lobe emotional disorders (Damasio & Van Hoesen, 1983); alexia without agraphia (Albert, 1979; Varney & Damasio, 1982); Balint's syndrome (DeRenzi, 1982); Charcot-Wilbrand syndrome (Critchley, 1953); callosal syndrome (Bogen, 1979); ideational/ideomotor apraxias (Heilman, 1979); reduplicative paramnesia (Benson, Gardner, & Meadows, 1976); misreaching or "optic ataxia" (Damasio & Benton, 1979; Rondot, de Recondo, & Dumas, 1977).

Also excluded from detailed consideration in this chapter are the aphasic disorders. In contrast to the rare disorders described above, the aphasic disorders are rather common and are highly localizing, most particularly in the context of a cerebrovascular accident (CVA) or stroke. The aphasic disorders, too, have practical and theoretical significance for clinical neuropsychology. Nevertheless, experience teaches that in order to perform the appropriate differential diagnosis in a reliable fashion, one must acquire a "tutored ear" under supervised clinical training. Also some special and still unresolved problems arise in the cognitive assessment of aphasic patients (Hamsher, 1981; Mohr, 1982). Therefore, the task of covering this very highly specialized area of neuropsychological assessment falls beyond the scope of this chapter. However, a number of resources are now available for the reader interested in the assessment and diagnosis of aphasic disorders (Albert, Goodglass, Helm, Rubens, & Alexander, 1981; Benson, 1979; Brown, 1972; Goodglass & Kaplan, 1983; Kertesz, 1979; Kirshner & Freemon, 1982; Sarno, 1981).

PURPOSE

Briefly stated, the purpose of every examination is to evaluate the differential diagnoses of the chief (presenting) complaint, to objectively establish the current status of the patient's general mentation, and to relay this information back to the referring source along with the corollary clinical significance of the findings. The clinical significance may be in the form of localization; it may relate to etiological issues and prognosis; it may show an indication for or against a particular treatment; the findings may bear on legal issues such as mental competency and the need for a legal guardian; there may be suggestions for patient management or rehabilitation; there may be

implications for discharge planning (such as to, or not to, return to work) and vocational retraining.

The latter forms of clinical significance are largely a function of common sense and foresightedness. For example, if a patient neglects stimuli on his left, then the bed in the hospital should be positioned so that visitors and medical personnel address the patient from his right. And such a patient should not drive nor return to a job as a mechanical inspector so long as this symptom persists. In contrast, the neurological implications of the neuropsychological findings are gleaned from clinical research. As the preponderance of this research has been published in the neurological, neurosurgical, and psychiatric literature, this area of knowledge may be beyond the pale of most traditionally educated psychologists. Furthermore, the extent of this literature is such that it cannot be conveyed in a week-long workshop. It would be a travesty to mislead enthusiastic, eager, or enterprising psychologists (and others) into believing otherwise.

DEFINING MENTAL STATES

Most important to the specialized approach to neuropsychological assessment is to define the basic mental status of the patient under examination. Much attention has been given to the specification of the psychological status of patients and clinical research subjects, that is, to denote when the subjects manifested psychoses or severe neuroses. This is because such conditions may invalidate neuropsychological test results. For reasons that may be unexplainable, when such conditions exist, the subjects may not heed the test instructions or they may bias their responses in an unpredictable way. Almost by definition, patients in psychotic states are not guided by the usual motivations and social demands of the examination situation (and the conditions under which the tests were standardized). However, in the absence of severe psychopathology, examiners can generally assume a patient's test responses are veridical and representative of current abilities.

Unfortunately, far less attention has been paid to the specification of patient's neurobehavioral status. Being syndrome oriented, the specialized approach has been more attentive to these issues. A very important role for clinical neuropsychology is to apply the scientific methodology for the study of cognitive behaviors to the problem of diagnosing disorders of mental status, that is, defining and identifying neurobehavioral syndromes. Thus, the specialized approach could be renamed the psychometric syndrome oriented approach.

DSM III

Most of the major neurobehavioral disorders have been well described in the neuropsychiatric literature. The recent revision (3rd edition) of the *Diagnostic and Statistical Manual of Mental Disorders* (DSM III) by the American Psychiatric Association (1980) has developed criteria in a manner much more acceptable to scientifically oriented clinicians than those given in previous editions. This is likely to further the recognition of the syndromes described in DSM III. Presently, however, the section on the Organic Brain Syndromes (Organic Mental Disorders) leaves much to be desired if the manual is to be generally applied so as to include the organic mental disorders seen in patients from neurological and neurosurgical services. The listed criteria are stated in general terms that lack specificity, such as what constitutes a "memory impairment." Furthermore, this catalog of mental disorders is too limited; even the aphasia syndromes are omitted. Moreover, if literally applied, most aphasic patients would be classified by DSM III criteria as having dementia. Such a diagnostic strategy would deprive the behavioral diagnosis of dementia from having any specific neurological import. If a diagnostic entity refers to all sorts of things, then it really means nothing.

In DSM III, one could take particular issues with the description of amnesia (Amnestic Syndrome) as involving a defect of both short-term and long-term memory. The problem arises from mixing the terminology of cognitive psychology with that of the clinical literature. The clinical literature has a tripartite view of memory derived from the observations of various types of memory disorders in neurologically impaired patients. These are immediate, recent, and remote memory. In this context, the term *short-term memory* has been inserted so as to contrast with the category of immediate memory, and it refers to the learning of a quantity of information (or the retention of information over a period of time) that exceeds one's immediate memory span (attention-concentration capacity). In cognitive psychology, however, the term *short-term memory* refers to

one's immediate memory span, and the phrase is intended to be contrasted with long-term memory (Cermak, 1982).

OVERVIEW

In summary, the basic goals of the psychometric syndrome oriented approach are fivefold. First, we begin by operationalizing the concepts of clinical neurology as they apply to disorders of cognition in accordance with psychometric principles. Then we evaluate the patient, respecting the technical and methodological principles of psychological testing (Anastasi, 1982). These data are then combined to classify the patient's general mental status according to a scheme of well-recognized and validated neurobehavioral (organic brain) syndromes. At the same time, we will want to investigate associated features and possible focal neuropsychological deficits. Finally, in a timely fashion, we must then be able to interpret the neurological and practical clinical significance of these efforts.

HISTORY AND DEVELOPMENT

The Benton Laboratory

Matarazzo has described the early history of the development of neuropsychology as a subspecialty of clinical psychology in the United States, beginning in the post-World War II era (Matarazzo, 1972). Notably there were two pioneers, Arthur L. Benton at the University of Iowa and Ralph Reitan at University of Indiana. Each went in his own direction. Reitan pursued the fixed battery approach, now called the Halstead-Reitan Battery (see Chapter 11), and Benton pursued the problem of blending traditional clinical neurology with psychology's scientific approach to the study and assessment of human behavior, especially cognitively mediated behaviors. In this section we shall review some of the developments that came from Benton's laboratory.

Benton came to the University of Iowa in 1948 as Professor of Psychology and Director of the Clinical Psychology Graduate Training Program. By 1950 he had established a small neuropsychological testing unit in the Department of Neurology, which then grew into one of the major centers for research and clinical training in neuropsychology. Even as a graduate student, Benton had a major interest in the relationships between intellectual functioning and neurological disease. So, he began a study of the neurological concepts of mental activity and the history behind the development of these concepts. Although there was no scarcity of tests of neuropsychologic function, clearly missing from this literature was the notion of standardization and the multiplicity of determinants of cognitive performance. Thus, he began his career by applying the methodology of experimental psychology to some of the neurological issues of the time. After some 10 years of controlled, systematic research on arithmetic ability, right-left discrimination, and finger localization, he applied this methodology to the popular notion of the Gerstmann syndrome. He found there was no scientific basis for calling this symptom tetrad (finger agnosia, right-left disorientation, acalculia, and agraphia) a syndrome (Benton, 1961, 1977c). In explaining the results, he pointed out how biased observations could lead to spurious concepts. This helped to establish new standards of acceptability for behavioral research in neurology.

At one time it may have been Benton's dream to see clinical neurology do away with the traditional bedside tests that were poorly constructed and unreliable and to substitute scientifically validated behavioral assessment instruments in their place. In any event, he always highlighted clinical utility. For example, in looking for ways to improve the reliability of the digit span test, a trade off between choosing elaborate psychophysical procedures versus a less time-consuming method suitable for routine clinical use was emphasized. (Blackburn & Benton, 1957). Another of the students in his laboratory demonstrated that, for the purposes of identifying patients with brain disease, one need not give the full Wechsler intelligence battery (Fogel, 1964). That is, no further information was to be gained from the full battery than what could be obtained from a single subtest or the combination of a few. With the limited availability of patient time, the decision to give the full battery would have to be at the expense of administering other tasks that could add new information. In the same study, Fogel demonstrated that by comparing a patient's obtained IQ with his expected IQ as estimated from the patient's educational background, predictive accuracy was significantly augmented as compared with using a single cutting score for all subjects. This finding continues to be replicated

(Overall & Levin, 1978; Wilson, Rosenbaum, & Brown, 1979).

It was also argued that in evaluating a test for neuropsychological assessment, the common practice of examining cutting scores and hit rates was, for the most part, off target. While appropriate for evaluating screening devices, such tests were not going to advance neuropsychology. Instead, progress was foreseen in:

> the prediction of a specific locus of lesion by the use of special methods according to neuropsychological hypotheses. As a rule, such techniques have little value as screening devices for the presence or absence of brain damage in general, although their contribution to the diagnostic evaluation of the individual patient may be of considerable importance. (Spreen & Benton, 1965, p. 332)

TEST DEVELOPMENT

The tests that were studied or developed in the Benton Laboratory of Neuropsychology were introduced either to test a hypothesis or as an aid to explore the nature of some established syndrome or symptom. For example, Benton, Levin, and Van Allen (1974) investigated the map localization test used to evaluate "disorders of spatial thought" (Critchley, 1953) that were commonly attributed to a right hemisphere lesion. Before this there had been no study that standardized the task or took into account the educational backgrounds of the subjects. The findings failed to show an association between defective performance and either right or left hemisphere lesions, and there was an overwhelming effect due to educational background. Thus, this task was not further developed for clinical use. On the other hand, the Facial Recognition Test (Benton & Van Allen, 1968) was introduced as an experimental device to study the syndrome of prosopagnosia. In this syndrome, patients are unable to recognize family members by their faces, and they appear unable to learn to recognize new faces such as those of their attending physician and ward staff. Although it was subsequently demonstrated that severely prosopagnosic patients could perform normally on this and related tasks (Benton, 1980a; Benton & Van Allen, 1972), the test proved to be a valid behavioral sign of acquired neurologic disability with localizing significance (Benton, Hamsher, Varney, & Spreen, 1983; Hamsher, Levin, &

Benton, 1979). A third example is that of the test of tactile form perception (Benton et al., 1983). It was originally introduced as a control task for subjects who failed tactile naming on the Neurosensory Center Comprehensive Examination for Aphasia (Spreen & Benton, 1969) so as to evaluate the sensory component of the defective performance. Later, defective performances were found to be associated with signs of spatial disturbances as well as contralateral sensorimotor deficits. Consequently, the test was developed for clinical use.

OVERVIEW

In summary, a prominent feature of the Benton Laboratory of Neuropsychology through many years of research was the development of objective tests to meet specific research needs. Since research topics often came from the clinical literature of neurology and neuropsychology, the transition from research tools to diagnostic instruments was a natural one. Empirical findings determined which tests would be developed for clinical use. Benton's program encompassed a wide variety of research topics. Thus, interest in the functional properties of the right hemisphere led to investigations such as motor impersistence and proprioception (Levin, 1973), facial recognition, tactile form perception, and constructional praxis (Benton et al., 1983). In assessing the validity of the "Gerstmann syndrome," objective measure of finger localization and right-left orientation came into being (Benton et al., 1983). Inquiries into the relationship between aphasic disorder and cognitive function led to development of two aphasia batteries (Benton & Hamsher, 1976; Spreen & Benton, 1969) and tests of pantomime recognition (Varney, 1978; Varney & Benton, 1982), phoneme discrimination (Varney & Benton, 1979), and sound recognition (Varney, 1980).

THEORY AND RESEARCH: BASIC PRINCIPLES

Nosological Problems

The concept of dementia dates back many centuries. It refers to a state of global deterioration in behavioral performances to such an extent that a person is rendered unable to discharge the respon-

sibilities associated with everyday life (Benton, 1980b). Unfortunately, this concept is very broad and vague. It sometimes takes on surplus meaning to include an image of drooling and the odors of incontinence. At the other extreme, it may be applied in the face of nearly any acquired cognitive defect, espcially in the elderly. Over the past 100 years, a number of distinct disorders have been distinguished from dementia, including the aphasias, amnesia, agnosia, and delirium (confusional states). The latter condition has also been variously called "acute organic brain syndrome" or "reversible dementia" (Cummings & Benson, 1983). Despite this history of taking a more differentiated view of disorders of mental status, there are others who have extended the concept of dementia to a condition characterized by preserved intellectual functioning but with impaired attention-concentration, psychomotor retardation, and a slowness in information retrieval, called the "subcortical dementias" (Albert, Feldman, & Willis, 1974; Benson, 1983; Joynt & Shoulson, 1979). If such trends were reinforced, we would suffer a loss of conceptual clarity in our diagnostic reasoning. The problem stems from competing interests in the purposes of diagnosis.

From the scientific method, one can infer two general purposes for diagnosis: classification and prediction. With regard to classification, one must keep in mind that this process is dependent upon technology. When we classify objects, chemicals, plants, diseases, and such, our goal is to sort like with like. But, while two objects may look alike with the naked eye, significant differences may be observed with a microscope, and this would cause us to refine our classification scheme. Thus, a limiting factor for any classification scheme is the assessment technology. A clinical classification scheme, or nosology, is intended to aid professional communication and to facilitate systematic inquiry. With regard to prediction and in the case of disease states, there are several objectives. We may wish to predict response to treatment, course or prognosis, etiology, and pathophysiological processes (Spitzer, Sheehy, & Endicott, 1977). No one classification schema may be able to accomplish all these goals at the same time. At any particular time, emphasis will be placed on one or another goal, depending upon current knowledge. With little available information about the etiology and pathophysiology of psychiatric disorders, Woodruff, Goodwin and Guze (1974) announced that for their diagnostic scheme, "the guiding rule was: *diagnosis is prognosis*" (p. ix). However, in closed head injuries, classification is based on clinical state, namely, coma, and prognosis is addressed in the subclassification or as an auxiliary diagnostic scheme, such as the Glasgow Coma Scale (cf. Levin, Benton, & Grossman, 1982; Teasdale & Jennett, 1974).

From these examples we can see that it would be foolish to state unequivocally that a particular approach to the development of diagnostic categories is the correct one for all time. As new information becomes available, conceptualizations may shift, and diagnostic categories may be split, refined, redefined, or erased. When clinical lore held that declining mentation in the elderly was the result of "hardening of the arteries of the brain," we had the concept of arteriosclerotic dementia. This concept no longer exists in the neurological nomenclature, as many of the cases that received this diagnosis in the past would now be considered examples of Alzheimer's disease; however, arteriosclerotic disease may contribute to the presentation of what is now commonly called multi-infarct dementia (Adams & Victor, 1981).

As noted above, disorders of mental status are primarily determined by the locus of lesion rather than the etiology of that lesion. Given this state of nature, it would seem reasonably prudent to avoid forcing our behavioral diagnoses into strict alignment with particular etiologies. Nevertheless, in some cases it is still too soon to strictly align behavioral diagnoses with presumptive lesion localizations. In particular, the concept of "subcortical dementia" seems rather ill-conceived. Albert's description of the disorder (Albert et al., 1974) seems similar to the presentation of patients described as having pseudodementia (Wells, 1979); that is, the late-life presentation of psychopathology, and other investigators have failed to replicate his findings in patients with progressive supranuclear palsy (Kimura, Barnett, & Burkhart, 1979). At the same time, there are disorders that principally involve subcortical ganglia, such as Wilson's disease and Huntington's disease, which result in mental changes similar to that seen in Alzheimer's disease rather than what has been described as the clinical presentation of "subcortical dementia" (Benson, 1983). Thus, mixing our diagnostic metaphors, that is, intermingling behavioral diagnostic terms with biologic entities, leads to conceptual confusion. Such an approach seems to ignore the fact that the behavioral presentation of a disease can change over time. For example, following moderate to severe closed head injuries, a person characteristically goes through a sequence of mental states, namely from coma to a confusional state to amnesia and then recovery (Levin, Benton, & Grossman, 1982). Thus, for conceptual clarity, it would be reasonable and appropriate to base our classification of mental states on our neuropsychological technology.

Nosological Refinements

Once objectively defined, we can develop the validity correlates of the diagnostic groups. Diagnoses can be subdivided when it is shown that the subdivision provides further information. For example, the clinical distinction between dementia of the primary degenerative type versus the multi-infarct type is based on elements of the clinical history that can be tabulated as an "Ischemic Score" (Rosen, Terry, Fuld, Katzman, & Peck, 1980). At this stage of subclassification, other types of data may be incorporated to make subtype distinctions that add to the validity correlates of the basic diagnoses. These other elements could include laboratory, radiological, or physical findings as well as specialized behavioral observations. In Alzheimer's disease, for example, it has been suggested that there is a characteristic form of perseverative error in the patient's speech called an intrusion (Fuld, Katzman, Davies, & Terry, 1982). If future research replicates this finding, this could be incorporated into a subclassification scheme.

MAJOR DISORDERS

The major neurobehavioral disorders are those in which disturbances of memory and attention are the prominent clinical features. These are dementia, confusional states, dementia with confusion, amnesia, psychogenic amnesia, material-specific memory/learning defects, and attentional dysfunction (or aprosexia). Included in the differential diagnosis (other diagnoses from which the condition should be differentiated by systematically comparing and contrasting their symptoms) are the aphasic disorders. Other disorders, which have yet to be defined as well-recognized syndromes by objective methodologies, include focal neuropsychological deficits implicating disease of either the right or left hemisphere (not accounted for by any of the above syndromes).

ASSESSMENT

The differential diagnosis relies on four types of measurements, assuming an aphasic disorder can be ruled out. In the clinical literature these are called remote memory, recent memory, short-term memory/new learning, and immediate memory. However, these concepts were derived from clinical observations rather than psychology's coherent body of knowledge about cognitive functioning. More in line with the terminology of the types of tests we shall use to measure these dimensions of mental funciton, we shall refer to these same constructs as (general) intelligence (psychometric g), recent memory and orientation, verbal and nonverbal learning, and attention-concentration, respectively. In cognitive psychology, what we call intelligence relates to semantic long-term memory, whereas our recent memory is akin to the notion of episodic long-term memory.

Intelligence, Attention, and Psychomotor Speed

The Wechsler Scale

For assessing intelligence, the Wechsler Adult Intelligence Scale (WAIS) (or its revised version, the WAIS-R) is recognized as the standard. As described above, one need not administer the entire battery for neurobehavioral diagnostic purposes. In choosing which subtests to select, we turn to the factor analysis studies. As reviewed by Matarazzo (1972), the general findings indicate two major factors and one or two additional factors. The first factor is defined by the Information, Comprehension, Similarities, and Vocabulary tests. We shall call it the verbal-conceptual factor, as its more common designation as "verbal comprehension" in the context of a neuropsychological assessment is likely to be confused with language conprehension, a dimension important to the diagnosis of aphasia but quite different from what is being assessed with the WAIS. The second major factor is defined by performances on Block Design, Object Assembly, Picture Arrangement, and Picture Completion. We shall arbitrarily call this the perceptual-constructional factor. The third factor is defined by performances on Digit Span and Arithmetic (occasionally Digit Symbol may load on this factor as well), which we shall designate attention-concentration (excluding Digit Symbol).

Within the first two factors, the combination of any two or three subtests will define the performance level with clinically adequate stability and reliability. That is, the subtests in the first two factors are highly intercorrelated, and all have substantial loadings on psychometric g. For report writing purposes, these scores can be described in terms of deviation quotients (DQs) by using the age-corrected scaled score equivalents, given in the back of the WAIS manual, and applying the formula of Tellegen and Briggs (1967). The advantage of this approach is to purify our measure of verbal and nonverbal intellectual functioning so as not to confound them with attention-concentration and psychomotor speed measures that may be selectively impaired in the brain damaged population. Relative impairments in attention-concentration and psychomotor speed performances on the WAIS also relate to the severity of psychopathology, when present (Overall, Hoffmann, & Levin, 1978). That is, it would be a mistake to identify a patient as manifesting general intellectual impairment when in fact the only performances to fall below expectations were on the attention-concentration and psychomotor speed tests. If averaged in with the other tests in the computation of the traditional Verbal, Performance, and Full Scale IQs, this could produce artifactual defective scores on the composite measures.

Because of the very high correlations between Information and Vocabulary, as well as between Block Design and Object Assembly, it would be redundant to include both in an abbreviated battery. Based on McFie's work (1975), looking at patterns of WAIS subtest performance in patients with focal brain lesions, the following selection would seem to provide the most information: Information and Similarities for the computation of the Verbal-conceptual DQ; Arithmetic and Digit Span for the computation of the Attention-concentration DQ; Block Design and Picture Arrangement for the computation of the Perceptual-constructional DQ, and Digit Symbol as a measure of psychomotor (or more precisely, graphomotor) speed. However, an atypical educational history or a history of a learning disability may be reflected in a significantly depressed score on Information (Zimmerman & Woo-Sam, 1973); in such instances it would be wise to include a third verbal-conceptual subtest for balance and stability of measurement.

Interpretation

Interpretation of these results involves a comparison of the obtained IQ (or DQ) values with the expected premorbid values (Benton, 1980b). Wilson et al. (1979) and Overall and Levin (1978) provide formulae for this purpose. Some accommodation may be needed to translate from the WAIS to the WAIS-R, since the two batteries do not give equivalent results (Wechsler, 1981). In my laboratory I found that if Wilson et al.'s recommendation for altering the educational coefficient were followed, then one could use the results from the WAIS-R. Specifically, comparing obtained DQ versus expected Verbal IQ in a sample of 212 non-neurologic hospital control patients, the results were as follows: (a) obtained verbal-conceptual DQ—expected Verbal IQ: $M = +0.2$; $SD = 8.4$; (b) obtained attention-concentration DQ—expected Verbal IQ: $M = -2.5$; $SD = 10.0$; (c) obtained verbal IQ—expected Verbal IQ: $M = -1.1$; $SD = 7.8$. In a subsample of 97 subjects, we found that the distribution for obtained perceptual-constructional DQ—expected Performance IQ had the following characteristics: $M = 3.9$; $SD = 10.9$. The subject population was representative of the demographic makeup of the city of Milwaukee and included about 24% from a poor, black inner city neighborhood. Obviously, local norms will always be more desirable for this prediction situation. It should be noted that in my laboratory, on the perceptual-constructional subtests, we depart from the manual of instructions; that is, as long as a subject works productively toward a correct solution to the problems, there is no penalty for exceeding the stated time limits. While this policy is deemed appropriate for the purposes of neuropsychological assessment, it would be inappropriate for application to psychiatrically normal and neurologically intact individuals whose intelligences were being evaluated for traditional purposes, such as for educational or occupational planning.

Caveat

A general principle to be followed in interpreting intellectual or neuropsychological test results in the context of a neurobehavioral evaluation is to keep one's eye keenly fixed on the referral question. Suppose one were assessing a 35-year-old patient with a focal seizure disorder and the patient's performance on the verbal and nonverbal scales of the WAIS fell significantly below expectations (often defined as being at or below the second percentile). We will stipulate that this patient is neither aphasic nor psychotic, and that malingering is not an issue in this case. The question is, have we demonstrated that the patient has dementia? The answer would, in great measure, depend upon the clinical history and the reason for the referral. If we were trying to explain a decline in mental status sufficient to produce significant psychosocial disability that interfered with social and occupational functioning, then the diagnosis of dementia would have to be entertained. Since a primary degenerative dementia would be unlikely at this age, one should look for an etiological event to support the diagnosis, such as a history of severe head trauma with prolonged coma, or severe hypotensive (anoxic-ischemic) cerebral damage (drowning, carbon monoxide poisoning), or infectious disease of the brain. However, without such a clinical history, the incidental finding of intellectual performances being significantly below expectations, based on the actuarial formulae, would not suggest dementia. Instead, it would raise the question of an error of prediction or call into question the information used to calculate the expected intellectual scores. Alternatively, such results could be an example of the obvious—that by definition, 2% of the general population (without a history or evidence of dementia) will score at or below the second percentile using these prediction formulae.

Comparison with Clinical Assessment

In the clinical (bedside) assessment of remote memory, examiners would inquire about the patient's early personal history; however, much of this information is difficult to verify and so this would not meaningfully contribute to a mental status assessment. In substitution, clinical examiners would inquire about various overlearned facts that are acquired in a grade school education, such as questions about major points in history, geography, or measurement (Strub & Black, 1977). As psychologists, we recognize this as assessing one's general fund of information, which, along with vocabulary, is an excellent predictor of general intelligence. Hence, we can substitute for the vaguely conceived clinical concept of remote memory, our elegant concepts, and measures of general intelligence. The only neuro-behavioral disorder in which there is a true defect of remote memory is dementia. In psychogenic amnesia, patients may claim to have lost their memory for childhood events or their own identity, but the absence of general intellectual impairment would indicate that this was not occurring on an organic basis (Pratt, 1977).

In the clinical mental status examination, attention-concentration is typically measured with a similar digit span task, by asking the patient to perform serial additions, subtractions, or other mental calculations, and by spelling common words backwards. For alternate psychometric measures of attention-concentration, as well as the other dimensions of mental functioning to be discussed in this chapter, the reader is referred to Lezak's book (1983). On the Wechsler Memory Scale, the Mental Control and Digits Forward and Digits Backward subtests tap the attention-concentration domain (Erickson & Scott, 1977). The Trail Making Test and the Symbol Digit Modalities Test (cf. Lezak, 1983) are commonly used tests that could be substituted for the Digit Symbol Test as measures of psychomotor speed.

Recent Memory and Orientation

Tests of recent memory are primarily intended to assess the contents of recent memory, whereas tests of verbal and nonverbal learning are intended to assess the processes by which such memories are acquired. Clinically, the examiner may ask the patient to explain the events leading up to his hospitalization or outpatient referral, to describe recent major news events, or to recount the recent presidents of the United States (Adams & Victor, 1981). Orientation to place and time are also typically included. A sharp division between what is recent memory and what is remote does not exist. Basically, the intent of recent memory testing is to assess the retention of material that is typically forgotten over the course of time through the process of normal forgetting. In this fashion one may be able to determine if there is an abnormal rate of forgetting. Many things influence recent memory capacity, including intellectual level, age, and the significance of the material to be assessed. A foreign war or the death of a foreign government leader may hold intellectual significance for the well educated and therefore be well remembered, but such may be of no consequence to the individual of less than average intelligence. A variety of questions assessing recent memory and orientation are included in the highly abbreviated mental status questionnaires (e.g., Pfeiffer, 1975).

Objective and well-standardized tests of recent memory are few in number. The test of temporal orientation by Benton, Van Allen, and Fogel (1964) is quick, easy to administer and score, and it has been extensively normed (Bental et al., 1983). A similar measure intended specifically for head injury victims is also available (Levin, O'Donnel, & Grossman, 1979). Other tests that may be taken from the experimental literature involve assessing memory for famous persons, news events, and television shows (Albert & Kaplan, 1980; Warrington, 1976). On the Wechsler Memory Scale, the Orientation and Information subtests tap this domain (Erickson & Scott, 1977). Defects in temporal orientation are common in patients with bilateral or diffuse cerebral disease (Benton et al., 1983) and in bilateral frontal lobe disease (Benton, 1968).

Learning

Tests of verbal and nonverbal learning are legion in the psychology and neuropsychology literature (see Lezak, 1983). On the Wechsler Memory Scale, the Logical Memory, Associate Learning and Visual Reproduction subtests would fall into these categories. With regard to clinical application, nearly all learning tests suffer from the same deficiency: They have not been well standardized. Since the speed of learning and the quantity of material that can be memorized are closely related to intelligence and age in neurologically intact individuals, the normative standards for learning tests must be adjusted according to such individual differences. Of all our demographic predictor variables, years of educational attainment show the closest relationship with IQ measures (Matarazzo, 1972). Therefore, tests of this sort should be minimally corrected (or separately normed) for educational background along with age. For a verbal learning test, the serial digit learning (or digit supraspan) test fulfills these requirements up through age 74 (Benton et al., 1983; Hamsher, Benton, & Digre, 1980). However, in some age-education categories, the test suffers from "floor effect," such that it can be used to identify normal performances but cannot adequately grade the severity of defective scores (i.e., just below normal limits versus grossly impaired). The Benton Visual Retention Test, Administration A (Benton, 1974) fulfills the essential normative criteria and can serve as a nonverbal learning test as, apparently, successful performance requires the subject to mentally rehearse the geometric designs. However, the test is also sensitive to disturbances of immediate memory. Performance on both the serial digit learning and visual retention tests drop precipitously with age (Benton, Eslinger, & Damasio, 1981). Both tests are frequently failed by patients with bilateral or diffuse cerebral diseases, whereas a minority of patients with unilateral disease perform defectively. There is only a slight bias for a higher failure rate on the verbal learning task by patients with left-sided unilateral lesions compared with right-sided unilateral lesions. On the nonverbal task, the bias is in the other direction, but again slight.

Differential Diagnosis

Dementia

From a neurobehavioral and psychometric standpoint, dementia is defined as a generalized decline in intellectual functioning that is associated with a significant impairment in psychosocial or occupational functioning (not due simply to physical limitations). On a reasonably comprehensive assessment battery, one should see widespread cognitive defects, although some aspects of cognitive performance may appear more severely affected than others (Benton, 1980b; Eslinger & Benton, 1983). However, aphasic patients are not intended to be classified in this category, even though they, too, may show multiple cognitive defects secondary to their linguistic disability. While patients with dementia eventually develop severe disorders of recent memory, orientation, and learning, only about 40% have such defects on their initial assessment when diagnosed in this fashion (Benton, Van Allen, & Fogel, 1964). Although attention-concentration may not be normal, it should be no worse than expected for the patient's current intellectual level. As a clinical rule of thumb, the attention-concentration DQ should not fall 15 or more points below the Verbal-conceptual DQ.

Confusional State

The hallmarks of a confusional state are disturbances in arousal and attention (Strub, 1982). The disturbances in arousal may cause the patient to be overly active (delirium or hyperkinetic confusional state) or underactive (mild lethargy or hypokinetic confusional state). Patients are inattentive and disoriented. Psychotic features are often present in the hyperkinetic phase, and speech may be mumbled or incoherent at times. Often, an inability to maintain a mental set requires that the examiner frequently prompt the patient so as to comply with the test instructions. Presumably, as a consequence of the impairment in attention-concentration, much information does not get registered, producing disturbances in recent memory and learning. Perceptual disturbances are also common. However, there is no loss of general information. While such patients are difficult to assess, when appropriately stimulated so as to maximize their attention, one finds that verbal-conceptual performances are not defective.

Dementia with Confusion

This is a rather common combination. These patients are easily identified because their mental impairments are global. Intelligence orientation and recent memory, learning, and attention-concentration all suffer. This condition has also been called "beclouded dementia" (Adams & Victor, 1981, pp. 281–282). A patient with a pre-existing but unidentified dementia very often comes to clinical attention when the features of an acute confusional state are superimposed. These are the patients who are best captured by the DSM III criteria for dementia and dementia with delirium.

Amnesia

These patients have no significant impairment of intellectual functioning, as in dementia, or of attention-concentration, as in a confusional state, but have a generalized (verbal and nonverbal) learning impairment with evidence of a recent memory defect, disorientation, or both.

Material-Specific Memory Disorder

This is a tenuous diagnostic category. It is intended to capture patients with unilateral temporal lobe lesions who show a disruption of either verbal or nonverbal learning, but not both, and who otherwise appear cognitively preserved. Primarily such disorders have been reported as a consequence of unilateral temporal lobectomy for the control of intractable seizures (Milner, 1974).

However, it has not been clearly established whether or not such patients simultaneously manifest associated temporal lobe symptoms, such as naming and other aphasic symptoms with left-sided lesions, or visuoperceptive and spatial disturbances in the case of right-sided lesions. If this were the case, then it may be difficult to parcel out a specific memory disorder that cannot be accounted for in terms of the associated symptomatology.

Attentional Dysfunction (Aprosexia)

Psychometrically, this disorder is characterized by impaired attention-concentration, with preserved intelligence. When severe, learning may also be mildly impaired, but there is no impairment of recent memory or orientation such as seen in confusional states and amnesia. Some psychomotor slowing and slowness in information retrieval are frequently associated symptomatology. This category of abnormal mental status has been overlooked in most modern nomenclatures. In the 1880s it was a recognized disorder, and it was given the name aprosexia (literally meaning a failure to heed). This disorder needs to be differentiated from the disorder of childhood and adolescence called the Attentional Deficit Disorder with or without hyperactivity. Therefore, it would seem appropriate to resurrect this now archaic term, *aprosexia*, and apply it to this diagnostic category. Aprosexia is defined in psychiatric dictionaries so as to mean precisely what we would wish it to mean: "Inability to maintain attention." The condition is common in organic states that affect the brain and psychiatric conditions" (Hinsie & Campbell, 1975, p. 60). Among neurology outpatients presenting with complaints of memory problems, this is the most frequent neuropsychologic finding. It is frequently associated with psychopathology.

Focal Deficits

Small or focal cerebral lesions are not likely to produce a general disturbance in one's cognitive status. In terms of the major neurobehavioral disorders, if the lesion were recent, then one may see an attentional dysfunction (aprosexia) that recedes over time. With focal lesions it would not be unusual to find no evidence of a significant disturbance of memory or attention. However, if the lesion were associated with diffuse pressure or brain edema, as is often the case with mass lesions, then the behavioral picture of diffuse dysfunction, characteristically expressed as a confusional state or pronounced aprosexia, may be present in addition to the focal features. Exceptions to this rule have been reported when the focal lesion involves certain regions of the thalamus (Castaigne, Lhermitte, Buge, Escourolle, Mauw, & Lyon-Caen, 1981; McFarling, Rothi, & Heilman, 1982) or polymodal association cortex in the right hemisphere (Mesulam, 1981; Mesulam, Waxman, Geschwind, & Sabin, 1976). In these situations, small lesions that were not associated with pressure or edema effects presented as confusional states with focal neuropsychological signs or emotional changes.

Before launching into an unwieldly investigation of neuropsychological signs of an unknown focal cerebral disease, one should formulate a hypothesis about the likelihood of the existence of a focal lesion and its location based on the history, neurological findings, radiographic data, clinical presentation, and the complaints of the patient. With ever-advancing technology in neurological medicine, it is becoming more common for the neuropsychologist to know where the lesion is before starting the examination. In such cases, the question may be, what is the significance of the lesion and in what behavioral context does it occur; that is, what is the patient's mental (or cognitive) status? In contrast, in non-neurological settings, one is often referred patients with a nonspecific history of some behavioral change that the patient either denies knowledge of or is only vaguely able to describe, with a lack of sufficient detail to suggest a particular problem for evaluation. In these cases, one may wish to rule out the major neurobehavioral disorders, screen the major domains of neuropsychological functions, and specifically address the issues of a disturbance of thought processes and personality functioning.

Neuropsychological tests are not direct measures of brain functioning. That is, we do not have tests that measure how well the left temporal or right temporal lobe is working. Likewise, a defective test score is not synonymous with an organic brain lesion. The tests can be thought of as challenges to the brain that are made to identify weaknesses and to elicit recognizable signs and symptoms of brain disease in addition to providing objective and quantified behavioral observations. Some of the signs come from incidental observations. For example, neurophysiological studies implicate a role for the superior parietal lobule in visually guided arm-hand movements (Hyvärinen, 1982), and clinical studies in man have shown that superior parietal lobule lesions may produce a characteristic sign called, among other names, misreaching (Damasio & Benton, 1979). Special tests would not be needed to evaluate this sign, since reaching is required in the performance of several neuropsychological tests, for example, in building three-dimensional block models.

The major realms of mental activity for which cognitive tests have been developed for clinical application include: speech and language, somatoperceptual functioning, visuoperceptive ability, spatial orientation, psycho-sensory and psychomotor functioning (Benton, 1977b, 1980b). Detailed reviews of the various psychometric signs and symptoms of focal cerebral lesions are provided by Freda Newcombe (1969) and Kevin Walsh (1978). Syndromes of neuropsychological impairment are reviewed in detail in the works of Hécaen and Albert (1978), Heilman and Valenstein (1979), and DeRenzi (1982). A comprehensive review of neuropsychological tests and their validity correlates is provided by Lezak (1983). Some of the tests developed in the Benton Laboratory are described in a recent book that also summarizes their validity data (Benton et al., 1983).

Speech and Language

Speech is assessed by listening to the patient during an examination. Rather than testing speech, it is rated in terms of various qualities such as fluency, articulation, and prosody, and by listening for errors, such as phonemic or semantic paraphasias. For this purpose, the rating scales for speech characteristics and aphasia severity from the Boston Diagnostic Aphasia Battery are most commonly used (Goodglass & Kaplan, 1983). Intrusions, perseverations, echolalia, and palilalia are other forms of speech disorders of central origin that may be seen in the absence of aphasia (Benson, 1979). Language functions that may be compromised in conditions other than aphasia, such as in dementia, confusional states, or with focal lesions of the left temporal or frontal lobe, include naming, word fluency, and comprehension (Barker & Lawson, 1968; Chédru & Geschwind, 1972; Mayeux, Brandt, Rosen, & Benson, 1980; Rosen, 1980; Seltzer & Sherwin, 1983). The visual naming, controlled oral word association, and Token Test subtests of the Multilingual Aphasia Examination (Benton & Hamsher, 1976) are useful for these purposes.

Somatoperceptual Functioning

Chief among these are tests of right-left orientation and finger localization (Benton et al., 1983). Both types of performance show a close relationship with aphasia and dementia. The right-left orientation task assesses this discrimination both in relation to the patient's body and that of a confronting person. A generalized defect on both parts of the test is associated with dementia and aphasia, whereas an isolated defect in pointing to a confronting person is found in right-hemisphere disease in addition to the other two major disorders (Ratcliff, 1982). The finger localization task assesses performance in both hands: Bilateral impairment is common in the presence of bilateral disease and aphasia. A unilateral defect on the side opposite the side of the lesion is the most common abnormal performance of nonaphasic patients with unilateral lesions, the majority of whom perform normally on this test.

Visuoperceptive Ability

A variety of visuoperceptive functions may be assessed in a neurobehavioral evaluation. Their localizing significance and historical background are reviewed by Benton (1979), and Ratcliff (1982), and the available tests are reviewed by Lezak (1983) and in Benton et al. (1983). Cancellation tests are used to identify visual inattention and lateralized neglect that may follow lesions of the right parietal lobe (Albert, 1973) or the frontal lobes and basal ganglia on either side (Damasio, Damasio, & Chui, 1980). Disorders of color perception are associated with bilateral occipitotemporal lesions (Damasio, Yamada, Damasio, Corbett, & McKee, 1980; Meadows, 1974), while disorders in associating colors with visual referents (e.g., what is the color of an apple?) are closely associated with aphasia (Damasio, McKee, & Damasio, 1979; Varney, 1982). Disturbances in facial recognition (i.e., the discrimination of unfamiliar faces) have two correlates when dementia has been excluded: Such impairment is seen in the context of aphasic language comprehension impairment and, thus, is associated with left hemisphere lesions; in the absence of a significant language comprehension deficit, the disorder is associated with focal right hemisphere lesions, with more frequent posterior than anterior involvement

(Hamsher, Levin, & Benton, 1979). Disorders of visual synthesis, pattern identification, and "closure" including the perception of subjective contours and the recognition of incomplete figures, have been associated with right hemisphere lesions (Hamsher, 1978a) with particular involvement of the temporal lobe (Newcombe & Russell, 1969). Disturbances in form discrimination appear sensitive to brain lesions in general (Benton et al., 1983), although there is a bias for patients with posterior parietal and temporal lobe lesions on the right to show more frequent and severe defects (Meier & French, 1965; Ratcliff, 1982). In the context of aphasia, the form discrimination test appears useful in the discrimination of two subtypes of alexia, by identifying a chiefly perceptual defect (Varney, 1981) that may be distinguished from a cognitive or semantic subtype (see below). Disorders of steroscopic perception (global stereopsis) in the absence of defects in steroacuity (local stereopsis) are associated with right hemisphere lesions, in fact, almost exclusively so (Hamsher, 1978b).

Spatial Orientation

Spatial ability is often assessed by asking patients to draw figures, copy geometric designs, and by assembling models, such as Block Design from the WAIS or three-dimensional block model constructions (Benton et al., 1983). The correlates of defective performance are similar to those noted above for facial recognition (Benton, 1973). Constructional apraxia as measured by the three-dimensional task is also a correlate of bilateral and unilateral right frontal lobe disease (Benton, 1968). More localizing is defective performance on the visual task of judging the spatial orientation of lines (Benton, Varney, & Hamsher, 1978), which, when performance is in the severely defective range, suggests right parietal lobe involvement. In the tactile modality, the identification of abstract tactile forms, i.e., tactile-visual pattern matching, appears quite sensitive to the presence of cerebral disease, both bilateral and unilateral (Benton et al., 1983). In addition to identifying a higher-level somesthetic defect in the hand contralateral to the lesion, bimanually defective performances appear to result from a generalized (or supramodal) spatial disability.

Psychosensory Functions

For neurobehavioral examination purposes, tests of sensory function are chiefly concerned with higher-level disorders of perception and extinction phenomena (i.e., when single stimuli on the right and left are adequately perceived, but double simultaneous stimulation results in a consistent suppression of responses on one side). Tests such as the finger localization and tactile form perception tests provide information about tactile perception in addition to their cognitive components. In the auditory modality, tests of dichotic listening may provide highly localizing information, in the absence of an auditory acuity defect (A.R. Damasio & H. Damasio, 1977; H. Damasio & A.R. Damasio, 1979); extinction on dichotic tests may be related to lesions in the geniculotemporal auditory pathway or in the transcallosal pathway that connects the superior temporal gyri from each hemisphere. Tests of the recognition of meaningful environmental sounds (Varney, 1980) and the discrimination of meaningless sounds (such as crackling or buzzing) (Vignolo, 1969) have demonstrated lateralizing value (left versus right hemisphere lesions, respectively). Also, the test of meaningful sound recognition has been useful in the differentiation of subtypes of language comprehension impairment. A perceptual subtype can be identified with a test of phoneme discrimination (Benton et al., 1983; Varney & Benton, 1979), whereas defective sound recognition in the context of preserved phoneme discrimination appears related to a cognitive or semantic subtype (Varney, 1980). Similarly, a test of the recognition of the import of pantomimes (Benton et al., 1983) has been helpful in identifying a subtype of alexia that appears related to a cognitive or semantic disturbance in the visual modality, as opposed to the perceptual subtype mentioned above (Varney & Benton, 1982).

Psychomotor Functioning

In the Benton Laboratory, emphasis was placed on the cognitive components of motor functioning. As a practical matter, it was felt that the neuropsychologist's distinctive contribution was in the assessment of cognitive functions, whereas tests of elementary sensory and motor function were somewhat redundant with the neurologic examination. Three aspects of psychomotor functioning that received considerable research attention were reaction time (Dee & Van Allen, 1971), motor impersistence (Levin, 1973), and gestural apraxia (Dee, Benton, & Van Allen, 1970). Although reaction time has been shown to be sensitive to brain disease in general (Dee & Van Allen,

1972), at the present it does not appear to contribute to differential diagnosis. However, several studies have found defective reaction times to be predictive of prognosis (e.g., Hamsher, Halmi, & Benton, 1981; Van Zomeran & Deelman, 1978). There are a number of unresolved issues concerning motor impersistence, that is, the inability to sustain voluntary motor acts (Benton et al., 1983). It shows a close relationship with dementia. In the context of unilateral cerebral lesions, it is related to proprioceptive disorders with lesions on the right, but not on the left. Likewise, studies of gestural apraxia have failed to resolve a number of conceptual and procedural issues relating to this putative disorder, which is primarily seen in the context of aphasia (Dee, Benton, & Van Allen, 1970). However, a special form of this disorder that only affects the performance of the left side of the body ("left-limb dyspraxia") has been well established, and it implicates involvement of the transcallosal motor pathways (Bogen, 1979).

FUTURE DIRECTIONS

Rehabilitation?

Costa (1983) has suggested an important direction for the future of clinical neuropsychology is in the delivery of rehabilitative services for acquired cognitive deficits. This will be called into question. If it were shown that behavioral intervention could significantly improve the course of recovery over what occurs with spontaneous recovery, this suggestion might indeed deserve further consideration. Convincing demonstrations of a truly therapeutic effect, however, are yet to be published. Certainly the research on aphasia therapy would not support a sanguine attitude (David, Enderby, & Bainton, 1982). On the other hand, the development of compensatory behavioral strategies for patients with specific cognitive defects may hold some promise (Finger & Stein, 1982; Gazzangia, 1978). For example, the spatially disoriented patient may benefit from the use of written instructions and verbal signs to overcome disturbances in topographic orientation. Nevertheless, one could still question whether or not rehabilitative work, which is quite time consuming, is an appropriate expenditure of a neuropsychologist's time. Given the educational costs and the amount of clinical training required to gain competency in this subspecialty area, a more appropriate allocation of resources may be in focusing on the issues of diagnosis and clinical

prediction. On the rehabilitative front, it might be more reasonable to encourage neuropsychologists to become involved in the education and clinical training of rehabilitative physicians, psychologists, and technologists (i.e., the physical, occupational, speech, and recreational therapists).

Diagnosis

Meier (1981) has stressed the need to establish standards of competency in neuropsychology based on educational and training requirements and a demonstration of current knowledge by objective testing and professional review. Equally important will be the development of a professional consensus of opinion on the standards of practice for neuropsychology (Matthews, 1981). What do we measure, how do we measure it, and what should we say in our interpretive reports? If we are all cognizant of the same body of scientific data, then why wouldn't there be a consensus? As a field develops, it is probably healthy for there to be a divergence of opinion on these issues, but at some point there should be enough data and experience to resolve these issues. I am not suggesting a rigid model that discourages further development and experimentation; nor am I suggesting that every examiner should be using identical testing instruments. Differences in patient populations, base rates, and the purposes for which the neuropsychological services are being requested, along with considerations, call for some rational diversity of approach in different settings. Hopefully, neuropsychology will continue to receive new and improved tests for clinical use that will sharpen our diagnostic and predictive capabilities, and such evolutionary changes should be encouraged. Perhaps the most serious criticism of the fixed battery approach, despite some of its advantages, is that it is quite resistant to technological and scientific developments on both sides of the brain-behavior equation.

Objective Criteria for Neurobehavioral Syndromes

Recommendations for the future of neuropsychology include the development of a basic framework for neuropsychological assessment geared to the identification of neurologically significant syndromes. Along with this we shall need to develop an objective nosology of neurobehavioral disorders. The chief goal of the nosology is to provide a brief summary statement about states of nature, namely, the congitive status of patients with brain disease or trauma. With these objective diagnostic categories in mind, we know what it is we are trying to predict from our assessment. This helps to establish a framework for diagnostic reasoning. Criteria for the diagnostic categories are not meant to be etched in stone. In fact, an objective nosology facilitates refinements and modifications of the criteria as new data are published. If an alteration in the criteria is shown to improve or add to the validity correlates for the diagnostic category, such should be adopted.

Once established, the diagnostic categories could be subtyped using objective behavioral or other findings that may be predictive of etiology, prognosis, reponse to a particular treatment, etc. The nosology would enhance both interprofessional and intraprofessional communications. It would also stimulate the professional development of the practice of neuropsychology by fostering uniform standards of practice based on sound propositions and scientific merit. Likewise, this would provide a focus for the further development of existing or new neuropsychological test instruments.

For research, the benefits would include an individualized control of mental status and demographic factors for both group and idiographic research designs. This would come with the use of standardized tests that took into account a patient's demographic background. In this fashion, demographic variables may be combined to predict an adjusted normal range of variability. Although such adjustments may not apply to all tests, such factors should be investigated in the development of all tests. An objective nosology, so devised, would provide a means by which investigators at different institutions could meaningfully contribute to the body of knowledge associated with each diagnostic category. Finally, this objective nosology would further the study of brain-behavior relationships because those relationships vary with the mental status of the subject. For example, if two patients each suffer a right parietal lobe stroke, but one happens to be demented and the other not, the outcomes are going to be quite different. Test measures that may correlate with each other in the context of dementia may show marked dissociation in the presence of certain focal cerebral lesions.

As a first step, neuropsychology should become receptive to, and encourage the development of, objective research criteria for the neurobehavioral syndromes. The major neurobehavioral disorders, defined above, would be a starting point, as they are already well recognized and validated syndromes despite there being some confusion in their differential diagnosis. To this list one would have to add the classical aphasia syndromes and the nonaphasic focal deficit syndromes of the left and right hemisphere. In recent years there has been a growing literature on atypical "aphasia" syndromes attributed to lesions in the internal capsule, basal ganglia, and the putamen (Damasio, Damasio, Rizzo, Varney, & Gersh, 1982; Naeser, Alexander, Helm-Estabrooks, Levine, Laughlin, & Geschwind, 1982), which now seem to have the potential for objective behavioral definition. Likewise, cognitive symptoms associated with thalamic lesions may eventually lead to their syndrome definition so as to differentiate them from other causes of similar symptomatology (Henderson, Alexander, & Naeser, 1982; Wallesch, Kornhuber, Kunz, & Brunner, 1983). Emotional changes, devoid of associated cognitive symptoms with localizing value, might one day be developed in an objective fashion so as to deserve the status of neurobehavioral syndrome designations and be added to our nosology. Although some of these emotional changes have been related to focal cerebral lesions, the behavioral concepts are in an early stage of development and still lack objective specificity (Bear, 1983; Damasio & Van Hoesen, 1983). Nevertheless, the future of clinical neuropsychology at this point in time looks quite promising and clearly has the potential for making a major impact on diagnostic conventions and the further study of brain-behavior relationships.

SUMMARY

In fixed test batteries for neuropsychological assessment the examiner is trained to administer the same set of tests to all patients. From these data a profile of results is established, and interpretations are derived from either what is known about the profile or some rational hypothesis, as formulated by the examiner, about what might account for the obtained pattern. In terms of diagnostic issues, the focus tends to be upon the localization of a focal lesion versus diffuse cerebral dysfunction. In contrast, in the specialized or flexible approach to neuropsychological assessment, the choice of tests is determined by the clinical context.

For example, if the presenting complaint were that the patient gets lost in familiar surroundings, such as in a local shopping mall, several clinical hypotheses would be formulated to account for this complaint. These hypotheses are derived from the literature of clinical neurology and they are summarized in the form of syndromes or neurobehavioral disorders, that is, conditions in which both the nature of the behavioral impairment and the responsible neurological condition are known to some extent. This particular presenting complaint would raise the question of a disturbance in spatial orientation, visual perception, or lateralized visual neglect, and tests of these functions would be administered accordingly. If the results indicated significantly defective performances on the tests of spatial orientation and visuoperception (based on comparisons with the performances of an appropriate normative group on the same tests) and there was no indication of lateralized neglect, one would consider the hypothesis of a spatial disorientation syndrome referrable to right hemisphere disease. Consideration would then turn to the differential diagnosis, which would include dementia, confusional state, and dementia with confusion. Had the spatial and visuoperceptual performances been normal, one would also consider an attentional disorder (aprosexia) or amnesia in the differential diagnosis. If our findings were negative or demonstrated the aprosexia syndrome, we would then investigate the possibility of psychopathology, as this is an associated risk for patients manifesting this cognitive syndrome, and it may also be treatable. If our findings indicated the patient were not demented (nor had any of the other major neurobehavioral disorders involving disturbances of memory and attention), we may want to elaborate on the psychological significance of the presumed lesion. In this situation our results might indicate a variety of signs of right parietal lobe disease, such as constructional apraxia, contralateral tactile sensory disturbances, and a left ear extinction on dichotic word listening.

Next, our attention might turn to other clinical issues, such as prognosis, treatment, or patient management. It would be risky to suggest a prognosis if we did not know the etiology. If it were a subdural hematoma, there is a chance that the condition could be reversible with neurosurgery. If it were a stroke, we would know that the lesion is likely to be static (barring another stroke). If a tumor were responsible, then a neuropsychologist would not be in a position to make a prognosis. This information would have to come from a neurologist, neurosurgeon, or some other medical specialist. If we knew that the patient suffered a stroke from the referral question, we would plan to consider tests that may be predictive of course of recovery under these circumstances, such as test of reaction time or motor impersistence.

This illustrative example helps to demonstrate the flexible or specialized approach to neuropsychological assessment. It is not all-inclusive of what a neuropsychologist might contribute in such a case, such as consideration of the disposition on discharge, helpful hints for the nursing and medical staff, approaches to rehabilitation, compensatory strategies for overcoming acquired cognitive deficits, etc. However, these considerations are not unique to the flexible approach. It is also worthwhile to note the omissions: In the course of considering the differential diagnosis, an examination of core linguistic functions typically would be included, but the patient would not have been worked up for an aphasia syndrome.

In the United States, this approach is most closely associated with Arthur Benton, his students, and associates. It is both clinical and experimental, and it is closely allied with the history, traditions, and practice of clinical neurology. Observations taken from clinical neurology on the types of cognitive deficits shown by patients with brain disease in its different varieties were the basis for the development of many of the tests. Other tests came from experimental work intended to explore the fundamental nature of the clinical symptoms. Those tests that showed promise for clinical applications were specifically developed for this purpose. Most have been extensively normed with careful attention to the possible influence of background or demographic variables on performance, such as age, sex, educational background, and others. This is one of the distinctive contributions that a neuropsychologist has to offer in the neurological evaluation of patients with known or suspected cerebral disease. Another distinctive contribution is the ability of the clinical neuropsychologist to deal with the issue of psychopathology. There are, of course, manifold ways in which psychopathology can intrude: It may occur as the patient's reaction to neurologic disease; it may be a direct expression of brain disease itself; it may masquerade as neurologic disease where no frank neurological disorder exists. Other contributions are described in Chapter 12.

This psychometric approach to neurobehavioral assessment stands in bold contrast to the "shot gun" approach, where the examiner sets out to assess everything a little bit (i.e., with one or a very few items). Most, but not all patients with brain disease have several cognitive defects; thus, if the behaviors we study are somewhat complex, it is likely that this "shot gun" approach will have demonstrable validity in separating patients with and without brain disease. But this is a crude distinction to make, and in many instances it can be done more efficiently and with less expense by other neurodiagnostic technologies, or simply by taking an adequate history and casually observing the patient. Also, while the "shot gun" approach yields many behavioral observations (because none were appropriately measured), we are left with little useful information about the patient's behavioral state. Neuropsychology has been defined as the study of brain-behavior relationships. To study behaviors without reference to the brain (Geschwind, 1980), or to study brain lesions without reference to their behavioral consequences, is just not neuropsychology as conceived by the founders of the field.

The specialized approach to neuropsychological assessment is, of course, interested in the localization of brain lesions in the appropriate case material for such study. However, it is also concerned with a broader perspective, which includes the specification of the patient's general mental status. Patients with dementia, for example, are not given an indemnity for focal brain damage. They, too, can be ushered into the hospital with a stroke, tumor, or subdural hematoma and be presented for neurological, including neuropsychological, evaluation. As yet, there are no laboratory tests for diagnosing Alzheimer's disease, the most common cause of dementia; it is diagnosed in the presence of dementia and in the absence of any evidence of another cause. In this case the CT scan can tell us of a focal lesion at some particular location in the brain. The observation of motor weakness on the left side may clinically localize this observable lesion. As neuropsychologists, however, we must go further, not only to document the signs and symptoms that may reasonably be attributed to the newly acquired focal lesion, but also to define the behavioral context in which they occur. This is done by determining the patient's mental status.

The flexible approach, being problem oriented, tries to arrive at an objective resolution of the nature of the patient's cognitive complaints. This may require the use of tests that are not generally applicable to patients with brain disease but can provide specific information in a given clinical context. A variety of issues may be dealt with in this fashion, not only diagnostic ones, but specialized tests may be applied for consideration of the issues of prognosis, predicting response to treatments, and others.

Efficiency in assessment is also stressed in the flexible approach. Lengthy examinations for acutely ill hospitalized patients very often cannot be justified unless the information is so critical that the physician cannot continue caring for the patient without it. The criteria of medical emergency does not often apply in considering the contributions of the clinical neuropsychologist. On the other hand, if the neuropsychologist's examination is reasonably well tailored to the current or presenting problem, and the examination can be completed in an hour or two, shortly followed by a consultative report, then there are many more situations in which the neuropsychologist can make a significant clinical contribution. Thus, choosing to administer one set of tests always means doing so at the expense of not giving other tests. Therefore it is incumbent upon the neuropsychologist to think ahead in terms of the categories of diagnosis to be considered.

Once again, one turns to the neurological literature to look for the categories of diagnosis. The major neurobehavioral disorders involving disturbances of memory and attention were described in psychometric terms. Examples of tests that may be used to identify focal cerebral lesions were briefly reviewed, particularly those tests used or developed in the Benton Laboratory of Neuropsychology. A psychometric approach for adapting the WAIS for neurobehavioral examination purposes was also described and its rationale explained.

Admittedly, the psychometrically defined neurobehavioral disorders described in this chapter are limited in scope. Some of these conditions can occur in combinations, for example, focal right hemisphere deficits and a confusional state. Clearly more work lies ahead in the enumeration of these disorders. Yet to be determined are more specific criteria, such as cutting points (e.g., which is most appropriate, the 1st, 2nd, or 5th percentile. However, such decisions must take into account which tests to use (which are best suited to the patient population under examination), base rates, and the import of the diagnostic decisions, all of which may vary from one setting to another. Likewise, it has yet to be determined if a single defect on a test of recent memory is adequate for inferring a recent memory disorder or whether several instances of such should be sought. Again, this will likely depend on the severity of the single defect. If it is December, 1984, but the patient says it is July, 1940, this may well be sufficient to deduce a disorder of recent memory (if not aphasia).

Future directions for neuropsychology were also considered. This is a controversial topic; predicting the future always is. The tradition of using neuropsychology to identify and localize focal cerebral lesions is a dying tradition in the face of other neurodiagnostic technologies. The question remains, should neurospychologists move toward a new role, such as that of a rehabilitative specialist, or should they embrace more tightly neuropsychology's history of providing psychometrically sound behavioral observations and combining these data to maximize its neurological and clinical import? Although the future will call for some redirection of neuropsychology's diagnostic efforts, the latter direction would continue the field's diagnostic tradition. A reading of the current neuropsychiatric literature clearly demonstrates burgeoning developments on the diagnostic front. Preoccupations with symptoms of cerebral disease are giving way to newer preoccupations with the role of the diencephalon and basal ganglia in determining cognitive deficits and emotional changes. Limited concepts of brain disease in the form of structural changes are being replaced with more physiological concepts, such as disorders of neurotransmitter metabolism. Such occult disorders have long been implicated in the origin of psychiatric disease and in some neurological disorders such as Parkinson's disease; now a neurotransmitter disorder is being held responsible for neuropsychology's most fundamental syndrome, dementia. All these observations support a strong diagnostic role in neuropsychology's future. No doubt, both rehabilitative and diagnostic avenues will be tried.

REFERENCES

Adams, R.D., & Victor, M. (1981). *Principles of neurology* (2nd ed.). New York: McGraw-Hill.

Albert, M.L. (1973). A simple test of visual neglect. *Neurology, 23,* 658–664.

Albert, M.L. (1979). Alexia. In K.M. Heilman & E. Valenstein (Eds.), *Clinical neuropsychology.* New York: Oxford University Press.

Albert, M.L., Feldman, R.G., & Willis, A.L. (1974). The subcortical dementia of progressive supranuclear palsy. *Journal of Neurology, Neurosurgery, and Psychiatry, 37,* 121–130.

Albert, M.L., Goodglass, H., Helm, N.A., Rubens, A.B., & Alexander, M.P. (1981). *Clinical aspects of dysphasia.* New York: Springer-Verlag.

Albert, M.S., & Kaplan, E. (1980). Organic implications of neuropsychological deficits in the elderly. In L.W. Poon, J.L. Fozard, L.S. Cermak, D. Arenberg, & L.W. Thompson (Eds.), *New directions in memory and aging.* Hillsdale, NJ: Erlbaum.

American Psychiatric Association. (1980). *Diagnostic and statistical manual of mental disorders* (3rd ed.). Washington, DC: Author.

Anastasi, A. (1982). *Psychological testing* (5th ed.). New York: Macmillan.

Barker, M.G., & Lawson, J.S. (1968). Nominal aphasia in dementia. *British Journal of Psychiatry, 114,* 1351–1356.

Bear, D.M. (1983). Hemispheric specialization and the neurology of emotion. *Archives of Neurology, 40,* 195–202.

Beaumont, J.S. (1983). *Introduction to neuropsychology.* New York: Guilford Press.

Benson, D.F. (1979). *Aphasia, alexia, and agraphia.* New York: Churchill Livingstone.

Benson, D.F. (1983). Subcortical dementia: A clinical approach. In R. Mayeux & W.G. Rosen (Eds.) *The dementias.* New York: Raven Press.

Benson, D.F., Gardner, H., & Meadows. J.C. (1976). Reduplicative amnesia. *Neurology, 26,* 147–151.

Benton, A.L. (1961). The fiction of the "Gerstmann Syndrome." *Journal of Neurology, Neurosurgery, and Psychiatry, 24,* 176–181.

Benton, A.L. (1968). Differential behavioral effects in frontal lobe disease. *Neuropsychologia, 6,* 53–60.

Benton, A.L. (1973). Visuoconstructive disability in patients with cerebral disease: Its relationship to side of lesion and aphasic disorder. *Documenta Ophthalmologica, 34,* 67–76.

Benton, A.L. (1974). *Revised visual retention test: Clinical and experimental applications* (4th ed.). New York: Psychological Corporation.

Benton, A.L. (1977a). Historical notes on hemispheric dominance. *Archives of Neurology, 34,* 127–129.

Benton, A.L. (1977b). Psychological testing. In A.B. Baker & L.H. Baker (Eds.), *Clinical neurology.* New York: Harper & Row.

Benton, A.L. (1977c). Reflections on the Gerstmann syndrome. *Brain and Language, 4,* 45–62.

Benton, A.L. (1979). Visuoperceptive, visuospatial and visuoconstructive disorders. In K.M. Heilman & E. Valenstein (Eds.), *Clinical neuropsychology.* New York: Oxford University Press.

Benton, A.L. (1980a). The neuropsychology of facial recognition. *American Psychologist, 35,* 176–186.

Benton, A.L. (1980b). Psychological testing for brain damage. In H.I. Kaplan, A.M. Freedman, & B.J. Badock (Eds.), *Comprehensive textbook of psychiatry/III. Vol. 1.* Baltimore: Williams & Wilkins.

Benton, A.L., Eslinger, P.J., & Damasio, A.R. (1981). Normative observations on neuropsychological test performance in old age. *Journal of Clinical Neuropsychology, 3,* 33–42.

Benton, A.L., & Hamsher, K. deS. (1976). *Multilingual aphasia examination*. Iowa City: University of Iowa.

Benton, A.L., Hamsher, K.deS., Varney, N.R., & Spreen, O. (1983). *Contributions to neuropsychological assessment: A clinical manual*. New York: Oxford University Press.

Benton, A.L., Levin, H.S., & Van Allen, M.W. (1974). Geographic orientation in patients with unilateral cerebral disease. *Neuropsychologia*, 12, 183–191.

Benton, A.L., & Van Allen, M.W. (1960). Impairment in facial recognition in patients with cerebral disease. *Cortex*, 4, 344–358.

Benton, A.L., & Van Allen, M.W. (1972). Prosopagnosia and facial discrimination. *Journal of the Neurological Sciences*, 15, 167–172.

Benton, A.L., Van Allen, M.W., & Fogel, M.L. (1964). Temporal orientation in cerebral disease. *Journal of Nervous and Mental Disease*, 139, 110–119.

Benton, A.L., Varney, N.R., & Hamsher, K.deS. (1978). Visuospatial judgment: A clinical test. *Archives of Neurology*, 35, 364–367.

Blackburn, H.L., & Benton, A.L. (1957). Revised administration and scoring of the digit span test. *Journal of Consulting Psychology*, 21, 139–143.

Bogen, J.E. (1979). The callosal syndrome. In K.M. Heilman & E. Valenstein (Eds.), *Clinical neuropsychology*. New York: Oxford University Press.

Brown, J.W. (1972). *Aphasia, apraxia and agnosia: Clinical and theoretical aspects*. Springfield: Charles Thomas.

Castaigne, P., Lhermitte, F., Buge, A., Escourolle, R., Hauw, J.J., & Lyon-Caen, O. (1981). Paramedian thalamic and midbrain infarcts: Clinical and neuropathological study. *Annals of Neurology*, 10, 127–148.

Cermak, L.S. (1982). The long and short of it in amnesia. In L.S. Cermak (Ed.), *Human memory and amnesia*. Hillsdale, NJ: Erlbaum.

Chédru, F., & Geschwind, N. (1972). Disorders of higher cortical functions in acute confusional states. *Cortex*, 8, 395–411.

Costa, L. (1983). Clinical neuropsychology: A discipline in evolution. *Journal of Clinical Neuropsychology*, 5, 1–11.

Critchley, M. (1953). *The parietal lobes*. London: Arnold.

Cummings, J.L., & Benson, D.F. (1983). *Dementia: A clinical approach*. Boston: Butterworth.

Damasio, A.R., & Benton, A.L. (1979). Impairment of hand movements under visual guidance. *Neurology*, 29, 170–178.

Damasio, A., & Damasio, H. (1977). Studies in dichotic listening: Contributions to neurophysiology. In F.C. Rose (Ed.), *Physiological aspects of clinical neurology*. Boston: Blackwell Scientific Publications.

Damasio, A.R., Damasio, H., & Chui, H.C. (1980). Neglect following damage to frontal lobe or basal ganglia. *Neuropsychologia*, 18, 123–131.

Damasio, A.R., Damasio, H., Rizzo, M., Varney, N., & Gersh, F. (1982). Aphasia with nonhemorrhagic lesions in the basal ganglia and internal capsule. *Archives of Neurology*, 39, 15–20.

Damasio, A.R., McKee, J., & Damasio, H. (1979). Determinants of performance in color anomia. *Brain and Language*, 7, 74–85.

Damasio, A.R., & Van Hoesen, B.W. (1983). Emotional disturbances associated with focal lesions of the limbic frontal lobe. In K.M. Heilman & P. Satz (Eds.), *Neuropsychology of human emotion*. New York: Guilford Press.

Damasio, A., Yamada, T., Damasio, H., Corbett, J., & McKee, J. (1980). Central achromatopsia: Behavioral, anatomic, and physiologic aspects. *Neurology*, 30, 1064–1071.

Damasio, H., & Damasio, A.R. (1979). "Paradoxic" ear extinction in dichotic listening: Possible anatomic significance. *Neurology*, 29, 644–653.

David, R., Enderby, P., & Bainton, D. (1982). Treatment of acquired aphasia: Speech therapists and volunteers compared. *Journal of Neurology, Neurosurgery, and Psychiatry*, 45, 957–961.

Davies, P. (1983). An update on the neurochemistry of Alzheimer disease. In R. Mayeux & W.G. Rosen (Eds.), *The dementias*. New York: Raven Press.

Dee, H.L., Benton, A.L., & Van Allen, M.W. (1970). Apraxia in relation to hemispheric locus of lesion and aphasia. *Transactions of the American Neurological Association*, 95, 147–150.

Dee, H.L., & Van Allen, M.W. (1971). Simple and choice reaction time and motor strength in unilateral cerebral disease. *Acta Psychiatrica Scandinavica*, 47, 315–323.

Dee, H.L., & Van Allen, M.W. (1972). Psychomotor testing as an aid in the recognition of cerebral lesions. *Neurology*, 22, 845–848.

Dee, H.L., & Van Allen, M.W. (1973). Speed of decision-making processes in patients with unilateral cerebral disease. *Archives of Neurology*, 28, 163–166.

DeRenzi, E. (1982). *Disorders of space exploration and cognition*. Chichester, England: Wiley.

Erickson, R.C., & Scott, M.L. (1977). Clinical memory testing: A review. *Psychological Bulletin*, 84, 1130–1149.

Eslinger, P.J., & Benton, A.L. (1983). Visuoperceptual performances in aging and dementia: Clinical and theoretical implications. *Journal of Clinical Neuropsychology*, 5, 213–220.

Finger, S., & Stein, D.G. (1982). *Brain damage and recovery*. New York: Academic Press.

Fogel, M.L. (1964). The intelligence quotient as an index of brain damage. *American Journal of Orthopsychiatry*, 34, 555–562.

Fuld, P.A., Katzman, R., Davies, P., & Terry, R.D. (1982). Intrusions as a sign of Alzheimer dementia: Chemical and pathological verification. *Annals of Neurology*, 11, 155–159.

Gazzaniga, M.S. (1978). Is seeing believing: Notes on clinical recovery. In S. Finger (Ed.), *Recovery from brain damage: Research and theory*. New York: Plenum.

Geschwind, N. (1980). Neurological knowledge and complex behaviors. *Cognitive Science*, 4, 185–193.

Goodglass, N., & Kaplan E. (1983). *The assessment of aphasia and related disorders* (2nd ed.). Philadelphia: Lea & Febiger.

Hamsher, K.deS. (1978a). Stereopsis and the perception of anomalous contours. *Neuropsychologia*, 16, 453–459.

Hamsher, K.deS. (1978b). Stereopsis and unilateral brain disease. *Investigative Ophthalmology & Visual Science*, 17, 336–343.

Hamsher, K. (1981). Intelligence and aphasia. In M.T. Sarno (Ed.), *Acquired aphasia*. New York: Academic Press.

Hamsher, K. (1983), Mental status examination in Alzheimer's disease: The neuropsychologist's role. *Postgraduate Medicine*, 73, 225–228.

Hamsher, K.deS., Benton, A.L., & Digre, K. (1980). Serial digit learning: Normative and clinical aspects. *Journal of Clinical Neuropsychology*, 2, 39–50.

Hamsher, K.deS., Haimi, K.A., & Benton, A.L. (1981). Prediction of outcome in anorexia nervosa from neuropsychological status. *Psychiatry Research*, 4, 79–88.

Hamsher, K.deS., Levin, H.S., & Benton, A.L. (1979). Facial recognition in patients with focal brain lesions. *Archives of Neurology*, 36, 837–839.

Hécaen, H., & Albert, M.L. (1978). *Human neuropsychology*. New York: Wiley.

Heilman, K.M. (1979). Apraxia. In K.M. Heilman & E. Valenstein (Eds.), *Clinical neuropsychology*. New York: Oxford University Press.

Henderson, V.W., Alexander, M.P., & Naeser, M.A. (1983). Right thalamic injury, impaired visuospatial perception, and alexia. *Neurology*, 32, 235–240.

Hinsie, L.E., & Campbell, R.J. (1975). *Psychiatric dictionary* (4th ed.). New York: Oxford University Press.

Hyvärinen, J. (1982). *The parietal cortex of monkey and man*. Berlin: Springer-Verlag.

Joynt, R.J., & Shoulson, I. (1979). Dementia. In K.M. Heilman & E. Valenstein (Eds.), *Clinical neuropsychology*. New York: Oxford University Press.

Kertesz, A. (1979). *Aphasia and associated disorders: Taxonomy, localization, and recovery*. New York: Grune & Stratton.

Kimura, D., Barnett, H.J.M., & Burkhart, G. (1979). *The psychological test pattern in progressive supranuclear palsy* (Research Bulletin #477, Department of Psychology). London, Canada: University of Western Ontario.

Kirshner, H.S., & Freemon, F.R. (Eds.). (1982). *The neurology of aphasia*. Lisse, The Netherlands: Swets & Zeitlinger.

Levin, H.S. (1973). Motor impersistence and proprioceptive feedback in patients with unilateral cerebral disease. *Neurology*, 23, 833–841.

Levin, H.S., Benton, A.L., & Grossman, R.G. (1982). *Neurobehavioral consequences of closed head injury*. New York: Oxford University Press.

Levin, H.S., O'Donnell, V.M., & Grossman, R.G. (1979). The Galveston orientation and amnesia test: A practical scale to assess cognition after head injury. *Journal of Nervous and Mental Disease*, 167, 675–684.

Lezak, M.D. (1983). *Neuropsychological assessment*. New York: Oxford University Press.

Lilly, R., Cummings, J.L., Benson, D.F., & Frankel, M. (1983). The human Kluver-Bucy syndrome. *Neurology*, 33, 1141–1145.

Lockard, I. (1977). *Desk reference for neuroanatomy: A guide to essential terms*. New York: Springer-Verlag.

Matarazzo, J.D. (1972). *Wechsler's measurement and appraisal of adult intelligence* (5th ed.). Baltimore: Williams & Wilkins.

Matthews, C.G. (1981). Neuropsychology practice in a hospital setting. In S.B. Filskov & T.J. Boll (Eds.), *Handbook of clinical neuropsychology*. New York: Wiley.

Mayeux, R., Brandt, J., Rosen, J., & Benson, D.F. (1980). Interictal memory and language impairment in temporal lobe epilepsy. *Neurology*, 30, 120–125.

McFarling, D., Rothi, L.J., & Heilman, K.M. (1982). Transcortical aphasia from ischaemic infarcts of the thalamus: A report of two cases. *Journal of Neurology, Neurosurgery, and Psychiatry*, 45, 107–112.

McFie, J. (1975). *Assessment of organic intellectual impairment*. London: Academic Press.

Meadows, J.C. (1974). Disturbed perception of colours associated with localized cerebral lesions. *Brain*, 97, 615–632.

Meier, M.J. (1981). Education for competency assurance in human neuropsychology: Antecedents, models, and directions. In S.B. Fillskov & T.J. Boll (Eds.), *Handbook of clinical neuropsychology*. New York: Wiley.

Meier, M.J., & French, L.A. (1965). Lateralized deficits in complex visual discrimination and bilateral transfer of reminiscence following unilateral temporal lobectomy. *Neuropsychologia*, 3, 261–272.

Mesulam, M.-M. (1981). A cortical network for directed attention and unilateral neglect. *Annals of Neurology*, 10, 309–325.

Mesulam, M.-M., Waxman, S.G., Geschwind, N., & Sabin, T.D. (1976). Acute confusional states with right middle cerebral artery infarctions. *Journal of Neurology, Neurosurgery, and Psychiatry*, 39, 84–89.

Milner, B. (1974). Hemispheric specialization: Scope and limits. In F.O. Schmitt & F.G. Worden (Eds.), *The neurosciences third study program*. Cambridge, MA: MIT Press.

Mohr, J.P. (1982). The evaluation of aphasia. *Stroke*, 13, 399–401.

Naeser, M.A., Alexander, M.P., Helm-Estabrooks, N., Levine, H.L., Laughlin, S.A., & Geschwind, N. (1982). Aphasia with predominantly subcortical lesion sites: Description of three capsular/putaminal aphasia syndromes. *Archives of Neurology*, 39, 2–14.

Newcombe, F. (1969). *Missile wounds of the brain: A study of psychological deficits*. London: Oxford University Press.

Newcombe, F., & Russell, W.R. (1969). Dissociated visual perceptual and spatial deficits in focal lesions of the right hemisphere. *Journal of Neurology, Neurosurgery, and Psychiatry*, 32, 73–81.

Overall, J.E., Hoffmann, N.G., & Levin, H. (1978). Effects of aging, organicity, alcoholism, and functional psychopathology on WAIS subtest profiles. *Journal of Consulting and Clinical Psychology*, 46, 1315–1322.

Overall, J.E., & Levin H.S. (1978). Correcting for cultural factors in evaluating intellectual deficit on the WAIS. *Journal of Clinical Psychology*, 34, 910–915.

Pfeiffer, E. (1975). SPMSQ: Short portable mental status questionnaire. *Journal of the American Geriatric Society*, 23, 433–441.

Pratt, R.T.C. (1977). Psychogenic loss of memory. In C.W.M. Whitty & O.L. Zangewill (Eds.), *Amnesia* (2nd ed.). London: Butterworths.

Ratcliff, G. (1982). Disturbances of spatial orientation associated with cerebral lesions. In M. Potegal (Ed.),

Spatial abilities: Development and physiological foundations. New York: Academic Press.

Rondot, P., de Recondo, J., & Dumas, J.L.R. (1977). Visumotor ataxia. *Brain*, 100, 355–376.

Rosen, W.G. (1980). Verbal fluency in aging and dementia. *Journal of Clinical Neuropsychology*, 2, 135–146.

Rosen, W.G., Terry, R.D., Fuld, P.A., Katzman, R., & Peck, A. (1980). Pathologic verification of the ischemic score in differentiation of dementias. *Annals of Neurology*, 7, 486–488.

Rubens, A.B. (1979). Agnosia. In K.M. Heilman & E. Valenstein (Eds.), *Clinical neuropsychology*. New York: Oxford University Press.

Sarno, M.T. (Ed.). (1981). *Acquired aphasia*. New York: Academic Press.

Seltzer, B., & Sherwin, I. (1983). A comparison of clinical features in early- and late-onset primary degenerative dementia. *Archives of Neurology*, 40, 143–146.

Spitzer, R.L., Sheehy, M., & Endicott, J. (1977). DSM-III: Guiding principles. In V.M. Rakoff, H.C. Stancer, & H.B. Kedward (Eds.), *Psychiatric diagnosis*. New York: Brunner/Mazel.

Spreen, O., & Benton, A.L. (1965). Comparative studies of some psychological tests for cerebral damage. *Journal of Nervous and Mental Disease*, 140, 323–333.

Spreen, O., & Benton, A.L. (1969). *Neurosensory Center Comprehensive Examination for Aphasia*. Victoria, B.C.: Neuropsychology Laboratory, Department of Psychology, University of Victoria.

Strub, R.L. (1982). Acute confusional state. In D.F. Benson & D. Blumer (Eds.), *Psychiatric aspects of neurologic disease. Volume II*. New York: Grune & Stratton.

Strub, R.L., & Black, F.W. (1977). *The mental status examination in neurology*. Philadelphia: F.A. Davis.

Teasdale, G., & Jennett, B. (1974). Assessment of coma and impaired consciousness: A practical scale. *Lancet*, 2, 81–84.

Tellegen, A., & Briggs, P.F. (1967). Old wine in new skins: Grouping Wechsler subtests into new scales. *Journal of Consulting Psychology*, 31, 499–506.

Van Zomeren, A.H., & Deelman, B.G. (1978). Long-term recovery of visual reaction time after closed head injury. *Journal of Neurology, Neurosurgery, and Psychiatry*, 41, 452–457.

Varney, N.R. (1978). Linguistic correlates of pantomime recognition in aphasic patients. *Journal of Neurology, Neurosurgery, and Psychiatry*, 41, 564–568.

Varney, N.R. (1980). Sound recognition in relation to aural language comprehension in aphasic patients. *Journal of Neurology, Neurosurgery and Psychiatry*, 43, 71–75.

Varney, N.R. (1981). Letter recognition and visual form discrimination in aphasic alexia. *Neuropsychologia*, 19, 795–800.

Varney, N.R. (1982). Colour association and "colour amnesia" in aphasia. *Journal of Neurology, Neurosurgery, and Psychiatry*, 45, 248–252.

Varney, N.R., & Benton, A.L. (1979). Phonemic discrimination and aural comprehension among aphasic patients. *Journal of Clinical Neuropsychology*, 1, 65–73.

Varney, N.R., & Benton, A.L. (1982). Qualitative aspects of pantomime recognition defect in aphasia. *Brain and Cognition*, 1, 132–139.

Varney, N.R., & Damasio, A.R. (1982). Acquired alexia. In R.N. Malatesha, & P.G. Aaron (Eds.), *Reading disorders: Varieties and treatments*. New York: Academic Press.

Vignolo, L.A. (1969). Auditory agnosia. In A.L. Benton (Ed.), *Contributions to clinical neuropsychology*. Chicago: Aldine.

Wallesch, C.W., Kornhuber, H.H., Kunz, T., & Brunner, R.J. (1983). Neuropsychological deficits associated with small unilateral thalamic lesions. *Brain*, 106, 141–152.

Walsh, K.W. (1978). *Neuropsychology: A clinical approach*. New York: Churchill Livingstone.

Warrington, E. (1976). Recognition and recall in amnesia. In J. Brown (Ed.), *Recall and recognition*. London: Wiley.

Wechsler, D. (1981). *WAIS-R manual*. New York: Harcourt Brace Jovanovich.

Wells, C.E. (1979). Pseudodementia. *American Journal of Psychiatry*, 136, 895–900.

Wilson, R.S., Rosenbaum, G., & Brown, G. (1979). The problem of premorbid intelligence in neuropsychological assessment. *Journal of Clinical Neuropsychology*, 1, 49–53.

Woodruff, R.A., Jr., Goodwin, D.W., & Guze, S.B. (1974). *Psychiatric diagnosis*. New York: Oxford University Press.

Zimmerman, I.L., & Woo-Sam, J.M. (1973). *Clinical interpretation of the Wechsler Adult Intelligence Scale*. New York: Grune & Stratton.

PART VI
INTERVIEWING

13 PSYCHIATRIC INTERVIEW AND MENTAL STATUS EXAMINATION

Iradj Siassi

INTRODUCTION

"The interview *is* the most important technical instrument of all those professions concerned with man and his social functioning" (Kolb, 1971, p. vii). Kolb's assertion is no less valid today than it was over a decade ago. Such is the case in an era characterized by the increasing use of computers and self- and technician-administered tests and rating scales, some of which have achieved broad acceptance and widespread applications (Endicott & Spitzer, 1978; Robins, Helzer, & Croughan, 1979; Wing, Birley, & Cooper, 1967).

There are, of course, a variety of ways to conceptualize psychiatric problems. And there also exist a vast number of contradictory psychiatric and social science theories. Thus, given that psychiatry is still without a *comprehensive* theory of behavior, ideally we should examine the patient from multiple perspectives, which include biologic, psychodynamic, sociocultural, and behavioral dimensions. Clearly, it would be impractical to devise *a* psychiatric interview and mental status examination equally acceptable by practitioners who are enamoured of conflicting and often contradictory theoretical persuasions. The best one can hope to accomplish in this context is an *out-line* that can be used to generate a set of clinical data containing sufficient information to fulfill the requirements of the currently mandated multiaxial psychiatric diagnostic system (APA, 1980). Such data can then serve as a common foundation for adherents of different theories and practices, to be augmented by additional information needed for their specific orientation and practice. The psychoanalyst, for example, may need a much more detailed assessment of the patient's ego strengths and weaknesses, defense mechanisms, and capacity for regression in his/her initial evaluation. Similarly, the behaviorist may require a much more detailed account of the antecedents and reinforcers of specific behaviors.

BACKGROUND

The psychiatric interview has undergone marked changes during this century. Early in the century, the psychiatric interview, as practiced by most American psychiatrists, was modeled after the medical history-taking of the time for physical illnesses. It was comprised chiefly of a question and answer format. With influences exerted first by Adolf Meyer (Gill, Newman, & Redlich, 1954;

Henrickson, Coffer, & Cross, 1954; Meyer, 1951; Muncie, 1974; Saul, 1957) and later by psychoanalytically oriented practitioners, much greater emphasis was placed on the *indirect* technique of interviewing, and a free-flowing exchange between the psychiatrist and the patient. In the past two decades, the theories and techniques of psychiatric interviewing have received much attention from researchers. Several structured interview schedules have been developed, and further attempts at refinements are still continuing. The modern psychiatric interview, at least as practiced in most American psychiatric facilities, is a combination of the earlier unstructured indirect techniques and a modified version of one or the other structured schedules.

The purposes of psychiatric interview and mental status examinations are to arrive at a diagnostic formulation and a rational treatment plan. As such, an attempt is made to discover the origin and evolution of the patient's mental disorder(s) by obtaining a biographical-historical account that can provide a psychological portrait of the patient. By securing knowledge concerning the personality, the forces that have played important parts in shaping it, and the situations in life that are anxiety-laden for the patient, the psychiatrist attempts to understand the illness and the meanings of symptoms. To study the patient's mental disorder(s) as an object of natural-history investigation requires that his/her difficulties be unraveled in the light of the fullest possible information concerning physical, biochemical, anatomical, physiological, pathological, social, psychological, and educational factors and influences. It is thus by means of both the cross-sectional method of mental status examination and the genetic-dynamic investigation of the patient's life history and developmental sequences that the clinician attempts to formulate his/her hypotheses regarding the patient's difficulties, whether they are primarily a particular form of thought disorder, affective disorder, behavior disorder, or psychophysiological disorder. Therefore, the psychiatrist, qua medical specialist, is expected to make a "diagnosis" in terms of some disease entity. In addition, however, he/she also seeks to reformulate the patient's particular difficulties by reconstructing the patient's life history through analysis of his/her life circumstances and the forces that have entered into the organization of his/her personality. The latter requires attention to significant personal relationships throughout the patient's life, particularly during the formative years of childhood. Specifically, one should look for development of persistent personality traits and methods for dealing with anxiety and stress, with special emphasis on their patterns during childhood and adolescence. The description of the patient's clinical picture, therefore, includes both diagnostic labels and a series of probable hypotheses to account for these labels. The psychiatrist attempts to posit orderly hypotheses regarding psychological and other factors that "explain" the dynamic relationship between past and present events and, to some degree, predict future ones.

The assessment of the patient's mental status requires: (a) discovering, describing, and classifying the manifestations of the patient's pathological mental reactions, (b) the meaning and significance of the psychopathological behaviors, and (c) the hypotheses regarding their motivations.

The assessment process, therefore, involves more than collection and codification of information. The psychiatrist integrates and collates the data obtained from the biological, psychological, social, and other fields of inquiry. For example, he/she arrives at a diagnosis of a personality disorder only when the data show a pattern or clustering, which, with few exceptions, is often repeated in the patient's life. These include certain themes, recurrent life issues, or conflicts prevailing through the patient's life history. Whenever possible, the data obtained from the patient should be supplemented by information from other sources (preferably more than one relative or friend to enhance the reliability of this information).

Most psychiatrists believe that the first interview is where the most satisfactory history can be secured, since typically both the patient and other informants are less likely to conceal important data.

THE PSYCHIATRIC INTERVIEW

General Considerations

The psychiatric interview discussed here is limited to the initial evaluation of a patient. This should usually be achieved in one interview. Whether the patient is being seen in an emergency room of a general hospital, the outpatient department of a psychiatric clinic, or in a private practitioner's office, the initial interview must be viewed quite seriously. No matter how trivial the patient's symptoms or complaints may appear on the surface, the practitioner must bear in mind that by the time the patient arrives for his initial contact with the psychiatrist, he/she has already been through several self-screenings. Whether the patient comes alone or is brought by relatives or friends, as a rule their support systems and other problem-solving resources have been exhausted. It is therefore incumbent upon the practitioner not only to treat the patient with the respect and understanding that professional ethics dictate, but to take the patient's complaints seriously. This means that the psychiatrist should respect the patient's assumptions about the importance, seriousness, and gravity of his or her symptoms.

It is my belief that the maximum relevant information should be obtained in the initial interview. Textbooks, chapters, and articles on the topic of psychiatric interview often exaggerate the difficulties of this and underplay its significance (Lazare, 1979; MacKinnon, 1980; Menninger, Mayman, & Pruyser, 1962; Whitehorn, 1944). However, the importance of obtaining the maximum relevant information during the initial interview cannot be overemphasized. There are many reasons for this. First, and most obvious, the patient may not be available for a *second* interview for a variety of reasons. Thus, important psychological or organic mental disorders may go untreated for indefinite lengths of time. Second, my own and other colleagues' experience indicates that typically the patient is often eager and quite willing to provide information in the first interview, even though this remains to be substantiated as an empirical claim. In the time between the first and second interview a great amount of resistance may develop, making the information that could have been available in the first interview no longer available. This also applies to relatives. For example, when relatives bring a patient to the admitting office of a psychiatric hospital, they usually are very eager to provide detailed information. However, once the patient is hospitalized and the original stress removed, they are frequently either unable or unwilling to provide the same amount of information. Often the guilt associated with taking part in the hospitalization of the patient and other factors mitigate against their being as open and objective informants as they would have been at the time of the initial contact.

It is also crucial to obtain *sufficient* information to formulate a rational plan after the first interview. For example, in the important area of dif-ferential diagnosis of organic mental disorders, by the end of the first interview there should have been at least some resolution of areas of concern and the arrangement for necessary laboratory or other ancillary diagnostic measures. Similarly, in the area of neuropsychological doubt or confusion, the differential diagnosis should have reached the stage where arrangements for obtaining additional testing could be discussed and suggested by the end of the first interview.

On the surface, it may appear a formidable task to obtain sufficient information to arrive at a diagnosis and to suggest steps for a treatment plan in one interview. However, I believe it is neither impossible nor even particularly difficult in the majority of cases to arrive at such a point, provided that the clinician has a clear idea of what constitutes pertinent and relevant information. Frequently, massive amounts of information are obtained over several interviews that contribute no more to definitive understanding of the problem nor to direction for further action than the information obtained in the single encounter.

The length of the initial interview depends upon the cooperativeness of the patient and on the interviewer's experience, capacity for cognitive and empathic observations, data-gathering skills, and collating and synthesizing abilities. It is my experience, however, that as a rule a period of 45 to 90 minutes is sufficient for obtaining the relevant information for tentative diagnosis, formulation, and planning. In the rare exception when more time might be advisable for the first interview, the clinician should make this time range available during the initial interview. Two common excuses for not obtaining comprehensive initial evaluations are the limitation of overcrowded emergency rooms or the extended time available in inpatient settings. It is paradoxical that *both* "too little" time and "too much" time are offered as excuses for failing to conduct proper initial evaluation.

Those who argue that the initial evaluation of the patient ought to extend over several interviews, run counter to the prevailing general practice, since the initial evaluation is completed in one interview in most situations. Nevertheless, the objection that the scope or extent of information obtained in one interview tends to be small, needs to be addressed. The typical claim is that the patient's state may change with the passage of time and that psychiatric observations will also change, thereby severely limiting the relevance of cross-sectional evaluation. It is difficult to argue that serial observations of the patient are superior to a single cross-sectional interview and mental status examination. However, this in no way detracts from the relevance or value of the data on a comprehensive mental status examination and review of the history of the patient at the time of the initial interview. If serial observations in the form of further interviews become available, they can always be compared with the existing data base. It is therefore essential to undertake a complex evaluation of the patient at the time of distress when the family and the patient are clearly different, than when the crisis is resolved by hospitalizing the patient. Indeed, the very fact that as time passes: (a) The patient's state may change, (b) his mental status may appear different, and (c) his account of his life history (i.e., the longitudinal account that supposedly was unchangeable) is also different because of different interpretations or different emphases by the patient all make it even more imperative that the initial evaluation be as complete as possible in order to provide a meaningful comparative data base.

I believe there is a definite distinction between diagnostic and therapeutic interviews in psychiatry. The notion that the psychiatrist becomes engaged in the treatment of the patient from the initial interview only makes sense if he/she is committed to a particular orientation that enables him/her to place every patient into that particular treatment modality. For example, if the psychiatrist already believes that all psychiatric difficulties can be explained in terms of behavior theory or psychoanalytic theory, and that the treatment of choice must be either behavior modification or psychoanalysis, respectively, then there is no need for demarcating the diagnostic interview from the subsequent therapeutic interviews. However, in the modern psychiatric practice in most public settings, university outpatient departments, or emergency rooms for psychiatric and general hospitals, the person who is involved in the initial evaluation of the patient is usually not the same person who becomes responsible for the treatment of the patient. To avoid ambiguity, it needs to be clearly stated that the initial interview is oriented only toward establishment of a diagnostic formulation and understanding of the patient's difficulties: in short, a working hypothesis for arriving at decisions regarding the future treatment steps to be taken. The patient and/or his relatives should be made aware that no treatment contract of any kind exists between the evaluator and the patient

until the nature of his/her difficulties are investigated, clarified, and delineated by the initial interview. Indeed, if the patient feels better as a result of the initial interview or the family's level of anxiety decreases, this should be attributed to the fact that some clear-cut direction has been provided for them regarding the next step.

Often, it is not very difficult to make many patients feel better by simply providing them or their families with false assurances, by sympathizing with their difficulties, or by allowing them to have an abreaction. However, this is not the primary task of the initial psychiatric interview. Even in private practice, where, as a rule, the psychiatrist seeing the patient for the first time typically decides to treat the patient, it is advisable to maintain the evaluation contract and treatment contract separately. Even in cases where psychotherapy is clearly indicated, it is important to keep initial evaluation completely distinct from the contract for psychotherapy. It is my experience that *cetris paribus*, the patient's acceptance of recommendations for any modality of treatment, is directly affected by how thoroughly he or she perceives the evaluation process to have been.

Several decades ago, it probably made little difference what specific diagnosis the patient was assigned, since the available treatments were highly limited and by necessity more or less applied to all patients. However, with the increasing availability of diagnostic-specific treatments, it has become imperative to view the initial interview as analogous to the kind of work-up routinely practiced in other medical specialties, leading to a diagnostic formulation and whenever possible to a diagnostic-specific treatment plan.

In a contrasting vein, many authors have drawn clear distinctions between the general medical interview and the psychiatric interview. Again, it is my experience that a good initial psychiatric interview and a good initial medical interview have much in common. In both the initial medical and the initial psychiatric interview the psychiatrist or the other medical specialist is being consulted because he/she is defined as an expert. Typically, the patient is suffering and desires relief; the psychiatrist or other medical practitioner is expected to know how to go about providing much relief. When the patient comes to a medical practitioner or a psychiatrist, it is with the hope of obtaining help to alleviate the suffering that motivated him to disclose his problems. In both situations this process is facilitated by the confidentiality of the doctor-patient relationship.

With the exception of patients who are uncooperative (due to either a medical or psychological disorder), the patient will communicate more or less freely any material that he or she feels may be pertinent to his/her difficulties. In medical or psychiatric situations it is a rational step to allow the patient to explain his/her difficulties at the beginning, since a great deal can be learned by merely listening to the patient. In both situations the patient has a right to expect more than a sympathetic listener. Both the psychiatrist and other medical specialists demonstrate their expertise by eliciting the type of information from the patient or relatives that will help in arriving at an understanding of the patient's difficulties and in planning subsequent steps. Both emphasize history-taking to obtain facts that will facilitate the establishment of a correct diagnosis and the institution of appropriate treatment. Usually, in both nonpsychiatric and psychiatric evaluations, the interview is organized around the chief complaint, present illness, past history, family and personal history, and a review of systems.

Beyond this general information that is obtained by all medical specialists, each specialist has specific questions related to his/her own speciality. An ophthalmologist, for example, has a series of specific questions and tests different from those a cardiologist uses. It is therefore not surprising that the data concerning the personality and personal life of the patient should be considered more important in the psychiatric interview than in a nonpsychiatric medical interview. Every specialist is interested in the patient's symptoms, their dates of onset, and whatever significant factors may contribute to understanding those symptoms. In most psychiatric cases, diagnoses and treatment planning depend as much on the total life history of the patient as on the present illness. Therefore, in the psychiatric history greater attention may be paid to the patient's life-style, self-appraisal, and psychological coping patterns than in other medical interviews.

A good psychiatric interview and a good nonpsychiatric interview have a great deal in common. Of course, it would be incorrect to claim that there are no differences between the two types of interviews. Psychiatric symptoms often involve defensive functions of the ego and represent unconscious psychological conflicts. To the extent that the patient is unaware of these conflicts, he/she cannot possibly share them with the interviewer. Furthermore, cultural factors, shame or embarrassment might make the patient conceal more from a psychiatrist than from another medical specialist. Because of this, it is possible that the reliability and validity of information obtained from the initial interview with the psychiatric patient may not be as high as with another medical specialist. This might also be due to the nature of the particular disorder. For example, a dependent patient might be as eager to obtain love and respect from the psychiatric examiner as in gaining relief from suffering and be unwilling to disclose any material that might put him/her in a bad light. Furthermore, the systems that are being reviewed specifically by a psychiatrist are much more difficult to review than the systems reviewed by a cardiologist or an ophthalmologist.

In the absence of adequate, reliable, and valid ancillary procedures, the psychiatrist has to depend more on his/her own powers of observation, judgment, and interpretation than almost any other medical specialist. Because the psychiatrist does not have the type of accurate and reliable laboratory tests and other paraclinical tools that most other medical specialists have, it is more difficult to arrive at a specific evaluation of the etiology of most psychiatric disorders. However, the process of arriving at a differential diagnosis prior to looking for extra-interview tools should be considered essentially similar.

Structured Versus Nonstructured Interviews

Concern over the lack of reliability (i.e., the consistency with which observations of patients are made among psychiatric practitioners) has in recent years led to the development of many structured interview schedules. The debate, however, is far from over. There is general agreement that the more structured the interview, the more reliability improves. That is, if two interviewers use a structured interview there is more chance of reliability than if they used indirect methods. However, the quality of the data obtained is also a matter of question. Those who argue for the indirect method of interviewing believe that the question-answer format of structured interviewing distorts the patient's picture, is useful only in certain diagnostic categories, and then only for arriving at a diagnosis. Nothing would be gained by joining this argument. The issue has been articulated extensively in the literature (Bartko & Carpenter, 1976; Endicott & Spitzer, 1972; Nemiah, 1961; Stevenson, 1959).

There is little argument, however, about the need for a common vocabulary of psychopathological behaviors and disorders. The general consensus about the need for a common language among psychiatrists has led to continuing efforts over the past several decades. The publication of the first diagnostic and statistical manual (DSM-I) (APA, 1952) in 1952, the changes that were made by developing the second (DSM-II) (APA, 1968) in 1968, and the further and major changes that were made before the third (DSM-III) (APA, 1980) was accepted as the official diagnostic nomenclature for American psychiatry in 1980, all reflect the search for a rational, uniform, and systematic vocabulary. The multiaxial diagnostic system, which is adopted in DSM-III and is now the official guide for American psychiatry, is in large measure a reflection of the ascendance of the biopsychosocial model of mental disorders. Clearly, the model is not universally accepted. However, since the multiaxial diagnostic formulations of the DSM-III depend on the assumptions of the psychobiosocial model in order to conform to the current official mandate, the following presentation on the initial interview and the development of a data base from the initial interview will be primarily based on the psychobiosocial model.

According to this model the simple formula of a person plus stress leading to reaction is used $(P + S \rightarrow R)$. The formula is a circular one, since the reaction itself might then act as further stress causing further reaction. However, for the purpose of simplicity we will use the formula as a linear one. Hence, the need for an understanding of the patient in terms of personality, life situation, and the possible stressors that might be acting on him and, in part, account for the reactions (symptoms). This is a formula that should be kept in mind.

With rare exceptions the patient and/or family who come for an initial evaluation are not aware of the information that is relevant for assessment and diagnosis. As stated earlier, in the majority of cases the combination of indirect and direct interviewing methods is used in order to complete the patient's initial evaluation. While using the indirect method, the interviewer should have a clear, structured organization of the data in mind and know what information is needed in order to have a complete initial evaluation and data base. As a rule, the patient provides the information without any given sequence. Once optimum information from indirect interviewing has been obtained, the interviewer might want to fill in the gaps that remain in the organization he keeps in his own mind prior to doing a formal mental status examination. The way that the material of the initial interview is typically organized does not differ greatly from one textbook to the other. However, there are some minor variations and different priorities. In my work with patients in different settings, I have found the following format for organizing the material to be quite acceptable.

Identifying Information

This should include the patient's name, age, sex, and other demographic variables, such as education, marital status, number of children, and employment. The number of previous psychiatric contacts and whether or not the patient has experienced previous psychiatric hospitalizations should be recorded here, with little detail. Referral and information sources (e.g., patient alone or patient with a given relative and/or previous charts) need to be recorded at the beginning of the organized evaluation.

Chief Complaint

Many textbooks discuss using the patient's exact words in recording the chief complaint. In some cases this might be sufficient, but in other cases the chief complaint may not be from the patient. Also, the patient may be totally resistant to sharing the chief complaint and may be unaware of it. Chief complaints comprise the symptoms that have led to the patient coming or being brought to the attention of the psychiatrist, and their intensity and duration need to be recorded. The importance of recording the length of time that each symptom has existed cannot be overemphasized. In psychiatry, as in other branches of medicine, primary attention should be given to any changes in quality and quantity from a previous state. Therefore, a chief complaint that the patient has crying spells has little meaning unless it is specified how long, how frequently, and under what circumstances they occur. Under "chief complaint," it is usually best to have a quotation from the patient. In cases where the patient is either unaware or reluctant to share the problems, the chief complaint has to be obtained from those who have brought the patient to the clinic or the psychiatrist's office. For example, the chief complaint of a psychotic patient that "there is nothing wrong with me, it is my wife who is sick and needs to be here" should be recorded. At the same time it should be recorded that the wife has complained that the patient has been barricading himself with a shotgun for four days in his bedroom. Once the chief complaint has been clearly stated, attention can be given to the present illness.

Present Illness

Keeping the formula $P + S \rightarrow R$ in mind, attempts are made to ascertain whether or not there were any precipitating factors leading to the chief complaint. When the patient is being seen for the first time and symptoms are of recent origin, the present illness would only go back as far as the onset of the symptoms. In situations where the present illness is a point in a continuum of a chronic psychiatric illness showing exacerbations and remissions, attempts should be made to elicit the stress or stresses that have led to these exacerbations. Frequently, however, clear-cut precipitating factors cannot be found for the patient's symptoms, and this itself is quite informative. There are times when the connection between the particular stress and symptoms is quite clear from a temporal point of view (e.g., connection between the recent death of a spouse and the symptoms of depression). However, there are many precipitating factors that are more subtle and require the clinician to draw on knowledge of behavior, psychodynamics, psychopathology, and medicine. For example, the patient may not have had any changes in his life in the period leading to his symptoms, but a significant person in his life may have died a decade before the patient began experiencing symptomatology. Such anniversary reactions may take place without the patient being consciously aware of them, and even if the patient is made aware, as a rule, he or she cannot emotionally understand the connection. On other occasions the death of a stranger might trigger symptoms because of its symbolic meaning. For example, a patient became depressed following the death of an old man in the neighborhood. She had no contact with this old man except for occa-

sional greetings. It became clear from her history, however, that the most significant person in her life had been her grandfather, whom she cared for greatly and who died when the patient was away in her early teens. The patient had not fully mourned the grandfather's death, and the death of the old man in the neighborhood had rekindled the unfinished mourning.

If the patient is being seen for the first time, a chronological account of difficulties from the time of their onset until the time the patient is seen for the interview must be noted. The actions taken by the patient in order to alleviate these difficulties, the medications used, and contacts with physicians or others form the substance of the present illness. Other kinds of information to be included are whether the patient's symptoms are becoming worse or improving and whether any maneuvers or medicines have helped the symptoms. In short, a detailed account is required. However, if the patient's present illness is one more episode in a continuing chronic intermittent disorder, a less detailed account will suffice. For example, if the patient has had a history of schizophrenia with several hospitalizations and is now being seen because of exacerbation of psychotic symptomatology, it is safe to assume that the present psychotic symptomatology is a point in the continuum of the patient's schizophrenic disorder. In this case, the present illness would be traced to the onset of the disorder. Here a detailed account of all that had been done for the patient from the beginning of the discovered schizophrenia is both tedious and superfluous. It would suffice to note the length and number of hospitalizations, what transpired between hospitalizations, what types of medications were taken by the patient, and whether or not the patient had been cooperative with previous treatment plans. It would also be helpful to see what triggers the patient's psychotic breaks. Is it, for example, discontinuation of maintenance neuroleptics, when he or she is threatened with a separation, or when the possibility of going to work is raised?

In cases where the patient has been seen for a different type of mental disorder in the past, the account should be confined to the present illness, and reference need only be made to the previous psychiatric difficulties. For example, if the patient is being now seen with symptoms of agoraphobia but previously had been seen for reactive depression, the latter should be discussed under past psychiatric history. The clinician therefore has in his mind a clear idea of the type of information that is needed in order to describe the present illness. As was mentioned earlier, this information does not have to be given in sequential order, and pieces of it may be obtained throughout the interview.

Past Psychiatric History

Any information regarding the patient's psychiatric illnesses in the past is recorded. Such information includes the type of disorder, the precipitating factors, if any, and the steps that were taken in order to alleviate it.

Medical History

Here any physical illnesses that might have a bearing on the patient's psychiatric disorder and any other serious illnesses should be recorded. Any periods of ill health, semi-invalidism, exhaustion, and inertia in the patient's life should also be recorded here. The reason for attention to periods of malaise and ill health is that psychiatric illnesses are often disguised by indefinite physical complaints.

Personal History

Having thus completed an orderly system of investigation of the patient's complaints and illnesses, both mental and physical, the psychiatric examiner turns to an assessment of the patient independently of ill health. All the information obtained about the longitudinal history of the patient (i.e., the patient's biography) is organized under the heading of personal history. Without such a biography the patient's state at the time of the examination (i.e., the cross-sectional view of the patient) is often difficult to understand. As the patient describes his/her life the interviewer is provided with an opportunity to see how the patient speaks, thinks, judges, and feels. Also revealed are ideas on religious, moral, and sexual questions, as well as the way the patient deals with the objective world and people. In organizing the data obtained in the interview, the usual practice is that the patient's personal history should come after the exhaustion of the material relating to past and present difficulties. This is logical, since in most psychiatric interviews the natural course of events is that the patient

describes recent life events and symptoms that have brought him/her for the interview first; it is only when the patient is relieved of the pressure of providing this information that he or she is able to give details of life history. This is also true when the patient is not accessible, and the interview is in large measure carried out with relatives who have brought him/her. The personal history begins with the family history. Short sketches should be obtained of parents, significant other relatives, and siblings. In each sketch there should be both objective information and the patient's subjective view. Objective information includes the age, or the age at the time of death and the cause of death, of family members, their level of education, and their occupations. The subjective information pertains to the patient's attitude and perception of each relationship. The information about parents or other family members who might have had significant influence on the patient's life would naturally be more detailed. However, some information needs to be obtained about each sibling. Usually, the recording of family history can begin with such statements as: "The patient is the third of four children. He has two older brothers and a younger sister. . . ."

Any history of psychiatric problems or severe medical illnesses in the family needs to be explored. The attention paid to manifest cases of psychoses, epilepsy, and addiction in parents or blood relatives is an important issue because of the clinical and research value of such information. The data base cannot be considered complete without such information.

Once the information about the parents and siblings has been recorded the personal history proceeds with a detailed account of the patient. Date and place of birth, the mother's condition during pregnancy, whether or not the patient was full term or premature, and whether the delivery was normal are recorded. Also, any difficulties with early feeding (whether healthy or sickly as a baby) and his/her progress through developmental milestones are recorded. Most psychiatrists put great emphasis on the first five years of life. Most patients, however, have little recollection of this period of their life and only occasionally have some recollection about their emotional relations with other members of the family at that time. However, as a rule, most patients have heard from their family whether or not they were colicky babies or had difficulties with feeding, and so on. Most patients know up to what age they were enuretic and when they became toilet trained. As part of this personal history, neurotic symptoms in childhood, such as temper tantrums, night terrors, stammering, mannerisms, or fear states need to be fully explored. The patient's health during childhood is also of interest, along with how the patient reacted to the first major change in his/her life (i.e., separation to attend school is of significance). A chronological account of the patient's school life, school performance, and relationship to schoolmates, teachers, and school authorities forms an integral and important part of the patient's biography. The patient's work history is equally important. The ability to obtain and hold employment, the type of jobs held in chronological order, the reasons for job change and the extent of progress and promotion in jobs, and how the patient related to fellow workers and authority figures are important areas of inquiry.

Attention should be paid to how the patient experienced the critical phase of puberty and sexual awareness. For females, the menstrual history is recorded as the age of the first period and the regularity, duration, and quantity of each period. Whether the patient's periods have been painful, whether psychic changes were experienced in premenstrum, and her attitude toward menstruation should be evaluated. The sexual history for both sexes also includes information about the source and kind of sexual information received. Inquiry also needs to be made about excessive masturbation or extensive and time-filling sexual fantasies, as well as the patient's sexual orientation, or sexual deviation, and his/her sexual experiences. If the patient is married the marital history is of great importance. Attention should be paid both to the sexual side of marriage as well as to the patient's handling of interpersonal problems of married life. If the couple is childless the reasons for that and the patient's feeling about it should be explored. If there are children, the attitude of the patient toward the children and how he/she handles them need to be noted. How the female patient has reacted to pregnancy and childbirth, and how the male or female patient has handled the advent of the first child is a very informative part of the personal history.

The personal history should provide the comprehensive portrait of the patient independently of his/her illness.

MENTAL STATUS EXAMINATION

The objective clinical observations of the interviewer are organized and described under the heading of the mental status examination. In the psychiatric evaluation the mental status examination is considered to be analogous to the physical examination in general medicine. Much of what will appear under this heading has already been gathered during the interview. For example, the patient's appearance, speech, mood, and affect have been observed while the patient was providing an account of his or her life or describing symptoms. While obtaining information about the present illness, we might have already found access to the existence of delusions, misinterpretations, or disorders of perception such as hallucinations. The anamnesis may have already given us information about the patient's memory, intelligence, general fund of knowledge, attention and concentration, and insight and judgment. In the case of most patients, the psychiatric interview provides the interviewer with some general idea about the disorder he/she is evaluating. In a number of patients, however, there is uncertainty regarding some of the most subtle issues. For example, even after obtaining the history of the present illness and the past history, one may not be certain as to whether or not the patient has perceptual difficulties or whether or not he/she is delusional. Specific questions need to be asked in order to narrow down the differential diagnosis. In addition to completing the mental status, direct questioning at the end of the psychiatric interview can provide the information required to complete the history or other data that was not provided in the free-flowing nondirective interview.

What happens under the mental status heading includes a description of the patient's general appearance and behavior, emotional state, thinking and perception, and higher intellectual functioning. Relevant observations are made throughout the interview, and it is only at the end of the interview that the psychiatrist will stop the free-flowing, open-ended style of history-taking and switch to asking direct formal questions regarding the mental state. As mentioned earlier, he/she will also use direct questioning in order to fill any gaps in the history or to cover any oversights. The formal testing of higher intellectual functions will complete the interview.

In situations where the patient is either totally uncooperative or confused, the mental status examination may be the sum total of the patient's psychiatric evaluation. At other times, as the interview progresses, the psychiatrist may begin to suspect that the patient is concealing information. Some patients wish to conceal their paranoid thinking or suicidal ideation. Elderly patients may be threatened or embarrassed over their concerns about failing memory or declining intellectual functioning and will not share these concerns in the interview. These suspicions can be dealt with through direct questioning at the time of conducting the formal part of the mental status examination. At the time of direct questioning for the mental status examination, the interviewer has the opportunity to obtain whatever data he/she feels are missing in order to arrive at a differential diagnosis, a formulation, and also a view of the need for further specialized investigation and possible relevant treatment.

The beginner often has difficulty accepting that he/she not only has the right, but the responsibility to ask intimate or at times seemingly painful and embarrassing questions. The interviewer must bear in mind that the psychiatric interview is not a social visit, and questions about sexual functioning *or* suicidal and homocidal ideation and intentions have to be asked, albeit in a matter-of-fact manner. Both the patient's statements and the clinician's observations are recorded under the mental status examination. It is, however, important to distinguish between observation and interpretation. The interpretation belongs to the formulation and does not fall under the mental status heading. Whenever possible, an exact and objective recording of what is observed should be made.

General Appearance and Behavior

Throughout the interview the clinician has the opportunity to make many observations regarding the patient's general appearance and behavior. The patient's physical appearance is described, and attention is paid to his/her dress, posture, gait, gestures, and the care of person and clothing. The patient's appearance often provides important clues to diagnostic formulation. These clues are sometimes quite obvious. For example, clues to drug intoxication or withdrawal are obvious when the patient has dilated pupils and is hallucinating or has pinpoint pupils and is stuporous. More subtle clues are provided by contradic-

tion of the story that the patient tells with what is observed. For example, a patient may deny delusions but his/her behavior gives strong suggestion that delusional concerns are present such as increased vigilance and poor eye contact. Another example is the patient who denies being depressed but upon observation exhibits slowness in movement and lack of spontaneity. The patient's level of activity throughout the interview should be noted. Is the patient restless and agitated at the beginning of the interview but gradually calms down, or does he/she remain restless throughout the interview or grow more agitated? Are there any disturbances in activity, such as stereotypy, mannerisms, ties, posturing, or grimacing? Is the patient hostile, resentful, friendly and cooperative, disinterested, or seductive toward the interviewer?

Speech and Thought

Whether the patient's speech is coherent, normal in progression, spontaneous and understandable, or whether speech abnormalities are present is described as observed. Does he speak spontaneously or only in answer? Is his speech slow or fast? Is there blocking present? Does he fall into sudden silences? Does he change topics without apparent rational reason? Does he have flights of ideas? Does he use strange words or syntax? Does he comment appropriately on what is being asked? At times, the presence of delusions and misinterpretations are quite obvious, and the patient makes no effort at concealment. At other times, the patient makes every effort to conceal delusional thinking from the interviewer, and much inquiry is needed to elicit the existence of delusions. This is done in an indirect fashion (e.g., by asking the patient about various people in his environment and his opinions about and attitude toward them). The patient's interpretation of what happens around him or what has happened to him can also be indicative of delusional thinking. The patient may deny having delusions but talk about how he's being persecuted, how various influences are being exerted on his body or mind, or how he's the subject of envy or contempt. The patient might depreciate himself, or he might be endowed with grandiose beliefs. Note is also made of whether or not the patient is frank or evasive, accessible or defensive, suspicious or ingratiating, irritable, aggressive, and assertive or submissive and meek, superior and condescending or self-deprecatory, sarcastic, abusive and opinionated, or indecisive.

Consciousness

The mental status examination proceeds by attention to the patient's level of consciousness. Is the patient's sensorium clear or clouded to varying degrees?

Mood and Affect

Patient's mood and affect are noted and recorded. The prevailing mood is often suggested by the patient's facial expression and bodily attitude. The patient's response to inquiries about his emotional state also can be revealing. The type of affect, its intensity, depth, and duration are observed and recorded. The appropriateness or inappropriateness of affect and oscillations such as euphoria, exhilaration, or irritability and empathy are noted. There are many varieties of mood in addition to happiness or sadness, including fearfulness, suspicion, irritability, restlessness, bewilderment, and worry. Also, the consistency of the patient's mood is noted. Changes in mood during the interview and what has caused them are recorded.

Perception

Disorders of perception, including hallucinations need to be ascertained. The circumstances of these experiences should also be noted. For example, when do the hallucinations occur (when falling asleep or when alone or in a special location)?

Obsessions and Compulsions

Any compulsive behavior and obsessional thoughts need to be noted. The quality of the experience is as much of interest as its occurrence. Does the patient realize or recognize the inappropriateness of the obsessional thoughts and the meaninglessness of the compulsive behavior, or does he believe in their reality and appropriateness?

Orientation

The patient's orientation to time, place, and person are usually intact except in severe cases of organic mental disorder or when the patient's sensorium is clouded.

Memory

The patient's memory is also an important subject of the mental status examination. The patient's distant memory can be tested by comparing his/her account of various life events with those obtained from other sources. Recent memory is tested by inquiring about recent events in the patient's life and checking the information elicited with other available information. The patient's ability to grasp, retain, and then recall a few minutes later an address or three names or a number can be tested easily. Digits are given to the patient to repeat forwards and backwards, with the numbers he/she repeats recorded. In reporting tests of memory, one always should record whether the patient was cooperative and attentive. Whenever there is selective impairment of memory for special incidents or particular periods in life of which the patient is aware, it also is useful to record the patient's attitude towards this forgetfulness and what has been forgotten.

Attention and Concentration

The patient's attention and concentration also are noted. Is his attention easily distracted, or does he show sustained attention? Is the patient preoccupied, therefore making it difficult to gain his full attention or to test his concentration? The serial subtraction of 7s from 100 is one of the tests for the patient's concentration.

General Information

The patient's general information also is part of the mental status examination. Answers should be recorded to a number of questions that normally should be known. The questions usually asked include the name of the President and his immediate predecessors. The patient is asked to name six large cities in the United States, to state the dates of the first and second world wars, and perhaps to name the capitals of a few countries.

Intelligence

A rough estimate of the patient's intelligence is also made from the evidence obtained from the interview, the level of education achieved, his fund of general knowledge, and his powers of reasoning. More accurate tests of intelligence are not part of the mental status examination and should be considered as additional tests to be used when indicated.

Insight and Judgment

Finally, the patient's insight and judgment are ascertained. The patient's attitude toward the difficulties that have led to seeking psychiatric help or psychiatric help being sought for him is usually indicative of his insight. Does the patient regard his state as an illness of an emotional, mental, or nervous nature? Does he regard his condition as needing treatment? His judgment is usually revealed by inquiring about his attitude toward social, ethical, and other problems. His past achievements or failures, the reasons for them, and his future plans are also the type of inquiry that gives important information about the patient's judgment.

Higher Intellectual Functioning

The patient's form of thinking (i.e., its logical or illogical character; his ability to abstract; the coherence of the material that the patient produces; and the quality of his associations) all provide important clues in this area. Brief clinical tests such as serial 7s and other calculations that are routinely used as part of the mental status examination to assess higher intellectual functioning are usually carried out in order to alert the clinician to the presence of organic disease. The structured nature of these brief tests of the sensorium, which have been in use since they were introduced by Adolf Meyer in 1902, gives them a high degree of reliability. However, it is important to be aware that they are not highly valid, since these brief tests may produce normal results in the presence of cerebral lesions and abnormal results in individuals with no organic pathology. For many cerebral lesions, there are no deficits in higher intellectual functioning discernible by these tests. There are a number of fairly brief standardized clinical tests of the sensorium that can provide more accurate indications of organic mental disorders. The best known are the Bender-Gestalt Test (Bender, 1938), The Set Test (Isaacs & Kennie, 1972), and the Mini-Mental State (Folstein, Folstein, & McHugh, 1976) examination. These are not a part of the usual mental status examination. However, in use with the elderly, where greater attention is needed for the detection of dementia, the inclusion of one or a combination of these tests has become a routine part of the examination. The Bender-Gestalt Visual Motor Test consists of showing the patient nine figures on a card and asking him to copy the design on a piece of paper. The available literature indicates that this test differentiates between patients with organic mental disorder and functional illness at a high level of significance (Brilliant & Gynther, 1963; Shapiro, Post, Lofving, &

Inglis, 1956). The Set Test was specifically designed for detection of dementia. The patient is asked to name ten terms in each of the four categories of colors, animals, fruits, and towns. Making allowances for intelligence or physical illness, test scores of 15 and less were shown to be highly correlated with dementia, and scores of 25 and less were suggestive of need for a dementia work-up (Roth, 1955). The Mini-Mental State examination is another practical method for grading the cognitive state of the patients. As mentioned before, these tests are not part of routine mental status examination, but may be used as supplementary tests when the psychiatric interview and routine mental status examination point to the possibility of an organic mental disorder (Anthony, LeResche, Niaz, Von Koniff, & Folstein, 1982).

Physical Examination and Other Steps

Some believe that a thorough physical examination is an integral part of each patient's initial assessment. In actual practice, physical examinations, like psychological tests and other ancillary investigations, are undertaken only when the clinical picture appears incomplete, except for hospitalized patients. In some organic psychiatric disorders where diagnosis is unclear, the best course may be a period of inpatient observation. In other cases a series of specialized tests at several points in time may be indicated. However, in the majority of psychiatric illnesses, the psychiatric interview and mental status examination provide the essential information for diagnostic formulation and initial clinical planning.

The objective-descriptive approach of the routine mental status examination makes it suitable for eliciting data about functional psychotic syndromes, such as the affective disorders and the schizophrenias, as well as for organic brain syndromes. It adds little to the information that is obtained from the psychiatric history in the assessment of psychoneurosis and personality disorders. Also, it is important to bear in mind that the clinician, prior to beginning the formal mental status examination at the end of the psychiatric interview, should already have arrived at explicit hypotheses concerning the patient's difficulties. He/she should have already placed the patient in one of the major diagnostic categories and used direct questioning only as a means of narrowing down the differential diagnoses.

Diagnostic Formulation

The clinical diagnosis should convey useful information concerning the disorder(s) and its probable course and prognosis. It is by taking all the data from the psychiatric interview and mental status examination into consideration that the interviewer arrives at a diagnostic formulation. In the case of organic mental disorders, the formulation as a rule attempts to be both descriptive and etiologic. In functional disorders, the diagnostic formulation usually encompasses complex multivariate relationships. In either case, the diagnostic classification utilized is that of the currently accepted clinical nomenclature. At this point in time, the criteria provided by the Third Edition of the Diagnostic and Statistical Manual (DSM-III) (APA, 1980) should be utilized for diagnostic classification. The DSM-III, using a multiaxial approach, mandates specific criteria for such diagnosis. The clinical data obtained from the psychiatric interview and mental status examination are recorded on each of five separate axes. All diagnosable mental disorders are assigned to Axes I and II. Personality disorders and specific developmental disorders are assigned to Axis II. The remaining mental disorders are assigned to Axis I. Relevant and/or important physical disorders are assigned to Axis III. The stresses that are judged to be relevant to the development or continuation of the patient's mental disorder(s) are assigned to Axis IV. The stress is coded as to its overall severity ranging from one (no psychosocial stress) to seven (catastrophic stress). The patient's highest level of adaptive funcitoning during the past year is recorded on Axis V. The scale used ranges from one (superior) to seven (grossly impaired).

RELATED RESEARCH

The development of the Research Diagnostic Criteria (RDC) (Feighner, Robins, Guze, Woodruff, Winokur, & Munoz, 1972) in the early 1970s and its subsequent revisions and tests of reliability (Spitzer, Endicott, & Robins, 1978) have been an important development. Furthermore, the structured psychiatric interview has already become the foundation of much modern clinical research. Much recent research in this area centers on testing the reliability and validity of the existing instruments (Anderson, Malm, Perris, Rapp, & Roman, 1974; Hodges, McKnew, Cytryn, Stern, & Kline, 1982; Kroll, Pyle, Zander, Martin, Lari, & Sines, 1981; Luria & McHugh, 1974; Soloff,

1981; Sturt, 1981), comparison of various interview schedules (Bech, Bolwig, Kramp, & Rafaelson, 1979; Hesselbrock, Stabanau, Hesselbrock, Mirkin, & Meyer, 1982; Luria & McHugh, 1974), specificity of various interview methods and rating scales for various disorders (Hughes, O'Hara, & Rehm, 1981; Newmark, Konanc, Simpson, Boren, & Prillaman, 1979; Orvaschel, Thompson, Belanser, Prusoff, & Kidd, 1982; Watts, 1973), transcultural application of various structured interviews (Okasha & Ashour, 1981; Yamamoto, Lam, Choi, Reece, Lo, Hahn, & Fairbanks, 1982), the use of various psychiatric instruments for epidemiological screening (Blumenthal, 1975; Blumenthal & Dielman, 1975; Roberts & Vernon, 1981; Schwartz, Myers, & Astracham, 1973), analysis of videotaped interviews (Fischer-Cornelssen & Abt, 1980; Jones & Pansa, 1979; Katz & Itil, 1974; Perris, Ericcson, Jacobsson, Lindstrom, & Perris, 1979), predictability of given symptoms for specific disorders (Manschreck, Maher, Rucklos, & White, 1979), development of new interview schedules and rating scales (Asberg, Montgomery, Perris, Schalling, & Sedvall, 1978), and comparison of traditional psychiatric interview with symptom-checklist-based histories (Climent, Plutchik, Estrada, Gaviria, & Arevalo, 1975; Duckworth & Kedward, 1978; Endicott & Spitzer, 1972).

Enthusiasm for structured interview schedules, however, is not universal. Many experienced clinicians question the validity of these schedules, and a few researchers have demonstrated the limitations of such schedules in comparison with the traditional psychiatric interview. They claim, for example, that the narrative record is superior because it can be reinterpreted at any time using different systems of psychopathological or nosological ideas (Brockington & Meltzer, 1982). Further, the conclusions drawn in regard to individual patients, especially the richness of the data from observed behavior, are often compromised when using research interviews (Carpenter, Sacks, Strauss, Bartko, & Rayner, 1976).

FUTURE DIRECTIONS

A historical review of psychiatric interview and mental status examinations shows that the body of data sought has remained remarkably constant over time (Donnolly, Rosenberg, & Fleeson, 1970). In the mental status examination, for example, the categories of information such as succinct descriptions of: (a) appearance, (b) behavior, attitudes and activities, (c) affect, both predominant and secondary, (d) mental activity, (e) cognitive functions, (f) adaptive capacities and so on, have remained constant since the day of Adolph Meyer as we have gradually progressed toward an automated (computerized) ideal. Only the means of arriving at the data have been subject to change. Psychiatry's efforts to discard the "art" designation and don a scientific mantle have necessitated the embracing of the goals of scientific analysis (i.e., the reduction of the role of interpretation to a minimum) (Kerlinger, 1973). Hence, the psychiatric interview and mental status examinations described in this chapter will likely be replaced in the future with the use of structured interview schedules for routine psychiatric evaluations. The direction is unmistakable. For many years now, there has been a growing trend in American psychiatry toward the use of operational criteria for psychiatric diagnosis (Feighner, et al., 1972) and well-defined taxonomies (Maultsby & Slack, 1971). The long-standing and almost exclusive use of structured examination in research settings (Spitzer, Endicott, Fleiss, & Cohen, 1970) and the growing influence of clinician-researchers have greatly accelerated this trend (Helzer, 1981). The demand for accountability has also forced a problem-oriented type of record keeping system in most institutions, with emphasis on branch-logic systems of psychiatric decision making, and progress notes that reflect resolution of symptom-syndromes and changes in problem status, rather than changes in psychodynamics. Finally, the impact of computers appears decisive. The narrative psychiatric interview cannot be computerized in a way that would allow for efficient retrieval of information. With the easy accessibility of minicomputers, even in private offices, clinicians are less willing to engage in retrieval of narrative information by normal search in the patient's paper chart. Furthermore, computers can be used to apply an algorithm to yield highly reliable diagnoses to raw diagnostic data. Fairly simple computer programs such as DIANO III (Spitzer, Endicott, & Cohen, 1974) and CATEGO (Wing, Cooper, & Sartorius, 1974) have been available for such diagnostic purposes for some time.

A separate but interesting development that may have future promise has been the psychiatric assessment of infants, which some maintain is increasing in importance and feasibility as new technologies become allied with interests in pre-ventive psychiatry. In this specialized area, there may be more analogies with adult assessment procedures than are at first imagined (Dowling & Wesner, in press). Suffice it to say that the field is moving rapidly beyond the stage of the bowl and tongue-blade used as exploration objects described by Winnocott (Winnocott, 1941).

SUMMARY

The purposes of this chapter have been threefold: (a) to present the basic concepts of psychiatric interview and mental status examination, (b) to delineate the framework within which psychiatric interview and mental status examination are conducted, and (c) to indicate the relevance of these concepts to the current practice of psychiatry. This chapter is intended as an introduction to what a psychiatrist does in the first encounter with a patient for those with little or no knowledge of the subject. As such, the focus has been on the broader concepts of the psychiatric interview and mental status examination and the fundamental principles of a particular approach to the evaluation of mental disorders. Finally, this framework should serve as a basis for the generation of a data base with sufficient information to make diagnostic formulations according to DSM-III criteria and arrive at some plan of action.

I have made no attempt to review the vast literature on the subject, nor to dwell on the development of a comprehensive schema for psychiatric history taking and examination. Nor was it my purpose to make this chapter a "how-to-do-it" manual by emphasizing the details of the techniques of interviewing—a subject adequately covered in numerous books and articles (Colby, 1951, Department of Psychiatry Teaching Committee, 1973; Deutsch & Murphy, 1955; Gill, Newman, & Redlich, 1954; MacKinnon & Michels, 1971; Whitehorn, 1944). Instead, I have emphasized the saliency of a type of clinical inquiry that follows the time honored principles of medical practice in general. The approach presented can, therefore, be viewed largely as atheoretical with regard to etiology, with the aim of eliciting those clinical features of the patient's disorder that are at the lowest order of inference necessary to describe its characteristics.

The psychiatric interview and mental status examination are the major evaluative tools in the understanding and diagnosis of mental disorders.

Their effective use requires considerable knowledge of psychiatry and familiarity with clinical hypotheses from several conceptual frameworks and theories. However, like any other skill, psychiatric interviewing cannot be mastered solely by reading. Intellectual mastery of psychiatric concepts and familiarity with diagnostic categories, necessary as they are, do not themselves produce clinical proficiency. Clinical skills are learned by practice under supervision and are refined through experience. At the same time, an organized framework is equally crucial for developing the habit of systematic study and conceptualization of the multiple factors that contribute to the etiology or phenomenology of mental disorders. Indeed, clinicians inexperienced in organizing the data base invariably exclude much essential material and include much extraneous data. It is through the disciplined generation of data and their organization in frameworks, such as the one proposed in this chapter, that the beginner can gradually become adept at discriminating relevant from extraneous data.

In sum, I have provided some specific guidelines regarding the content and organization of a clinically "optimal" data base. This includes the organization and selection of historical and observational data according to a closed system of clinical hypotheses which are called "diagnoses." The clinician is thus forced to consider the relationship between data and clinical inference, with the specific guidelines of the multiaxial criteria of DSM-III as the frame of reference. The record thus produced should allow the reader to assess which hypotheses have been considered and whether there are adequate data for their confirmation. Moreover, the narrative should also be amenable to reinterpretation by clinicians of different theoretical persuasions and should permit them to augment the data base by additional information as required by their specific needs and conceptual orientation.

REFERENCES

American Psychiatric Association. (1952). *Diagnostic and statistical manual of mental disorders* (1st ed.). Washington, DC: Author.

American Psychiatric Association. (1968). *Diagnostic and statistical manual of mental disorders* (2nd ed.). Washington, DC: Author.

American Psychiatric Association. (1980). *Diagnostic and statistical manual of mental disorders* (3rd ed.). Washington, DC: Author.

Anderson, K., Malm, V., Perris, C., Rapp, W., & Roman, G. (1974). The inter-rater reliability of scales for rating symptoms and side-effects in schizophrenic patients during a drug trial. *Acta Psychiatrica Scandinavia*, (Suppl.), 249, 38–42.

Anthony, J.C., LeResche, L., Niaz, U., Von Koroff, M.R., & Folstein, M.F. (1982). Limits of the "minimental state" as a screening test for dementia and delirium among hospital patients. *Psychological Medicine*, 12, 397–408.

Asberg, M., Montgomery, S.A., Perris, C., Schalling, D., & Sedvall, G. (1978). A comprehensive psychopathological rating scale. *Acta Psychiatrica Scandinavia* (Suppl.), 271, 5–27.

Bartko, J.J., & Carpenter, W.T. (1976). On the methods and theory of reliability. *Journal of Nervous and Mental Disease*, 163, 307–406.

Bech, P., Bolwig, T.G., Kramp, P., & Rafaelsen, O.J. (1979). The Bech-Rafaelsen Mania Scale and the Hamilton Depression Scale. *Acta Psychiatrica Scandinavia*, 59, 420–430.

Bender, L. (1938). *A visual motor gestalt test and its clinical use*. New York: American Orthopsychiatric Association.

Blumenthal, M.D. (1975). Measuring depressive symptomatology in a general population. *Archives of General Psychiatry*, 32, 971–978.

Blumenthal, M.D., & Dielman, T.E. (1975). Depressive symptomatology and role function in a general population. *Archives of General Psychiatry*, 32, 985–991.

Brilliant, P., & Gynther, M. (1963). Relationship between performance on three tests for organicity and selected patient variables. *Journal of Consulting Psychology*, 27, 474–479.

Brockington, I.F., & Meltzer, H.Y. (1982). Documenting an episode of psychiatric illness: Need for multiple information sources, multiple raters, and narrative. *Schizophrenia Bulletin*, 8, 485–492.

Carpenter, W.T., Sacks, M.H., Strauss, J.S., Bartko, H.H., & Ryner, J. (1976). Evaluating signs and symptoms: Comparison of structured interview and clinical approaches. *British Journal of Psychiatry*, 128, 397–403.

Climent, C.E., Plutchik, R., Estrada, H., Gaviria, L.F., & Arevalo, W. (1975). A comparison of traditional and symptom-checklist-based histories. *American Journal of Psychiatry*, 132, 450–453.

Colby, K.M. (1951). *A primer for psychotherapists*. New York: Wiley.

Department of Psychiatry Teaching Committee; The Institute of Psychiatry, London. (1973). *Notes on eliciting and recording clinical information*. London: Oxford University Press.

Deutsch, F., & Murphy, W.F. (1955a). *The clinical interview: Volume 1*. New York: International Universities Press.

Deutsch, F., & Murphy, W.F. (1955b). *The clinical interview: Volume 2*. New York: International Universities Press.

Donnolly, J., Rosenberg, M., & Fleeson, W. (1970). The evolution of the mental status—Past and present. *American Journal of Psychiatry*, 26, 997–1002.

Dowling, J., & Wesner, D. (in press). The concept of an infant mental status examination. *Psychiatry*.

Duckworth, G.S., & Kedward, I.B. (1978). Man or machine in psychiatric diagnosis. *American Journal of Psychiatry*, 135, 64–68.

Endicott, J., & Spitzer, R.L. (1972). Current and past psychopathology scales: Rationale, reliability, and validity. *Archives of General Psychiatry*, 27, 678–687.

Endicott, J., & Spitzer, R.L. (1978). A diagnostic interview: The schedule for affective disorders and schizophrenia. *Archives of General Psychiatry*, 35, 837–844.

Endicott, J., & Spitzer, R.L. (1982). The value of the standardized interview for the evaluation of psychopathology. *Journal of Personality Assessment*, 8, 410–417.

Feighner, J.P., Robins, E., Guze, S.B., Woodruff, R.A., Winokur, G., & Munoz, R. (1972). Diagnostic criteria for use in psychiatric research. *Archives of General Psychiatry*, 26, 57–63.

Fischer-Cornelssen, K.A., & Abt, K. (1980). Videotaping recording in psychiatry and psychopharmacology. Review and presentation of a new method. *Acta Psychiatrica Scandinavia*, 61, 228–238.

Folstein, M.H., Folstein, S.E., & McHugh, P.R. (1976). Mini-mental state—A practical method for grading the cognitive state of patients for the clinician. *Journal of Psychiatric Research*, 12, 189–198.

Gill, M.M., Newman, R., & Redlich, F.C. (1954). *The initial interview in psychiatric practice*. New York: International Universities Press.

Helzer, J.E. (1981). The use of a structured diagnostic interview for routine psychiatric evaluations. *Journal of Nervous and Mental Disease*, 169, 45–49.

Henrickson, W.J., Coffer, R.H., & Cross, T.N. (1954). The initial interview. *Archives of Neurology*, 71 24–30.

Hesselbrock, V., Stabanau, J., Hesselbrock, M., Mirkin, P., & Meyer, P. (1982). A comparison of two interview schedules. The schedule for affective disorders and schizophrenia-lifetime and the National Institute for Mental Health Diagnostic Interview Schedule. *Archives of General Psychiatry*, 39, 674–677.

Hodges, K., McKnew, D., Cytryn, L., Stern, L., & Kline, J. (1982). The Child Assessment Schedule (CAS) diagnostic interview: A report on reliability and validity. *Journal of American Academy of Child Psychiatry*, 21, 468–473.

Hughes, J.R., O'Hara, M.W., & Rehm, L.P. (1981). Measurement of depression in clinical trials: An overview. *Journal of Clinical Psychiatry*, 43, 85–88.

Isaacs, B., & Kennie, A. (1972). The Set Test as an aid to the detection of dementia in old people. *British Journal of Psychiatry*, 123, 474–479.

Jones, J.H., & Pansa, M. (1979). Some nonverbal aspects of depression and schizophrenia occurring during the interview. *Journal of Nervous and Mental Disease*, 167, 402–409.

Katz, M.M., & Itil, T.M. (1974). Video methodology for research in psychopathology and psychopharmacology: Rationale and application. *Archives of General Psychiatry*, 31, 204–210.

Kerlinger, F. (1973). *Foundations of behavioral research* (2nd ed.). New York: Holt, Rinehart, & Winston.

Kolb, L.C. (1971). Foreword. In R.A. MacKinnon & R. Michels (Eds.), *The psychiatric interview in clinical practice*. Philadelphia: W.B. Saunders.

Kroll, H., Pyle, R., Zander, J., Martin, K., Lari, S., & Sines, L. (1981). Borderline personality disorder: In-

terrater reliability of the diagnostic interview for borderlines. *Schizophrenia Bulletin*, 7, 269–272.

Lazare, A. (Ed.). (1979). *Outpatient psychiatry*. Baltimore: Williams & Wilkins.

Luria, R.E., & McHugh. (1974). Reliability and clinical utility of the "Wing" Present State Examination. *Archives of General Psychiatry*, 30, 866–871.

MacKinnon, R.A. (1980). Psychiatric interview. In H.I. Kaplan, A.M. Freedman, & B.J. Sadock (Eds.), *Comprehensive textbook of psychiatry: III*. Baltimore: Williams & Wilkins.

MacKinnon, R.A., & Michels, R. (1971). *The psychiatric interview in clinical practice*. Philadelphia: W.B. Saunders.

Manschreck, T.C., Maher, B.A., Rucklos, M.E., & White, M.T. (1979). The predictability of thought disordered speech in schizophrenic patients. *British Journal of Psychiatry*, 134, 595–601.

Maultsby, M.C., & Slack, W.V. (1971). A computer-based psychiatric history system. *Archives of General Psychiatry*, 25, 570–572.

Menninger, K.A., Mayman, M., & Pruyser, P.W. (1962). *A manual for psychiatric case study*. New York: Grune and Stratton.

Meyer, A. (1951). Outlines of examinations. In E. Winters (Ed.), *Collected papers: Volume III*. Baltimore: Johns Hopkins Press.

Muncie, W.S. (1974). The psychological approach. In S. Arietti (Ed.), *American handbook of psychiatry* (2nd ed.). New York: Basic Books.

Nemiah, J.C. (1961). *Foundations of psychopathology*. New York: Oxford University Press.

Newmark, C.S., Konanc, J.T., Simpson, M., Boren, R.B., & Prillaman, K. (1979). Predictive validity of the Rorschach Prognostic Rating Scale with schizophrenic patients. *Journal of Nervous and Mental Disease*, 167, 135–143.

Okasha, A., & Ashour, A. (1981). Psycho-demographic study of anxiety in Egypt: The PSE in its Arabic version. *British Journal of Psychiatry*, 139, 70–73.

Orvaschel, H., Thompson, W.D., Belanser, A., Prusoff, B.A., & Kidd, K.K. (1982). Comparison of the family history method to direct interview. Factors affecting the diagnosis of depression. *Journal of Affective Disorders*, 4, 49–59.

Perris, C., Ericcson, U., Jacobsson, L., Lindstrom, H., & Perris, H. (1979). Interprofessional communicability and reliability of the Comprehensive Psychopathological Rating Scale (CPRS) as assessed by video-taped interviews. *Acta Psychiatrica Scandinavia*, 60, 144–148.

Roberts, R.E., & Vernon, S.W. (1981). Usefulness of the PERI Demoralization Scale Screen for psychiatric disorder in a community sample. *Psychiatry-Research*, 5, 183–193.

Robins, L., Helzer, J., & Croughan, J.L. (1979). *NIMH-Diagnostic Interview*. Bethesda, MD: National Institute of Mental Health.

Roth, M. (1955). The natural history of mental disorder in old age. *Journal of Mental Science*, 101, 281–301.

Saul, L.J. (1957). The psychoanalytic diagnostic interview. *Psychoanalysic Quarterly*, 26, 79–90.

Schwartz, C.C., Myers, J.K., & Astrachan, B.M. (1973). Comparing three measures of mental status:

A note on the validity of estimates of psychological disorder in the community. *Journal of Health and Social Behavior*, 14, 265–273.

Shapiro, M.B., Post, F., Lofving, B., & Inglis, J. (1956). Memory functions in psychiatric patients over sixty: Some methodological implications. *Journal of Mental Science*, 102, 233–246.

Soloff, P.H. (1981). Concurrent validation of a diagnostic interview for borderline patients. *American Journal of Psychiatry*, 138, 691–693.

Spitzer, R.L., & Endicott, J. (1975). *Schedule for affective disorders and schizophrenia-lifetime version.* New York: Biometrics Research: New York State Psychiatric Institute.

Spitzer, R.L., Endicott, J., & Cohen, J. (1974). Constraints on the validity of computer diagnosis. *Archives of General Psychiatry*, 31, 197–203.

Spitzer, R.L., Endicott, J., Fleiss, J.L., & Cohen, J. (1970). The psychiatric status schedule. *Archives of General Psychiatry*, 23, 41–55.

Spitzer, R.L., Endicott, J., & Robins, E. (1978). Research diagnostic criteria: Rationale and reliability. *Archives of General Psychiatry*, 35, 773–782.

Stevenson, I. (1959). The psychiatric interview. In S. Arieti (Ed.), *American Handbook of Psychiatry.* New York: Basic Books.

Sturt, E. (1981). Hierarchical patterns in the distribution of psychiatric symptoms. *Psychological Medicine*, 11, 783–792.

Watts, G.P. (1973). The Carkhuff Discrimination Scale as a predictor of accurate perception of others. *Journal of Consulting and Clinical Psychology*, 41, 202–206.

Whitehorn, J.C. (1944). Guide to interviewing and clinical personality study. *Archives of Neurology and Psychiatry*, 52, 197–209.

Wing, J.K., Birley, J.L.T., & Cooper, J.E. (1967). Reliability of a procedure for measuring and classifying present psychiatric state. *British Journal of Psychiatry*, 113, 449–515.

Wing, J.K., Cooper, J.E., & Sartorius, N. (1974). *Description and classification of psychiatric symptoms.* Cambridge, England: Cambridge University Press.

Winnocott, D. (1941). The observation of infants in a set situation. *The International Journal of Psychiatry*, 22, 229–249.

Yamamoto, H., Lam, H., Choi, W.I., Reece, S., Lo, S., Hahn, D.S., & Fairbanks, A.L. (1982). The psychiatric status schedule for Asian Americans. *American Journal of Psychiatry*, 139, 1181–1184.

14 STRUCTURED PSYCHIATRIC INTERVIEWS FOR CHILDREN AND ADOLESCENTS*

Craig Edelbrock
Anthony J. Costello

INTRODUCTION

The interview has long been the cornerstone of child clinical assessment, but this traditional information-gathering procedure has only recently been refined to the point of yielding valid and reliable data. The unstructured interview of the parent, which has been the dominant method of assessing child psychopathology, is being rapidly replaced by structured interviewing procedures that yield a more comprehensive and reliable picture of the child's behavioral and emotional functioning. The development of structured interview procedures for children has been spurred by successes in the adult area. The unreliability of adult psychiatric diagnoses prompted the development of structured interviews, such as the Diagnostic Interview Schedule (Robins, Helzer, Croughan, & Ratcliff, 1981) and the Schedule for Affective Disorders and Schizophrenia (Endicott & Spitzer, 1978), which have been found to substantially reduce the "information variance" inherent in the diagnostic process and to boost diagnostic reliability (see Matarazzo, 1983, for a review). Researchers interested in child and adolescent disorders were quick to follow suit, and, in fact, many child interview schedules are downward extrapolations of adult interviews. Additional impetus for stan-

dardizing child diagnostic procedures was gained from the advent of more highly differentiated taxonomies of childhood disorders which employ more explicit diagnostic criteria (e.g., American Psychiatric Association, 1980). Such criteria demand more precision and quantification of symptom data than afforded by unstructured interview procedures.

The development of structured psychiatric interviews for children and adolescents has been marked by two major trends. One move has been toward increasing structure and specialization of the interview. Increasing structure has reduced the role of clinical judgment in eliciting information from the interviewee and has resulted in greater comparability of data across cases. Specialization has resulted in a variety of interview materials and procedures designed for different purposes, age ranges, and disorders. The other major trend has been to view the *child as informant* regarding his or her own feelings, behaviors, abilities, and social relationships. The assessment of child psychopathology has traditionally depended on reports and ratings by adults, particularly parents. This is reasonable, since parents are the most common instigators of child mental

*Preparation of this chapter was supported by NIMH Research Scientist Development Award #MH00403 to the first author and by grant #MH37372 and contract #278-81-0027 from NIMH. The generous support of the William T. Grant Foundation is also gratefully acknowledged.

health referrals, and their perceptions are often crucial in the implementation of treatments and the evaluation of treatment outcomes. Until recently, however, one perspective has been conspicuously lacking in child psychiatric assessment: that of the *child*. The assumptions that children could not understand the concept of an anamnestic or symptom-oriented interview and could not report on their own symptoms and behaviors have been largely overthrown. This is not to say that children's reports are more reliable or valid than those of other informants, but the value of the child's report in the assessment and diagnosis of childhood disorders is now more widely recognized, and many interview schedules have been designed for direct questioning of the child.

DESCRIPTION

A structured psychiatric interview is essentially a list of target behaviors, symptoms, and events to be covered, and some guidelines or rules for conducting the interview and recording the data. Interview schedules differ markedly in degree of structure imposed on the interview. Some schedules offer only general and flexible guidelines, whereas others involve strict and detailed rules. In general, it is useful to distinguish between *semistructured* and *highly structured* interviews. A highly structured interview specifies the exact sequence and wording of questions and provides well-defined rules for recording and/or rating the subject's responses. With highly structured interviews, the interviewer is regarded as an interchangeable part of the assessment machinery. The role of clinical judgment in eliciting and recording information is minimized and, given the same respondent, different interviewers should obtain the same information. Semistructured interviews, on the other hand, are less restrictive and permit the interviewer some flexibility in conducting the interview. Clinical judgment plays more of a role in determining what is asked, how questions are phrased, and how responses are recorded. Given the same respondent, different interviewers should cover the same target phenomena when using a semistructured interview, but they may do so in different ways and may end up with slightly different results. It is not yet clear if a high degree of structure yields consistently better data. Both types of interviews appear to have advantages. Highly structured interviews reduce the role of clinical inference and interpretation in the assessment and diagnostic process, and they typically yield more objective and quantifiable raw data. Alternatively, semistructured interviews are less stilted and permit a more spontaneous interview that can be tailored to the client.

The structured interviews discussed in this chapter vary in ways other than degree of structure. Most of the instruments and procedures we will cover have been developed for interviewing the parent about the child's behavior and development, but—consistent with the trend to view the child as informant—many parent interviews have parallel versions for directly questioning the child. Interviews also differ in terms of length, organization, time requirements, diagnostic coverage, and age appropriateness. Lastly, interviews differ in terms of their intended purpose. Some were designed specifically for screening nonreferred populations for psychiatric disorders, whereas others were intended to serve descriptive and diagnostic functions.

In the following sections, we briefly trace the history and development of structured psychiatric interviews for children aged 3 through 18, and we describe some of the more commonly used instruments and procedures. The reliability and validity of currently available interview schedules is reviewed, and a discussion of future directions is offered.

HISTORY AND DEVELOPMENT

Prior to 1968 and the publication of the second edition of the Diagnostic and Statistical Manual (DSM-II) (American Psychiatric Association, 1968) differential diagnosis of childhood disorders was not common practice. Although adult diagnoses embodied in the first edition of the DSM (APA, 1956) could be applied to children, the vast majority of children referred to psychiatric clinics were either undiagnosed or labeled "Adjustment Reactions" (Rosen, Bahn, & Kramer, 1964). Researchers were struggling with two fundamental questions: What constitutes psychiatric disorder in children? And how can one reliably differentiate among such disorders? The tools necessary to answer these questions were not yet available. There were no accepted definitions of pathognomonic symptoms and behaviors in children, and scientific knowledge regarding the prevalence and patterning of behavioral and emotional problems in childhood was almost totally lacking. Screening and diagnostic efforts in child psychiatry were handicapped by the absence of a basic taxonomic framework, not to mention the lack of standardized assessment and diagnostic procedures for children.

In the spring of 1955, Lapouse and Monk (1958, 1964) undertook a survey aimed at determining the prevalence and patterning of problem behaviors among a representative sample of non-referred children. Two major decisions were made in this pioneering effort. First, mothers were used as the source of information regarding their children's behavior. Despite the subjective and potentially biased nature of maternal reports, it was necessary to "begin somewhere," and it was felt that mothers are exceptionally well qualified to report on all aspects of their children's functioning. Second, the decision was made to use a standardized interview focused on the child's behavior. The standardized interview schedule served many purposes. It reduced the role of clinical judgment in eliciting information from the parent and yielded more objective and quantifiable data than possible with an unstructured interview. It also insured that comparable data would be obtained on all subjects. Lastly, since the interview was focused on specific behaviors and abilities, unresolved questions regarding the existence and definition of child psychiatric disorders were circumvented. In other words, the goal was to *describe* children's behavioral and emotional problems, rather than to detect prespecified syndromes and disorders.

Systematic interviews were conducted with mothers of 482 children aged 6–12, drawn from randomly selected residences in Buffalo. In addition, for a selected sample of 193, 8- to 12-year-olds, children and their mothers were interviewed separately. The 1½-hour interview covered 200 questions pertaining to clinically relevant behaviors. Most items entailed a yes/no response, but some involved rating the frequency or intensity of target behaviors.

A number of findings in this early study have emerged time and again in more recent analyses of interview data. Reinterview of mothers, for example, indicated high test-retest reliability (>90% agreement) for concrete, easily observable behaviors such as thumb sucking, bed wetting, and stuttering, but low to moderate reliability (52–87% agreement) for behaviors requiring more subjective judgments (e.g., fears and worries) or precise estimates of frequency (e.g., number of temper tantrums). Mother-child agreement was high for behaviors such as

bed wetting, temper tantrums, and biting fingernails but was low for many other behaviors. Analysis of discrepancies between mother and child reports revealed the following pattern: Mothers tended to report more overt behaviors that are particularly irksome to adults (e.g., bedwetting, restlessness, overactivity), whereas children tended to report more covert problems (e.g., fears and worries, nightmares). This general pattern has been replicated in several recent studies involving structured interviews of parent and child.

In another pioneering effort, Rutter and Graham (1968) recognized the need to standardize procedures for directly interviewing the *child* regarding his or her own behaviors, feelings, and abilities. This represented a departure from prevailing thought and clinical practice at the time. Direct interview of the child was predominantly used as a *therapeutic* rather than *diagnostic* tool. Moreover, diagnostic uses of the interview were largely restricted to uncovering unconscious wishes, fears, conflicts, and fantasies (cf. Group for the Advancement of Psychiatry, 1957). In contrast, the interview procedures developed by Rutter and his colleagues (Graham & Rutter, 1968; Rutter & Graham, 1968) involved direct questioning of the child (and parent) about abnormalities in the child's behavior, emotions, and social relationships.

The parent and child versions of this interview schedule are not identical, but parallel one another in terms of content and rating procedures. Both are "semistructured" interviews designed for clinically sophisticated interviewers. The exact wording of questions is not specified, and the rating of many items requires clinical judgment. The child interview includes approximately 80 background questions covering areas such as friendships and activities outside school, involvement in organized activities, and behavior with parents. The section on psychiatric symptoms comprises 31 questions about antisocial behavior, anxiety, depression, and ideas of reference. In general, the time frame for each question is specified and ranges from 1 week to 1 year. The interview ends with 10 questions about school performance and future plans. The interviewer then rates the child's behavior and mental status and makes an overall judgment of whether he/she has *no psychiatric impairment, some impairment, or definite or marked impairment.*

The parent interview follows a similar outline, but begins with a general question about the child's behavior and employs a time frame of the past year. Problems reported by the parent are explored to determine severity, duration, action taken, presumed cause, and expected course. The next section covers 36 questions pertaining to symptomatology. Questions may be skipped if they were covered in the first part of the interview. Overall, the interview is straightforward and easy to use. The technique of semistructured interviewing is quite easy for a trained clinician to learn.

Two findings in this early work have been borne out in more recent studies. First, many structured interviews yield reliable information regarding global psychiatric status, but not regarding specific syndromes or disorders. Rutter and Graham (1968), for example, found the overall rating of psychiatric impairment based on separate interviews of the child by clinicians to be highly reliable ($r = .84$). However, interrater reliability was mediocre for items pertaining to attention and motor behavior (average $r = .61$) and social relations (average $r = .64$), and it was low for items pertaining to anxiety and depression (average $r = .30$). Second, reliability is generally higher for more overt problems such as antisocial behavior and overactivity, than for more covert phenomena such as fears, anxiety, and depression.

The clinical and research utilty of these semistructured interviews has also been demonstrated in a series of epidemiological investigations (Rutter, Cox, Tupling, Berger, & Yule, 1975; Rutter, Tizard, & Whitmore, 1970; Rutter, Tizard, Yule, Graham, & Whitmore, 1976). In one study, a *multistage screening procedure* was employed to identify psychiatrically disturbed children (Rutter et al., 1970). Teachers and parents completed brief screening questionnaires, and children whose scores exceeded predetermined cut-off points on either instrument were selected for interviews. This procedure precludes calculation of sensitivity and specificity of the interview alone, but sheds some light on relations between different assessment methods and informants. Among children finally diagnosed as abnormal, for example, only 29.4% were judged deviant on the basis of the child interview, whereas 83% were judged deviant on the basis of the parent interview. This suggests, at least, that parental reports are more valuable in screening efforts, or alternatively that parent reports are given more weight in formulating diagnoses.

Summary

The pioneering studies by Lapouse and Monk and by Rutter and his colleagues broke new ground in the clinical assessment of the child and introduced several innovations, including: (a) use of standardized interview schedules covering specific content areas and symptoms, (b) use of prespecified categories and scales for recording and rating responses of the interviewee, (c) focus on the phenomenology of the child's behavior, feelings, and abilities, rather than psychodynamic states, (d) direct questioning of the child, and (e) development of parallel interview schedules for parent and child. Research in the last 15 years has amplified and improved upon these methodological innovations, and a diverse array of structured psychiatric interviews for children and adolescents is now available.

A major trend has been toward increasing specialization of interviewing materials and procedures. Specialization of *purpose*, for example, has resulted in screening inventories aimed at identification of disturbed children. Alternatively, diagnostic interviews have been developed to differentiate among disorders. Specialization in terms of *age range* has yielded interviews designed for preschool-aged children, grade schoolers, and older adolescents. Interview schedules also differ in terms of diagnostic coverage and focus. The majority of structured interviews for children cover a broad array of symptoms and behaviors, but some are focused on specific syndromes or disorders such as childhood depression. Lastly, there has been increasing specialization with respect to the *interviewer*. Structured interviews are now tailored to the qualifications and training of the interviewer and differ in terms of the degree of clinical sophistication required for administration and scoring.

RESEARCH FINDINGS

Our discussion of research findings is organized according to specific interview schedules, which were categorized as being either *screening procedures* or *diagnostic tools*. In general, instruments are discussed in chronological order of their development. However, most are undergoing constant revision and refinement, and few have reached definitive form. Each interview schedule is described in terms of style and degree of structure, content and organization, procedure for recording and/or rating responses, respondent (i.e., parent or child), age range, time frame, training and qualifications of interviewers, and time requirements. The reliability and validity of the interviews are reported in as much detail as the published literature allows. In addition, we have attempted to evaluate the performance of the interview schedules in terms of *sensitivity* (percentage of "true" positive cases which are identified as positives according to the measure) and *specificity* (percentage of "true" negative cases which are identified as negatives). A major problem is that there is no definitive criterion for child psychopathology. The identification of "true" cases and non-cases is based on various criteria, which are admittedly fallible. Nevertheless, this comparative evaluation seems justified. Most structured interview schedules have been evaluated against clinical judgment or referral for services, which reflect important decisions made about children's mental health. Sensitivity and specificity are also directly relevant to the evaluation of screening inventories designed to identify children manifesting psychiatric disorders. Moreover, validation of diagnostic interviews commonly involves comparisons between psychiatrically referred and nonreferred populations or some other comparison related to screening efficiency.

Screening Procedures

There have been two noteworthy efforts to develop structured interviews for identifying disturbed children in the general population. Both involve interview of the parent about the child, and both have met with moderate success.

The Behavioural Screening Questionnaire

Richman and Graham (1971) developed the Behavioural Screening Questionnaire (BSQ) to identify psychiatrically disturbed preschool-aged children. The BSQ, which has been published in its entirety (Richman & Graham, 1971), is a parent interview comprising approximately 60 questions concerning the health, behavior, and development of the child. The time frame varies from the previous month to previous year depending on the target behavior. But for some questions the time frame is not defined, with the wording being "Does [child's name] do that *now*?" Questions are designed to be read as written, but "can be supplemented until the interviewer feels confident about the rating" (Richman & Graham,

1968, p. 7). Parents' responses are rated on a 0-1-2 scale, where 0 indicates the behavior is *absent*, 1 indicates the behavior occurs *sometimes or to a mild degree*, and 2 indicates the behavior occurs *frequently or to a marked degree*. The wording of most questions is clearcut and should be easily understood by parents. The BSQ requires about 20–30 minutes for the average child, and although it is suitable for lay interviewers it has typically been administered by trained clinicians.

The behavior scale of the BSQ was constructed from the 12 behavioral items that discriminated best between clinically referred and nonreferred children. Interrater reliability for scores on the behavior scale was .77 based on separate interviews of the parent, and it was .94 based on independent ratings of taped interviews. Unfortunately, reliabilities for individual items are low (average $r = .44$; range $= .15-.77$). Validity of the BSQ behavior scale has been supported by significant discrimination between clinically referred and nonreferred samples. A cut-off score of 11 out of a possible 24 points on the behavior scale resulted in good separation between 20 children referred for psychiatric services and 57 normal controls. Given referral for services as a criterion, the behavior scale achieved a sensitivity of 70% and a specificity of 91.2%.

The BSQ has become one of the most widely researched interview procedures and has been used in numerous epidemiological investigations (Earls, 1980a, 1980b; Earls, Jacobs, Goldfein, Silbert, Beardslee, & Rivinus, 1982; Earls & Richman, 1980a, 1980b; Richman, 1977; Richman, Stevenson, & Graham, 1975). Overall, these studies have supported the validity of the BSQ. Earls et al. (1982), for example, reported a correlation of .74 between scores on the BSQ behavior scale and clinicians' ratings of psychiatric impairment based on observations of the child's behavior in the home, parent ratings, and a summary of the entire interview with the parent. Using clinicians' ratings as a criterion for psychiatric disorder, a cut-off score of 11 on the behavior scale yielded a sensitivity of 64% and specificity of 98% for a sample of 70 preschoolers. Dropping the cut-off score to 8 resulted in a sensitivity of 100%, but specificity was reduced to only 70%. Richman (1977) has also developed a paper-and-pencil version of the behavior scale, which parallels the interview version in terms of items and rating format. Four-week test-retest reliability of the checklist version was $r = .81$, which is slightly higher than the .77 reliability obtained for the BSQ. Using referral for services as the criterion, the checklist version yielded a sensitivity of 70%, which is considerably lower than that reported for the BSQ, and a specificity of 87.4%, which is comparable to that achieved by the BSQ.

The Child Screening Inventory

A screening inventory for assessing psychiatric impairment in children aged 6–18 has been developed by Langner, Gersten, McCarthy, Eisenberg, Greene, Herson, and Jameson (1976). The screening measure was derived from a 2–3 hour structured interview of the parent covering the child's behavior and development, family background, the marital relationship, and child rearing practices. Interviewers with some training in psychology or social work administered the entire interview to two samples: a *cross-sectional sample* of 1,034 randomly selected children aged 6–18 residing in Manhattan and a *welfare* sample of 1,000 children of the same age range.

The Child Screening Inventory was constructed in the following way. The initial pool of 654 items tapping children's behavior was reduced to 287 items by eliminating low frequency items and by combining similar items (e.g., items about fears were combined into a single fear score). Factor analysis of the reduced item pool yielded seven factors, and each was represented by its five highest loading items. These factors were labeled Self-Destructive Tendencies, Mentation Problems, Conflict with Parents, Regressive Anxiety, Fighting, Delinquency, and Isolation.

The resulting 35-item screening inventory requires only 15–20 minutes to administer and yields a global screening score as well as scores on seven factor-based scales. The scales have been found to have low-moderate internal consistency (coefficient alpha averaged .49), whereas the total screening score has somewhat higher internal consistency (alpha = .76). Scores on the 35-item screening scale correlated .69 with the total impairment rating derived from the entire interview. But it correlated only .33 with psychiatrists' ratings of psychiatric impairment based on direct interview of the child and only .49 with treatment referral status. Screening efficiency of the total score has also been evaluated with respect to psychiatrists' ratings of impairment based on the entire 2–3 hour structured interview. These ratings were trichotomized into categories reflecting the *well or mildly impaired child*, *moderate impair-*

ment, and *marked or severe impairment*. Scores on the 35-item screening inventory were trichotomized in the same way. Taking psychiatrists' ratings of *marked or severe impairment* as the criterion for psychiatric disorder, the screening inventory had a sensitivity of only 67.2% and a specificity of 91.8% for the cross-sectional sample. For the welfare sample, specificity of 95.9% was achieved, but sensitivity was only 38.5%. This inventory has therefore been recommended for use primarily as a descriptive tool, rather than as a screening procedure (Langner et al., 1976).

Diagnostic Interviews

In the past few years, numerous diagnostic interview schedules for children and adolescents have been developed, some of which are tied directly to a diagnostic system such as that embodied in the DSM-III (American Psychiatric Association, 1980). Others do not address specific diagnostic criteria, but nevertheless yield information relevant to psychiatric evaluation and diagnosis.

The Kiddie-SADS

The Kiddie-SADS (Puig-Antich & Chambers, 1978) is a semistructured psychiatric interview for children aged 6–17, modeled after the Schedule for Affective Disorders and Schizophrenia (SADS), a structured interview for adults developed by Endicott and Spitzer (1978). The K-SADS covers episodes of current psychopathology and is scorable in terms of Research Diagnostic Criteria (cf. Feighner, Robins, Guze, Woodruff, Winokur, & Munoz, 1972) and DSM-III diagnostic criteria. Despite its title, the K-SADS taps more than affective disorders and schizophrenia and includes questions about a broad range of child psychiatric diagnoses, such as conduct disorders, separation anxiety, phobias, and obsessive-compulsive disorders. The K-SADS is administered by clinically sophisticated interviewers who must be familiar with the administration and scoring of the interview as well as the RDC and DSM-III diagnostic criteria.

The parent and child are interviewed separately. The parent is usually interviewed first regarding the psychiatric status of the child, and in the subsequent interview of the child, any discrepancies between parent and child reports are addressed. The interviewer may confront the child directly about such discrepancies and attempt to resolve them before making final ratings.

The K-SADS begins with an unstructured interview lasting 15–20 minutes in which the interviewer establishes rapport with the respondent, obtains a history of the present illness, and inquires about major presenting symptoms and their periodicity. The interviewer then determines the mode of onset and duration of the current disorder and records the amount and type of treatment received. The remainder of the K-SADS comprises more structured sections on psychiatric symptomatology. Each section includes an item to be rated by the interviewer (e.g., depressed mood). Items are rated on a 1–7 scale ranging from *not at all* to *very extreme*. Each section also includes a series of questions (e.g., Have you felt sad? Have you cried?), which serve as guidelines for the interview. Interviewers have considerable flexibility in determining the number, type, and wording of specific questions, however, and they are encouraged to ask as many questions as necessary to substantiate symptom ratings.

The K-SADS also embodies a *skip structure*, whereby sections can be omitted if the initial screening questions or "probes" yield no evidence of symptomatology. If depressed mood is not evident, for example, subsequent questions in that section can be skipped. This substantially reduces interviewing time, while minimizing loss in information.

Following the section on psychiatric symptomatology, the interviewer rates 11 observational items (e.g., appearance, affect, attention, motor behavior) and rates the reliability and completeness of the entire interview. Finally, the interviewer completes a global assessment scale reflecting degree of symptomatology and impairment.

Although the K-SADS is widely cited and used within the field of child psychiatry, there are little published data on its reliability or validity. Of course, the interview has strong content validity in that it was designed to tap prespecified diagnostic criteria. Other than that, validation of the K-SADS rests upon its ability to identify children with major affective disorders (cf. Puig-Antich, Blau, Marx, Greenhill, & Chambers, 1978). There are two other lines of evidence supporting the validity of the K-SADS, but both arise from preliminary studies that are provocative, but far from conclusive. First, children identified by the K-SADS as meeting RDC for major depression have reportedly demonstrated overnight and 24-hour cortisol hypersecretion—a neuroendocrine

abnormality characteristic of approximately 50% of adult depressive patients. However, this finding is based on only four subjects, and only two showed the abnormality. Moreover, of the two who showed cortisol hypersecretion, only one had been diagnosed via the K-SADS (Puig-Antich, Chambers, Halpern, Hanlon, & Sachar, 1979). Moreover, cortisol hypersecretion is of questionable validity as an indicator of depression, in that sensitivity is only about 50% among adults and specificity, at least in children, is largely unknown. Second, the K-SADS has been shown to be sensitive to imipramine treatment of major affective disorders in prepubertal children (Puig-Antich, Perel, Lupatkin, Chambers, Shea, Tabrizi, & Stiller, 1979). However, the findings in this pilot study pertain only to a small subset of K-SADS items, and significance was obtained only in analyses of a selected subsample of subjects.

An epidemiological version of the K-SADS (K-SADS-E) has been developed to assess both past and current psychopathology in children aged 6–17 (Orvaschel, Puig-Antich, Chambers, Tabrizi, & Johnson, 1982). The K-SADS-E parallels the K-SADS, but taps a broader range of symptoms relevant to DSM diagnoses, and the focus is on lifetime symptomatology. The time frame for the K-SADS-E thus depends on the age of the child, and most questions are worded: "Have you *ever* done X." Validity has been investigated by comparing diagnoses based on initial K-SADS interview with diagnoses based on retrospective report (K-SADS-E) 6 months to 2 years later. For 17 subjects, all but one obtained the same diagnosis by the K-SADS-E as by the original interview. Agreement between parents and their children has been reported for 14 depressive symptoms and for 7 other symptoms and disorders (e.g., hallucinations, phobias). For 17 cases, kappa averaged .61, suggesting moderate parent-child agreement. However, the standard K-SADS interview procedure involves attempts to reconcile discrepancies between parent and child reports, so this level of agreement may be inflated.

Diagnostic Interview for Children and Adolescents

Herjanic and her colleagues at Washington University have developed a highly structured psychiatric interview in which the order and specific wording of questions, as well as the response coding, are specified. The Diagnostic Interview for Children and Adolescents (DICA), which can be administered to either parent or child, covers general background characteristics of the child and the frequency and duration of a broad range of symptoms relevant to DSM diagnoses. Most of the interview is organized thematically (e.g., behavior at home, behavior at school, relationships with peers), but some sections are organized according to content areas (e.g., drugs and alcohol abuse), while other sections follow a syndromic structure (e.g., affective disorders, mania, anxiety disorders, etc.).

The DICA embodies a more elaborate skip structure than most other interview schedules. The complex skip structure involves choices between alternative lines of questioning both *within* and *between* items. For example, the main question may be: "Have you ever been placed in a special class?" The skip structure could indicate the following lines of questioning: IF NO, skip to the next item. IF YES, ask "When did this first happen?" and "When did it happen last?" In some sections (e.g., alcohol abuse) negative response to the first few questions permits the interviewer to skip numerous subquestions.

In terms of validity, Herjanic and Campbell (1977) found that the number of symptoms computed from DICA interviews with parent and child discriminated significantly between children referred to a psychiatric clinic and a matched sample of children referred to a pediatric clinic ($n = 50$ for each group). Items pertaining to relationship and academic problems provided the best discrimination, whereas items pertaining to neurotic and somatic symptoms yielded the poorest discrimination. Despite these significant differences, there was considerable overlap between criterion groups in terms of number of symptoms, particularly among younger children (i.e., 6- to 8-year-olds). Herjanic and Campbell (1977) did not report the screening efficiency of total number of symptoms scored for the DICA, but sensitivity and specificity can be calculated for content areas. For relationship problems, which provided the best discriminative power, number of DICA symptoms yielded 72% sensitivity and 76% specificity. Screening efficiency for academic problems was comparable, but was much lower for number of school problems, neurotic symptoms, and somatic symptoms (Herjanic & Campbell, 1977).

Other studies with the DICA have focused on agreement between mother and child. Agreement has averaged 80% for the 207 DICA items (Herjanic, Brown, & Wheatt, 1975), but this figure is misleading. The majority of DICA items refer to psychiatric symptoms that are of low prevalence, even among referred samples. High percentages of agreement are therefore expected by chance. The statistic kappa (Cohen, 1960), which corrects for chance level of agreement, provides a more realistic picture of agreement between parent and child. For the 168 DICA items tapping psychiatric symptoms, kappa averaged only .22 (Herjanic & Reich, 1982). Agreement on diagnoses was only slightly better, with the majority being below .40 (Reich, Herjanic, Welner, & Gandhy, 1982).

Mental Health Assessment Form

Kestenbaum and Bird (1978) have developed a format, called the Mental Health Assessment Form (MHAF), for recording the results of a semistructured interview with children aged 7 to 12. Unlike the other interviews we have reviewed, the MHAF provides only a general outline of topics to be covered, and an indirect method of eliciting information about symptoms is recommended. Questions about fears and worries, for example, are slipped into a section on fantasy life, which begins: "Sometimes when you're bored at school and look out the window, what do you think about?"

The MHAF consists of 168 items organized into two major parts. Part I is a standard mental status exam in which the interviewer rates physical appearance, motor behavior and speech, relatedness, affect, and language and thinking as observed during the interview. Part II deals with affective symptoms, interpersonal relations, dreams and fantasies, self-concept, conscience, and general level of adaptation. Most items are rated on a 1–5 scale, ranging from *no deviation* to *marked deviation* from expected. Brief examples of expected behaviors and responses are given for most items, but the interviewers' clinical experience and theoretical musings must still be invoked to determine if the child deviates from the "norm."

Reliability was determined for 35 videotaped interviews that were rated by three child psychiatrists. Interrater reliabilities ranged from .43 to .94 and averaged only .72, which is low for assessments based on taped interviews. Moreover, given the loose structure of the interview and the degree of clinical inference involved in rating items, it is likely that reliability would be lower when comparing ratings by clinicians differing in professional training and experience. To date, there is little empirical evidence supporting the validity of the MHAF.

The Interview Schedule for Children

The Interview Schedule for Children (ISC) (Kovacs, 1982) is a structured, symptom-oriented interview for children aged 8–17, designed to be administered by clinicians familiar with the ISC items and rating procedures. It is focused primarily on depressive symptoms, and although it yields symptom ratings rather than diagnoses, ISC data are scorable in terms of operational diagnostic criteria. Questions are designed for face-to-face interview of the child, which is limited to a total of 40–60 minutes. With appropriate changes in the phrasing of questions, the ISC is used to interview the parent about the child.

The ISC begins with a brief unstructured interview focused on the duration and chronicity of any recent problems. The interviewer then proceeds with the more structured portion of the interview. The ISC has been thoughtfully designed, and it has several unique features. For one, the order in which questions are asked may vary. If during the unstructured interview the interviewee spontaneously mentions symptoms or behaviors covered by the ISC, the interviewer may turn to that section and follow the specified

line of inquiry. The interviewer may then return to the unstructured format or proceed to other sections. Another feature of the ISC is "double check" questions, which are follow-up questions designed to explore and confirm the child's initial responses before making symptom ratings. Another feature of the ISC is that standard inquiries are abbreviated on the rating form. For example, the abbreviation "?Feeling" stands for "Are you (or have you been) feeling that way?," whereas "?Yesterday" signifies "Did you feel (or do) that yesterday? The skip structure employed in the ISC is also *implicit*, rather than *explicit* as in other interviews such as the DICA. If the interviewer feels that answers to the initial questions provide sufficient information to make the rating, the subsequent questions can be skipped, but these options are not built into the interview schedule format.

Table 14.1 portrays a sample item from the ISC concerning irritability that illustrates many of the ISC design features. The first four questions directly concern irritability. If they elicit negative replies, the interviewer may skip the remaining questions and make the rating. If some evidence of irritability is obtained, standard inquiries, given in abreviated form, are asked (e.g., Does that happen a lot? How many times does this happen?). The next question, "Do you feel like

TABLE 14.1. SAMPLE ITEM FROM KOVACS' INTERVIEW SCHEDULE FOR CHILDREN (ISC).

IRRITABILITY

Do things bother you, "get on your nerves"? Have you been feeling cranky/crabby? Have you been upset a lot? ?Get into arguments easily. Do you "snap" at your parents/siblings/friends?

?a lot. ?many times. Once in a while?

?feel like your parents/friends "hassle" you. (?) *Do you yell/cry/get upset when you feel cranky/hassled? *Can you make the feeling go away? How? Are you this way everyday? ?many days. ?a few days. *Have your friends/parents said anything about your being "snappy," or *"hard to get along with"*? [?]

0 *None*; not at all.

1 *Minimal*; infrequent, occasional crankiness/irritability
2 (1–3/week) but transient and not marked; not a problem.

3 *Mild*; irritable/snappy more than 3 times/week or less
   frequent but acute episodes; gets upset; evident to others
4 but not pervasive; can be modulated; somewhat of a
   problem in social functions.

5 *Moderate*; considerable/evident irritability; snappy/upset
   more often than not; irritated by a wide range of stimuli;
6 interferes with social functioning.

7 *Severe*; pronounced irritability; irritable almost all the
   time; gets upset very easily with most situations; feeling
8 is out of control; disrupts social functioning.

9 Not assessed; inadequate data.

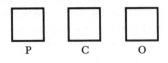

P   C   O

your parents/friends hassle you?" is followed by two "double check" questions and seven follow-up questions. The section ends with a "?" indicating to ask "How come?" or "Why does this happen?" The interviewer then rates the symptom (irritability) on a 0–8 scale ranging from *none* to *severe*. Space is provided for three ratings per form: parent (P), child (C), and interviewer (O). The interviewer's rating is based on clinical appraisal of all evidence and does not have to agree with the rating based on either the parent or child interview.

Following the sections on psychiatric symptoms, the interviewer rates the child's speech, motor behavior, attention, and so on, as observed during the interview and rates the child's grooming, cooperation, likability, degree of empathy, and level of social maturity. The interviewer also records diagnostic impressions for Axis I and II of the DSM-III.

Data on the validity of the ISC are not yet available, but reliability has been evaluated by comparing ratings made by the clinician who conducted the interview with those of another clinician who observed and coded through a one-way mirror. For 46 interviews, the intraclass correlation between ratings of the current disorder was .86. Comparisons of parent and child interviews have reportedly revealed high concordance, with the highest agreement on items related to conduct disorder, and lower concordance for items about affective, cognitive, and vegetative symptoms (Kovacs, 1982).

The Child Assessment Schedule

The Child Assessment Schedule (CAS, Hodges, McKnew, Cytryn, Stern, & Kline, 1982) (Hodges, Kline, Stern, Cytryn, & McKnew, 1982) is a semistructured interview for children aged 7 through 12, comprising 75 questions about topics such as school, friends, and family, and 53 items that the interviewer rates after the interview. The interview appears to have been designed for trained clinicians and requires 45–60 minutes for the typical child. The child's responses are coded in a Yes/No format, with three alternative codes: Ambiguous, No Response, and Not Applicable. The CAS is organized thematically and begins with questions about school, followed by family and friends, then more direct questions about feeling and behaviors. The interview concludes with questions about delusions, hallucinations, and related symptoms.

The CAS relies on clinical judgment for both administration and interpretation. The specific line of questioning is left to the discretion of the interviewer, and certain sections (e.g., schizophrenia) can be skipped entirely. Interpretation of the results is quite flexible, and the CAS is intended to facilitate evaluation of the child's functioning in various areas and to aid the formulation of diagnostic impressions. Rather than yielding diagnoses, the CAS is scorable in terms of 11 content areas and nine "symptom complexes" (see Table 14.2). A total score reflecting number of symptoms is also obtained.

TABLE 14.2. CONTENT AREAS AND SYMPTOM COMPLEXES SCORED FROM THE CHILD ASSESSMENT SCHEDULE (CAS).

Content Areas
School
Friends
Activities
Family
Fears
Worries
Self-Image
Mood
Somatic Concerns
Expression of Anger
Thought Disorder

Symptom Complexes
Attention Deficit with Hyperactivity
Attention Deficit without Hyperactivity
Undersocialized Conduct Disorder-Aggressive
Undersocialized Conduct Disorder-Unaggressive
Socialized Conduct Disorder
Separation Anxiety
Overanxious
Oppositional
Depression

Note. From Hodges et al. (1982a). "The development of a child assessment interview for research and clinical use." *Journal of Abnormal Child Psychology,* 10, 173–189.

Independent ratings of 53 interviews yielded a reliability of $r = .90$ for total score, but consistent with earlier findings, reliability was lower for both content areas (average $r = .73$) and symptom complexes (average $r = .69$). In addition, reliability was lower for fears, worries, and anxiety (average $r = .60$). Reliability for individual items is also mediocre. For selected pairs of raters, kappa averaged only .57.

The CAS has undergone more complete validation than any other structured interview for children. Total pathology score, for example, has been shown to discriminate significantly between inpatient, outpatient, and normal control groups and has correlated significantly ($r = .53$, $p < .001$) with the total behavior problem score derived from the Child Behavior Checklist (CBCL) (Achenbach, 1978; Achenbach & Edelbrock, 1979) completed by mothers. Scores on the over-anxious symptom complex correlated significantly ($r = .54$, $p < .0001$) with Speilberger's (1973) State-Trait Anxiety Inventory for Children. In addition, scores on the CAS depression scale correlated significantly ($r = .53$, $p = < .001$) with the Child Depression Inventory, a self-report measure developed by Kovacs and Beck (1977).

Using referral for inpatient or outpatient psychiatric services as a criterion for disorder, the CAS total score achieved a sensitivity of 78% and

specificity of 83.8% based on discriminant analysis (cf. Hodges et al., 1982). In comparison, the CBCL total score yielded a sensitivity of 86.7% and specificity of 94.6% for the same sample. Combining both the CAS and CBCL scores in one discriminant analysis yielded a sensitivity of 93.3% and specificity of 100% (no false positives). This suggests that use of both a structured interview and behavioral checklist is a superior method of detecting psychopathology in children.

The Diagnostic Interview Schedule for Children

Lastly, NIMH has recently commissioned the development and testing of the Diagnostic Interview

TABLE 14.3. DSM-III DIAGNOSES OBTAINED FROM THE PARENT AND CHILD VERSIONS OF THE DIAGNOSTIC INTERVIEW SCHEDULE FOR CHILDREN (DISC).

Attention Deficit Disorder	Schizophrenic Disorders
with hyperactivity	disorganized
without hyperactivity	paranoid
residual type	undifferentiated
Conduct Disorder	residual
undersocialized, aggressive	Affective Disorders
undersocialized, nonaggressive	Bipolar disorder
socialized, aggressive	mixed
socialized, nonaggressive	manic
atypical	depressed
Anxiety Disorders	Major depression
separation anxiety disorder	single episode
avoidant disorder	recurrent
overanxious disorder	Other Specific Affective Disorders
Other disorders	Cyclothymic disorder
elective mutism (parent interview only)	Dysthymic disorder
oppositional disorder	Atypical Affective Disorders
Eating Disorders	atypical bipolar disorder
anorexia nervosa	atypical depression
bulimia	Anxiety Disorders
pica (parent interview only)	agoraphobia
Stereotyped Movement Disorders	with panic attacks
(parent interview only)	without panic attacks
transient tic disorder	social phobia
chronic motor tic disorder	simple phobia
Tourette's disorder	panic disorder
atypical tic disorder	obsessive-compulsive disorder
atypical stereotyped movement disorder	Somatoform Disorders (parent interview only)
Other disorders with physical manifestations	somatization (not fully generated)
functional enuresis	conversion disorder
functional encopresis	hypochondriasis
Pervasive Developmental Disorders	Dissociative Disorders (parent interview only)
(parent interview only)	psychogenic amnesia
infantile autism	psychogenic fugue
childhood onset PDD	Psychosexual disorders
atypical PDD	transsexualism
Substance Abuse Disorders	gender identity disorder
	atypical gender identity disorder

Note. From *The NIMH Diagnostic Interview Schedule for Children* by Costello et al., 1982.

Schedule for Children (DISC), a highly structured interview for children aged 6–18 (Costello, Edelbrock, Kalas, Kessler, & Klaric, 1982). The child version of the DISC comprises 264 items and takes an average of 50–60 minutes for referred children. The parent version includes 302 items and takes an average of about 60–70 minutes to administer. DSM-III diagnoses, which are generated by computer algorithms applied to the DISC data, are listed in Table 14.3. As shown in this table, the DISC covers a broader range of diagnoses than previous interview schedules for children. For problems where the child's report may be questionable or unattainable (e.g., pica, autism, pervasive developmental disorder), diagnoses are derived from the parent interview alone.

The main goal of the DISC project is to develop a comprehensive diagnostic interview that can be administered by lay interviewers with little or no previous clinical training or interviewing experience. The interview will then be used in large scale epidemiological surveys of nonreferred populations—an endeavor that has been hampered by the prohibitive costs and unavailability of trained diagnosticians. The DISC is therefore a highly structured instrument in which the order and wording of questions are completely specified. The role of clinical judgment in selecting a line of inquiry, choosing specific wording of questions, and recording responses has been minimized through the use of predetermined response codes and a very explicit skip structure. Some descriptive material about the child's behavior is recorded during the DISC interview, but most questions involve a 0–1–2 coding, where 0 indicates the item is not true, 1 indicates it is somewhat or sometimes true, and 2 indicates it is very

often true. The "Yes/No" questions are coded simply 0–2.

Table 14.4 portrays a section from the child version of the DISC, which illustrates item wording, coding, and skip structure. The first question "Have you ever run away from home?," is coded 0–1–2. The skip structure indicates IF YES (i.e., 1 or 2), the subquestions "Did you stay out overnight?" should be asked. Positive responses lead successively to three more subquestions regarding the frequency and chronicity of running away. The last subquestion, "When was that?" is recorded in terms of months ago, and 6 months duration is listed in parentheses to remind the interviewer of the diagnostic criterion. The second items illustrates the hierarchical skip structure, which for this item begins with an IF NO followed by an IF YES. A "DESCRIBE" prompt is also illustrated, which instructs the interviewer to record the child's response verbatim.

The DISC project, which is scheduled for completion in 1984, involves detailed comparisons between data derived from parents and their children and comparisons between lay interviewers and trained clinicians. Two- to three-week test-retest reliability is being evaluated for both parent and child reports. In addition, extensive analyses of relations between DISC data and a wide variety of behavioral measures, cognitive tests, medical criteria, and indices of school performance and academic achievement are being undertaken.

Summary of Findings

Most structured psychiatric interviews for children and adolescents yield global indices that are reliable enough for detecting the presence or absence of disorder, but few yield dependable

---

TABLE 14.4. SAMPLE ITEMS FROM THE CHILD
VERSION OF THE DIAGNOSTIC INTERVIEW
SCHEDULE FOR CHILDREN (DISC).

Have you ever run away from home?	0 1 2
IF YES, Did you stay out overnight?	0 1 2
IF YES, Was that more than once?	0 1 2
IF YES, How many times? (SPECIFY): _____	
IF YES, When was that? (SPECIFY): (6 mos.) _____	
Sometimes kids don't tell the truth. Do you tell a lot of lies?	0 1 2
IF NO, Are there any times when you tell lies?	0 1 2
IF YES, Tell me more about that. (DESCRIBE): _____	

information about specific behaviors or syndromes. As foretold in early studies, reliability has generally been higher for more overt behaviors than for more covert phenomena, such as fears, worries, and anxieties. Reliability has also been low for items requiring precise estimates of frequency or complex inferences by either the interviewer or respondent. To date, most studies have focused on rather trivial forms of reliability, such as interrater agreement on taped interviews. Such procedures sidestep many major sources of information variance inherent in the diagnostic process, such as temporal instability of the interviewee's responses and differences in the line of inquiry and wording of questions offered by the interviewer. It seems likely therefore that the levels of reliability reported for many interviews is much higher than would be obtained in clinical practice.

Validation of most interviews is weak and rests primarily on "face" validity and the ability to discriminate between vastly different groups, such as psychiatrically referred and nonreferred samples. Outside of the work by Hodges et al. (1982a), few researchers have compared assessments based on structured interviews with data derived via other methods, such as self-report inventories or standardized behavioral checklists. Moreover, there has been little validation of interview-based diagnoses with respect to the etiology, course, prognosis, or treatment responsiveness of childhood disorders. The one exception here is the provocative preliminary work with the K-SADS.

Comparisons between interviews of parents and children have generally revealed mediocre to poor agreement, but this is not an indictment of either informant. Parents and children may differ in their sensitivity to and awareness of different phenomena as well as in their willingness to report certain problems and events. The failure to agree on specific behaviors and symptoms does not necessarily indicate that one informant is "right" and the other "wrong." Moreover, given the differences in their perspectives and biases, it is probably not advisable to seek high levels of parent-child agreement. Instead, it would be more profitable to determine who can provide reliable and predictive information about which phenomena.

FUTURE DIRECTIONS

Structured psychiatric interviews are here to stay, and it seems likely that they will become the standard assessment and diagnostic tools in clinical research and epidemiology. In addition, they will probably become more closely integrated into the training of mental health professionals and the delivery of services to disturbed children. The interviews themselves will continue to evolve along the lines of increasing specialization of purpose, coverage, age range, degree of structure, and interviewer qualifications. As taxonomies of childhood disorders evolve and become more differentiated, structured interviews will necessarily change in terms of their content. More importantly, we can expect results obtained via structured interviews to precipitate change in the diagnostic systems and criteria applied to children.

In terms of reliability and validity, more comprehensive and methodologically sound studies are needed to identify major sources of information variance in child psychiatric assessment and diagnosis. Both the strengths and weaknesses of structured interview schedules in eliciting information about childhood symptoms and disorders must be evaluated and compared to alternative assessment procedures, such as psychological testing, behavioral assessment, and self-report inventories. Validation of structured interviews must also be extended to a broader array of clinically relevant criteria, including etiology, course, prognosis, and treatment responsiveness.

Two other trends are likely to continue over the next several years and, in our view, both will yield increasing rewards. The first involves the synergistic combination of assessment methods and procedures. Preliminary analyses (e.g., Hodges et al., 1982a; Richman, 1977) indicate a closer correspondence than first expected between data derived from structured interviews and other methods, such as checklists, rating scales, and self-report inventories. Studies to date also suggest that multimethod assessment yields a more comprehensive, reliable, and valid picture of the child's behavioral and emotional functioning. The second trend involves the application of computers to the asessment and diagnosis of childhood disorders. We do not necessarily advocate "computer diagnosis" of child psychiatric disorders, but "*computer assisted diagnosis*," which involves the use of the computer to sift through numerous bits of data relevant to diagnostic decision-making— is on the horizon.

SUMMARY

Structured diagnostic interviews are new tools for clinicians and researchers interested in disorders of childhood and adolescence. Their development has emulated that of successful adult psychiatric interviews and has paralleled the advent of a more differentiated taxonomy of childhood disorders. Numerous interview schedules are now available. They differ in terms of their intended purpose (screening versus diagnosis), diagnostic coverage, the informant (parent or child), degree of structure, and age appropriateness. They also differ in terms of the level of training required of the interviewer and in technical features, such as skip structure, wording of questions, and coding of responses.

Overall, reliability of these interview procedures is adequate for identifying children with psychiatric disorders, but not for precise diagnostic formulations. The validity of most interviews is largely undocumented. Despite the fact that such procedures reduce information variance in the clinical assessment of the child, the promise of providing a more reliable and valid basis for detecting and differentiating among childhood disorders has yet to be fulfilled. Nevertheless, rapid progress has been made in the last few years, and, if anything, there are now even greater expectations regarding the value and potential contributions of structured interviews to research and clinical practice.

REFERENCES

Achenbach, T.M. (1978). The child behavior profile: I. Boys aged 6–11. *Journal of Consulting and Clinical Psychology, 46*, 478–488.

Achenbach, T.M., & Edelbrock, C.S. (1979). The child behavior profile: II. Boys aged 12–16 and girls aged 6–11 and 12–16. *Journal of Consulting and Clinical Psychology, 47*, 223–233.

American Psychiatric Association. (1952). *Diagnostic and statistical manual, mental disorders.* Washington, DC: Author.

American Psychiatric Association. (1968). *Diagnostic and statistical manual, mental disorders* (2nd ed.). Washington, DC: Author.

American Psychiatric Association. (1980). *Diagnostic and statistical manual, mental disorders* (3rd ed.). Washington, DC: Author.

Cohen, J.A. (1960). A coefficient of agreement for nominal scales. *Educational and Psychological Measurement, 20*, 37–46.

Costello, A.J., Edelbrock, C., Kalas, R., Kessler, M.D., & Klaric, S. (1982). *The NIMH Diagnostic Interview Schedule for Children (DISC).* Pittsburgh: Author.

Earls, F. (1980a). The prevalence of behavior problems in three-year-old children: A cross-national replication. *Archives of General Psychiatry, 37*, 1153–1157.

Earls, F. (1980b). The prevalence of behavior problems in three-year-old children: Comparison of reports of mothers and fathers. *Journal of the American Academy of Child Psychiatry, 19*, 439–452.

Earls, F., & Richman, N. (1980a). The prevalence of behavior problems in three-year-old children of West Indian-born parents. *Journal of Child Psychology and Psychiatry, 21*, 99–107.

Earls, F., & Richman, N. (1980b). Behavior problems of preschool children of West Indian-born parents: A re-examination of family and social factors. *Journal of Child Psychology and Psychiatry, 21*, 108–117.

Earls, F., Jacobs, G., Goldfein, D., Silbert, A., Beardslee, W., & Rivinus, T. (1982). Concurrent validation of a behavior problems scale for use with 3-year-olds. *Journal of the American Academy of Child Psychiatry, 21*, 47–57.

Endicott, J., & Spitzer, R.L. (1978). A diagnostic interview: The Schedule for Affective Disorders and Schizophrenia. *Archives of General Psychiatry, 35*, 837–844.

Feighner, J.P., Robins, E., Guze, S.B., Woodruff, R.A., Winokur, G., & Munoz, R. (1972). Diagnostic criteria for use in psychiatric research. *Archives of General Psychiatry, 26*, 57–63.

Graham, P., & Rutter, M. (1968). The reliability and validity of the psychiatric assessment of the child: II. Interview with the parent. *British Journal of Psychiatry, 114*, 581–592.

Group for the Advancement of Psychiatry. (1957). *The diagnostic process in child psychiatry.* New York: Author.

Herjanic, B., & Campbell, W. (1977). Differentiating psychiatrically disturbed children on the basis of a structured interview. *Journal of Abnormal Child Psychology, 5*, 127–134.

Herjanic, B., Herjanic, M., Brown, F., & Wheatt, T. (1975). Are children reliable reporters? *Journal of Abnormal Child Psychology, 3*, 41–48.

Herjanic, B., & Reich, W. (1982). Development of a structured psychiatric interview for children: Agreement between child and parent on individual symptoms. *Journal of Abnormal Child Psychology, 10*, 307–324.

Hodges, K., Kline, J., Stern, L., Cytryn, L., & McKnew, D. (1982a). The development of a child assessment interview for research and clinical use. *Journal of Abnormal Child Psychology, 10*, 173–189.

Hodges, K., McKnew, D., Cytryn, L., Stern, L., & Kline, J. (1982b). The Child Assessment Schedule (CAS) Diagnostic Interview: A report on reliability and validity. *Journal of the American Academy of Child Psychiatry, 21*, 468–473.

Kestenbaum, C.J., & Bird, H.R. (1978). A reliability study of the Mental Health Assessment Form for school-age children. *Journal of the American Academy of Child Psychiatry, 7*, 338–347.

Kovacs, M. (1982). The longitudinal study of child and adolescent psychopathology: I. The semi-structured psychiatric interview schedule for children (ISC). Unpublished manuscript.

Kovacs, M., & Beck, A.T. (1977). An empirical-clinical approach toward a definition of childhood depression. In J.G. Schulterbrandt & A. Raskin (Eds.), *Depression in childhood: Diagnosis, treatment, and conceptual models.* New York: Raven Press.

Langner, T.S., Gersten, J.C., McCarthy, E.D., Eisenberg, J.G., Greene, E.L., Herson, J.H., & Jameson,

J.D. (1976). A screening inventory for assessing psychiatric impairment in children 6 to 18. *Journal of Consulting and Clinical Psychology*, 44, 286–296.

Lapouse, R., & Monk, M.A. (1958). An epidemiologic study of behavior characteristics of children. *American Journal of Public Health*, 48, 1134–1144.

Lapouse, R., & Monk, M.A. (1964). Behavior deviations in a representative sample of children: Variations by sex, age, race, social class, and family size. *American Journal of Orthopsychiatry*, 34, 436–446.

Matarazzo, J.D. (1983). The reliability of psychiatric and psychological diagnosis. *Clinical Psychology Review*, 3, 103–145.

Orvaschel, H., Puig-Antich, J., Chambers, W., Tabrizi, M.A., & Johnson, R. (1982). Retrospective assessment of prepubertal major depression with the Kiddie-SADS-E. *Journal of the American Academy of Child Psychiatry*, 21, 392–397.

Puig-Antich, J., Blau, S., Marx, N., Greenhill, L.I., & Chambers, W. (1978). Pre-pubertal major depressive disorder: A pilot study. *Journal of the American Academy of Child Psychiatry*, 17, 695–707.

Puig-Antich, J., & Chambers, W. (1978). *The Schedule for Affective Disorders and Schizophrenia for school-aged children*. New York: New York State Psychiatric Institute.

Puig-Antich, J., Chambers, W., Halpern, F., Hanlon, C., & Sachar, E.J. (1979). Cortisol hypersection in prepubertal depressive illness: A preliminary study. *Psychoneuroendocrinology*, 4, 191–197.

Puig-Antich, J., Perel, J.M., Lupatkin, W., Chambers, W., Shea, C., Tabrizi, M.A., & Stiller, R.L. (1979). Plasma levels of imipramine (IMI) and desmethylimipramine (DMI) and clinical response in prepubertal major depressive disorder: A preliminary report. *Journal of the American Academy of Child Psychiatry*, 18, 616–627.

Reich, W., Herjanic, B., Welner, Z., & Gandhy, P.R. (1982). Development of a structured psychiatric interview for children: Agreement on diagnosis comparing parent and child. *Journal of Abnormal Child Psychology*, 10, 325–336.

Richman, N. (1977). Short-term outcome of behavioral problems in preschool children. In P. Graham (Ed.), *Epidemiological approaches in child psychiatry*. London: Academic Press.

Richman, N., & Graham, P. (1968). A behavioural screening questionnaire for use with three-year-old children: Prelminary findings. *Journal of Child Psychology and Psychiatry*, 12, 5–33.

Richman, N., Stevenson, J., & Graham, P. (1975). Prevalence of behavior problems in three-year-old children: An epidemiological study in a London borough. *Journal of Child Psychology and Psychiatry*, 16, 277–287.

Robins, L.N., Helzer, J.E., Croughan, J., & Ratcliff, K.S. (1981). National Institute of Mental Health Diagnostic Interview Schedule. *Archives of General Psychiatry*, 38, 381–389.

Rosen, B.M., Bahn, A.K., & Kramer, M. (1964). Demographic and diagnostic characteristics of psychiatric clinic patients in the USA, 1961. *American Journal of Orthopsychiatry*, 34, 455–468.

Rutter, M., Cox, A., Tupling, C., Berger, M., & Yule, W. (1975). Attainment and adjustment in two geographical areas: I. The prevalence of psychiatric disorder. *British Journal of Psychiatry*, 126, 493–509.

Rutter, M., & Graham, P. (1968). The reliability and validity of the psychiatric assessment of the child: I. Interview with the child. *British Journal of Psychiatry*, 11, 563–579.

Rutter, M., Tizard, J., & Whitmore, K. (1970). *Education, health, and behaviour*. London: Longmans.

Rutter, M., Tizard, J., Yule, W., Graham, P., & Whitmore, K. (1976). Isle of Wight studies, 1964–1974. *Psychological Medicine*, 6, 313–332.

Spielberger, C.D. (1976). *Manual for the State-Trait Anxiety Inventory for Children*. Palo Alto: Consulting Psychologists Press.

15 STRUCTURED PSYCHIATRIC INTERVIEWS FOR ADULTS

Duane G. Spiker
Joan G. Ehler*

INTRODUCTION AND HISTORICAL REVIEW

Structured interviews can be seen as a recent step in the long evolving history of mankind's attempts to understand the mentally ill. Disorders that today are called mental retardation, schizophrenia, depression, mania, and acute and chronic organic brain syndromes have affected humanity for a very long time. What has changed over the millennia is how society has perceived these disorders. What is particularly striking are the changes in concepts of classification, etiology, appropriate treatment, and the effect of these on determining what information is collected and, indeed, who collects it.

In ancient Greece, extreme imbalances of passion and reason, violent aberrant behavior, hallucinations, and wandering around the countryside were considered signs of mental illness (Mora, 1980). As in many early societies, the popular view of mental illness was that it had a supernatural origin. A man was possessed by evil spirits because he had angered the gods. In contrast, the Hippocratic medical concepts of madness described an imbalance between the four basic humors of the body, which were derived from the two basic polarities of nature of dry-moist and warm-cold. What we would today call signs and

symptoms of psychiatric illnesses were described as "intemperance in drink and food, in sleep and in wakefulness, the endurance of toil either for the sake of certain passions . . . passionate outbursts, strong desires . . . fears, shame and pain" (Goshen, 1967, pp. 6–7).

The Greeks also described hysteria, which was felt to result from the movement of the uterus to various parts of the body. This would result in a variety of symptoms including inability to swallow, seizures, headaches, paralysis, or abnormal menstruation. Case histories were usually restricted to the patient's account of the illness (Mora, 1980).

Several of the works of Caelius Aurelianus (ca. 500 A.D.?) and Galen (ca. 138–201 A.D.) are extant and provide insight into the Roman approach to mental illness. Caelius Aurelianus was an obscure African physician who translated the works of Aretaeus of Cappadocia (ca. 100 A.D.) and Soranus of Ephesus into Latin. His two books, *On Acute Disease* and *On Chronic Diseases*, have been translated into English (University of Chicago Press, Chicago, 1950). He describes mania as a chronic illness without fever in which there is an impairment of reason.

*The authors would like to express their appreciation to Jane Cofsky Weiss, M.S.W., Sheila Pearlman, M.S., and Janet Solarczyk for their assistance in conducting the research project presented in this chapter.

This impairment of reason is in some cases severe, in others mild, it differs in the various cases in its outward form and appearance, though its nature and character are the same. For when mania lays hold of the mind, it manifests itself now in anger, now in merriment, now in sadness or futility and now, as some relate in an overpowering fear of things, which are quite harmless. (Goshen, 1967, p. 21)

He recognized that patients were sometimes delusional and may at times have brief remissions of illness. Physical symptoms such as bulging and bloodshot eyes, bulging facial veins, and "hardness of the body," were also commonly associated with mental illness. Mania was contrasted with phrenitis, which was an acute illness accompanied by fever. The signs of approaching melancholy were mental anguish and distress, dejection, silence, animosity toward members of the household, sometimes a desire to live and at other times a longing for death, suspicion on the part of the patient that a plot was being hatched against him, weeping without reason, meaningless muttering, and again, occasional joviality. In the remission there is an abatement of these symptoms, or at least a clearing up of most of them (Goshen, 1967).

Galen expanded the Hippocratic theories and emphasized the four basic qualities of warm-cold and dry-moist (Jackson, 1969). The four humors, blood, black bile, yellow bile, and phlegm, were characterized by the four degrees (McVaugh, 1969). Disease resulted from an excess of one humor leading to an imbalance, from various mixtures of the humors, or from an accumulation of the humors in certain organs (Ellenberger, 1974). Therapy was based on choosing a substance (food, medicine, or herb) with the appropriate degree of qualities to correct the imbalance (Kroll, 1973). Although this was not based on a pure empirical approach to mental illness, it did have an elaborate theoretical basis and did encourage some experimentation with treatment regimes.

Galen was a towering figure in the history of medicine, and his influence continued for the next 1,000 years. Indeed, his biological explanation of the etiology of mental illness continued to have some followers. In the 13th century, Bartholomaeues wrote a widely distributed manuscript that discussed mental illness in terms of natural causes (Kroll, 1973). English legal documents still extant from the 13th through the 17th century

show that the mentally ill were classified into at least two categories. Idiocy was recognized as being present from birth. Lunacy was commonly described as a mental incompetency brought on by natural disease (Neugebauer, 1979).

Other popular explanations regarding the etiology of mental illness were based on astrology, sinfulness, and demonology. For example, Paracelsus (ca. 1493–1541 A.D.) described the effects of various phases of the moon on the bodily humors and the subsequent effects on the mind (Goshen, 1967). "Sloth" was considered one of the seven deadly sins and was characterized by "boredom, depression, obsessions, anxiety and a variety of psychosomatic signs" (Mora, 1980, p. 34). Demonology, witchcraft, and possession have a long history as explanations for mental illness (Mora, 1980). However, that explanation probably reached its height in 1484 with the publication of Pope Innocent VIII of the papal bull *Summis Desiderantes Affectibus*, which strongly urged the civil and religious authorities of Northern Germany to assist "Our dear sons Henry Kramer and James Sprenger, . . . [who] have been by Letters apostolic delegated as Inquisitors of these heretical practices in Northern Germany" (Summers, 1928, p. xiv). It was followed by the publication of *Malleus Maleficarum* (The Witches' Hammer) by Kramer and Sprenger in 1486 (Summers, 1928).

This lengthy and extremely detailed book opens with a clear statement that anyone who does not believe in witchcraft is either naive or "is rightly considered to be a heretic" (Summers, 1928, p. 4). Thus, early physicians who dared to put forward the idea that some of these people might be mentally ill ran the risk of being tried themselves as heretics. The book goes on to discuss how witches should be indicted, tried, and punished, usually by burning. The numerous sections on how to identify a witch describe signs and symptoms of what we would today call mental illness.

"Statements of one's hallucinations or delusions were considered a valid confession" of being a witch (Zilboorg, 1935, p. 45). "Suddenness of onset of illness, but particularly chronicity, were considered pathognomonic of the work of the devil" (Zilboorg, 1935, p. 47). Other signs of the devil were mutism, "especially under torture," hysterical anesthesia, speaking in a strange language, frenzy, and murmuring profanities in a church. Strange rituals were particularly suspect.

However, as noted earlier, this was not the only approach to the mentally ill in the early part of the 16th century. Some scholars and physicians, such as Levinus Lemnius (1505–1568), Paracelsus (1493–1541), and Cornelius Agriyspa (1486–1535) (Horms, 1967; Zilboorg, 1935) continued to advocate a more rational approach to the patients and to seriously question the concept of witchcraft to explain the psychopathology seen in these people. However, Johannes Weyer (1515–1588) was probably the most vocal critic of the witch hunt and used a clinical approach in his examination of the mentally ill. "My object is also medical in that I have to show that those illnesses whose origins are attributed to witches come from natural causes" (Zilboorg, 1935, p. 117). He then went on to describe a variety of cases that today would be recognized as malingering, hysteria, scurvy, erysipelas, and pseudocyesis. He recognized auditory and visual hallucinations as symptoms of an ailment (Zilboorg, 1935). He also clearly attributed some delirious fantasies to atropine which was found in various salves and described manic patients with grandiose delusions (Zilboorg, 1935). Weyer advocated a positive, empirical, and medical point of view.

> We ought to resort now to other means than those which heretofore have been held by custom as unassailable. . . . First of all and before anything else is done, as soon as one observes some ailment which is engendered against the order of nature, one should resort to . . . one who understands various modalities, their differences, their signs, their causes. (Zilboorg, 1935, p. 119)

Later in the 16th century, the medical man who was concerned with the mentally ill was still a rarity. Felix Platter (1536–1614) was one of the few exceptions. He went into the dungeons and cellars where the mentally ill were kept and described their case histories. This practice of collecting clinical information was quite rare at the time, as most writers used descriptions from the classics when writing about illnesses (Ellenberger, 1974). Platter also provided a new classification system that had four major divisions—mental deficiency and dementia, disturbances of consciousness, psychosis, and mental exhaustion (Menninger, 1963). These had various subdivisions, and he described symptoms, causes, and treatment (Ellenberger, 1974).

In the 17th century, certain disorders such as idiocy, cretinism, and epilepsy began to be accepted as appropriate areas of interest for the medical profession (Zilboorg, 1941). Although the field of psychiatry still did not exist, the concepts of Galenism began to decline, and the area of disturbances of the nervous system as a cause of mental disorder began to be accepted. The interest in classification increased. In 1621, Paolo Zacchias (1584–1659) published a book in which he expounded a new system of classification of mental disorders (Menninger, 1963). In 1667 and 1672, Thomas Willis (1625–1675) published two books that contained chapters on melancholia, mania, idiocy, apoplexy, and other mental disorders. Although he continued to be influenced by Galen's ideas of humor, he did lay the foundation of neuroanatomy and neurophysiology as partial explanations of psychopathology (Menninger, 1963).

In the 18th century, various religious organizations began to advocate a more humane approach to the treatment of the mentally ill. Although most of the patients were still confined in deplorable conditions in prisons, more humane institutions, such as the Charetè of Senlis outside of Paris, were established (Ellenberger, 1974). In 1763, Francois Boissier de Sauvages (1705–1767) published *Noslogia Methodica*, which included a section on mental diseases. He followed the lead of Sydenham and attempted to classify mental illnesses as "diseases" much as botanists classified flowers. Mental illnesses were classified in four orders and 23 species (Menninger, 1963).

Philippe Pinel (1745–1826) is best known for his dramatic reforms at Bicêtre where he released the mentally ill from their chains during the French revolution and where he advocated the "moral treatment" of patients. In 1801 he published *A Treatise on Insanity*, in which he classified mental illnesses into five forms—melancholia, mania without delirium, mania with delirium, dementia, and idiocy (Mora, 1980). Although these terms have different meanings today, his approach was similar. He examined a large number of cases himself, defined terms, and classified the patients primarily according to clinical presentation, course, and presumed etiology. During the rest of the 19th century, this approach, which can be traced back at least to Weyer and Platter, was continued by a large number of physicians in both Europe and the United States. Pinel also greatly expanded the concepts of taking clinical histories and advocated the use of hospitals to study the mentally ill. His case histories were very detailed and the result of observations of patients over extended periods of time. He initiated procedures at Bicêtre and later at Salpêtrière that led to the establishment of permanent case records (Zilboorg, 1941). This procedure continues today at virtually every psychiatric hospital or clinic.

In the rest of the 19th century and the early part of the 20th century, there was an explosive growth in the number of people interested in various aspects of the diagnosis, treatment, and etiology of mental illnesses. Since this is beyond the scope of this chapter, the interested reader is referred to the works of Zilboorg (1941), Menninger (1963), Ellenberger (1974), and Mora (1980). Only a few trends pertinent to the understanding of the background of structured interviews will be discussed here. Jean-Etienne Esquirol (1772–1840) was a student of Pinel and continued his philosophical approach to the mentally ill. He continued the practice of keeping careful case records and initiated the use of asylum statistics to aid the study of the causes, course, and prognosis of mental disease (Ellenberger, 1974). In his 1838 textbook, *Des Maladies Mentales*, he expanded Pinel's classification of mental disorder and defined signs and symptoms of psychiatric illness, such as hallucinations and illusions, which are still used today (Mora, 1980).

In the early part of the 19th century, the mentally ill were clearly an acceptable area of investigation and study for medicine. Masses of statistics were compiled, and numerous competing systems of classification were developed. Some, like those of David Skae (1814–1873), were based on symptoms (Zilboorg, 1941). Other symptoms, such as that of H. Maudsley, were based on presumed etiology (Zilboorg, 1941). The discovery of syphilis as the cause of general paralysis strongly reinforced the idea that "mental diseases are physical illnesses of the central nervous system" (Zilboorg, 1941, p. 398). Wilhelm Griesinger (1817–1868) was a leading advocate of this approach in Germany. He believed that neuropathology and psychopathology were one and the same. He emphasized descriptive psychiatry but viewed these as simply manifestations of the underlying disease (Zilboorg, 1941).

Emil Kraepelin (1855–1926) can be considered the epitome of modern clinical descriptive psychiatrists. He collected the life histories of literally thousands of patients, sorting out what they had in common and what was different. His major contribution to psychiatry was to show that the major psychoses that his predecessors had divided into a multitude of entities consisted only of two major mental illnesses: dementia praecox and manic-depressive psychosis (Kraepelin, 1919). Kraepelin's influence is still apparent today in such nosological systems as the Research Diagnostic Criteria (RDC) (Spitzer, Endicott, & Robins, 1978b), and DSM-III (American Psychiatric Association, 1980). Many of his criteria for making a diagnosis, such as phenomenology, age of onset, and course of illness are incorporated into structured interviews in use today (e.g., the Schedule for Affective Disorders and Schizophrenia) (SADS) (Endicott & Spitzer, 1978).

Kraepelin's nosological system for dividing the major psychoses into two major groups, dementia praecox and manic-depressive psychosis, was not universally accepted, especially in the United States. Adolph Meyer felt Kraepelin was making a serious mistake: ". . . physicians and students sort out patients, not the facts, and label the men and women as cases of 'manic-depressive insanity,' or 'dementia praecox' and a few other entities, created by Kraepelin in a fit of indignation . . ." (Meyer, 1951, p. 50). As an alternative he recommended a "psychobiological" approach in which diagnosis "is no longer a process of diagnostic identification of a case or a patient with a standard entity, but a formulation of the available facts of each case in terms of 'an experiment of nature' " (Meyer, 1951, p. 65). His "Outline of Examinations" (Meyer, 1951) is some 30 pages long and divides the examination into several parts: Family History, Personal History, Present Illness, Physical Examination, and Mental Status. Although he does allow a diagnosis to be given in clear-cut cases, he clearly preferred a "concise statement of the symptom complex, or the reaction type, exactly as it occurs in the patient regardless of whether it accords with the customary types" (p. 224). Adolph Meyer's advice against premature closure of the diagnosis is still valid today. His outline of a recommended psychiatric evaluation, with minor revision, is still widely used. His admonition to psychiatrists to be aware of the multiple aspects of a person and his/her problems and not to focus solely on the major psychiatric diagnosis to some extent foreshadows the multiaxial diagnostic system used in DSM-III.

Sigmund Freud (1856–1939) was a contemporary of both Kraepelin and Meyer and one of the most influential figures in psychiatry in the 20th century. His life, works, and influence are beyond the limits of this chapter to discuss. However, for the purposes of understanding the development of structured interviews, a few points are relevant.

Freud was not primarily concerned with developing diagnostic criteria (Stoller, 1977), but rather with describing and understanding the internal dynamic processes of the mind. His concepts and approaches expanded the concepts of mental disorders to include what we today call neuroses and personality disorders.

Eugene Bleuler (1857–1939) made a major contribution to psychiatry by conceptualizing the "Group of Schizophrenias" as a psychopathological reaction in which some patients deteriorated and others recovered with or without defect. He introduced the idea of a hierarchy of primary and secondary symptoms. The primary symptoms were disturbances of affect, association, and volition. Secondary symptoms included such things as hallucinations and delusions. His concepts and, indeed, the word schizophrenia are still in use today (Lehmann, 1975).

In the 1950s and 1960s, interest in psychiatric diagnosis was stimulated by the discovery of several psychoactive drugs. Clinicians and researchers recognized the need to be able to describe patients in terms that were readily understandable to others. Unfortunately, several authors pointed out that the current systems had very poor reliabiliy (Kreitman, 1961; Spitzer & Fleiss, 1974; Ward, Beck, Mendelson, Mock, & Erbaugh, 1962; Zubin, 1967). The major source of unreliability of psychiatric diagnosis was shown to be criterion variance (Kreitman, 1961; Ward et al., 1962), which has been defined as the formal inclusion and exclusion criteria used to summarize patient data into psychiatric diagnoses (Spitzer, Endicott, & Robins, 1978a). This ultimately led to the development of nosological systems with precise criteria for each diagnostic entity, such as the "Feighner" criteria of the St. Louis group (Feighner, Robins, Guze, Woodruff, Winokur, & Munoz, 1972) and the Research Diagnostic Criteria (RDC) (Spitzer et al., 1978b). As investigations continued, it became apparent that the reliability of diagnosis could be even further improved by systematically collecting information deemed to be appropriate (Saghir, 1971; Wietzel, Morgan, Gugden, & Robinson, 1973). This led to the development of structured interviews as we know them today.

THEORETICAL POINTS

There are several principles that form the theoretical background for the development of categorical nosological systems and consequently structured interviews. Most of them are concerned with the value of separating patients into different groups (diagnostic entities) and with increasing the reliability and validity of those diagnoses. These issues are discussed in detail elsewhere (Grove, Andreasen, McDonald-Scott, Keller, & Shapiro, 1981; Helzer, Robins, Taibleson, Woodruff, Reich, & Wish, 1977; Kendell, 1975; Spitzer & Fleiss, 1974). A group of principles or goals that are the basis for a classification of mental disorders follows.

1. *Mental illness exists.* Although it is probably not possible to clearly differentiate mental illness from mental health, the general public and mental health professionals recognize certain conditions "associated with discomfort, pain, disability, death or an increased liability to these states" as constituting a disease (Guze, 1978, p. 52). These conditions are not simply problems regarding the relationship of the person to society. The concept *mental illness* also implies that these diseases are undesirable, and that therefore there should be methods of preventing or treating the condition (Spitzer & Williams, 1980).

2. *The evaluation and study of mental illness should be based on a scientific empirical approach.* This implies an openness to criticism and the expectation of evolution as new information becomes available (Roth, 1978). Although on the surface this seems more than reasonable, historically, as discussed earlier, this has not always been the case.

3. *A nosological system is of critical importance.* This allows patients to be classified into groups, which aids clinicians and researchers to investigate and answer questions regarding "epidemiology, etiology, pathogenesis, prognosis, effectiveness of treatment, and presentation" (Guze, 1978, p. 52) of illness. In other words, it is of vital importance to know whether a patient is suffering from schizophrenia, alcohol withdrawal, or senile dementia. Implicit in this is the notion that additional information about a patient is gained by identifying the patient as being a member of a certain diagnostic group (Spitzer & Williams, 1980). This is really another way of saying that the ability to predict accurately is a goal of diagnosis.

4. *The various categories in the nosological system should be separate diagnostic entities.*

This implies that there are significant differences among the illnesses. These differences may have to do with one or more of several possibilities, such as etiology, pathogenesis, course, response to treatment or associated familial psychopathology (Guze, 1978). Although most current diagnostic entities do not meet the requirements of discontinuity, it should be vigorously pursued (Kendell, 1975). A corollary of this notion is that arrangements should be made to take care of unclear cases by establishing an "undiagnosed" category (Akiskal, 1978; Kendell, 1975).

5. *There is a hierarchy in the diagnostic classes.* This concept can be traced back to Karl Jasper (Roth, 1978) and implies that "a category in a class high in the hierarchy may have features found in classes that are lower, but the reverse is not true" (Spitzer & Williams, 1980, p. 1036).

6. *Diagnostic entities should be defined with specific operational criteria and not simply by a general description of the syndrome.* This necessitates an explicit unambiguous statement of the specific features, including the degree of severity of the symptoms, that must be present for a diagnosis to be made (Kendell, 1975).

7. *The specific criterion used in operational definitions of the diagnostic entities should be able to be ascertained with a high degree of reliability* (Sanson-Fisher & Martin, 1981). For example, the criterion "ambivalence" has a low reliability and is therefore seldom found in operational definitions today (Corbett, 1978).

STRUCTURED INTERVIEWS

As the development of nosological systems with operational criteria decreased the unreliability arising from criterion variance, interest became focused on the development of structured interviews to decrease other sources of unreliability (Burgoyne, 1977; Sanson-Fisher & Martin, 1981). Several writers have described certain features that should be considered when evaluating structured interviews:

1. *The sources of information should be specified.* This will reduce information variance, which is the unreliability resulting from using various sources of information (Spitzer & Williams, 1980).

2. *Structured interviews should define terms so that clinicians are consistent in their use of them.*

3. *Guidelines for determining the presence or absence of specified signs and symptoms should be given* (Spitzer & Williams, 1980).

4. *Structured interviews should prompt clinicians to gather information to determine whether the criteria for a particular diagnosis are present by specifying what questions should be asked.* This can be viewed as increasing the construct validity of the diagnosis (Kendell, 1975).

5. *Structured interviews should collect information in a format so that diagnoses can be made in a logical fashion, so that the same data will always yield the same diagnosis.* This can be facilitated by the use of computer programs (Spitzer & Williams, 1980).

Several of the following interviews were developed for use with a particular nosological system and have evolved as the nosological system has changed. Indeed, several of the following systems are still being tested for reliability and validity. Interested readers are advised to contact the principal investigator of each interview for the most current version. The following list is not exhaustive and is limited to those interviews that currently seem to hold the most promise for widespread use by researchers and clinicians.

Present State Examination (PSE)

The PSE was developed by Wing, Cooper, and Sartorius (1974) and is a structured interview consisting of 145 items. Although suggested probing questions are given, the interviewer may ask further clarifying questions. Each symptom is rated present or absent; and if present, the degree of severity is noted. The time period covered is 1 month prior to the interview. A glossary of the symptoms is included. A computer program entitled CATEGO is available, which successively derives 35 syndromes from the 140 symptoms, 6 descriptive categories from the syndromes, and 1 CATEGO class from the categories. This can then be converted into the International Classification of Diseases—8 nosology.

The PSE was used in the US-UK Diagnostic Project (Cooper, Kendell, Gurland, Sharpe, Copeland, & Simon, 1972) and in the World

Health Organization (WHO) International Pilot Study of Schizophrenia (WHO, 1973). It has been shown to have good reliability (Cooper, Copeland, Brown, Harris, & Gourley, 1972; Luria & Berry, 1979; Wing, Nixon, Mann, & Leff, 1977). However, Wing and his colleagues do note that it has some limitations with organic symptoms, historical information, and behavioral observations during the interview (Wing et al., 1974). It is widely used in Europe and meets many of the criteria described as desirable for a structured interview.

Diagnostic Interview Schedule (DIS)

This is a highly structured interview designed to be used by lay interviewers in epidemiological studies (Robins, in press). It collects information to make diagnoses using DMS-III (American Psychiatric Association, 1980), the Feighner criteria (Feighner et al., 1972), and the Research Diagnostic Criteria (RDC) (Spitzer et al., 1978b). It takes about 1 hour to administer. Using the results of a DIS interview by a trained psychiatrist as the "correct" diagnosis, lay interviewers have been shown to have good reliability, sensitivity, and specificity for most diagnoses (Robins, Helzer, Croughan, & Ratcliff, 1981; Robins, Helzer, Ratcliff, & Seyfried, 1982). Studies are currently being conducted with a revised version.

Renard Diagnostic Interview (RDI)

The RDI was designed to be used by nonphysician interviewers as a diagnostic tool in a clinical setting. Specific questions are noted to evaluate each symptom. Further probes are recommended to establish the severity of the symptoms if present and to ascertain if the symptom is a result of a medical illness or alcohol, or drug ubuse (Helzer, Robins, Croughan, & Welner, 1981). The Feighner criteria are used as the diagnostic criteria (Feighner et al., 1972). In an elaborate study utilizing a traditional interview by psychiatrists, the RDI by two psychiatrists, RDI by a psychiatrist and a lay interviewer, and the RDI by two lay interviewers for a suitable sample of patients, the reliability and procedural validity were found to be quite acceptable for most diagnostic entities (Helzer et al., 1981).

The Schedule for Affective Disorders and Schizophrenia (SADS)

This semistructured interview was developed by Endicott, Spitzer and Robins (Endicott & Spitzer, 1978) and is divided into two sections. The first part deals with the present episode, while the second deals with past episodes of illness and lifetime diagnoses. There is also a lifetime version called SADS-L, which is basically the second half of the SADS (Endicott & Spitzer, 1978). Diagnoses are made using the Research Diagnostic Criteria (RDC) (Spitzer et al., 1978b). The SADS and RDC are currently being widely used in the United States; there have been several studies showing that the RDC have good reliability using the SADS or SADS-L (Andreasen, Grove, Shapiro, Keller, Hirschfeld, & McDonald-Scott, 1981; Andreasen, McDonald-Scott, Grove, Keller, Shapiro, & Hirschfeld, 1982; Endicott & Spitzer, 1978; Keller, Lavori, Andreasen, Grove, Shapiro, Sheftner, & McDonald-Scott, 1981; Keller, Lavori, McDonald-Scott, Sheftner, Andreasen, Shapiro, & Croughan, 1981; Spitzer et al., 1978b). One additional study evaluating the SADS and RDC recently completed by the authors is described in the following section of this chapter.

THE RESEARCH PROJECT

Although the reliability of the RDC is quite good when the SADS is used, only a few of the studies described above used the test-retest method in which a patient is interviewed separately by two different interviewers after a brief period. This is felt to be the most rigorous methodological approach to use when evaluating the reliability of psychiatric diagnoses (Helzer et al., 1977). The first goal of this research project was to attempt to replicate the reliability studies of the RDC (Keller et al., 1981a, 1981b).

One other aspect of diagnosis that has received little attention, with the exception of Helzer and associates (1981), is what Spitzer calls procedural validity (Spitzer & Williams, 1980). In essence, this compares the method of collecting the information used to make diagnoses against some "golden standard." For example, the diagnoses given by an experienced clinician using a structured interview may be considered the "golden standard" to use to compare the diagnoses given by a clinician using an unstructured interview format. The instructions to the RDC tell the clinician to use the "best available" information to make diagnoses and to screen patients to exclude subjects with medical illnesses that may be causing the psychiatric disturbance (Spitzer et al., 1978b). There have been studies done of the incidence of medical illnesses in psychiatric patients (Hall, Gardner, Popkin, Lecann, & Stickney, 1981; Maguire & Granville-Grossman, 1968). However, the investigators were not aware of any study demonstrating the value of using "best available information" instead of just the results of a single interview. Indeed, not obtaining this information probably contributes to the variance in interrater reliability (Keller et al., 1981b). The second goal of this project was to demonstrate the procedural validity of the inclusion of best available information for making diagnostic judgments.

Methods

At the time this project began, the two psychiatrists in this project had worked together on the same inpatient unit for about 6 months. The residency training of one, JGE, had been basically psychoanalytic, but she had subsequently worked for many years on an acute care inpatient unit where rapid diagnosis and proper psychopharmacological intervention were highly valued and carried out on a daily basis. The other psychiatrist, DGS, trained at Washington University School of Medicine in St. Louis, where the "Feighner Criteria" originated, and subsequently had worked for several years on a clinical research unit where the major research interests were in the evaluation and treatment of patients with major depressive disorders. Thus, the two psychiatrists came from substantially different backgrounds.

Because of their research interests, both psychiatrists had independently begun to use the RDC with only casual discussion about the diagnostic criteria. Both were using the SADS as part of their regular clinical research. Up to that point in time, there had been no formal effort to check reliability. When the decision was made to begin this project, they jointly interviewed 10 patients with the SADS. After independently diagnosing the patients using the RDC, each item in the SADS was reviewed point by point. Then the current and life-time diagnoses were compared, and any discrepancies were discussed and resolved to their mutual satisfaction. The only significant problem that arose from that review was the timing of the onset of the present episode. After discussion, this and other minor discrepancies were also satisfactorily resolved.

All of the patients in this project were inpatients at Western Psychiatric Institute and Clinic (WPIC). Almost all of the patients were on the Clinical Research Unit (CRU) on the service of one or the other of the psychiatrists in this study. To decrease the time to reach a reasonable sample size, a small number of patients on another inpatient unit were also interviewed shortly after their admission. For purposes of this project, the psychiatrist who first interviewed the patients was designated the "primary psychiatrist," and except for the six patients on the other unit was the psychiatrist who actually cared for them during their hospitalization. The first SADS was done by the patient's primary psychiatrist within one working day of admission. The second psychiatrist then reinterviewed the patient within the next 24 hours. Patients were taken on a "catch as catch can" basis. The limiting factor was the availability of the second psychiatrist to reinterview the patient within 24 hours.

The degree of interrater reliability for the diagnoses given by the two psychiatrists was determined by using the kappa (κ) coefficient (Fleiss, 1971). Kappa is an index of agreement that corrects for chance agreement (Helzer et al., 1977). Although it generally meets the needs of this investigation, it does have some limits. It should not be used where the frequency of the diagnosis is less than 5% (Grove et al., 1981), nor where the proportion of the cases in one of the cells where both raters agree is less than 10% of the proportion of cases in the other cell when both raters agree (Janes, 1979). In the latter cases, a more appropriate statistic may be the Random Error Coefficient of Agreement (R.E.) (Janes, 1979; Maxwell, 1977).

The second phase of this investigation was concerned with the validity of the diagnosis given by the patient's primary psychiatrist. The usual practice on the CRU is to observe the patient drug free for at least a few days, and in many cases up to 14 days. During this period, the patient undergoes a variety of tests to rule out a general medical cause of their psychiatric illness. These include a physical examination, routine blood and urine tests, an electroencephalogram, thyroid function tests, and

TABLE 15.1. CURRENT DIAGNOSES.

Diagnoses	Rater A* +	+	−	−	Frequency of diagnosis (%)	κ	R.E.
	Rater B* +	−	+	−			
Schizophrenia	4	2	3	53	11	.57	.84
Schizoaffective, Depressed	1	3	2	56	6	.24	.84
Manic Disorder	4	1	0	57	7	.88	.97
Major Depressive Disorder	36	1	3	22	61	.86	.87
Episodic Minor Depressive Disorder	2	0	1	59	5	.79	.97
Chronic & Intermittent Depressive Disorder	4	4	2	52	11	.52	.84
Drug Abuse	2	3	0	57	6	.55	.90

*(+) = present; (−) = absent

any other laboratory test indicated based on the patient's medical history or physical examination. In addition, past medical and psychiatric records are reviewed, family members are interviewed to obtain corroborative history, and the patient's type and severity of psychopathology is observed by the unit staff. This information is then synthesized by the patient's primary psychiatrist, and the patient is given his best RDC diagnosis. A total of 66 patients were approached and asked to be in this protocol. Two patients refused, while the rest gave informed consent after the procedure was explained to them. An additional two patients did not complete the study because they refused to be reinterviewed by the second psychiatrist, leaving a final sample size of 62. The sample included 6 black and 22 white males, and 5 black and 29 white females. Their ages ranged from 19–65, with the mean age (± SD) of 35.5 ± 13.7 years.

Results

Table 15.1 shows the reliability data for the current diagnoses. Frequency of diagnosis was given.

For example, the diagnosis of Major Depressive Disorder was made in 61% of the 124 interviews. For reasons given previously, κ was not calculated for diagnoses that have a frequency of diagnoses of less than 5%. As seen in Table 15.1, the kappa for most of the diagnoses was acceptable to very good, except for Schizoaffective Disorder-Depressed. However, the raters agreed that it was present in only 1 (1.6%) case and that it was absent in 56 (90.3%) cases. Thus, the R.E. may be a more appropriate statistical expression of reliability, and for Schizoaffective Disorder-Depressed it was .84. Table 15.2 shows the reliability data for the Life-time Diagnoses, which are also quite good, using κ or R.E. as appropriate.

Table 15.3 shows the reliability data for the subtypes of Major Depressive Disorder.

The procedural validity of an experienced psychiatrist, using the SADS during only one interview to collect data to make diagnoses using the RDC, was only moderately good. As Table 15.4 shows, there were 15 patients, 24.2% of the 62, for whom the process of reviewing old records, observing them drug free, and talking with family members made what the investigators felt was a

TABLE 15.2. LIFE-TIME DIAGNOSES.

Diagnoses	Rater A* +	+	−	−	Frequency of diagnosis (%)	κ	R.E.
	Rater B* +	−	+	−			
Bipolar 1	4	0	1	57	7	.88	.97
Bipolar 2	4	3	1	54	10	.63	.87
Recurrent Unipolar	16	4	2	40	31	.77	.81
Labile Personality	3	6	1	52	11	.41	.77
Antisocial Personality	4	1	0	57	7	.88	.97

*(+) = present; (−) = absent

TABLE 15.3. SUBTYPES OF MAJOR DEPRESSIVE DISORDER.

Diagnoses	Rater A* +	+	−	−	Frequency of diagnosis (%)	κ	R.E.
	Rater B* +	−	+	−			
Primary	21	5	3	33	40	.73	.74
Secondary	8	3	7	44	21	.52	.68
Psychotic	2	1	3	56	7	.47	.87
Incapacitating	4	1	23	34	26	.13	.23
Endogenous	24	9	3	26	52	.77	.61
Agitated	6	9	2	45	20	.75	.65
Retarded	2	13	3	44	22	.58	.48
Situational	17	8	4	33	37	.59	.61
Simple	18	7	3	34	37	.66	.68

*(+) = present; (−) = absent

"significant change" in their diagnosis. The investigators chose to define "significant change" as a change in the Present or Life-time diagnosis as defined in the RDC, which would result in a change in treatment for the patient. The most common change was the result of uncovering information that led to an additional psychiatric diagnosis in a patient who was previously felt to only have a Primary Major Depressive Disorder. The most common additional diagnosis was alcoholism. Additional information obtained from observation revealed that three other patients with a Major Depressive Disorder were psychotically depressed when they initially had not been given that diagnosis.

Another advantage of the drug-free observation period is that a certain percentage of the depressed patients will have a remission of their depressive symptoms during that time. In this study, this occurred in 5 (13.9%) of the 36 patients diagnosed by both psychiatrists as having a Major Depressive Disorder. In all of the cases, this occurred within 5–6 days of admission, and most were within the first 48 hours.

Obtaining routine laboratory tests to rule out general medical illness causing the psychiatric symptoms is also important. In this study, of the 36 patients diagnosed as having Major Depressive Disorder by both psychiatrists at the time of admission, 4 (11.1%) had a previously undiagnosed general medical or physical illness affecting their central nervous system. There were two cases of temporal lobe epilepsy, and two patients had severe hypertension. One was secondary to a staghorn calculus of her left kidney, and the other was in a 24-year-old male who had essential hypertension. In the 26 patients with a diagnosis other than Major Depressive Disorder, none had any significant medical illness affecting his central nervous system.

TABLE 15.4. CHANGES IN DIAGNOSIS BASED ON INFORMATION
FROM A SADS INTERVIEW VERSUS BEST AVAILABLE INFORMATION.

Initial diagnosis	Final diagnosis	Number of patients
1. MDD, Primary Subtype	MDD, Secondary Subtype (Alcoholism)	3
	Obsessive-Compulsive Disorder	1
	Drug Abuse and Phobic Disorder	1
2. MDD, Secondary Subtype (Alcoholism)	MDD, Primary Subtype	2
3. MDD, Not Psychotic Subtype	MDD, Psychotic Subtype	3
4. Not Bipolar I	Bipolar I	1
5. MDD	Unspecified Functional Psychoses	1
6. Other Psychiatric Disorder	Schizoaffective Disorder—Depressed	1
	MDD—Psychotic Subtype	1
7. Unspecified Functional Psychoses	Schizoaffective Disorder—Depressed	1
	Total	15

Discussion

The interpretation of reliability data is not simple. The maximum possible kappa depends on the sensitivity, specificity, and base rate of the diagnostic category under consideration. Basically, as either of those factors decrease, the maximum possible kappa also decreases. For a more detailed discussion, the reader is referred to Grove et al. (1981) and others (Carey & Gottesman, 1978; Janes, 1979). The error that must be avoided in interpreting the data on reliability generated by this project is falsely rejecting a relatively low kappa as unreliable when in fact it might be quite good considering the base rate, sensitivity, and specificity of the diagnostic category under consideration. With this note in mind, a conservative evaluation of the diagnoses in Tables 15.1–3 is that most of them are acceptable to quite good, with the possible exceptions of Schizoaffective Disorder-Depressed and the Incapacitating subtype of Major Depressive Disorder.

Although the κ for Schizoaffective Disorder-Depressed is low, the R.E. is .84. The low kappa is probably explained by the 1:56 ratio of cases where the two psychiatrists agreed on the diagnosis being present, compared to the diagnosis being absent. However, an even closer look at the five cases discordant for the diagnosis of Schizoaffective Disorder-Depressed is instructive. In all five cases, both psychiatrists felt the patients were psychotic. However, in three cases, one psychiatrist felt that the patients did not have a depressive syndrome, but only had a few depressive symptoms. In those cases, the diagnosis of Schizophrenia was given. In the other two cases, one psychiatrist felt that two patients did not have the types of delusions consistent with a Schizoaffective Disorder and therefore give the diagnosis of Major Depressive Disorder, Psychotic subtype, instead of Schizoaffective Disorder-Depressed. There was no constant pattern as to which of the two psychiatrists made the discordant diagnosis. Thus, the problem seems to be with the reliability of the diagnostic criteria for those patients who have a mixture of affective and psychotic symptoms.

The low reliability of the Incapacitating subtype of Major Depressive Disorder arises from a different source. As seen in Table 15.3, Rater B coded this diagnostic category present in 23 cases, while Rater A rated it absent. Clearly, Rater B had a different threshold for scoring this category present than Rater A. This low κ for the Incapacitating subtype is not new. At least two previous studies have also reported a low kappa for this diagnostic category for the current episode (Andreasen et al., 1981, 1982). It appears that the criteria for this entity should be changed; if the reliability does not improve after several changes, perhaps the category should be dropped.

The data in this study indicate that the procedural validity of deriving a diagnosis only on the basis of a one time SADS interview is not good. Indeed, the authors of the RDC recommend using best available information, and the results of this research study strongly support that position. Almost one of every four patients in this study had a significant change in his or her diagnosis when best available information was used instead of the information from just a single interview. Although reliability of a structural interview like the SADS is undoubtedly better than an unstructured one (Beckett, Grisell, Crandall, & Gudobba, 1967; Weitzel et al., 1973), it should be supplemented by other sources of information such as past records, interviews with family, and if possible, a drug free observation period by trained personnel.

Ruling out medical illnesses that affect the central nervous system and may account for the patient's psychiatric symptomatology is important for both clinical management and research purposes. In this study, four patients had a previously undiagnosed medical illness affecting their central nervous systems. The two patients with temporal lobe epilepsy had clearly abnormal electroencephalograms and were both treated with anticonvulsants. The other two patients had diastolic blood pressures that were consistently above 110 mm Hg. Although this does not exclude the possibility of the diagnosis of Major Depressive Disorder, it does reinforce the recommendation of other investigators on the importance of looking for medical illness in psychiatric patients (Hall et al., 1981; Maguire & Granville-Grossman, 1968).

One final group that has received little attention in the literature is the five patients with Major Depressive Disorder who had a spontaneous remission of their symptoms shortly after being hospitalized. This constitutes 13.9% of the 36 patients who both psychiatrists diagnosed as having a Major Depressive Disorder. Although quick remission of symptoms does not negate the diagnosis, it does raise questions for future research. There are several possible explanations for this remission of symptoms. Some patients with a situational problem may benefit from even a short hospitalization by being taken out of a difficult situation and put in a therapeutic environment. Other patients may have a rapidly cycling variant of bipolar illness or a personality disorder with a fluctuating course. The investigators also felt that some may be women who have a premenstrual tension syndrome, which remits with the onset of their menses in the hospital. Still another possibility is that some patients may be denying symptoms so they can be discharged from the hospital quickly. Obviously, this group of "spontaneous" or "quick remitters" requires further attention in order for the phenomena to be better understood.

Thus this study, which utilized a test-retest methodology to evaluate the SADS and RDC, basically supports the work of other investigators showing that the RDC has good reliability. However, the authors have also shown that the procedural validity of the SADS can be substantially increased by using multiple sources of information and by performing laboratory tests and a physical examination to rule out medical causes of the patient's symptoms.

FUTURE DIRECTIONS

Categorical nosological systems are going to be with us for the foreseeable future. Other alternatives such as the dimensional approach, in which patients are assigned positions on one or more axes or dimensions, are unlikely to replace the categorical approach (Kendell, 1975). However, it is equally safe to say that the diagnostic entities in the various categorical systems will continue to change and evolve as new information is developed. As that occurs, structured interviews will also change.

Many clinicians doubt that the structured interviews currently available will ever be widely used because they are felt to be cumbersome (Burgoyne, 1977; Helzer, 1981). Many find the process of flipping through pages of an interview disruptive to developing a therapeutic alliance with the patient. In addition, by their inquiry into multiple areas of potential psychopathology, they are felt to take longer to complete than a traditional psychiatric evaluation. To some extent, these are valid criticisms. However, structured interviews clearly have an advantage in clinical research settings and in epidemiological studies. They substantially increase the reliability of diagnoses by reducing the error arising from differences in interviewer techniques of questioning, interviewer

expectations, and differences in definition of terms (Kendell, 1975). It is imperative for good research and clinical care that interviewers give the same diagnoses to patients with similar symptoms. Clinicians must weigh the advantages of structured interviews against the time and effort needed to use them. Hopefully, those developing structured interviews will find the proper balances necessary to make them attractive to nonresearch clinicians. Helzer (1981) has shown that this goal is probably obtainable.

SUMMARY

There have been major changes over the last two millennia in the attitudes of society toward the mentally ill, and there have been significant changes in the conceptual approach regarding etiology of psychopathology. Innumerable systems have been developed to classify, categorize, subdivide, lump, or split these patients into groups that make it easier for humans to make sense out of the seemingly random presentation of patients. There has also been tremendous variation in the type of information considered essential to categorize these patients and the determination of who should collect it. There have been many ebbs and flows, blind alleys, and occasionally some advances in our understanding of psychopathology. Today, structured interviews do seem to be of some help in this process. Hopefully, future generations will look more favorably on our efforts than we look on those of some of our predecessors.

REFERENCES

Akiskal, H. (1978). The joint use of clinical and biological criteria for psychiatric diagnosis. I. A historical and methodological review. In H. Akiskal & W.L. Webb (Eds.), *Psychiatric diagnosis: Exploration of biological predictors.* New York: S.P. Medical and Scientific Books.

American Psychiatric Association. (1980). *Diagnostic and statistical manual of mental disorders* (3rd ed.). Washington, DC: Author.

Andreasen, N.C., Grove, W.M., Shapiro, R.W., Keller, M.B., Hirschfeld, R.M.A., & McDonald-Scott, P. (1981). Reliability of lifetime diagnosis: A multicenter collaborative perspective. *Archives of General Psychiatry, 38,* 400–405.

Andreasen, N.C., McDonald-Scott, P., Grove, W.M., Keller, M.B., Shapiro, R.W., & Hirschfeld, R.M.A. (1982). Assessment of reliability in multicenter collaborative research with a videotape approach. *American Journal of Psychiatry, 139,* 876–882.

Beckett, P.G.S., Grisell, J., Crandall, R.G., & Gudobba, R. (1967). A method of formalizing psychiatric study. *Archives of General Psychiatry*, 16, 407–415.

Burgoyne, R.W. (1977). The structured interview—An aid to compiling a clear and concise data base. *International Journal of Mental Health*, 6, 37–48.

Carey, G., & Gottesman, I.I. (1978). Reliability and validity in binary ratings. *Archives of General Psychiatry*, 35, 1454–1459.

Cooper, J.E., Copeland, J.R.M., Brown, G.W., Harris, T., & Gourley, A.J. (1972). Further studies in interviewer training and interrater reliability of the present state examination (PSE). *Psychological Medicine*, 7, 517–523.

Cooper, J.E., Kendell, R.E., Gurland, B.J., Sharpe, L., Copeland, J.R.M., & Simon, R. (1972). *Psychiatric diagnosis in New York and London*. London: Oxford University Press.

Corbett, L. (1978). Clinical differentiation of the schizophrenic and affective disorders: A comparison of the Bleulerian and phenomenological approaches to diagnosis. In H.S. Akiskal & W.L. Webb (Eds.), *Psychiatric diagnosis: Exploration of biological predictors*. New York: S.P. Medical and Scientific Books.

Ellenberger, H.F. (1974). Psychiatry from ancient to modern times. In S. Arieti (Ed.), *American handbook of psychiatry* (Vol. 1). New York: Basic Books.

Endicott, J., & Spitzer, R.L. (1978). A diagnostic interview: The schedule for affective disorders and schizophrenia. *Archives of General Psychiatry*, 35, 837–844.

Feighner, J., Robins, E., Guze, S.B., Woodruff, R.A., Winokur, G., & Munoz, R. (1972). Diagnostic criteria for use in psychiatric research. *Archives of General Psychiatry*, 26, 57–63.

Fleiss, J.L. (1971). Measuring nominal scale agreement among many raters. *Psychological Bulletin*, 76, 378–382.

Goshen, C.E. (1967). *Documentary history of psychiatry*. New York: Philosophical Library.

Grove, W.M., Andreasen, N.C., McDonald-Scott, P., Keller, M.B., & Shapiro, R.W. (1981). Reliability studies of psychiatric diagnosis: Theory and practice. *Archives of General Psychiatry*, 38, 408–413.

Guze, S.B. (1978). Validating criteria for psychiatric diagnosis: The Washington University approach. In H. Akiskal & W.L. Webb (Eds.), *Psychiatric diagnosis: Exploration of biological predictors*. New York: S.P. Medical and Scientific Books.

Hall, R.C.W., Gardner, E.R., Popkin, M.K., Lecann, A.F., & Stickney, S.K. (1981). Unrecognized physical illness prompting psychiatric admission: A prospective study. *American Journal of Psychiatry*, 138, 629–635.

Helzer, J.E. (1981). The use of a structured interview for routine psychiatric evaluations. *Journal of Nervous and Mental Disease*, 169, 45–49.

Helzer, J.E., Robins, L.E., Croughan, J.L., & Welner, A. (1981). Renard diagnostic interview: Its reliability and procedural validity with physicians and lay interviewers. *Archives of General Psychiatry*, 38, 393–398.

Helzer, J.E., Robins, L.E., Taibleson, M., Woodruff, R.A., Reich, T., & Wish, E.D. (1977). Reliability of psychiatric diagnosis I. A methodological review. *Archives of General Psychiatry*, 34, 129–133.

Horms, E. (1967). *Origins of modern psychiatry*. Springfield: Charles C. Thomas.

Jackson, S.W. (1969). Galen on mental disorders. *Journal of the History of the Behavioral Sciences*, 5, 365–384.

Janes, C.L. (1979). Agreement measurement and the judgment process. *Journal of Nervous and Mental Disease*, 167, 343–347.

Keller, M.B., Lavori, P.W., Andreasen, N.C., Grove, W.M., Shapiro, R.W., Scheftner, W., & McDonald-Scott, P. (1981a). Test-retest reliability of assessing psychiatrically ill patients in a multi-center design. *Journal of Psychiatric Research*, 16, 213–227.

Keller, M.B., Lavori, P.W., McDonald-Scott, P., Scheftner, W.A., Andreasen, N.C., Shapiro, R.W., & Croughan, J. (1981b). Reliability of lifetime diagnoses and symptoms in patients with a current psychiatric disorder. *Journal of Psychiatric Research*, 16, 229–240.

Kendell, R.E. (1975). *The role of diagnosis in psychiatry*. Oxford: Blackwell Scientific Publications.

Kraepelin, E. (1914) *Dementia praecox and paraphrenia* (R.M. Barclay, trans.). Edinburgh: E. & S. Livingston.

Kraepelin, E. (1921). *Manic depressive insanity and paranoia* (R.M. Barclay, trans.). Edinburgh: E. & S. Livingston.

Kreitman, N. (1961). The reliability of psychiatric diagnosis. *Journal of Mental Sciences*, 107, 876–886.

Kroll, J. (1973). A reappraisal of psychiatry in the middle ages. *Archives of General Psychiatry*, 32, 276–283.

Lehmann, H.E. (1975). Schizophrenia: Introduction and history. In A.M. Freedman, H.I. Kaplan, & B.J. Sadock (Eds.), *Comprehensive textbook of psychiatry II*. Baltimore: Williams & Wilkins.

Luria, R.E., & Berry, R. (1979). Reliability and descriptive validity of PSE syndromes. *Archives of General Psychiatry*, 36, 1187–1195.

Maguire, G.P., & Granville-Grossman, K.L. (1968). Physical illness in psychiatric patients. *British Journal of Psychiatry*, 115, 1365–1369.

Maxwell, A.E. (1977). Coefficients of agreement between observers and their interpretation. *British Journal of Psychiatry*, 130, 79–83.

McVaugh, M. (1969). Quantified medical theory and practice on the 14th century. *Montpellier Bulletin of Medical History*, 3, 397–413.

Menninger, K. (1963). *The vital balance*. New York: The Viking Press.

Meyer, A. (1951). The collected papers of Adolph Meyer. In E.E. Winters (Ed.), *Medical teaching* (Vol. 2). Baltimore: The Johns Hopkins Press.

Mora, G. (1980). Historical and theoretical trends in psychiatry. In H.I. Kaplan, A.M. Freedman, & B. J. Sadock (Eds.), *Comprehensive textbook of psychiatry III*. Baltimore/London: Williams & Wilkins.

Neugebauer, R. (1979). Medieval and early modern theories of mental illness. *Archives of General Psychiatry*, 35, 477–483.

Robins, L.N. (in press). The development and characteristics of the NIMH diagnostic interview schedule. In M.M. Weissman & J.K. Meyers (Eds.), *Epidemiological community surveys*. New York: Prodist Neale Watson Academic Press.

Robins, L.N., Helzer, J.E., Croughan, J., & Ratcliff, K.S. (1981). The NIMH diagnostic interview schedule: Its history, characteristics and validity. *Archives of General Psychiatry*, 38, 381–389.

Robins, L.N., Helzer, J.E., Ratcliff, K.S., & Seyfried, W. (1982). Validity of the diagnostic interview schedule, version II: DSM-III diagnoses. *Psychological Medicine*, 12, 855–870.

Roth, M. (1978). Psychiatric diagnosis in clinical and scientific settings. In H.S. Akiskal & W.L. Webb (Eds.), *Psychiatric diagnosis: Exploration of biological predictors*. New York: S.P. Medical and Scientific Books.

Saghir, M.T. (1971). A comparison of some aspects of structured and unstructured interviews. *American Journal of Psychiatry*, 128, 72–76.

Sanson-Fisher, R.W., & Martin, C.J. (1981). Standardized interviews in psychiatry: issues of reliability. *British Journal of Psychiatry*, 139, 138–143.

Spitzer, R.L., Endicott, J., & Robins, E. (1978a). Reliability of clinical criteria for psychiatric diagnosis. In H.S. Akiskal & W.L. Webb (Eds.), *Psychiatric diagnosis: Exploration of biological predictors*. New York: S.P. Medical and Scientific Books.

Spitzer, R.L., Endicott, J., & Robins, E. (1978b). Research diagnostic criteria: Rationale and reliability. *Archives of General Psychiatry*, 35, 773–782.

Spitzer, R.L., & Fleiss, J.L. (1974). A re-analysis of the reliability of psychiatric diagnosis. *British Journal of Psychiatry*, 125, 341–347.

Spitzer, R.L., & Williams, J.B.W. (1980). Classification of mental disorders and DSM-III. In H.I. Kaplan, A.M. Freedman, & B.J. Sadock (Eds.), *Comprehensive textbook of psychiatry III*. Baltimore: Williams & Wilkins.

Stoller, R.J. (1977). Psychoanalytic diagnoses. In V.M. Rakoff, H.C. Stancer, & H.B. Kedward (Eds.), *Psychiatric diagnosis*. New York: Brunner/Mazel.

Summers, M. (trans.) (1928). *Malleus Maleficarum*, H. Kramer, & J. Sprenger 1486 (Eds.), London: The Pushkin Press.

Ward, C.H., Beck, A.T., Mendelson, M., Mock, J.E.; & Erbaugh, J.K. (1962). The psychiatric nomenclature. *Archives of General Psychiatry*, 7, 198–205.

Weitzel, W.D., Morgan, D.W., Gugden, T.F., & Robinson, J.A. (1973). Toward a more efficient mental status examination: free form or operationally defined. *Archives of General Psychiatry*, 28, 215–218.

Wing, J.K., Cooper, J.E., & Sartorius, N. (1974). *The measurement and classification of psychiatric symptoms*. Cambridge, MA: Cambridge University Press.

Wing, J.K., Nixon, J.M., Mann, S.A., & Leff, J.P. (1977). Reliability of the PSE. *Psychological Medicine*, 7, 505–516.

World Health Organization. (1973). *International pilot study of schizophrenia*. Geneva: WHO.

Zilboorg, G. (1935). *The medical man and the witch during the renaissance*. New York: Cooper Square.

Zilboorg, G. (1941). *A history of medical psychology*. New York: W.W. Norton.

Zubin, J. (1967). Classification of the behavior disorders. In P.R. Farnsworth & O. McNemar (Eds.), *Annual Review of Psychology*. Palo Alto, CA: Annual Reviews.

PART VII

PERSONALITY ASSESSMENT

16 OBJECTIVE PERSONALITY ASSESSMENT

James N. Butcher
Laura S. Keller

INTRODUCTION

In his analysis of the impact of technological change on individuals and society, Mesthene (1970) described two extreme views of technology: It can be seen as an "unalloyed blessing for man and society" or alternatively as "an almost unmitigated curse" (pp. 16–17). Those who favor the latter view stress the impersonal and potentially dehumanizing aspects of technology; proponents of technological change emphasize its promise for "freeing man to pursue creative productivity" (Williams, 1977, p. 108). As an important component of psychology's technology, objective personality assessment has been both criticized and praised on the basis of such extreme value positions as those above. Realistically, however, technological developments have value only in their relevance and utility for the achievement of valued goals. Objective methods of personality assessment and their logical outgrowth, automated assessment methods, are particularly well-suited to the achievement of practical goals in both research and applied psychological settings.

Objective assessment devices are characterized by the structured and standardized nature of their test stimuli, response options available to the subject, and scoring and interpretive strategies. The vast majority of structured personality tests are *self-report inventories*, which consist of "conventional culturally crystallized questions to which the subject must respond in one of a few fixed ways" (Meehl, 1945, p. 296). The proliferation of use and development of such tests in the last half century attests to their practical advantages. Objective tests can be reliably and accurately administered, scored, and in many cases even interpreted by nonprofessional workers or even by a machine. The latter is possible because of the huge amount of research data available on popular instruments such as the Minnesota Multiphasic Personality Inventory (MMPI). These data have been incorporated into standardized systems of interpretive rules that relate test scores to meaningful extratest criteria. The reliability and standardization of data collected through objective self-report inventories are obviously ideal for research applications. In addition, the efficiency of such assessment methods is increasingly important in applied settings: Limited funding and the current emphasis on accountability are making the cost/benefit ratios of various psychological technologies a standard concern.

DEVELOPMENT OF SELF-REPORT INVENTORIES

The first self-report inventories were developed in applied settings to aid psychologists in practical decision-making tasks. The Woodworth Personal Data Sheet (PDS) was constructed during World War I for mass psychiatric screening of military draftees (Woodworth, 1920). Designed to function as a standardized clinical interview, the PDS was a paper-and-pencil test consisting of questions about neurotic symptoms. The subject's score on this test was the total number of symptoms he or she endorsed. After the war, many other inventories were developed for a variety of predictive purposes and by a variety of methods. Many, like the PDS, were developed through *rational* methods. Items were selected, written, and/or grouped according to the test developer's theory of which items and scales should work for his or her purpose. However, researchers began to find that à priori predictions of how particular items would relate to criteria of interest were often disconfirmed in practice.

A different method of test construction, the *empirical criterion keying* approach, deals with this problem by asserting that a person's response "constitutes an intrinsically interesting and significant bit of verbal behavior, the non-test correlates of which must be discovered by empirical means" (Meehl, 1954, p. 297). Rather than grouping items into scales according to preconceived theoretical notions, the empirical test constructor uses the *method of contrasted groups* to select items according to their significance in distinguishing between groups of people differing on the criterion of interest. For example, in constructing the Depression scale for the MMPI, the responses of a group of diagnosed depressives were contrasted with those of a group of "normals." Items for which the frequency of endorsement differed significantly between the two groups were included in the scale. The MMPI and its "normal" personality counterpart, the California

Psychological Inventory (Gough, 1975), were both constructed largely through methods of empirical criterion keying. Construction and validation of the MMPI will be described in more detail later in this chapter.

A third method of personality test construction has gained popularity as the computer technology necessary for its execution has become available. In the *factor analytic* or *internal consistency* approach to test construction, homogeneous scales are developed by factor analyzing the interitem correlations among a large pool of personality items. This approach is best exemplified in the work of Raymond Cattell, the developer of the Sixteen Personality Factor Questionnaire or "16PF" (Cattell, Eber, & Tatsuoka, 1970). Cattell attempted to provide a comprehensive description of personality by factor analyzing ratings of individuals on a set of trait items derived from the set of all personality trait names in the English dictionary and the psychiatric literature. Cattell described the resultant factors as "primary source traits" of personality, which Anastasi (1976) noted is "a designation that seems to imply more universality and stability of results than appear justified by the antecedent research" (p. 508). More recently, the 16PF has been extended to include dimensions of pathological personality functioning as well. This new instrument, the Clinical Analysis Questionnaire (CAQ), is designed to provide a comprehensive assessment of every meaningful dimension of both normal and pathological functioning (Krug, 1980). McNair's review of the instrument, however, casts doubt on the sufficiency of present research evidence to support the criterion validity or even the internal consistency validity of the CAQ (McNair, 1978).

CONTEMPORARY STATUS OF SELF-REPORT PERSONALITY TESTS

Contemporary test construction efforts have tended to combine several strategies in a multistep developmental process. Jackson (1971) presented a model test construction strategy involving rational-theoretical selection of items, followed by scale refinement through internal consistency checks, and finally empirical validation against external criteria. Jackson's Personality Research

Form (Jackson, 1967–1974) and Differential Personality Inventory (Jackson, 1972) were both constructed through this combination of rational, internal consistency and empirical validation methodology. Both inventories consist of sets of relatively independent scales with high content homogeneity and have also been designed to minimize the distorting effects of certain subject response styles. Unfortunately, however, neither instrument has generated enough validation research to justify its use in applied settings at this time.

This dearth of published validation research characterizes another of the "contenders to replace the MMPI monopoly" (Kleinmuntz, 1982, p. 242) as well: Theodore Millon's Clinical Multiaxial Inventory (MCMI). Like the PRF and DPI, the MCMI was developed using a mixture of scale construction methods. Item and scale content are linked to Millon's own clinical personality theory, but selection of the final item pool and scale composition were refined through a combination of internal consistency methods and external criterion checking. Millon set out to "draw upon the best features of the MMPI, minimize its limitations, and move forward to develop instruments that reflect advances of the past quarter of a century in psychopathology, diagnostic assessment, and test construction" (Millon, 1982, p. 1). Accordingly, the MCMI is distinguished by its brevity compared to comparable instruments, its link to a systematic clinical theory, the coordination of its interpretations with the current official psychiatric diagnostic system, its attempt to separate enduring personality characteristics from acute clinical symptom pictures, and its purported ability to discriminate among psychiatric groups. Because it was constructed with the latter goal in mind, the instrument is not recommended for use in "normal" populations or "for purposes other than diagnostic screening or clinical assessment" (Millon, 1982, p. 3).

It should be evident from our comments above that although new developments in objective personality assessment may hold promise for the future, the present lack of criterion-relevant validation research seriously limits the contemporary practical utility of these instruments. Butcher and Owen (1978), in their comprehensive survey of research literature on four clinical assessment instruments, found that 84% of the articles published between 1972 and 1977 utilized a 40-year-old test: the MMPI. The 16PF came in a not very close second, and the new DPI and MCMI had extremely little published research coverage to validate their practical utility beyond the original empirical studies the authors had utilized in constructing the tests.

In reviewing the literature on these four instruments since Butcher and Owen's survey, we found that the pattern has changed very little. (Our survey of research on the MMPI, MCMI, DPI, and 16PF included all references obtained from a computer search [MEDLINE and PSYCH ABSTRACTS] of the published literature from 1978 to 1982. We recognize that some publications may have been missed inadvertently, and that the delay between publication and listing in these data bases has forced us to exclude some of the literature published since mid-1982.) Our survey indicates that of the literature published between 1978 and 1982 incorporating any of these four tests, roughly 87% utilized the MMPI. The 16PF again came in second, showing up in approximately 100 of the nearly 800 studies we found, and there were less than 10 reports utilizing either the MCMI or the DPI. These results show clearly that despite new developments in test construction that may hold promise for the future, the contemporary status of objective personality assessment is still largely synonymous with the contemporary status of the MMPI. Accordingly, the next major section of this chapter will describe this popular instrument in more detail, including its original construction, subsequent scale and interpretive developments, a brief survey of contemporary research and clinical applications, problems with the instrument, and plans for the future restandardization and redevelopment of the test. This discussion of the MMPI as the prototypal example of contemporary objective personality assessment technology will be followed by the final portion of our chapter, which takes a look at the role of computer technology in the future of objective personality assessment.

THE MMPI: PAST, PRESENT, AND FUTURE

Original Item and Scale Development

In 1940 Hathaway and McKinley published the first of a number of articles detailing the development of a new paper-and-pencil personality test, the Minnesota Multiphasic Personality Inventory (MMPI), which was devised as an objective means of obtaining clinical-diagnostic information about clients in psychiatric and general medical settings. Unlike most existing personality inventories, scale development work on the MMPI was, for the most part, empirical. That is, the items selected for the scales were not obtained according to some theoretical plan of the test developers, but through empirical item analysis procedures. The collection of empirically based psychometric scales was devised to assess clinically relevant problem behaviors, such as depression, hypochondriasis, sociopathy, schizophrenia, and hypomania, and to aid the clinician in arriving at a clinical diagnosis.

The test authors initially collected over 1,000 items from a variety of sources, including clinical cases, textbooks, and previously published tests. These items were reduced to a pool of 504 items by eliminating those that were considered redundant or not promising for other reasons. This item pool was administered to a group of individuals referred to as the "Minnesota normals": mostly visitors to the University of Minnesota Hospitals who were not presently under a doctor's care. The clinical scales were developed by determining which items actually differentiated the normal group from various clinical reference groups. These reference groups were made up of individuals who had been diagnosed as having the symptoms or problems defined by the diagnostic categories in use at the time: for example, Depression or Schizophrenia. Care was taken in the accumulation of clinical cases in each group to assure that the clinical problems were homogeneous and clearly defined by the diagnostic criteria used in the study. An additional 46 items (on the Mf and Si scales) were later included, bringing the total number to 550 for the full MMPI. On the later-developed Group Form booklet for the MMPI there are 566 items, since 16 items are repeated. The MMPI validity scales, clinical scales, and some special scales are described in Table 16.1.

Subsequent Developments

Although early MMPI research development and clinical application emphasized empirical correlates and reliance upon objective interpretation of

profiles, there were also advocates of *content based interpretation* (Grayson, 1951; Harris & Lingoes, 1968; Koss & Butcher, 1973; Wiggins, 1969). Content interpretation assumes that the subject, in answering test items, is reacting and responding to the item meaning and content. Consequently, the content of MMPI items might represent an important source of information that is not available through empirical test interpretation procedures. Several approaches to interpretation of MMPI content have been developed.

The Factor-analytic Approach

Several researchers have attempted to develop keys for factor dimensions within the MMPI. Welsh (1956) and Block (1965) developed factor scales by intercorrelating the standard MMPI scales. Others (Comrey, 1957; Johnson, Butcher, Null, & Johnson, in press; Stein, 1968) attempted to factor analyze the MMPI item pool using item intercorrelations to arrive at homogeneous factor scales. While the factor analytic approach is not specifically oriented toward obtaining "pure" content dimensions, the research has produced a number of scales with homogeneous content.

The Rational Approach to Content Analysis

Several efforts to develop content scales by rational analysis have been attempted. One set of content scales, the Harris-Lingoes subscales for the MMPI (Harris & Lingoes, 1968), has become widely used in clinical and computerized MMPI interpretation. The Harris-Lingoes subscales are subsets of MMPI items on several MMPI scales: *D,Hy, Pd, Pa,SC*, and *Ma*. The subscales were developed by reading through the items and placing "similar" items into content groups. A more systematic approach to developing content scales (Wiggins, 1969) included all of the MMPI items in the pool of potential contents and developed 13 homogeneous content scales for the MMPI. These scales are: *HEA* (Health), *DEP* (Depression), *ORG* (Organic Symptoms), *FAM* (Family Problems), *AUT* (Authority Conflict), *FEM* (Feminine Interests), *REL* (Religious Fundamentalism), *HOS* (Manifest Hostility), *MOR* (Poor Morale), *PHO* (Phobias), *PSY* (Psychoticism), *HYP* (Hypomania), and *SOC* (Social Maladjustment). High

TABLE 16.1. SUMMARY OF CORRELATES OF THE MMPI VALIDITY, CLINICAL AND SELECTED SPECIAL SCALES.

MMPI SCALE	EMPIRICAL SCALE CORRELATES
Validity Scales	
?	The number of omitted items. Suggests uncooperativeness or defensiveness if over 30 items are left unanswered.
L	Measures the tendency to claim an excessive amount of virtue. High scores reflect a tendency to present an overly favorable self-image.
F	Measures the tendency to endorse rare or unusual attributes. High scores may suggest faking, confusion, disorganization or severe disturbance.
K	Measures an individual's unwillingness to disclose personal information. High scores reflect defensiveness or the individual's unrealistic view of himself or herself.
Clinical Scales	
1 (Hs)	Measures the neurotic tendency to develop or claim somatic problems. High scorers have many vague physical complaints. They are described as unhappy, complaining, demanding, hostile, and attention-seeking.
2 (D)	Low mood, low self-esteem and feelings of inadequacy are reflected in high scores on this scale. High scorers are described as shy, moody, pessimistic, despondent, over-controlled, guilt-ridden and depressed.
3 (Hy)	High scorers rely on repression and denial to manage conflict. They tend to develop physical symptoms under stress. They are described as naive, gullible, outgoing, visible, demanding, manipulative and noninsightful.
4 (Pd)	Scale 4 measures anti-social behavior such as impulsivity, poor social judgment, disregard for rules and authority, hostility, and aggressiveness. High scorers are found to be extraverted, likable, exhibitionistic, controlling and manipulative in social situations, immature, and to have difficulties in interpersonal relationships.
5 (Mf)	This scale measures sex role attitudes and behavior. High scoring males are viewed as being passive, sensitive, effeminate and as having broad interests; conflicts over heterosexual behavior are often found. High scoring females are viewed as masculine, aggressive, adventurous, and as having narrow interests.
6 (Pa)	This scale reflects characteristics such as suspiciousness, aloofness, shrewdness, and guardedness that are found among paranoid individuals. High scorers tend to be hostile, argumentative, angry, resentful and tend to externalize blame.
7 (Pt)	This scale measures anxiety, obsessive-compulsive behavior and general maladjustment. Individuals who score high on this scale are seen as tense, worried, preoccupied, and phobic. They tend to intellectualize and ruminate about problems.
8 (Sc)	High scorers on this scale have unconventional, schizoid and alienated life styles. They are withdrawn, moody, feel confused and have unusual ideas. Very high scores reflect bizarre mentation, personality disorganization, delusions and hallucinations.
9 (Ma)	High scores reflect energetic, sociable, impulsive, overly optimistic characteristics. These individuals tend to be irritable, moody, impatient and grandiose. Some evidence of mood disturbance and flight of ideas may be present in very high scoring individuals.
Si	High scores on this scale suggest social introversion. Characteristics of overcontrol, shyness, lethargy, tension, guilt proneness, and withdrawal are present for high scorers. Low scoring individuals are viewed as extraverted. They are outgoing, undercontrolled, visible, socially forward, aggressive and impulsive.
Special Scales	
A (Anxiety)	This scale marks the first factor of the MMPI and measures anxiety or general maladjustment. High scorers are tense, anxious, and lacking in self confidence.
R (Repression)	This scale marks the second major MMPI factor and measures the tendency to use repression and overcontrol to deal with anxiety. High scorers tend to avoid problems and are generally uninsightful.
Es (Ego Strength)	This scale measures the ability to withstand stress and to deal effectively with problems.
Mac (MacAndrew Alcoholism Scale)	This scale measures an individual's proneness to becoming addicted to alcohol or other substances.

scores on the content scales reflect high degrees of endorsement of the themes represented in the content scales.

The Critical Item Approach to Content Interpretation

This approach assumes that individuals disclose personal problems through their response to individual items and suggests that certain item groups are more significant than others for reflecting important problem areas. Grayson (1951) first recommended use of specific MMPI items as important sources or signs of psychopathology. The items he suggested as "critical" for the assessment of psychopathology have been referred to as the "MMPI Critical Items" and have received widespread use despite the lack of empirical verification of their validity as problem indices. More recently, Koss and Butcher (1973) and Koss, Butcher, and Hoffman (1976) have published empirically based critical items. Use of such critical items for "fleshing out" MMPI interpretations has gained wide acceptance. Although there are some problems with this interpretive approach (Koss, 1980), particularly the low reliability of single items, this content-based procedure may add considerably to the empirical method of test interpretation.

Current research and practice with the MMPI rely primarily on use of validity scales, clinical scales, content scales, and a number of *Special scales* or experimental scales. Several hundred additional scales have been developed for the MMPI, primarily for specific purposes, such as measuring characteristics like Dominance or Prejudice, or for predicting various symptom patterns such as Drug Abuse or Low Back Pain. Most of these additional scales have not attained wide use or acceptability. However, a few of the Special scales have been widely researched and used clinically to such an extent as to warrant inclusion on the new MMPI profile sheet. These "experimental" scales now included on the standard profile sheet are: The Ego Strength Scale (Es), a measure of ego strength or tolerance for stress (Barron, 1953); the Welsh Anxiety scale (A), designed as a measure of general maladjustment or anxiety (Welsh, 1956); the Welsh repression scale (R), designed as a measure of overcontrol; and the MacAndrew Alcoholism scale (Mac), a measure of an individual's proneness to addiction (MacAndrew, 1965).

Administration and Scoring of the MMPI

In most situations the MMPI is administered in a reusable booklet form (either the Group Form or Form R) with an answer sheet that can be hand or machine scored. (MMPI booklets, answer forms, scoring templates and other MMPI materials are available through National Computer Systems (NCS), P.O. Box 1416, Minneapolis, MN 55440.) Other administration formats are available for special circumstances. These include: the Box Form, in which each item is printed on a card and the subject is required to sort the cards into groups according to whether the items are True or False; the Audio Form; and the Computer Administered Version. Although there are some MMPI computer scoring programs available through commercial outlets, there is no assurance that these programs generate scores that match those in the MMPI Handbook. Unverified scores should be used only with caution.

The answer sheet can be hand scored by placing scoring templates or scoring keys on the answer form and counting the number of item responses appearing through the punched holes on the stencil. The raw scores for each scale are then transformed into T-score units (standard scores with a mean of 50 and standard deviation of 10) when they are plotted on the profile sheet (see Figure 16.1). Scale elevations above two standard deviations from the mean (a score elevated above a T-score of 70) are generally considered clinically significant.

Computer scoring of MMPI records is becoming increasingly popular. There are several approaches to computer scoring of the subject's responses. Printed answer sheets can be keypunched onto data cards or optically scanned and stored on a magnetic data tape, then entered into a scoring program. Alternatively, subject responses can be scored as the subject is taking the MMPI interactively by computer. Computer processing of MMPI records, both scoring and interpretation, will be discussed in more detail later in this paper.

Interpreting the MMPI

Initially it was thought that simple individual scale elevations would serve as direct measures of various types of psychopathology. For example, depressed patients would be expected to show

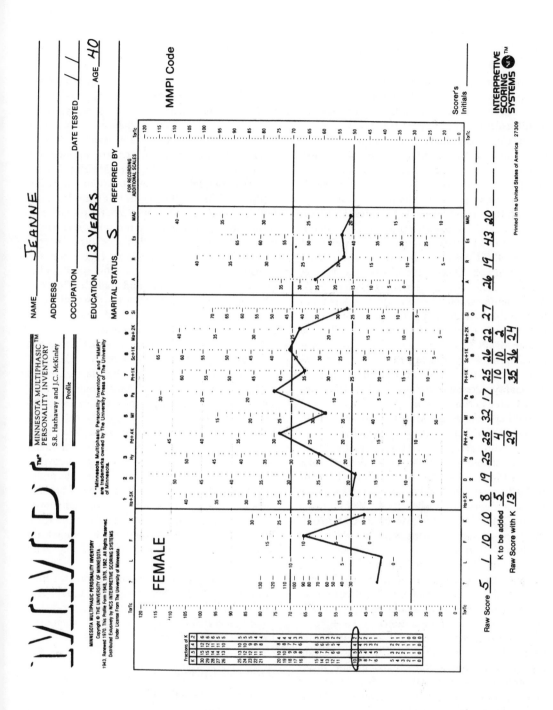

Figure 16.1. Sample MMPI profile form

313

elevations on Scale 2 (the Depression scale), but not on Scale 8 (the Schizophrenia scale). In practice, however, it was often found that several MMPI scales may be elevated together. Clinicians found that individuals with common MMPI profile patterns were similar in terms of manifest problems, symptoms, and personality characteristics. The pattern or *configural approach* to MMPI interpretation came to be the preferred interpretive strategy (Halbower, 1955; Meehl, 1954). Several subsequent research programs have delineated actuarially based empirical descriptions of various MMPI patterns referred to as *code types* (Gilberstadt & Duker, 1965; Lewandowski & Graham, 1972; Marks, Seeman, & Haller, 1974). A substantial amount of empirical research has been published detailing the descriptive and symptomatic features of patients classified by similar MMPI codes. This work serves as the empirical basis of objective MMPI profile interpretation underlying many of the computerized personality assessment systems, such as those discussed later in this chapter.

Another strategy for MMPI interpretation involves use of *objective rules* or *objective indexes* to arrive at clinical decisions. This interpretation approach can use either actuarially derived rules such as the Goldberg Index (Goldberg, 1965) or clinically compiled classification rules such as the Henrichs Rules (Henrichs, 1964, 1966) or the Meehl-Dahlstrom Rules (Meehl & Dahlstrom, 1960) for distinguishing between neurotics and psychotics. In this approach the test interpreter, after scoring the record and drawing the profile, computes the index or classifies the profile according to decision rules. The particular decision recommended by the index would be reported. For example, if the Goldberg Index (L + Pa + Sc − Hy − Pt) is greater than 45 the individual would be diagnosed as psychotic, or if the classification rules confirm that a correctional inmate meets Megargee's "I" classification in his system for grouping criminal offenders (Megargee & Bohn, 1977), then the correlates and predictions relevant to that felony group would be applied to the case. An advantage of the objective classification approach is that it can readily be applied by a clerical worker or by a computer.

Interpretation of the MMPI, whether by clinician or computer, is objective and is based on applying the established empirical correlates of the scales, code types, and test indices. The test interpreter compares the individual's profile and scale scores with the established empirical correlates of those of well-defined clinical reference groups. The personality characteristics, symptom patterns, typical problem behaviors, etc. that have been established for scale elevations or particular profile configurations are applied for "new" cases. For example, if the MMPI profile to be interpreted has prominent elevations on Scales 4 (Pd), 6 (Pa), and 9 (Ma), as in Figure 16.1, the test interpreter could refer to several possible reference sources and employ the published sets of empirical descriptions available for this code type. If the profile shown in Figure 16.1 meets the classification rules of either the Gilberstadt-Duker (1965) or Marks, Seeman, and Haller (1974) classification systems, the actuarial descriptions of clinical cases they provide could guide the test interpreter in preparing the report.

MMPI interpretation for a case such as the one presented in Figure 16.1 might also include analysis of content themes from the Harris-Lingoes MMPI subscales or the Wiggins Content scales. There have been relatively few studies establishing empirical correlates for the content scales. Thus, their interpretation is based upon rational or "intuitive" analysis of the scales by examining the "meanings" of the content dimensions reflected in the elevated scale. The interpreter might also wish to examine the content of particularly significant items endorsed by the individual. Checking the subject's endorsements of the Koss-Butcher Critical Items would provide some leads about significant problem areas to be followed up in interview.

Later in this chapter we will illustrate the integration and application of all these interpretive methods to the case in Figure 16.1, through a report generated by the senior author's computerized interpretive system.

Survey of Current MMPI Use

It is not possible in the allotted space of this chapter to provide a detailed evaluation of recent MMPI research and clinical applications. Instead, we will try to provide a brief overview of general areas of current MMPI use.

In the 6 years since Butcher and Owen (1978) published their survey of objective personality assessment, the MMPI has continued to be the most widely used and researched personality assessment instrument. There are several hundred new publications a year on the MMPI, and the number of clinical applications involving the test appears to be growing substantially. International applications of the MMPI, for example, have dramatically increased in the past 10 years. There have been over 90 foreign language translations of the MMPI (Butcher, 1984), and the test is presently being used for clinical and research purposes in many countries, including such unlikely nations as the Soviet Union (Valsiner, 1982) and China (Song, 1981), which in the past have not been open to using personality scales for individual assessment.

Even a cursory look at the current clinical literature indicates that the MMPI or one or more of its scales are used as criterion measures for clinical research on a routine basis. The instrument is often used as the standard against which other devices are compared, and many current psychotherapeutic treatment outcome studies use some aspect of the MMPI as part of their assessment strategy. Changes in MMPI indexes from pretreatment to posttreatment are often employed as measures of treatment efficacy, and many studies utilize pretreatment MMPI administrations to investigate the relationship between personality factors or level/type of psychopathology and subsequent treatment outcome.

The major areas of MMPI research reviewed by Butcher and Owen in 1978 included, among others: detection of alcohol and drug problems, use with medical patients, cross-cultural and subcultural applications, and development of various short forms and alternative forms of the instrument. These content domains have continued to attract research interest. In particular, alcohol and drug abuse have been heavily researched. Much of the work continues to center on validation of the MacAndrew scale across diverse populations, although many other scales and strategies for differentiating alcoholics and/or drug addicts from various other groups are reported and sometimes compared to the MAC scale. The search continues for useful MMPI typologies to identify subgroups of chemical abusers sharing common treatment-relevant characteristics.

The current research on alcoholism is illustrative of a trend that can be seen across all the areas of MMPI research: namely, the growing concern with demographic/cultural differences that might modify the validity of MMPI predictors. Many of the research reports we saw were investigations of the generalizability of MMPI scales or typologies to different socioeconomic classes, ethnic groups,

and to other nationalities, as well as across age and sex.

The MMPI has been heavily used and researched in the medical field, particularly in investigating the psychogenic component of such problem areas as chronic pain, asthma, coronary heart disease, and even cancer. Studies include attempts at discovering personality types prone to develop certain conditions, as well as differentiating groups that may require different treatment strategies. The latter approach, used in applications such as predicting surgery outcome for chronic pain patients, is aimed at identifying subgroups of patients suffering from a particular physical disorder who share a common etiology, particularly separating functional versus organic causes. The MMPI has also been used to predict treatment outcome for other problems commonly encountered in behavioral medicine, such as obesity, anorexia, bulimia, smoking, and sexual dysfunction. Interestingly, there were quite a few studies in the last several years on the pre-post psychological adjustment of patients undergoing transsexual surgery.

Short forms of the MMPI continue to be widely used in the clinical literature as criterion measures of psychological functioning, despite the general lack of external validity data justifying their use as equivalent forms of the MMPI. Most of the studies we examined still evaluated the validity of short forms through correlations with long form scores, rather than looking at whether similar clinical decisions would be made based on the results of short versus long forms. Computerized forms of the MMPI were utilized in a few studies, but in general the research on validity of automated systems was scanty in our sample.

Research on MMPI use in forensic settings has burgeoned in the last few years. Typological systems and special scales have been developed to predict recidivism, assess potential aggressiveness, and judge the legal competence of felons. Prediction of institutional adjustment using the Megargee classification of personality types has received some further validational work, and other scales and configural rules have been researched as descriptors of major subtypes within the "criminal personality." In a somewhat related area, there were several reports on the utility of the MMPI as a screening device for police applicants.

The research and clinical areas mentioned above provide a sample of the broad and varied current uses of the MMPI. Many more specific studies were reported. Other topic areas such as adolescent adjustment, family problems, relationship of MMPI indices to other psychometric data, and prediction of response to psychopharmacologic treatment are too numerous to mention in this brief survey.

Problems with the MMPI

In their overview of recent developments in the use of the MMPI, Butcher and Owen (1978) noted a number of problems and criticisms of the MMPI. Some of these problems involved the test itself and centered around the apparent need for a revision and restandardization of the inventory. Butcher and Owen called for updating and broadening the MMPI item pool, as well as restandardizing the test on a broader, more representative contemporary normal sample. Other problems involved the failure of the test distributor to keep up with the existing MMPI technology and to provide necessary new interpretive materials that have been developed for the MMPI.

Since that review, a number of changes have taken place in the publication and distribution of the MMPI that may serve to rectify some of these problems. The major administrative change was that the University of Minnesota Press, the MMPI copyright holder, resumed responsibility for research and development of the instrument. The University Press has contracted with the National Computer Systems of Minneapolis to be the licensed distributor of the MMPI and to develop new profile sheets, scoring sheets, and other MMPI related materials to enhance clinical use of the test. The profile form illustrated in Figure 16.1 is an example of these updated materials, incorporating the four well-researched scales *Es*, *A*, *R*, and *MAC* as well as the standard validity and clinical scales that appeared on the old form.

New Standardization of the MMPI

Future plans for the MMPI include a new test restandardization initiated by the University of Minnesota Press and begun in 1983. The University Press will also encourage and sponsor continuing international test research and development. Redevelopment and restandardization will be designed to eliminate some of the difficulties noted above. For example, the item pool has been broadened to include other important clinical problems and personality factors in the test. Some of the goals of the redevelopment project for the MMPI are:

1. To maintain the integrity of the existing validity, clinical, and widely used special scales of the test;
2. To broaden the item pool to include other contents not represented in the original version, for example, treatment compliance, amenability to change, relationship problems, and so on;
3. To revise and reword the language of some of the existing items that are out of date, awkward, or sexist;
4. To develop new, up-to-date norms to replace those based on the "Minnesota normals" of 40 years ago. Regional normative samples collected in West Virginia by Diehl (1977) and in southern Minnesota by Colligan, Osborne, Swenson, and Offord (1984) have indicated that the old norms are probably not representative of response patterns of contemporary "normal" people, but no nationwide standardization has ever been undertaken. Data collection for the University Press' restandardization includes a broad national sample selected to be representative of the U.S. population characteristics reported in the 1980 census;
5. To include separate forms of the MMPI for adults and adolescents. New items will be included for the adolescent form of the MMPI that are specific to problems of adolescents.

Comments

MMPI scale development and interpretive strategies have increasingly incorporated methods, such as content analysis and factor analysis, that range far from the test's original strict empirical-criterion-keyed roots. However, the rationale for inclusion of these new methods, as well as the rationale for revision of the MMPI, remains the same: to provide a more efficient, accurate, reliable, and valid tool to aid psychologists in practical decision making. Many of the new developments with the MMPI, as well as with other assessment devices, would not have been possible without the aid of another tool: the computer. The last section of our chapter will focus on the role of automation in the contemporary status and the future direction of objective personality assessment.

AUTOMATED PERSONALITY ASSESSMENT

Greist and Klein (1981) reported that although 70% of state departments of mental health and 50% of community mental health centers use computers, very few of these employ them for clinical uses. Instead, computer technology has been introduced into these settings to meet management needs for information on resources, materials, facilities, staff, finances, patient population characteristics, and services provided. Traditionally, administrative and fiscal operations have been seen as much more amenable to automation than the less well-understood, less structured, and less specific techniques of clinical practice. Nevertheless, computers have been utilized as tools for assistance in clinical as well as administrative decision making.

Johnson, Giannetti, and Williams (1976) described the history of computer use in mental health care delivery as a progression from (a) automated patient data systems, to (b) development of automated clinical techniques, to (c) the development of interventionally relevant, decision-oriented strategies. Early computer applications, such as patient data management, test scoring, and interpretive programs designed to mimic traditional clinical practice, capitalized mainly on the speed, objectivity, and enormous memory capacity of the computer. More recent innovative applications have begun to utilize the flexibility and unique adaptive capabilities of computers, modifying old assessment strategies and developing new ones.

Automated Test Scoring and Interpretation

Automated scoring of objective test answer sheets was one of the first clinical applications of computer technology, followed by computerized interpretation of standard psychological tests. Objective inventories such as the MMPI are particularly amenable to automation because of their limited and structured response options and the standardized nature of interpretive rules for these tests. The computer can store and access a much larger fund of interpretive literature and base rate data than any individual clinician could master, contributing to the accuracy, objectivity, and validity of computerized reports.

Rome, Swenson, and colleagues at the Mayo Clinic developed the first computerized scoring and interpretive system for the MMPI (Rome, Swenson, Mataya, McCarthy, Pearson, Keating, & Hathaway, 1962). Since that time, their system has been expanded, and other more complicated computerized MMPI interpretive systems have been developed. At least seven computerized MMPI interpretive systems were commercially available in 1978 when Adair and Butcher provided reviews of automated MMPI assessment for Buros' *Eighth Mental Measurements Yearbook* (Adair, 1978; Butcher, 1978).

Figures 16.2 and 16.3 present the case description and an example of a computer generated report for the woman whose MMPI profile follows. This particular automated system, the Minnesota Report (National Computer Systems, 1982), is one of the newest commercially available computerized scoring and interpretive program. It incorporates all of the interpretive strategies described earlier in this chapter, including code type and individual scale interpretation, content analysis using the Wiggins scales, and utilization of well-researched special scales. Profiles are plotted for the standard validity and clinical scales and for the special scales included in the interpretation. Indexes and decision rules such as the Goldberg Index and Henrichs Rules are reported, along with a list of the Koss-Butcher Critical Items the client endorsed. The computer program tailors interpretive statements according to the subject's population (mental health outpatient or inpatient, medical, adult correctional, personnel, or college counseling) and according to demographic data such as education, marital status, and ethnicity, which research has shown to be modifiers of interpretive rules.

Many other assessment instruments have also been automated, including psychiatric screening devices and both intellectual and personality tests. Evidence has accumulated that even less structured and seemingly less computer-adaptable tests might be amenable to automation. For example, Piotrowski (1980) recently presented "a system of automated interpretation of coded visual-motor responses elicited by horizontally symmetrical, ambiguous, and indeterminate visual stimuli, i.e. by the ten Rorschach inkblots" (p. 85). Morf, Alexander, and Feurth (1981) developed an automated version of the Picture Preference Test employing visual stimuli to predict diagnosis.

On-line Assessment Using
Standard Clinical Techniques

Although most automated testing systems have merely scored and interpreted test forms that were hand-administered, the computer is increasingly being utilized as test administrator as well. Lushene, O'Neil, and Dunn (1974) first described an on-line MMPI administration, scoring, and interpretive system, and several large clinical settings, such as the Salt Lake City VA (Johnson & Williams, 1980), now routinely use computer-administered assessment devices including the MMPI. *Teleprocessing of test responses* is possible through scoring services such as those offered by National Computer Systems. Users can enter subjects' test responses into a remote terminal and have the data transmitted to the central scoring service via regular phone lines, receiving almost instant turn-around on the test results. Alternatively, the test can be administered directly

to the subject via the terminal and her or his responses can be sent to the scoring service without the need for an intermediary data entry step.

According to Johnson, Giannetti, and Williams' review (1976), "automation has been applied to such psychiatric techniques as the psychiatric examination, diagnostic decisionmaking, and computer-conducted patient interviewing" (p. 85). Notable in this field is the work by Spitzer and Endicott of the New York State Psychiatric Institute, who have developed a series of DIAGNO computer programs that generate psychiatric diagnoses from structured interview data (Spitzer & Endicott, 1969, 1974). Although their schedule is completed by a mental health worker who then enters the data into the computer, other systems have utilized direct data collection through the patient's interaction with an on-line terminal. Erdman and colleagues reviewed 21 studies of computerized patient interviews and concluded that they are "reliable,

Case Description

Jeanne, a 40-year-old woman employed as an office machine mechanic, was self-referred for a psychological evaluation. She expressed concern that her memory and intellectual functioning had been deteriorating since a motorcycle accident a year and a half ago. She had left a party after smoking marijuana and having a number of drinks, and drove her motorcycle into another vehicle. She was knocked unconscious for about a half an hour and suffered a broken leg and abrasions on her head. Jeanne wondered if her accident had caused permanent brain damage.

Jeanne was an attractive, slight woman who came to the interview dressed in a demin jacket and jeans. She was extremely open in presenting her life history and approached the assessment in an unguarded manner.

In interview she reported a long history of personal and legal difficulties that dated back to the 1960s when she was a "flower child" in Califoria. During that period she was a heavy user of LSD, marijuana and other drugs and had experienced a number of difficult life circumstances. She had been divorced three times and had four children whom she had given up for adoption. She had an extensive court record, mostly for petty crimes such as shoplifting and drug-related offenses. Her most serious legal problem involved a charge of drug dealing, for which she had received a suspended sentence. At the time of evaluation Jeanne was having difficulties in her job, which she had held for five years. Her supervisor apparently did not trust her and checked up on her constantly, "following her around." Jeanne was receiving poor performance ratings because she was considered unreliable.

For the past 20 years Jeanne had been a member of several motorcycle gangs, and in interview she said that she considered herself a confirmed "biker" and would probably never give it up. During the period of her psychological evaluation Jeanne failed to show up for one of her sessions because, as she explained latter, she met a guy (a truck driver) who she liked and they took off for the weekend together.

On intellectual, memory and construction tasks Jeanne performed at a high level of ability. Her Wechsler Adult Intelligence Scale (WAIS) Verbal IQ was 135 and her Performance IQ was 135. Her Full Scale WAIS IQ was 135. Jeanne's performance on the Wechsler Memory Scale and the Bender-Gestalt Visual Motor Test was excellent; she showed no evidence of intellectual impairment as measured by these instruments.

Figure 16.2.

THE MINNESOTA REPORT ^{TM*} Page 1

for the Minnesota Multiphasic Personality Inventory ^{TM}: Adult System

By James N. Butcher, Ph.D.

Client No. : 98765432101   Gender : Female
Setting : Medical   Age :   40
Report Date : 1-NOV-83
ISS Code Number : 00021987 002 0002

PROFILE VALIDITY

    This is a valid MMPI profile. The client's responses to the MMPI
validity items suggest that she cooperated with the evaluation enough to
provide useful interpretive information. The resulting clinical profile is
an adequate indication of her present personality functioning.

SYMPTOMATIC PATTERN

    Individuals with this MMPI profile tend to be chronically maladjusted.
Narcissistic and rather self-indulgent, the client is somewhat dependent
and demands attention from others. She appears to be rather hostile and
irritable and tends to resent others.

    She has great trouble showing anger and may express it in
passive-agressive ways. She may have a problem with acting-out behavior
and may have experienced difficulty with her sexual behavior in the past.
She tends to blame her own difficulties on others and refuses to accept
responsibility for her own problems.

    Her response content also suggests that she may feel somewhat estranged
from people--somewhat alienated and concerned over the actions of others--
and may blame others for her negative frame of mind. She views the world
as a threatening place, sees herself as having been unjustly blamed for
others' problems, and feels that she is getting a raw deal out of life.
These characteristics are reflected in the content of her responses. The
items she endorsed include content suggesting that her thinking is confused
and bizarre. She feels that others do not understand her and are trying to
control her . She is also tending toward withdrawal into a world of
fantasy.

INTERPERSONAL RELATIONS

    She is experiencing great difficulty in her social relationships, and
feels that others do not understand her and do not give her enough
sympathy. She is somewhat aloof, cold, non-giving, and uncompromising, and
attempts to advance herself at the expense of others. Her lack of trust
may prevent her from developing warm, close relationships.

BEHAVIORAL STABILITY

    This profile reflects a pattern of long-standing poor adjustment. Her
anger may produce periods of intense interpersonal difficulty.

DIAGNOSTIC CONSIDERATIONS

NOTE: This MMPI interpretation can serve as a useful source of hypotheses
about clients. This report is based on objectively derived scale indexes
and scale interpretations that have been developed in diverse groups of
patients. The personality descriptions, inferences and recommendations
contained herein need to be verified by other sources of clinical
information since individual clients may not fully match the prototype.
The information in this report should most appropriately be used by a
trained, qualified test interpreter. The information contained in this
report should be considered confidential.

Figure 16.3. Sample MMPI Automated Interpretive Report

Client No. : 98765432101   Report Date :   1-NOV-83   Page   2

     An individual with this profile is usually viewed as having a
Personality Disorder, such as a Passive-Aggressive or Paranoid Personality.
The possibility of a Paranoid Disorder should be considered, however.

TREATMENT CONSIDERATIONS

     Individuals with this profile tend not to seek psychological treatment
on their own, and they are usually not good candidates for psychotherapy.
They resist psychological interpretation, argue, and tend to rationalize
and to blame others for their problems. In addition, they frequently leave
therapy prematurely.

THE MINNESOTA REPORT   Page 3

for the Minnesota Multiphasic Personality Inventory : Adult System

By James N. Butcher, Ph.D.

CLINICAL PROFILE

Client No. : 98765432101   Gender : Female
Setting : Medical   Age :   40
Report Date : 1-NOV-83

| | 1 | 2 | 3 | 4 | 5 | 6 | 7 | 8 | 9 | 0 |
| ? L F K | Hs | D | Hy | Pd | Mf | Pa | Pt | Sc | Ma | Si |

(Clinical profile graph, T-scores 30–110)

Clinical Profile Scores:

	?	L	F	K	Hs	D	Hy	Pd	Mf	Pa	Pt	Sc	Ma	Si
					1	2	3	4	5	6	7	8	9	0
Raw	5	1	10	10	8	19	25	25	32	17	25	26	22	27
K-Correction					5			4			10	10	2	
T	41	40	66	46	50	49	61	74	59	76	66	71	68	52

Percent True :   46   F - K (Raw)   :   0

Profile Elevation :   64.4
(Hs,D,Hy,Pd,Pa,Pt,Sc,Ma)

Welsh Code :   648'973-501/2:   F-K?L:

The Minnesota Multiphasic Personality Inventory
SUPPLEMENTAL PROFILE
Client No. : 98765432101   Report Date :   1-NOV-83   Page   4

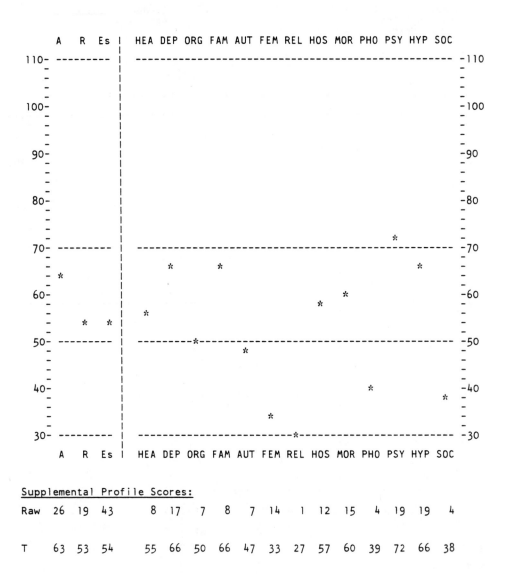

Supplemental Profile Scores:

	A	R	Es	HEA	DEP	ORG	FAM	AUT	FEM	REL	HOS	MOR	PHO	PSY	HYP	SOC
Raw	26	19	43	8	17	7	8	7	14	1	12	15	4	19	19	4
T	63	53	54	55	66	50	66	47	33	27	57	60	39	72	66	38

The Minnesota Multiphasic Personality Inventory

EXTENDED SCORE REPORT

Client No. : 98765432101   Report Date : 1-NOV-83   Page 5

Supplementary Scales:	Raw Score	T Score
Dependency (Dy)	31	57
Dominance (Do)	19	62
Responsibility (Re)	19	43
Control (Cn)	31	64
College Maladjustment (Mt)	24	63
Overcontrolled Hostility (O-H)	10	37
Prejudice (Pr)	13	52
Manifest Anxiety (MAS)	22	60
MacAndrew Addiction (MAC)	20	51
Social Status (St)	23	62

Depression Subscales (Harris-Lingoes):		
Subjective Depression (D1)	8	49
Psychomotor Retardation (D2)	4	40
Physical Malfunctioning (D3)	4	55
Mental Dullness (D4)	6	68
Brooding (D5)	3	50

Hysteria Subscales (Harris-Lingoes):		
Denial of Social Anxiety (Hy1)	5	59
Need for Affection (Hy2)	4	47
Lassitude-Malaise (Hy3)	7	67
Somatic Complaints (Hy4)	2	43
Inhibition of Aggression (Hy5)	4	54

Psychopathic Deviate Subscales (Harris-Lingoes):		
Familial Discord (Pd1)	3	57
Authority Problems (Pd2)	7	76
Social Imperturbability (Pd3)	9	58
Social Alienation (Pd4a)	15	85
Self Alienation (Pd4b)	10	74

Masculinity-Femininity Subscales (Serkownek):		
Narcissism-Hypersensitivity (Mf1)	11	75
Stereotypic Feminine Interests (Mf2)	4	24
Denial of Stereo. Masculine Interests (Mf3)	7	58
Heterosexual Discomfort-Passivity (Mf4)	1	23
Introspective-Critical (Mf5)	4	55
Socially Retiring (Mf6)	4	44

Paranoia Subscales (Harris-Lingoes):		
Persecutory Ideas (Pa1)	7	75
Poignancy (Pa2)	5	69
Naivete (Pa3)	3	47

Schizophrenia Subscales (Harris-Lingoes):		
Social Alienation (Sc1a)	7	64
Emotional Alienation (Sc1b)	2	50
Lack of Ego Mastery, Cognitive (Sc2a)	4	66
Lack of Ego Mastery, Conative (Sc2b)	4	59
Lack of Ego Mastery, Def. Inhib. (Sc2c)	3	58
Bizarre Sensory Experiences (Sc3)	4	55

Hypomania Subscales (Harris-Lingoes):		
Amorality (Ma1)	1	47
Psychomotor Acceleration (Ma2)	10	92
Imperturbability (Ma3)	3	51
Ego Inflation (Ma4)	5	64

Social Introversion Subscales (Serkownek):		
Inferiority-Personal Discomfort (Si1)	11	59
Discomfort with Others (Si2)	2	35
Staid-Personal Rigidity (Si3)	7	29
Hypersensitivity (Si4)	3	42
Distrust (Si5)	7	66
Physical-Somatic Concerns (Si6)	3	60

The Minnesota Multiphasic Personality Inventory

CRITICAL ITEM LISTING

Client No. : 98765432101   Report Date : 1-NOV-83   Page 6

        The following Critical Items have been found to have possible
significance in analyzing a client's problem situation. Although these
items may serve as a source of hypotheses for further investigation,
caution should be taken in interpreting individual items because they may
have been inadvertently checked. Critical item numbers refer to The
Group Form test booklet. Corresponding item numbers for Form R (only
items 367-566 differ) can be found in the MMPI "Manual" or Volume I of
"An MMPI Handbook." Corresponding item numbers for the Roche Testbook
can be found in "The Clinical Use of the Automated MMPI."

ACUTE ANXIETY STATE   (Koss-Butcher Critical Items)

    3.   I wake up fresh and rested most mornings. (F)
   13.   I work under a great deal of tension. (T)
   72.   I am troubled by discomfort in the pit of my stomach every
         few days or oftener. (T)
  238.   I have periods of such great restlessness that I cannot sit
         long in a chair. (T)
  337.   I feel anxiety about something or someone almost all the time.
         (T)
  543.   Several times a week I feel that something dreadful is about
         to happen. (T)
  555.   I sometimes feel that I am about to go to pieces. (T)

DEPRESSED SUICIDAL IDEATION   (Koss-Butcher Critical Items)

   41.   I have had periods of days, weeks, or months when I couldn't take care
         of things because I couldn't "get going". (T)
   76.   Most of the time I feel blue. (T)
   84.   These days I find it hard not to give up hope of amounting to
         something. (T)
  107.   I am happy most of the time. (F)
  259.   I have difficulty in starting to do things. (T)
  301.   Life is a strain for me much of the time. (T)
  379.   I very seldom have spells of the blues. (F)
  526.   The future seems hopeless to me. (T)

THREATENED ASSAULT   (Koss-Butcher Critical Items)

   39.   At times I feel like smashing things. (T)
   97.   At times I have a strong urge to do something harmful
         or shocking. (T)
  145.   At times I feel like picking a fist fight with someone. (T)
  234.   I get mad easily and then get over it soon. (T)
  381.   I am often said to be hotheaded. (T)

MENTAL CONFUSION   (Koss-Butcher Critical Items)

   33.   I have had very peculiar and strange experiences. (T)
   50.   My soul sometimes leaves my body. (T)
   66.   I see things or animals or people around me that others
         do not see. (T)
  345.   I often feel as if things were not real. (T)

PERSECUTORY IDEAS   (Koss-Butcher Critical Items)

   16.   I am sure I get a raw deal from life. (T)
   35.   If people had not had it in for me I would have been much more
         successful. (T)
  110.   Someone has it in for me. (T)
  121.   I believe I am being plotted against. (T)
  278.   I have often felt that strangers were looking at me
         critically. (T)
  284.   I am sure I am being talked about. (T)

CHARACTEROLOGICAL ADJUSTMENT -- ANTISOCIAL ATTITUDE
(Lachar-Wrobel Critical Items)

38. During one period when I was a youngster, I engaged in
     petty thievery. (T)
118. In school I was sometimes sent to the principal for cutting
     up. (T)

CHARACTEROLOGICAL ADJUSTMENT -- FAMILY CONFLICT
(Lachar-Wrobel Critical Items)

21. At times I have very much wanted to leave home. (T)

SEXUAL CONCERN AND DEVIATION (Lachar-Wrobel Critical Items)

37. I have never been in trouble because of my sex behavior. (F)
74. I have often wished I were a girl.(Or if you are a girl) I have
     never been sorry that I am a girl. (T-Males, F-Females)
133. I have never indulged in any unusual sex practices. (F)
179. I am worried about sex matters. (T)

SOMATIC SYMPTOMS (Lachar-Wrobel Critical Items)

55. I am almost never bothered by pains over the heart or in my
     chest. (F)
62. Parts of my body often have feelings like burning, tingling,
     crawling, or like "going to sleep." (T)
72. I am troubled by discomfort in the pit of my stomach every few
     days or oftener. (T)
281. I do not often notice my ears ringing or buzzing. (F)
330. I have never been paralyzed or had any unusual weakness of any
     of my muscles. (F)
544. I feel tired a good deal of the time. (T)

NCS Interpretive Scoring Systems P.O. Box 1416, Mpls, MN 55440

MINNESOTA MULTIPHASIC PERSONALITY INVENTORY
Copyright THE UNIVERSITY OF MINNESOTA
1943, Renewed 1970. This Report 1982. All rights reserved.
Scored and Distributed Exclusively by NCS INTERPRETIVE SCORING SYSTEMS
Under License From The University of Minnesota

accurate, and highly acceptable to most patients"
(Erdman, Greist, Klein, Jefferson, & Getto, 1981,
p. 394). In general, concerns about the imper-
sonality of such interactions have not proved to be
justified; reports show that patients usually enjoy
the process and have often revealed *more* sensitive
data to a computer than to a human interviewer
(Greist & Klein, 1980, 1981; Johnson & Williams,
1980; Space, 1981).

Applications such as these and the many others
described in the contemporary literature illustrate
automated technology's potential for streamlining
traditional procedures. Computers can increase
the accuracy and reliability of standardized administration, data collection, data storage, and
application of objective decision rules. However,
on-line technology also offers the possibility of
more innovative uses than simply duplicating existing manual procedures. Some new uses include
programming computers to mimic the human
judgmental process and using the computer's capabilities for dynamic, branched, adaptive systems of analysis to improve human decision
making in applied settings.

Dynamic, Adaptive Assessment Strategies

Although Holtzman (1960) claimed that the clinician's uniquely human adaptive, creative, and
intuitive judgment could never be reproduced by
a machine, Kleinmuntz and McLean (1968) listed
flexibility as one of the three main advantages of a
computer, along with speed and objectivity. According to them, "the ability of the computer to
alter its activity as the result of the environment in
which it is working is its greatest strength" (p. 75).
In the case of an on-line test administration or
interview, the computer can be programmed to
choose one of several alternative content areas as a
function of an individual's prior responses, much
as a human interviewer would. Such a capability
could be very useful in psychiatric screening, both
in tailoring specific assessment devices to maximize information about particular patients and
in adapting a standardized interview sequence to
the characteristics and needs of the individual
subject. In addition, the flexibility and perfect
memory of the computer make it possible for it to
evaluate its own performance according to specified criteria and modify subsequent decisions
and actions accordingly.

Branched Interviews

Most of the work utilizing flexible assessment
strategies has involved adaptive interview strategies. The growing utilization of large automated
patient data systems requires collection of great
quantities of information on each individual, but
administration of the same lengthy interview
schedule to every subject may often be a wasteful
and inefficient procedure. Certain responses make
other questions inappropriate or, on the other
hand, may indicate the need for more detailed
questioning in specific topic areas. For example,
asking an unemployed patient a series of questions
relating to job performance would be an inefficient use of patient and interviewer time.

Several automated interview systems have been
designed to deal with these problems. Stillman,
Roth, Colby, and Rosenbaum (1969) described
one of the first on-line psychiatric inventories, the
Computer-Assisted Special Enquirer (CASE) developed at Stanford. The clinician entered interview questions and branching options into a
terminal, using both multiple choice and narrative format items. This interview network was
then presented to patients via an on-line terminal.
Any particular patient received only about 50%
of the total item pool due to the branching options. A computer-generated report indicated to
the clinician which items were presented and
what the responses to these were.

The extensive patient data systems in use at the
University of Wisconsin and at the Salt Lake City
VA also employ branched strategies to good advantage. For example, Greist and Klein (1980) at
Wisconsin have described adaptive administration of their computerized Social Adjustment Interview, which collects patient history
information and evaluates current role functioning. Detailed questions later in the interview are
conditioned upon earlier answers to a standard set
of initial demographic items and the patient's
choice of "two areas that are most involved in
your problems right now" (p. 165). Although the
interview as a whole consists of more than 650
questions, the average unmarried patient is likely
to be presented with only about 150 of these
items.

Adaptive Test Administration

Adaptive administration of objective personality
tests is not as well researched as flexible interview

strategies. Although theoretically the branching ability of the computer could make it possible to produce personality tests "tailored to each individual's needs and abilities" (Patience, 1977), thus far such adaptive testing strategies have been primarily utilized in achievement and ability testing (English, Reckase, & Patience, 1977; Vale & Weiss, 1975; Weiss, 1973). Whether the psychometric assumptions underlying adaptive ability testing can be met by personality measures may be questionable, especially for tests with such internally heterogeneous scales as the MMPI. However, the basic strategy of providing an individually tailored test seems to be transferable to personality assessment. For example, Kleinmuntz and McLean (1968) presented a model for a branched, interactive computerized MMPI short form. Their program presented the subject with a subset of 5 items from each of the 15 scales to be estimated, on the basis of which a T-score was computed for each scale. Additional items were administered only for those scales that could not be clearly classified as "normal" or "abnormal" based on these T-scores, and the test ended when all scales could be so classified. Kleinmuntz and McLean's system cut the MMPI administration time drastically, but the correlations of their scale scores with the long form scores were not impressive.

Clavelle and Butcher (1977) utilized an adaptive typological approach to predict MMPI code type membership, rather than estimating long form scale scores as Kleinmuntz and McLean had done. Hoffman and Butcher (1975) had pointed out that even though good prediction of long form scale elevations could be achieved by several popular MMPI short forms, the congruence between code type classification based on the two forms was generally too low to be useful for practical clinical decision making. They suggested that instead of attempting to predict long form scale elevations, "a more fruitful clinical approach might be to use multivariate techniques, such as the discriminant function, to select a small subset of items for direct prediction of selected criteria or for specific decision problems" (p. 38).

Clavelle and Butcher implemented this suggestion by examining item responses for a large group of outpatients whose MMPI profiles fell into one of nine selected code type groups. Sixty-nine items that showed significant differences in endorsement frequency between these groups were used

as predictor variables in a stepwise multiple discriminant function analysis with code type as the criterion. Accuracy of classification was assessed after administration of each block of 10 items. Results showed that classification accuracy tended to reach an asymptotic level after administration of a relatively small number of items, and in addition, certain blocks of code types tended to form higher order groups that were retained or excluded together. Clavelle and Butcher concluded that:

> Rather than continue with the administration of items of increasingly dubious discriminant value, it seems that a more efficient strategy would be to branch out to another set of items capable of providing the most additional information pertinent to a differentiation among the remaining code types. (p. 857)

Very few other studies have examined the utility of applying adaptive strategies to traditional personality assessment devices. Some notable preliminary efforts in this area include a dissertation by Sapinkopf (1977) examining the application of Weiss' tailored testing techniques to estimation of CPI scale scores, a report by Lyons and Brown (1981) of a computer algorithm for predicting MMPI scale scores from an individually tailored short form, and an adaptive version of the Picture Preference Test developed by Morf, Alexander, and Fuerth (1981).

Development of New Assessment Strategies

In their description of the comprehensive automated Patient Assessment Unit (PAU) presently in use at the Salt Lake City VA, Johnson, Giannetti, and Williams (1979) noted that automation of standard clinical techniques does not take full advantage of the computer's capabilities and data bank. Accordingly, they attempted to construct a new inventory specifically designed for the computer. They took all the items in the PAU data base (approximately 2,500 questions based on a battery of standardized tests that required from 5 to 7 hours to administer) and had expert clinicians rationally categorize them into content areas. They also took suggestions for items to be added for under-represented content areas, and deleted redundant or over-repeated questions. The full question list was then administered to normal and psychiatric samples, and factor analysis was used to extract the empirical factors within each content domain. Only the items with the highest loadings on these factors were retained in the item pool. Johnson's group also added demographic and historical items at the beginning of the test as a basis for branching through the rest of the item pool and empirically derived a dissimulation index to check on response validity. The preliminary verison of the Psychological Systems Questionnaire (PSQ) consisted of 24 multiple choice demographic and branching items, 18 true-false dissimulation index items, and 729 true-false items that were scored on several factor-analytically derived scales.

Although the PSQ is still in a developmental stage, several aspects of its functioning illustrate the tremendous future potential of interactive computer assessment. First, the demographic items at the beginning save time by allowing elimination of later items that are irrelevant or inappropriate. Second, the computer's ongoing computational ability allows it to continually calculate the individual's current standing on each scale throughout the entire test administration and to respond appropriately. For example,

> When a respondent is found to have scored high on a particular scale, he/she is asked for comments . . . the computer might say, 'Mr. Jones, your test responses seem to indicate that you are very depressed. Would you care to make any comments about this?' These comments are then taken free-form from the typewritten keyboard. (Johnson, Giannetti, & Williams, 1979, p. 259)

This continuous scale-scoring ability may prove to be particularly useful in evaluating the validity of the patient's responses to the interactive self-report questionnaire. The PSQ program will print out cautionary reminders to the subject if the dissimulation index is getting high. If the response pattern seems completely invalid, the computer will terminate the test prematurely. Stout (1981) reports an even more sophisticated use of computer capabilities in ongoing evaluation of response validity. He suggests incorporation of ancillary data such as response latencies and key pressure into the computer's decision scheme. If certain latency patterns are found to be reliable indicators of invalidity or other unusual testing

events, the computer could respond to these patterns appropriately. Stout lists examples, such as sudden high-speed responding as an indicator of randomness or progressively longer response latencies as an indicator of fatigue. The computer could respond to such patterns either passively by marking potentially invalid responses or actively by recommending a rest break, encouraging better cooperation and then readministering items, inserting extra items to check on the validity of earlier ones, switching to an alternate form more appropriate for the subject's capabilities, or signaling to a human examiner that something is amiss in the testing situation.

Finally, one of the most important advantages of computerized testing systems, such as the prototypal PSQ, is the computer's ability to utilize empirical data to modify its decision rules. If the computer is provided with information on the accuracy and utility of its decisions, it could be programmed to continually evaluate the relative contribution of particular items, actuarial formulas, and so on, and drop or add variables and decision rules as appropriate. Computer systems will be ideal "testing grounds" for new measures and assessment strategies (Giannetti, Klingler, Johnson, & Williams, 1976).

SUMMARY

D.J. Smail (1971) criticized what he saw as psychology's infatuation with technology by commenting that

> by becoming dazzled by statistical sophistication and technological efficiency, he [the psychologist] may forget to question the basis of his science and the ultimate purpose of his actions. In consequence he stands in danger of building around him an artificial world which, although possibly beautifully efficient within its own boundaries and elegant in its design, may bear no relation to anything that matters. (p. 173)

This review has attempted to show that, despite Smail's claims, personality assessment technology can and does have relevance to many things that matter. We pointed out at the beginning of this chapter that the value of technology lines in its utility as a tool to achieve valued goals. The extensive research and clinical literature on objective tests such as the MMPI attests to the practical value of these tools for contemporary psychological applications. Future developments, including new test construction methods and the increasing use of computer technology, will have to face the same empirical tests as have made or broken past assessment strategies. However, we believe that objective tests and their logical extension, automated methods, will play a major, successful role in the future of personality assessment technology.

REFERENCES

Adair, L.F. (1978). Review of MMPI computer services. In O. Buros (Ed.), *Eighth mental measurements yearbook*. Highland Park, NJ: Gryphon Press.

Anastasi, A. (1976). *Psychological testing* (4th ed.). New York: Macmillan.

Barron, F. (1953). An ego-strength scale which predicts response to psychotherapy. *Journal of Consulting Psychology*, 17, 327–333.

Block, J. (1965). *The challenge of response sets: Unconfounding meaning, acquiescence, and social desirability in the MMPI*. New York: Appleton-Century-Crofts.

Butcher, J.N. (1978). Present status of computerized MMPI reporting services. Review in O. Buros (Ed.), *Eighth mental measurements yearbook*. Highland Park, NJ: Gryphon Press.

Butcher, J.N. (1984). Current developments in MMPI use: An international perspective. In J.N. Butcher & C.D. Spielberger (Eds.), *Advances in personality assessment* (Vol. 4). Hillsdale, NJ: Erlbaum.

Butcher, J.N., & Owen, P.L. (1978). Objective personality inventories: Recent research and some contemporary issues. In B. Wolman (Ed.), *Handbook of clinical diagnosis of mental disorders*. New York: Plenum.

Cattell, R.B., Eber, H.W., & Tatsuoka, M.M. (1970). *Handbook for the Sixteen Personality Factor Questionnaire (16PF)*. Champaign, IL: Institute for Personality and Ability Testing.

Clavelle, P.R., & Butcher, J.N. (1976). An adaptive typological approach to psychiatric screening. *Journal of Consulting and Clinical Psychology*, 45, 851–859.

Colligan, R.C., Osborne, D., Swenson, W.M., & Offord, K.P. (1984). *The MMPI: A contemporary normative study*. New York: Praeger.

Comrey, A.L. (1957). Factors in the items of the MMPI. *American Psychologist*, 12, 437.

Diehl, L.A. (1977). The relationship between demographic factors, MMPI scores and the social readjustment rating scale. *Dissertation Abstracts Interntional*, 38 (5-B), 2360.

English, R.A., Reckase, M.D., & Patience, W.M. (1977). Application of tailored testing to achievement measurement. *Behavior Research Methods and Instrumentation*, 9, 158–161.

Erdman, H.P., Greist, J.J., Klein, M.H., Jefferson, J.W., & Getto, C. (1981). The computer psychiatrist: How far have we come? Where are we heading? How far dare we go? *Behavior Research Methods and Instrumentation*, 13, 393–398.

Giannetti, R.A., Klingler, D.E., Johnson, J.H., & Williams, T.A. (1976). The potential for dynamic assessment systems using on-line computer technology. *Behavior Research Methods and Instrumentation*, 8, 101–103.

Gilberstadt, H., & Duker, J. (1965). *A handbook for clinical and actuarial MMPI interpretation*. Philadelphia: W.B. Saunders.

Goldberg, L.R. (1965). Diagnosticians vs. diagnostic signs: The diagnosis of psychosis vs. neurosis from the MMPI. *Psychological Monographs*, 79, (Whole No. 602).

Gough, H.G. (1975). *California Psychological Inventory* (revised manual). Palo Alto, CA: Consulting Psychologists Press.

Grayson, H.M. (1951, June). Psychological admissions testing program and manual. Los Angeles: Veterans Administration Center, Neuropsychiatric Hospital.

Greist, J.H., & Klein, M.H. (1980). Computer programs for patients, clinicians, and researchers in psychiatry. In J.B. Sidowski, J.H. Johnson, & T.A. Williams (Eds.), *Technology in mental health care delivery systems*. Norwood, NJ: Ablex Publishing Corporation.

Greist, J.H., & Klein, M.H. (1981). Computers in psychiatry. In S. Arieti (Ed.), *American handbook of psychiatry* (2nd ed., Vol. 7). New York: Basic Books.

Halbower, C.C. (1955). *A comparison of actuarial versus clinical prediction to classes discriminated by MMPI*. Unpublished doctoral dissertation, University of Minnesota.

Harris, R.E., & Lingoes, J.C. (1968). *Subscales for the Minnesota Multiphasic Personality Inventory*. Unpublished manuscript, San Francisco: The Langley Porter Clinic.

Henrichs, T. (1964). Objective configural rules for discriminating MMPI profiles in a psychiatric population. *Journal of Clinical Psychology*, 20, 157–159.

Henrichs, T. (1966). A note on the extension of MMPI configural rules. *Journal of Clinical Psychology*, 22, 51–52.

Hoffman, N.G., & Butcher, J.N. (1975). Clinical limitations of three Minnesota Multiphasis Personality Inventory short forms. *Journal of Consulting and Clinical Psychology*, 43, 32–39.

Holtzman, W.H. (1960). Can the computer supplant the clinician? *Journal of Clinical Psychology*, 16, 119–122.

Jackson, D.N. (1971). The dynamics of structured personality tests: 1971. *Psychological Review*, 78, 229–248.

Jackson, D.N. (1967–1974). *Personality research form*. Port Huron, MI: Research Psychologists Press.

Jackson, D.N. (1972). *Differential personality inventory*. London, Ontario: Author.

Johnson, J.H., Butcher, J.N., Null, C., & Johnson, K.N. (in press). A replicated item level factor analysis of the full MMPI. *Journal of Personality and Social Psychology*.

Johnson, J.H., Giannetti, R.A., & Williams, T.A. (1976). Computers in mental health care delivery: A review of the evolution toward interventionally relevant on-line processing. *Behavior Research Methods and Instrumentation*, 8, 83–91.

Johnson, J.H., Giannetti, R.A., & Williams, T.A. (1979). Psychological Systems Questionnaire: An objective personality test designed for on-line computer presentation, scoring, and interpretation. *Behavior Research Methods and Instrumentation*, 11, 257–260.

Johnson, J.H., & Williams, T.A. (1980). Using on-line computer technology to improve service response and decision-making effectiveness in a mental health admitting system. In J.B. Sidowski, J.H. Johnson, & T.A. Williams (Eds.), *Technology in mental health care delivery systems*. Norwood, NJ: Ablex Publishing Corporation.

Kleinmuntz, B. (1982). *Personality and psychological assessment*. New York: St. Martin's Press.

Kleinmuntz, B., & McLean, R.S. (1968). Computers in behavioral science: Diagnostic interviewing by digital computer. *Behavioral Science*, 13, 75–80.

Koss, M.P. (1980). Assessing psychological emergencies with the MMPI. *Clinical notes on the MMPI*, Roche Psychiatric Service Institute Monograph Series.

Koss, M.P., & Butcher, J.N. (1973). A comparison of psychiatric patients' self-report with other sources of clinical information. *Journal of Research in Personality*, 7, 225–236.

Koss, M.P., Butcher, J.N., & Hoffman, N.G. (1976). The MMPI critical items: How well do they work? *Journal of Consulting and Clinical Psychology*, 44, 921–928.

Krug, S.E. (1980). *Clinical analysis questionnaire manual*. Champaign, IL: Institute for Personality and Ability Testing.

Lewandowski, D., & Graham, J.R. (1972). Empirical correlates of frequently occurring two-point MMPI code types: A replicated study. *Journal of Consulting and Clinical Psychology*, 39, 467–472.

Lushene, R.E., O'Neil, H.F., & Dunn, T. (1974). Equivalent validity of a completely computerized MMPI. *Journal of Personality Assessment*, 38, 353–361.

Lyons, J.P., & Brown, J. (1981). Reduction in clinical assessment time using computer algorithms. *Behavior Research Methods and Instrumentation*, 13, 407–412.

MacAndrew, C. (1965). The differentiation of male alcoholic outpatients from nonalcoholic psychiatric patients by means of the MMPI. *Quarterly Journal of Studies on Alcohol*, 26, 238–246.

Marks, P.A., Seeman, W., & Haller, D. (1974). *The actuarial use of the MMPI with adolescents and adults*. Baltimore: Williams & Wilkins.

McNair, D.M. (1978). Review of the Clinical Analysis Questionnaire (CAQ). In O.K. Buros (Ed.), *Eighth mental measurements yearbook*. Highland Park, NJ: Gryphon Press.

Meehl, P.E. (1945). The dynamics of "structured" personality tests. *Journal of Clinical Psychology*, 1, 296–303.

Meehl, P.E. (1954). *Clinical versus statistical prediction: A theoretical analysis and review of the evidence*. Minneapolis: University of Minnesota Press.

Meehl, P.E., & Dahlstrom, W.G. (1960). Objective configural rules for discriminating psychotic from neurotic MMPI profiles. *Journal of Consulting and Clinical Psychology*, 24, 375–387.

Megargee, E.I., & Bohn, M.J. (1977). A new classification for criminal offenders, IV: Empirically determined characteristics of the ten types. *Criminal Justice and Behavior*, 4, 149–210.

Mesthene, E.G. (1970). *Technological change: Its impact on man and society*. New York: The New American Library.

Millon, T. (1982). *Millon Clinical Multiaxial Inventory* (2nd ed.). Minneapolis: National Computer Systems.

Morf, M., Alexander, P., & Fuerth, T. (1981). Fully automated psychiatric diagnosis: Some new possibilities. *Behavior Research Methods and Instrumentation*, 13, 413–416.

National Computer Systems. (1982). *User's guide for the Minnesota Report*. Minneapolis: National Computer Systems.

Patience, W.M. (1977). Description of components in tailored testing. *Behavioral Research Methods and Instrumentation*, 9, 153–157.

Piotrowski, Z.A. (1980). CPR: The psychological X-ray in mental disorders. In J.B. Sidowski, J.H. Johnson, & T.A. Williams (Eds.), *Technology in mental health care delivery systems*. Norwood, NJ: Ablex Publishing Corporation.

Rome, H.P., Swenson, W.M., Mataya, P., McCarthy, C.E., Pearson, J.S., Keating, F.R., & Hathaway, S.R. (1962). Symposium on automation technics in personality assessment. *Proceedings of the Staff Meetings of the Mayo Clinic*, 37, 61–82.

Sapinkopf, R.C. (1978). A computer adaptive testing approach to the measurement of personality variables. *Dissertation Abstracts International*, 38, 4993.

Smail, D.J. (1971). Statistical prediction and "cookbooks": A technological confidence trick. *British Journal of Medical Psychology*, 44, 173–178.

Song, W.Z. (1981). *Application of the Minnesota Multiphasic Personality Inventory in some areas of the People's Republic of China*. Paper given at the Seventh International Conference on Personality Assessment, Honolulu, Hawaii.

Space, L.G. (1981). The computer as psychometrician. *Behavior Research Methods and Instrumentation*, 13, 595–606.

Spitzer, R.L., & Endicott, J. (1969). DIAGNO II: Further developments in a computer program for psychiatric diagnosis. *American Journal of Psychiatry*, (supp), 125, 12–21.

Spitzer, R.L., & Endicott, J. (1974). Can the computer assist clinicians in psychiatric diagnosis? *American Journal of Psychiatry*, 131, 523–530.

Stein, K.B. (1968). The TSC scales: The outcome of a cluster analysis of the 550 MMPI items. In P. McReynolds (Ed.), *Advances in psychological assessment* (Vol. 1). Palo Alto, CA: Science and Behavior Books.

Stillman, R., Roth, W.T., Colby, K.M., & Rosenbaum, C.P. (1969). An online computer system for initial psychiatric inventory. *American Journal of Psychiatry*, (supp), 125, 8–11.

Stout, R.L. (1981). New approaches to the design of computerized interviewing and testing systems. *Behavior Research Methods and Instrumentation*, 13, 436–442.

Vale, C.D., & Weiss, D.J. (1975, October). *A study of computer-administered stradaptive ability testing*. (Research Report 75-5). Minneapolis: University of Minnesota, Psychometric Methods Program.

Valsiner, J. (1982). Use of the MMPI in the Soviet Union. Unpublished mimeographed materials.

Weiss, D.J. (1973, September). *The stratified adaptive computerized ability test*. (Research Report 73-3). Minneapolis: University of Minnesota, Psychometric Methods Program.

Welsh, G.S. (1956). Factor dimensions A and R. In B.S. Welsh & W.G. Dahlstrom (Eds.), *Basic readings on the MMPI in psychology and medicine*. Minneapolis: University of Minnesota Press.

Wiggins, J.S. (1969). Content dimensions in the MMPI. In J.N. Butcher (Ed.), *MMPI: Research developments and clinical applications*. New York: McGraw-Hill.

Williams, T.A. (1977). Computer technology in mental health care: "Toys" or tools? *Behavior Research Methods and Instrumentation*, 9, 108–109.

Woodworth, R.S. (1920). *Personal data sheet*. Chicago: Stoelting.

17 RORSCHACH ASSESSMENT

Philip Erdberg
John E. Exner, Jr.

INTRODUCTION

The assessment technique that Hermann Rorschach introduced in 1921 has had its share of critics, but even they must acknowledge the resilience and durability of an instrument that, against considerable odds, has now survived into its second half-century. After Rorschach's tragically early death the year following its publication, the fledgling test was maintained by a few of his associates and then brought to America, only to find itself with five groups of increasingly diverging adoptive parents whose differences ultimately became so extensive as to threaten its unitary identity. Methodological criticism came from outside the Rorschach community as well, changing priorities within clinical psychology decreased the value placed on projective assessment, and there were even suggestions that the test be discarded entirely. But by the mid-1970s a new consolidation had integrated into the mainstream of psychometric methodology the best of what had been learned during the half-century of divergence. New research directions were expanding the test's applications, and the Rorschach now appears to have entered what may well turn out to be its healthiest years to date. The history of the test's development, a review of its elements and

their clinical utility, and some descriptions of new directions coming into focus are the subjects of this chapter.

HISTORY AND DEVELOPMENT

The idea that an individual's associations to ambiguous visual stimuli could provide keys for understanding that person is an ancient one. Early writings suggest that the classical Greeks were interested in the interaction of ambiguity and the person's depiction of reality (Piotrowski, 1957), and by the 15th century, both Da Vinci and Botticelli were postulating a relationship between creativity and the processing of ambiguous materials (Zubin, Eron, & Schumer, 1965). The use of inkblots as stimuli for imagination achieved substantial popularity in Europe during the 19th century. A parlor game called Blotto asked people to create responses to inkblots and designs, and a book by Justinius Kerner (1857) contained a collection of poetic associations to inkblot-like designs.

As the 19th century ended, several workers in the professional community turned their attention to the utilization of inkblots in the study of a variety of psychological traits. Krugman (1940) reports Binet and Henri's interest as early as 1895 in inkblots as a way of studying visual imagination, and Tulchin (1940) describes Dearborn's work at Harvard (which resulted in 1897 and 1898 publications) discussing the use of inkblots in an experimental approach to the study of consciousness. Another American investigator, Whipple (1910), was also utilizing a series of inkblots as a way of studying what he called "active imagination." Rybakow (1910), working in Moscow, developed a series of eight blots to tap imaginative function, and Hens (1917), working at Bleuler's clinic in Zurich, used inkblots with a series of children, normal adults, and psychiatric patients.

Thus, young Swiss psychiatrist Hermann Rorschach was not the first to utilize inkblots in the study of psychological processes. However, the work that he began intermittently in 1911 and devoted himself to much more intensively from 1917 and 1920 was qualitatively different from anything that had preceded it in its establishment of a framework from which personality descriptions of substantial scope could be generated. Rorschach's preliminary but remarkably far-sighted *Psychodiagnostik* was published in 1921. He died within a year, at the age of 38, of complications of appendicitis.

It was three of Rorschach's friends, Walter Morgenthaler, Emil Oberholzer, and George Roemer, who insured that the insights and challenges of *Psychodiagnostik* were not lost. Morgenthaler had championed the book's publication against some resistance from the Bircher publishing house, Oberholzer followed up by making sure that an important posthumous elaborative paper was published (1923), and all three continued to teach the test and encourage adherents. One of Oberholzer's students, David Levy, took the test to Chicago, where he established the first American Rorschach seminar in 1925.

Although each perhaps could have, neither Oberholzer nor Levy moved into a clear position as Rorschach's successor, and once in America, the test was adopted by five psychologists of very different backgrounds—Samuel Beck, Bruno Kloper, Zygmunt Piotrowski, Marguerite Hertz, and David Rapaport. Of the five, only Beck, through the opportunity of a year's fellowship with Oberholzer in Zurich, was able to spend a significant amount of time with someone who had

worked directly with Rorschach. Thus, with little in the way of common heritage, the five Americans soon began moving independently in directions consistent with their differing theoretical orientations. Each ultimately produced a separate Rorschach system that attracted adherents and generated a body of published literature and clinical lore. The history of the Rorschach from the late 1920s to the early 1970s is the history of the development and elaboration of these five systems.

Beck completed the first American Rorschach dissertation in 1932, followed it with a number of journal articles, and published his *Introduction to the Rorschach Method* in 1937. He completed the elaboration of his system with additional books in 1944, 1945, and 1952, with revised editions published through 1967. Klopfer had his first direct contact with the Rorschach in 1933, and after a series of articles, which included a description of a scoring system (Klopfer & Sender, 1936), he published *The Rorschach Technique* with Douglas Kelley in 1942. Elaborations of his system occurred in books in 1954, 1956, and 1970. Piotrowski was a member of a seminar offered by Klopfer in 1934, but within two years he was moving toward an independent system, which culminated in his publication of *Perceptanalysis* in 1957. Hertz, after a relatively brief interaction with Levy and Beck, utilized the Rorschach in her dissertation research in 1932 and continued researching the test for the decade after at the Brush Foundation in Cleveland. Sadly, the nearly 3,000 cases she had amassed and the almost completed manuscript describing her system were inadvertently destroyed when the Foundation closed, and she never produced another book. However, her steady stream of journal articles and her ongoing seminars led to the clear existence of a Hertz system by 1945. Rapaport became interested in the Rorschach in the late 1930s and published a paper that described it in detail as part of a review of projective techniques in 1942. The first volume of *Diagnostic Psychological Testing* was published with Merton Gill and Roy Schafer in 1945, with the second volume following a year later. Schafer extended the system with additional books in 1948, 1954, and 1967, and Robert Holt edited a revised edition of the original two volumes in 1968.

With publication of Piotrowski's book in 1957, all five of the systems were essentially complete and so different in their details that the picture painted in a comprehensive review (Exner, 1969b) was of five overlapping but clearly discrete Rorschachs. Each of the systematizers had taken the 10 inkblots chosen by Rorschach and utilized some of the ideas in *Psychodiagnostik* to fashion an instrument consistent with his or her theoretical training and professional interests. Each asked the subject to associate to the 10 cards, although with differences in the exact instructions given, and each attempted some sort of inquiry as a way of specifying various aspects of the free association. Each had developed a format for coding various aspects of the subject's responses, and at this "scoring" level, there were at least as many differences as similarities among the systems (Exner, 1969b; Toomey & Rickers-Ovsiankina, 1977). These differences can at least partially be ascribed to the differing methodologies each had used in developing the coding function. Beck's rigorous positivism and behavioral training emerged in his insistence on normative and validational backing for the various scoring elements. Klopfer's phenomenological background allowed him to give examiners greater leeway to use their own experience for reference in coding the same material. Rapaport, Hertz, and Piotrowski used methodological approaches somewhere in-between Beck and Klopfer. Finally, each systematizer made an interpretation of the, by now, somewhat diverging data that each had developed, and at this level of inference the differences among the systems became substantial. In particular, Rapaport's extensive utilization of psychoanalytic concepts separates his work from the somewhat less stringently "theory-based" interpretive strategies of the other four systematizers.

Thus, there were significant differences at all levels from administration to interpretation among the five American Rorschach systems, but a distinction suggested by Weiner (1977) and Exner and Weiner (1982) can be of value in cutting across these various details and levels. They suggest that the Rorschach can be conceptualized either as a perceptual-cognitive task or as a stimulus to fantasy. The perceptual-cognitive stance assumes that the basic Rorschach task is to structure and organize an ambiguous stimulus field and that the way a person accomplishes this task is directly *representative* of behavior that could be expected in other situations requiring the same sort of structuring and organizing operations. As an example, a person who dealt with the inkblots by breaking them into details that he/she then

combined into meaningful relationships could be expected to deal with other elements of his/her world in a similarly energetic, synthesizing manner. The focus in the perceptual-cognitive conceptualization of the Rorschach is not on the words but rather the structure of the person's response, such as choice of location or use of color or imposition of organization. These reliably quantifiable descriptions of response structure are then utilized to generate descriptions of *how* the person tends to behave elsewhere, taking advantage of the large body of validity studies that link the structural variables with a variety of non-Rorschach behavior.

The stimulus to fantasy approach, on the other hand, assumes that the basic Rorschach task is for the person to project material about need states onto the ambiguity of the blot, and the person's productions are seen as *symbolic* of internal dynamics. As an example, the percept of "a terribly angry and disappointed woman" might be utilized to postulate and then explain some sort of interpersonal conflict. The focus in the stimulus to fantasy approach is on the actual words, and these verbalizations are utilized to generate explanations of *why* the person tends to behave in particular ways, taking advantage of the interpreter's theoretical framework of linkages between symbols and dynamics.

There is some question about where Rorschach himself should be placed in terms of the perceptual-cognitive versus stimulus-to-fantasy distinction, but it is likely that he would have taken a middle-ground position that combined the two approaches. He had specifically criticized Hens' 1917 inkblot work for its focus solely on verbalizations and imagination, differentiating himself from Hens and, by implication, from most of the earlier inkblot work on imagination by noting that his primary interest was what he called "the pattern of perceptive process" and not the content of subjects' responses. *Psychodiagnostik* itself is almost totally in the perceptual-cognitive camp, with Rorschach devoting attention to issues of form, movement, and color. The 1923 posthumous paper added the structural element of shading. And yet Rorschach was well trained in the work of Freud and Jung. He almost certainly would have been comfortable with an elaboration of Freud's 1896 description of projection as a mechanism by which an individual could endow external material with aspects of his or her own dynamics, and with Frank's classic 1939 paper, which suggested that stimuli such as inkblots could serve as "projective methods" for eliciting the process. Indeed, Roemer (1967) states that Rorschach saw value in content analysis, citing a 1921 letter that suggests that Rorschach envisioned his technique as combining both structural and symbolic material in making diagnostic formulations.

If we review their actual work in dealing with Rorschach material, we find that all five of the American systematizers also saw the data as having both perceptual-cognitive and symbolic components, with Beck perhaps staying closest to the structural aspects, Rapaport most willing to place emphasis on the verbalizations, and the other three at varying points in between. The systems differ in the methdologies with which they were developed, in their theoretical emphases, and prosaically but importantly on a day-to-day basis, in their details and terminology. As each system solidified and developed a specialized literature, psychologists schooled in one approach could not communicate easily with those trained in some other system, because increasingly they lacked a shared language and body of knowledge.

The purpose of Exner's development of the Comprehensive System (1974, 1978, 1982) was to provide the fragmented Rorschach community once more with a common methodology, language, and literature. The accumulated literature of all five systems was reviewed, and some new research was undertaken. Using reliability and validity as criteria for inclusion, this program yielded a constellation of empirically defensible elements that forms the structural aspect of the system. Analysis of the verbalizations is a secondary but significant part of the Comprehensive System, and the approach to the handling of data as symbolic material can be characterized as dynamic but not specifically linked to any single theory of personality operation. What follows is a description of the elements of the Comprehensive System.

THE RORSCHACH ELEMENTS

A very frequent role of the Rorschach psychologist is to act as consultant to the helping process, offering data that can be useful to the professional responsible for providing "treatment," whatever the setting. Typically it is this professional who makes the referral, in the hope that psychodiagnostic assessment will supplement the data acquired in the clinical interaction and thus provide additional understanding of the client and guidance about treatment decisions and strategies. Since this is the way the Rorschach is typically employed, it seems useful to organize this review of its elements and their supporting literature in terms of the kinds of questions to which the test can validly be addressed. We will begin with a series of questions designed to provide a picture of the person's psychological operation and then consider a few illustrative clinical issues.

What is the Person's Preferred Style of Coping with Need States?

Faced with stressful situations, some individuals tend to utilize their internal resources to cope, while others are more apt to seek interaction with some aspect of their world. The Erlebnistypus (EB) first proposed by Rorschach (1921) provides an extraordinarily valuable indicator of which of these response tendencies is more likely for a particular individual. A substantial number of studies (Molish, 1967; Singer & Brown, 1977, provide reviews) have lent support to Rorschach's hypothesis that individuals who use a preponderance of human movement (M) in formulating their Rorschach percepts (introversives) tend to utilize inner resources to deal with needs, while those who involve proportionately more chromatic color (FC, CF, and C) as determinants for their responses (extratensives) are more likely to seek interaction with the environment during need states. Rorschach also demarcated a third response style, the ambiequal or ambitent, a person who does not have a clearly skewed introversive or extratensive profile.

A study by Exner, Bryant, and Leura (1975) is illustrative of some behavioral correlates of the three styles and also provides a point of departure for contrasting them. A logical analysis task in which each move could potentially provide increasingly specific information about the combination of moves necessary to reach a solution was given to academically matched college students whom the Rorschach had identified as either introversive, ambiequal, or extratensive. The students were scored on total moves to solution, total errors, total repeated moves, time between moves, and time to solution. The introversive group was characterized by fewer moves, longer times between moves, and fewer repeated moves and errors. The extratensive group had more moves and shorter time between moves, and the ambitent group took more time to get to solution. We can speculate from these data that the introversive group responded to this problem-solving situation with a more "thoughtful" approach, processing feedback internally and thus needing less of it to come to solution, while the extratensive group utilized more interaction with the environment and less internal processing time to deal with the same task. If we use time to solution as a measure of the efficiency of the two problem-solving styles, it is important to note that they appear to be equally effective although very different. Using the time to solution criterion, it is only the ambitents who are less efficient, and the investigators speculate about this group's being more "unsure" in their problem-solving strategy.

The issue of problem-solving style has far-ranging implications for the clinician. For example, we can hypothesize that extratensive individuals might move more easily into some sort of "helping relationship," since their preferred problem-solving style is one that is accustomed to utilizing interaction with others during stressful situations. Introversive individuals, on the other hand, might have a more difficult time involving another person in the processing of coping with a problematical situation. Another speculation might be that spouses whose styles are different would have difficulty when they needed to confront a problem as a couple, since one member's style of using interaction to "talk the problem through" could interfere with the other member's need for solitude to "think the problem through." These speculations await validational support, but they do not stray far from the substantial body of data about coping styles.

How Likely is the Person's Preferred Coping Style to Work and What Kinds of Problems Will it Encounter?

Although the introversive and extratensive approaches are stylistically different, they both represent organized approaches to dealing with a need state, volitional strategies that the individual decides to call up to handle a given situation. Indeed, most individuals have both approaches in their behavioral repertoire, with the direction of their EB providing a probability statement about which style is more likely to be utilized. Consequently, Beck (1960) suggested that the summation of human movement and color determinants

(EA) could be utilized as a measure of the person's organized psychological resources, those coping strategies the individual could decide to apply to some sort of stressful situation. A clue as to whether these organized strategies can be expected to work for the individual is provided by considering another summation, the *ep*, and its relationship to EA.

The *ep*, a measure developed by Exner (1974), encompasses the totality of unorganized psychological material that impinges on the person in unexpected and often disorganizing ways. Using EA as a measure of accessible coping strategies and *ep* as a measure of nondeliberate, intrusive psychological material, Exner (1978) summarizes their relationship as follows ". . . if *ep* is greater than EA, the person will be less able to exert direction and/or control in coping situations, whereas the high EA individual is more able to do so because more resources are available for use" (p. 94). An interesting study (Wiener-Levy & Exner, 1981) compared EA > *ep* and *ep* > EA individuals in their handling of a very frustrating pursuit-rotor task, and in analyzing the significant differences, concluded that ". . . in those instances where EA exceeds *ep*, it seems likely that the person will have greater psychological command in the formulation of actions" (p. 122).

If the *ep* represents the totality of unorganized psychological material tapped by the Rorschach, a review of its components can be of value in describing more specifically the quality of the variables that have the potential for interfering with the person's deliberate coping style, be it introversive, extratensive, or ambiequal. Two Rorschach elements, animal movement (FM) and inanimate movement (m), appear to be associated with disruptive ideation, and four elements that involve the use of shading or achromatic color in formulating the response appear to be associated with intrusive affect. We will discuss each of these components of the *ep* in detail.

Although less validational data have been developed for the animal movement (FM) determinant than for most Rorschach variables, it appears to be associated with the unexpected experience of relatively unorganized ideation about need states intruding into consciousness with an intensity that demands action. What happens, then, may well depend on the extensiveness of the person's coping strategies for dealing with the need state to which he/she has been alerted.

When the unorganized ideation reflected by FM is greater than the organized ideational style associated with M, the probability of more impulsive or "primitive" behavior may go up. Two studies (Exner & Murillo, 1975; Exner, Murillo, & Cannavo, 1973) found that when FM is greater than M, the likelihood of posthospitalization relapse is greater for a variety of psychiatric patients. We can speculate that one of the reasons for the relapsers' inability to operate outside the hospital involved the ongoing experience of their being alerted to need states for which they did not have sufficient coping and delaying strategies and to which they thus responded impulsively and inappropriately.

Another sort of disruptive ideation is that which appears to be associated with the use of inanimate movement (m) in formulating Rorschach percepts. While the FM experience seems to involve ideation about internal need states, (m) is reflective of ideation about the experience of external, situational stress over which the individual feels little control. Thus, subject groups as varied as Navy personnel under severe storm conditions, depressed psychiatric inpatients the day before a first ECT treatment, trainees the day before their first parachute jump, and hospital patients the day before surgery all showed more (m) in the Rorschachs they produced at these times than in records taken from them at some less situationally stressful period (Armbruster, Miller, & Exner, 1974; Exner, Armbruster, Walker, & Cooper, 1975; Exner & Walker, 1973; Shalit, 1965). A series of temporal consistency studies (Exner, 1978) also supports the conceptualization of (m) as a situational or "state" variable.

The next group of components making up the individual's unorganized psychological material appears to be associated with the experience of painful emotion as opposed to painful ideation. Each component is reflective of a somewhat different type of distressing emotional experience, and it will be helpful to discuss each separately.

The use of the shading features of the blots to formulate a percept involving texture (T) appears to reflect the experience of a need for affective interpersonal contact that has more of an "unconditional" than an "intellectual" quality. Exner and Bryant (1974a), for example, found that individuals who had been recently separated or divorced and had not yet established new "emotional" relationships produced 2.7 times as much (T) in their

records as a group of demographically matched controls who rated their marriages at least average for stability and happiness. (T) is the most frequent of the shading determinants, with most nonpatients producing one or two percepts involving texture. On the other hand, a review of a series of studies (Exner, 1978) suggests that the distribution of (T) for several patient groups may have a more "bimodal" quality, with members of these groups producing either more or less (T) than would be expected. We can speculate that these extremes are associated with disruptions in effective interpersonal function, with the high-(T) individuals manifesting "needy" behavior and the (T)-less individuals "burnt out" on seeking relationships that have a meaningful affective component.

Another Rorschach variable that can contribute to the amount of painful emotion impinging on the person involves the use of the shading features to formulate a percept of depth or dimensionality (V). The use of this determinant appears to reflect the kind of introspection that produces a negative self-evaluation. Exner and Wylie (1977), Exner (1978), and Arffa (1982) have found that this generally rare variable is frequently present in the records of suicidal adults, adolescents, and children, and we can speculate about the intense pain that the negative introspection reflected by V must involve.

A third source of disruptive emotion is the experience associated with the use of the light-dark features of the blots (Y). This appears to involve a feeling of resignation or helplessness in the face of a stressful situation, which demands action. Exner (1978) studied a group of subjects whom he postulated from other Rorschach variables (presence of (m) and $ep > EA$) should be feeling a sense of helplessness, since their organized coping strategies were likely inadequate to deal with the situational stress they were experiencing. This group had significantly more (Y) in their Rorschachs than controls whose records had no m and thus who were probably not experiencing a sense of helplessness. Exner, Wylie, and Kline (1977b) followed psychotherapy patients in a longitudinal study and found that those who were able to terminate by 18 months were characterized by significant decreases in the amount of (Y) in their records, while patients still in therapy at that time had about the same amount of (Y) as when they had begun treatment. We can hypothesize from all of these studies that (Y) is associated with at least some experience of inadequacy in dealing with stressful demands.

The final Rorschach variable that contributes to disruptive emotion impinging on the individual involves the utilization of the white-gray-black features of the blot (C') in formulating a response. This determinant appears to be related to the experience of containing affect as opposed to allowing its discharge into the world. Exner (1974) demonstrated that several groups of individuals who could be expected to contain affect (depressives who did not make suicide attempts, psychosomatics, obsessive-compulsives, and schizoids) were characterized by significantly more (C') in their Rorschachs than individuals whose behavior manifested less containment of affect (personality disorders and depressives who made suicide attempts). It would appear that (C') is representative of the internalization of affect, and the pressure and disequilibrium that this painful limiting of the overt expression of emotion can produce is substantial.

These, then, are the sources of disorganizing, intrusive ideation and emotion that appear to have Rorschach correlates. When these disruptive, nonvolitional elements predominate in a person's psychological operation, they can interfere significantly with the ability to utilize organized coping strategies effectively.

How Likely is the Person to Function Objectively?

The sole use of the shape feature of the blots (F) in formulating percepts may well represent a psychological operation different from that of any of the other determinants of Rorschach responses. We can hypothesize that the (F) activity is a relatively affect-free one in which the person is able to ignore the more emotional aspects of his/her own psychology and deal with the task in a primarily objective manner. A number of studies (Exner, 1974; Exner & Murillo, 1973; Goldman, 1960; Sherman, 1955) have found that schizophrenics have less (F) in their records during acute phases than during periods of remission and recovery. If we view F as the most affect-free determinant, then it is helpful to contrast its occurrence with that of all the other Rorschach determinants, which are felt to involve more influx of the person's psychology. Lambda, which is calculated as the ratio of (F) responses to all other responses in the record, allows this contrast. As Lambda goes

up, the record would have a high proportion of F responses, and as it goes down, proportionately few (F) responses. How much a person is willing to allow his/her own emotional material to mix with his/her logical operations may vary on a situational basis. Exner, Armbruster, and Mittman (1978) found a lower Lambda range for patients who were tested by the therapist they had seen for 20 to 40 sessions than for a similar group of patients who were tested by a stranger. There is some suggestion (Exner, 1978) that extremes may be associated with maladaptive behavior. We can speculate that, in general, optimal psychological function involves being able to allow some—but not too much and not too little—of one's own psychology to mix with purely objective operation.

How Mature and Complex are the Person's Psychological Operations?

There are a variety of ways to approach the inkblots, some of them involving substantially more complexity than others, and these distinctions appear to be of value in describing the sophistication of the person's psychological operations in other situations. Meili-Dworetzki (1939, 1956) found that as children increase in age, their location, selection and integration of blot details become more complex. In a more recent study, Smith (1981) classified second- and sixth-grade students using the Piagetian stages of cognitive development and found that children at the higher stages more frequently chose the whole blot as the location for their percepts and integrated various details into some meaningful relationship ("Two women stirring food in a pot") than did children at earlier stages of cognitive maturity. Exner and Weiner (1982) found that these organized responses increased from 17% in their 5-year-old normative sample to 28% for their sixteen-year olds, while vague percepts ("Some kind of a cloud") decreased from 32% to 7%. In the Comprehensive System (Exner, 1974), the scoring of developmental quality encompasses a range from complex integration to quite diffuse and arbitrary approaches to the blots and may thus provide data about the sophistication with which the person approaches the world.

The use of blends, percepts in which more than one determinant is used in formulating the response, appears to be associated with the complexity of the person's psychological operations.

Exner (1974) did find that the number of blends in a record is correlated with intelligence for nonpatients but not for psychiatric outpatients. He suggests that, although there may be some relation to intelligence, what blends probably reflect more specifically is the complexity of the person's psychological operations. He goes on to suggest that either a very large or very small number of blends may be problematical, with the large numbers associated with an immobilizingly overcomplex style and the low numbers reflecting insufficient ability to entertain complex alternatives when responding to demands.

What is the Extent and Quality of the Person's Self-focus?

There is some suggestion that a person's use of the symmetrical properties of the inkblots to generate percepts involving reflections (Fr) or pairs (2) may be associated with narcissism or egocentricity. Although it is difficult to specify precisely what the behavioral correlates of self-focus would be, Exner (1973, 1974) found that pair and reflection responses were positively associated with self-focusing answers on a sentence completion task and with mirror-looking behavior in a group of engineering job applicants waiting for an interview. These findings led to the establishment of an egocentricity index, a weighted percentage of the number of reflections and pairs in a person's record. As with some of the other Rorschach variables we have considered, we can speculate with the egocentricity index that too much or too little self-focus may be associated with maladaptive function. Thus, Exner (1974, 1978) found that adult character disorders, schizophrenics, and psychiatric outpatients tended to have egocentricity indexes higher than a nonpatient group, while depressives and suicidal individuals tended to be lower. Children and adolescents with behavior problems tended to be higher than nonpatients on this index, while withdrawn children and adolescents were lower. Although there are many exceptions, a variety of studies (Exner, 1974, 1978; Exner & Murillo, 1973, 1977) would suggest that movement from either of the extremes into the midrange is associated with ratings of success in treatment.

It would appear that one of the components of the egocentricity index, the use of reflections, represents a somewhat more primitive and intense form of self-focus. Although frequencies for all groups are low, Exner and Weiner (1982) found that the percentage of reflection responses in the records of their nonpatient five-year-olds was more than twice that of the eleven-year-olds. Reflection responses are very rare for adults, except those with significant sex role confusion, character disorders, or schizophrenia (Exner, 1969a, 1974; Raychaudhuri & Mukerji, 1971). Exner, Wylie, and Bryant (1974) found that individuals with reflection responses in their records were ranked negatively by their outpatient group peers on items such as "would seek advice from" or "would tell problems to." We can speculate that reflections represent a particularly intense "closed system" sort of self-focus that can make for distortion of perception, especially in interpersonal situations.

What is the Quality of the Person's Reality Testing?

The individual's ability to converge on percepts that are frequently seen or can be easily seen by others is a Rorschach indicator thought to be representative of accuracy in reality testing. Although there have been different methodologies used in the establishment of this indicator (Exner, 1974; Kinder, Brubaker, Ingram, & Reading, 1982), it is fair to say that Rorschach and all the systematizers since have viewed "form quality" as an important variable, descriptive of the individual's ability to operate conventionally and realistically in the world. This skill manifests very early in normal development, and it is fascinating to note that the perceptual accuracy of nonpatient 5-year-olds is virtually identical to that found for 16-year-olds and for adults (Exner & Weiner, 1982). Exner (1974) provides an extensive review suggesting that significant deficits in Rorschach form quality are associated with psychosis, organic dysfunction, and limited intellectual operation.

Rorschach's original recommendation was that percepts be differentiated into categories on the basis of "good" and "poor" form. Elaborations of this basic dichotomy have allowed for greater specificity in describing the individual's reality testing. Using a modification of an approach suggested by Mayman (1966, 1970), Exner (1974) divides good form responses into those involving superior articulation and those that are merely ordinary and divides poor form responses into those that "bend" reality and those that distort it in arbitrary and very inaccurate ways. This sort of distinction can be of substantial value, as for example in the assessment of schizophrenia, where the specification of how badly reality is distorted may be diagnostic. Harder and Ritzler (1979), for example, found that a good form versus poor form dichotomy was unable to differentiate between psychotics and nonpsychotics in their inpatient sample, while approaches that made finer gradations within the good and poor form categories could differentiate the two groups quite accurately.

Another elaboration that may have substantial value in describing the person's reality testing is the distinction between perceptual accuracy in relatively affect-free situations (F + %) and accuracy in situations involving more affect (X + %). Typically, these two indicators are highly correlated, but when they differ markedly, the divergence may have clinical significance. Thus, Exner (1974) found that his inpatient non-schizophrenic group, which contained a large number of individuals with affective disorders, was characterized by many records in which the F + % was much higher than the X + %, suggesting that for this group affective intrusion and significant potential for disrupting perceptual accuracy. We can speculate that individuals whose affect-free reality testing is significantly better than their reality testing in emotionally toned situations might do well in relatively structured hospital settings but would tend to have difficulty if they were discharged into much more ambiguous and complex environments.

With What Frequency and Efficiency Does the Person Attempt to Organize the Environment?

Faced with the Rorschach blots, an individual can either take a sort of "conservation of energy" approach in which percepts are limited to a single detail or attempt to "organize" the blot more energetically, utilizing either the whole blot or synthesizing two or more details into a meaningful relationship. With one possible exception (the whole percept for Card V), responses involving wholes or the integration of details appear to represent a more organizationally challenging, energy-consuming process. The frequency with which the person attempts this sort of organization (Zf) may provide a useful representation of his/her style in approaching the elements of his world. Although (Zf) does have a modest correla-

tion with intelligence (Exner, 1974), it would appear that other variables, such as psychopathology, must play at least as great a part in determining how likely it is that the individual will attempt the analytic, synthesizing sorts of operations that this index reflects. For example, Exner (1978) hypothesizes that low (Zf) could be associated either with cognitive limitations or with some constellation of psychological factors creating reluctance to attempt a synthesis of the environment.

Whatever the frequency of the individual's organizational attempts, it is perhaps even more important to know whether each is likely to be efficient or not, and an index developed by Exner (1974) can be of substantial value in describing the quality of the person's integrative efforts. This index, the (Zd), provides a measure of whether, for any given number of organizational attempts, the overall complexity of an individual's integrative operation is greater, less, or about the same as that of a primarily nonpatient group studied by Wilson and Blake (1950). Individuals with a high positive (Zd) tend to bring in more complexity per organizational attempt than the Wilson and Blake sample, and they can be described as overincorporators, while a high negative (Zd) implies that the individual has involved less complexity in organizational attempts than the normative sample did, an underincorporative style. A series of studies suggests that the Rorschach finding of overincorporative or underincorporative style is associated with some quite consistent behavioral tendencies, whether the subjects were 8- and 9-year-olds playing Simon Says, high school students doing a perceptual-spatial task, college sophomores guessing from incomplete verbal data, or adults doing a serial learning problem (Bryant & Exner, 1974; Exner & Bryant, 1975; Exner & Caraway, 1974; Exner & Leura, 1974). The underincorporators were characterized by fast speed but many errors, responding before they had fully scanned and processed the data, and guessing early as opposed to waiting for the appearance of additional data. The overincorporators tended to be much more cautious in their response style, waiting much longer before acting and needing much more data, sometimes to the point of redundancy, to prompt their decisions. Both of these extreme styles can be maladaptive, with the underincorporator running the risk of inappropriate action because he/she has not scanned and processed all the available relevant elements of a situation, while the overincorporator's need for "all the data" before acting can be immobilizing.

With What Balance of Activity and Passivity Does the Person Interact with the World?

A differentiation of whether the person's human, animal, and inanimate movement responses are active ("a bird building a nest") or passive ("a bird gliding through the sky") appears to have substantial promise as a way of describing a variety of important non-Rorschach behaviors. Exner (1974) found that acute schizophrenics, patients hospitalized for characterological disorders, and patients with a variety of diagnoses but having a common history of assaultiveness were characterized by significantly more active movement responses, while chronic schizophrenics and depressives had significantly more passive movement percepts. Even more important, though, was the finding that approximately 70% of psychiatric patients have a skewed active-passive mix (active percepts three or more times greater than passive percepts or *vice versa*), while about the same percentage of nonpatients had a more balanced mix of the two kinds of movement responses.

If the individual's active-passive mix is skewed one way or the other, a series of studies suggests that he/she may be characterized by a sort of cognitive inflexibility in a wide variety of situations. Exner (1973) found that when the progress of adolescents who had been treated for behavioral problems was evaluated by significant others, most of those rated as improved had shifted from a skewed to a more balanced active-passive ratio, while almost all of those rated as behaviorally unimproved had not made this shift. Women whose active-passive mix was skewed on the Rorschach were also characterized by a relatively rigid style when the actions of the central figure of their daydreams were evaluated, while women with more balanced active-passive ratios shifted much more frequently between active and passive modes for their daydream's central figure (Exner, 1974). Exner and Wylie (1974) found that psychoanalytically oriented therapists rated patients with skewed active-passive ratios lower for insight, progress, and overall session effectiveness and higher for redundancy than they did a group of patients with a more even distribution of active to passive percepts. A study by Exner and Bryant

(1974b) found that high school students with balanced active-passive ratios were able to come up with significantly more unusual or "creative" uses for familiar objects both singly and in combination than an academically matched group of students with very skewed active-passive ratios. The common theme in all these studies is that the Rorschach finding of a skewed distribution of active and passive percepts appears to be associated with a sort of cognitive rigidity that may limit the variety of the person's coping behaviors.

Two studies are of interest in suggesting correlates of the particular Rorschach finding of more passive than active percepts. Exner (1978) developed a measure that evaluated behavioral passivity and administered it to the significant others of two groups of outpatients—those with passive exceeding active percepts by more than one and those not showing this finding. Ratings for the two groups differed very significantly, with the Rorschach passive group scoring much higher for a variety of passive behaviors. Even more specifically, it would appear that when passive percepts for human movement exceed active percepts by more than one, the person's deliberate ideational operation may be characterized by a sort of "magical thinking," which awaits the intervention of others at stressful times. Exner, Armbruster, and Wylie (1976) compared two groups of nonpatient adults, assigned on the basis of whether they had more active than passive human movement or whether their passive human movement percepts exceeded their active percepts by more than one. Subjects were asked to write endings for TAT stories in which the central character was portrayed as being in a problematical situation of some sort. The Rorschach passive individuals brought new persons into the endings with significantly greater frequency, and these "interveners," not the central characters, were significantly more often instrumental in initiating some sort of resolution.

How Does the Person Respond to the Affective Aspects of his World?

It has been suggested (Beck, 1961; Klopper, 1942) that the proportion of responses a person gives to the three fully chromatic blots may provide data about responsiveness to emotionally charged stimuli throughout his world. Exner (1962) has shown that the fully chromatic features of these three cards generate more responses than when the cards are modified to make them achromatic.

Nonpatients typically give about 40% of the responses they produce for the ten inkblots on these three cards (Exner, 1978). The affective ratio (Afr) provides an index of how the person has responded to the fully chromatic blots, and it is formulated so that high scores mean that the person has been proportionately overresponsive to these blots and low scores mean that he/she has "backed away" from them and given proportionately fewer responses. As the affective ratio goes up, it would appear, so do receptivity to emotional stimuli and willingness to process this material and make it a part of the basis on which the person ultimately acts (Exner, 1974; Exner & Leura, 1977; Exner, Leura, Armbruster, & Viglione, 1977).

It is noteworthy that patient groups tend to be at the extremes of the affective ratio, with bimodal distributions suggesting that they have either under- or overresponded to the chromatic blots (Exner, 1978). When tested again after treatment, those patients who were rated by significant others as improved had moved into the normal range with much greater frequency than those rated as unimproved (Exner, Wylie, & Kline, 1977a). It would appear that either under- or overresponsiveness to the emotionally loaded aspects of experience has potential for generating maladaptive function.

If we view the affective ratio as providing a probability statement about how likely it is that emotional stimuli will be processed and responded to, then an important next question concerns how well controlled the response will be when it does occur. The person's combination of form and color on the Rorschach appears to be reflective of this sort of control, with FC percepts (form-dominated color such as "a red butterfly") associated with well-mediated affective responding, and CF and C percepts (color-dominated form or pure color such as "a blazing fire" or "blood") associated with less well-controlled displays of affect. Gill (1967) found that ability to delay responses in a problem-solving task was associated with significantly more FC percepts and that individuals who could not delay their responses were characterized by significantly more CF and C. Adult nonpatients typically have about twice as much FC as CF and C in their records, while several patient groups all had more CF and C (Exner, 1978). Several studies, involving patients in a variety of diagnostic categories, have suggested that a shift to more FC than CF and C is associated

with evaluations of improvement in treatment and less likelihood of relapse (Exner & Murillo, 1975; Exner, Murillo, & Cannavo, 1973; Exner, Wylie, & Kline, 1977b).

The configuration of the two kinds of data—one reflecting responsiveness to affective stimuli and the other describing how well controlled the resulting responses are likely to be—can be of value in predicting the person's overall approach to the emotional parts of his/her world. For example, we could speculate that a person who is overresponsive to the affective aspects of experience (high Afr) and who does not mediate this material well (CF and C greater than FC) would be likely to manifest relatively frequent episodes of poorly controlled, "emotional" behavior.

The next questions are associated with diagnostic issues in which Rorschach data can be of value. The scope of this chapter does not allow a complete review of the Rorschach's utilization in diagnosis, but two illustrative areas—schizophrenia and suicide potential—have been chosen because of their substantial clinical significance.

Is It Likely that the Person Is Schizophrenic?

The evaluation of schizophrenia is a complex process, and a study by Exner and Weiner (1982) suggests that judges with test data *and* clinical/historical material are more accurate in their identification of independently diagnosed schizophrenic children than either judges or a computer using only test data. As far as the test material itself is concerned, an approach presented by Weiner (1966, 1971) is of value in formulating a strategy for the use of Rorschach data in the identification of schizophrenia. The first step in this strategy is the articulation of the defining elements of schizophrenia, and Weiner suggests that these are disordered thinking, poor reality testing, limited interpersonal effectiveness, and poor emotional control. The second step is the identification of Rorschach variables that appear to be representative of these behavioral features. Five elements that the Comprehensive System calls Special Scorings (Exner, Weiner, & Schuyler, 1976) appear to be closely associated with disordered thinking. These categories involve language or logic outside of generally accepted usage and percepts in which the person forms increasingly strained and inappropriate juxtapositions of details. Weiner and Exner (1978) found that withdrawn adolescents and schizophrenic adults showed significantly more of these indicators of cognitive slippage than did nonpatient and nonschizophrenic controls. As previously described, poor Rorschach form quality, particularly when gross distortions predominate over less serious perceptual "bending," is a useful measure of problems with reality testing. Exner and Weiner (1982) suggest that a limited number of whole human percepts can provide an indicator of interpersonal difficulties, and that the presence of unmodulated color (C as opposed to CF or FC) is suggestive of problems with emotional control.

Exner (1978) and Exner and Weiner (1982) note that presence of the Special Scoring indicators of disordered thinking is almost certainly the most critical Rorschach finding associated with schizophrenia, identifying high percentages of schizophrenics and few nonschizophrenic controls. Poor Rorschach form quality also manifests with much higher frequency in schizophrenics than controls. Although the indicators of interpersonal difficulties and poor emotional control are frequently seen in schizophrenics, they also appear with substantial frequency in other types of psychopathology and thus become supporting as opposed to identifying data. Exner (1978) suggests that utilizing the configuration of Rorschach indicators associated with the defining characteristics of schizophrenia represents a conservative diagnostic approach, likely to misidentify only very low numbers of "false positives."

Is it Likely that the Person Is Suicidal?

Although there have been continuing efforts to utilize both Rorschach and MMPI data in the assessment of suicide potential, until quite recently they have been of little clinical value because of unacceptably high levels of both false positive and false negative findings (Clopton, 1979; Exner, 1978). A study by Exner and Wylie (1977) marks a significant turning point and suggests that Rorschach data may have some clinical utility in the evaluation of suicide potential. They compared adult Rorschachs taken within 60 days before attempted or effected suicide with those of nonsuicidal patient and nonpatient controls and found a constellation of 11 variables that appeared more frequently in the suicidal groups. The presence of any eight of the variables identified 75% of the effected suicides, while bringing in as false positives only 20% of a nonsuicidal

inpatient depressed group, 12% of an inpatient schizophrenic group, and none of the nonpatient controls. Exner (1978) provides a useful summary of the interpretive significance of the suicide constellation variables:

> When the information about all 11 variables is integrated, a picture emerges of a person who is introspective, probably negatively so; who does not, or cannot, express emotions easily or directly and who often aborts them because of that uneasiness or uncertainty; whose emotions tend to "get out of hand" when they are displayed; who does not regard himself or herself very highly in social comparisons; whose resources are not easily or fully available for coping; who may be overly concerned with convention—or may, conversely, have reached a point where convention is disregarded; who does not organize perceptual inputs efficiently, tending to misinterpret stimuli more often than is affordable; who may be quite negative; who has difficulty in creating or maintaining interpersonal relations; and who may be psychologically and/or motorically retarded or inhibited. (p. 209)

A similar study with children and adolescents (Exner, 1978) yielded a constellation of eight variables, with the presence of any seven identifying 71% of effected suicides, 22% of nonsuicidal withdrawn youngsters, and no nonpatient controls. Other recent studies (Arffa, 1982; Kendra, 1979) have also utilized constellations of Rorschach variables in the assessment of suicide potential, and this multiple sign approach appears to have the greatest promise of any psychometric technique at present in its ability to identify relatively high percentages of suicidal individuals while including relatively few false positives. Farberow and Schneidman (1961) have shown significant relationships between demographic/behavioral variables and effected suicide, and Exner (1978) cautions that it is very unlikely that psychological tests, used alone, will ever be able to improve on this sort of data in the prediction of suicide potential. It remains to be seen whether test findings account for a "different part of the variance" than that associated with the demographic/behavioral variables. If they do, a combination of the two approaches could be of substantial value in the assessment of suicidal risk.

FUTURE DIRECTIONS

The basic nature of the Rorschach—whether it is a perceptual-cognitive task or a stimulus to fantasy—continues to be an important issue, and any discussion of the Rorschach's future must look at the current status of this question. A number of workers hold that the test's most valuable contributions are those that come when it is used to explore the uniquely personal aspects of the individual. Taking this approach, Aronow, Reznikoff, and Rauchway (1979) suggest that the Rorschach's greatest value lies in its ability to provide a rich idiographic data source, and they have proposed an interview-like administration technique that encourages the production of as much personalized material as possible. After an extensive analysis, Shaffer, Duszynski, and Thomas (1981) conclude that most of the variance in the Rorschach's structure can be accounted for by a relatively small number of factors. They question the use of many of the structural scoring categories and speculate that the idiographic and not the nomothetic material derived from the test may turn out to be more helpful in understanding the individual. Schwartz and Lazar (1979) hold that clinicians interpret projective test data in semantic, not probabilistic, ways and that concepts of psychometric validity are thus inappropriate, since assessment is a psycholinguistic as opposed to a predictive enterprise. Singer (1977) views the Rorschach as a conversational transaction and presents a technique for describing the person's style of communication and evaluating various kinds of "communication deviances." Although all of these workers advocate the utilization of some structural data, they are clearly suggesting that other aspects of the Rorschach are more likely to provide useful sources of understanding.

Exner (1980) notes that it has been customary to view the structural data derived from the perceptual-cognitive approach to the Rorschach as providing information about basic psychological styles and the content data gained from the stimulus-to-fantasy approach as providing information about the more personal, idiographic aspects of the person. He suggests that this distinction may be somewhat oversimplistic. A relatively new area of study—the way responses are generated—may cut across the structure versus content dichotomy and many of the issues raised by the workers described above by focusing on how it comes to be that a particular response is delivered. Some recent studies suggest that the blot is scanned very quickly and that the person processes substantially more percepts than he reports (Exner, 1980; Exner & Armbruster, 1974; Exner, Armbruster, & Mittman, 1978). It is also known that some aspects of the blot, such as achromatic color, are rarely reported, although they are quite important to the production of many percepts (Baughman, 1954, 1959; Exner, 1959). What happens in the interim between the person's scanning of the blot and his articulation of a response appears to involve a very complex interaction of forces. The response the person decides to articulate is chosen from a much wider set of possibilities, with need states, concern for perceptual accuracy, and evaluation of the range of responses that are socially "acceptable" within the particular test situation all contributing to the decision (Exner, 1978). This focus on the response generation process recognizes that the Rorschach is simultaneously a perceptual-cognitive problem-solving task, a social transaction, and an often highly effective way of eliciting uniquely idiographic material. The explication of this response generation process is clearly one of the most important new directions in Rorschach research.

Another important new topic involves the utilization of the Rorschach in treatment planning and evaluation. A study by Exner, Wylie, and Kline (1977a) provides some promising initial data in this area. They followed adult outpatients involved in seven different types of psychotherapy over a 28-month period and identified differences in treatment course as a function of both type of treatment and the individual's pretreatment psychological organization as described by the Rorschach EA-*ep* contrast. Further studies may ultimately result in the Rorschach's having substantial utility in the specification of treatment modality and the prediction and monitoring of treatment course.

SUMMARY

Perhaps the survival of Rorschach's deceptively simple technique can be traced to its unexpectedly comprehensive ability to tap the complexity of human psychological operation. At the same time, it has been this very richness of data that has made for sometimes immobilizing controversies as various workers have attempted to decide how best to conceptualize and process the test's varied yield. Hopefully some of the new developments such as the Comprehensive System and the focus on response production will serve an integrative function in turning these controversies into what it increasingly looks as if they often are: alternative and complementary approaches to a field whose breadth we are still charting after more than half a century.

REFERENCES

Arffa, S.M. (1982). Predicting adolescent suicidal behavior and the order of Rorschach measurement. *Journal of Personality Assessment*, 46, 563–568.

Armbruster, G. L., Miller, A.S., & Exner, J.E. (1974). Rorschach responses of parachute trainees at the beginning of training and shortly before their firstjump. Workshops study No. 201 (unpublished). Bayville, NY: Rorschach Workshops.

Aronow, E., Reznikoff, M., & Rauchway, A. (1979). Some old and new directions in Rorschach testing. *Journal of Personality Assessment*, 43, 227–234.

Baughman, E.E. (1954). A comparative analysis of Rorschach forms with altered stimulus characteristics. *Journal of Projective Techniques*, 18, 151–164.

Baughman, E.E. (1959). An experimental analysis of the relationship between stimulus structure and behavior on the Rorschach. *Journal of Projective Techniques*, 23, 134–183.

Beck, S.J. (1937). Introduction to the Rorschach method: A manual of personality study. *American Orthopsychiatric Association Monograph*, No. 1.

Beck, S.J. (1944). *Rorschach's test. I. Basic processes.* New York: Grune & Stratton.

Beck, S.J. (1945). *Rorschach's test. II. A variety of personality pictures.* New York: Grune & Stratton.

Beck, S.J. (1952). *Rorschach's test. III. Advances in interpretation.* New York: Grune & Stratton.

Beck, S.J. (1960). *The Rorschach experiment: Ventures in blind diagnosis.* New York: Grune & Stratton.

Beck, S.J., Beck, A.G., Levitt, E., & Molish, H.B. (1961). *Rorschach's test. I. Basic processes* (3rd ed.). New York: Grune & Stratton.

Beck, S.J., & Molish, H.B. (1967). *Rorschach's test. II. A variety of personality pictures.* New York: Grune & Stratton.

Bryant, E.L., & Exner, J.E. (1974). Performance on the Revised Minnesota Paper Form Board Test by under and overincorporators under timed and nontimed conditions. Workshops study No. 188 (unpublished). Bayville, NY: Rorschach Workshops.

Clopton, J.R. (1979). The MMPI and suicide. In C.S. Newmark (Ed.), *MMPI clinical and research trends.* New York: Praeger.

Exner, J.E. (1959). The influence of chromatic and achromatic color in the Rorschach. *Journal of Projective Techniques*, 23, 418–425.

Exner, J.E. (1962). The effect of color on productivity in cards VIII, IX, X of the Rorschach. *Journal of Projective Techniques*, 26, 30–33.

Exner, J.E. (1969a). Rorschach responses as an index of narcissism. *Journal of Projective Techniques and Personality Assessment*, 33, 437–455.

Exner, J.E. (1969b). *The Rorschach systems.* New York: Grune & Stratton.

Exner, J.E. (1973). The Self Focus Sentence Completion: A study of egocentricity. *Journal of Personality Assessment*, 37, 437–455.

Exner, J.E. (1974). *The Rorschach: A comprehensive system Vol. 1.* New York: Wiley.

Exner, J.E. (1978). *The Rorschach: A comprehensive system. Vol. 2: Current research and advanced interpretation.* New York: Wiley.

Exner, J.E. (1980). But it's only an inkblot. *Journal of Personality Assessment*, 44, 563–577.

Exner, J.E., & Armbruster, G.L. (1974). Increasing R by altering instructions and creating a time set. Workshops study No. 209 (unpublished). Bayville, NY: Rorschach Workshops.

Exner, J.E., Armbruster, G.L., & Mittman, B.L. (1978). The Rorschach response process. *Journal of Personality Assessment*, 42, 27–38.

Exner, J.E., Armbruster, G.L., Walker, E.J., & Cooper, W.H. (1975). Anticipation of elective surgery as manifest in Rorschach records. Workshops study No. 213 (unpublished). Bayville, NY: Rorschach Workshops.

Exner, J.E., Armbruster, G.L., & Wylie, J.R. (1976). TAT stories and the Ma:Mp ratio. Workshops study No. 225 (unpublished). Bayville, NY: Rorschach Workshops.

Exner, J.E., & Bryant, E.L. (1974a). Rorschach responses of subjects recently divorced or separated. Workshops study No. 206 (unpublished). Bayville, NY: Rorschach Workshops.

Exner, J.E., & Bryant, E.L. (1974b). Flexibility in creative efforts as related to three Rorschach variables. Workshops study No. 187 (unpublished). Bayville, NY: Rorschach Workshops.

Exner, J.E., & Bryant, E.L. (1975). Serial learning by over and underincorporators with limited and unlimited numbers of training trials. Workshops study No. 194 (unpublished). Bayville, NY: Rorschach Workshops.

Exner, J.E., Bryant, E.L., & Leura, A.V. (1975). Variations in problem solving by three EB types. Workshops study No. 217 (unpublished). Bayville, NY: Rorschach Workshops.

Exner, J.E., & Caraway, E.W. (1974). Identification of incomplete stimuli by high positive Zd and high negative Zd subjects. Workshops study No. 186 (unpublished). Bayville, NY: Rorschach Workshops.

Exner, J.E., & Leura, A.V. (1974). "Simon says" errors and the Zd scores in young children. Workshops study No. 204 (unpublished). Bayville, NY: Rorschach Workshops.

Exner, J.E., & Leura, A.V. (1977). Rorschach performances of volunteer and nonvolunteer adolescents. Workshops study No. 238 (unpublished). Bayville, NY: Rorschach Workshops.

Exner, J.E., Leura, A.V., Armbruster, G.L., & Viglione, D. (1977). A focal study of temporal consistency. Workshops study No. 253 (unpublished). Bayville, NY: Rorschach Workshops.

Exner, J.E., & Murillo, L.G. (1973). Effectiveness of regressive ECT with process schizophrenics. *Diseases of the Nervous System*, 34, 44–48.

Exner, J.E., & Murillo, L.G. (1975). Early prediction of posthospitalization relapse. *Journal of Psychiatric Research*, 12, 231–237.

Exner, J.E., & Murillo, L.G. (1977). A long term follow-up of schizophrenics treated with regressive ECT. *Diseases of the Nervous System*, 38, 162–168.

Exner, J.E., Murillo, L.G., & Cannavo, F. (1973). Disagreement between patient and relative behavioral reports as related to relapse in nonschizophrenic patients. Washington, D.C: Eastern Psychological Association.

Exner, J.E., & Walker, E.J. (1973). Rorschach responses of depressed patients prior to ECT. Workshops study No. 197 (unpublished). Bayville, NY: Rorschach Workshops.

Exner, J.E., & Weiner, I.B. (1982). *The Rorschach: A comprehensive system. Vol. 3: Assessment of children and adolescents*. New York: Wiley.

Exner, J.E., Weiner, I.B., & Schuyler, W. (1976). *A Rorschach workbook for the Comprehensive System*. Bayville, NY: Rorschach Workshops.

Exner, J.E., & Wylie, J.R. (1974). Therapist ratings of patient "insight" in an uncovering form of psychotherapy. Workshops study No. 192 (unpublished). Bayville, NY: Rorschach Workshops.

Exner, J.E., & Wylie, J.R. (1977). Some Rorschach data concerning suicide. *Journal of Personality Assessment*, 41, 339–348.

Exner, J.E., Wylie, J.R., & Bryant, E.L. (1974). Peer preference nominations among outpatients in four psychotherapy groups. Workshops study No. 199 (unpublished). Bayville, NY: Rorschach Workshops.

Exner, J.E., Wylie, J.R., & Kline, J.R. (1977a). Variations in Rorschach performance during a 28 month interval as related to seven intervention modalities. Workshops study No. 240 (unpublished). Bayville, NY: Rorschach Workshops.

Exner, J.E., Wylie, J.R., & Kline, J.R. (1977b). A long term study of treatment effects as manifest in Rorschach performance. Workshops study No. 240 (unpublished). Bayville, NY: Rorschach Workshops.

Farberow, N.L., & Shneidman, E.S. (Eds). (1961). *The cry for help*. New York: McGraw-Hill.

Frank, L.K. (1939). Projective methods for the study of personality. *Journal of Psychology*, 8, 343–389.

Gill, H.S. (1966). Delay of response and reaction to color on the Rorschach. *Journal of Projective Techniques and Personality Assessment*, 30, 545–552.

Goldman, R. (1960). Changes in Rorschach performance and clinical improvement in schizophrenia. *Journal of Consulting Psychology*, 24, 403–407.

Harder, D.W., & Ritzler, B.A. (1979). A comparison of Rorschach developmental level and form-level systems as indicators of psychosis. *Journal of Personality Assessment*, 43, 347–354.

Hens, S. (1917). Szynon phantasieprufung mit formlosen klecksen be, schulkindern, normalen erwachseuen und genteskranken. Unpublished dissertation. Zurich.

Kendra, J.M. (1979). Predicting suicide using the Rorschach Inkblot Test. *Journal of Personality Assessment*, 43, 452–456.

Kerner, J. (1857). Klexographien. In R. Pissen (Ed.), *Kerners werke*. Berlin: Boag and Co.

Kinder, B., Brubaker, R., Ingram, R., & Reading, E. (1982). Rorschach form quality: A comparison of the Exner and Beck systems. *Journal of Personality Assessment*, 46, 131–138.

Klopfer, B., & Sender, S. (1936). A system of refined scoring symbols. *Rorschach Research Exchange*, 1, 19–22.

Klopfer, B., & Kelley, D. (1942). *The Rorschach technique*. Yonkers, NY: World Book.

Klopfer, B., Ainsworth, M.D., Klopfer, W.G., & Holt, R.R. (1954). *Developments in the Rorschach technique. Vol. I. Technique and theory*. Yonkers-on-Hudson, NY: World Book.

Klopfer, B. Ainsworth, M.D., Klopfer, W.G., & Holt, R.R. (1956). *Developments in the Rorschach technique. Vol. II. Fields of application*. Yonkers, NY: World Book.

Klopfer, B., Meyer, M.M., & Brawer, F. (1970). *Developments in the Rorschach technique. Vol. III. Aspects of personality structure*. New York: Harcourt Brace, Jovanovich.

Krugman, M. (1940). Out of the inkwell. *Rorschach Research Exchange*, 4, 91–101.

Mayman, M. (1966). *Measuring reality-adherence in the Rorschach test*. Paper presented at the Psychological Association, New York.

Mayman, M. (1970). Reality contact, defense effectiveness, and psychopathology in Rorschach form-level scores. In B. Klopfer (Ed.), *Developments in the Rorschach technique. III. Aspects of personality structure*. New York: Harcourt Brace Jovanovich.

Meili-Dworetzki, G. (1939). Le test Rorschach et l'evolution de la perception. *Archives of Psychology*, 27, 111–127.

Meili-Dworetzki, G. (1956). The development of perception in the Rorschach. In B. Klopfer, (Ed.), *Developments in the Rorschach technique. II. Fields of application*. Yonkers, NY: World Book.

Molish, H.B. (1967). Critique and problems of the Rorschach. A survey. In S.J. Beck & H.B. Molish (Eds.), *Rorschach's test. II. A variety of personality pictures*. New York: Grune & Stratton.

Piotrowski, Z. (1957). *Perceptanalysis*. New York: Macmillan.

Rapaport, D., Gill, M., & Schafer, R. (1945, 1946). *Diagnostic psychological testing*. 2 Vols. Chicago: Yearbook Publishers.

Rapaport, D., Gill, M., & Schafer, R. (1968). *Diagnostic psychological testing*. (rev. ed.). In R.R. Holt (Ed.). New York: International Universities Press.

Raychaudhuri, M., & Mukerji, K. (1971). Homosexual-narcissistic "reflections" in the Rorschach: An examination of Exner's diagnostic Rorschach signs. *Rorschachiana Japonica*, 12, 119–126.

Roemer, G. (1967). The Rorschach and Roemer symbol test series. *Journal of Nervous and Mental Disorders*, 144, 185–197.

Rorschach, H. (1921). *Psychodiagnostik*. Bern: Bircher. (English translation, Bern: Hans Huber, 1942.)

Rorschach, H., & Oberholzer, E. (1923). The application of the form interpretation test. *Zeitschrift fur die Gesamte Neurologie und Psychiatrie*, 82. (Also in H. Rorschach (1942). *Psychodiagnostik*. Bern: Hans Huber.)

Rybakow, T. (1910). *Atlas for experimental research on personality.* Moscow: University of Moscow.

Schafer, R. (1948). *The clinical application of psychological tests.* New York: International Universities Press.

Schafer, R. (1954). *Psychoanalytic interpretation in Rorschach testing.* New York: Grune & Stratton.

Schafer, R. (1967). *Projective testing and psychoanalysis.* New York: International Universities Press.

Schwartz, F., & Lazar, Z. (1979). The scientific status of the Rorschach. *Journal of Personality Assessment*, **43**, 3–11.

Shaffer, J.W., Duszynski, K.R., & Thomas, C.B. (1981). Orthogonal dimensions of individual and group forms of the Rorschach. *Journal of Personality Assessment*, **45**, 230–239.

Shalit, B. (1965). Effects of environmental stimulation on the M, FM, and m responses in the Rorschach. *Journal of Projective Techniques and Personality Assessment*, **29**, 228–231.

Sherman, M.H. (1955). A psychoanalytic definition of Rorschach determinants. *Psychoanalysis*, **3**, 68–76.

Singer, J.L., & Brown, S.L. (1977). The experience type: Some behavioral correlates and theoretical implications. In M.A. Rickers-Ovsiankina (Ed.), *Rorschach psychology.* Huntington, NY: Robert E. Krieger Publishing Company.

Singer, M.T. (1977). The Rorschach as a transaction. In M.A. Rickers-Ovsiankina (Ed.), *Rorschach psychology.* Huntington, NY: Robert E. Krieger Publishing Company.

Smith, N.M. (1981). The relationship between the Rorschach whole response and level of cognitive functioning. *Journal of Personality Assessment*, **45**, 13–19.

Toomey, L.C., & Rickers-Ovsiankina, M.A. (1977). Tabular comparison of scoring systems. In M.A. Rickers-Ovsiankina (Ed.), *Rorschach psychology.* Huntington, NY: Robert E. Krieger Publishing Company.

Tulchin, S.H. (1940). The pre-Rorschach use of inkblot tests. *Rorschach Research Exchange*, **4**, 1–7.

Weiner, I.B. (1966). *Psychodiagnosis in schizophrenia.* New York: Wiley.

Weiner, I.B. (1971). Rorschach diagnosis of schizophrenia: Empirical validation. *Rorschachiana*, **9**, 913–920.

Weiner, I.B. (1977). Approaches to Rorschach validation. In M.A. Rickers-Ovsiankina (Ed.), *Rorschach psychology.* Huntington, NY: Robert E. Krieger Publishing Company.

Weiner, I.B., & Exner, J.E. (1978). Rorschach indices of disordered thinking in patient and nonpatient adolescents and adults. *Journal of Personality Assessment*, **42**, 339–343.

Whipple, G.M. (1910). *Manual of mental and physical tests*, Baltimore: Warwick & York.

Wiener-Levy, D., & Exner, J.E. (1981). The Rorschach EA-*ep* variable as related to persistence in a task frustration situation under feedback conditions. *Journal of Personality Assessment*, **45**, 118–124.

Wilson, G., & Blake, R. (1950). A methodological problem in Beck's organizational concept. *Journal of Consulting Psychology*, **14**, 20–24.

Zubin, J., Eron, L.D., & Schumer, F. (1965). *An experimental approach to projective techniques.* New York: Wiley.

PART VIII

BEHAVIORAL ASSESSMENT

18 BEHAVIORAL ASSESSMENT OF CHILDREN

Thomas H. Ollendick
Alice E. Meador

INTRODUCTION

Although treatment strategies based on behavioral principles have a long and rich tradition in clinical psychology (e.g., Holmes, 1936; Jones, 1924; Watson & Rayner, 1920), psychological assessment procedures based on these principles have lagged significantly behind. This situation is surprising, since the development and evaluation of efficacious treatment procedures depend on the development of sound assessment devices. In recent years, attempts to address this imbalance have been evident, as witnessed by a proliferation of books (e.g., Ciminero, Calhoun, & Adams, 1977; Cone & Hawkins, 1977; Haynes, 1978; Hersen & Bellack, 1976; Keefe, Kopel, & Gordon, 1978; Mash & Terdal, 1976; Nay, 1979), journals (*Behavioral Assessment, Journal of Behavioral Assessment*), and research articles. Most of these recent developments have been directed toward assessment of adults and their behavior disorders; unfortunately, behavioral assessment of children and their disorders has been even slower to evolve. Furthermore, most behavioral assessment procedures for children have been adopted, sometimes indiscriminately, from those used with adults. This practice is of dubious merit and has frequently led to questionable findings. Only very recently have concerned efforts been made to develop and systematically evaluate behavioral

assessment procedures for children (e.g., Mash & Terdal, 1981; Ollendick & Herson, 1984).

As first described by Mash and Terdal (1981) and expanded upon more recently by Ollendick and Hersen (1984), child behavioral assessment can best be viewed as *an exploratory, hypothesis-testing process in which a range of specific procedures is used in order to understand a given child, group, or social ecology and to formulate and evaluate specific intervention strategies*. As such, child behavioral assessment entails more than identification and observation of highly discrete and specific target behaviors and their controlling variables. While the importance of systematic observation of target behaviors should not be underestimated, more recent advances in child behavioral assessment have incorporated a variety of assessment procedures including behavioral interviews, self-reports, ratings by significant others, self-monitoring, *and* behavioral observations. Such an approach can be described as a multimethod one in which a "picture" of the child is obtained that is informative and useful in the understanding and modification of child behavior disorders (Ollendick & Cerny, 1981).

Two other primary features characterize child behavior assessment procedures: *First*, they must be sensitive to rapid developmental changes in children, and *second*, they must be empirically validated. Probably the most distinguishing characteristic of children is developmental change. Whether such change is based on hypothetical stages of growth or derived from precise principles of learning, it has direct implications for the selection of specific assessment procedures and their use in the evaluation of response to treatment. Behavioral interviews, self-reports, other-reports, self-monitoring, and behavioral observation are all affected by rapidly changing developmental processes. For example, interviews may be more difficult to conduct with very young children, self-reports may be less reliable, other-reports may be biased due to unclear or exaggerated expectancies, and self-monitoring and behavioral observations may be differentially reactive at varying ages. Age-related constraints are numerous and must be taken into consideration when selecting specific methods of assessment.

Just as child behavioral assessment procedures must be developmentally sensitive, they must also be empirically validated. All too frequently, professionals working with children have used assessment methods of convenience without due regard for psychometric issues related to reliability, validity, and clinical utility. Although child behavior assessors have fared somewhat better in this regard, they too have tended to design and use highly idiosyncratic tools for assessment. As we have noted elsewhere (Ollendick & Hersen, 1984), comparison across studies is extremely difficult, if not impossible, and the advancement of an assessment technology, let alone an understanding of child behavior disorders, is not realized with such an idiosyncratic approach.

While a multimethod approach that is based on developmentally sensitive and empirically validated procedures is espoused, it should be clear that a "test battery" approach is not being recommended. The specific devices to be used depend upon a host of factors, including the nature of the referral question and the personnel, time, and resources available (Ollendick & Cerny, 1981). Nonetheless, given the inherent limitations of the various procedures, as well as the desirability of obtaining as complete a "picture" of the child as possible, we recommend multimethod assessment whenever feasible. Any single procedure, including direct behavioral observation, is not sufficient to provide this picture of the child. The multimethod approach is not only helpful in assessing specific target behaviors and in determining re-

sponse to behavior change, but in understanding child behavior disorders and advancing our database in this area of study.

Based on these considerations, the following summary statements regarding child behavioral assessment are offered (Ollendick & Hersen, 1984).

1. Children are a special population. The automatic extension of adult behavioral assessment methods to children is not warranted and is often inappropriate. Age-related variables affect the choice of methods as well as the procedures employed.

2. Given rapid developmental change in children, normative comparisons are required to ensure that appropriate target behaviors are selected and that change in behavior is related to treatment, not to normal developmental change. Such comparisons required identification of suitable reference groups and information about the "natural course" of child behavior problems.

3. Thorough child behavioral assessment involves multiple targets of change, including overt behavior, affective states, and cognitions. Further, such assessment entails determining the context (e.g., familial, social, cultural) in which the child's behavior occurs and the "function" that the targeted behaviors serve.

4. Given the wide range of targets for change, multimethod assessment is desirable and necessary. Multimethod assessment should not be viewed simply as a "test battery" approach; rather, methods should be selected on the basis of their appropriateness to the referral question. Regardless of the measures used, they should be developmentally sensitive and empirically validated.

HISTORY AND DEVELOPMENT

As indicated earlier, adequate assessment of children's behavior problems requires a multimethod assessment approach, gathering information from self- and other-report sources as well as from direct behavioral observation. This allows for important information from the cognitive and affective modalities to be combined with overt behavioral data in order to obtain a more complete picture of the child. In addition, a multimethod approach to assessment provides the clinician with necessary information regarding the perceptions and reactions of significant others in the child's environment (e.g., parents, teachers) to the ostensible problematic behaviors. However, this comprehensive assessment approach is of a relatively recent origin in the area of child behavioral assessment.

In its earliest stages, behavioral assessment of children (Ullmann & Krasner, 1965) relied exclusively on the identification and specification of discrete and observable target behaviors. As such, assessment was delimited to gathering information from the motoric response modality. This early assessment approach followed logically from the theoretical assumptions of the operant school of thought in vogue at the time. Early on, behaviorally oriented psychologists posited that the only appropriate behavioral domain for empirical study was that which was directly observable (Skinner, 1953). Contending that the objective demonstration of behavior change following intervention was of utmost importance, behaviorists relied upon data that could in fact be objectively measured. Hence, frequency, rate, and duration measures of the behaviors of interest were obtained. Although the existence of organismic cognitions and affective states was acknowledged, these were not deemed appropriate subject matter for experimental analysis.

As treatment approaches with children broadened to include cognitive and self-control techniques (e.g., Bandura, 1977; Kanfer & Phillips, 1970; Kendall & Hollon, 1980; Meichenbaum, 1977), it became apparent that assessment strategies would likewise have to expand into the cognitive and affective domains. Furthermore, even though operant techniques have proven highly efficacious in effecting behavior change under controlled conditions, the clinical significance and social validity of these changes were less easily addressed through sole reliance on direct assessment of specific behaviors. This state of affairs prompted behaviorists to take into account information from a variety of sources (e.g., significant other-report measures), even though these sources provided only indirect measures of behavior (Cone, 1978). The issue of the clinical significance of behavior change is especially crucial in child behavioral assessment, since children are invariably referred for treatment by adults (e.g., parents, teachers). Once the treatment goals have been adequately identified, the ultimate index of treatment efficacy lies in the referral source's perceptions of change. Hence, other-report measures become as important as direct observational ones.

More recently, the scope of behavioral assessment has broadened even further to incorporate the impact of large-scale social systems (e.g., schools, sociocultural influences) on the child's behavior (Patterson, 1976; Wahler, 1976). Although inclusion of these additional factors serves to complicate the assessment process, it is an integral part of assessment, because the ideologies and expectations of these seemingly distal social systems often have profound and immediate effects on individual behavior.

In sum, child behavioral assessment has progressed from sole reliance on measurement of target behaviors in its inchoate state to a broader approach that takes into account the cognitive and affective processes of the child that mediate behavior change and the social context in which the child exists. The assessment techniques that accompany this approach include indirect behavioral measures, such as the behavioral interview, and self- and other-report instruments. These measures are utilized in addition to direct behavioral observation, which remains the cornerstone of behavioral assessment (Mash & Terdal, 1981; Ollendick & Hersen, 1984).

THEORETICAL UNDERPINNINGS

Although behaviorism has had a historical development of its own independent of the historical course of the psychodynamic school of thought, it is fair to say that a major impetus for the increased poularity of behavioral psychology in the last three decades has been the growing dissatisfaction with the psychodynamic approach. This is reflected in the fact that virtually all discussions of behavioral assessment are carried out through comparison and contrast with traditional assessment approaches (e.g., Bornstein, Bornstein, & Dawson, 1984; Cone & Hawkins, 1977; Goldfried & Kent, 1972; Mash & Terdal, 1981; Mischel, 1968; Ollendick & Hersen, 1984). Though such comparisons often result in oversimplification of both approaches, they are nevertheless useful and serve to elucidate the theoretical underpinnings of the behavioral approach. In this section, we will therefore contrast the theoretical assumptions that guide behavioral and traditional assessment and discuss the practical implications of these assumptions for assessment.

The most fundamental difference between traditional and behavioral assessment approaches lies in the conception of personality and behavior. In the traditional assessment approach, personality is viewed as a reflection of underlying and enduring traits. Behavior is assumed to be caused by these internal personality characteristics. In contrast, behavioral approaches have generally avoided references to underlying personality constructs, focusing instead on what the child does under specific circumstances. From the behavioral perspective, the term *personality* refers to patterns rather than causes of behavior. Furthermore, behavior is viewed as a response to current environmental stimuli, be they extraorganismic and environmental or intraorganismic and cognitive or affective in nature.

It is important not to oversimplify the behavioral view of the causes of behavior. It has often been erroneously asserted that the behavioral approach focuses on external determinants of behavior at the exclusion of organismic states or internal cognitions and affects. To be sure, behavioral views of childhood disorders have emphasized the significant role of environmental factors in the manifestation of behavior. However, intraorganismic variables that influence behavior are not ignored. This is evidenced by the array of self-report instruments tapping cognitive and affective modalities currently utilized in behavioral assessment. A thorough behavioral assessment should attempt to identify controlling variables, whether environmental or organismic in nature. As Mash and Terdal (1981) point out, "the relative importance of organismic and environmental variables and their interaction . . . should follow from a careful analysis of the problem" (p. 23).

The traditional conception of personality as comprised of stable and enduring traits implies that behavior will be relatively consistent across situations and over time. The behavioral view, in contrast, has been one of situational specificity; that is, since behavior is in large part a function of situational determinants, a child's behavior will change as these situational factors are altered. Similarly, consistency of behavior across the temporal dimension is not necessarily expected. Hence, an aggressive act, such as a child hitting another child, would be seen from the traditional viewpoint as a reflection of underlying hostility, which, in turn, is related to early life experiences or intrapsychic conflicts. Little or no attention is given to specific situational factors or the environmental context in which the aggressive act occurred. From the behavioral perspective, an attempt is made to identify those variables that elicit and maintain the aggressive act in that particular situation. That the child may aggress in a variety of situations is explained in terms of his or her learning history where reinforcing consequences have been obtained for past aggressive acts, and not in terms of an underlying personality trait of hostility. From this analysis, it is evident that the actual behavior is of utmost importance to behaviorists, since it represents a sample of the child's behavioral repertoire in a given situation. From the traditional viewpoint, the behavior assumes importance only insofar as it represents an underlying cause.

These differing assumptions have implications for the assessment process. In behavioral assessment, the emphasis on situational specificity necessitates an assessment approach that samples behavior across a number of settings. Hence, assessment of the child's behavior at home, in school, and/or on the playground is important in addition to information obtained in the clinic setting. Furthermore, the information obtained from these various settings likely will not, and in fact is not necessarily expected to, be consistent. The child may behave aggressively in school and on the playground but not at home. This lack of consistent findings would be more problematic for the traditional approach but would not likely occur, since traditional assessment generally takes place solely within the clinic setting. Similarly, the notion of temporal inconsistency necessitates that the child's behavior be assessed at several points in time, whereas this generally is not required from the traditional assessment standpoint.

At one point, it was relatively easy to differentiate behavioral from traditional assessment on the basis of the methods employed. Direct behavioral observation was the defining characteristic and often the sole assessment technique of the behavioral approach, whereas interviewing and projective techniques characterized traditional assessment. However, as behavioral assessment has expanded to include a wider repertoire of assessment methods, it has become increasingly difficult to differentiate behavioral and traditional assessments simply on the basis of assessment methods utilized. It is not uncommon for behaviorists to utilize information from interviews, self-report instruments, or even (though less commonly) projective techniques in assessment. Thus, there is much overlap in the actual assessment practices. The difference between traditional and behavioral assessment lies then not in the methods employed but rather in the manner in which data from assessment sources are utilized. Traditional approaches interpret assessment data as signs of underlying personality functioning. These data are used to diagnose and classify the child and to make prognostic statements. From the behavioral perspective, assessment data are utilized to identify target behaviors and their maintaining conditions (again, be they overt or covert). Information obtained from assessment serves as a sample of the child's behavior under specific circumstances. This information guides the selection of appropriate treatment procedures. Further, since behavioral assessment is ongoing, this information serves as an index by which to continually evaluate the effects of treatment and to make appropriate revisions in treatment. Since assessment data are viewed as samples of behavior, the level of inference required is low, whereas a high level of inference is required when one attempts to make statements about one's personality functioning from his responses to interview questions or test items.

In sum, traditional and behavioral assessment approaches operate under different assumptions regarding the child's behavior. These assumptions, in turn, have implications for the assessment process. Of paramount importance for child behavior assessors is the necessity of tailoring the assessment approach to the specific difficulties of the child in order to accurately identify the problem, specify treatment, and evaluate treatment effectiveness. This requires ongoing assessment from a number of sources under appropriately diverse stimulus situations.

DESCRIPTION OF ASSESSMENT PROCEDURES

Multimethod behavioral assessment of children entails the use of a wide range of specific procedures. As behavioral approaches with children evolved from sole reliance on operant procedures to those involving cognitive and self-control procedures, the methods of assessment changed accordingly. The identification of discrete target behaviors has been expanded to include the specification of individual cognitions and affects, as well as large scale social systems that impact upon the child (e.g., families, schools, communities).

Information regarding these additional areas can be obtained most efficiently and productively

through behavioral interviews, self-reports, and other-reports. Cone (1978) has described these assessment methods as indirect ones; that is, while they may be used to measure the behaviors of clinical relevance, they are obtained at a time and place different from that when the actual behaviors occurred. In both behavioral interviews and self-report questionnaires, a verbal representation of the behaviors of interest is obtained. Other-reports or ratings by others are also included in the indirect category because they involve retrospective descriptions of behavior. Generally, a significant person in the child's environment (e.g., parent, teacher) is asked to rate the child based on previous observations (recollections).

As noted by Cone (1978), ratings such as these should not be confused with direct observation methods, which assess the behaviors of interest at the time and place of their occurrence. Of course, information regarding cognition and affects, as well as the situations or settings in which they occur, can also be obtained through direct behavioral observations, either by self-monitoring or through trained observers. Cone (1978) labels these latter two procedures as direct methods of assessment. In the sections that follow both indirect and direct methods will be briefly discussed.

Behavioral Interviews

The first method of indirect assessment to be considered is the behavioral interview. Of the many procedures employed by behavioral clinicians, the interview is the most widely used (Swan & MacDonald, 1978) and is generally considered an indispensable part of assessment (Gross, 1984; Linehan, 1977). Behavioral interviews are structured to obtain detailed information about the target behaviors and their controlling variables, to begin the formulation of specific treatment plans, and to develop a relationship with the child and his or her family (Ollendick & Cerny, 1981). While the primary purpose of the behavioral interview is to obtain information, we have found that traditional "helping" skills including reflections, clarifications, and summary statements help put the child and his or her family at ease and greatly facilitate the collection of this information.

The popularity of the behavioral interview may be due in part to a number of practical considerations, as well as to advantages it offers over other procedures (Gross, 1984). While direct observations of target behaviors are the hallmark of behavioral assessment, such observations are not always practical or feasible. At times, especially in outpatient therapy, the clinician must rely upon the child's self-report as well as that of his or her parents, to initiate assessment and treatment. Further, the interview allows the clinician to obtain a broad band of information regarding overall functioning as well as detailed information about specific areas. The flexibility inherent in the interview also allows the clinician to build a relationship with the child and his or her family and to obtain information that might otherwise not be revealed. As noted by Linehan (1977), some family members may be more likely to divulge information verbally in the context of a professional relationship than to write it down on a form to be entered into a permanent file. Finally, the interview allows the clinician the opportunity to observe firsthand verbal and nonverbal behaviors of the family in reaction to a variety of topics. Such information can be used to form an initial description of the family context in which the problem behaviors occur and to assess resources within the family that might be involved to assist in treatment planning and implementation.

When conducting behavioral interviews with children and their families, two special problems should be considered (Evans & Nelson, 1977; Ollendick & Cerny, 1981). First, children rarely refer themselves for treatment; invariably, they are referred by adults (parents, teachers, physicians) whose perceptions of problems may not coincide with those of the referred children. In fact, it is not unusual for children to maintain that they have no problem. A second problem, related to the first, is the determination of when child behaviors are problematic and when they are not. Normative developmental comparisons are useful in this regard. It is not uncommon for parents to refer 5-year-olds who reverse letters, 3-year-olds who wet the bed, and 13-year-olds who are concerned about their physical appearance. Frequently, these referrals are based on parental uneasiness or unrealistic expectations rather than genuine problems. For these reasons, we approach the initial interview with caution and do not blindly accept that a "problem" exists in the child. Rather, upon occasion, parents, siblings, and/or systems have become the "clients."

In sum, an attempt is made during the initial behavioral interview to obtain as complete a picture of the child and his or her family as possible. While the interview is focused around specific target behaviors, caution is exercised to ensure that an accurate description is obtained as well as the perceptions of the various family members. The information obtained should be considered tentative and used primarily to formulate hypotheses about the target behaviors and their controlling variables and to select additional assessment methods to explore the target behaviors in greater depth (e.g., rating scales, self-reports, self-monitoring, and behavioral observations). The behavioral interview is only the first step in the assessment process.

Ratings and Checklists

Following the initial interview and the clarification of presenting complaints, significant others in the child's environment may be requested to complete rating forms or checklists. In general, these forms are useful in providing an overall description of the child's behavior, in specifying dimensions or response clusters that characterize the child's behavior, and in serving as outcome measures for the effectiveness of treatment. Many of these forms contain items related to such diverse areas of functioning as school achievement, peer relationship, activity level, and self-control. As such, they provide a potentially comprehensive and cost-effective picture of the child and his or her overall level of functioning. Further, the forms are useful in eliciting information that may have been missed in the behavioral interview (Novick, Rosenfeld, Block, & Dawson, 1966). Finally, the forms might prove useful in the search for the best "match" between various treatments (e.g., systematic desensitization, cognitive restructuring, and self-control) and "types" of children as described on these forms (Ciminero & Drabman, 1977).

The popularity of these rating forms and checklists is attested to by the number of forms currently available (McMahon, 1984; Ollendick & Cerny, 1981). Two of the more frequently used forms will be briefly described. The most frequently used and widely researched scale is the Behavior Problem Checklist (Quay & Peterson, 1967, 1975). Based on Peterson's (1961) early efforts to directly sample diverse child behavior problems, the scale consists of 55 items, each rated on a 3-point severity scale. While some of the items are quite general and require considerable inference (e.g., lacks self-confidence, jealous), others are more specific (e.g., cries, sucks thumb). Three primary dimensions or response clusters of child behavior have been identified on this scale: conduct problems, personality problems, and inadequacy-immaturity problems. A fourth cluster, socialized delinquency, has been found in adolescent delinquent samples but not in students in public school classes or in children referred to child guidance clinics. Interestingly, the conduct and personality problem clusters are similar to those found in numerous factor analytic studies of other rating forms and checklists as well. These two factors or response clusters represent consistent dimensions of child behavior problems, reflecting externalizing (e.g., acting out) and internalizing (e.g., anxiety, withdrawal) dimensions of behavior (Achenbach, 1966).

While the Behavior Problem Checklist has a rather lengthy history and is the most researched scale, it does not include the rating of positive behaviors and, hence, does not provide a basis on which to evaluate more appropriate behaviors. A scale that does assess appropriate behaviors, as well as inappropriate ones, is the Child Behavior Checklist (Achenbach, 1978; Achenbach & Edelbrock, 1979). The scale, designed for both parents and teachers, is comprised of both social competency and behavior problem items. Further, separate editions of the scale are available for boys and girls in each of three age ranges (4–5, 6–11, and 12–16 years), with considerable normative data available. Social competency items examine the child's participation in various activities (e.g., sports, hobbies, chores), social organizations (e.g., clubs, groups), and school (e.g., grades, placement, promotions). Responses to each item are scored on a 3-point scale that reflects both the quantity and quality of competency-related behaviors. The behavior problem scale of the checklist consists of 118 items, each also rated on a 3-point scale. As with Quay and Peterson's Behavior Problem Checklist, some of the items are general and require considerable inference (e.g., feels worthless, acts too young, and fears own impulses), while others are more specific and easily scored (e.g., wets bed, sets fires, and destroys own things). Factor analyses have revealed a variety of response clusters that differ with the age and sex of the child; nonetheless, broad-band groupings of the factors reflect the aforementioned internalizing and externalizing behavioral dimensions. This checklist, while less

researched at this time, holds considerable promise in child behavioral assessment.

In addition to these more general rating forms, highly specific rating forms are also available for use in child behavioral assessment. Among these is the Louisville Fear Survey Schedule for Children (Miller, Barrett, Hampe, & Noble, 1972). This scale is comprised of 81 items that cover an extensive array of fears and anxieties found in children and adolescents. Each item is rated on a 3-point scale by the child's parents. Responses to specific fear items can be used to "subtype" fearful children. For example, Miller et al. (1972) were able to differentiate among various subtypes of school phobic children on the basis of this instrument.

In sum, a variety of other-report instruments are available. As noted earlier, these forms must be considered indirect methods of assessment, since they rely on retrospective descriptions of the child's behavior. For all of these scales, the person is asked to rate the child based on past observations of that child's behavior. The primary asset of these scales is that they provide a comprehensive sampling of potential behavior problems. Unfortunately, this asset might also be considered a deficit; that is, they do not provide highly specific information about the behaviors of direct interest. Nonetheless, they do provide useful information in the formulation and evaluation of treatment programs.

Self-Report Instruments

Coincident with the collection of other-reports regarding the child's behavior, self-reports of attitudes, feelings, and behaviors may also be obtained from the child himself or herself. Early behaviorists eschewed such data, maintaining that the only acceptable piece of data was observable behavior. To a large extent, this negative bias against self-report was an outgrowth of early findings indicating that reports of subjective states did not always coincide with observable behaviors (Finch & Rogers, 1984). While synchrony in responding is, in fact, not always observed, contemporary researchers have cogently argued that the child's perceptions of his or her behavior and its consequences may be as important for behavior change as the behavior itself (Finch, Nelson, & Moss, 1983; Ollendick & Hersen, 1984). Furthermore, as we have stated earlier, although different assessment procedures may yield slightly different information, data from these sources should be compared and contrasted in order to produce the best picture of the child and to derive meaningful treatment procedures and goals. Although self-report instruments have specific limitations, they provide valuable information about the child and can be used as an index of change following treatment.

A wide variety of self-report instruments have been developed for use with children. Among these are specific measures of anger (Nelson & Finch, 1978), anxiety (Spielberger, 1973), assertion (Deluty, 1979), depression (Kovacs, 1978), and fear (Scherer & Nakamura, 1968). Each of these instruments has been carefully developed and empirically validated. Three of the more frequently used instruments will be briefly described.

Spielberger's State-Trait Anxiety Inventory for Children (1973) consists of 20 items that measure "state" anxiety and 20 items that measure "trait" anxiety. The state form is used to assess the more transient aspects of anxiety, while the trait form is used to measure the more generalized aspects of anxiety. Combined, the two scales provide both process and outcome measures of change in self-reported anxiety. That is, the state form can be used productively to determine session-by-session changes in anxiety, while the trait form can be used as a pre, post, and follow-up measure of reduction in generalized anxiety. A clear advantage of this instrument is that the state scale is designed so that responses to relatively specific anxiety-producing situations can be determined. For example, the child can be instructed to indicate how he or she feels "at this moment" about standing up in front of class, leaving home for summer camp, or being ridiculed by peers. Further, cognitive, motoric, and physiologic indicants of anxiety can be endorsed by the child (e.g., feeling upset, scared, mixed up, jittery, or nervous). Reponses to the items are scored on a 3-point scale (e.g., "I feel very scared . . . scared . . . not scared"). Finally, the extent of generalization of the anxiety response can be measured by the trait form. The Spielberger scales are most useful for middle-aged children (9–12), but have been used with both younger children and older adolescents as well.

A second instrument that has been used frequently in child behavioral assessment is the Fear Survey Schedule for Children (Scherer & Nakamura, 1968) and its recent revision (Ollendick, 1983). In the revised scale, designed to be used with younger and middle-age children, the child is instructed to rate his or her fear level to each of 80 items on a 3-point scale. Children are asked to indicate whether a specific fear item (e.g, having to go to school, being punished by father, dark places, riding in a car) frightens them "not at all," "some," or "a lot." Factor analysis of the scale has revealed five primary factors: fear of failure or criticism, fear of the unknown, fear of injury and small animals, fear of danger and death, and medical fears. Further, it has been shown that girls report greater fear than boys, that specific fears change developmentally, and that the most prevalent fears of boys and girls have remained unchanged over the past 30 years. Such information is highly useful when determining whether a child of a specific age and gender is excessively fearful. Further, the instrument can be used to differentiate "subtypes" of specifically phobic youngsters whose fear of school is related to separation anxiety (e.g., death, having parents argue, being alone) from those whose fear is due to specific aspects of the school situation (e.g., taking a test, making a mistake, being sent to the principal). When information from this instrument is combined with that from parents on the Louisville Fear Survey Schedule for Children (Miller et al., 1972), a relatively complete picture of the child's characteristic fear pattern is obtained.

The final self-report instrument to be briefly reviewed is Kovacs' (1978) Children's Depression Inventory. Within the last 10 years no other area in clinical child psychology has received more attention than depression in children. A multitude of issues regarding its existence, nature, assessment, and treatment have been examined (Cantwell, 1983). One of the major obstacles to systematic investigations in this area has been the absence of an acceptable self-report instrument. The Children's Depression Inventory, though still in its research form, appears to meet this need. The instrument is a 27-item severity measure of depression based on the well-known Beck Depression Inventory. Each of the 27 items consists of three response choices designed to range through normally to definite but probably not clinically significant depression, to fairly severe and clinically significant symptoms. Kovacs reports that the instrument is suitable for middle-aged children or through adolescence (8–17 years of age). We have found the instrument to be useful with younger children as well, especially when the items are read aloud and the response choices are depicted on a bar graph. However, as noted by Finch and Rogers (1984), considerably more work is needed on this instrument before it can be widely used. Until additional reliability and cross-validational studies are completed, caution should be exercised in the routine use of this instrument.

In sum, a variety of self-report instruments are available. As with other-report forms, self-reports should be used with appropriate caution and due regard for their specific limitations. Since they generally involve the child's retrospective rating of attitudes, feelings, and behaviors, they too, must be considered indirect methods of assessment (Cone, 1978). Nevertheless, they do provide valuable information regarding the child's own perception of his or her behavior.

Self-Monitoring

Self-monitoring differs from self-report in that it constitutes an observation of *the* clinically relevant target behavior at the time of its occurrence (Cone, 1978). As such, it is a direct method of assessment. Self-monitoring requires the child to observe his or her own behavior and then to systematically record its occurrence. Typically, the child is asked to keep a diary, place marks on a card, or push the plunger on a counter as the behavior occurs or immediately thereafter. Although self-monitoring procedures have been used with both children and adults, at least three considerations must be attended to when such procedures are used with younger children (Shapiro, 1984): The behaviors should be clearly defined, prompts to use the procedures should be readily available, and rewards for their use should be provided. Younger children may have difficulty remembering exactly what behaviors to monitor and how those behaviors are defined. For these reasons, it is generally considered desirable to provide the child a brief description of the target behavior, or better yet a picture of it, and to have the child record only one or two behaviors at a time. In an exceptionally sensitive application of these guidelines, Kunzelman (1970) recommended the use of COUNTOONS, simple stick figure drawings that depict the specific behaviors to be self-monitored. Children are instructed to place a tally mark next to the picture when the behavior occurs. For example, a girl monitoring hitting her younger brother may be given an index card with a drawing of a girl hitting a younger boy and instructed to mark each time she does what the girl in the picture is doing. Of course, in a well-designed program, the girl might also be provided a picture of a girl and a younger boy sharing toys and asked to mark each time she emits the appropriate behavior as well. Such pictorial cues serve as visual prompts for self-monitoring. Finally, children should be reinforced following the successful use of self-monitoring.

In general, methods of self-monitoring are highly variable and dependent upon the behavior being monitored and its place of occurrence. For example, Shapiro, McGonigle, and Ollendick (1980) had mentally retarded and emotionally disturbed children self-monitor on-task behavior in a school setting by placing gummed stars on assignment sheets, while Ollendick (1981) had child ticquers simply place tally marks contingent on occurrences of tics on a colored index card carried in the child's pocket. In our clinical work, we have also used wrist counters with children whose targeted behaviors occur while they are "on the move." Such a device is not only easy to use, but serves as a visual prompt to self-record. The key to successful self-monitoring in children is the use of recording procedures that are uncomplicated.

In sum, self-monitoring procedures represent a direct means to obtain information about the target behaviors as well as their antecedents and consequences. While specific monitoring methods may vary, any procedure that allows the child to record presence of the targeted behaviors can be used. When appropriate procedures are used, self-monitoring represents a direct and elegant method of assessment.

Behavioral Observations

Direct observation of the child's behavior in the natural environment is the hallmark of child behavioral assessment. As described by Johnson and Bolstad (1973), the development of naturalistic observation procedures represents *the* major contribution of the behavioral approach to assessment and treatment of children. Naturalistic observations provide a direct sample of the child's behavior at the time and place of its occurrence. As such, it is the least inferential of the assessment methods described. However, behavioral observations in the naturalistic environment should not necessarily be viewed as "better" than these other methods of assessment. Rather, they should be viewed as complementary to the other methods, with each providing slightly different but valuable information.

In behavioral observation systems, a single behavior or set of behaviors that have been identified as problematic (generally through the aforementioned procedures) are operationally defined, observed, and recorded in a systematic fashion. In addition, the events that precede and follow the behaviors of interest are recorded and subsequently used the development of specific treatment programs. Although Jones, Reid, and Patterson (1975) have recommended the use of "trained impartial observer-coders" for collection of these data, this is not always possible in child behavioral assessment. Frequently, time constraints, lack of trained personnel, and insufficient resources mitigate against the use of highly trained and impartial observers. In some cases behavioral clinicians have used significant others in the child's environment (e.g., parents, teachers, siblings) or the children themselves as observers of their own behavior. Although not impartial, these observers can be adequately trained to record clearly defined observable behaviors in the natural environment. In other cases, behavioral clinicians have resorted to laboratory or analogue settings that are analogous to, but not the same as, the natural environment. In these simulated settings, the child may be asked to behave "as if" he or she is angry with his or her parents, to role play assertive responding, or to approach a highly feared object. Behaviors can be directly observed or taped and reviewed retrospectively. The distinguishing characteristic of behavioral observations, whether they be obtained in the naturalistic environment or in simulated settings, is that a direct sample of behavior is obtained.

A wide variety of target behaviors have been examined using behavioral observation procedures. These behaviors have varied from relatively discrete behaviors like enuresis and tics that require simple recording procedures to complex social interactions that require extensive behavioral coding systems (e.g., O'Leary, Romanczyk, Kass, Dietz, & Santogrossi, 1971; Patterson, Ray, Shaw, & Coff, 1969; Wahler, House, & Stambaugh, 1976).

The utility of behavioral observations in naturalistic and simulated settings is nicely illustrated in Ayllon, Smith, and Rogers' (1970) behavioral assessment of a school phobic girl. In this case study, impartial observers in the child's home monitored the stream of events occurring on school days in order to better delineate the actual "school phobic" behaviors and to determine the antecedent and consequent events associated with them. In this single parent family, it was noted that the mother routinely left for work about one hour after the targeted girl (Valerie) and her siblings were to leave for school. Although the siblings left for school without incident, Valerie was observed to "cling" to her mother and refuse to leave the house and go to school. As described by Ayllon et al. "Valerie typically followed her mother around the house, from room to room, spending approximately 80% of her time within 10 feet of her mother. During these times there was little or no conversation" (p. 128). Given her refusal to go to school, the mother took Valerie to a neighbor's apartment for the day. However, when the mother attempted to leave for work, Valerie followed her at a 10-foot distance. Frequently the mother had to return to the neighbor's apartment with Valerie in hand. This daily pattern was observed to end with the mother "literally running to get out of sight of Valerie" so that she would not follow her to work. During the remainder of the day, it was observed that Valerie could do whatever she pleased: "her day was one which would be considered ideal by many grade school children—she could be outdoors and play as she chose all day long. No demands of any type were placed on her" (p. 129). Clearly, it appeared from these observations that Valerie's separation anxiety and refusal to attend school were related to her mother's attention and to the reinforcing environment of the neighbor's apartment where she could play all day.

However, since Valerie was reported to be afraid of school itself, Ayllon et al. designed a simulated school setting in the home to determine the extent of anxiety or fear toward specific school-related tasks. (Obviously, observation in the school itself would have been desirable but was impossible, since she refused to attend school.) Little or no fear was evinced in the simulated setting; in fact, Valerie performed well and appeared to enjoy the school-related setting and tasks. In this case, these detailed behavioral observations were useful in ruling upon differential hypotheses related to school refusal. Importantly, they led directly to a specific and efficacious treatment program based on shaping and differential reinforcement principles. The utility of behavioral observations for accurate assessment and treatment programming has been noted in numerous other studies as well (e.g., Ollendick & Gruen, 1972; Smith & Sharpe, 1971).

A major disadvantage of behavioral observations in the natural environment is that the target behavior may not occur during the prearranged observation periods. In such instances, simulated settings that occasion the target behaviors can be used. Simulated observations are especialy helpful when the target behavior is of low frequency, when the target behavior is not observed in the naturalistic setting due to reactivity effects of being observed, or when the target behavior is difficult to observe in the natural environment due to practical constraints. Ayllon et al.'s use of a simulated school setting illustrates this approach under the latter conditions. A study by Matson and Ollendick (1976) illustrates this approach for low frequency behaviors. In this study, parents reported that their children bit either the parent or siblings when they "were unable to get their way or were frustrated." Direct behavioral observations in the home confirmed parental report, but it was necessary to observe the children for several hours prior to witnessing one incident of the behavior. Further, parents reported that their children were being "nice" while the observers were present and that the frequency of the biting behavior was much less than its usual rate. Accordingly, parents were trained in observation procedures and instructed to engage their children in play for four structured play sessions per day. During these sessions, the parents were instructed to occasion biting behavior by deliberately removing a preferred toy. As expected, the removal of favored toys in the structured situations resulted in increases in target behaviors, which were then possible to eliminate through behavioral procedures. The structured, simulated play settings maximized the probability that biting would occur and that it could be observed and treated under controlled conditions.

In sum, direct behavioral observation—either in the natural or controlled simulated environment—provides valuable information for child behavioral assessment. When combined with information gathered through behavioral interviews, self- and other-reports, and self-monitoring, a comprehensive picture of the child and his or her behaviors, as well as its controlling variables, is obtained. As with other assessment procedures, however, direct behavioral observation alone is not sufficient to meet the various behavioral assessment functions required for a thorough analysis of a child's problem behavior.

RESEARCH FINDINGS

As noted earlier, the use of assessment instruments and procedures that have been empirically validated is one of the primary characteristics of child behavioral assessment. However, the role of conventional psychometric standards in evaluating child behavioral assessment procedures is a controversial one (e.g., Cone & Hawkins, 1977; Mash & Terdal, 1981). Given the theoretical underpinnings of child behavioral assessment and the basic assumptions regarding situational specificity and temporal instability of behavior, traditional psychometric standards would appear to be of little or no value. After all, how can behaviors thought to be under the control of highly specific antecedent and consequent events be expected to be similar in different settings and at different times? Yet, if there is no consistency in behavior across settings and time, the prediction of behavior is impossible and the generalizability of findings obtained from any one method of assessment is meaningless. Such an extreme idiographic stance precludes meaningful assessment, except of a highly discrete behavior in a particular setting and at a specific point in time (Ollendick & Hersen, 1984).

Recent research findings suggest that we need not totally dismiss the notions of cross-situational and cross-temporal consistency of behavior (e.g., Bem & Allen, 1974). Although a high degree of behavioral consistency cannot be expected, we can expect a moderate degree of behavioral consistency across situations that involve increasingly similar stimulus and response characteristics and are temporally related. When the various procedures of the multimethod approach are used under these constraints, we can expect a modest relationship among the measures and a fair degree of predictability and generalizability. Under such circumstances, application of conventional psychometric standards to evaluation of child behavioral assessment procedures is less problematic and increasingly useful (Cone, 1977; Ollendick & Hersen, 1984). The value of psychometric principles has already been demonstrated for certain classes of behavior when measured through diverse methods like behavioral observation (e.g., Olweus, 1979), self-report (e.g., Ollendick, 1981), and other-report ratings (e.g., Cowen, Pederson, Barbigian, Izzo, & Trost, 1973). Further, when multiple methods of behavioral assessment have been used in the same studies, a modest degree of both concurrent and predictive validity has been reported (e.g., Gresham, 1982).

It is beyond the scope of the present chapter to review specific research findings related to the reliability, validity, and utility of the various procedures espoused in the multimethod approach. Nonetheless, brief mention will be made of specific directions of research and ways of enhancing the psychometric qualities of each procedure.

Behavioral Interviews

As noted by Evans and Nelson (1977), data based on retrospective reports obtained during the interview may possess both low reliability (agreement among individuals interviewed may differ and responses may vary over time) and low validity (reported information may not correspond to the "facts"). Such inaccurate or "distorted" recollections may result not only in delayed clarification of the presenting complaints, but in faulty hypotheses about causal agents and maintaining factors. For example, Chess, Thomas, and Birch (1966) reported that parents inaccurately reported that certain behavior problems developed at times predicted by popular psychological theories. For instance, problems with siblings were recalled to have begun with the birth of a younger sibling, and problems with dependency were reported to have begun when the mother became employed. In actuality, these behaviors were present prior to these events. In a similar vein, Schopler (1974) has noted that many parents inaccurately blame themselves for their child's problematic behaviors and that many therapists inadvertently "buy into" this notion that "parents are to blame." Such scapegoating accomplishes little in the understanding, assessment, and treatment of the child's problematic behavior (Ollendick & Cerny, 1981).

While the reliability and validity of general information about parenting attitudes and practices are suspect, recent findings suggest that parents and children can be reliable and valid reporters of current, specific information about problematic behaviors (e.g., Graham & Rutter, 1968; Gross, 1984; Herjanic, Herjanic, Brown, & Wheatt, 1973). The reliability and validity of the information are directly dependent upon the recency of the behaviors being discussed and the specificity of the information obtained. Thus, careful specification of precise behaviors and the conditions under which they are occurring is more

reliable and valid than vague descriptions of current behaviors or general recollections of early childhood events (Ciminero & Drabman, 1977). When the interview is conducted along such guidelines, it is useful in specifying behaviors of clinical interest and in determining appropriate therapeutic interventions. As we have noted, however, it is only the first step in the hypothesis-generating process that is characteristic of child behavioral assessment.

Ratings and Checklists

As with behavioral interviews, issues related to reliability and validity are also present with ratings and checklists. Cronbach (1960) has noted that the psychometric quality of rating scales is directly related to the number and specificity of the item rated. Further, O'Leary and Johnson (1979) have identified four factors associated with item response characteristics and raters that enhance the reliability and validity of such scales: (a) the necessity of using clearly defined reference points on the scale (i.e., estimates of frequency, duration, or intensity), (b) the inclusion of more than two reference points on the scale (i.e., reference points that quantify the behavior being rated), (c) a rater who has had extensive opportunities for observing the child being rated, and (d) more than one rater who has equal familiarity with the child.

The rating forms and checklists described earlier (Behavior Problem Checklist, Child Behavior Checklist, and the Louisville Fear Survey Schedule for Children) incorporate these item and response characteristics and are generally accepted as reliable and valid instruments. For example, the interrater reliability of the Behavior Problem Checklist is quite high when raters are equally familiar with the children being rated and when ratings are provided by raters within the same setting (Quay, 1977). Further, the stability of these ratings has been reported over 2-week and 1-year intervals. These findings have been reported for teachers in the school setting and parents in the home setting. However, when ratings of teachers are compared to parents, interrater reliabilities are considerably lower. While teachers seem to agree with other teachers and one parent tends to agree with the other, there is less agreement between parents and teachers. Such differences may be due to differential perception of behavior by parents and teachers or to the situational specificity of behavior, as discussed earlier. In the least, these findings support the desirability of obtaining information about the child in as many settings as possible.

The validity of the Behavior Problem Checklist has been demonstrated in numerous ways. It has been shown to distinguish clinic-referred children from nonreferred children, to be related to psychiatric diagnosis, other measures of behavioral deviances, prognosis, and the differential effectiveness of specific treatment strategies, and to reflect specific changes following therapeutic intervention (see Ollendick & Cerny, 1981, for a discussion of these findings).

Similar findings to the Behavior Problem Checklist have been reported for the Child Behavior Checklist and the Louisville Fear Survey Schedule. These rating forms and checklists, as well as select others, have been shown to possess sound psychometric qualities and to be clinically useful. They not only provide meaningful data about the child's adaptive and problem behaviors; in addition, they are useful in orienting parents, teachers, and significant others to specific problem or asset areas and in alerting them of the need to accurately observe and record specific behaviors.

Self-Report Instruments

Of the various methods used in child behavioral assessment, the self-report method has received the least attention and empirical support. Traditionally, behavioral assessors have eschewed the use of self-report instruments, largely on the basis of their suspected low reliability and validity. As we have noted, however, such data can be meaningfully used to understand and describe the child, plan treatment, and evaluate treatment outcome.

As with interview and checklist or rating data, self-report of specific behaviors or events is more reliable and valid than more general, global reports of life experiences (Ollendick & Cerny, 1981). Such self-reports of specific states can be used to specify discrete components of more general constructs (e.g., determining the exact fears of a fearful child and the exact situations that produce withdrawn behavior in an unassertive child). Illustratively, Scherer and Nakamura's (1968) Fear Survey Schedule for Children and its recent variation (Ollendick, 1983) can be used to pinpoint very specific fears and classes of fear.

Further, it has been shown to be reliable over time, to possess internal consistency and a meaningful factor stucture, to distinguish between phobic and nonphobic children, and to discriminate among subtypes of phobic youngsters within a particular phobic group.

Clearly, more research is needed in this area before the routine use of self-report instruments can be endorsed. Nonetheless, those instruments that measure specific aspects of behavior rather than global traits hold considerable promise for child behavioral assessment.

Self-Monitoring

In self-monitoring, the child observes his or her own behavior and then systematically records its occurrence. As with other measures, concerns related to the reliability and validity of this procedure remain. What is the extent of interobserver agreement between a child who is instructed to monitor his or her own behavior and an objective observer? How accurate is the child in recording actual occurrences of behavior? How reactive is the process of self-monitoring?

The literature in this area is voluminous (see Shapiro, 1984, for an excellent review). Even though all necessary studies have not been completed, the findings are in general agreement. *First*, children can be trained to be reliable and accurate recorders of their own behavior. The specific behaviors should be clearly defined, prompts to self-record should be available, and reinforcment for self-monitoring should be provided. Under such conditions, children's recordings closely approximate those obtained from observing adults. For example, in a study examining the effects of self-monitoring and self-administered overcorrection in the treatment of nervous tics in children, Ollendick (1981) showed that children who were provided clear prompts to self-record highly discrete behaviors were able to do so reliably. Estimates of occurrence very closely paralleled those reported by parents and teachers, even though children were unaware that these adults were recording their nervous tics. In another study, Shapiro and Ackerman (in press) demonstrated the accuracy of children's self-monitoring. Accuracy of self-monitoring was determined by comparing self-recorded data with a permanent product measure (the number of units produced in a work setting).

Second, self-monitoring may result in behavior change due to the self-observation process and result in altered estimates of the target behaviors. This effect is known as reactivity. Numerous factors have been shown to influence the occurrence of reactivity: specific instructions, motivation, goal setting, nature of the self-recording device, and the valence of the target behavior (e.g., Nelson, 1977, 1981). Among the more important findings, it has been shown that desirable behaviors (e.g., study habits, social skills) increase, while undesirable behaviors (e.g., nervous tics, hitting) decrease following self-monitoring and that the more obtrusive the self-recording device the greater the behavior change. For example, Nelson, Lipinski, and Boykin (1978) found that hand-held counters produced greater reactivity than belt-worn counters. Holding a counter in one's hand was viewed as more obtrusive, contributing to pronounced reactivity. Reactivity is a concern in the assessment process, since it affects the actual occurrences of behavior. However, if one is aware of the variables that contribute to the reactive effects, it can be used as a simple and efficient mechanism for data collection (Shapiro, 1984).

In short, self-monitoring has been found to be useful in the assessment of a wide range of child behavior problems across a wide variety of settings. When issues related to the reliability, accuracy, and reactivity of measurement are addressed, self-monitoring represents a clinically useful strategy that is highly efficient.

Behavioral Observation

As with other assessment strategies, behavioral observation procedures must possess adequate psychometric qualities and be empirically validated before their routine use can be endorsed. Although early behaviorists accepted the accuracy of behavioral observations based on their deceptively simplistic face validity, recent investigations have enumerated a variety of problems associated with their reliability, validity, and clinical utility (e.g., Johnson & Bolstad, 1973; Kazdin, 1977). These problems include the complexity of the observation code, the exact recording procedures to be used (e.g., frequency counts, time-sampling, etc.), observer bias, observer drift, and the reactive nature of the observation process itself (see Barton & Ascione, 1984, for a recent discussion of

these issues). From our experience, the greatest threat to the utility of observational data comes from the reactive nature of the observational process itself, especially when the observer is present in the natural setting. It is well known that the presence of an observer affects behavior, usually in socially desirable directions. Two strategies have been found to be useful in reducing such reactive effects: (a) recruiting and training observer-coders already present in the natural setting (e.g., a teacher or parent), or (b) if this is not possible, planning extended observations so that children can habituate to the observers and so that the effects of reactivity are allowed to dissipate. However, it should be noted that several sessions of observations are required, since reactive effects have been observed for as long as six sessions (Johnson & Lobitz, 1974). Reactive effects, combined with the aforementioned practical issues of personnel, time, and resources, have led us to place greater emphasis upon recruiting observer-coders already present in the children's natural environment or training the children themselves as recorders of their own behavior.

In brief, behavioral observations are the most direct and least inferential method of assessment. Even though a variety of problems related to their reliability and validity are evident, they are highly useful strategies and represent the hallmark of child behavioral assessment.

FUTURE DIRECTIONS

A number of directions for future research and development in child behavioral assessment may be evident to the reader. What follows is our attempt to highlight some of the more relevant areas that appear highly promising and in need of greater articulation.

First, it seems to us that greater attention must be given to developmental factors as they affect the development, selection, and evaluation of child behavioral assessment procedures. Although we have argued that child behavioral assessment procedures should be developmentally sensitive, child behavioral assessors have frequently not attended to, or have ignored, this admonition. As we noted earlier, the most distinguishing characteristic of children is developmental change. Such change encompasses basic biological growth and maturity as well as affective, behavioral, and cognitive fluctuations that characterize children at different age levels. While the importance of accounting for developmental level when assessing behavior may be obvious, ways of integrating developmental concepts and principles into child behavioral assessment are less clear. Edelbrock (1984) has noted three areas for the synthesis of developmental and behavioral principles: (a) the use of developmental fluctuations in behavior to establish normative baselines of behavior, (b) the determination of age and gender differences in the expression and covariation of behavioral patterns, and, (c) the study of stability and change in behavior over time as related to such variables as age of onset and situational influences. Clearly, these areas of synthesis and integration are in their infancy and in need of considerably greater articulation (e.g., Harris & Ferrari, 1983; Ollendick & Hersen, 1983).

Second, and somewhat related to the first, greater attention must be focused upon the incremental validity of the multimethod approach when used for children of varying ages. Throughout this chapter, we have espoused a multimethod approach consisting of interviews, self- and other-reports, self-monitoring, and behavioral observations. Quite obviously, some of these procedures may be more appropriate at certain age levels than at others. Further, the psychometric properties of these procedures may vary with age. If these procedures are found to be less reliable or valid at different age levels, their indiscriminate use with "children" should not be endorsed. Inasmuch as these strategies are inadequate, the combination of them in a multimethod approach would only serve to compound their inherent limitations (Mash & Terdal, 1981). The *sine qua non* of child behavioral assessment is that the procedures be empirically validated.

Third, more effort must be directed toward the development of developmentally sensitive and empirically validated procedures for the assessment of cognitive processes in children. In recent years, child behavioral assessors have become increasingly interested in the relationship of children's cognitive processes to observed behaviors and affective experiences. The need for assessment in this area is further evidenced by the rapid increase of cognitive-behavioral treatment procedures with children (e.g., Kendall, Pellegrini, & Urbain, 1981; Meador & Ollendick, in press). As noted by Kendall et al. (1981), a particularly pressing need is to develop procedures that can

examine the very cognitions and processes that are targeted for change in these intervention efforts. For example, the reliable and valid assessment of self-statements made by children in specific situations would go a long way toward the empirical evaluation of cognitive-behavioral procedures like self-instructional training and cognitive restructuring.

Fourth, we must concentrate additional effort on the role of the child in child behavioral assessment. All too frequently, "tests are administered *to* children, ratings are obtained *on* children, and behaviors are observed *in* children" (Ollendick & Hersen, 1984). This process views the child as a passive responder, someone who is largely incapable of actively shaping and determining the behaviors of clinical relevance. Although examination of these organismic variables is only beginning, it would appear that concerted and systematic effort must be directed to their description and articulation.

Fifth, and finally, we must begin to turn our attention to ethical issues in child behavioral assessment. A number of ethical issues regarding children's rights, proper and legal consent, professional judgment, and social values are raised in the clinical practice of child behavioral assessment (Rekers, 1984). Are children capable of granting full and proper consent to a behavioral assessment procedure? At what age are children competent to give such consent? Is informed consent necessary? Or, might not informed consent be impossible, impractical, or countertherapeutic in some situations? What ethical guidelines surround the assessment procedures to be used? Current professional guidelines suggest that our procedures be reliable, valid, and clinically useful. Do the procedures suggested in this chapter, and others, meet these professional guidelines? What are the rights of parents? Of society? It should be evident from these questions that a variety of ethical issues exist. Striking a balance among the rights of parents, society, and children is no easy matter but is one that takes on added importance in our increasingly litigious society.

In short, the future directions of child behavioral assessment are numerous and varied. Even though a technology for child behavioral assessment has evolved and is in force, we need to begin to explore the issues raised before we can conclude that the procedures are maximally productive and in the best interests of children.

SUMMARY

Child behavioral assessment strategies have been slow to evolve. Only recently has the chasm between child behavior therapy and assessment been narrowed. Increased awareness of the importance of developing assessment procedures that provide an adequate representation of child behavior disorders has spurred research into assessment procedures and spawned the generation of a plethora of child behavioral assessment techniques. The growing sophistication of child behavioral assessment is witnessed by the appearance of self- and other-report strategies that take into account developmental, social, and cultural influences as well as cognitive an affective mediators of overt behavior. At the same time, attention to psychometric properties of assessment procedures has continued.

Certain theoretical assumptions guide child behavioral assessment. Foremost among these is the premise that behavior is a function of situational determinants and not a "sign" of underlying personality traits. To adequately assess the situational determinants and obtain as complete a picture of the child as possible, a multimethod assessment approach is recommended utilizing both direct and indirect measures of behavior. Direct measures include behavioral observation by trained observers in naturalistic or analogue settings and self-monitoring. Indirect measures include behavioral interviewing and self- and other-report measures. These sources of information are considered indirect ones because they involve retrospective reports of previous behavior.

Even though direct behavioral observation remains the hallmark of child behavioral assessment, information from these other sources is considered not only valuable, but integral in the understanding and subsequent treatment of child behavior disorders. Hence, whereas the identification and specification of discrete target behaviors was once considered sufficient, thorough behavioral assessment involves serious consideration and systematic assessment of cognitive and affective aspects of the child's behavior and of developmental, social, and cultural factors that influence the child as well as direct observation of the problematic behavior.

Several areas of future research remain. These include clearer specification of developmental variables, a closer examination of the utility of the multimethod approach at different age levels, de-velopment of specific measures to examine cognitive processes in children, articulation of the role of the child in child behavioral assessment, and the development of ethical guidelines. While the basis for a technology of child behavioral assessment exists, much fine-tuning remains.

REFERENCES

Achenbach, T.M. (1966). The classification of children's psychiatric symptoms: A factor analytic study. *Psychological Monographs*, 80, 1–37.

Achenbach, T.M. (1978). The Child Behavior Profile—I. Boys aged 6–11. *Journal of Consulting and Clinical Psychology*, 46, 478–488.

Achenbach, T.M., & Edelbrock, C.S. (1979). The Child Behavior Profile—II. Boys aged 12–16 and girls aged 6–11 and 12–16. *Journal of Consulting and Clinical Psychology*, 47, 223–233.

Aries, P. (1962). *Centuries of childhood*. New York: Vintage Books.

Ayllon, T., Smith, D., & Rogers, M. (1970). Behavioral management of school phobia. *Journal of Behavior Therapy and Experimental Psychiatry*, 1, 125–138.

Bandura, A. (1977). Self-efficacy: Toward a unifying theory of behavioral change. *Psychological Review*, 84, 191–215.

Barton, E.J., & Ascione, F.R. (1984). Direct observations. In T.H. Ollendick & M. Hersen (Eds.), *Child behavioral assessment: Principles and procedures*. New York: Pergamon Press.

Bem, D.J., & Allen, A. (1974). On predicting some of the people some of the time: The search for cross-situational consistencies in behavior. *Psychological Review*, 81, 506–520.

Bornstein, P.H., Bornstein, M.T., & Dawson, B. (1984). Integrated assessment and treatment. In T.H. Ollendick & M. Hersen (Eds.), *Child behavioral assessment: Principles and procedures*. New York: Pergamon Press.

Cantwell, D.P. (1983). Childhood depression: A review of current research. In B.B. Lahey & A.E. Kazdin (Eds.), *Advances in clinical child psychology* (Vol. 5). New York: Plenum.

Chess, S., Thomas, A., & Birch, H.G. (1966). Distortions in developmental reporting made by parents of behaviorally disturbed children. *Journal of the American Academy of Child Psychiatry*, 5, 226–231.

Ciminero, A.R., Calhoun, K.S., & Adams, H.E. (Eds.) (1977). *Handbook of behavioral assessment*. New York: Wiley-Interscience.

Ciminero, A.R., & Drabman, R.S. (1977). Current developments in the behavioral assessment of children. In B.B. Lahey & A.E. Kazdin (Eds.), *Advances in clinical child psychology* (Vol. 1). New York: Plenum.

Ciminero, A.R., Nelson, R.O., & Lipinski, D.P. (1977). Self-monitoring procedures. In A.R. Ciminero, K.S. Calhoun, & H.E. Adams (Eds.), *Handbook of behavioral assessment*. New York: Wiley-Interscience.

Cone, J.D. (1977). The relevance of reliability and validity for behavioral assessment. *Behavior Therapy*, 8, 411–426.

Cone, J.D. (1978). The behavioral assessment grid (BAG): A conceptual framework and taxonomy. *Behavior Therapy*, 9, 882–888.

Cone, J.D., & Hawkins, R.P. (Eds.) (1977). *Behavioral assessment: New directions in clinical psychology*. New York: Brunner/Mazel.

Cowen, E.L., Pederson, A., Barbigian, H., Izzo, L.D., & Trost, M.A. (1973). Long-term follow-up of early detected vulnerable children. *Journal of Consulting and Clinical Psychology*, 41, 438–445.

Cronbach, L.J. (1960). *Essentials of psychological testing*. New York: Harper & Row.

Deluty, R.H. (1979). Children's Action Tendency Scale: A self-report measure of aggressiveness, assertiveness, and submissiveness in children. *Journal of Consulting and Clinical Psychology*, 47, 1061–1071.

Edelbrock, C. (1984). Developmental considerations. In T.H. Ollendick & M. Hersen (Eds.), *Child behavioral assessment: Principles and procedures*. New York: Pergamon Press.

Evans, I.M., & Nelson, R.O. (1977). Assessment of child behavior problems. In A.R. Ciminero, K.S. Calhoun, & H.E. Adams (Eds.), *Handbook of behavioral assessment*. New York: Wiley-Interscience.

Finch, A.J., Nelson, W.M., III, & Moss, J.H. (1983). A cognitive-behavioral approach to anger management with emotionally disturbed children. In A.J. Finch, W.M. Nelson, & E.S. Ott (Eds.), *Cognitive behavioral approaches to treatment with children*. Jamaica, NY: Spectrum Publications.

Finch, A.J., & Rogers, T.R. (1984). Self-report instruments. In T.H. Ollendick & M. Hersen (Eds.), *Child behavioral assessment: Principles and procedures*. New York: Pergamon Press.

Goldfried, M.R., & Kent, R.N. (1972). Traditional versus behavioral personality assessment: A comparison of methodological and theoretical assumptions. *Psychological Bulletin*, 77, 409–420.

Graham, P., & Rutter, M. (1968). The reliability and validity of the psychiatric assessment of the child— II. Interview tih the parents. *British Journal of Psychiatry*, 114, 581–592.

Gresham, F.M. (1982). Social interactions as predictors of children's likeability and friendship patterns: A multiple regression analysis. *Journal of Behavioral Assessment*, 4, 39–54.

Gross, A.M. (1984). Behavioral interviewing. In T.H. Ollendick & M. Hersen (Eds.), *Child behavioral assessment: Principles and procedures*. New York: Pergamon Press.

Harris, S.L., & Ferrari, M. (1983). Development factors in child behavior therapy. *Behavior Therapy*, 14, 54–72.

Haynes, S.N. (1978). *Principles of behavioral assessment*. New York: Gardner.

Herjanic, B., Herjanic, M., Brown, F., & Wheatt, T. (1973). Are children reliable reporters? *Journal of Abnormal Child Psychology*, 3, 41–48.

Hersen, M., & Bellack, A.S. (1976). *Behavioral assessment: A practical handbook*. New York: Pergamon Press.

Holmes, F.B. (1936). An experimental investigation of a method of overcoming children's fears. *Child Development*, 1, 6–30.

Johnson, S.M., & Bolstad, O.D. (1973). Methodological issues in naturalistic observations: Some problems and solutions for field research. In L.A. Hammerlynck, L.C. Handy, & E.J. Mash (Eds.), *Behavior change: Methodology, concepts, and practice*. Champaign, IL: Research Press.

Johnson, S.M. & Lobitz, G.K. (1974). Parental manipulation of child behavior in home observations. *Journal of Applied Behavior Analysis*, 1, 23–31.

Jones, M.C. (1924). The elimination of children's fears. *Journal of Experimental Psychology*, 7, 382–390.

Jones, R.R., Reid, J.B., & Patterson, G.R. (1975). Naturalistic observation in clinical assessment. In P. McReynolds (Ed.), *Advances in psychological assessment* (Vol. 3). San Francisco: Jossey-Bass.

Kanfer, F.H., & Phillips, J.S. (1970). *Learning foundations of behavior therapy*. New York: Wiley.

Kazdin, A.E. (1977). Artifact, bias, and complexity of assessment: The ABCs of reliability. *Journal of Applied Behavior Analysis*, 4, 7–14.

Keefe, F.J., Kopel, S.A., & Gordon, S.B. (1978). *A practical guide to behavioral assessment*. New York: Springer.

Kendall, P.C., & Hollon, S.D. (Eds.) (1980). *Cognitive-behavioral intervention: Assessment methods*. New York: Academic Press.

Kendall, P.C., Pellegrini, D.S., & Urbain, E.S. (1981). Approaches to assessment for cognitive-behavioral interventions with children. In P.C. Kendall & S.D. Hollon (Eds.), *Assessment strategies for cognitive-behavioral interventions*. New York: Academic Press.

Kovacs, M. (1978). *Children's Depression Inventory (CDI)*. Unpublished manuscript, University of Pittsburgh.

Kunzelman, H.D. (Ed.) (1970). *Precision teaching*. Seattle: Special Child Publications.

Linehan, M. (1977). Issues in behavioral interviewing. In J.D. Cone & R.P. Hawkins (Eds.), *Behavioral assessment: New directions in clinical psychology*. New York: Brunner/Mazel.

Mash, E.J., & Terdal, L.G. (1981). Behavioral assessment of childhood disturbance. In E.J. Mash & L.G. Terdal (Eds.), *Behavioral assessment of childhood disorders*. New York: The Guilford Press.

Matson, J.L., & Ollendick, T.H. (1976). Elimination of low frequency biting. *Behavior Therapy*, 7, 410–412.

McMahon, R.J. (1984). Behavioral checklists and rating forms. In T.H. Ollendick & M. Hersen (Eds.), *Child behavioral assessment: Principles and procedures*. New York: Pergamon Press.

Meador, A.E., & Ollendick, T.H. (in press). Cognitive behavior therapy with children: An evaluation of its efficacy and clinical utility. *Child and Family Behavior Therapy*.

Meichenbaum, D.H. (1977). *Cognitive-behavior modification*. New York: Plenum.

Miller, L.C., Barrett, C.L., Hampe, E., & Noble, H. (1972). Comparison of reciprocal inhibition, psychotherapy, and waiting list control for phobic children. *Journal of Abnormal Psychology*, 79, 269–279.

Mischel, W. (1968). *Personality and assessment*. New York: Wiley.

Nay, W.R. (1979). *Multimethod clinical assessment*. New York: Gardner Press.

Nelson, R.O. (1977). Methodological issues in assessment via self-monitoring. In J.D. Cone & R.P. Hawkins (Eds.), *Behavioral assessment: New directions in clinical psychology.* New York: Brunner/Mazel.

Nelson, R.O. (1981). Theoretical explanations for self-monitoring. *Behavior Modification,* 5, 3–14.

Nelson, R.O., Lipinski, D.P., & Boykin, R.A. (1978). The effects of self-recorders training and the obtrusiveness of the self-recording device on the accuracy and reactivity of self-monitoring. *Behavior Therapy,* 9, 200–208.

Nelson, W.M., III, & Finch, A.J., Jr. (1978). *The Children's Inventory of Anger.* Unpublished manuscript. Xavier University.

Novick, J., Rosenfeld, E., Bloch, D.A., & Dawson, D. (1966). Ascertaining deviant behavior in children. *Journal of Consulting and Psychology,* 30, 230–238.

O'Leary, K.D., & Johnson, S.B. (1979). Psychological assessment. In H.C. Quay & J.S. Werry (Eds.), *Psychopathological disorders of children.* New York: Wiley.

O'Leary, K.D., Romanczyk, R.G., Kass, R.E., Dietz, A., & Santogrossi, D. (1971). *Procedures for classroom observations of teachers and parents.* Unpublished manuscript, State University of New York at Stony Brook.

Ollendick, T.H. (1981). Self-monitoring and self-administered overcorrection: The modification of nervous tics in children. *Behavior Modification,* 5, 75–84.

Ollendick, T.H. (1983). Reliability and validity of the Revised-Fear Survey Schedule for Children (FSSC-R). *Behaviour Research and Therapy,* 21, 685–692.

Ollendick, T.H, & Cerny, J.A. (1981). *Clinical behavior therapy with children.* New York: Plenum.

Ollendick, T.H., & Gruen, G.E. (1972). Treatment of a bodily injury phobia with implosive therapy. *Journal of Consulting and Clinical Psychology,* 38, 389–393.

Ollendick, T.H., & Hersen, M. (1979). Social skills training for juvenile delinquents. *Behaviour Research and Therapy,* 17, 547–554.

Ollendick, T.H., & Hersen, M. (Eds.) (1983). *Handbook of child psychopathology.* New York: Plenum.

Ollendick, T.H., & Hersen, M. (Eds.) (1984). *Child behavioral assessment: Principles and procedures.* New York: Pergamon Press.

Olweus, D. (1979). Stability of aggressive reaction patterns in males: A review. *Psychological Bulletin,* 86, 852–875.

Patterson, G.R. (1976). The aggressive child: Victim and architect of a coercive system. In E.J. Mash, L.A. Hammerlynck, & L.C. Hardy (Eds.), *Behavior modification and families:* New York: Brunner/Mazel.

Patterson, G.R., Ray, R.S., Shaw, D.A., & Cobb, J.A. (1969). *Manual for coding family interaction* (6th ed.). Unpublished manuscript, University of Oregon.

Pederson, D.R. (1961). Behavior problems of middle childhood. *Journal of Consulting and Clinical Psychology,* 25, 205–209.

Quay, H.C. (1977). Measuring dimensions of deviant behavior: The Behavior Problem Checklist. *Journal of Abnormal Child Psychology,* 5, 277–287.

Quay, H.C., & Peterson, D.R. (1967). *Manual for the Behavior Problem Checklist.* Champaign, IL: University of Illinois.

Quay, H.C., & Peterson, D.R. (1975). *Manual for the Behavior Problem Checklist.* Unpublished manuscript.

Rekers, G.A. (1984). Ethical issues in child behavioral assessment. In T.H. Ollendick & M. Hersen (Eds.), *Child behavioral assessment: Principles and procedures.* New York: Pergamon Press.

Rie, H.E. (Ed.) (1971). *Perspectives in child psychopathology.* Chicago: Aldine-Atherton.

Scherer, M.W., & Nakamura, C.Y. (1968). A fear survey schedule for chldren (FSS-FC): A factor analytic comparison with manifest anxiety (CMAS). *Behaviour Research and Therapy,* 6, 173–182.

Schopler, E. (1974). Changes of direction with psychiatric children. In A. Davids (Ed.), *Child personality and psychopathology: Current topics* (Vol. I). New York: Wiley.

Shapiro, E.S. (1984). Self-monitoring. In T.H. Ollendick & M. Herson (Eds.), *Child behavioral assessment: Principles and procedures.* New York: Pergamon Press.

Shapiro, E.S., & Ackerman, A. (in press). Increasing productivity raters in adult mentally retarded clients: The failure of self-monitoring. *Applied Research in Mental Retardation.*

Shapiro, E.S., McGonigle, J.J., & Ollendick, T.H. (1980). An analysis of self-assessment and self-reinforcement in a self-managed token economy with mentally retarded children. *Journal of Applied Research in Mental Retardation,* 1, 227–240.

Skinner, B.F. (1953). *Science and human behavior.* New York: Macmillan.

Smith, R.E., & Sharpe, T.M. (1970). Treatment of a school phobia with implosive therapy. *Journal of Consulting and Clinical Psychology,* 35, 239–243.

Spielberger, C.D. (1973). *Preliminary Manual for the State-Trait Anxiety Inventory for Children ("How I Feel Questionnaire").* Palo Alto, CA: Consulting Psychologist Press.

Swann, G.E., & MacDonald, M.L. (1978). Behavior therapy in practice: A rational survey of behavior therapists. *Behavior Therapy,* 9, 799–807.

Ullman, L.P., & Krasner, L. (Eds.) (1965). *Case studies in behavior modification.* New York: Holt, Rinehart & Winston.

Wahler, R.G. (1976). Deviant child behavior in the family: Developmental speculations and behavior change strategies. In H. Leitenberg (Ed.), *Handbook of behavior modification and behavior therapy.* Englewood Cliffs, NJ: Prentice-Hall.

Wahler, R.G., House, A.E., & Stambaugh, E.E. (1976). *Ecological assessment of child problem behavior: A clinical package for home, school, and institutional settings.* New York: Pergamon Press.

Watson, J.B., & Rayner, R. (1920). Conditioned emotional reactions. *Journal of Experimental Psychology,* 3, 1–14.

19 BEHAVIORAL ASSESSMENT OF ADULTS*

Stephen N. Haynes

INTRODUCTION

Assessment is an indispensable component in the analysis and treatment of adult behavior disorders. It provides the bases for diagnosis and classification, identification of causal factors, selection of intervention target behaviors and goals, development of intervention strategies, and evaluation of intervention outcome. Most importantly, assessment is necessary for the continuing development of more powerful intervention procedures and the refinement of the conceptual models upon which those interventions are based (Goldfried, 1977; Haynes, 1978).

Behavioral assessment is one of many assessment systems (e.g., projective, neuropsychological) and refers to a set of methods and concepts derived from and closely tied to behavioral construct systems (Bandura, 1969; Kanfer & Philips, 1970). It includes diverse methods, such as naturalistic and analogue observation, self-monitoring, psychophysiological measurement, interviews and questionnaires, product of behavior measures, manipulation, and critical event sampling. It is most frequently identified with an emphasis on observable and minimally inferential constructs, environmental determinism, and the quantification of psychological constructs (Haynes, 1983).

Impact

Behavioral assessment is an active area of research and application. The most obvious indices of its status are the proliferation of books, published articles, symposia, and presentations at scientific conventions that have behavioral assessment as their focus. Although no behavioral assessment books were published prior to the mid-1970s, several (Barlow, 1981; Ciminero, Calhoun, & Adams, 1977; 1984; Cone & Hawkins, 1977; Haynes, 1978; Haynes & Wilson 1979, Hersen & Bellack, 1981; Keefe, Kopel, & Gordon, 1978; Mash & Terdal, 1981; May, 1979; Nelson & Hayes, 1984) have recently appeared. Two journals (*Behavioral Assessment*, *Journal of Behavioral Assessment*) were begun in 1979 and publish primarily original research and methodological and review articles on behavioral assessment. In a limited survey of the literature in 1977 and 1978, Haynes and Wilson (1979) reviewed over 900 articles involving psychological interventions that used behavioral assessment procedures. Furthermore, an increasing number of graduate level courses in psychology, education, and rehabilitation focus on behavioral assessment (Hay, 1982; Prinz, 1980). The impact of behavioral assessment is spreading to a number of behavioral science disciplines, such as clinical psychology

*Preparation of this chapter was supported, in part, by the Clinical Center, Southern Illinois University at Carbondale. The author would like to thank Linda Gannon, C. Chrisman Wilson, and Karen Clark for their assistance in the preparation of this manuscript.

(Hersen, Kazdin, & Bellack, 1983), behavioral medicine (Melamed & Siegel, 1980), psychiatry (see *Journal of Behavioral Therapy and Experimental Psychiatry*), social work (Special Poster Presentation, Association for Advancement of Behavior Therapy, Los Angeles, 1982), cognitive psychology (Merluzzi, Glass, & Genest, 1981), community psychology (Nietzel, Winett, MacDonald, & Davidson, 1977), and program evaluation (Alevizos, De Risi, Liberman, Eckman, & Callahan, 1978).

Derivation and Development

The historical derivations of behavioral assessment reflect the diversity of its methods. Naturalistic and analogue behavioral observation were used in early Pavlovian, Watsonian, and other experimental psychological studies and can be traced back to Hellenic and Egyptian eras (Alexander & Selesnick, 1966; Kazdin, 1978). These technologies for scientific inquiry have been adopted and refined by behavior analysis. Methodological refinements to behavioral observation, as well as other assessment procedures, have also come from adjunctive disciplines such as ethology, social psychology, developmental psychology, and experimental psychology (e.g., Achenbach, 1974; Hutt & Hutt, 1970).

Other methods of behavioral assessment, such as questionnaires and interviews, have been adapted from traditional applied psychological disciplines such as educational, developmental, and clinical psychology. Their content and focus have been modified and refined by behavioral analysts in order to increase their methodological and conceptual congruence with behavioral construct systems.

The development and application of behavioral assessment procedures have been strongly influenced by the methods and foci of behavioral interventions (Haynes, 1983; Kazdin, 1979; Miller, 1981; Russo, Bird, & Masek, 1980). Although interventions with adult disorders based upon behavioral paradigms occurred in the 1950s and earlier (Kazdin, 1978), extensive applications of behavioral paradigms did not take place until the 1960s (Bachrach, 1962; Bandura, 1969; Ullmann & Krasner, 1965; Wolpe, 1958). These interventions emphasized the manipulation of the client's interaction with his or her environment and necessitated use of assessment procedures that differed procedurally and conceptually from those followed in traditional clinical interventions. In

particular, traditional assessment methods, such as projective or global questionnaire measures, were not sufficiently congruent with this new emphasis on environmental determinism.

Behavioral assessment methods and foci have also been influenced by advances in behavioral construct systems, particularly by an increasingly comprehensive functional analysis of the characteristics and determinants of behavior disorders. For example, the recently hypothesized roles of stimulus-control factors in sleep disorders (Youkilis & Bootzin, 1981), cognitive factors in phobic disorders (Taylor & Agras, 1981), behavior chains in child behavior problems (Voeltz & Evans, 1982), temporally noncontiguous events in marital distress (Margolin, 1981), and situational specificity in many behavior disorders (Kazdin, 1982; McFall, 1982) have affected the methods and foci of assessment procedures used with these disorders.

Another impetus for the development of behavioral assessment has been a dissatisfaction with traditional clinical assessment instruments and their underlying conceptual systems. The perceived stagnation of traditional clinical psychology — its failure to evolve more powerful conceptual models and intervention strategies — has been attributed, in part, to its emphasis on unobservable and inferential intrapsychic processes and causal factors. This emphasis was manifested in an almost exclusive reliance on verbal psychotherapies, the psychodynamic orientation of the prevalent diagnostic systems (DSM I; DSM II), and in the type of assessment instruments employed (Wolman, 1978). Highly inferential assessment instruments of questionable psychometric qualities were frequently used to identify hypothesized intrapsychic causal mechanisms and to provide trait-based personality descriptions.

Chapter Focus

The focus of this chapter is limited to one of the many applications of behavioral assessment — the assessment of adult behavior disorders. However, its widespread applicability renders such a limited focus artificial. Many advances in assessment occur first in limited areas of application before becoming more generalized. For example, a *systems perspective* was initially adopted in behavioral conceptualizations of family interaction and dysfunction (Vincent, 1980; Wahler, 1981), but has obvious relevance for the assessment of adult behavior disorders (e.g., Haynes & Chavez, 1983;

Miller, 1981). Therefore, advances in evaluation concepts and methods in other behavioral assessment applications will be considered when relevant to the assessment of adult behavior disorders.

The following section introduces the conceptual and methodological assumptions that influence the roles, foci, and methods of behavioral assessment. The functions of behavioral assessment are then considered, and the various behavioral assessment methods are described. Subsequent sections consider evaluative dimensions and some current directions in behavioral assessment.

THEORETICAL AND METHODOLOGICAL BASES OF BEHAVIORAL ASSESSMENT

The goals, methods, and foci of every assessment system are influenced by three sets of assumptions: (a) those concerning the characteristics of behavior disorders, (b) those concerning the causes of behavior disorders, and (c) those concerning epistemology, that is, which investigative strategies are most effective for studying behavior. In this section attention is directed to the conceptual and epistomological assumptions that underlie behavioral assessment. More extensive presentations of these issues can be found in publications by Bandura (1969), Haynes (1978), Kanfer and Philips (1970), Mischel (1968), Nelson and Hayes (1984), and Wiggins (1973).

Assumptions Concerning the Characteristics of Behavior Disorders

There are several assumptions concerning the characteristics of behavior disorders which affect behavioral assessment strategies: (a) Behavior disorders can be expressed in cognitive, verbal, overt behavioral and physiological response modes, (b) these response modes may demonstrate fractionation or a low level of covariation, (c) the degree of response mode covariation varies across individuals, modes, and disorders, (d) there are individual differences in the topography of a behavior disorder, (e) topographically dissimilar behaviors may demonstrate common variance (i.e., function as a "response class"), and (f) many behaviors are interdependent, and modification of one behavior is likely to affect others (Bandura, 1969, 1981;

Haynes, 1978; Haynes & Wilson, 1979; Kanfer & Phillips, 1970; Rimm & Masters, 1979).

The multimodel nature of many adult behavior disorders suggests the need for assessment strategies with multiple foci. Anxiety disorders, for example, may involve overt avoidance or escape behaviors, verbalizations of subjective fear and discomfort, indices of autonomically-medicated arousal, and/or cognitive intrusions or distortions (Taylor & Agras, 1981). Therefore, a comprehensive assessment necessitates use of methods that are capable of targeting multiple components. The importance of multimodal assessment is further enhanced because the various components of behavior disorders frequently demonstrate low levels of covariation (Borkovec, Weerts, & Bernstein, 1977; Gannon, 1983; Haynes & Wilson, 1979; Kaloupek & Levis, 1980). Inferences about one mode cannot be confidently drawn from measures of another, and intervention programs may have differential effects across components.

There also are differences across individuals in the degree of covariation among response components and in the significance of the modes. Even though the level of covariation among response modes is a partial function of the manner in which the modes are measured, some individuals demonstrate a much higher degree of covariation among components than others (e.g., some phobics, but not others demonstrate high correlations among physiological, verbal, and overt behavioral modes). Also, the component that is the defining characteristic of a behavior disorder for one individual (e.g., cognitive factors in depression) may play a relatively minor role for other individuals with the same disorder. Because of this variance, intervention targets and methods will vary across individuals, and the importance of multiple assessment procedures and multiple foci is evident (Lazarus, 1976).

The preceding discussion focused on multiple elements of a particular behavior disorder. However, covariation among structurally dissimilar behaviors (e.g., stealing, alcohol intake, and verbal aggression) also is frequently observed. Intervention effects are more likely to generalize to behaviors that covary or function as a response class. However, response covariation cannot be assumed, and the degree of covariation is likely to vary as a function of situational factors and across individuals and intervention strategies (Patterson & Bechtel, 1977). In some cases, covariation among topographically dissimilar behaviors can facilitate assessment because some members of the response class may be more amenable than others to assessment. For example, high frequency behaviors may sometimes be more easily assessed than their low-frequency covariates (Wahler, 1975).

A significant advance in the conceptual foundations of behavioral construct systems has been the recognition of the interdependence of behaviors and behavior-environment interactions within their larger social systems. Behavior problems cannot be viewed independently from their environmental context. For example, the financial status, level, and type of social support from family members, and extramarital relationships can affect an individual's level of marital distress (Stuart, 1980). Perhaps more importantly, it is recognized that intervention programs can be affected by the client's social system and can also have unintended effects (e.g., reductions in the level of heterosexual anxiety of a college student may affect his or her study behavior and interaction with same-sex friends). This systems perspective (Vincent, 1980) requires a significant deviation from the more limited focus thus far associated with behavioral assessment. It demands, instead, incorporation of a client's social system and adds to the mandate for a broad spectrum assessment.

Assumptions about the Causes of Behavior Disorders

The most important determinants of the methods and focus of an assessment system are causal assumptions about sources of variance of behavior and behavior disorders. Because most intervention programs attempt to modify hypothesized controlling factors, identification of those factors is a primary goal of assessment. The assumptions of causality underlying behavioral assessment emphasize: (a) environmental interactionism, (b) operation of mediational variables, (c) situational determinants of behavior, and (d) multiple and idiosyncratic determinism.

The most important causal assumption is that of *environment interactionism* or *reciprocal determinism* (Bandura, 1981; Nelson & Hayes, 1979): The probability, type, topography, intensity, and duration of behavior disorders is significantly affected by environmental events such as social contingencies, cues, environmental stressors, and classical conditioning experiences. These, in turn,

are influenced by the behavior of the individual. For example, depression has been hypothesized to be precipitated or exacerbated by social reinforcement decrements that can be precipitated by the behavior of the depressed individual toward members of his or her social environment (Lewinsohn, 1975). Similarly, insomnia may be a function of inappropriate stimulus conditions associated with the bed and bedroom, conditions resulting from the presleep behaviors of the insomniac (Youkilis & Bootzin, 1981).

The attribution of causal properties to environmental events does not preclude the possibility that behavior disorders may also be a function of genetic, physiological, or cognitive dysfunctions. Indeed, evidence for significant organic involvement in behavior disorders such as depression (Anisman & LaPierre, 1982), schizophrenia (Shapiro, 1981), and ulcers (Walker & Sandman, 1981) is quite strong. Behavior disorders must be considered final manifestations of multiple causal pathways. At the same time, an emphasis on the assessment of the functional relationships between a behavior disorder and environmental variables will, in many cases, result in the identification of important sources of behavioral variance.

The presumed causal role of behavior-environmental interactions partially accounts for the emphasis on assessment methods, such as naturalistic observation and self-monitoring, which target behavior-environment interactions. It also dictates the *focus* of assessment procedures, since potential environmental controlling factors are frequent assessment targets in interviews and questionnaires.

Congruent with a stress on environmental interactionism is an emphasis on the *behavioral skills* of clients. It is assumed that a client's behavioral repertoire (excesses, deficits, topography, content, timing) not only defines many behavior disorders, but also affects the probability, type, or degree of behavior disorders. For example, a behavior skills analysis might identify deficits in social initiation skills for withdrawn or depressed individuals, verbal communication or negotiation skills for marital distress, time-management skills for habit problems (e.g., academic achievement, procrastination), sexual interaction skills for male or female sexual dysfunctions or disorders, or stress-reducing skills for sleep disorders and headaches. The alleviation of identified skill deficits frequently becomes a major goal of intervention.

An emphasis on reciprocal rather than passive determinism also suggests that *mediational variables* can play an important role in the genesis of behavior disorders (Bandura, 1981; Miller, 1981). The probability of an individual manifesting depressive, ingestive, or psychosomatic disorders in the presence of biological or environmental precipitating stimuli is influenced not only by the individual's behavioral skills, but also by social support systems, cognitive coping strategies, and/or previous exposure to particular environmental events that mediate the effects of those stimuli (Haynes & Wilson, 1984). The assessment of mediational variables is an important but frequently omitted component in the analysis of behavior disorders. It can facilitate the identification of intervention targets and also provide basic data for the development of prevention programs.

Behavioral construct systems also assume that a significant proportion of the variance in behavior can be accounted for by variance in *situational stimuli* (Haynes, 1979; Kazdin, 1979; O'Leary, 1979; Patterson & Bechtel, 1977). This is in contrast to the trait conceptualizations underlying most traditional clinical assessment procedures, which presume a higher degree of cross-situational consistency of behavior (Hogan, DeSoto, & Solano, 1979; McFall, 1982; Messick, 1981; Mischel, 1980).

Situational and trait models are not necessarily dichotomous, and neither can claim satisfactory predictive validity. Some degree of behavioral consistency is not incompatible with situationally controlled variance, and a *person × situation interactive model* is probably a more accurate representation of behavioral variance than a model based on either component alone. Although situational factors exert considerable control over behavior, cross-situational consistencies in behavior probabilities and topography can and frequently do occur.

Further complicating the issue of behavioral consistency is the observation that the degree of situational control varies across behaviors, individuals, and situations (Haynes, 1979; Nelson, 1980). As noted by Nelson (1980), behaviors such as arithmetic abilities or automobile driving, which are associated with similar contingencies (or eliciting stimuli) across situations, are likely to demonstrate greater cross-situational stability than are behaviors such as social initiations or alcohol intake, which are associated with significant cross-situational variance in contingencies.

Similarly, individuals with a history of stable contingencies for a particular behavior across situations (such as a person who has received consistent contingencies for aggressive behaviors at home, school, restaurants, and supermarkets) are more likely to demonstrate cross-situational behavioral stability than those with a less consistent contingency history. The person × situation interactive model of behavioral variance suggests that cross-situational behavioral stability, while possible, cannot be assumed. Therefore, assessment procedures must sample a variety of potential antecedent and eliciting situations (Eisler, Hersen, Miller, & Blanchard, 1975; Galassi & Galassi, 1980; Stuart, 1980).

A causal assumption that affects not only the focus of behavioral assessment but also enhances the role of assessment in the behavioral intervention process is that of *multiple and idiosyncratic determinism*: There are multiple determinants of behavior disorders, and determinants vary across disorders and individuals. Univariate causal models cannot satisfactorily account for the onset, topography, duration, temporal and situational variance, or intensity of behavior disorders; they are usually the product of several interacting causal factors. Attempts to account for a behavior disorder through reference only to an isolated parameter such as contingencies, eliciting stimuli, cognitive processes, environmental stressors or biochemical dysfunctions, in isolation, will usually result in an inadequate functional analysis.

Behavior determinants are presumed to vary across disorders and across individuals manifesting the same disorder. This assumption of idiographic causality contrasts with most nonbehavioral models (e.g., psychodynamic, gestalt, biochemical), which assume less variant models of causality. For example, in behavioral construct systems the determinants of migraine headaches are presumed to differ significantly from those of depression or phobias. In addition, the etiological role of potential causal factors (e.g., social contingencies, aversive environmental stimuli, decrements in environmental reinforcement, biochemical factors, and cognitive self-statements) will vary across individuals manifesting the same disorder.

The presumption of multiple and idiosyncratic determinism increases the importance of preintervention behavioral assessment. With unitary causal models, classification of a behavior disorder is sufficient to indicate an intervention strategy (Taylor, 1983). In behavioral construct systems, however, classifications of behavioral syndromes, such as "depression," or "paranoia" is insufficient because diagnosis only indicates a vague picture of current functioning and a domain of potential causal factors (Haynes, 1979, 1984). The behavior analyst must carefully evaluate the role of many possible determinants before an intervention program aimed at modifying these determinants can be designed.

Epistemological Assumptions

Construct systems differ not only in their assumptions about the characteristics and causes of behavior, but also in their epistemology —assumptions about which *methods* of inquiry are more heuristic. The epistemology of behavioral construct systems emphasize empirical hypothesis-testing (Hay, 1982); hypotheses are developed about target behaviors, goals, determinants of behavior disorders, and preferred intervention strategies. Assessment is the basis for both hypothesis generation and testing.

The preferred method for hypothesis evaluation is through the application of empirical or scientific methods (Hersen & Barlow, 1976: Kazdin, 1982, Kratochwill, 1978; Sidman, 1960). This involves an emphasis on careful measurement of variables, the use of instruments of known psychometric properties, careful control of measurement conditions, and serial measurement concomitant with systematic manipulation of independent variables.

This empirical hypothesis-testing paradigm strongly affects the role, methods, and focus of behavioral assessment. It mandates quantification of variables, the continuing psychometric evaluation of assessment instruments, use of minimally inferential constructs and measurement procedures, and assessment and intervention within controlled conditions. Quantification is stressed because it minimizes susceptibility to interpretative biases inherent in the the use of qualitative inferences and enhances confidence in the evaluation of causal hypotheses and intervention outcome. Therefore, behavioral interviewers request information about the rates, durations, and intensities of target behaviors and particularly about

their *conditional probabilities* (the probability that a specified behavior will occur given the occurrence of other events).

The most sensitive indicator of the viability of psychological construct systems is their degree of evolution over time. Construct systems based upon an heuristic epistemology will evolve; others will not. The conceptual stagnation of traditional psychological construct systems has been attributed, in part, to their use of highly inferential constructs and causal explanations. In contrast, behavior analysts have emphasized an epistemology that minimizes the use of such constructs. Behavioral construct systems are more likely to focus on observable, consensually verifiable behaviors, behavioral goals, and causal relationships. The causal role of inferential variables such as conflicts, complexes, impulses, and feelings is minimized. Assessment methods such as naturalistic observation and behavioral self-monitoring attain increased status because they can focus more on what clients do than on their psychological states.

Despite this emphasis on observables, inferential concepts are not alien to behavioral construct systems and are frequently the focus of behavioral assessment efforts. For example, behavior analysts make inferences about "cognitive events" by measuring verbal and overt motor behavior (Merluzzi et al., 1981), "brain functioning" through neuropsychological assessments (Boll, 1981), or "anxiety" through behavioral avoidance tests or questionnaires (Haynes & Wilson, 1979).

The emphasis on empiricism in behavioral assessment has been closely associated not only with particular assessment foci and the use of particular assessment instruments, but also with careful control of the temporal and situational conditions of their administration and the designs within which intervention strategies occur. Experimental designs such as reversal, replication, multiple baseline, simultaneous treatment, alternating treatment, and changing criterion, which are suited for clinical situations involving intensive study of individuals over extended periods of time have received particular attention (Hersen & Barlow, 1976; Kazdin, 1982; Kratochwill, 1978). Behavior analysts have also adopted the statistical procedures applicable to the analysis of those time-series designs (Glass, Wilson, & Gottman, 1975; Gorsuch, 1983; Hartmann, Gottman, Jones, Gardner, Kazdin, & Vaught, 1980;

Kratochwill & Levin, 1979; Wolery & Billingsley, 1982). The renewed emphasis in applied psychology on the intensive longitudinal study of single clients under systematically controlled conditions has been a major contribution of behavioral assessment.

The empirical emphasis has had an indirect but important effect on the delivery of psychological services by accentuating the importance of accountability of professionals (Lloyd, 1983; O'Leary, 1979) and providing a technology for the evaluation of service delivery and intervention outcome. Application of psychometrically evaluated assessment instruments within appropriate research designs can provide a strong test of the validity of clinical hypotheses and the efficacy of intervention.

An overzealous adoption of methodological empiricism, however, can have negative ramifications for a construct system. As noted by Glass and Kliegl (1983), many outcome measures in intervention research involve trivial quantification (e.g., use of "fear thermometers") and assessment procedures that are devoid of psychometric validity and social or practical importance. Such exaggerated attempts at quantification demean methodological behaviorism and contribute to the perception of a focus on trivial events.

An excessive reliance on quantification can also reduce the creativity of psychological inquiry. Our knowledge of functional relationships among behaviors and environmental events is elementary; such an early stage of scientific development requires an openness to new concepts and relationships. Although empiricism is the preferred method of evaluating hypotheses, and while the close examination of data can serve as a stimulus for new hypotheses, many ideas are generated from simply qualitative observations of phenomena. By supplementing quantitative with qualitative analyses, behavior analysts can insure that creative processes are not hindered by an excessive reliance on empiricism.

Despite the dangers, the importance of the empirical methodological bases of behavioral assessment cannot be understated. *Psychological construct systems must be based on methods of inquiry rather than on conceptual assumptions.* Psychological construct systems such as gestalt, transactional analysis, Rogerian, and most psychoanalytic schools have remained essentially unchanged for the past three decades because they are *defined* by conceptual assumptions rather than methodological paradigms. By contrast, the rapid evolution of the conceptual elements of behavioral construct systems can be attributed to its stronger emphasis on a set of *methods* for studying behavior rather than an emphasis on a set of concepts about behavior or the best methods of modifying it.

FUNCTIONS

Assessment systems may differ not only in their underlying construct system and methods, but also in their functions or the purpose for which they are applied. These functions affect the focus as well as the methods of assessment and can vary across settings, clients, behavior problems and the investigative intent (e.g., clinical outcome evaluation vs. demonstrating a new intervention strategy) (Hawkins, 1979). Behavioral assessment has a number of interdependent functions which are outlined below.

Identification of Target Behaviors

Clients frequently present multiple behavior problems or are unable to pinpoint specific behavior problems. One major goal of the assessment process is to select behavior(s) (desirable and undesirable) upon which to focus intervention efforts (Wilson & Evans, 1983). The bases for target behavior selection include the frequency, intensity, duration, and magnitude of the behavior, the centrality of particular behaviors to the client's problems in living, the degree to which they maximize or minimize the client's reinforcers, the values of the client and behavior analyst, the degree of danger to the client or others presented by the behavior, the probability of successful intervention, and a task analysis of treatment goals (Keefe et al., 1978; Krasner, 1969; Myerson & Hayes, 1978; Nelson & Barlow, 1981).

Identification of Alternative Behaviors

In many cases the task of the behavior analyst is not confined to identification of undesirable target behaviors (such as excessive drinking or exhibitionism). It may also involve selection of behaviors that are positive alternatives to undesirable target behaviors or the selection of behaviors which reduce the probability or functional utility of problem behaviors (Goldfried, 1982). For example, positive coping self-statements may be desirable alternatives to deprecatory self-statements of depressives; enhanced assertive skills may be associated with a reduction in behaviors such as aggressive outbursts or social avoidance, and self-induced relaxation skills may allow self-control of sleep-onset, headaches, and fear reactions. Focusing efforts on assessment through positive behavioral goals may increase the use of positive rather than negative contingencies, facilitate social acceptability, and increase the probability of successful reduction of the targeted problem behaviors.

Identification of Causal Variables

Perhaps the most important function of any psychological assessment system is the identification of causal variables. Those variables are frequently the target of intervention efforts. Reciprocal environmental determinism and methods of causal analysis in a behavioral construct system were discussed earlier in this chapter and are discussed in greater depth in Haynes (1984).

Development of a Functional Analysis

A functional analysis is the conceptual integration of results from preintervention assessment. It is a summary of problem behaviors, interacting behavioral, cognitive and physiological components and chains, associated behavioral assets and deficits, situational sources of variance, the social system within which the client is embedded, and other mediational variables. Even though the functional analysis is the ultimate determinant of intervention goals and strategies, it is the most complex, subjective, and least investigated aspect of behavioral assessment (Cooke & Meyers, 1980; Curran & Wessberg, 1981; Haynes, 1984; Lewinsohn & Lee, 1981).

The Design of Intervention Strategies

Preintervention assessment is an integral part of the behavioral intervention process because it has a significant impact upon design of intervention strategies. Intervention progams vary across and within classes of behavior disorders as a function of their characteristics and determinants identified in the preintervention assessment process. Intervention decisions are also influenced by the relative effectiveness of interventions, their potential side-effects, the availability of alternate interventions, ethical and social validity considerations, and a cost-efficiency analysis (Haynes, 1984). The components of intervention strategies must also be selected. Examples of intervention components include specific items in desensitization hierarchies, instructional or situational variables in behavior rehearsal, or specific reinforcers in contingency management programs.

Evaluation and Modification of Intervention

Consistent with an empirical hypothesis-testing and accountability epistemology, a major function of behavioral assessment is the evaluation of intervention outcome. This evaluation most frequently occurs through serial administration of assessment instruments before, during, and following interventions administered within carefully controlled conditions (Hersen & Barlow, 1976; Kazdin, 1982; Kratochwill, 1979). Intervention outcome is evaluated on the basis of its side-effects and generalization across situations, behaviors, and persons in addition to changes in the main target behaviors. Assessment throughout the intervention process can also suggest when modification of an intervention program is required. Intervention program modification may involve changes in target behaviors, intervention strategies, or components of intervention programs.

Facilitating Client-Therapist Interaction

The previously delineated functions of behavioral assessment have focused on its role in data acquisition and program evaluation. However, a major and frequently overlooked function of assessment is to establish a facilitative relationship between the client and behavior analyst. Clients' perceptions of the assessment-intervention process and its underlying assumptions, and their perceptions and reactions to the behavior analyst, can significantly affect their cooperation in the intervention process, the probability of successful intervention, and even the probability of clients' continued involvement in the intervention process. The major vehicle for establishing a positive client-assessor relationship is through the preintervention assessment interview (Haynes & Chavez, 1983), although the variables affecting such a relationship have not been systematically studied.

Summary

Behavioral assessment has multiple functions; the relationship between these functions and the methods of assessment is complex. The functions of assessment vary among clients, disorders, and the intent of the behavior analyst and assessment instruments are differentially applicable to these functions. For example, behavioral observation can be a powerful method of evaluating intervention outcome but is of limited use in facilitating client-assessor interactions. In contrast, the behavioral interview is an excellent vehicle for gathering historical data and evaluating clients' perceptions of the intervention process, but may be less applicable for deriving quantitative indices of intervention outcome.

There are functions of behavioral assessment other than the ones described. These include providing the data for differential diagnosis, gathering historical data on clients and their behavior problems, and gathering demographic or epidemiological data. These are secondary functions of the behavioral assessment of adult disorders, because they only indirectly contribute to the development of a functional analysis and the design and evaluation of intervention strategies.

METHODS OF BEHAVIORAL ASSESSMENT

An appreciation of behavioral assessment methods and underlying concepts should be enhanced by delineation of the boundaries between behavioral and nonbehavioral assessment. However, these boundaries are increasingly indistinct and permeable. During the preparation of a book on behavioral assessment (Haynes, 1978) between 1974 and 1977, it was not difficult to distinguish behavioral from nonbehavioral assessment procedures. At that time there was considerable consensus among behavior analysts that behavioral assessment methods included naturalistic observation, analogue observation, self-monitoring, participant-observation, psychophysiological methods, behavioral interviewing, and behavioral questionnaires.

Behavioral assessment is becoming more inclusive. Perusal of recently published behaviorally oriented books and journal articles indicates that many of the assessment procedures used or advocated here have not been traditionally associated with a behavioral construct system and are sometimes inconsistent with its underlying concepts. For example, in an edited book on the behavioral assessment of adult disorders (Barlow, 1981), assessment procedures presented included neuropsychological assessment (Boll, 1981), diaries (Blanchard, 1981), a projective method involving interpretation of patients' stories (Lewinsohn & Lee, 1981), traditional trait-based personality tests such as the IE scale, MMPI, the Beck Depression Inventory, and tests of academic achievement. Also, the former editor of *Behavioral Assessment* advocated the use of intelligence tests by behavior analysts (see Nelson, 1980).

The increasingly diffuse boundaries between behavioral and nonbehavioral assessment have several roots. First, behavior analysts are more frequently focusing on variables (e.g., cognitions, physiology, affect) that were excluded from earlier behavioral paradigms. This expanding focus has necessitated the use of a larger array of assessment instruments, many with greater inferential qualities. Second, there has been a moderation in the tendency of behavior analysts to automatically reject any assessment procedure identified with traditional clinical psychology. This has been replaced with a more reasoned appraisal of the applicability and psychometric qualities of traditional assessment instruments. Third, an early exclusionary emphasis on situational control of behavior has been replaced by a *person × situation interactionist* model. This conceptual modification has led to introduction into behavior assessment of some trait-based assessment instruments.

A more disturbing determinant of the growing inclusiveness of behavioral assessment methods is an apparent reduction in the conceptual and methodological rigor of behavior analysts. Many seem unaware of the conceptual assumptions underlying the assessment procedures they use. For example, assumptions inherent in administering an assessment instrument that provides a single "score" of some multifactored construct (e.g., depression, internality) are frequently unacknowledged. Similarly, there are frequently unacknowledged interpretative problems in administering an assessment instrument that provides a highly inferential or indirect measure of a construct (e.g., measures of irrational beliefs or cognitive distortion) or in administering an assessment instrument with unknown psychometric properties for the target population to which it is applied. Many behavior analysts also do not acknowledge the conceptual difficulties in interpreting data from an assessment instrument, which was developed under a conceptual framework different from, and often incompatible with, a behavioral construct system (e.g., providing behavioral interpretations of scores from a locus-of-control scale) (Jensen & Haynes, in press). Conceptual unsophistication is a particular concern because of its eventual impact on the evolution, viability, and empirical rigor of the construct system.

In view of these definitional difficulties, the focus of this chapter has been limited to those methods that have been traditionally associated with behavioral assessment or those methods that, although infrequently used, are congruent with behavioral construct systems. More extensive descriptions of behavioral assessment instruments can be found in books by Ciminero et al. (1977, 1984), Cone and Hawkins (1977), Haynes (1978), Haynes and Wilson (1979), Hersen and Bellack (1981), and Nay (1979).

Behavioral assessment methods have been divided into three classes: (a) those primarily associated with behavioral construct systems, (b) those frequently used by behavior analysts but adopted from traditional nonbehavioral assessment systems, and (c) those less frequently used by behavior analysts but consistent with behavioral construct systems.

Assessment Methods Primarily Associated with Behavioral Construct Systems

Naturalistic Observation

The assessment method most congruent with behavioral construct systems is naturalistic observation using nonparticipant observers (observers who are not normally part of the natural environment) (Hartmann & Wood, 1982; McIntyre et al., 1983). Typically, two or more trained observers enter the client's natural environment (e.g., hospital ward, home, classroom, bar, restaurant) several times on a predetermined schedule and systematically record occurrence or nonoccurrence of preselected and predefined behaviors. Each observation session is divided into smaller time-sampling periods (eg., 10-, 15-, or 30-second

periods). The observers may record occurrence or nonoccurrence of specified client behaviors (e.g., pain-reference verbalizations or physical activity in a case of chronic pain) that occur during all or part of the sampling interval, behavior chains (e.g., sequential interaction between a depressed client and family members), of behaviors that are occurring at predetermined points in time (e.g., the behavior being emitted by a psychiatric inpatient at the end of serial 15-second intervals).

Behaviors sampled are those that: (a) have potential etiological significance for identified behavioral problems (e.g., verbal contingencies emitted during distressed marital interaction), (b) provide a sensitive measure of problem behaviors and intervention outcome (e.g., frequency of social interaction by a depressed psychiatric inpatient), (c) indicate side-effects and generalization of intervention, and/or (d) are goals or positive alternatives to undesirable behaviors. In all cases, these *behavior samples* are carefully selected and defined prior to observation (Hartmann & Wood, 1982). Although observers usually focus on only one individual at a time, the interaction between two or more individuals is frequently monitored, and observation targets may be sequentially or randomly sampled from a group of potential subjects (e.g., rotation of targeted subjects among several individuals in a group or on a ward).

The training of observers and their method of observation have an important effect on the validity of derived data (Foster & Cone, 1980; Hartmann & Wood, 1982). Observers must be systematically trained to a satisfactory level of accuracy prior to observing target subjects. To reduce the probability of bias, drift, and other observer errors, interobserver agreement should be evaluated frequently on a random schedule, retraining should be initiated when necessary, composition of observer teams should be changed, and observer awareness of the client's status (e.g., pre- or posttreatment) should be minimized (Haynes, 1978).

In open environments, such as a home, some constraints are often placed on the behavior of targeted individuals (McIntyre et al., 1983). For example, a dissatisfied marital couple being observed at home might be requested to remain within two rooms, to refrain from long phone conversations, watching T.V., and visits from friends during the observation sessions. While such constraints compromise the naturalness of the assessment environment and, therefore, the generalizability of the obtained data, they are sometimes necessary to increase the efficiency of the observation process.

Naturalistic observation has been used in the assessment of a wide range of behavior problems, populations, and environments (Haynes & Wilson, 1979). Targeted behavior problems have included interactions of distressed marital couples (Follingstad & Haynes, 1981), eating patterns of obese individuals (Brownell, 1981), pain talk in cases of chronic pain (Fordyce, 1976), drinking behaviors of alcoholics (Griffiths, Bigelow, & Liebson, 1977), stuttering (James, 1981), leisure behavior of handicapped adults (Schleien, Wehman, & Kiernan, 1981), behaviors of institutional staff (Bassett & Blanchard, 1977) and foster grandparents (Fabrey & Reid, 1978), restaurant skills of disabled individuals (Van den Pol, Iwata, Ivancic, Page, Neef, & Whitley, 1981), social interaction of depressed individuals (Lewinsohn & Lee, 1981), approaches to feared or phobic objects (Waranch, Iwata, Wohl, & Nidiffer, 1981), self-help and work behaviors of institutionalized retarded and psychiatric inpatients (Cuvo, Leaf, & Borakove, 1978; Kazdin, 1982), behaviors of parents of problem children (Lytton, 1977), and aggressive behaviors of schizophrenics (Matson & Stephens, 1977). Environments in which naturalistic observation has occurred include homes (Jacobson, Elwood, & Dallas, 1981), schools, (Fagot, 1978), institutions for developmentally disabled psychiatric or geriatric patients (Kazdin, 1980), restaurants and cafeterias (Brownell, 1981), prisons (Bassett & Blanchard, 1977), hospital labor rooms (Anderson & Standley, 1977), and bathrooms (Cuvo et al., 1978).

Several types of data can be derived from observation measures. Most frequently they are used to provide a quantitative sample of the rate or frequency of targeted behaviors (actually, the percentage of sampling intevals in which a behavior occurs). More importantly, they can provide measures of the *conditional probabilities* of behaviors (the probability that a behavior will occur given the occurrence of other behavior or events or given a particular situation or environment). For example, observation of marital interaction in the home can provide data on positive or negative reciprocity (the probability that one spouse will emit a positive or negative behavior following a positive or negative behavior emitted by the other) (Jacobson & Margolin, 1979; Stuart, 1980).

Behavioral observation can also provide *qualitative information* (Weinrott, Reid, Bauske, & Brumett, 1981). Informal observation of clients can be a rich source of hypotheses concerning problem behaviors, response classes (behaviors that demonstrate a high degree of covariance and functional similarity), behavior chains, behavior deficits, and other characteristics and determinants of behavior problems. Inclusion of a qualitative component to observation assessment can significantly facilitate functional analyses.

Naturalistic observation is probably the most powerful method of intervention outcome evaluation for many behavior problems. Its congruence with behavioral construct systems derives from its focus on behavior in the natural environment, its utility in detecting and measuring behavior-environment interactions, the quantitative properties of the obtained information, and the minimal level of inference associated with its use. However, like all assessment instruments, it varies in its applicability across behavior disorders and assessment functions.

There are several sources of error variance in data obtained from naturalistic observation (Baum, Forehand, & Zegoib, 1979; Fiske, 1978; Foster & Cone, 1980; Haynes, 1978; Haynes & Horn, 1982; Johnson & Bolstad, 1973; Sackett, 1978; Wasik & Loven, 1980; Wildman & Erikson, 1977). These include: (a) variance in the situational context in which observation occurs, (b) observer inaccuracy, bias, and drift, (c) error variance in time or behavior sampling, and (d) insufficient definitional precision of codes.

A major source of error in all assessment procedures, but particularly in naturalistic observation, is *reactivity*. An assessment process is reactive when it transiently or permanently modifies the targets of assessment. For example, staff, spouses, and parents may behave differently when observers are present than when they are not present. Therefore, reactivity is a threat to the external validity or situational and temporal generalizability of the acquired data. In the cases of exceptionally socially sensitive behaviors (e.g., sexual or antisocial behaviors), naturalistic observation may be sufficiently reactive as to preclude its use. Conceptual frameworks within which reactive effects of observation can be viewed and possible methods of minimizing them have been discussed in greater detail by Baum et al. (1979) and Haynes and Horn (1982).

Analogue Observation

Analogue observation involves the systematic observation of target subjects in *analogue situations*—controlled environments that vary from the natural environment of the client (Haynes, 1978). For example, to evaluate possible communication difficulties, a distressed marital couple might be requested to discuss a problem in their relationship while being observed from behind a one-way mirror in an outpatient clinic (Jacobson et al., 1981). Similarly, an individual with heterosexual anxieties might be observed in a clinic waiting room while attempting to initiate and maintain a conversation with a confederate-stranger (cf. Bellack, Hersen, & Lamparski, 1979).

One form of analogue assessment frequently used in the evaluation of social skills is *role playing*, in which a client is placed in an analogue situation and responds to social stimuli typical of those encountered in the natural environment. Trained confederates are frequently used to provide carefully controlled stimuli to the client. For example, Greenwald (1977) presented heterosocially anxious females with audiotaped scenarios depicting social interaction with a male friend at a fast-food restaurant and other situations. The subjects role played each of these situations by responding to stimuli provided by the audiotape and a male confederate.

Another frequently used variation of analogue assessment is the *behavior avoidance test (BAT)*, in which subjects are asked to approach a feared object (Bernstein, 1973; Haynes & Wilson, 1979). For example, Cohen (1977) requested acrophobic subjects to approach a railing and plate glass window on the 14th and 15th floor of a building. Observation measures of approach behavior and questionnaire measure of discomfort were taken.

Occasionally, analogue assessment involves *behavior analogues*: The observed behavior is assumed to covary with the behavior of primary interest. For example, Lindsley (1960) monitored level presses of psychiatric inpatients on a human operant response panel. Carter and Thomas (1973) had spouses in distressed marriages indicate the impact and intent of their verbal communication by pressing designated buttons. In these examples, the monitored responses (lever and button presses) were presumed to function as more easily observed and quantified analogue measures or covariates of behaviors of primary interest (psychotic behavior and marital communication patterns).

Analogue observation has been used in the assessment of a variety of behavior problems, such as nonspecific social anxiety and social skills def-

icits (Bellack, 1979; Curran & Wessberg, 1981), dental anxietey (Wroblewski, Jacob, & Rehm, 1977), stuttering (James, 1981), heterosexual anxiety (Greenwald, 1977), alcohol ingestion, (Miller, 1981), assertive responses of the elderly (Edinberg, Karoly, & Gleser, 1977), parent-child interaction (Hughes & Haynes, 1978), marital interaction (Haynes, Jensen, Wise, & Sherman, 1981), speech anxiety (Fremouw & Zitter, 1978), small animal phobias (Barrera & Rosen, 1977), test anxiety (Goldfried, Linehan, & Smith, 1978), and eating disorders (Brownell, 1981).

A variety of measures have been taken in analogue assessments. Most analogue assessments involve direct observation of behavior using codes, sampling parameters, and procedures similar to those described for naturalistic observation. However, physiological, verbal self-report, questionnaire, qualitative observer impressions of observers, and self-monitoring measures also are frequently taken.

The main advantage of analogue assessment is that it provides a cost-efficient method of behavioral observation. The assessment environment and stimuli are arranged to increase the probability of occurrence of targeted behaviors and hypothesized etiological variables. This increases the cost efficiency of the assessment method relative to that of naturalistic observation. Attempts to gather similar data in the natural environment can be extremely time-consuming and costly, and many behaviors (e.g., social initiations by socially anxious clients) occur at a rate sufficiently low to preclude naturalistic observation. Analogue assessment procedures also reduce the degree of situational variance in observation measures. Because the physical environment and social stimuli associated with assessment are more carefully controlled than in naturalistic observation, behavioral variance attributable to situational stimuli is reduced, although external validity is concomitantly reduced.

Several sources of error have been identified in analogue assessment (Bellack, 1979; Bellack, Hersen, & Lamparski, 1979; Forehand & Atkinson, 1977; Haynes, 1978; Haynes & Wilson, 1979; Hughes & Haynes, 1978; Kazdin, Esveldt-Dawson, & Matson, 1983). These include: (a) instructional variables, (b) variance in situational stimuli, (c) reactivity, (d) demand factors, and (e) errors associated with the observers, sampling parameters, or other aspects of the data acquisition process.

The primary drawback to analogue observation is that it is only an indirect measure of the individual's behavior in the setting of greatest importance—the natural environment. Although some studies have demonstrated significant correlations between behaviors emitted in analogue and naturalistic settings, other studies have found low levels of correlation (see reviews by Haynes & Wilson, 1979). Generalization of behavior between naturalistic and analogue settings cannot be assumed. Further, the degree or probability of generalization is likely to vary across subjects, target behaviors, settings, and observation methods.

Self-Monitoring

Self-monitoring involves the systematic self-observation and recording of the occurrence (or nonoccurrence) of specified behaviors and events (Ciminero, Nelson, & Lipinski, 1977; Kanfer, 1970; Nelson, 1977). Typically, the events to be recorded are first specified by the client and behavior analyst, and a recording form is developed. For low rate behaviors (e.g., seizures, migraine headaches) clients may record every occurrence of the behavior. For high rate or continuous behaviors (e.g., tics, high blood pressure), monitoring most frequently occurs within specified time periods. When appropriate, topographic data (e.g., headache location and symptoms) or antecedent or consequent events (e.g., situations in which binge eating occurs and social reactions to attempt at social initiation also are monitored.

Self-monitoring has been used in the assessment of numerous behaviors and behavior problems such as the eating patterns of obese individuals (Brownell, 1981; Jeffrey & Knauss, 1981), cognitions (Merluzzi et al., 1981), smoking (Glasgow, Klesges, Godding, & Gegelman, 1983), bruxism (Rosen, 1981), blood pressure (Beiman, Graham, & Ciminero, 1978), caffeine intake (Bernard, Dennehy, & Keefauver, 1981), fuel conservation (Foxx & Hake, 1977), startle responses (Fairbank, DeGood, & Jenkens, 1981), deviant sexual behavior (Foote & Laws, 1981), Raynaud's symptoms (Keefe, Surwit, & Pilon, 1981), hair pulling (Ottens, 1981), arthritic pain (Varni, 1981), alcohol intake (Miller, 1981), drug intake (Thompson & Conrad, 1977), seizures (Lubar & Shouse, 1977), and sleeping patterns of insomniacs (Bootzin & Engle-Friedman, 1981).

Several types of data can be acquired through self-monitoring. Clients can monitor overt motor behavior, verbal behavior, occurrence of environmental events associated with their behavior, physiological responses, cognitions, and affective responses. Durations and intensities, as well as frequencies, can be monitored.

Self-monitoring has many advantages. It is applicable to a wide range of behavior problems, it is inexpensive, it is not time consuming, it can be used to gather data in the natural environment, and it can be used to derive quantitative indices of multiple response modalities. It is one of the most cost efficient and clinically useful behavioral assessment procedures.

However, like other assessment devices, self-monitoring is subject to several general and idiosyncratic sources of error (Ciminero et al., 1977; Haynes, 1978; Nelson, 1977). Perhaps the most significant of those is observer bias, in which the recordings can be influenced by the expectancies and biases of the client, the social sensitivity associated with the targeted behavior, and the contingencies associated with the recordings. In some cases these biases may be so great as to compromise the validity of the data. For example, significant biases have been noted in the self-reported drinking behavior of alcoholics and eating behavior of obese individuals (Brownell, 1981; Miller, 1981).

Other sources of error variance include degree of prior training of the client in self-monitoring procedures, degree of specification of target behaviors, methods of time sampling and recording, contingencies associated with self-monitoring or submission of the acquired data to the behavior analyst, reaction from the client's social environment to the self-recording procedures, and characteristics (e.g., rate, duration) of the targeted behaviors. As with other observation methods of assessment, reactivity is a particularly potent source of variance. The reactive impact of self-monitoring is frequently so great that self-monitoring is sometimes used as a method of intervention with clients. (Broden, Hall, & Mitts, 1971).

Participant Observation

Participant observation is a form of naturalistic observation in which observers are normally part of the natural environment (Haynes & Wilson, 1979). Although the sampling and recording methods are similar to those described in "naturalistic observation," participant observers are usually less well trained than external observers and focus on a more restricted range of target events. For example, a staff member on a psychiatric ward might monitor the frequency and targets of social initiations by a depressed person during mealtime and recreation periods.

Although most frequently used in the assessment of children and institutionalized individuals, participant observation has also been used in the assessment of marital distress (Price & Haynes, 1980), food intake (Epstein & Martin, 1977), heterosexual social behaviors (Arkowitz, Lichtenstein, Mcgovern, & Hines 1975), family interactions (Weinrott et al., 1981), caffeine intake (Bernard et al., 1981), alcohol intake (Garlington & Dericco, 1977), deviant sexual behavior (Foote & Laws, 1981), phobic behavior (Warnach et al., 1981), aggressive behavior (Matson & Stephens, 1977), and sexual dysfunction (Zeiss, 1978).

Reactive effects of participant observation are likely but have been infrequently studied (e.g., Price & Haynes, 1980). If the variables influencing reactivity outlined by Baum, Forehand, and Zegoib (1979) and Haynes and Horn (1982) apply to participant observation, their reactive effects should be less than nonparticipant observers, as participant observation involves minimal changes in the natural environment. However, the method of monitoring and the relationship between the observer and the target individual may affect the probability or degree of reactivity. There are many situations (e.g., an individual monitoring the sexual or ingestive behavior of a spouse) in which participant observation might be expected to result in significant alterations of the monitored behavior or in social interaction between the observer and target.

The advantages of participant observation are similar to those of self-monitoring: It is inexpensive, applicable to a wide range of problem behaviors, populations, and environmental events, and can be used to gather data from the natural environment. Like self-monitoring, the acquired data can also reflect biases on the part of the observer (Christensen, Sullaway, & King, 1983; Margolin, 1983). Other sources of error include the degree of training of observers, the degree of specification of observation targets, and the methods of sampling and recording. Concern with possible biases and errors in participant

monitoring and insufficient investigation of its psychometric properties has confined its use to an adjunctive rather than primary assessment instrument (Haynes & Wilson, 1979).

Psychophysiological Measures

An increasing use of psychophysiological methods in behavioral assessment can be attributed to three trends: (a) an increasing focus on physiological components of behavior problems, (b) an increasing involvement of behavior analysts in the analysis and treatment of medical-psychological disorders, and (c) an increasing use of intervention procedures designed to modify physiological processes. The focus of behavior analysts upon physiological as well as cognitive and motoric components of behavior problems has encouraged the adoption of psychophysiological (or electrophysiological) measurement methods. For example, obsessive-compulsive behavior problems (Mavissakalian & Barlow, 1981) have multiple components, frequently including automatically and centrally mediated physiological responses such as peripheral vasomotor constriction, heart rate acceleration, increases in skeletal muscle tension, and/or increases in skin conductance. As noted earlier in this chapter, physiological, cognitive, and motoric components of a syndrome frequently do not significantly covary, and assessment of all components is necessary for a valid description, functional analysis, and intervention evaluation.

Impetus for the use of psychophysiological measurement techniques has also come from the increasing involvement of behavior analysts in the evaluation and treatment of psychosomatic and medical-psychological disorders (Davison & Davison, 1980; Haynes & Gannon, 1981; Melamed & Siegel, 1980). There is an increasing recognition of the etiological and mediational role of environmental and psychological factors in many organic disorders (see DSM III) and of the significant psychological consequences frequently associated with organic disorders (Boll, 1981). The concepts and technology of behavioral construct systems are uniquely suited to the investigation and modification of these factors.

Psychophysiological measures used most frequently in behavioral assessment include brain wave patterns, eye movements, peripheral temperature, blood volume pulse, muscle tension, respiration, penile erections, skin conductance, and blood pressure. Most of these methods have been borrowed from the discipline of psychophysiology (Martin & Venables, 1980). With some notable exceptions (e.g., Henson, Rubin, & Henson 1979), behavior analysts have made only minimal methodological contributions.

Medical-psychological disorders that have been assessed by behavior analysts with psychophysiological measurement methods include muscle-contraction headache (Blanchard et al., 1983; Haynes, 1981), migraine headache (Sturgis, Adams, & Brantley, 1981), essential hypertension (Elder, Geoffray, & McAfee, 1981), asthma (Alexander, 1981), dermatitis (Haynes, Wilson, & Britton, 1979), insomnia (Bootzin & Engle-Friedman, 1981), sexual dysfunctions (Heiman & Hatch, 1981), gastrointestinal dysfunctions (Walker & Sandman, 1981), diabetes (Green, 1978), pain (Chapman & Wykoff, 1981), hemophilia (Varni, 1981), and Raynaud's symptoms (Keefe et al., 1981). Psychophysiological methods have also been used in the assessment of behavior problems such as speech anxiety (Gatchel et al., 1978), smoking (Hynd, Severson, & O'Neil, 1976), pedophilia (Foote & Laws, 1981), bruxism (Rosen, 1981), hyperactivity (Wells, Conners, Imber, & Delamater, 1981), rape (Quinsey, Chaplin, & Varney, 1981), phobias (Taylor & Agras, 1981), obsessive-compulsive disorders (Mavissakalian & Barlow, 1981), social-anxiety (McFall, 1982), and depression (Doyne, Chambless, & Beutler, 1983).

Many behavioral interventions such as biofeedback, desensitization, relaxation training, operant conditioning of physiological responses, flooding (implosive) treatment, and specific imagery are intended to modify some aspect of physiological functioning. Psychophysiological assessment methods are necessary to evaluate intervention outcome and also facilitate the monitoring of the intervention process.

Each psychophysiological measurement method has common and unique sources of error associated with its technology (e.g., sensitivity, movement artifact, filtering, sensor placement, surface resistance). In addition, the generalizability of the obtained data is limited by the idiosyncracy of laboratory situations, sensor placement, time-sampling parameters, and reactivity. For example, the setting and temporal generalizability of laboratory occlusive measures of blood pressure of a hypertensive client will be influenced by the characteristics of the laboratory environment, the position of the client while blood pressure is ta-

ken, the placement and size of the occlusion cuff, exercise and dietary factors occurring immediately prior to measurement, types of stressors or other stimuli presented, methods of recording, and time-sampling parameters used.

Assessment Instruments Adapted from Traditional Clinical Assessment

Two behavioral assessment procedures (the interview and questionnaire) have been adapted from traditional applied psychological disciplines. In both cases there are significant differences in format and content between behavioral and traditional applications that reflect differences in the underlying conceptual systems.

Because of the self-report nature of interviews and questionnaires and their association with traditional clinical psychology, they have been viewed skeptically and used sparingly by many behavior analysts. It was presumed that the probability of error, particularly biases in self-report, and the degree of inference inherent in their interpretation was sufficient to render them of little value as a primary data source. This blanket skepticism is being replaced by a recognition that error variance in questionnaires and interviews differs from, but probably does not exceed, that of other behavioral assessment methods. Furthermore, they can be useful adjuncts in a behavioral assessment program.

Behavioral Assessment Interviews

The interview is probably the most frequently used assessment instrument (Cormier & Cormier, 1979; Haynes 1978; Haynes & Chavez, 1983; Haynes & Jensen, 1979; Haynes & Wilson, 1979; Linehan, 1977; Matarazzo & Wiens, 1972; Morganstern, 1976; Sanson-Fisher & Martin, 1981; Wiens, 1981). Almost every behavioral intervention involves preintervention verbal interaction with clients or significant individuals (e.g., teachers, staff, parents) from the client's environment.

The importance of the interview is a result of its multiple functions. Other assessment instruments have as their primary goal the derivation of data on the client's behavior or interactions with his or her environment. The assessment interview serves these functions. Additionally, it is used to screen clients for therapy, evaluate and enhance clients' motivations for further assessment and intervention, select additional assessment strategies, facilitate client-assessor interaction, inform clients about the assessment-intervention process, and gather historical information (Haynes & Chavez, 1983). Thus, the assessment interview has a multiple and profound impact on assessment and intervention.

There are significant differences in the content and format of behavioral and nonbehavioral assessment interviews. Compared to nonbehavioral interviews, behavioral interviews tend to be more: (a) systematic and structured, (b) focused on overt behavior and behavior-environment interactions, (c) attentive to situational sources of behavioral variance, (d) focused on current rather than historical behaviors and determinants, and (e) quantitative in orientation.

It is in the interview that a systems perspective of behavioral assessment is most apparent. Assessment foci are becoming less confined to the analysis of discrete target behaviors and contingent and antecedent factors. Instead, the client is more frequently evaluated in the context of his or her larger social system. Other interactions in the client's social system, collateral changes potentially associated with intervention (such as changes in family interactions or occupational patterns), sources of social support, mediational events, and behaviors that may covary with the targeted behaviors (response classes) are also evaluated in the interview.

Despite its importance, the interview has been the assessment instrument least subjected to empirical evaluation (Haynes & Jensen, 1979; Haynes & Wilson, 1979; Linehan, 1977). Although it has been subjected to intermittent investigation for other purposes (Sanson-Fisher & Martin, 1981; Wiens, 1976) its psychometric properties as a behavioral assessment instrument have been infrequently studied (Haynes, Jensen, Wise, & Sherman, 1981).

Questionnaires

The questionnaire is probably the second most frequently used instrument in behavioral assessment (Emmelkamp, 1981; Wade, Baker, & Hartmann, 1979). Like the interview, it has been applied to the assessment of almost all adult behavior disorders (see reviews by Barlow, 1981; Bellack & Herson, 1977; Haynes & Wilson, 1979; Jensen & Haynes, in press; Nay, 1979).

Many questionnaires used by behavior analysts (e.g., depression scales, marital satisfaction scales) are unaltered adoptions of those employed in traditional psychological assessment. Although some provide useful data to the behavior analyst, many have been adopted without sufficient attention to their underlying assumptions, psychometric properties, or applicability to targeted populations. Most traditional questionnaires are designed to measure some "personality trait" (e.g., intelligence, neuroticism) and do not satisfactorily attend to the situational variance of behavior. In addition, many are based on psychodynamic etiological assumptions and do not provide measures of multimodal components and determinants of specific targeted responses. Traditional questionnaires also frequently provide a single summary score of a multifaceted syndrome. As a result, they are sometimes appropriate for screening or as a vague index of program outcome but seldom have utility for most of the other functions of behavioral assessment.

Other questionnaires have been developed by behavior analysts. These target specific adult behavior problems such as social skills deficits (Curran & Wessberg, 1981), obsessive-compulsive behaviors (Hodgson & Rachman, 1977), fears and phobias (Geer, 1965), anger (Novaco, 1975), marital distress and dysfunction (Weiss & Cerrato, 1980), ingestive disorders (Brownell, 1981; Miller, 1981), sexual dysfunctions (Lopiccolo & Steger, 1974), and menstrual dysfunctions (Cox, 1977). Most have face validity, focus on more specific behaviors and events, and attend to situational determinants of behavior. However, their development and application have frequently violated standard psychometric principles. Many are rationally rather than empirically derived, were not subject to internal homogeneity or factor analyses, and did not undergo multimethod validity evaluation prior to application. Such psychometric deficiencies hinder interpretation of their resultant scores.

When properly developed, evaluated, and applied, questionnaires can be an efficient and useful source of data. They are inexpensive to administer and score, have face validity for clients, and their analysis and interpretation can be simplified through computer administration and scoring. However, because of the significant possibility of reporting biases, and the inferential difficulties in interpreting derived scores, questionnaire-derived, as well as interview-derived, data should be corroborated by data from other assessment procedures.

Adjunctive Methods

There are several other assessment methods that are less frequently used in behavior assessment but are consistent with its underlying concepts. These include product-of-behavior measures, manipulation, critical-event sampling, and computer-assisted assessment.

Product-of-Behavior Measures

Product-of-behavior measures are temporary or permanent records generated by target behaviors (Haynes & Wilson, 1979). For example, weight is a frequently used product-of-behavior measure for eating behavior and is frequently used in the evaluation of behavioral interventions with obesity (Brownell, 1981). Other product-of-behavior measures include tokens acquired and spent (as a measure of social and work behaviors of psychiatric inpatients) (Kazdin, 1984), grades or workbook performance (as measures of study behaviors), and blood urine composition (as measures for smoking or drug intake) (Glasgow et al., 1983; Stitzer et al., 1982).

Most product-of-behavior measures have the advantages of being relatively unobtrusive, permanent (or long lasting), and easily accessible. In many cases, these measures are minimally reactive and provide a quantitative index of behaviors emitted in the natural environment.

There are difficulties in interpreting product-of-behavior measures, however. Because the product-of-behavior index may reflect behaviors other than those targeted, the relationship between the product-of-behavior measure and the targeted behavior is frequently unclear. For example, weight changes may reflect targeted changes in eating patterns, but may also reflect changes in caloric expenditure, the intake of fluids or diuretics, hormonal changes, or the intake of stimulant medication or appetite suppressants. Because of these inferential problems, the external validity of the measures cannot be assumed. Also, because of the latency between some target behaviors and their products, a number of product-of-behavior measures may be insufficiently sensitive to behavior change.

Manipulation

One of the most potentially useful but least frequently used methods of assessment is manipulation of hypothesized controlling events. Changes in dependent variables which occur concomitantly with manipulation of hypothesized causal factors is a powerful basis for deriving causal inferences (Haynes, 1984). This has been a prime method of causal analysis of many empirically biased psychological disciplines such as experimental psychology (Kling & Riggs, 1971), experimental psychopathology (Maher, 1966), and the experimental analysis of behavior (Honig, 1966).

Although manipulation is consistent with an hypothesis testing epistemology, it has been infrequently used in behavioral assessment. Several examples of manipulation were reviewed by Mavissakalian and Barlow (1981) in their discussion of behavioral assessment strategies for obsessive-compulsive disorders. For example, in studies by Rachman, compulsive hand washers first touched contaminated objects. They were then allowed to either wash their hands immediately afterwards, were forced to delay hand-washing, or had their hand-washing interrupted. Multimethod assessment was used to evaluate the effects of these manipulations. Manipulation has also been used to assess the effect of social stimuli on the drinking behavior of alcoholics by systematically manipulating these stimuli in simulated bars (Miller, 1981).

Manipulation of hypothesized antecedent stimuli can also be useful in the functional analysis of medical-psychological disorders. For example, the exposure of headache clients to various stressors in a laboratory while simultaneously monitoring electromyographic responses from multiple cephalic sites may help identify specific antecedents and localized muscle tension responses associated with head pain. Controlled presentation of laboratory stimuli may also help identify precipitants of blood pressure increases of hypertensives, anxiety-arousing stimuli for fearful subjects, or the efficacy of potential reinforcers.

The greatest advantage of assessment via manipulation is that it can provide confirmatory or disconfirmatory data on hypothesized controlling stimuli, both antecedent and consequent. Alternative methods of evaluating these relationships are limited to self-report unless they occur at a rate sufficient for observation. The primary disadvantages of this assessment method reside in threats to its internal and external validity. Care must be taken in designing the manipulation strategies (e.g., controlling sequence, duration, intensity, expectancy factors) so that valid causal inferences may be drawn. More importantly, the external validity or setting generality of the observed relationships cannot be assumed when manipulations occur in analogue settings.

Computer-assisted Assessment

Computer-assisted assessment is similar in content and procedure to both interviews and questionnaires. Typically, a client sits in front of a video monitor upon which questions or other visual stimuli are presented. His or her responses are made via an adjacent keyboard. The interactive computer system operates as a decision-tree, and stimuli presented are a function of previous client responses. For example, if a client indicates problems with sleep-onset insomnia, a series of questions might be presented concerning the client's sleeping environment, presleep cognitions, or diet.

Preliminary research (Angle, 1981; Angle, Ellinwood, Hay, Johnson, & Hay, 1977; Angle, Hay, Hay, & Ellinwood, 1977; Kleinmuntz, 1972) suggests that computer-assisted assessment can facilitate the collection and analysis of massive amounts of data and is well received by clients. In addition, errors associated with bias, fatigue or procedural variance in assessment interviews are reduced.

The main drawbacks to computer-assisted assessment appear to be technological and financial. The initial investment for a computer and its programming can be considerable, although it may be cost efficient over an extended period of time. In addition, because computer programs tend to be somewhat specialized, it is difficult to develop an interactive program with sufficient sensitivity and flexibility to satisfactorily address the myriad of problems and controlling variables presented in most clinical situations.

Critical Event Sampling

Another potentially useful but infrequently used method of behavioral assessment involves automated recording in the natural environment during problematic periods for clients (Haynes, 1978; Margolin, 1981). For example, tape recorders can be self-actuated by a distressed marital couple during verbal altercations at home or by a heterosocially anxious individual while on a date.

Critical event sampling can be cost and time efficient because sampling is limited to periods when there is a high probability of problematic

interactions in the natural environment. Similar information would be costly to acquire through naturalistic observation. Quantitative indices may be derived from these recordings, and they can also provide a rich source of qualitatively derived hypotheses.

Because there has been no psychometric evaluation of this assessment procedure, sources and degree of error can only be estimated. As with many other assessment instruments, critical event sampling may have significant reactive effects. For example, critical event sampling of verbal altercations of distressed marital couples was attempted in one study (Follingstad, 1981), but the procedure had obvious reactive effects on marital interaction. Furthermore, the audio tapes returned to the investigators were not random samples of marital altercations—couples sometimes erased recordings or failed to record at designated times.

EVALUATION

The applicability of classical psychometric principles to behavioral assessment is a subject of debate (Cone, 1984; Nelson, 1983). However, assessment systems and instruments can be evaluated on a number of important dimensions, including applicability and utility, reliability, validity, and sources of error variance. The evaluation of any assessment instrument is complicated by the fact that its psychometric properties cannot be assumed stable and are not necessarily generalizable across populations, settings, or assessment functions. The psychometric evaluation of behavioral assessment is rendered even more difficult because it is composed of a set of divergent procedures, each of which is associated with idiosyncratic attributes and psychometric characteristics. Because of this complexity, the following section only highlights major evaluative dimensions in behavioral assessment. More comprehensive examinations of particular assessment methods can be found in books by Cone and Hawkins (1977), Ciminero et al., (1977), Haynes (1978), Haynes and Wilson (1979), and Nay (1979).

Applicability and Utility

The applicability and utility of an assessment instrument refers to the degree to which it is useful for assessing particular populations or behaviors or behavior disorders, its applicability in particular situations, and the degree to which it is useful for particular assessment purposes. In considering the applicability and utility of behavioral assessment instruments, several evaluative dimensions such as clinical utility, cost-efficiency, utility for developing a functional analysis, and utility for DSM III (APA, 1980) diagnoses are particularly important considerations.

There can be little doubt that behavioral assessment instruments have *empirical utility* — they provide powerful methods of multimethod and multimodal evaluation of intervention effects and hypothesized functional relationships. In contrast, the *utility* of behavioral assessment has been questioned in *clinical* situations where *service delivery* rather than research is the prime focus (Barlow, 1980; Emmelkamp, 1981; Haynes, 1983; Margolin, 1981; Swan & MacDonald, 1979; Wade et al., 1979). Surveys of behavior therapists in clinical practice have suggested that their use of behavioral assessment instruments is frequently limited to interviews and questionnaires (Swan & MacDonald, 1978).

The limited clinical application of behavioral assessment methods can be attributed to several factors (Haynes, 1984): (a) Many behavioral assessment instruments (particularly psychophysiological and observational methods) are costly to apply and have a relatively unfavorable cost-effectiveness ration (Alvizos et al., 1978; McIntyre et al., 1983; Wickramesekera, 1981), (b) many behavior analysts are inadequately trained in the application of behavioral assessment instruments (O'Leary, 1979), (c) the type of information provided by the assessment instruments (e.g., observed behavior rates) is not always useful in formulating functional analyses and designing intervention programs (Foster & Cone, 1980), (d) adequate assessment instruments have not been developed for many problem behaviors encountered by clinicians (such as paranoia, hypochondriasis, psychosomatic disorders) (Haynes & Wilson, 1984), and (e) the financial contingency systems operating in private practice and social service agencies reward client contracts for therapy more than for assessment.

Several additional issues in the clinical utility of behavioral assessment are worthy of consideration. First, like all assessment instruments, behavioral assessment instruments are differentially useful across disorders. Perhaps the most important determinant of an instrument's utility in deriving a functional analysis for a particular disorder is the degree to which the disorder has a functional relationship with environmental variables. For some behavior disorders (such as marital distress, phobias, and aggression), evidence supports a strong functional relationship between the disorder and behavioral and environmental variables. For other disorders (such as depression or migraine headaches), controlling variables appear to be shared among environmental organic factors. For many behavior disorders (such as schizophrenia, paranoia, or asthma), a functional relationship with behavioral-environmental factors is possible but undemonstrated (Haynes & Wilson, 1985). Therefore, the utility of behavioral assessment (and any psychological assessment) in deriving pretreatment functional analyses is a function of the proportion of variance in the targeted disorder accounted for by variance in environmental factors of behavioral-environmental interactions. However, even when environmental determinants play a minor role, behavioral assessment is a very powerful system for intervention evaluation.

Second, specific behavioral assessment instruments are differentially useful in formulating functional analyses and in their applicability for the other purposes of assessment (Haynes, 1984; Nelson & Hays, 1979). Some instruments, such as the interview, are more useful for developing than for testing hypotheses. Others, such as naturalistic observation, are more suitable for hypothesis testing than for hypothesis development.

Third, there is an increasing emphasis on the use of DSM III (APA, 1980), which is simply a multiaxial system primarily for differential diagnosis (Boll, 1981; Nathan, 1980; Neale & Oltmanns, 1981; Nelson & Barlow, 1981). It should be emphasized that behavioral assessment is primarily a method of data acquisition. Because the validity of diagnoses cannot exceed the validity of data upon which diagnostic decisions are made, behavioral assessment can make a particularly important contribution to DSM III diagnoses. Behavioral assessment is especially suited to deriving data for axis IV — examining psychosocial factors contributing to behavior disorders. However, there are important differences in the conceptual systems underlying psychiatric classificatory systems and behavioral assessment (Taylor, 1983). Behavioral assessment remains more descriptive than classificatory. As discussed elsewhere (Haynes, 1979, 1984), in most cases classification is insufficient to indicate behavioral intervention strategies. A more fine-grained analysis of target behaviors and controlling variables is necessary.

Considering the alternatives (nonbehavioral interviews and objective and projective tests), behavioral assessment is, despite its deficiencies, the most powerful and clinically useful assessment system. It provides the clinician with a *set* of procedures amenable to the multimethod and multimodal assessment of most adult disorders, in most settings and for most purposes. No other assessment system approaches such diversity of utility. Because of its empirical analysis, it is particularly suited to the clinician who adopts a hypothesis-testing and accountability orientation (O'Leary, 1979).

Reliability

Reliability is a complex concept reflecting the stability of measures derived from repeated administrations of a measurement instrument (*external reliability*) or from the degree or pattern of covariance of elements within an instrument (*internal reliability*). Reliability is a particularly important attribute of an instrument because it sets the upper limit to its validity.

The application of traditional reliability concepts to behavioral assessment poses difficulties because of differences between traditional and behavioral conceptual systems in assumptions about the situational and temporal stability of behavior (Haynes, 1978, 1979). Coefficients of reliability for measures of a presumably stable phenomenon (e.g., IQ, neuroticism, locus of control) provide one index of the validity or degree of error variance of those measurement instruments. Coefficients of reliability for measures of events demonstrating situational or temporal instability (e.g., eating patterns, marital interaction, autonomic arousal) may be indicative either of error variance associated with the measurement instruments or of true variance in the phenomenon measured.

For example, staff observations of a psychiatric inpatient may demonstrate considerable day-to-day variability in the frequency with which he or she initiates social interaction with other patients. This measured variability may accurately reflect the patient's behavior or may reflect varying levels of diligence by the observers, the use of different observers on different days, variance in the times or settings in which the patient's social behavior is sampled, or insufficient specification of the observation code "social initiations."

The probability that measured variance is a function of true behavior variability rather than error variance in the measurement instrument can be enhanced by careful control of sources of error. Thus, care in construction and application of assessment instruments, such as the use of highly trained observers, careful training of patients in self-monitoring procedures, careful specification of target events, specifically worded questionnaire and interview items, and consistency in the timing and setting of assessment can reduce the impact of methodological errors. Also, use of criterion measures (such as a second observer) can help evaluate sources of error variance attributable to the measurement instruments.

Criterion-Referenced Validity

Because assessment instruments differ in the degree to which they accurately measure the phenomena they are intended to measure, their validity is frequently evaluated by comparing resulting indices with those derived from other independently evaluated assessment instruments. This process is referred to as criterion-referenced validity evaluation and can be either concurrent or predictive. Concurrent validity is the degree of correlation between two instruments administered at the same time. For example, the *concurrent validity* of an interview with a female reporting orgasmic dysfunctions might be indicated by the degree of correlation between the interview, questionnaires, or sexual partner reports of sexual behavior. *Discriminant validity* is a form of concurrent validity measuring the degree to which an assessment instrument can differentiate groups classified on the basis of naturally occurring phenomenon. For example, the disriminant validity of an analogue measure of marital communication might be the degree to which it could successfully discriminate couples seeking marital therapy from those not seeking marital therapy. *Predictive validity* is the degree to which an assessment instrument can differentiate groups classified on the basis of naturally occurring phenomena. For example, the later time. For example, the predictive validity of a self-monitoring measure of time spent practicing relaxation might be indicated by the degree to which it is associated with a measure of the outcome of relaxation training.

There is considerable variability in the extent to which behavioral assessment instruments have been subjected to criterion-referenced validity evaluations. Some, such as interviews (Haynes & Chavez, 1983) and naturalistic observation (Hartmann & Wood, 1982) have undergone very little criterion validity evaluation. Others, such as behavioral questionnaires (Bellack & Hersen, 1977) and analogue observation (Bellack, 1979) have been the subject of more extensive evaluation (see reviews in Ciminero et al., 1977, 1984; Haynes & Wilson, 1979; Nelson & Hayes, 1984). The results of these evaluations have been mixed, reflecting both the methodological difficulties inherent in applying this psychometric concept to behavioral assessment instruments and the early developmental stage of most behavioral assessment instruments. For example, several validity evaluations of analogue assessment procedures (Bellack, 1979; Curran, Monti, Corriveau, Hay, Hagerman, Zwick, & Farrell, 1980; Jacobson, Ellwood, & Dallas, 1981) have noted problems in the external validity or setting generalizability of the obtained measures. In particular, analogue measures of social behavior frequently do not correlate highly with other measures of the same phenomenon or with the same measure administered in a different setting.

Behavior analysts have frequently ascribed an inherent validity to behavioral observation. Observation measures were presumed to be valid because they are minimally inferential and were assumed to simply reflect the behavior of the targeted individual at the time of observation. Differences between behavioral observation and another measure of the same phenomenon (e.g., discrepancies between questionnaire measured phobic behavior and an individual's motor behavior in the presence of a phobic stimulus) were presumed to be indicative of invalidity of the non-observation measure. However, behavioral observation measures are no longer presumed to be inherently valid. Measures derived from behavioral observation can reflect methodological variance as well as true behavior variance, and low coefficients of agreement with other measures can as readily be indicative of error in the observation measure.

In summary, a large number of studies have reported data indicating that behavioral assessment instruments can provide data with a satisfactory degree of criterion-referenced validity (Ciminero et al., 1977; Haynes & Wilson, 1979).

However, inferences of validity of any assessment instrument should be drawn cautiously. Validity and reliability are not stable properties of an assessment instrument. Neither can automatically be generalized across populations, settings, methods of administration, or functions of assessment. Furthermore, low indices of criterion validity have been reported in some studies, and many behavioral assessment instruments have undergone insufficient validity evaluation (Conger & Keane, 1981).

Content Validity

Content validity refers to the degree to which the content of an assessment instrument (items on a questionnaire, situation sampled codes in an observation system) adequately samples the targeted construct (Goldfried, 1982; Haynes, 1978; Linehan, 1980). For example, a behavioral interview with adequate content validity for preintervention assessment of depressed clients should focus on typical sources of reinforcers, recent modification of reinforcement rate or stimulus control parameters, social consequences for depressive behavior, associated congitive or attributive behaviors, environmental stimuli preceding depressive episodes, coping behaviors, and social supports (Lewinsohn & Lee, 1981). In addition, content validity is also affected by methods of sampling, data reduction and data analysis used by the assessor (Linehan, 1980).

The structure and content of a content valid instrument varies with the purposes of assessment. For example, an observational system to assess the effects of a token system on the self-care behaviors of hospitalized schizophrenics should adequately sample those self-care behaviors, but should also sample potential side-effects or mediating variables such as token stealing or staff-patient interactions. Different behaviors might be sampled in an observation system directed at the same patients but intended to evaluate the general and specific effects of pharmacological intervention.

Although content validity is a qualitative dimension of an assessment instrument, it can be enhanced through careful instrument construction and evaluation. Most behavioral assessment instruments are constructed rationally or analytically—the developer selects elements of the instrument (e.g., questions, observation codes) on the basis of his or her theoretical preconceptions (Conger, Wallander, Mariotto, & Ward, 1980).

As a result, the instruments sometimes more closely reflect these preconceptions than empirically determined characteristics and determinants of the targeted behavior problem. Rational derivations can be supplemented with alternative methods of constructing assessment instruments involving examination of previously used items or comparing groups varying on the dimension of interest (e.g., comparing social initiation responses of socially skilled with those of socially unskilled individuals). The social and external validity of identified items can also be examined, and tests for redundancy and internal homogeneity can be conducted (Conger et al., 1980; Spence, 1981).

Content validity of a behavioral assessment instrument decreases over time because the instrument is based on an evolving conceptualization of the targeted disorder. As our understanding of the characteristics and determinants of behavior problems increases over time, the content validity of assessment instruments based on earlier conceptualizations diminishes.

Generalizability is an alternative conceptual and statistical process for identifying sources of variance in an obtained score (Coates & Thoresen, 1978; Cronbach, Gleser, Nanda, & Rajaratnam, 1972; Foster & Cone, 1980; Hartmann & Wood, 1982). Through analysis of variance procedures, proportions of variance can be assigned to sources (facets), such as observers, situations, or time. Although still infrequently used in behavioral assessment, generalizability theory presents an alternative psychometric model of conceptualizing and analyzing the reliability and validity of an assessment instrument and identifying and isolating sources of error variance.

TRENDS

Behavioral assessment is an *evolutionary* conceptual and methodological system characterized by an ongoing process of refinement. Compared to the 1980s, behavioral assessment in the 1990s will have a significantly greater empirical basis, clinical applicability, and conceptual sophistication. These changes stimulate, as well as reflect, developments in behavioral construct systems. There are two major areas of change in behavioral assessment: (a) an expanding focus of assessment and (b) the increased application of psychometric and research design principles.

An Expanding Focus

The focus of behavioral assessment reflects the expanding array of variables, relationships, and target behaviors included in behavioral construct systems. There is an increased focus on behavioral chains, temporally extended and discontiguous determinants, predictor and mediating variables, community and environmental settings, cognitive variables, and treatment generalization and side effects. In addition, behavioral assessment is being used with an expanding range of adult behavioral disorders.

As noted earlier in this chapter, there has been a strong emphasis in behavioral assessment on a SORC (stimulus, organism, response, contingency) model (Goldfried, 1982; Goldfried & Sprafkin, 1976; Nelson & Barlow, 1981). This model identifies four potential determinants of behavior disorders and has been used as a descriptive system for behavior problems, suggesting intervention targets and strategies. The SORC model has served to contrast behavioral with traditional conceptual systems, which focused primarily on the etiological role of organismic, particularly intrapsychic, variables. The SORC model has also served to emphasize the multifaceted qualities and determinants of behavior problems.

Recent conceptual advances suggest that the SORC model, although originally heuristic, may unnecessarily limit the range of identifiable behavioral relationships and controlling variables. For example, a number of studies have pointed to the etiological importance of *extended interactions* or *behavioral chains* (Cromwell & Peterson, 1981; Gottman, 1979; Haynes, 1983; Margolin, 1981, 1983; McFall, 1982; Miller, 1981; Vincent, 1980; Voeltz & Evans, 1982) and the clinical utility of examining *response classes* (Mash, 1979; Miller, 1981). For example, marital satisfaction and distress may be predicted more accurately from an analysis of extended periods of interactions (Margolin, 1981) than from assessment of only recent interactions. Similarly, paranoid ideation may be functionally related to multiple interactions across a range of interpersonal interactions (Haynes & Wilson, 1985) rather than to transient or situationally specific interpersonal experiences. Voeltz and Evans (1982) also noted that analyses limited to stimulus-response or response-consequence relationships may omit important controlling variables. In many cases, *chains* or reponses may reliably precede behavior problems (such as cognitive and behavioral chains preceding aggressive behaviors, overeating, or social avoidance).

Behavioral etiological conceptualizations and assessments have stressed controlling variables in close temporal proximity to the target behavior (Russo, Bird, & Masek, 1980). For example, most systems for naturalistic observation attend to those antecedent stimuli that immediately (e.g., within 60 seconds) precede target responses. In fact, the structure of most behavioral observation systems and associated methods of data analysis make it difficult to identify controlling events that occur more than a few minutes prior to a target behavior. More recently, the etiological role of controlling events that are less temporally contiguous to target behaviors is being recognized (Haynes, 1983, 1984; Margolin, 1981). Many adult behavior disorders such as obsessive ruminations, sleep disorders, elevated blood pressure, or sexual dysfunctions may be associated with events that occurred hours, days, or months previously.

An emphasis on cost-efficiency evaluations of interventions and a recognition of the idiosyncratic nature of behavior disorders and individuals' responses to intervention have resulted in a greater interest in identifying and measuring variables that predict or mediate intervention outcome (Blanchard, 1981; Cooke & Meyers, 1980). A wide range of predictors or mediators have been suggested, including social supports, cognitive factors, previous intervention experiences, self-reinforcement and self-control skills, and etiology-intervention congruence (Haynes, 1984). The focus on predictors and mediators has two potential benefits. First, psychological services can be disseminated more efficiently, and clients can be matched more effectively to intervention programs. Second, the potential effectiveness of interventions can be increased through identification and modification of mediational factors.

One important mediational variable that has come under closer scrutiny is *treatment compliance* (sometimes called *procedural reliability*) (Billingsley, White, & Munson, 1980; Blanchard, 1981; Brownell, 1981; Epstein & Martin, 1977; Johnson, Wildman, & O'Brien, 1980; Peterson, Homer, & Wonderlich, 1982; Shapiro & Shapiro, 1983) or the degree to which clients emit the prescribed behaviors designed to effect modification of the target problem(s). Examples of behav-

ioral intervention prescriptions include practicing relaxation at home for treatment of anxiety or psychosomatic disorders and altering the stimulus-control aspects of the home environment in treatments of insomnia or obesity. Assessment of compliance with intervention prescriptions is particularly important because: (a) Treatment compliance is a major determinant of intervention outcome, (b) it helps identify sources of variance in the targeted behavior problems, and (c) it contributes to the understanding of the etiology of targeted disorders.

Behavior analysts also have expanded the focus of *outcome evaluations*. In early intervention studies, evaluation of outcome was usually limited to effects on the main target variables (Ullmann & Krasner, 1965). However, a complete evaluation of interventions cannot be limited to their effects on the primary target behaviors. Interventions must also be evaluated on the basis of their degree of *generalization* of the treatment effects across behaviors, persons, or settings (Blanchard, 1981; Russo, Cataldo, & Cushing, 1981), other *side-effects* of the intervention (Epstein & Martin, 1977), the *perceived validity* or significance by the client of the associated behavior changes (Kazdin, 1977; Lebow, 1982; Wolf, 1978), and the *cost efficiency* of intervention (Haynes, 1984).

An emphasis on intervention outcome predictor variables, the increased use of cognitive intervention strategies (e.g., "rational" interventions, covert modeling, and covert reinforcement), and the increased emphasis on the etiological role of cognitions have been associated with increased attention to cognitive factors in behavioral assessment (Cooke & Meyers, 1980; Doyne et al., 1983; Van Egeren, Haynes, Franzen, & Hamilton, 1983; Lewinsohn & Lee, 1981; Merluzzi et al., 1981; Miller, 1981; Rimm et al., 1977). Cognitions are assumed to function as antecedent stimuli of behavior (e.g., self-deprecatory thoughts preceding social withdrawal), as consequences for behavior (e.g., self-delivered punishment following failure experiences), as the primary defining characteristics of behavior problems (e.g., obsessive ruminations), and/or as significant mediators of treatment outcome (e.g., perceived credibility of an intervention).

The recent emphasis on cognitive factors in psychological construct systems has been the subject of criticism (Sampson, 1981). Their role, significance, and assessment must remain highly inferential. Moreover, they are frequently assumed to be the terminal point rather than simply elements in causal chains. Behavior analysts sometimes forget that cognitions also function as dependent variables and neglect to search for their social learning or situational determinants.

The focus of behavioral assessment also reflects the expanding applications of behavioral interventions. For example, interventions in the community (Alevizos et al., 1978; Carr, Schnelle, & Kirchner, 1980; Foxx & Hake, 1977; Hawkins, 1979; Jones, 1979; Lloyd, 1983; Nietzel et al., 1977; O'Donnell, 1977; Palmer, Lloyd, & Lloyd, 1977) have focused on such problems as energy conservation, police activities, pollution, facility utilization, and program evaluation. While such interventions may seem irrelevant to the current focus on adult behavior disorders, behaviors are identified as problematic on the basis of an evolving social consensus; behaviors that are not socially problematic at one point in time (such as energy wastage) may be defined as socially problematic at another.

Behavioral assessment strategies also are being applied to an expanding number of clinical behavior problems. These include pain (Chapman & Wykoff, 1981), dermatological disorders (Haynes et al., 1979), obsessive-compulsive disorders (Emmelkamp & Kwee, 1977), post-traumatic startle responses (Fairbank et al., 1981), hemophilia (Varni, 1981), hemodialysis (Maher, 1981), and problems of the elderly (Edinburg et al., 1977).

These are exciting advances in the conceptual bases and clinical applicability of behavioral assessment. Although they significantly complicate the assessment process and the functional analysis of behavior problems, there can be little doubt that the resulting benefits of more powerful conceptual analyses and intervention power outweigh the cost of increased assessment time by the behavior analyst.

Epistemological Advances

The most important elements of a psychological construct system are not the assumptions about behavior and its determinants, but the methods of inquiry that enabled the derivation of those concepts. Although there is an obvious interdependence between concepts and methodology, such advances in *methods of inquiry* ultimately determine the utility and viability of a psychological construct system. It is this methodological emphasis that most forcefully discriminates behavioral from most nonbehavioral construct systems.

The empirical orientation of behavioral construct systems has promoted a close examination of the temporal and situational structure within which measurement and intervention occur. Confidence in the inferences derived from assessment is influenced not only by the validity of the instruments used, but also by the degree to which threats to internal and external validity are minimized by the structure of their administration.

The empirical bases of behavioral assessment are evolving in several areas: a more frequent investigation of the psychometric properties of behavioral assessment instruments, an emphasis on standardization and norm development, a refinement of procedures for the statistical analysis of time-series designs, and the development of research designs useful in clinical situations.

As noted earlier in this chapter, an initial emphasis on the face validity of assessment instruments and a rejection of traditional psychometric principles was partly responsible for the early proliferation of behavioral assessment instruments (rationally constructed without attention to psychometric principles of development and evaluation). This has been replaced with a more judicious application of psychometric principles to the development and evaluation of assessment instruments. Behavior analysts are increasingly concerned with principles such as internal and external reliability (Haynes et al., 1979; Jacobson et al., 1981), factor structure (Galassi & Galassi, 1980), criterion and content validity (Bellack et al., 1979; Foster & Cone, 1980), applicability and utility (Barlow, 1980), and sources of error (Baum, Forehand, & Zegoib, 1979). Although there are difficulties in applying traditional psychometric concepts to behavioral assessment methods, their thoughtful application can increase confidence in the validity and applicability of derived measures.

The need for standardization of measurement instruments and development of norms has been noted by a number of authors (Goldfried, 1982; Hartmann, Roper, & Bradford, 1979; Haynes & Chavez, 1983; Korchin & Schulberg, 1981; Mash, 1979; McFall, 1977; O'Leary, 1979). There are significant differences across researchers in the assessment instruments used, and normative data for most assessment instruments are unavailable.

The result is that data derived from most behavioral assessment instruments must be interpreted subjectively rather than empirically. This condition is probably unavoidable in early phases of any technological enterprise. But a movement toward standardization and development of norms is now beginning.

There also is increasing attention to the development and application of statistical procedures, particularly for deriving inferences about intervention outcome and behavior causality (Asher, 1976; Edgington, 1982; Gardner, Hartmann, & Mitchell, 1982; Gorsuch, 1983; Hartmann et al., 1980; Horne, Yang, & Ware, 1982; Jones, Vaught, & Weinrott, 1977; Kaplan & Litrownik, 1977; Kratochwill & Piersel, 1983; Notarius, Krokoff, & Markham, 1981). Although there is appropriate concern that increased reliance on statistical inference might be accompanied by less careful control of sources of experimental variance (Michael, 1974; Sidman, 1960), the judicious use of statistical procedures within carefully controlled experimental designs can frequently facilitate a more sensitive evaluation of treatment effects and causal relationships.

In summary, an epistemology that stresses the use of an empirically based scientific method for evaluating intervention effects and the functional analysis of behavior and behavior problems is one of the most exciting attributes of behavioral assessment and behavioral construct systems. Although an emphasis on method rather than theory has been criticized, it is this epistemological orientation that is responsible for the continued viability and evolution of behavioral methods and concepts.

SUMMARY

Behavioral assessment is an increasingly viable conceptual and methodological system. It is the topic of many books, research and review articles, journals, symposia, and graduate level courses and is having an impact on many fields of applied psychology. The derivations of behavioral assessment reflect the diversity of its methods and have been influenced by traditional technologies of scientific inquiry, traditional methods of clinical assessment, the methods and focus of behavioral intervention, and a dissatisfaction with traditional clinical construct systems.

There are a number of assumptions that have a strong impact upon the methods, focus, and goals of behavioral assessment. These include presumptions of: (a) low levels of covariation among multimodal components of behavior disorders, (b) interdependence of many behaviors, (c) individual differences in behavioral covariations, (d) environmental interactionism, (e) the importance of mediational and situational factors as sources of behavior control, (f) multiple and idiosyncratic determinants of behavior disorders, and (g) the heuristic value of methodological empiricism.

Assessment methods and foci are also affected by their functions. These include: (a) identification of target behaviors, (b) indentification of alternative behaviors, (c) identification of causal variables, (d) development of a functional analysis, (e) design of intervention strategies, (f) evaluation of target behaviors, (b) identification of alternative behaviors, (c) identification of causal functions vary across clients, disorders, and the intent of the behavior analyst. Furthermore, the various assessment methods are differentially applicable to these functions.

The boundaries between behavioral and nonbehavioral assessment methods are becoming increasingly indistinct and permeable. This appears to be a result of the growing focus on unobservable variables, a more reasoned appraisal of traditional clinical assessment instruments, and a reduction of the conceptual and methodological rigor of behavior analysts. Assessment methods most often associated with or consistent with a behavioral paradigm include naturalistic observation, analogue observation, self-monitoring, participant observation, psychophysiological measures, behavioral interviews, behavioral questionnaires, product-of-behavior measures, manipulation, critical-event-sampling, and computer assisted assessment. Each assessment method is associated with idiosyncratic areas of applicability, utility, and sources of error. The reactive effects sometimes associated with assessment are a particularly salient source of error for many instruments.

An early emphasis on the inherent and face validity of behavioral instruments is being replaced by judicious psychometric evaluations. Particular attention is being focused on their applicability, utility, reliability, criterion-related validity, content validity, and generalizability. Although the application of some psychometric principles is problematic, the clinical utility, content validity, and external validity of certain instruments is of particular concern.

Perhaps the greatest asset of behavioral measurement systems is that they are conceptually and methodologically evolutionary. This is reflected in an expanding focus of behavioral assessment to include a wider array of controlling and covarying events, especially extended interactions, behavioral chains, response classes, noncontemporaneous controlling events, and mediational variables. Intervention outcome variables have also been expanded to include generalization, side effects, predictors, and cost-efficiency evaluations. Behavioral assessment methods are also being applied to an increasing number of target disorders. The empirical bases of behavioral assessment are also expanding through increased application of psychometric principles, a recognition of the need for standardization and norm development, and the application of statistical and design principles.

REFERENCES

Achenback, T.M. (1974). *Developmental psychopathology.* New York: Ronald.

Alevizos, P., DeRissi, W., Liberman, R., Eckman, T., & Callaghan, E. (1978). The behavior observation instrument: A method of direct observation for program evaluation. *Journal of Applied Behavior Analysis,* 11, 243–257.

Alexander, A.N. (1981). Asthma. In S.N. Haynes & L.R. Gannon (Eds.), *Psychosomatic disorders: A psychophysiological approach to etiology and treatment.* New York: Praeger.

Alexander, F.G., & Selesnick, S.T. (1966). *The history of psychiatry: An evaluation of psychiatric thought and practice from prehistoric times to the present.* New York: Harper & Row.

Anderson, B.J., & Standley, K. (1977). Manual for naturalistic observation of the childbirth environment. *Catalog of Selected Documents in Psychology,* 7, 6.

Angle, H.V. (1981). The interviewing computer: A technology for gathering comprehensive treatment information. *Behavior Research Methods & Instrumentation,* 13, 607–612.

Angle, H.V., Ellinwood, E.H., Hay, W.M., Johnson, T., & Hay, L.R. (1977). Computer-aided interviewing in comprehensive behavioral assessment. *Behavior Therapy,* 8, 747–754.

Angle, H.V., Hay, L.R., Hay, W.M., & Wllinwood, E.H. (1977). Computer assisted behavioral assessment. In J.D. Cone & R.P. Hawkins (Eds.), *Behavioral assessment: New directions in clinical psychology.* New York: Brunner/Mazel.

Anisman, H., & LaPierre, Y. (1982). Neurochemical aspects of stress and depression: Formulations and caveats. In R.W.J. Neufeld (Ed.), *Psychological stress and psychopathology.* New York: McGraw-Hill.

Annis, H.M. (1979). Self-report reliability of skid-row alcoholics. *British Journal of Psychiatry,* 134, 459–465.

Arkowitz, H., Lichtenstein, E., McGovern, K., & Hines, P. (1975). The assessment of social competency in males. *Behavior Therapy,* 6, 3–14.

Asher, H.B. (1976). *Causal modeling.* Beverly Hills: Sage Publications.

Bachrach, A.J. (Ed.). (1962). *Experimental foundations of clinical psychology.* New York: Basic Books.

Bandura, A. (1969). *Principles of behavior modification.* New York: Holt, Rinehart & Winston.

Bandura, A. (1981). In search of pure unidirectional determinants. *Behavior Therapy,* 12, 30–31.

Barlow, D.H. (1980). Behavior therapy: The next decade. *Behavior Therapy,* 11, 315–328.

Barlow, D. (Ed.). (1981). *Behavioral assessment of adult disorders.* New York: Guilford Press.

Barrera, M., Jr., & Rosen, G.M. (1977). Detrimental effects of a self-reward contracting program on subjects' involvement in self-administered desensitization. *Journal of Consulting and Clinical Psychology,* 45, 1180–1181.

Bassett, J.E., & Blanchard, E.B. (1977). The effect of the absence of close supervision on the use of response cost in a prison token economy. *Journal of Applied Behavioral Analysis,* 10, 375–379.

Baum, C.G., Forehand, R., & Zegoib, L.E. (1979). A review of observer reactivity in adult-child interactions. *Journal of Behavioral Assessment,* 1, 167–177.

Beiman, J., Graham, L.E., & Ciminero, A.R. (1978). Self-control progressive relaxation training as an alternative nonpharmacological treatment for essential hypertension: Therapeutic effects in the natural environment. *Behaviour Research and Therapy,* 16, 371–375.

Bellack, A.S. (1979). A critical appraisal of strategies for assessing social skill. *Behavioral Assessment,* 1, 157–176.

Bellack, A.S., & Hersen, M. (1977). Self-report inventories in behavioral assessment. In J.D. Cone & R.P. Hawkins (Eds.), *Behavioral assessment: New directions in clinical psychology.* New York: Brunner/Mazel.

Bellack, A.S., Hersen, M., & Lamparski, D. (1979). Role-play tests for assessing social skill: Are they valid? Are they useful? *Journal of Consulting and Clinical Psychology,* 47, 335–342.

Bernard, M.E., Dennehy, S., & Keefauver, L.W. (1981). Behavioral treatment of excessive coffee and tea drinking: A case study and partial replication. *Behavior Therapy,* 12, 543–548.

Bernstein, D.A. (1973). Situational factors in behavioral fear assessment: A progress report. *Behavior Therapy,* 4, 41–48.

Billingsley, F., White, O.R., & Munson, R. (1980). Procedural reliability: A rationale and an example. *Behavioral Assessment,* 2, 229–241.

Blanchard, E.B. (1981). Behavioral assessment of psychophysiologic disorders. In D.H. Barlow (Ed.), *Behavioral assessment of adult disorders.* New York: Guilford Press.

Blanchard, E.B., Andrasik, F., Arena, J.G., Neff, D.F., Saunders, N.L., Jurish, S.E., & Teders, S.J. (1983). Psychophysiological responses as predictors of response to behavioral treatment of chronic headache. *Behavior Therapy,* 14, 374–375.

Boll, T.J. (1981). Assessment of neuropsychological disorders. In D.H. Barlow (Ed.), *Behavioral assessment of adult disorders*. New York: Guilford Press.

Bootzin, R.R., & Engle-Friedman, M. (1981). The assessment of insomnia. *Behavioral Assessment, 3,* 107–126.

Borkovec, T.D., Weerts, T.C., & Bernstein, D.A. (1977). Assessment of anxiety. In A.R. Ciminero, K.S. Calhoun, & H.E. Adams. (Eds.), *Handbook of behavioral assessment*. New York: Wiley.

Broden, M., Hall, R.F., & Mitts, B. (1971). The effect of self-recording on the classroom behavior of two eighth-grade students. *Journal of Applied Behavior Analysis, 4,* 191–199.

Brownell, K.D. (1981). Assessment of eating disorders. In D.H. Barlow (Ed.), *Behavioral assessment of adult disorders*. New York: Guilford Press.

Carr, A.F., Schnell, J.F., & Kirchner, R.E., Jr. (1980). Police crackdowns and slowdowns: A naturalistic evaluation of changes in police traffic enforcement. *Behavioral Assessment, 2,* 33–41.

Carter, R.D., & Thomas, E.J. (1973). Modification of problematic marital communication using corrective feedback and instruction. *Behavior Therapy, 4,* 100–109.

Chapman, C.R., & Wyckoff, M. (1981). The problem of pain: A psychobiological perspective. In S.N. Haynes & L.R. Gannon (Eds.), *Psychosomatic disorders: A psychophysiological approach to etiology and treatment*. New York: Praeger.

Christensen, A., Sullaway, M., & King, C.E. (1983). Systematic error in behavioral reports of dyadic interaction: Egocentric bias and content effects. *Behavioral Assessment, 5,* 129–140.

Ciminero, A.R., Calhoun, K.S., & Adams, H.E. (Eds.). (1977). *Handbook of behavioral assessment*. New York: Wiley.

Ciminero, A.R., Calhoun, K.S., & Adams, H.E. (Eds.). (in press). *Handbook of behavioral assessment* (2nd ed.). New York: Wiley.

Ciminero, A.R., Nelson, R.O., & Lipinski, D.P. (1977). Self-monitoring procedures. In A.R. Ciminero, K.S. Calhoun, & H.E. Adams (Eds.), *Handbook of behavioral assessment*. New York: Wiley.

Coates, T.J., & Thoresen, C.E. (1978). Using generalizability theory in behavioral observation. *Behavior Therapy, 9,* 157–162.

Cohen, D.C. (1977). Comparison of self-report and overt-behavioral procedures for assessing acrophobia. *Behavior Therapy, 8,* 17–23.

Cone, J.D. (1981). Psychometric considerations. In M. Hersen, & A.S. Bellack, (Eds.), *Behavioral assessment: A practical handbook* (2nd ed.). New York: Pergamon Press.

Cone, J.D., & Hawkins, R.P. (Eds.). (1977). *Behavioral assessment: New directions in clinical psychology*. New York: Brunner/Mazel.

Conger, J.C., & Keane, S.P. (1981). Social skills intervention in the treatment of isolated or withdrawn children. *Psychological Bulletin, 90,* 478–495.

Conger, A.J., Wallander, J.L., Mariotto, M.J., & Ward, D. (1980). Peer judgments of heterosexual-social anxiety and skill: What do they pay attention to anyhow? *Behavioral Assessment, 2,* 243–259.

Cooke, C.J., & Meyers, A. (1980). The role of predictor variables in the behavioral treatment of obesity. *Behavioral Assessment, 2,* 59–69.

Cormier, W.H., & Cormier, L.S. (1979). *Interviewing, strategies for helpers: A guide to assessment, treatment, and evaluation*. Monterey, CA: Brooks/Cole.

Cox, D.J. (1977). Menstrual symptom questionnaire: Further psychometric evaluation. *Behaviour Research and Therapy, 15,* 506–508.

Cromwell, R.E., & Peterson, G.W. (1981). Multisystem-multimethod assessment: A framework. In E.E. Filsinger, & R.A. Lewis (Eds.), *Assessing marriage: New behavioral approaches*. Beverly Hills: Sage Publications.

Cronbach, L.J., Gleser, C.C., Nanda, H., & Fajaratnam, N. (1972). *The dependability of behavioral measurements: Theory of generalizability for scores and profiles*. New York: Wiley.

Curran, J.P., Monti, P.M., Corriveau, D.P., Hay, L.R., Hagerman, S., Zwick, W.R., & Farrell, A.D. (1980). The generalizability of a procedure for assessing social skills and social anxiety in a psychiatric population. *Behavioral Assessment, 2,* 389–401.

Curran, J.P., & Wessberg, H.W. (1981). Assessment of social inadequacy. In D.H. Barlow (Ed.), *Behavioral assessment of adult disorders*. New York: Guilford Press.

Cuvo, A.J., Leaf, R.B., & Borakove, L.A. (1978). Teaching janitorial skills to the mentally retarded: Acquisition, generalization, and maintenance. *Journal of Applied Behavior Analysis, 11,* 345–355.

Davidson, P.O., & Davison, S.M. (1980). *Behavioral medicine: Changing health lifetstyles*. New York: Brunner/Mazel.

Doyne, E.J., Chambless, D.L., & Buetler, L.E. (1983). Aerobic exercise as a treatment for depression in women. *Behavior Therapy, 14,* 434–440.

Edgington, E.S. (1982). Nonparametric tests for single-subject multiple schedule experiments. *Behavioral Assessment, 4,* 83–91.

Edinberg, M.A., Karoly, P., & Gleser, G.C. (1977). Assessing assertion in the elderly: An application of the behavioral-analytic model of competence. *Journal of Clinical Psychology, 33,* 869–874.

Eisler, R.M., Hersen, M., Miller, P.M., & Blanchard, E.B. (1975). Situational determinants of assertive behavior. *Journal of Consulting and Clinical Psychology, 43,* 330–340.

Elder, S.T., Geoffray, D.J., & McAfee, R.D. (1981). Essential hypertension: A behavioral perspective. In S.N. Haynes & L.R. Gannon (Eds.), *Psychosomatic disorders: A psychophysiological perspective on etiology and treatment*. New York: Praeger.

Emmelkamp, P.M.G. (1981). The current and future status of clinical research. *Behavioral Assessment, 3,* 249–253.

Emmelkamp, P.M.G., & Kwee, K.C. (1977). Obsessional ruminations: A comparison between thought stopping and prolonged exposure in imagination. *Behaviour Research and Therapy, 15,* 441–444.

Epstein, L.H., & Martin, J.E. (1977). Compliance and side effects of weight regulation groups. *Behavior Modification, 1,* 551–558.

Fabray, P.L., & Reid, D.H. (1978) Teaching foster grandparents to train severely handicapped persons. *Journal of Applied Behavior Analysis*, 11, 111–123.

Fagot, B.I. (1978). Reinforcing contingencies for sex-role behaviors: Effect of experience with children. *Child Development*, 49, 30–36.

Fairbank, J.A., DeGood, D.E., & Jenkins, C.W. (1981). Behavioral treatment of a persistent post-traumatic startle response. *Journal of Behavior Therapy and Experimental Psychiatry*, 12, 321–324.

Fiske, D.W. (1978). *Strategies for personality research: The observation versus interpretation of behavior.* San Francisco: Jossey-Bass.

Follingstad, D.R., & Haynes, S.N. (1981). Naturalistic observation in assessment of behavioral marital therapy. *Psychological Reports*, 49, 471–479.

Foote, W.E., & Laws, D.R. (1981). A daily alternation program for organismic reconditioning with a pedophile. *Journal of Behavior Therapy and Experimental Psychiatry*, 12, 267–273.

Fordyce, W.E. (1976). *Behavioral methods for chronic pain and illness.* Saint Louis: C.V. Mosby Company.

Forehand, R., & Atkeson, B.M. (1977). Generality of treatment effects with parents as therapists: A review of assessment and implementation procedures. *Behavior Therapy*, 8, 575–593.

Foster, S.L., & Cone, J.D. (1980). Current issues in direct observation. *Behavioral Assessment*, 2, 313–338.

Foxx, R.M., & Hake, D.R. (1977). Gasoline conservation: A procedure for measuring and reducing the driving of college students. *Journal of Applied Behavior Analysis*, 10, 61–74.

Fremouw, W.J., & Zitter, R.E. (1978). A comparison of skills training and cognitive restructuring—relaxation for the treatment of speech anxiety. *Behavior Therapy*, 9, 248–259.

Galassi, M.D., & Galassi, J.P. (1980). Similarities and differences between two assertion measures: Factor analysis of college self-expression scale and the Rathus assertiveness inventory. *Behavioral Assessment*, 2, 43–57.

Gannon, L.R. (1983). *Response desynchronization in psychosomatic disorders.* Unpublished manuscript.

Gardner, W., Hartmann, D.P., & Mitchell, C. (1982). The effects of serial dependence on the use of χ^2 for analyzing sequential data in dyadic interactions. *Behavioral Assessment*, 4, 75–82.

Garlington, W.K., & DeRicco, D.A. (1977). The effect of modeling on drinking rate. *Journal of Applied Behavior Analysis*, 10, 207–211.

Gatchel, R.J., Korman, M., Weis, C.B., Smith, D., & Clark, L. (1978). A multiple-response evaluation of EMG biofeedback performance during training and stress-induction conditions. *Psychophysiology*, 15, 253–258.

Geer, J.H. (1965). The development of a scale to measure fear. *Behaviour Research and Therapy*, 3, 45–53.

Glasglow, R.E., Klesges, R.C., Godding, P.R., & Gegelman, R. (1983). Controlled smoking, with or without carbon monoxide feedback, as an alternative for chronic smokers. *Behavior Therapy*, 14, 386–397.

Glass, G.V., & Kliegl, R.M. (1983). An apology for research integration in the study of psychotherapy. *Journal of Consulting and Clinical Psychology*, 51, 28–41.

Glass, G.V., Wilson, V., & Gottman, J.M. (1975). *Design and analysis of time-series experiments.* Boulder, CO: Colorado Associated University Press.

Goldfried, M.R. (1977). Behavioral assessment in perspective. In J.D. Cone & R.P. Hawkins (Eds.), *Behavioral assessment: New directions in clinical psychology.* New York: Brunner/Mazel.

Goldfried, M.R. (1982). Behavioral assessment: An overview, In A.S. Bellack, A.E. Kazdin, & M. Hersen (Eds.), *International handbook of behavior and modification and therapy.* New York: Plenum.

Goldfried, M.R., Linehan, M.M., & Smith, J.L. (1978). Reduction of test anxiety through cognitive restructuring. *Journal of Consulting and Clinical Psychology*, 46, 32–39.

Goldfried, M.R., & Sprafkin, J.N. (1976). Behavioral personality assessment. In J.T. Spence, R.C. Carsons, & J.W. Thibaut (Eds.), *Behavioral approaches to therapy.* Morristown, NJ: General Learning Press.

Gorsuch, R.L. (1983). Three methods for analyzing limited time-series (N of 1) data. *Behavioral Assessment*, 5, 141–145.

Gottman, J.M. (1979). *Marital interaction: Experimental investigation.* New York: Academic Press.

Green, L. (1978). Temporal and stimulus factors in self-monitoring by obese persons. *Behavior Therapy*, 9, 328–341.

Greenwald, D.P. (1977). The behavioral assessment of differences in social skill and social anxiety for female college students. *Behavior Therapy*, 8, 925–237.

Griffiths, R.R., Bigelow, G., & Liebson, I. (1977). Comparison of social time-out and activity time-out procedures in suppressing ethanol self-administration in alcoholics. *Behaviour Research and Therapy*, 15, 329–336.

Hartmann, D.P., Gottman, J.M., Jones, R.R., Gardner, W., Kazdin, A.E., & Vaught, R.S. (1980). Interrupted time series analysis and its application to behavioral data. *Journal of Applied Behavior Analysis*, 13, 543–559.

Hartmann, D.P., Roper, B.L., & Bradford, D.C. (1979). Some relationships between behavioral and traditional assessment. *Journal of Behavioral Assessment*, 1, 3–21.

Hartmann, D.P., & Wood, D.D. (1982). Observation methods. In A.S. Bellack, A.E. Kazdin, & M. Hersen (Eds.), *International handbook of behavior modification and therapy.* New York: Plenum.

Hawkins, R.P. (1979). The functions of assessment: Implications for selection and development of devices for assessing repertoires in clinical educational and other settings. *Journal of Behavioral Assessment*, 12, 501-516.

Hay, L.R. (1982). Teaching behavioral assessment to clinical psychology students. *Behavioral Assessment*, 4, 35–40.

Haynes, S.N. (1978). *Principles of behavioral assessment.* New York: Gardner Press.

Haynes, S.N. (1979) Behavioral variance, individual differences and trait theory in a behavioral construct system: A reappraisal. *Behavioral Assessment*, 1, 41–49.

Haynes, S.N. (1981). Muscle contraction headache. In S.N. Haynes & L.R. Gannon (Eds.), *Psychosomatic disorders: A psychophysiological approach to etiology and treatment*. New York: Praeger.

Haynes, S.N. (1983). Behavioral assessment. In M. Hersen, A.E. Kazdin, & A.S. Bellack (Eds.), *The clinical psychology handbook*. New York: Pergamon Press.

Haynes, S.N. (1984). Behavioral assessment in the design of intervention programs. In R.O. Nelson & S. Haynes (Eds.), *Conceptual foundations of behavioral assessment*. New York: Guilford Press.

Haynes, S.N., & Chavez, R. (1983). The interview in the assessment of marital distress. In E.E. Filsinger (Ed.), *A sourcebook of marriage and family assessment*. Beverly Hills: Sage Publications.

Haynes, S.N., Follingstad, D.R., & Sullivan, J.C. (1979). Assessment of marital satisfaction and interaction. *Journal of Consulting and Clinical Psychology*, 47, 789–791.

Haynes, S.N., & Gannon, L.R. (1981). *Psychosomatic disorders: A psychophysiological approach to etiology and treatment*. New York: Praeger.

Haynes, S.N., & Horn, W.F. (1982). Reactive effects of behavioral observation. *Behavioral Assessment*, 4, 369–385.

Haynes, S.N., & Jensen, B.J. (1979). The interview as a behavioral assessment instrument. *Behavioral Assessment*, 1, 97–106.

Haynes, S.N., Jensen, B.J., Wise, E., & Sherman, D. (1981). The marital intake interview: A multimethod criterion validity assessment. *Journal of Consulting and Clinical Psychology*, 43, 379–387.

Haynes, S.N., & Wilson, C.C. (1979). *Behavioral assessment*. San Francisco: Jossey-Bass.

Haynes, S.N., & Wilson, C.C. (1984). *Psychopathology: An advanced text*. Unpublished manuscript.

Haynes, S.N., Wilson, C.C., & Britton, B.T. (1979). Behavioral intervention with atopic dermatitis. *Biofeedback and Self-Regulation*, 4, 195–209.

Heiman, J.R., & Hatch, J.P. (1981). Conceptual and therapeutic contributions of psychophysiology to sexual dysfunction. In S.N. Haynes & L.R. Gannon (Eds.), *Psychosomatic disorders: A psychophysiological approach to etiology and treatment*. New York: Praeger.

Henson, D.E., Rubin, H.B., & Henson C. (1979). Consistency of the labial temperature change of human female eroticism. *Behaviour Research and Therapy*, 17, 226–240.

Hersen, M., & Barlow, D.H. (1976). *Single case experimental designs: Strategies for studying behavior change*. New York: Pergamon Press.

Hersen, M., & Bellack, A.S. (Eds.). (1976). *Behavioral assessment: A practical handbook*. New York: Pergamon Press.

Hersen, M., & Bellack, A.S. (1977). Assessment of social skills. In A.R. Ciminero, K.R. Calhoun, & H.E. Adams (Eds.), *Handbook of behavioral assessment*. New York: Wiley.

Hersen, M., & Bellack, A.S. (Eds.). (1981). *Behavioral assessment: A practical handbook* (2nd ed.). New York: Pergamon Press.

Hersen, M., Kazdin, A.E., & Bellack, A.S. (Eds.). (1983). *The clinical psychology handbook*. New York: Pergamon Press.

Hodgson, R., & Rachman, S. (1977). Obsessional-compulsive complaints. *Behaviour Research and Therapy*, 15, 389–395.

Hogan, R., DeSoto, C.B., & Solano, C. (1977). Traits, tests, and personality research. *American Psychologist*, 81, 255–264.

Honig, W.K. (1966). *Operant behavior: Areas of research and application*. New York: Appleton-Century-Crofts.

Horne, G.P., Yang, M.C.K., & Ware, W.B. (1982). Time series analysis for single-subject designs. *Psychological Bulletin*, 91, 178–189.

Hughes, H.M., & Haynes, S.N. (1978). Structured laboratory observation in the behavioral assessment or parent-child interactions: A methodological critique. *Behavior Therapy*, 9, 428–447.

Hutt, S.J., & Hutt, C. (1970). *Direct observation and measurement of behavior*. Springfield, IL: Charles C. Thomas.

Hynd, G.W., Severson, H.H., & O'Neil, M. (1976). Cardiovascular stress during the rapid smoking procedure. *Psychological Reports*, 39, 371–375.

Jacobson, N.S., Elwood, R.W., & Dallas, M. (1981). Assessment of marital dysfunction. In D.H. Barlow (Ed.), *Behavioral assessment of adult disorders*. New York: Guilford Press.

Jacobson, N.S., & Margolin, G. (1979). *Marital therapy: Strategies based on social learning and behavior exchange principles*. New York: Brunner/Mazel.

James, J.E. (1981). Behavioral self-control of stuttering using time-out from speaking. *Journal of Applied Behavior Analysis*, 14, 25–37.

Jeffrey, D.B., & Knaus, M.R. (1981). The etiologies, treatments, and assessments of obesity. In S.N. Haynes & L.R. Gannon (Eds.), *Psychosomatic disorders: A psychophysiological approach to etiology and treatment*. New York: Praeger.

Jensen, B.J., & Haynes, S.N. (in press). Behavioral questionnaires. In A.R. Ciminero, K. Calhoun, & H.E. Adams (Eds.), *Handbook of behavioral assessment* (2nd ed.). New York: Wiley.

Johnson S.M., & Bolstad, O.D. (1973). Methodological issues in naturalistic observation: Some problems and solutions for field research. In L.A. Hammerlynck, L.C. Handy, & E.J. Mash (Eds.), *Behavior change: Methodology, concepts, and practice*. Champaign, IL: Research Press.

Johnson, W.G., Wildman, H.E., & O'Brien, T. (1980). The assessment of program adherence: The achilles' heel of behavioral weight reduction? *Behavioral Assessment*, 2, 297–301.

Jones, R.R. (1979). Program evaluation design issues. *Behavioral Assessment*, 1, 51–56.

Jones, R.R., Vaught, R.S., & Weinrott, M.L. (1977). Time-series analysis in operant research. *Journal of Applied Behavior Analysis*, 10, 151–166.

Kamens, L., Haynes, S.N., Hamilton, J., & Franzen, M. (in press). The role of presleep cognitions in sleep-onset insomnia. *Journal of Behavioral Medicine*.

Kanfer, F.H. (1970). Self-monitoring: Methodological limitations and clinical applications. *Journal of Consulting and Clinical Psychology*, 61, 341–347.

Kanfer, F., & Phillips, J. (1970). *Learning foundations of behavior therapy*. New York: Wiley.

Kaplan, R.M., & Litrownik, A.J. (1977). Some statistical methods for the assessment of multiple-outcome criteria in behavioral research. *Behavior Therapy*, 8, 383–392.

Kaloupek, D.B., & Levis, D.J. (1980). The relationship between stimulus specificity and self-report indices in assessing fear of heterosexual social interaction: A test of the unitary response hypothesis. *Behavioral Assessment*, 2, 267–281.

Kazdin, A.E. (1977). Assessing the clinical and applied importance of behavior change through social validation. *Behavior Modification*, 1, 427–452.

Kazdin, A.E. (1978). *History of behavior modification*. Baltimore: University Park Press.

Kazdin, A.E. (1979). Situational specificity: The two-edged word of behavioral assessment. *Behavioral Assessment*, 1, 57–75.

Kazdin, A.E. (1982a). Symptom substitution, generalization, and response covariation: Implications for psychotherapy outcome. *Psychological Bulletin*, 91, 349–365.

Kazdin, A.E. (1982b). *Single-case research designs: Methods for clinical and applied settings*. New York: Oxford University Press.

Kazdin, A.E., Esveldt-Dawson, K., & Matson, J.L. (1983). The effects of instructional set on social skills performance among psychiatric inpatient children. *Behavior Therapy*, 14, 413–423.

Kazdin, A.E. (1984). *Behavior modification in applied settings*. Homewood, IL: The Dorsey Press.

Keefe, F.L., Kopel, S.A., & Gordon, S.B. (1978). *A practical guide to behavioral assessment*. New York: Springer.

Keefe, F.J., Surwit, R.S., & Pilon, R.N. (1981). Collagen vascular disease: Can behavior therapy help? *Journal of Behavior Therapy and Experimental Psychiatry*, 12, 171–175.

Kleinmuntz, B. (1972). *Computer in personality assessment*. Morristown, NJ: General Learning Press.

Kling, J.W., & Riggs, L.A. (1971). *Experimental psychology*. New York: Holt, Rinehart, & Winston.

Korchin, S.J., & Schulberg, D. (1981). The future of clinical assessment. *American Psychologist*, 36, 1147–1158.

Krasner, L. (1969). Behavior modification—values and training: The perspective of a psychologist. In C.M. Franks (Ed.), *Behavior therapy: Appraisal and status*. New York: McGraw-Hill.

Kratochwill, T.R. (Ed.). (1978). *Single subject research: Strategies for evaluating change*. New York: Academic Press.

Kratochwill, T.R., & Levin, J.R. (1979). What time-series designs may have to offer educational researchers. *Contemporary Educational Psychology*, 3, 273–329.

Kratochwill, T.R., & Piersel, W.C. (1983). Time-series research: Contributions to empirical clinical practice. *Behavioral Assessment*, 5, 165–176.

Lazarus, A.A. (1976). *Multimodal behavior therapy*. New York: Springer.

Lebow, J. (1982). Consumer satisfaction with mental health treatment. *Psychological Bulletin*, 91, 244–259.

Lewinsohn, P.M. (1975). The behavioral study and treatment of depression. In M. Hersen, R.M. Eisler, & P.M. Miller (Eds.), *Progress in behavior modification: Volume 1*. New York: Academic Press.

Lewinsohn, P.M., & Lee, W.M. (1981). Assessment of affective disorders. In D.H. Barlow (Ed.), *Behavioral assessment of adult disorders*. New York: Guilford Press.

Lindsley, O.R. (1960). Characteristics of the behavior of chronic psychotics as revealed by free-operant conditioning methods. *Diseases of the Nervous System*, 21, 66–78.

Linehan, M.M. (1977). Issues in behavioral interviewing. In J.D. Cone & R.P. Hawkins (Eds.), *Behavioral assessment: New directions in clinical psychology*. New York: Brunner/Mazel.

Linehan, M.M. (1980). Content validity: Its relevance to behavioral assessment. *Behavioral Assessment*, 2, 147–159.

Lloyd, M.E. (1983). Selecting systems to measure client outcome in human service agencies. *Behavioral Assessment*, 5, 55–70.

LoPiccolo, J., & Steger, J.C. (1974). The sexual interaction inventory: A new instrument for assessment of sexual dysfunction. *Archives of Sexual Behavior*, 3, 585–595.

Lubar, J.R., & Shouse, M.N. (1977). Use of biofeedback in the treatment of seizure disorders and hyperactivity. In B. Lahey & A.E. Kazdin (Eds.), *Advances in clinical child psychology*. New York: Plenum.

Lytton, H. (1977). Do parents create, or respond to, differences in twins? *Developmental Psychology*, 13, 456–459.

Maher, B. (1966). *Introduction to research in psychopathology*. New York: McGraw-Hill.

Maher, B. (1981). Psychological intervention in haemodylasis. Invited address at Southern Illinois University, Carbondale, Illinois.

Margolin, G. (1981). Practical applications of behavioral marital assessment. In E.E. Filsinger & R.A. Lewis (Eds.), *Assessing marriage: New behavioral approaches*. Beverly Hills: Sage Publications.

Margolin, G. (1983). An international model for the behavioral assessment of marital relationships. *Behavioral Assessment*, 5, 103–127.

Martin, I., & Venables, P.H. (Eds.). (1980). *Techniques in psychopathology*. New York: Wiley.

Mash, E.J. (1979). What is behavioral assessment? *Behavioral Assessment*, 1, 23–29.

Mash, E.J., & Terdal, L.G. (1981). *Behavioral assessment of childhood disorders*. New York: Guilford Press.

Matarazzo, J.D., & Wiens, A.N. (1972). *The interview: Research on its anatomy and structure*. Chicago, IL: Aldine-Atherton.

Matson, J.L., & Stephens, R.M. (1977). Overcorrection of aggressive behavior in a chronic psychiatric patient. *Behavior Modification*, 1, 559–564.

Mavissakalian, M.G., & Barlow, D.H. (1981). Assessment of obsessive-compulsive disorders. In D.H. Barlow (Ed.), *Behavioral assessment of adult disorders*. New York: Guilford Press.

McFall, R.M. (1977). Behavioral training: A skill acquisition approach to clinical problems. In J.T. Spence, R. Carson, & J. Thibaut (Eds.), *Behavioral approaches to therapy*. Morristown, NJ: General Learning Press.

McFall, R.M. (1982). A review and reformulation of the concept of social skills. *Behavioral Assessment*, 4, 1–33.

McIntyre, T.J., Bornstein, P.H., Isaacs, C.D., Woody, D.J., Bornstein, M.T., Clucas, T.J., & Long, G. Naturalistic observation of conduct-disordered children: An archival analysis. *Behavior Therapy*, 14, 375–385.

Melamed, B.G., & Siegel, L.J. (1980). *Behavioral medicine: Practical applications in health care*. New York: Springer.

Merluzzi, T.V., Glass, C.R., & Genest, M. (1981). *Cognitive assessment*. New York: Guilford Press.

Messick, S. (1981). Constructs and their vicissitudes in educational and psychological measurement. *Psychological Bulletin*, 89, 575–588.

Michael, J. (1974). Statistical inference for individual organism research: Some reactions to a suggestion by Gentile, Roden, and Klein. *Journal of Applied Behavior Analysis*, 7, 627–628.

Miller, P.M. (1981). Assessment of alcohol abuse. In D.H. Barlow (Ed.), *Behavioral assessment of adult disorders*. New York: Guilford Press.

Mischel, W. (1968). *Personality and assessment*. New York: Wiley.

Mischel, W. (1980). *Introduction to personality*. New York: Holt, Rinehart & Winston.

Morganstern, K.P. (1976). Behavioral interviewing: The initial stages of assessment. In M. Hersen & A.S. Bellack (Eds.), *Behavioral assessment: A practical handbook*. New York: Pergamon Press.

Myerson, W.A., & Hayes, S.C. (1978). Controlling the clinician for the client's benefit. In J.E. Krapfl & E.A. Vargas (Eds.), *Behaviorism and ethics*. Kalamazoo, MI: Behavioredelia.

Nathan, P. (1980). Symptomatic diagnosis and behavioral assessment: A synthesis. In D.H. Barlow (Ed.), *Behavioral assessment of adult disorders*. New York: Guilford Press.

Nay, W.F. (1979). *Multimethod clinical assessment*. New York: Gardner Press, Inc.

Neale, J.M., & Oltmanns, T.F. (1981). Assessment of schizophrenia. In D.H. Barlow (Ed.), *Behavioral assessment of adult disorders*. New York: Guilford Press.

Nelson, R.O. (1977). Methodological issues in assessment via self-monitoring. In J.D. Cone & R.P. Hawkins (Eds.), *Behavioral assessment: New directions in clinical psychology*. New York: Brunner/Mazel.

Nelson, R.O. (1977). Assessment and therapeutic functions in self-monitoring. In M. Hersen, R.M. Eisler & P.M. Miller (Eds.), *Progress in behavior modification: Volume 5*. New York: Academic Press.

Nelson, R.O. (1980). The use of intelligence tests within behavioral assessment. *Behavioral Assessment*, 2, 417–423.

Nelson, R.O. (1983). Behavioral assessment: Past, present, and future. *Behavioral Assessment*, 5, 195–206.

Nelson, R.O., & Barlow, D.H. (1981). Behavioral assessment: Basic strategies and initial procedures. In D.H. Barlow (Ed.), *Behavioral assessment of adult disorders*. New York: Guildford Press.

Nelson, R.O., & Hayes, S.C. (1979). Some current dimensions of behavioral assessment. *Behavioral Assessment*, 1, 1–16.

Nelson, R.O., & Hayes, S.C. (1984). *Conceptual foundations of behavioral assessment*. New York: Guilford Press.

Nietzel, M.T., Winett, R.A., MacDonald, M.L., & Davidson, W.S. (1977). *Behavioral approaches to community psychology*. New York: Pergamon Press.

Notarius, C.I., Krokoff, L.J., & Markham, H.J. (1981). Analysis of observational data. In E.E. Filsinger & R.A. Lewis (Eds.), *Assessing marriage: New behavioral approaches*. Beverly Hills: Sage Publications.

Novaco, R.W. (1975). *Anger control: The development and evaluation of an experimental treatment*. Lexington, MA: Lexington Books.

O'Donnell, C.R. (1977). Behavior modification in community settings. In M. Hersen, R.M. Eisler & P.M. Miller (Eds.), *Progress in behavioral modification: Volume 4*. New York: Academic Press.

O'Leary, K.D. (1979). Behavioral assessment. *Behavioral Assessment*, 1, 31–36.

Ottens, A.J. (1981). Multifaceted treatment of compulsive hair pulling. *Journal of Behavior Therapy and Experimental Psychiatry*, 12, 77–80.

Palmer, M.H., Lloyd, M.E., & Lloyd, K.E. (1977). An experimental analysis of electricity conservation procedures. *Journal of Applied Behavior Analysis*, 10, 665–671.

Patterson, G.R., & Bechtel, C.G. (1977). Formulating the situational environmental in relation to states and traits. In R.B. Cattell & P.M. Greger (Eds.), *Handbook of modern personality therapy*. Washington, DC: Halstead.

Peterson, L., Homer, A.L., & Wonderlich, S.A. (1982). The integrity of independent variables in behavior analysis. *Journal of Applied Behavior Analysis*, 15, 477–492.

Price, M.G., & Haynes, S.N. (1980). The effects of participant monitoring and feedback on marital interaction and satisfaction. *Behavior Therapy*, 11, 134–139.

Prinz, R.J., Roberts, W.A., & Hantman, E. (1980). Dietary correlates of hyperactive behavior in children. *Journal of Consulting and Clinical Psychology*, 48, 760–769.

Quinsey, V.L., Chaplin, T.C., & Varney, G. (1981). A comparison of rapists' and non-sex offenders' sexual preference for mutually consenting sex, rape, and physical abuse of women. *Behavioral Assessment*, 3, 127–135.

Rimm, D.C., Janda, L.H., Lancaster, W., Nahl, M., & Dittmar, K. (1977). An exploratory investigation of the origins and maintenance of phobias. *Behaviour Research and Therapy*, 15, 231–238.

Rimm, D.C., & Masters, J.C. (1979). *Behavior therapy, techniques, and empirical findings*. New York: Academic Press.

Rosen, J.C. (1981). Self-monitoring in the treatment of diurnal bruxism. *Journal of Behavior Therapy and Experimental Psychiatry*, 12, 347–350.

Russo, D.C., Bird, B. L., & Masek, B.J. (1980). Assessment issues in behavioral medicine. *Behavioral Assessment*, 2, 1–18.

Russo, D.C., Cataldo, M.F., & Cushing, P.J. (1981). Compliance training and behavioral covariation in the treatment of multiple behavior problems. *Journal of Applied Behavior Analysis*, 14, 209–222.

Sackett, G.P. (Ed.). (1978). *Observing behavior, Volume II: Data collection and analysis methods.* Baltimore, MD: University Park Press.

Sampson, E.E. (1981). Cognitive psychology as ideology. *American Psychologist, 36,* 730–743.

Sanson-Fisher, R.W., & Martin, C.J. (1981). Standardized interviews in psychiatry: Issues of reliability. *British Journal of Psychiatry, 139,* 138–143.

Schleien, S.J., Wehman, P., & Kiernan, J. (1981). Teaching leisure skills to severely handicapped adults: An age-appropriate darts game. *Journal of Applied Behavior Analysis, 14,* 513–519.

Shapiro, D.A., & Shapiro, D. (1983). Comparative therapy outcome research: Methodological implications of meta-analysis. *Journal of Consulting and Clinical Psychology, 51,* 42–53.

Shapiro, S.A. (1981). *Contemporary theories of schizophrenia.* New York: McGraw-Hill.

Sidman, M. (1960). *Tactics of scientific research.* New York: Basic Books.

Spence, S.H. (1981). Validation of social skills of adolescent males in an interview conversation with a previously unknown adult. *Journal of Applied Behavior Analysis, 14,* 159–168.

Stitzer, M.L., Bigelow, G.E., Liebson, I.A., & Hawthorne, J.W. (1982). Contingent reinforcement for benzodiazepine-free urine: Evaluation of a drug abuse treatment intervention. *Journal of Applied Behavior Analysis, 15,* 493–503.

Stuart, R.B. (1980). *Helping couples change.* New York: Guilford Press.

Sturgis, E.T., Adams, H.E., & Brantley, P.J. (1981). The parameters, etiology, and treatment of migraine headaches. In S.N. Haynes & L. Gannon (Eds.), *Psychosomatic disorders: A psychophysiological approach to etiology and treatment.* New York: Praeger.

Swan, G.E., & MacDonald, M.L. (1979). Behavior therapy in practice: A national survey of behavior therapists. *Behavior Therapy, 9,* 799–807.

Taylor, C.B. (1983). DSM-III and behavioral assessment. *Behavioral Assessment, 5,* 5–14.

Taylor, C.B., & Agras, S. (1981). Assessment of phobia. In D.H. Barlow (Ed.), *Behavioral assessment of adult disorders.* New York: Guilford Press.

Thompson, M.S., & Conrad, P.L. (1977). Multifaceted behavioral treatment of drug dependence: A case study. *Behavior Therapy, 8,* 731–737.

Ullmann, L.P., & Krasner, L. (1965). *Case studies in behavior modification.* New York: Holt, Rinehart & Winston.

Van den Pol, R.A., Iwata, B.A., Ivancic, M.T., Page, T.J., Neef, N.A., & Whitley, F.P. (1981). Teaching the handicapped to eat in public places: Acquisition, generalization, and maintenance of restaurant skills. *Journal of Applied Behavior Analysis, 14,* 61–69.

Van Egeren, L., Haynes, S.N., Franzen, M., & Hamilton J. (1983). Presleep cognitions and attributions in sleep-onset insomnia. *Journal of Behavioral Medicine, 6,* 217–232.

Varni, J.P. (1981). Self-regulation techniques in the management of chronic arthritic pain in hemophilia. *Behavior Therapy, 12,* 185–194.

Vincent, J.P. (1980). *Advances in family intervention, assessment, and theory.* Greenwich, CT: Aijai Press.

Voeltz, L.M., & Evans, I.M. (1982). The assessment of behavioral interrelationships in child behavior therapy. *Behavioral Assessment, 4,* 131–165.

Wade, T.C., Baker, T.B., & Hartmann, D.P. (1979). Behavior therapists' self-reported views and practices. *The Behavior Therapist, 2,* 3–6.

Wahler, R.G. (1975). Some structural aspects of deviant child behavior. *Journal of Applied Behavior Analysis, 8,* 27–42.

Wahler, R.G. (1981). Insularity. Invited address presented at Southern Illinois University, Carbondale, Illinois.

Wahler, R.G., House, A.W., & Stambaugh, E.E. (1976). *Ecological assessment of child problem behavior: A clinical package of home, school, and institutional settings.* New York: Pergamon Press.

Walker, B.B., & Sandman, C.A. (1981). Disregulation of the gastrointestinal system. In S.N. Haynes & L.R. Gannon (Eds.), *Psychosomatic disorders: A psychophysiological approach to etiology and treatment.* New York: Praeger.

Waranch, H.R., Iwata, B.A., Wohl, M.K., & Nidiffer, F.D. (1981). Treatment of a regarded adult's mannequin phobia through *in vivo* desensitization and shaping approach responses. *Journal of Behavior Therapy and Experimental Psychiatry, 12,* 359–362.

Wasik, B.H., & Loven, M.D. (1980). Classroom observation data: Sources of inaccuracy and proposed solutions. *Behavioral Assessment, 2,* 211–227.

Weinrott, M.R., Reid, J.B., Bauske, B.W., & Brumett, B. (1981). Supplementing naturalistic observations with observer impressions. *Behavioral Assessment, 3,* 151–159.

Weiss, R.L., & Cerrato, M.C. (1980). The marital status inventory: Development of a measure of dissolution potential. *American Journal of Family Therapy, 8,* 80–85.

Wells, K.C., Connors, C.K., Imber, L., & Delamater, A. (1981). Use of single-subject methodology in clinical decision-making with a hyperactive child on the psychiatric inpatient unit. *Behavioral Assessment, 3,* 359–369.

Wickramesekera, I.E. (1981). Clinical research in a behavioral medicine private practice. *Behavioral Assessment, 3,* 265–271.

Wiens, A.N. (1981). The assessment interview. In I.B. Wiener (Ed.), *Clinical methods in psychology.* New York: Wiley.

Wiggins, J.S. (1973). *Personality and prediction: Principles of personality assessment.* Reading, MA: Addison-Wesley.

Wildman, B.G., & Erikson, M.T. (1977). Methodological problems in behavioral observation. In J.D. Cone & R.P. Hawkins (Eds.), *Behavioral assessment: New directions in clinical psychology.* New York: Brunner/ Mazel.

Wilson, F.E., & Evans, I.M. (1983). The reliability of target-behavior selection in behavioral assessment. *Behavioral Assessment, 5,* 15–32.

Wolery, M., & Billingsley, F.F. (1982). The application of Revulsky's R_n test to slope and level changes. *Behavioral Assessment, 4,* 93–103.

Wolfe, M.M. (1978). Social validity: The case for subjective measurement or how applied behavior analysis is finding its heart. *Journal of Applied Behavior Analysis*, 11, 203–214.

Wolman, B.B. (1978). *Clinical diagnosis of mental disorders*. New York: Plenum.

Wolpe, J. (1958). *Psychotherapy by reciprocal inhibition*. Stanford, CA: Stanford University Press.

Wolpe, J., & Lazarus, A.A. (1966). *Behavior therapy techniques: A guide to the treatment of neuroses*. Oxford, England: Pergamon Press.

Wroblewski, P.F., Jacob, T., & Rehm, L.P. (1977). The contribution of relaxation to symbolic modeling in the modification of dental fears. *Behaviour Research and Therapy*, 15, 113–117.

Youkilis, H.D., & Bootzin, R.R. (1981). A psychophysiological perspective of the etiology and treatment of insomnia. In S.N. Haynes & L.R. Gannon (Eds.), *Psychosomatic disorders: A psychophysiological approach to etiology and treatment*. New York: Praeger.

Zeiss, R.A. (1977). Self-directed treatment of premature ejaculation: Primary case reports. *Journal of Behavior Therapy and Experimental Psychiatry*, 8, 87–91.

Zeiss, R.A. (1978). Self-directed treatment for premature ejaculation. *Journal of Consulting and Clinical Psychology*, 46, 1234–1241.

PART IX

ASSESSMENT AND INTERVENTION

20 PSYCHOLOGICAL ASSESSMENT IN TREATMENT*

J. R. Wittenborn

INTRODUCTION

At one time most therapy for problem behavior was organized and directed on the supposition that the problem behavior per se served some basic, underlying disposition, possibly motivational, possibly neurochemical in nature. It was supposed that: (a) Problem behavior could serve to express or implement the underlying predisposition, (b) the elimination of one implementing behavior would not necessarily prevent the emergence of another expression that could also be a problem, and (c) the proper object of treatment must be the modification of the underlying predisposition. Recently, it has become acceptable to regard some explicit delimited behavior as the object of treatment. With this shift from an emphasis on hypothesized disposition to concern for the actual problem behavior, it has become possible to compare the efficacy of various treatments with respect to the attainment of the specified behavioral objective.

Usually therapies or treatments imply a course of action that has a corrective, restorative, or remedial role with respect to some overt behavioral objective. Basic initial instruction in motor skills, communication via spoken or written language, and factual knowledge are generally considered educational objectives and not included

among the aims of treatment. Any listing of behavioral objectives that might be called goals of treatment is arbitrary and certainly incomplete. Nevertheless, some major classes of objectives may be noted: (a) the modification of affect that is inappropriate for the circumstances, (b) the elimination of unnecessary and maladaptive behavior and the acquisition of adaptive modes of response, (c) the modification of affect or specifiable behaviors that are regarded as symptomatic of a diagnosable psychopathology whether or not the symptom behavior is maladaptive, and (d) skills that have been lost or were not acquired under the conditions in which such learning usually occurs. The functional significance of the behavior, not necessarily the behavior itself, may determine whether its modification should be considered treatment. For example, modification of behavior that is a source of distress to the individual or others, that is alien to the patient's normal personality, that is a pronounced exaggeration of some aspect of his/her normal personality, or that is contrary to the requirements of law or the conventions of society may be considered treatment.

Most studies of therapeutic efficacy offer some description of the method of treatment. Some

*The preparation of this manuscript was supported in part by a grant from the Cape Branch Foundation, Dayton, New Jersey. The author wishes to thank C.M. Franks, Rutgers University, for his critical reading of the finished manuscript.

405

studies compare procedures that are limited to a specific describable psychotherapeutic method or pharmaceutical intervention. Other comparisons may involve the concurrent or sequential use of more than one therapeutic principle or specifiable method.

The present review is concerned with controlled investigations of adults who have been treated by psychotherapy or psychotropic drugs. The review does not attempt to survey the assessment devices that have been used to show therapeutic effects in samples of children or adolescents.

The Sample

The selection of devices appropriate for the assessment of treatment-related change, as well as the interpretation of the findings, must be approached with an awareness of the characteristics of the sample. Such characteristics of patients as their age, sex, social relationships, economic commitments, opportunities, marital status, friendships, and familial associations can play a role that has supportive, limiting, or provocative functions. In addition to specifying pertinent features of any clinical sample, it is conventional to provide a diagnosis for each patient. Diagnoses, although controversial, serve to remind the clinician of features of the illness that may have been overlooked, provide a guide to prognostic speculation, and afford some economics of description.

Limitations in the patient's competence should be considered in designing the investigation, selecting practicable assessment devices, and maintaining the therapeutic regimen. The relevant limiting factors may include memory faults, failures in orientation, delusional disorders, sensory-motor impairments, or social-emotional predispositions. The conditions under which the patient lives and the presence of responsible others can also impose realistic limitations on both the treatment and the assessment of its effects.

All clinical samples are heterogeneous, and the degree of this hetrogeneity, as well as its sources, can be important. Unrecognized and uncorrected heterogeneity in the sample reduces the sensitivity of all research. If sources of heterogeneity pertinent to the efficacy of treatment are known before the trial, some effort is usually made to eliminate them. If pretreatment heterogeneities cannot be eliminated from the sample, some investigators seek to randomize them so that the biasing influence will be equally distributed among the treatments under comparison. Other investigators, however, will choose to stratify identifiable sources of heterogeneity and to assign them equally to treatments under comparison. With such provisions, their contribution to changes in the patient may be calculated, their tendency to interact with any treatment identified, and their confounding with intertreatment comparisons minimized by statistical procedures.

Thus, pertinent characteristics of the sample not only include the kinds of behaviors that are the immediate causes for the patient's being in treatment and may be accepted as criteria of efficacy, but also suggest behaviors that are not a target of therapy but may qualify therapeutic effect. Such behaviors should be assessed so that their biasing effect may be weighed and eliminated by appropriate data analysis.

The Selection of Assessment Devices

Standard test performances, ratings of observed behavior, and inventories for self-description can reflect some of the behavioral changes expected from theoretical considerations or from prior experience with the proposed treatment. Self-descriptive inventories and observer rating scales often have the same descriptive titles and highly similar, if not identical, content for their behavioral referents. Despite this similarity in content, they do not distinguish between individuals in the same way, and one should not be regarded as an equivalent or substitute for the other. Ad hoc inventories or checklists that represent pertinent aspects of behavior not represented by standard assessment devices sometimes are desirable for evaluating treatment-related behavior changes.

Most investigators tend to rely heavily on a common group of assessment devices. A common pool of assessment devices may confer the advantage of a degree of comparability among studies. This possible advantage is only incidental, however, and investigators must remain critically evaluative of the appropriateness of any assessment considered for their particular purposes. Uncertainty concerning the practicability of an assessment procedure for the sample of patients or the conditions of the study should be resolved before any selection becomes final.

It is important to select assessment procedures that not only reflect the behavioral content of the patient's symptoms, but also discriminate within a sufficiently broad range of severity to show either an increase or a decrease. If the range of severity sampled by the test cannot show an appreciable increase or decrease for the level of severity that the sample presents, the scope of the test is insufficient for the task.

All tests and assessment procedures considered for inclusion in the investigation should be pretested on a small sample of the population proposed for the investigation. Such pretesting provides guidance for anticipating the qualifications of personnel necessary for the assessment, for estimating the amount of training and supervision they must have, and for providing the general conditions under which reliable assessments can be made. If pretesting reveals that the proposed assessment procedures will be impracticable under the conditions of the inquiry, the investigator will be spared by embarrassment and loss of time and effort that would have been involved if this very practical aspect of the investigation had been disregarded.

Investigators should consider the characteristics of their samples, the context in which the treatment is conducted, and the behavior to be modified when they select devices to assess therapeutic efficacy. Usually it is possible to choose assessment devices that have been used by prior investigators in similar situations to reflect changes consequent to the treatment, and these findings can provide some basis for anticipating the possible results when these assessment devices are applied in the proposed investigation.

The number of assessment devices can be critical. If too few are applied, they will not reflect all the pertinent changes that may occur during the course of treatment. If the parsimonious selection of the criteria is unfortunate, the study may fail to detect any of the ways in which the therapy is efficacious, and a potentially effective treatment may go unrecognized. If too many assessment devices are applied, the administrative burden may be excessive, and the probability that some of the scores will not reflect the drug-related changes is increased.

Data Analysis and Interpretation

When numerous assessments have been made and only a modest portion of them shows a significant drug effect, the investigator may have difficulty in deciding whether the observed discriminations are true and verifiable evidence of therapeutic effect or merely the kind of chance contrasts that occur in most series of trials. In such cases, a multivariate discriminant analysis is often used to show whether the set of tests generates a significant discrimination. If the entire set of tests is a significant discriminator, then some of the individual tests that meet a criterion for statistical significance are probably truly significant discriminators and not fortuitous unconfirmable events. The number of assessment devices or separate scores should not exhaust the number of degrees of freedom available for testing the significance of a multivariate discriminator. In general, the larger the number of separate scores to be analyzed, the larger the number of patients that should be available for the analysis.

When the exploratory nature of an investigation has resulted in the inclusion of many criteria of efficacy, some investigators have found it practical to reduce the number of potential criteria by factor analysis. This step in data reduction can lead to the use of factor scores as criteria of efficacy. It can also provide the identification of criteria that are the best measures of the factors and lead to the restriction of analyses to these criteria. In exploratory studies, it can be useful also to use two independent measures of each expected change. Mutually confirmatory findings can be reassuring to the investigator, while inconsistent findings alert the investigator to the hazard of overconfident generalization.

There are numerous advantages to providing both a representative set of promising criteria and a sufficiently large sample, particularly when the investigation is exploratory in nature and there are no applicable precedents to guide the way. For example, samples of ample size offer the advantage of permitting the group to be split into two comparable subsamples for analytical purposes. If the two subsamples generate corresponding, mutually confirming indications of change in some particular respect, the investigator's belief that the finding is not a sampling artifact is strengthened.

One persisting problem in the comparison of the efficacy of treatments is the interpretation of negative results. What does it mean when the inquiry reveals no difference between two treatments? It could mean that the treatments are equally effective, that neither treatment is effective, that the criteria of treatment effect were inappropriate, or that the assessments were conducted in an improper manner and would be unable to show consistent differences between any treatment groups. Other interpretations of negative results could be applicable. Perhaps the two treatment groups were exposed to confounding influences that would obscure any differences. Perhaps the assessments were delayed until a spontaneous remission had erased all contrasts. The difficulties in interpreting inconclusive results and the logical impossibility of proving the null hypothesis strongly suggest that investigators avoid experimental designs where a substance under assessment is compared with a standard treatment of known efficacy and no placebo comparison is included. An investigational treatment may have therapeutic merit even though it is inferior to the standard treatment, and under these conditions an answer to the efficacy question requires a placebo comparison. If an investigational treatment happens to be superior to a standard treatment control, the implications are unambiguously supportive, regardless of the availability of a placebo control.

PHARMACOTHERAPY

The effect of pharmacotherapy is usually shown in a diversity of ways. In addition to the anticipated and desired effects, there also may be effects that were not anticipated and that may or may not be regarded as desirable. Major undesirable effects of treatment are not predictable for the individual, and their manifestation under the prescribed conditions of treatment are usually regarded as idiosyncratic.

When selecting criteria for efficacy of pharmacotherapies, the investigators should be aware of pharmacological, neurochemical, and possible behavioral effects of the treatment chosen. With increasing pharmacologic and neurochemical sophistication, there is a growing tendency to regard medication from the standpoint of its pharmacodynamics, pharmacokinetics, and its mode of action, including the neurotransmitters involved. Unfortunately, the metabolic basis for behavioral disorders is not sufficiently known to permit the selection of treatment on the basis of its pharmacologic effects, and the probable behavioral effects of a drug may involve a diverse spectrum, only a part of which corresponds with any current generally accepted constellation of psychopathology.

When psychopathology is ameliorated by pharmacotherapeutic intervention, it is often surmised that the psychopathology was a manifestation of some metabolic disorder that was corrected by the pharmacotherapeutic intervention. In most cases, this seems to be a gratuitous inference. A pharmacologic intervention that happens to modify certain behavioral capacities in a therapeutically desirable manner may be no more than a fortunate coincidence and need tell us nothing about the etiology of the disorder or of its implementing physiology. Nevertheless, some knowledge of the mode of action of pharmacotherapeutic substances can be of value in anticipating the possible spectrum of behavioral effects and selecting criteria for the assessment of these effects. Some of the medications seem to have a relatively direct effect on behavior via their influence on mediating brain structures. For example, some drugs appear to affect the metabolism of certain brain cells; others affect the mobilization or removal of some neurotransmitters. The study of neurotransmitters is currently of great interest in pharmacotherapy, possibly because it helps account for the behavioral distinctions between the effects of some drugs, and for this reason may be useful in selecting devices for the assessment of efficacy.

Studies of the efficacy of psychotropic drugs have far exceeded studies of the efficacies of psychotherapies in number and until recently, perhaps, in the quality of design, execution, and data analysis as well. The great burst of research activity in clinical psychopharmacology during the last two decades was an inevitable consequence of two major factors: The market potential for effective psychotropic medication brought forth a substantial flow of substances that were candidates for proprietary use, and the FDA insisted that marketable drugs must be supported by sound research evidence of efficacy and safety. The minimal requirements for proper clinical investigation of psychotropic substances have been set forth by an international committee (Wittenborn, 1977), and, with minor modifications, have been accepted by investigators in most nations that support an appreciable pharmaceutical industry. This and other publications (Wittenborn, 1971) illuminate current criteria for the development of evidence to support a claim of efficacy for new psychotropic medications.

In general, studies of psychotropic substances are focused on some recognized, diagnostically sanctionable mental disease entity, whereas psychotherapy may be committed to modification of specific observable behaviors. Psychotropic medication is assessed in terms of the alleviation of symptoms and judgments of overall improvement. An overall judgment of improvement implies that an underlying diagnosable psychopathological disease has, at least in part, remitted. In contrast, many of the psychotherapeutic trials are assessed in terms of the amelioration of specific behaviors. In consequence, the criteria of therapeutic efficacy most frequently used in clinical psychopharmacology may be expected to differ from those most frequently used in the assessment of psychotherapeutic effects.

Because of the great number and diversity of reports of drug trials, a comprehensive list of the assessments that have been used to show treatment-related changes would exceed the limits of the present review. The Early Clinical Drug Evaluation Units Program (ECDEU) of the U.S. Mental Health Administration has provided a manual (Guy, 1976) describing assessment devices recommended for use in the assessment of psychotropic substances. These devices are concerned with the symptoms of functional, as contrasted with organic, disorders and are presented under several headings. The devices listed in Table 20.1 are from the ECDEU Manual (Guy, 1976) and were selected because of their common use in studies of adult patients.

Almost all studies of the effect of psychotropic substances include some provision for assessing undesired effects. The procedures commonly used for this purpose vary with the type of drug under investigation. In addition to measures of vital signs, kidney function, and blood chemistry, investigators commonly include various other metabolic and behavioral assessments. For example, there may be methods for assessing adverse neurological effects, such as represented by the Abnormal Involuntary Movement Scale from the ECDEU Manual (Guy, 1976) and a diversity of devices for assessing other undesired central nervous system effects that can impair everyday behavior, particularly its psychomotor aspects.

TABLE 20.1. SELECTED ASSESSMENTS FROM THE ECDEU MANUAL.

Observer Rating Scales for Adult Patients	Source of Assessment Device
Brief Psychiatric Rating Scale (BPRS)	Overall & Gorham, 1962
Hamilton Depression Scale (HAMD)	Hamilton, 1967
Hamilton Anxiety Scale (HAMA)	Hamilton, 1959
Wittenborn Psychiatric Rating Scale (WITT)	Wittenborn, 1955
Nurses' Observation Scale for Inpatient Evaluation	Honigfeld & Klett, 1965
Self-Descriptive Inventories	
Self-Report Symptom Inventory (SCL-90)	Derogatis, 1977
Self-Rating Anxiety Scale (SAS)	Zung, 1971
Beck Depression Inventory (BECK)	Beck & Beamesderfer, 1974
Clyde Mood Scale (CLYDE)	Clyde, 1963
Hopkins Symptom Checklist (HSCL)	Derogatis, Lipman, Rickels, Uhlenhuth, & Covi, 1973
Profile of Mood States (POMS)	McNair, Lorr, & Droppleman, 1971
Scales for Geriatric Patients	
Crichton Geriatric Rating Scale (CRICHT)	Robinson, 1964
Sandoz Clinical Assessment—Geriatric (SCAG)	Shader, Harmatz, & Salzman, 1974
Standard Tests	
Wechsler Adult Intelligence Scale (WAIS)	Wechsler, 1955
Wechsler Memory Scale (WMEM)	Wechsler & Stone, 1945
Memory for Designs Test	Graham & Kendall, 1960

Undesired behavioral effects may be surveyed by a simple checklist, but additional procedures are usually required.

In a review of controlled studies of behavioral toxicity, Wittenborn (1980) reported the incidence with which various assessments showed detracting behavioral changes in consequence of different classes of psychotropic medication. The findings for sedative-hypnotic drugs and benzodiazepine tranquilizers are of particular interest and are summarized in Table 20.2. These studies, published between 1968 and 1978, were based on initial day of standard dosage applied to normal volunteers and provided tests of significance of difference of drug effect between treatment and placebo groups. Table 20.2 gives the portion of studies in which the drug was more detracting than placebo relative to the number of studies that met the criteria for inclusion in the review.

Other classes of psychotropic substances have been shown to be associated with significant behavioral impairment. For example, Wittenborn, Flaherty, McGough, Bossange, and Nash (1976) reported a study in which normal subjects were used to show that a standard daily dose of imipramine had a significantly detracting effect on such practical performances as Digit Symbol Substitution Test (DSST) and latency and accuracy of response in a vigilance test. Psychomotor responses to psychotropic medication are not invariably detracting, however, They can vary with the aspect of behavior examined, as well as with the drug under scrutiny. As early as 1961, Wittenborn, Plante, Burgess, and Livermore reported that in depressed patients iproniazid had an enhancing effect on such behaviors as performance on the WAIS Similarities, Numerical Ability as represented by the Differential Aptitude Test (DAT), and latency of response in a reaction time situation. Obviously, standard tests of mental ability and psychomotor performance have a place in the assessment of psychotropic substances. Whether such tests show ameliorating or toxic effects of medication will depend upon the drug, the patient's condition (the therapeutic effect may be confounded with the detracting effects of the drug), as well as numerous other factors. The literature is voluminous and difficult to organize (Wittenborn, 1978, 1979).

Most commonly used drugs have a detracting effect on performance on mental tests, particularly those that measure psychomotor components. To the extent that these drugs may alleviate symptoms that in themselves have a significant detracting effect, assessment in patients may or may not show a loss, but among normal controls detracting effects can be expected. Among the possible exceptions, particularly for certain behaviors, are the stimulants. Among 15 comparisons involving stimulants cited in a recent review (Wittenborn, 1980), 6 showed a significant gain, particularly in performance involving speed, such as DSST, tapping, and cancellation. The various psychomotor tests considered here cannot claim to represent the entire universe of practical behavior, and published reports of drug effects on driving and endurance under stress (e.g., flying) comprise a separate literature.

Current investigations of the efficacy of psychotropic substances can draw upon a large and diversified literature of prior studies. Some caveats are implicit in this literature. For example, the meaning of a rating scale score can depend upon the professional role and orientation of the

TABLE 20.2. PORTION OF STUDIES IN WHICH SIGNIFICANT
LOSS RELATIVE TO PLACEBO WAS REPORTED.

Type of Measure	Hypnotic/Sedative		Benzodiazepine		Difference
	Incidence	No. of studies	Incidence	No. of studies	
Reaction time	.33	3	.17	12	.14
DSST	.69	16	.60	10	.09
Hand-eye coordination	.17	6	.50	8	− .33
Tapping	.55	11	.38	8	.17
Visual-perceptual	.40	10	.10	10	.30
Cancellation	.57	7	.44	9	.13
Card sorting	.75	12	.43	7	.32
CFF	.63	8	1.00	5	− .37
Immediate memory	.50	4	1.00	4	− .50

user (Wittenborn, Plante, & Burgess, 1961), and there are cultural differences in symptom constellations (Wittenborn, 1966a). There is a large literature on factors that qualify the efficacy of medication, for example, the importance of the presence or absence of a dependent self-critical personality in depressed women treated with imipramine (Wittenborn, 1966b) or the importance of class status in response to antidepressant medication (Downing & Rickels, 1972).

PSYCHOTHERAPY

Definitions of psychotherapy appear to have varied over time. The term *psychotherapy* once referred to the nonphysical interventions of a psychiatrist or, in some quarters, a psychoanalyst. Later, psychotherapy included the interventions of psychologists, particularly if they were working in a medical setting or under the direction of a psychiatrist. Eventually, psychotherapy was practiced by psychologists working independently, usually under the licensure of a state. The implicit, if not explicit, goal of psychotherapy was often described as strengthening or fulfilling the potential of the patient's personality. This growth or restructuring of the personality was expected to bring some amelioration, if not remission, of psychopathological symptoms and the emergence of behavior forms that were satisfactory from the standpoint of the patient or others. During this period there seemed to be as much concern for philosophical orientation as for method per se.

Method, to whatever extent it was explicated, followed a well-elaborated point of view, for example, the nondirective method developed by Rogers and his associates (Rogers, 1942), the classical psychoanalytic methods or their modifications (Freud, 1935), or the eclectic Meyerian psychobiological orientation (Meyer, 1951). In most traditional psychotherapeutic interventions, the procedure involved a series of interviews between the therapist and patients and was only secondarily concerned with the objective content of the presenting problem behavior. Instead, the focus was on affect and motive, and the objective for patients was the acquisition of a new understanding of their behavior ("insight") and the development of a more effective life style than they had before therapy. The efficacy of these various interventions was assumed, and, with one or two exceptions, controlled evaluations of such procedures were virtually nonexistent.

Among the various alternative psychotherapeutic procedures that emerged, there were methods that focused on the modification of specifiable problem behaviors. Although the patient's psychopathology may be characterized by more than one concurrent manifestation, the methods described as "behavior modification" usually distinguished among discrete problem behaviors (Franks & Barbrack, 1983). When the goal of therapy was approached as modification of one or more discrete target behaviors, reports of controlled systematic assessment of psychotherapeutic efficacy began to appear in the literature. One important procedure for such focused intervention became known as desensitization. This acquisition of an aversive or nonresponse in a context that formerly provoked symptomatic problem responses was effected by means of a program, often ad hoc, contrived by the therapist, wherein responses avoidant or incompatible with the problem behavior were elicited and reinforced. Some greatly circumscribed aversive learning is reminiscent of some of the early methods of Watson (1925). Desensitization and other methods that focus on the avoidance of undesired responses and place relatively little emphasis on insight and motivational modifications could be truly called a program of behavior modification. Other programs, often referred to as cognitive, were concerned with modifying the manner in which patients viewed themselves and their problem behavior, but did not necessarily involve the patient in the circuitry of dynamic formulations and motivational modifications.

The present review of psychotherapy was limited to controlled investigations that provided tests of the significance of intertreatment differences in assessed changes. It was necessary, moreover, that the assessment methods be sufficiently standard, explicit, and describable for the reader of the report to repeat the inquiry if desired. This review of controlled studies of psychotherapeutic efficacy could not presume to be comprehensive, but it is usefully representative of the kinds of studies that meet the present criteria. Most of the acceptable studies described changes based upon some specified method, and most of them were directed toward limited prestated objectives. The 25 studies selected for review were roughly classified in terms of both the method (desensitization, cognition, or neither) and objectives (reduction of anxiety manifestations, reduction of phobic, obsessive, compulsive symptoms, reduction of depression, or objective unspecified).

In most of the studies, certain assessment procedures failed to show a significant contrast between the respective methods under comparison. This failure could be due to many factors other than the possibility that the method was not effective for the behavior assessed, particularly in the sample under investigation. For this reason, assessment procedures that offered no discriminations will be disregarded. For the present purposes, the de facto objective of therapy was the behavior shown to be responsive to the procedure. It is of interest, therefore, to review the assessments that offered some discrimination, but it must be recognized that it may not be possible to replicate all of the findings.

With few exceptions the psychotherapeutic studies selected for review are well designed, well conducted, and intelligently reported, and they contrast favorably with the comparable literature published prior to 1960. The quality of the recent research appears to be a consequence of four developments: (a) the general acceptance of group psychotherapy, which makes it relatively easy to form a sample of patients exposed to a common psychotherapeutic situation; (b) the development and acceptance of relatively limited explicit therapeutic procedures; (c) the acceptance of limited therapeutic goals comprising behavioral changes specifiable prior to therapy; and (d) the general acceptance of multivariate concepts and methods of analysis among clinical investigators.

The various methods of desensitization are conspicuous among the widely accepted explicit psychotherapeutic interventions. Among the 10

TABLE 20.3. ASSESSMENTS THAT DISTINGUISHED DESENSITIZATION
EFFECTS ON ANXIOUS, PHOBIC, OR COMPULSIVE MANIFESTATIONS.

Assessment	Frequency of use	Source of Procedure
Grade Point Average	4	From school records
Anxiety Differential	3	Husek & Alexander, 1963
Adjective Checklist for Anxiety	2	Zuckerman, 1960
*Personal Report of Confidence of a Speaker	1	Paul, 1966
Worry-Emotionality Scale (Worry)	1	Liebert & Morris, 1967
Cognitive Interference Questionnaire	1	Sarason, unpublished, 1976
Exam Behavior Scale from Effective Study Test	1	Brown, 1975
10-item Anagram Test	1	ad hoc, Kirkland & Hollandsworth, Jr., 1980
Suinn Test Anxiety Behavior Scale	1	Suinn, 1969
Test Anxiety Scale	1	Sarason, 1972
Timed Behavioral Checklist for Performance Anxiety	1	Paul, 1966
Word Count	1	From Recorded Speech Sample
Duration of Silences	1	From Recorded Speech Sample
Number of "ah" Statements	1	From Recorded Speech Sample
Social Anxiety Scale	1	Watson & Friend, 1969
*Beck Depression Inventory	1	Beck & Beamesderfer, 1974
*State-Trait Anxiety Inventory Trait Anxiety Scale	1	Spielberger, Gorsuch, & Lushene, 1970
Complaints	1	ad hoc, McLean & Hakstian, 1979
Goals	1	ad hoc, McLean & Hakstian, 1979
Social	1	ad hoc, McLean & Hakstian, 1979
Average Satisfaction	1	ad hoc, McLean & Hakstian, 1979
Mood	1	ad hoc, McLean & Hakstian, 1979
Dropout Rate	1	
Stress Tolerance Test in Standard Situation	1	Lazarus, 1961
Washing Time in Standard Situation	1	Foa, Steketee, & Milby, 1980
Digit Symbol	1	Brown, 1969
Digit Symbol	1	Meichenbaum, 1972
Achievement Anxiety Test-Debilitating Anxiety	1	Alpert & Haber, 1960
Frustration Thermometer Scores	1	McReynolds & Tori, 1972
Fear Rating	1	Tori & Worell, 1973
Approach Test	1	ad hoc, Tori & Worell, 1973

*Assessments that distinguished both desensitization and cognitive methods studies in which the therapeutic objective was behaviorally explicit, desensitization was a principal method in 9. In each of these inquiries, the efficacy of desensitization was compared with one to four other methods, usually including a nontherapy control. For eight of these nine studies, the objective was the amelioration of handicapping anxiety, for example, in written examinations, in public speaking, or in the elimination of a phobic or compulsive reaction. These manifestations yielded to the method of desensitization, and the assessment procedures that displayed one or more significant contrasts are listed in Table 20.3 according to the frequency of their use. Since most of these assessments were used and found to be discriminating in only one of the studies included in the present review, they may not all prove to be discriminating in other similar inquiries. Nevertheless, it is apparent that many assessment procedures can be sensitive to the differential effects of various therapeutic approaches. These assessment procedures would seem to be promising candidates for further use when the desensitization approach is applied to the amelioration of the particular neurotic manifestations modified in the studies under review.

A second major approach that lends itself to controlled inquiry is concerned with patients' recognition and reconceptualization of their problem behaviors. These approaches are somewhat diversified in their specifics and range from the approach advocated by Beck (1967) to the rational-emotive approach endorsed by Ellis (1962). Eight studies involved a cognitive type approach. These studies are of particular interest because they suggest that the cognitive approaches have been preferred for the psychotherapy of depressed affect. In contrast, among the studies presently reviewed the desensitization approach was applied one time only to the treatment of depression, despite the fact that desensitization was frequently used for the amelioration of symptoms often accompanying depression, that is, anxious, phobic, or compulsive behaviors. Since desensitization has been applied to the elimination or modification of neurotic behavior and the cognitive approach has been applied most often to the amelioration of depression, it is not surprising to learn that the effects of these contrasting methods have been shown by different assessment procedures. With few exceptions, the devices that have proven sensitive when the cognitive approach has been compared with

other approaches (Table 20.4) are different from those found to be differentiating in the desensitization studies (Table 20.3).

An explicitly defined behavioral objective or a definite, well-specified procedure is not necessary to compare the efficacy of various psychotherapies. There were four acceptable studies that had no definite behavioral objective and methods that were either described vaguely or conformed with neither of the two major classes of approach. The discriminating assessments for these studies are listed in Table 20.5.

TREATMENT-RELATED CHANGES IN GERIATRIC SAMPLES

Pharmacotherapy

Within the last two decades there have been conspicuous changes in the way in which people over 60 years of age view themselves and are viewed by others. The average life expectancy for most persons has increased, and accordingly, there is an increased itnerest in the treatment of behavioral problems among the old.

The usual diversity of mental problems may be found among the old, but age brings an important shift in the relative prevalence of problems. For the most part, behavioral difficulties of the elderly seem to be related to impairment of mental faculties. Conspicuous also are dysphoric changes in affect that may be realistic responses to the accelerating loss in their capacities and the diminished significance of the role they can play. Since diminution of mental faculties, particularly memory, is probably the single most common basis for a concern on the part of patients and their associates, many treatments have been sought and evaluated from the standpoint of their potential for retarding, ameliorating, and possibly reversing what had appeared to be an irreversible deteriorating process.

It is amply evident that most therapists regard drugs as the treatment of choice for the problems of the elderly and do not consider them to be desirable candidates for psychotherapy (Kucharski, White, & Schratz, 1979). In addition to the antipsychotic, antidepressant, and antianxiolytic medications that are prescribed for the general population, there are several substances that offer some promise for ameliorating those deteriorating mental changes that, for most persons, become a part of advancing years.

TABLE 20.4. ASSESSMENTS THAT DISTINGUISHED
THE EFFECTS OF COGNITIVE APPROACHES.

Assessment	Frequency of use	Source of Procedure
*Beck Depression Inventory	4	Beck & Beamesderfer, 1974
Hamilton Rating Scale for Depression	3	Hamilton, 1967
Anxiety Scale	2	Similar to Walk's fear thermometer, 1956
MMPI-D	2	Hathaway & Meehl, 1951
*Personal Report of Confidence	2	Paul, 1966
MMPI-Sc	1	Hathaway & Meehl, 1951
Hopelessness Scale	1	Heimberg, 1961
Miskimins Self-Goal-Other II	1	Miskimins, 1972; Miskimins & Braucht, 1971
Discussion for Therapy Group 10-minutes	1	ad hoc, Fuchs & Rehm, 1977
Pleasant Events Schedule	1	MacPhillamy & Lewinsohn, 1972
Self-Evaluation Questionnaire	1	ad hoc, Fuchs & Rehm, 1977
Self-Reinforcement	1	ad hoc, Fuchs & Rehm, 1977
Self-Control Attitudes and Beliefs Test	1	ad hoc, Fuchs & Rehm, 1977
*State-Trait Anxiety Inventory Trait Anxiety Scale	1	Spielberger, Gorsuch, & Lushene, 1970
Eysenck Personality Inventory Neuroticism Scale	1	Eysenck & Eysenck, 1968
Item 4 from Fear Survey Scale	1	Reynolds, 1967
Irrational Beliefs Test	1	Jones, 1969
Idea Inventory	1	Kassinove, Crisci, & Tiegerman, 1977
Multiple Affect Adjective Check List:		
Anxiety Scale, Depression Scale	1	Zuckerman, Lubin, & Robins, 1965
Approach Behavior Test	1	ad hoc, Biran & Wilson, 1981
Efficacy Expectations	1	Bandura, Adams, & Beyer, 1977
Performance Fear	1	ad hoc, Biran & Wilson, 1981
Heart Rate	1	
Skin Potential	1	

*Assessments that distinguished both desensitization and cognitive methods

TABLE 20.5. ASSESSMENTS THAT DISTINGUISHED
THE EFFECTS OF METHODS OTHER THAN DESENSITIZATION OR COGNITIVE.

Assessment	Frequency of use	Source of Procedure
Acceptance of Other Scale	1	Guerney, 1977
Self-Feeling Awareness Scale	1	Guerney, 1977
Mother-Daughter Situation Questionnaire Expressive Skill	1	Ely, Guerney, & Stover, 1973
Adolescent-Parent Communication Checklist	1	Beaubien, 1970
Personal Orientation Inventory	1	Shostrom, 1966
Secord-Jourard Body-Cathexis Scale	1	Jourard & Remy, 1957
Dosamentes-Alperson Expressive Movement Scale	1	Dosamentes-Alperson, 1975
Post Session Questionnaire	1	Soeken, Manderscheid, Flatter, & Silbergeld, 1981
Semistructured Interview of Basic Demography	1	ad hoc, Meyer, Derogatis, Miller, Reading, Cohen, Park, & Whitmarsh, 1981
Hopkins Symptom Checklist	1	Derogatis, Lipman, Rickels, Uhlenhuth, & Covi, 1973

The literature presents considerable diversity in the kinds of behavioral losses experienced by old people, the medications that have been subject to clinical trial, and the findings that have been reported. Reports of a comprehensive review of this literature (Wittenborn, 1981a, 1981b) lend themselves to our present interest. This review was limited to studies of the efficacy of pharmacotherapy for samples of patients over 65 years of age. All of the samples comprised persons described as experiencing some degree of impairment, which ranged from minimal to major. Samples of primarily psychotic patients or patients suffering from functional disorders uncomplicated by evidence of mental impairment were excluded, as were samples of patients whose impairment was a consequence of stroke, trauma, or toxic influences. Only controlled investigations that provided explicit tests of statistical significance of intertreatment group contrasts were included. Because of the large volume of relevant literature, a large number of significant contrasts were reported. Many of these contrasts could not be confirmed in the reports reviewed. Only those treatment effects that were found in at least one half of the studies of a drug and were mutually confirming in at least two studies were included for review.

Table 20.6 identifies the 28 tests that discriminated in at least one study and indicates the frequency with which they discriminated. The literature identified 42 additional tests that failed to discriminate. Formal mental tests were not major contributors to the evidence of therapeutic efficacy. This modest evidence of the pertinence of mental tests for displaying drug-related behavioral changes in the elderly may be partly due to the kinds of studies in which the tests were applied. Subjects able to take most mental tests may not have enough impairment to show a significant treatment-related change, and persons who are most likely to change may be unable to meet the requirements for the proper use of the test. Regardless of the explanation for these particular results, the value of mental tests for assessing pharmacotherapy for the old remains to be shown and may require approaches relating population characteristics to test requirements in a way that was not always provided by studies included in the present series.

The review distinguished the rating scales and inventories on the basis of whether the device was sufficiently standard to have a name or whether it was an ad hoc procedure designed to serve the needs of the investigation. There were 24 named scales. Ten were used more than once, and 14 were used one time only. The 10 named scales used more than once (Table 20.7) provided some significant discriminations in one half of the studies in which they were applied. The named scales

TABLE 20.6. TESTED BEHAVIOR THAT DISTINGUISHED* BETWEEN THE RESPONSES OF DRUG AND PLACEBO GROUPS.

Score	Used	Discriminated	Score	Used	Discriminated
Orientation	13	5	Wechsler Adult Intelligence		
Digit Span	12	2	Scale-Comprehension	1	1
Digit Symbol Substitution Test	7	2	Wechsler Memory-Visual	1	1
Abstractions	6	2	Paired Associate-Pictorial	1	1
Writing Performance	5	1	Digit Copying	1	1
General Information	5	1	Bourdon-Wiersma		
Successive Subtractions	5	1	Cancellation	1	1
Wechsler Memory Learning					
Associates	5	1	Spoke Test	1	1
Gottschaldt Hidden Figures	2	1	Figure Perception	1	1
Bender-Gestalt	4	1			
Raven	4	1	Yerkes-Spatial Visualizing	1	1
Vocabulary	4	1	Delayed Recall	1	1
			Object Memory	1	1
Finger Tapping	3	2	Apraxia	1	1
Critical Flicker Fusion	3	2			
Similarities	3	1			
Short-term Memory	3	1			
Krakau Visual Acuity Test	2	2			

*42 scored behaviors were tested without any significant discriminations

TABLE 20.7. INCIDENCE OF DISCRIMINATING USE.

Rating Scale	Number of Scales	Number of Comparisons*	Comparisons with Significant Discrimination	Portion with Significant Discrimination
Named scales— Multiple use	10	36	18	.50
Named scales— Single use	14	14	3	.21
Unnamed scales	16	17	12	.71

*More than one scale might be applied in a single study

that were used in a single study were significant discriminators in only 3 (21%) of the 14 studies in which they were used. The 16 unnamed or ad hoc scales were significant discriminators in 71% of the applications. These findings suggest that investigators may sometimes resort to the use of a known procedure despite the fact that it may not be wholly appropriate for their purposes. The findings further suggest that an ad hoc assessment designed to reflect the anticipated changes can be discriminating, despite the fact that it is without the benefit of the great background of successful use that often supports the familiar named procedures.

Findings for the named scales are summarized in Table 20.8. It is strikingly apparent that only observer rating scales were effective in showing significant differences between treatment groups and that none of the well known self-report inventories provided any discrimination. There are various possible explanations for the failure of

self-report inventories in the studies of the elderly. Perhaps they were too distractible in the testing situation or their comprehension was limited. It is also possible that old people are particularly unrealistic in identifying the specific nature of their failures and recognizing specific improvements.

Psychotherapy

Despite the fact that old patients may be regarded by many psychiatrists as undesirable candidates for psychotherapy (Ford & Sbordone, 1980; Kucharski et al., 1979), there is an appreciable literature describing psychotherapeutic-like interventions in the care of elderly who suffer from behavioral disturbances or disabilities. Much of this literature describes how such intervention might be or has been conducted. Unfortunately, most of these accounts have an anectodal quality, present few if any systematic comparisons, and do not qualify as reports of controlled investigations.

TABLE 20.8. NAMED RATING SCALES USED IN MORE THAN ONE
PLACEBO-CONTROLLED STUDY OF PSYCHOTROPIC DRUG EFFECTS IN OLD PEOPLE.

Rating Scale	Number of Studies Involved	Studies with at Least One Modified Behavior*	Portion with at Least One Modified Behavior*
Nurses' Observation Scale for Inpatient Evaluation (NOSIE)	7	3	.43
Profile of Mood Scales (POMS)**	5	0	.00
Sandoz Clinical Assessment-Geriatrics (SCAG)	4	4	1.00
Brief Psychiatric Rating Scale (BPRS)	3	2	.67
Crichton Royal Behavior Scale	2	2	1.00
Stockton Geriatric Rating Scale	2	0	.00
Barabee-Hyde Hospital Adjustment Rating Scale	2	0	.00
Beck Depression Rating Scale**	2	0	.00
Taylor Manifest Anxiety Scale (TMAS)**	2	0	.00
SCAG-like Scales	7	7	1.00

*At least one scorable component with a significant drug-placebo contrast in change
**Self-descriptive

In addition to this literature, which usually refers to small samples or illustrative case descriptions, there are a few reports of systematic studies based on adequate samples, conventional designs, and analyses of the significance of intergroup differences in mean change. The literature of relatively strong studies is quite small, however, and the present review is based on the strongest available reports. Two studies were concerned with reality orientation therapy, but the methods used differed somewhat. A third study was concerned with the efficacy of individualized treatment for patients approached from the standpoint of their excess disabilities. The fourth study described the use of brief psychotherapy providing sessions limited to 15 minutes, and the fifth study examined the efficacy of a daily program of physical stimulation wherein patients were maintained in an enriched program of activity. In these five investigations, improvement in the patients' performance in practical respects such as self-care, communication, and social interaction, as well as the diminution of affective disturbance and various indications of dementia, were central among the therapeutic objectives. The discriminating assessments indicating therapeutic efficacy are listed in Table 20.9.

It is not suggested, nor should it be inferred, that the five studies on which Table 20.9 is based comprise all of the appropriate studies that might be found in the literature. Nevertheless, they were the best studies available to the present reviewer and may be regarded as sufficient to assure the reader that there are benefits that can result from psychotherapy with geriatric patients and that these differentiating benefits may be detected by the use of formal assessment procedures.

COMMENTS ON THE FUTURE

As therapeutic innovations modify additional aspects of human behavior, procedures for assessing these behavior changes will emerge. Current behavior modification therapies have not exhausted the possibilities implicit in traditional behavior theory, and there is a constant search for new psychotropic substances to change behaviors that current psychotropic drugs do not modify satisfactorily.

There are reasons for hoping that we are now at the threshold of important new knowledge of the relationships between neurochemical changes and behavior changes. The properties of behavior that are included in these new relationships may be different from those that form the content of current assessments. The application of this advanced understanding to the development of psychotropic substances may require assessment procedures that do not now exist.

The assessment of therapies will surely be influenced by the growing availability of automated electronic surveillance and the potential of computers for reducing this surveillance to scores and other quantities reflective of therapeutic influence. By such means, trends and components of behavior now imprecisely described may be subject to exact quantification.

Related to the assessment of therapeutic effects per se are the identification and quantification of factors, particularly characteristics of the patient, which modify therapeutic effects. If interest in individual differences in treatment response matures in consequence of the development of new treatment and assessment procedures, there will

TABLE 20.9. ASSESSMENTS SENSITIVE TO PSYCHOTHERAPIES IN GERIATRIC SAMPLES.

Assessment	Frequency of use	Source of Procedure
Mental Status Exam	1	Bower, 1967
Therapist's Rating	1	ad hoc, Godbole & Verinis, 1974
Zung Depression Scale	1	Zung, 1965
Scale of Excess Disability	1	Brody, Kleban, Lawton, & Silverman, 1971
Test of Reality Orientation with Geriatric Patients (TROG)	1	Johnson, McLaren, & McPherson, 1981
Florida State Hospital Behavior Rating Sheet	1	Harris, 1976

be interest in assessment procedures for those pretreatment individual differences that are associated with differences in therapeutic response.

The behavioral effects of either psychopharmacological or psychological treatments may diminish shortly after the termination of treatment. Thus, it is often said that these treatments provide more control than cure. It is possible that the future will bring research to illuminate the nature of any underlying predisposition toward behavioral problems. If it is found that predispositions have an existence independent of their implementing responses, particularly if the potential of these predispositions for generating problem behavior can be assessed, the choice between traditional psychotherapy and behavior modification may assume a new dimension.

REFERENCES

Alpert, R., & Haber, R.N. (1960). Anxiety in academic achievement situations. *Journal of Abnormal and Social Psychology,* 61, 207–215.

Bandura, A., Adams, N.E., & Beyer, J. (1977). Cognitive processes mediating behavioral change. *Journal of Personality and Social Psychology,* 35, 125–129.

Beck, A.T. (1967). *Depression: Clinical, experimental and theoretical aspects.* New York: Harper & Row.

Beck, A.T., & Beamesderfer, A. (1974). Assessment of depression: The depression inventory. In P. Pichot (Ed.), *Psychological measurement in pharmacopsychiatry* (Vol. 7). Basel: S. Karger.

Baubien, C.O. (1970). *Adolescent-parent communication styles.* Unpublished doctoral dissertation, Pennsylvania State University.

Biran, M., & Wilson, G.T. (1981). Treatment of phobic disorders using cognitive and exposure methods: A self-efficacy analysis. *Journal of Consulting and Clinical Psychology,* 49, 886–899.

Bower, H.M. (1967). Sensory stimulation and the treatment of senile dementia. *Medical Journal of Australia,* 1, 1113–1119.

Brody, E.M., Kleban, M.H., Lawton, M.P., & Silverman, H.A. (1971). Excess disabilities of mentally impaired aged: Impact of individualized treatment. *Gerontologist,* 11, 124–133.

Brown, M. (1969). *A set of eight parallel forms of the digit symbol test.* Unpublished set of tests, University of Waterloo, Waterloo, Ontario, Canada.

Brown, W.F. (1975). Effective study test: Manual of directions. San Marcos, TX: Effective Study Materials.

Clyde, D.J. (1963). *Manual for the Clyde Mood Scale.* Miami: Clyde Computing Service.

Derogatis, L.R. (1977). *SCL-90, administration, scoring, and procedures manual for the revised version.* Baltimore, MD: Johns Hopkins University School of Medicine.

Derogatis, L.R., Lipman, R.S., Rickels, K., Uhlenhuth, E.H., & Covi, L. (1973). The Hopkins Symptom Checklist (HSCL): A Measure of primary symptom dimensions. In P. Pichot (Ed.), *Psychological measurement in pharmacopsychiatry* (Vol. 7). Basel: S. Karger.

Dosamantes-Alperson, E. (1975). *The Dosamantes-Alperson Expressive Movement Scale.* Unpublished test, California State University, Los Angeles, California.

Downing, R.W., & Rickels, K. (1972). Predictors of amitriptyline response in outpatient depressives. *The Journal of Nervous and Mental Disease,* 154, 248–263.

Ellis, A. (1962). *Reason and emotion in psychotherapy.* New York: Lyle Stuart.

Ely, A., Guerney, B.G., Jr., & Stover, L. (1973). Efficacy of the training phase of conjugal therapy. *Psychotherapy: Theory, research and practice,* 10, 201–207.

Eysenck H.J., & Eysenck, S.B.G. (1968). *Manual: Eysenck Personality Inventory.* San Diego: Educational and Industrial Testing Service.

Foa, E.B., Steketee, G., & Milby, J.B. (1980). Differential effects of exposure and response prevention in obsessive-compulsive washers. *Journal of Consulting and Clinical Psychology,* 48, 71–79.

Ford, C.V., & Sbordone, R.J. (1980). Attitudes of psychiatrists toward elderly patients. *American Journal of Psychiatry,* 137, 571–575.

Franks, C.M., & Barbrack, C.R. (1983). Behavior therapy with adults: An integrative approach. In M. Hersen, A.E. Kazdin, & A.S. Bellack (Eds.), *The clinical psychology handbook.* New York: Pergamon Press.

Freud, S. (1935). *A general introduction to psychoanalysis.* New York: Liveright Publishing Corp.

Fuchs, C.Z., & Rehm, L.P. (1977). A self-control behavior therapy program for depression. *Journal of Consulting and Clinical Psychology,* 45, 206–215.

Godbole, A., & Verinis, J.S. (1974). Brief psychotherapy in the treatment of emotional disorders in physically ill geriatric patients. *Gerontologist,* 14, 143–148.

Graham, F.K., & Kendall, B.S. (1960). Memory for Designs Test: General revised manual. *Perceptual and Motor Skills,* Monograph Supplement, 11, 147–188.

Guerney, B.G., Jr. (1977). *Relationship enhancement: Skill-training programs for therapy, problem prevention, and enrichment.* San Francisco: Jossey-Bass.

Guy, W. (Ed.). (1976). *ECDEU Assessment manual for psychopharmacology* (rev. ed.). (DHEW Publication No. ADM 76-338). Washington, DC: U.S. Government Printing Office.

Hamilton, M. (1959). The assessment of anxiety states by rating. *British Journal of Medical Psychology,* 32, 50–55.

Hamilton, M. (1967). Development of a rating scale for primary depressive illness. *British Journal of Social and Clinical Psychology,* 6, 278–296.

Harris, C. (1976). The Florida State Hospital Patient Behavior Rating Sheet. In J. Cone & R. Hawkins (Eds.), *Behavior assessment: New directions in clinical psychology.* New York: Brunner-Mazel.

Hathaway, S.R., & Meehl, P.E. (1951). *An atlas for the clinical use of the MMPI.* Minneapolis: University of Minnesota Press.

Heimberg, L. (1961). *Development and construct validation for an inventory for the measurement of future time perspective.* Unpublished master's thesis, Vanderbilt University.

Honigfeld, G., & Klett, C. (1965). The Nurses' Observation Scale for Inpatient Evaluation (NOSIE): A new scale for measuring improvement in chronic schizophrenia. *Journal of Clinical Psychology, 21,* 65–71.

Husek, T., & Alexander, S. (1963). The effectiveness of anxiety differential in examination stress situations. *Educational Psychological Measurement, 23,* 309–318.

Johnson, C.H., McLaren, S.M., & McPherson, F.M. (1981). The comparative effectiveness of three versions of 'classroom' reality orientation. *Age and Ageing, 10,* 33–35.

Jones, R.G. (1969). *A factored measure of Ellis' irrational belief system, with personality and maladjustment correlates.* Doctoral dissertation, Texas Technological College. (University Microfilms, No. 69-6443)

Jourard, S.M., & Remy, R.M. (1957). Individual variance scores: An index of the degree of differentiation of the self and the body image. *Journal of Clinical Psychology, 13,* 62–63.

Kassinove, H., Crisci, R., & Tiegerman, S. (1977). Developmental trends in rational thinking. *Journal of Community Psychology, 5,* 266–274.

Kirkland, K., & Hollandsworth, J.G., Jr. (1980). Effective test taking: Skills-acquisition versus anxiety reduction techniques. *Journal of Consulting and Clinical Psychology, 48,* 431–439.

Kucharski, L.T., White, R.M., Jr., & Schratz, M.S. (1979). Age bias, referral for psychological assistance and the private physician. *Journal of Gerontology, 34,* 423–428.

Lazarus, A.A. (1961). Group therapy of phobic disorders by systematic desensitization. *Journal of Abnormal and Social Psychology, 63,* 504–510.

Liebert, R.M., & Morris, L.W. (1967). Cognitive and emotional components of test anxiety: A distinction and some initial data. *Psychological Reports, 20,* 975–978.

MacPhillamy, D.J., & Lewinsohn, P.M. (1972, September). *The measurement of reinforcing events.* Paper presented at the meeting of the American Psychological Association, Honolulu.

McLean, P.D., & Hakstian, A.R. (1979). Clinical depression: Comparative efficacy of outpatient treatments. *Journal of Consulting and Clinical psychology, 47,* 818–836.

McNair, D.M., Lorr, M., & Droppleman, L.F. (1971). *Manual for the Profile of Mood States.* San Diego: Educational and Industrial Testing Services.

McReynolds, W.T., & Tori, C. (1972). A further assessment of attention-placebo effects and demand characteristics in studies of systematic desensitization. *Journal of Consulting and Clinical Psychology, 38,* 261–264.

Meichenbaum, D.H. (1972). Cognitive modification of test anxious college students. *Journal of Consulting and Clinical Psychology, 39,* 370–380.

Meyer, A. (1951). The collected papers of Adolf Meyer. In E.E. Winters (Ed.), *Mental Hygiene,* Vol. 4. Baltimore: The Johns Hopkins Press.

Meyer, E., III, Derogatis, L.R., Miller, M.J., Reading, A.J., Cohen, I.H., Park, L.C., & Whitmarsh, G.A. (1981). Addition of time-limited psychotherapy to medical treatment in a general medical clinic. *The Journal of Nervous and Mental Disease, 169,* 780–790.

Miskimins, R.W. (1972). *Manual: MSGO II.* Fort Collin, CO: Rocky Mountain Behavioral Science Institute.

Miskimins, R.W., & Braucht, G.N. (1971). *Description of the Self.* Fort Collins, CO: Rocky Mountain Behavioral Science Institute.

Overall, J.E., & Gorham, D.R. (1962). The Brief Psychiatric Rating Scale. *Psychological Reports, 10,* 799–812.

Paul, G.L. (1966). *Insight vs. desensitization in psychotherapy: An experiment in anxiety reduction.* Stanford: Stanford University Press.

Reynolds, D.J. (1967). *The Temple Fear Survey Inventory.* Unpublished manuscript, Temple University.

Robinson, R.A. (1964). The diagnosis and Prognosis of dementia. In W.F. Anderson (Ed.), *Current achievements in geriatrics.* London: Cassell.

Rogers, C.R. (1942). *Counseling and psychotherapy.* Boston: Houghton Mifflin.

Sarason, I.G. (1972). Experimental approaches to test anxiety: Attention and the use of information. In C.D. Speilberger (Ed.), *Anxiety: Current trends in theory and research* (Vol. 2). New York: Academic Press.

Sarason, I.G. (1976). *Cognitive Interference Questionnaire.* Unpublished instrument. University of Washington, Seattle, Washington.

Shader, R.I., Harmatz, J.S., & Salzman, C. (1974). A new scale for clinical assessment in geriatric populations: Sandoz Clinical Assessment Geriatric (SCAG). *Journal of American Geriatric Society, 22,* 107–113.

Shostrom, E.L. (1964). A test for the measurement of self-actualization. *Educational and Psychological Measurement, 24,* 207–218.

Soeken, D.R., Manderscheid, R.W., Flatter, C.H., & Silbergeld, S. (1981). A controlled study of quantitative feedback in married-couples brief group psychotherapy. *Psychotherapy: Theory, Research and Practice, 18,* 204–215.

Spielberger, C., Gorsuch, R., & Lushene, R. (1970). *The State-Trait Anxiety Inventory (STAI) test manual.* Palo Alto, CA: Consulting Psychologists Press.

Suinn, R.M. (1969). The STABS, a measure of test anxiety for behavior therapy: Normative data. *Behaviour Research and Therapy, 7,* 335–339.

Tori, C., & Worrell, L. (1973). Reduction of human avoidant behavior: A comparison of counterconditioning, expectancy, and cognitive information approaches. *Journal of Consulting and Clinical Psychology, 41,* 269–278.

Walk, R.D. (1956). Self-ratings of fear in a fear-invoking situation. *Journal of Abnormal and Social Psychology, 52,* 171–178.

Watson, J.B. (1925). *Behaviorism.* New York: Norton.

Watson, D., & Friend, R. (1969). Measurement of social-evaluative anxiety. *Journal of Consulting and Clinical Psychology, 33,* 448–457.

Wechsler, D. (1955). *Manual for the Wechsler Adult Intelligence Scale.* New York: Psychological Corporation.

Wechsler, D., & Stone, C.P. (1945). Manual for Wechsler Memory Scale. *Journal of Psychology*, 19, 87–95.

Wittenborn, J.R. (1955). *Manual: Wittenborn Psychiatric Rating Scales*. New York: Psychological Corporation.

Wittenborn, J.R. (1966a). Psychiatric syndromes as a cultural phenomenon. *Proceedings of the 5th International Congress of the Collegium Internationale Neuropsychopharmacologicum, Washington 1966, Excerpta Medica International Congress Series 129*.

Wittenborn, J.R. (1966b). The assessment of clinical change. In J.O. Cole & J.R. Wittenborn (Eds.), *Pharmacotherapy of Depression*. Springfield, IL: Charles C. Thomas.

Wittenborn, J.R. (1971). The design of clinical trials. In J. Levine, B.C. Schiele, & L. Bouthilet (Eds.), *Principles and problems in establishing the efficacy of psychotropic agents*. Washington, DC: U.S. Government Printing Office. Public Health Service Publication No. 2138.

Wittenborn, J.R. (Ed.). (1977). Guidelines for clinical trials of psychotropic drugs. *Pharmakopsychiatrie Neuro-Psychopharmakologie*, 4, 205–264.

Wittenborn, J.R. (1978). Behavioral toxicity in normal humans as a model for assessing behavioral toxicity in patients. In M.A. Lipton, A. DiMascio, & K.F. Killam (Eds.), *Psychopharmacology: A generation of progress*. New York: Raven Press.

Wittenborn, J.R. (1979). Effects of benzodiazepines on psychomotor performance. *British Journal of Clinical Pharmacology*, 7, 61S–67S.

Wittenborn, J.R. (1980). Behavioral toxicity of psychotropic drugs. *The Journal of Nervous and Mental Disease*, 168, 171–176.

Wittenborn, J.R. (1981a). The assessment of behavioral changes in geriatric patients. *Psychopharmacology Bulletin*, 17, 96–103.

Wittenborn, J.R. (1981b). Pharmacotherapy for age-related behavioral deficiencies. *Journal of Nervous and Mental Disease*, 169, 139–156.

Wittenborn, J.R., Flaherty, C.F., Jr., McGough, W.E., Bossange, K.A., & Nash, R.J. (1976). A comparison of the effect of imipramine, nomifensine, and placebo on the psychomotor performance of normal males. *Psychopharmacology*, 51, 85–90.

Wittenborn, J.R., Plante, M., & Burgess, F. (1961). A comparison of physicians' and nurses' symptom ratings. *Journal of Nervous and Mental Disease*, 133, 514–518.

Wittenborn, J.R., Plante, M., Burgess, F., & Livermore, N. (1961). The efficacy of electroconvulsive therapy, iproniazid and placebo in the treatment of young depressed women. *The Journal of Nervous and Mental Disease*, 133, 316–332.

Zuckerman, M. (1960). The development of an affect adjective checklist for the measurement of anxiety. *Journal of Consulting Psychology*, 24, 457–462.

Zuckerman, M., Lubin, B., & Robins, S. (1965). Validation of the Multiple Affect Adjective Check List in clinical situations. *Journal of Consulting Psychology*, 29, 594.

Zung, W.W.K. (1965). A Self-Rating Depression Scale. *Archives of General Psychiatry*, 12, 63–70.

Zung, W.W.K. (1971). A rating instrument for anxiety disorders. *Psychosomatics*, 12, 371–379.

21 TESTING AND INDUSTRIAL APPLICATION

Robert Perloff
James A. Craft
Evelyn Perloff

INTRODUCTION

It is generally acknowledged that psychological testing has much, if not a lion's share, of its roots in what is generally characterized as the industrial setting, where this setting goes beyond employment testing for businesses and corporations. This setting includes the determination of individual differences and the use of an objective interpretation of these differences in the "real world" in general — the military establishment, local governments and community agencies, the vast federal bureaucracy in Washington, as well as the private sector of business and industry. Clinical and educational settings in which tests are used are described elsewhere in this handbook, while this chapter is confined to a selective overview of testing instruments and broadly defined procedures that are used in industrial or profit-making organizations.

The idea of profit making is very important. For our purposes its importance reaches beyond the association of profits with our capitalistic, entrepreneurial system. What is of considerable significance in seeking to persuade the reader of the credibility of testing in industry is that even though industry is far from perfect, it is striking to note that the use of testing in industry has an honorable history of nearly three-quarters of a

century. When one bears in mind the fact that business leaders covet zealously the "bottom line" in seeking to reduce costs while maximizing income, this says a lot for the viability of industrial testing. Thousands of studies have been conducted over the years showing that testing procedures more often than not save organizations hundreds of thousands of dollars and more annually. The use of tests and related procedures reduce training time, accidents, dysfunctional performance, and other behaviors. On the income side of the ledger, using testing procedures for selection, classification, and training assignments very frequently has positive effects on productivity. That is, testing helps organizations to do a better job of providing more goods and services, which in turn contributes to an enhancement of organizational revenues. The point is that testing is not merely used in industrial settings because it is a scientific procedure or because it is humanitarian to place the right person in the right job, but because it enhances productivity and reduces costs.

Of course, this is not to say that testing is foolproof or immune to abuses, incompetencies, or misuse of test result interpretation. Ethical procedures and highly detailed and comprehensive compendia for constructing, using, and interpreting results of tests have been adopted by a number of scientific and professional organizations (APA, 1981; Committee to Develop Joint Technical Standards for Educational and Psychological Testing, 1983). Many individuals who work for these organizations, for example, psychologists, also happen to be members of the American Psychological Association. And this is true of other professionals in other organizations, who naturally feel obliged to adhere to the ethical and technical tenets of their professional societies.

The first major section of this review is a treatment of what is probably the primary use of testing in industry—the area of personnel selection and classification. We examine biodata and the interview, psychological tests in general, and newer procedures such as the assessment center. The second major section is a fairly thorough overview of a ubiquitous measure permeating the industrial setting: job satisfaction. We have selected job satisfaction for this rather comprehensive scrutiny not only because it is used very commonly in industry, but also because job satisfaction gives an individual an opportunity to tell how he/she feels about a variety of job dimensions. Of equal importance is the fact that job satisfaction measures are frequently viewed as dependent or criterion variables for validating psychological instruments and assessing employee morale.

Because of space constraints, our coverage of testing in organizations has been generally limited to private sector organizations, but there are other organizations where tests are heavily used, and these include the military and governmental organizations from municipal through federal levels. We were unable to cover explicitly the psychology of testing in these environments, but we are comfortable with the fact that there is considerable overlap between these environments and the industrial setting, which we have scrutinized in some detail.

Another area we have not covered, and one that can be as objective and technically complex as tests and testing procedures, is performance evaluation (used in determining an individual's performance over a given period of time, say annually). Such ratings are of the first importance because of their influence upon employees as motivators for future performance, and because they provide feedback to the employee as to how he or she is perceived by his/her supervisor in a systematic way. An informative and thorough review of performance ratings is provided by Landy and Farr (1980).

PERSONNEL SELECTION AND CLASSIFICATION

Personnel selection and classification efforts in industry presuppose that individual workers will vary in their actual and potential job performance. Psychological assessment is conducted to differentiate among candidates for available positions. It helps to identify those who possess the qualifications to be successful on the job and to match persons to the jobs for which they are qualified. Beyond the initial acquisition and placement decisions, however, it plays a role in the promotion and transfer of employees to jobs that have requirements consistent with their aptitudes, achievements, and experience. The objective of assessment is to assist the organization by enhancing efficiency and improving productivity, but equally important, it helps the individual employee by providing opportunities for greater job satisfaction, better work adjustment, and possibly greater earnings. It facilitates improved utilization and conservation of human resources (Paterson, 1957).

The use of psychological assessment in industry can be traced to the early part of this century when Hugo Munsterberg formulated a program to apply psychology to industrial problems (Munsterberg, 1913; Viteles, 1932). He pointed out the importance of psychology to work adjustment and efficiency and developed the first test for selection of personnel for a specific job in his experiments in choosing motormen for a Boston railway. However, the modern era of personnel selection began during World War I, when 1,728,747 men were tested in the army for selection, classification, and assignment purposes (Scott, Clothier, & Spriegel, 1949). While there was limited use of psychological assessment in business and industry after World War I (spread by the Scott Company, the Psychological Corporation, and individuals who had been in the Army Division of Psychology), it was not until World War II that the use of testing and other assessment procedures became widespread and reached a reasonably high degree of sophistication. Today most firms enjoy some type of assessment procedure to determine the fit between prospective employees and the jobs that are available. These assessment activities, however, are covered by Title VII of the Civil Rights Act of 1964 and other legislation, which prohibit any type of employment discrimination on the basis of race, sex, national origin, color, religion, and other factors (Arvey, 1979). This, along with good practice, requires that all assessment procedures and instruments have demonstrated job related-ness and validity.

There are a variety of different procedures and devices that can be used to assess the abilities, aptitudes, traits, and achievements of job appli-cants. In the review presented here, we will describe and summarize the research based knowledge relating to a few of the most widely used assessment methods, including biodata and the interview, conventional testing, and multiple assessment procedures. We will be particularly interested in validity, usefulness, and fairness in regard to equal employment opportunity implica-tions.

Biodata and the Interview

Biodata (i.e., personal history/biographical data) and the personnel interview are probably two of the most widely used selection assessment proce-dures in industry today. Both rely heavily on the behavioral consistency concept (Wernimont & Campbell, 1968), in that they collect and use the past history and behavior information about a person to predict future behavior. The assumption is that a person will exhibit basically the same characteristics, traits, abilities, and behaviors in the future that have been exhibited in the past. Both of these methods allow the investigator to learn about the person quickly—questions replace observation over time (Guion, 1965). The inter-view may go somewhat further, however, and the trained interviewer may attempt to make appro-priate assessments of the candidate's personal characteristics during the interview process.

Biodata

Almost all employers collect these types of data in some form from prospective employees on appli-cation blanks, biographical information blanks, or life history forms. In some cases, biodata is considered to be only information that is historical and verifiable (Asher, 1972), but it may include unverifiable self-reports relating to memory, be-havior, or interpretation as well (Reilly & Chao, 1982).

In regard to the quality of the information pro-vided on biodata forms, research suggests that it is quite accurate, at least for verifiable questions. Data given by job applicants when checked against available records indicate little falsifica-tion and rather high consistency with correlations at .9 and above (Cascio, 1975; Mosel & Cozan, 1952; Owens, 1976). In particular, the likelihood of faking biodata appears to be minimal if respon-dents are warned of the presence of a lie scale (Schrader & Osburn, 1977).

Even though the process of quantifying and weighting biodata for prediction purposes can be based on hypotheses, it is often an exercise in raw empiricism. Using a large group of current or former employees divided into successful and un-successful workers, each item is assessed in terms of how well it predicts particular criteria of success. Differential weights are established for the various responses to each item in regard to its predictiveness. When in use, a composite score for all items is computed for each person, and this can be used for selection (England, 1971; Guion, 1965).

As far as validity is concerned, biodata have a lengthy history as a useful predictor of turnover, job success, and numerous other criteria in a va-riety of occupations (England & Paterson, 1960). In a review by Asher (1972), it was found that biodata had "vastly superior validity" to other predictors such as intelligence, aptitude, and per-sonality tests. Using 31 validity coefficients from 11 cross-validated studies, he found that 97% of the correlations were .30 or above, 74% were .40 or higher, 55% were .50 or more, and 35% were .60 and higher. Another more recent review of cross-validated coefficients from 58 studies found that the average coefficients for each of five types of criteria (i.e., tenure, training, ratings, produc-tivity, salary) ranged from .32 to .46 (Reilly & Chao, 1982). These and other studies support the relative validity of biodata in personnel selection (Owens, 1976). In addition, it appears that in some cases biodata validity may hold up over decades (Brown, 1978) and have predictability across national boundaries for some jobs (Hinrichs, Haanpera, & Sonkin, 1976). Finally, recent research suggests that biodata may be quite useful in assessing individuals and classifying them into subgroups for purposes of better place-ment and utilization (Owens & Schoenfeldt, 1979; Schoenfeldt, 1974).

As far as equal employment opportunity is concerned, the rather sparse research available suggests that biodata will likely be valid and fair for both majority and minority groups (Reilly & Chao, 1982). However, some findings indicate that different scoring keys may be necessary for men and women (Reilly & Chao, 1982). Where there are large differences in criterion means between groups (e.g., race, age), adverse impact is likely, since fewer of certain protected class persons may be selected with valid biodata predictors. The empirical weighting process can compound the difficulty in defending biodata if adverse impact occurs, since it may be difficult to show a logical relationship between predictor items and the criterion they predict. The best strategy seems to be to eliminate those items that identify specific groups on the basis of protected class characteristics (e.g., sex, age) before scoring the biodata and to try to use items that appear to have a rational relationship to the job and criterion being considered (Pace & Shoenfeldt, 1977).

Interview

The basic objective of the selection interview is to gather relevant information about candidate qualifications and experience for an available job. It may involve collecting data on the person's background, work experience, attitudes, expectations, and assessment of characteristics that can be determined in a face-to-face situation (e.g., poise, interpersonal skills). It is a communication process involving one or more interviewers and an interviewee. The interview process may range from unstructured approaches with little or no consistency in specific questions asked and direction taken, to highly structured procedures whereby all candidates are asked precisely the same questions in an identical manner and order. Interviews may also vary in regard to their systematic nature. A systematic interview involves careful planning with clear statements of objectives, planned approaches to obtain and evaluate the necessary information, and the use of trained interviewers (Ghiselli & Brown, 1955).

Research and experience suggest that information obtained in the interview may include more errors and distortions than from biodata. There appears to be a tendency for people to upgrade aspects of their previous work experience, and this may require that it be checked against outside sources (Cascio, 1982; Weiss & Dawis, 1960).

In regard to reliability, intrarater consistency seems to be satisfactory, but most research reviews indicate that there is usually very low interrater reliability (Hakel, 1982; Wagner, 1949; Webster, 1964). In unsystematic interviews, the interviewers often hold differing stereotypes and expectations regarding acceptable candidates and may have different levels of knowledge about the job and its requirements. Even if various interviewers have all the relevant data presented to them, they often process the data differently and reach varying conclusions regarding candidates (Valenzi & Andrews, 1973). It does appear, however, that reliability can be significantly increased through the use of more systematic and structured interview procedures (Mayfield, Brown, & Hamstra, 1980; Schwab & Heneman, 1969).

In order to better understand the interview as an assessment and decision-making process, a great deal of psychological research has been conducted over the last 15 years (Carlson, Thayer, Mayfield, & Peterson, 1971; Schmitt, 1976; Webster, 1964). Some important findings suggest that: Interviewers tend to make decisions about candidates very early in the interview (primacy effect); negative information about an interviewee seems to be weighted more heavily than positive information; visual cues are more important than verbal cues; an applicant's rating in the interview is partially dependent on the other individuals being rated at the same time (contrast effects); sex, race, or other similarities of interviewee to interviewer may lead to somewhat more favorable evaluations; without proper recording of responses, many interviewers cannot recall all the relevant information given by a candidate during an interview; substantial day-to-day interviewing experience apparently does not enhance the effectiveness of an interviewer; situational pressures will affect the interviewer's judgment regarding the acceptability of interviewees.

Given the above information, it is not surprising that literature reviews over the years have generally found there are few encouraging data on the validity of the interview (Mayfield, 1964; Ulrich & Trumbo, 1965; Wagner, 1949). Current experience tends to be consistent with these traditional findings. For example, in a recent review of 12 interview validation studies, using supervisory ratings as criteria, the average coefficient was estimated at .19 (Reilly & Chao, 1982). However, the prospects for the interview as an assessment tool may not be as bleak as the literature reviews suggest. For years there has been evidence that more systematic, job related, and structured interviews have had respectable validities (Ghiselli, 1966b; McMurray, 1947). Recently, a study using the situational interview, with specific questions based on job related critical incidents, has shown reliabilities generally over .70 and validities with performance appraisal criteria ranging from .30 to .46 (Latham et al., 1980). It appears that there is reasonable hope for the interview as an assessment tool if the content is focused on job related situational questions, job knowledge questions, job sample questions, worker requirements questions (Pursell, Campion, & Gaylord, 1980), and if the interviewer is aware of effective interviewing practices (Hakel, 1982) and is trained to avoid rating errors (Latham, Wexley, & Pursell, 1975).

With regard to equal employment opportunity, a review of the very sparse existing research provides little if any evidence that people are evaluated unfairly on the basis of race in the interview (Arvey, 1979). This review did suggest, however, that females tend to be evaluated lower than males, but this may vary with the job and situational factors. Clearly, the issue of fairness should be of concern whenever the interview is used, but particularly in unsystematic and unstructured interview processes.

Psychological Tests

Psychological tests are employed in numerous business firms to assess the abilities, traits, and achievements of job applicants and current employees. These assessments are used to predict future job performance and/or to evaluate the psychological characteristics related to the performance level of present employees. Theoretically, these tests represent a sample of a person's behavioral repertoire or provide a sign that a person is predisposed to behave in certain ways. They are useful to the degree that they do in fact represent broader areas of behavior. Psychological tests are considered more objective than alternative assessment procedures because they are objectively scored (using an agreed upon set of rules) and can be interpreted in terms of a specific set of norms. They are generally deemed to have greater reliability (test-retest, parallel form, internal consistency) than other methods due to standardization and uniformity of procedures. In addition, given

decades of experience with tests, we know more about them than many other assessment procedures.

Any meaningful industrial testing program for selection and placement begins with an analysis of the job and a determination of the psychological characteristics needed to perform effectively. Subsequently, the tests used to assess these characteristics in current and prospective employees may be developed particularly for the organization and job, or the firm may choose to use commercially available instruments that measure appropriate constructs.

In this brief review, we will focus on occupational aptitude tests and content oriented achievement tests.

Aptitude Tests

These tests assess the basic capacities of persons for acquiring the necessary knowledge and skills to perform effectively on the job. They measure potential rather than accomplishment. Such tests may be pencil-and-paper instruments requiring a response to written questions by writing or marking an answer, or they may be performance tests in which the individual is required to manipulate apparatus or equipment. In general, occupational aptitude tests include tests of intellectual, spatial, mechanical, and motor abilities, perceptual accuracy, and personality traits (Ghiselli, 1966a).

In regard to validity, Ghiselli (1966a, 1973) has conducted some monumental work summarizing available validity information for a 50-year period. Over a wide range of jobs (21 classes), it was found that "for every job there is at least one type of test which has at least moderate validity" (Ghiselli, 1973, p. 477). While results varied among tests and occupations, it was found that the overall average validity coefficient across all jobs was .39 for training criteria and .22 for proficiency criteria. The overall average of the *maximal* validity coefficients for all jobs was .45 and .35 for training and proficiency criteria, respectively. Except for executives, aptitude tests generally had higher validity coefficients for training criteria than for proficiency critieria. In regard to the size of validity coefficients with proficiency criteria, it must be noted that Ghiselli's study used only single test measures (not test batteries), criteria were often global assessments (complex constructs), and the concurrent validation model was used in many of the studies summarized. These factors clearly attenuated the results, and the findings must be considered underestimates of the predictive power of aptitude tests.

In more recent research using a new method of cumulating results across validity studies and using combinations of cognitive and psychomotor ability tests, a reported predictive validity of .53 was obtained across a variety of jobs (Hunter & Schmidt, 1982; Schmidt & Hunter, 1977). Other reviews have shown that aptitude tests have a very high proportion ("significant batting averages") of validity coefficients that are statistically significant (Lent et al., 1971). Reviews of personality test validities, however, indicate that there is little *generalizable* evidence that they can be used as practical and effective tools in employee selection (Ghiselli & Barthol, 1953; Guion & Gottier, 1965; Locke & Hulin, 1962).

Traditionally, the observed variability in aptitude test validity coefficients, even when the tests and jobs seemed to be reasonably similar, led to the belief that validity is situationally and/or job specific (Albright, Glennon, & Smith, 1963; Guion, 1965). A growing body of recent research, however, presents evidence to suggest that much of this variability was due to sampling error, differences in criterion reliability, test reliability, range restriction, and other factors (Schmidt & Hunter, 1981; Schmidt, Hunter & Pearlman, 1981). It is now being argued that validities of cognitive aptitude tests are generalizable and that there is no factual basis for requiring a validation study in each situation or for each separate job in a job family. In addition, there is evidence to suggest that aptitude tests are *equally* valid for training and proficiency criteria (Perlman, Schmidt, & Hunter, 1980).

In regard to equal employment opportunity, some research after the enactment of the Civil Rights Act indicated that cultural differences might lead to valid results for majority but not minority test takers (single group validity). There was also concern that aptitude tests, if valid for both groups, might have significantly different validities for minority and majority persons (differential validity). Substantial research now indicates that such results are the exception rather than the rule in adequately controlled validation studies (Arvey, 1979; Dunnette & Borman, 1979; Linn, 1978).

Achievement Tests

These are used to assess proficiency in regard to job knowledge or performance. Job knowledge tests may be oral or written. They generally consist of a series of questions regarding job activity or processes that will differentiate among testees in terms of level of experience and skill (e.g., journeyman, apprentice, no experience). Job performance or work sample tests, on the other hand, require that the candidates perform an actual sample of the job tasks under standardized procedures and conditions for a fixed time or until a given number of work items are completed. Such performance tests may be classed as "motor" tests if they basically entail physical manipulation of things or "verbal" if the tasks are essentially language- or people-oriented (Asher & Sciarrino, 1974). The interest in job performance tests appears to have been stimulated in the last decade. This is partly due to their attractiveness in terms of fair employment practices. They are job analysis based, have high content validity, and appear to be nondiscriminatory, since people are evaluated on whether they can do the job tasks, not on an aptitude test score. Also, they can be used with relatively small numbers of applicants. A person cannot bluff his/her way through the tests. Applicants may be able to get immediate feedback. Moreover, the tests are perceived as fair by the candidates, since they have high face validity (Cascio & Philips, 1979; Schmidt et al., 1977). On the negative side, they are often difficult and costly to develop, and they may require special equipment and facilities to administer.

In regard to the validity of performance tests, it appears that appropriately developed and standardized work samples consistently yield higher validities than aptitude tests (Dunnette & Borman, 1979). In a review of validity research, it was found that motor performance tests had validities second only to biographical information when related to proficiency criteria. Forty-three percent of motor test validities were above .50 and 70% were above .40. Verbal performance tests also were good predictors of proficiency criteria, but not as effective as motor tests. Twenty-one percent of verbal test validity coefficients were over .50, and 41% over .40. When using success in training as the criterion, verbal performance samples had more significant validity coefficients than did motor tests. For example, 39% of the verbal test coefficients met or exceeded .50, and 65% were .40 and above, while the comparable figures for motor tests were 29% and 47%, respectively (Asher & Sciarrino, 1974). In a well-designed and executed study comparing performance test results with pencil-and-paper aptitude tests, it was found that the work sample had significant concurrent validities of .42, .46, and .66 on three proficiency criteria, while none of the aptitude test scores provided meaningful indications of validity (Campion, 1972). Specific validity data on job knowledge tests are not widely published. However, some early information suggests that they can be effective tools for differentiating among persons with varying knowledge and skill levels in particular occupations (McCormick and Winstanley, 1950; Stead et al., 1940), and the U.S. Employment Service has made effective use of them (Guion, 1965).

Finally, as far as equal employment opportunity issues are concerned, the research data at this time indicate job performance tests have little if any adverse impact. In one city, using job performance tests covering a range of jobs, a careful analysis found no adverse impact in any job category (Cascio & Phillips, 1979). Another study found no racial bias in the evaluation of testees when they were assessed on tasks representing job relevant behavior and when raters used behavioral recording forms (Brugnoli, Campion, & Basen, 1979). A carefully conducted study comparing job sample tests with written aptitude tests found less adverse impact with work samples and also reported that minorities perceived these to be fairer and clearer than written tests (Schmidt et al., 1977). It would be expected that job sample tests will show racial differences no greater than actual job performance differences.

The Assessment Center

The most well known and widely employed multiple assessment procedure in industry is the assessment center. It is generally used to evaluate the potential of candidates for promotion to first or middle level management positions, to diagnose employee developmental needs, and/or to identify the long-range potential of assessees (Boehm, 1982; Kraut, 1976). The key aspect of an assessment center is that the candidate's behavior and performances on several standardized assessment exercises are recorded and evaluated systematically by multiple trained observers. These observations and judgments are subsequently pooled, discussed, and used by the assessors to formulate an overall evaluation of each assessee (Task Force on Assessment Center Standards, 1980).

The exercises constitute the core elements of the assessment center. They are developed after a thorough job analysis of the position for which the assessment is to be made. The exercises must represent the "types, complexities and difficulty level of activities that are actually required on the job" (Byham, 1980, p. 30). At least one of these exercises must be a simulation, which requires the assessee to respond behaviorally to situational stimuli resembling those in the target job. Some common examples of individual and group exercises used in assessment centers are: In-Basket test, leaderless group discussions, oral presentations; group gaming; paper-and-pencil tests (aptitude, personality or achievement); and interviewing (Boehm, 1982; Byham, 1970; Finkle, 1976). The particular set of exercises will depend upon the job involved, the objective of the assessment, and the nature of the organization.

The assessors are responsible for observing the candidates' behavior during the assessment center activity and recording their observations on predefined job-related dimensions. These assessment dimensions are developed from the job analysis and represent categories that may be used to examine and classify observed behavior. They must be defined so that they are observable, relevant to the situation, and quantifiable (Jaffee & Cohen, 1980). Some commonly used assessment dimensions include: Organizing and Planning, Oral Communication Skill, Decision-Making, Judgment, and Creativity (Byham, 1980; Finkle, 1976). The assessors are usually managers one to three levels above the job for which the candidates are being assessed. They are trained to observe and evaluate behaviors relevant to the target job. Upon completion of the assessment cycle, the assessors pool their findings and discuss as a group the strengths and weaknesses of each assessee. They reach a judgment, formulate an overall evaluation of each candidate, and write a thorough report regarding their findings.

It appears that trained managers and professional psychologists do about equally well in performing assessor tasks (Byham, 1970; Huck, 1973). Research findings also indicate that there is significant interrater reliability among the assessors (Parker, 1980), even before discussions of assessee performance (Schmitt, 1977). In a review of available data, it was found that interrater reliability in various studies ranged from .60 to .98, with most apparently over .75 (Howard, 1974). In addition, there is evidence suggesting that ratings made by successive assessor teams participating in the same assessment center are stable over time (Sackett & Hakel, 1979).

Various reviews of assessment center performance indicate that the overall assessments of candidates have high predictive validities (Cohen, Moses, & Byham, 1971; Howard, 1974; Huck, 1973). One reviewer noted that in comparison with traditional methods for predicting managerial success, "the *average* validity of the assessment center is about as high as the *maximum* validity attained by use of these traditional methods" (Norton, 1977, pp. 442–443). Another analyst, examining 22 studies of company operated assessment centers, found that this method was *more* effective than other approaches in 21 cases (with validity ranging as high as .64) and was *as effective* in only one case. In no case was it less effective (Byham, 1970). It is to be noted, however, that assessment centers tend to be better predictors of criteria reflecting managerial progress (e.g., promotions received, salary level) and managerial potential than of actual performance. This is reflected in a review of 19 research studies showing the median validity coefficient for job potential criteria was .63, for job progress criteria was .40, and for predicting job performance was .33 (Cohen et al., 1974; see also Parker, 1980). In fact, a word of caution has been strongly offered by some analysts. Noting that high validities have been obtained generally using management progress and advancement criteria, the assessment center may simply capture the *preferences* of upper level managers who make promotion and salary decisions rather than assessing potential *performance* (Klimoski & Strickland, 1977). Another concern is that most studies of assessment center validity are flawed, since the criteria are often contaminated because candidate assessments are generally known by those persons making recommendations for salary increases and promotions. Nevertheless, there have been two studies, both conducted at AT&T, in which the assessment center evaluations were carefully withheld from subsequent decision makers. In one of these studies, there was a strong relationship of assessment to management progress (Bray & Grant, 1966); in the other there was a strong relationship between assessments and performance criteria (Bray & Campbell, 1968).

Regarding equal employment opportunity, it seems logical to suspect that there would be little problem because the assessment center exercises are based on specific job analysis, the activities are face valid for the most part, and evaluations are based on observed behavior rather than inferences. The research evidence generally supports this expectation. In a study examining the assessments of several thousand men and women, it was found that distributions of ratings for the two sexes were quite similar. In addition, the assessment evaluation was equally valid for men and women in the study (Moses & Boehm, 1975). There is some evidence indicating that black and white males perform similarly in exercises that are typically used in assessment centers (Jaffee, Cohen, & Cherry, 1972). Also, in a study of black and white women, the assessment center validities were similar for both (Huck & Bray, 1976). However, in this study, black women had significantly lower overall assessments than did white women but also performed less well in terms of global criterion ratings—hence, similar validities. This, of course, could result in adverse impact. Nevertheless, the overall evidence suggests that assessment center evaluations are valid and promising predictors for all groups, regardless of sex or minority status.

JOB SATISFACTION: A PERVASIVE MEASURE IN THE INDUSTRIAL SETTING

A recently published compilation of 249 measures for assessing occupational experiences (Cook, Hepworth, Wall, & Warr, 1981) illustrates the many and varied constructs applicable to industrial settings that have used a testing approach. These constructs include: beliefs about work, group atmosphere, job attachment, job characteristics, job complexity, job context, job involvement, job motivation, job needs, job-related stress, job satisfaction, leadership style, organizational climate, organizational commitment, supervisory behavior, work alienation, work ethic, work facilitation, work group functioning, work preferences, work-related expectancies, work role, and work values. Testing approaches here referred almost exclusively to paper-and-pencil, multiple-item Likert scales.

Since space does not permit attention to all relevant constructs, we will report on a single construct, job satisfaction, which has received extensive industrial attention. Following a discussion of current measurement issues, we will consider various measures available for determining employee job satisfaction.

Measurement Issues

A major area of concern to both employees and employers has always been a variant "of the central theme 'how much do you like your job?' " (Cook et al., 1981). Earliest survey studies can be traced to Hoppock's (1935) work, which provided the first published, multiple-item measure of job satisfaction, and the celebrated Hawthorne studies (Roethlisberger & Dickson, 1939). The Hoppock scale included four items, with 7-point responses, which yielded a single overall job satisfaction score varying from a low of 4 to a high of 28. From this beginning a large number of far more sophisticated and complex measures have been developed (Chun, Cobb, & French, 1975; Cook et al., 1981; Lake, Miles, & Earle, 1973; Miller, 1977; Robinson, Athanasion, & Head, 1969; Robinson & Shaver, 1973). Review of even a sample of instruments in these volumes indicates immediately that differences exist not only with regard to format, but also with regard to their content.

Although effective measurement has always been fraught with conceptual, methodological, and operational problems, assessment of job satisfaction has been especially difficult. The two primary issues to be addressed here are (a) difficulties of obtaining efficient and comparable measures and (b) varying results due to application of different research strategies.

Concerns with defining job satisfaction are still very much with us. Thus, some investigations have assessed workers' job satisfaction by asking: "On the whole, how satisfied are you with your job?" Other studies have addressed worker satisfaction with a number of specific job features where scales not only differ widely in constructs and language, but also vary from assessment of a single job feature about subordinates (McFillen, 1978) to covering as many as 28 specific job features (Dawis, Pinto, Weitzel, & Nezzer, 1974). Among the more popular specific satisfactions measured have been those with coworkers, promotion opportunities, pay, supervision, working conditions, security, nature of work, subordinates, intrinsic/extrinsic rewards, amount of work, and company identification. Furthermore, scales proposing to measure identical job features can differ in significant ways, particularly with regard to item content and phraseology. For example, Hackman and Oldham's (1975) pay subscale asks the following two questions, with responses on a 7-point scale of 1 to 7 (Extremely dissatisfied, Dissatisfied, Slightly dissatisfied, Neutral, Slightly satisfied, Satisfied, Extremely satisfied):

How satisfied are you with this aspect of your job?
- The amount of pay and fringe benefits I receive.
- The degree to which I am truly paid for what I contribute to the organization.

In contrast, Quinn and Staines' (1979) Financial Rewards subscale includes the following three items, with four responses scored from 1 to 4 (Not at all true, A little true, Somewhat true, Very true):

Financial Rewards
- The pay is good.
- The job security is good.
- My fringe benefits are good.

As pointed out by Barnowe, Mangione, and Quinn (1973), there are a number of different research strategies that have been used to study worker job satisfaction. The simplest strategy has been to ask workers to consider a list of job facets (aspects) and then to evaluate them in terms of what they believe are "good jobs," "ideal jobs," or jobs they would "most like to have." This strategy was not only among the first to be followed, but continues in use. Not surprising, then, is Barnowe et al.'s (1973) preference for an experimental design strategy, which they consider, on the one hand, most appropriately valid but, on the other hand, most costly. This approach, of course, involves experimental manipulation of job facets to effect the desired outcome of significantly improving job satisfaction. Unfortunately, but realistically, this strategy has neither been nor is likely to be a popular approach in view of the demands it makes on research investigators and employers.

The third strategy asks employees to specify major reasons for their job satisfaction or dissatisfaction and offers no indication of any validity "between the job satisfaction criterion and the quality of employment predictors" (Barnowe et al., 1973, p. 4). Although this approach is weak, its ease of implementation probably assures continued usage.

An approach comparable to factor analyses previously used to analyze satisfaction judgments (Quinn & Cobb, 1971) has recently been suggested by Billings and Cornelius (1980) for a better understanding of work outcomes. They proposed use of multidimensional scaling (MDS) to uncover "the latent spatial structure inherent in the perceptual judgments that subjects give to a set of objects" (p. 152). Although their study used MDS to verify underlying dimensional structure of work outcomes commonly labeled extrinsic or intrinsic, this methodology is highly generalizable for determining perceptual organization of other work outcomes across samples of workers. Regarding findings of the Billings and Cornelius study, the latent spatial structure (for 21 work outcomes investigated) consisted of three dimensions, not only the intrinsic/extrinsic dichotomy usually proposed. However, among the three dimensions, two (underlying needs and inherent in the work itself) corresponded to intrinsic and extrinsic factors, with a third dimension reflecting societal values (anchored by prestige on the high end and enjoyment of work itself on the low end).

The fifth strategy uses survey methodology to obtain relationships between job facets and some outcome or criterion, which is most commonly job satisfaction. This approach defines the importance of a job facet by the extent to which it accounts for criterion variance. As noted by Barnowe et al. (1973), this nonexperimental strategy cannot, of course, provide evidence of causality, but it is probably a most realistic and reasonable procedure for currently assessing what job satisfaction entails.

In fact, Barnowe et al. (1973) used this strategy to identify significant facets of job satisfaction from a national probability sample of 1,533 employed persons. That is, 33 different job facets that measured four employment factors (Challenge, Resources, Comfort, and Financial Rewards) were correlated with a single criterion of overall job satisfaction in order to develop an empirical model for explaining job satisfaction. The results showed that:

(a) the final form of the 33-predictor quality of employment model was able to explain 53 percent of the variance of the study's job satisfaction criterion measure . . . [and]

(b) none of the 33 job facets stood out as a major determinant of job satisfaction . . . [but] most contributed a modest amount to job satisfaction, and the aggregation of all 33 contributed a great deal. (Barnowe et al., 1973, pp. 62, 65)

Another model for linking predictors to a criterion of job satisfaction has been described by Schmitt, Coyle, White, and Rauschenberger (1978). They hypothesized direct relationships from sex and socioeconomic status to individual needs to job perceptions to job satisfactions. Their research strategy again relied on relating a set of predictors (sex, socioeconomic status, individual needs, job perceptions) to a criterion measure (job satisfaction). The Schmitt et al. (1978) model, however, stressed the effect of individual difference variables on perceptions of job characteristics (facets), which they suggest are "primary determinants of job satisfaction" (p. 891).

Schmitt et al. (1978) used a mailed questionnaire to survey 411 recent high school graduates who were either jobholders or were still jobhunting. The questionnaire included multi-item scales to assess the predictors and criterion measure. The results indicated that:

> The data fit the proposed model reasonably well and are generally consistent with results from past studies. . . . The fit could be better, however, and the generally low multiple R's suggest [that] a major portion of the job satisfaction variance remains unexplained . . . [with] the R of .57 for satisfaction . . . perhaps somewhat inflated because the job perception and job satisfaction variables were measured at the same point in time. (Schmitt et al., 1978, pp. 897–898)

In contrast, James and Jones (1980) recently proposed a model to test a hypothesis of reciprocal causation between job satisfaction and three job perceptions (challenge, autonomy, importance). Questionnaires included measures on: (a) individual characteristics (i.e., self-esteem, job involvement, achievement motivation), (b) demographic variables (age and education), (c) job attributes/work group structure, and, of course, (d) job perceptions and job satisfaction. Results of administration of these measures to over 1,200 supervisory and nonsupervisory personnel indicated that:

higher-order job perceptions and job satisfaction are reciprocally and dynamically related . . . [and] job satisfaction appeared to be a stronger cause of the job perceptions than vice-versa. (James & Jones, 1980, p. 127)

Finally, James and Jones (1980) recommended a descriptive (job perception) versus affective (job satisfaction) dichotomy for distinguishing between the two constructs rather than the generally assumed unidirectional flow of job perceptions to job satisfaction, as suggested by Schmitt et al. (1978).

Available Measures

Two categories of measuring instruments have been selected for review here: overall job satisfaction and specific job satisfaction. Again, in view of space limitations, we will be highly selective in the report of available measures that follows.

Overall Job Satisfaction

The 17 measures presented by Cook et al. (1981) are representative of what have been used over the past 50 years to determine job satisfaction. More particularly, they reflect what measures have been reported in studies published in 15 principal international journals from 1974 to mid-1980. These 17 measures, spanning over 45 years of development, vary in length from 4 items in Hoppock's Overall Job Satisfaction scale, to 38 items on Quinn and Staine' Overall Job Satisfaction measure. The measures also vary widely with regard to their effectiveness, specifically validity and reliability. Since it is unreasonable to describe all available scales here, we have prepared a tabular summary to highlight 10 of the most frequently used measures. Thus, Table 21.1 lists scale, author(s), publication date, number of items, and primary orientation tapped by each measure.

As Table 21.1 indicates, these 10 measures were developed from different orientations, although they were developed to measure job satisfaction.

TABLE 21.1. SUMMARY FEATURES OF 10 MEASURES OF OVERALL JOB SATISFACTION.

Scale	Author(s)	Publication Date	Number of Items	Primary Orientation
Attitude Toward the Job	Vroom	1960	3	Supervisory staff issues
Facet-free Job Satisfaction	Quinn & Staines	1979	5	Affective reactions to the job
General Job Satisfaction	Hackman & Oldham	1975	5	Extent to which employee is "satisfied" and "happy" with his/her job
General Satisfaction	Taylor & Bowers	1972	7	Construct of central "organizational functioning"
Minnesota Satisfaction Questionnaire	Weiss, Dawis England, & Lofquist	1967	100 Long Form 20 Short Form	Need to maintain correspondence with "work environment" (performance) and "personal environment" (satisfaction)
Overall Job Satisfaction	Brayfield & Rothe	1951	18	Wide range of "evaluative reactions" applicable to many jobs
Overall Job Satisfaction	Bullock	1952	10	"Social factors" relating to job satisfaction
Overall Job Satisfaction	Cammann, Fichman, Jenkins, & Klesh	1979	3	Affective responses to jobs
Overall Job Satisfaction	Hoppock	1935	4	General "liking of" and "satisfaction with" one's job
Overall Job Satisfaction	Warr, Cook, & Wall	1979	15	Extrinsic and intrinsic features of blue-collar jobs

Note. Information from *The experience of work* by Cook et al., 1981. New York: Academic Press.

Review of their items indicates quite clearly that all measures have face validity; items inquire about specific job features and working conditions. Three of the above scales (Bullock, 1952; Cammann, Fichman, Jenkins, & Klesh, 1979; Quinn & Staines, 1979) stress workers' affective responses to their jobs; two measures (Taylor & Bowers, 1972; Vroom, 1960) assess job satisfaction by tapping reactions to organizational or supervisory functioning; and one scale was specifically developed to cover extrinsic and intrinsic features of blue-collar jobs. The remaining four scales are more representative of those developed to determine the extent to which workers find their jobs satisfying.

Just as these 10 measures differ in number and kind of items, they also vary in statistical assessment of reliability and validity; more specifically, in the nature of reliability and validity information available. Since it is again inappropriate to present all published evidence about the measures, we will first highlight salient findings on their reliability and then on their validity.

Reliability reports have primarily consisted of internal consistency measures (coefficient alpha, Spearman-Brown, Hoyt, Kuder-Richardson) and have varied between $r = .75$ and $r = .95$. Bullock (1952) also reported a test-retest correlation coefficient of $r = .94$ over a 6-week interval for his Overall Job Satisfaction Scale, but this was obtained with students for previously held jobs. Miles (1975), however, did find a test-retest correlation of $r = .80$ over a 4-month interval, whereas a test-retest correlation of only $r = .55$ was noted for the General Satisfaction Scale of Taylor and Bowers (1972). Vroom (1960) reported a test-retest coefficient of $r = .75$ over six months for his Attitude Toward the Job Scale.

Validity information on these measures is more varied, depending on the particular measure and criterion variables with which it is correlated. Most studies report criterion and construct validity but rarely provide the complete information necessary for assessing convergent and discriminant validity (Cook et al., 1981). This latter requirement is not reported because journals cannot "reasonably be expected to contain so much material" (Cook et al., 1981), and also because these assessments rarely exist.

Review of validity information on these 10 overall measures of job satisfaction indicates the following selected relationships (Cook et al., 1981):

1. Stahl, Manley, and McNichols (1978) correlated Hoppock's (1935) Overall Job Satisfaction Scale with their Work Satisfaction and Pay Satisfaction subscales and obtained coefficients of $r = .73$ and $r = .16$, respectively.

2. Stone, Mowday, and Porter (1977) obtained a correlation of $r = .38$ between Brayfield and Rothe's (1951) Overall Job Satisfaction Scale and the Job Scope Measure (perceived Variety, Autonomy, Task Identity, Feedback). Similarly, Stone (1976) recorded $r = .43$ for 594 varied employees. Again, we see correlation of this measure with the Job Descriptive Index of Smith, Kendall, and Hulin's (1969) where the Work Itself scale correlated .73, but the Pay Satisfaction scale correlated only .18.

3. A correlation of $r = .71$ was reported by Wanous (1974) for General Satisfaction scores of the Minnesota Satisfaction Questionnaire and total Job Descriptive Index scores. Schriesheim and Murphy (1976) obtained a correlation of $r = -.25$ between the General Satisfaction scores and unit size.

4. Quinn and Staines' (1979) Facet-free Job Satisfaction measure was found to correlate $-.22$ and .43 with a measure of role ambiguity and Quinn and Shepard's (1974) Depressed Mood at Work Scale.

5. Although only a 3-item scale of Overall Job Satisfaction, this measure by Cammann et al. (1979) correlated $r = .35$ and $r = .58$ with these authors' measures of Job Involvement and Intention to Turn Over.

6. Hollon and Chesser (1976) used Vroom's Attitude Toward the Job measure as a measure of overall job satisfaction and found it correlated $r = -.43$ with desired increase in personal influence, $r = -.49$ with the Job-related Tension Scale of Kahn, Wolfe, Quinn, Snoeck, and Rosenthal (1964), and $r = -.32$ with the Job Involvement measure of Lodahl and Kejner (1965).

7. The Overall Job Satisfaction measure by Warr, Cook, and Wall (1979) was found to correlate $r = .58$ with Organizational Commitment (Cook & Wall, 1980) and $r = -.29$ with the General Health Questionnaire.

In summary, then, these overall job satisfaction measures do apparently account for some of the variance of job satisfaction, but the current results are far from adequate. Significant next steps should surely include attention to: (a) developing a theory of work, including appropriate measurement issues, and (b) implementing discriminant and convergent assessment.

Specific Job Satisfaction

Cook et al. (1981) present 29 measures designed to evaluate the contribution of various specific job features to job satisfaction. In contrast to the early appearance of an overall job satisfaction scale (Hoppock, 1935), these measures reflect a more recent measurement approach, with a majority of scales developed after 1970. Although several measures contain as few as three items, most measures of specific satisfactions contain many more. We will again use a tabular summary format to highlight the major features of these measures. Table 21.2 presents 11 frequently used scales, by subscales and corresponding number of items. Table 21.3 again lists scale, author(s), publication date, total number of items, and primary orientation tapped by each measure.

The 11 measures presented in Table 21.2 again show a variety of differences. These scales include as few as 3 items and a single subscale (Social Rewards Satisfaction and Pay Satisfaction) to as many as 77 items (Managerial Opinion Survey) and eight subscales (Index of Organizational Reactions). The three specific job satisfactions (subscales) most frequently tapped by the 11 measures were Pay $(n = 8)$, Promotions $(n = 6)$, and Supervision $(n = 6)$. In contrast, six subscales (Esteem Needs, Subordinates, Intrinsic rewards, Extrinsic rewards, Friends' attitudes, Family attitudes) appeared only once in these measures.

Although descriptions of these 11 instruments of specific satisfactions may suggest measurement of a number of different features, factor analytic studies indicate considerable overlapping of measures. The scales represent a recent measurement trend, with the earliest scale (Index of Organizational Reactions) having been developed in 1962, and a majority $(n = 6)$ constructed within the past

TABLE 21.2. SPECIFIC JOB SATISFACTION MEASURES* BY SUBSCALE AND CORRESPONDING NUMBER OF ITEMS.

Scale	Total Number of Items	Supervision	Company as a whole	Nature of work	Extent of work	Co-workers	Working conditions	Pay	Promotions	Security	Social needs	Autonomy	Personal growth	Esteem needs	Subordinates	Intrinsic rewards	Extrinsic rewards	Friends' attitudes	Family attitudes
Facet-specific satisfaction	33	11	—	—	—	3	7	3	3	—	—	—	6	—	—	—	—	—	—
Index of organizational reactions	42	6	5	6	4	5	6	5	5	—	—	—	—	—	—	—	—	—	—
Intrinsic and extrinsic rewards	6	—	—	—	—	—	—	—	—	—	—	—	—	—	—	3	3	—	—
Job descriptive index	72	18	—	18	—	18	—	9	9	—	—	—	—	—	—	—	—	—	—
Job expectations	28	—	—	4	—	—	—	4	4	4	—	4	—	—	—	—	—	4	4
Managerial opinion survey	77	13	12	15	—	10	—	7	8	—	—	—	—	12	—	—	—	—	—
Need satisfaction questionnaire	13	—	—	—	—	—	—	—	—	1	2	4	3	3	—	—	—	—	—
Pay satisfaction	3	—	—	—	—	—	—	3	—	—	—	—	—	—	—	—	—	—	—
Social rewards satisfaction	3	—	—	—	—	—	—	—	—	—	3	—	—	—	—	—	—	—	—
Specific satisfactions	14	3	—	—	—	—	—	2	—	2	—	3	4	—	—	—	—	—	—
Worker opinion survey	48	8	8	8	—	8	—	8	8	—	—	—	—	—	—	—	—	—	—

Note. Information from *The experience of work* by Cook et al., 1981. New York: Academic Press.

TABLE 21.3. SUMMARY FEATURES OF 11 MEASURES OF SPECIFIC JOB SATISFACTION.

Scale	Author(s)	Publication Date	Number of Items	Primary Orientation
Facet-specific Job Satisfaction	Quinn & Staines	1979	33	Specific job satisfactions measured, with items speaking to "facets"
Index of Organization Reactions	Smith	1962	42	Item content speaks to relationship between job features and performance
Intrinsic and Extrinsic Rewards Satisfaction	Cammann et al.	1979	6	Taps satisfaction toward intrinsic and extrinsic rewards
Job Descriptive Index	Smith, Kendall, & Hulin	1969	72	Measures principal, specific job satisfactions, with respondents describing their work (not feelings about work) in evaluative terms
Job Expectations Questionnaire	Stodgill	1965	28	Measures satisfaction of seven specific job features
Managerial Opinion Scale	Warr & Routledge	1969	77	Measures principal, specific job satisfactions relevant to supervisors and managers, with items referring to job features rather than to respondents
Need Satisfaction Quesionnaire	Porter	1961	13	Emphasis is on personal needs rather than job features
Pay Satisfaction	Cammann et al.	1979	3	Assesses satisfaction with pay
Social Rewards Satisfaction	Cammann et al.	1979	3	Measures satisfaction with social rewards
Specific Satisfactions	Hackman & Oldman	1975	14	Assesses specific job satisfactions that speak to work context and personal development
Worker Opinion Survey	Cross	1973	48	Measures principal, specific job satisfactions related only to shop-floor workers

Note. Information from *The experience of work* by Cook et al., 1981. New York: Academic Press.

decade. A final difference among these scales relates to their length, which varies from a total of only 3 items (Social, Rewards, and Pay Satisfaction) to a high of 48 items (Worker Opinion Survey).

Analysis of reliability and validity assessments of specific job satisfaction scales indicates values similar to those for overall job satisfaction measures, but with greater variability due to broader coverage of job features. That is, most instruments included in this group provide several subscales, each of which seeks to assess a different aspect of work. Subscales vary in length from a single item to as many as 75 items, and as such, can significantly differ in reliability.

Reliability information for the 11 specific job satisfaction measures discussed above is similar to that presented for the overall satisfaction instruments. Calculations do, however, stress subscale reliabilities and, as such, are the commonly calculated internal consistency measures. The correlation coefficients generally run well above rs of .70, which is not surprising because each scale seeks to include a homogeneous sample of items. Although some authors do not recommend obtaining total scores, if internal reliability coefficients are calculated for an entire scale, correlations will, of course, be even higher. In fact, coefficient alphas of over .90 for all 72 items of the Job Descriptive Index have been consistently reported (Cook et al., 1981). Test-retest reliability correlations reported for both subscale and total scores do, of course, run lower, Thus, test-retest correlations across 12 months on Porter's Need Satisfaction Questionnaire for 59 machine operators and 35 managers were $r = .45$ and $r = .67$, respectively. Similarly, test-retest stability correlations for the Pay subscale (JDI) have varied over 12 months from a low of $r = .29$ to a high of .73.

Two approaches are generally followed for determining validity assessment: correlation among subscales and correlations with other job satisfaction measures. For example, correlations among the eight subscales of Smith's Index of Organizational Reactions ranged from $r = .32$ to $r = .77$, which Cook et al. (1981) considered on the high side. They add, however, that "factor analyses to confirm the intended structure of the scale were encouraging, with clearly identifiable factors for each of the subscales . . ." (p. 41). Studies of the Job Descriptive Index by Smith et al. (1969) provide similar data for subscale relationships but tend to average lower correlations. Total validity information obtained by correlating the subscales and total job satisfaction scores of specific job satisfaction measures indicates that these associations are strong. Most particularly here, we refer to the Smith Index of Organizational Reactions and Smith et al.'s Job Descriptive Index (JDI). Both measures have had extensive research by the authors and many other researchers who have used the scales to measure how employees feel about their jobs. To illustrate, we cite the following: (a) Correlations of subscales of the Index of Organization Reactions with corresponding subscales of the Job Descriptive Index and Minnesota Satisfaction Questionnaire varied from $r = .39$ for Career Future to $r = .51$ for Kind of Work, and $r = .61$ for Co-Workers to $r = .71$ for Supervision, respectively. An interesting study by Smith (1977) reported that correlations of the Index of Organizations Reactions' subscales and managers' attendance levels varied as a function of weather and travel problems. Thus, correlations for 27 work groups averaged around $r = .45$ for the day following a severe snow storm, but $r = .00$ when weather and travel in another city presented no

problems, "indicating that attitudes and behavior are likely to be linked only in conditions where a person's freedom of choice is salient" (Cook et al., 1981, p. 41). (b) The five subscales of the JDI have been validated against three of the Overall Job Satisfaction measures listed earlier: Brayfield-Rothe, Hoppock, and Minnesota Satisfaction Questionnaire. Correlations vary for subscales, from a low of $r = .16$ to a high of $r = .73$. Similar relationships were found by Newman (1975) and Saal (1978) with the Lodahl and Kejners (1965) Job Involvement Scale. These studies represent just a few of the many investigations that have employed the Job Descriptive Index. And, as Cook et al. (1981) point out:

> The Job Descriptive Index will deservedly find a place in future research, but it is not without limitations. It was devised in the 1960's, before the upsurge of interest in intrinsic job characteristics, and its emphasis is therefore upon Extrinsic Satisfaction. (p. 58)

In summary, investigations on reliability and validity of specific job satisfaction scales again indicated that the numerous available scales varied not only in content coverage, but also in discriminability and consistency. Review of these findings clearly indicated that specific job satisfaction measures will continue to require analysis and development if we are to design and measure the "real" features of work associated with job satisfaction.

WHAT ABOUT THE FUTURE?

The Computer

Notwithstanding the incredible proliferation of computers in offices and homes, we believe that it is still a bit too early to forecast what effect the availability of computer technology will have on testing theory and practice in the industrial setting. Obviously, one consequence would be for the use of hierarchies of testing variables or clusters in the same fashion as in programmed instruction several years ago, where an individual, having demonstrated his/her proficiency at a particular level, is then instructed by the computer to go on to a higher level of question asking. This certainly is possible now with the use of computers and will probably be an increasing phenomenon in the next few years. A far wider range of abilities and predispositions might well be available to industrial decision makers through the use of questions and rich behavioral scenarios that are readily programmed on computers.

One of the major unsolved problems in testing, not only in industry but in other user domains, is the use of personality or noncognitive tests, discussed elsewhere in this volume. It is well known that a rather large number of failures, especially at the executive level, is due to personality factors rather than lack of competence or intellectual ability. Yet, personality related tests, inventories, schedules, and scales are considerably less creditable psychometrically than are the cognitive, intellectual, aptitude, or achievement tests. It is quite likely that this state of affairs will be ameliorated through the greater range of affective dimensions and the number of questions that can be asked on computer testing accessories, and this represents still another potential contribution of the computer to testing.

Individual Counseling

An effort has been made to argue on behalf of the propositions that increased counseling of employees, especially at the management level, might well enhance overall life satisfaction and increase job satisfaction (Perloff, 1982). If the individual were helped to see what his or her skills and potentials are *beyond* the job, this might help the employee feel better about the organization, less disgruntled, and even result in an increment to his or her productivity. We would think that more formal and comprehensive efforts on the part of psychologists, probably counseling psychologists, in industry would have these salutary effects, and we are hoping that such efforts will be made during the next decade or two.

CONCLUSION

In summary, we believe that this review has shown that psychologists and others involved in the human resource enterprise in industry have served their employers and workers well by the use of the objective procedures highlighted in this review. We are confident that we have seen only the tip of the iceberg, and that continued and expanded use of objective procedures in industry will help management and workers alike achieve their respective organizational and personal goals.

REFERENCES

Albright, L.E., Glennon, J.R., & Smith, W.J. (1963). *The uses of psychological tests in industry.* Cleveland: Allen.

American Psychological Association. (1981). *Ethical principles of psychologists.* Washington, DC: Author.

Arvey, R.D. (1979). *Fairness in selecting employees.* Reading, MA: Addison-Wesley.

Asher, J.J. (1972). The biographical item: Can it be improved? *Personnel Psychology,* 25, 251–269.

Asher, J.J., & Sciarrino, J.A. (1974). Realistic work sample tests: A review. *Personnel Psychology,* 27, 519–533.

Barnowe, J., Mangione, T.W., & Quinn, R.P. (1973). An empirically derived model of job satisfaction. In R.P. Quinn & T.W. Mangione (Eds)., *The 1969–70 survey of working conditions: Chronicle of an unfinished enterprise.* Ann Arbor, MI: Institute for Social Research.

Billings, R.S., & Cornelius, E.T., III. (1980). Dimensions of work outcomes: A multi-dimensional scaling approach. *Personnel Psychology,* 33, 151–162.

Boehm, V.R. (1982). Assessment centers and management development. In K.M. Rowland & G.R. Ferris (Eds.), *Personnel management.* Boston: Allyn & Bacon.

Bray, D.W., & Campbell, R.J. (1968). Selection of salesmen by means of an assessment center. *Journal of Applied Psychology,* 52, 36–41.

Bray, D.W., & Grant, D.L. (1966). The assessment center in the measurement of potential for business management. *Psychological monographs,* 80, (17, Whole No. 625).

Brayfield, A.H., & Rothe, H.F. (1951). An index of job satisfaction. *Journal of Applied Psychology,* 35, 307–311.

Brown, S.H. (1978). Long-term validity of a personal history item scoring procedure. *Journal of Applied Psychology,* 63, 673–676.

Brugnoli, G.A., Campion, J.E., & Basen, J.A. (1979). Racial bias in the use of work samples for personnel selection. *Journal of Applied Psychology,* 64, 119–123.

Bullock, R.P. (1952). Social factors related to job satisfaction: A technique for the measurement of job satisfaction. Columbus, OH: Bureau of Business Research, Ohio State University.

Byham, W.C. (1970). Assessment centers for spotting future managers. *Harvard Business Review,* 48, 150–167.

Byham, W.C. (1980). Starting an assessment center the correct way. *Personnel Administrator,* 25, 27–32.

Cammann, C., Fichman, M., Jenkins, D., & Klesh, J. (1979). *The Michigan Assessment Questionnaire.* Unpublished manuscript, University of Michigan, Ann Arbor, MI.

Campion, J.E. (1972). Work sampling for personnel selection. *Journal of Applied Psychology,* 56, 40–44.

Carlson, R.E., Thayer, P.W., Mayfield, E.C., & Peterson, D.A. (1971). Improvements in the selection interview, *Personnel Journal,* 50, 268–275.

Cascio, W.F. (1975). Accuracy of verifiable biographical information blank responses. *Journal of Applied Psychology,* 60, 767–769.

Cascio, W.F. (1982). *Applied psychology in personnel management* (2nd ed.). Reston, VA: Reston Publishing Company.

Cascio, W.F., & Phillips, N. (1979). Performance testing: A rose among thorns? *Personnel Psychology*, 32, 751–766.

Chun, K., Cobb, S., & French, J.R.P., Jr. (1975). *Measures for psychological assessment: A guide to 3,000 original sources and their application.* Ann Arbor, MI: Institute for Social Research.

Cohen, S.L., Moses, J.L., & Byham, W.C. (1974). *The validity of assessment centers: A literature review.* Monograph II. Pittsburgh: Development Dimensions International.

Committee to Develop Joint Technical Standards for Educational and Psychological Testing. (1983). *Joint technical standards for educational and psychological testing.* Washington, DC: American Psychological Association.

Cook, J., & Wall, T.D. (1980). New work attitude measures of trust, organizational commitment and personal need non-fulfillment. *Journal of Occupational Psychology*, 53, 39–52.

Cook, J.D., Hepworth, S.J., Wall, T.D., & Warr, P.B. (1981). *The experience of work.* New York: Academic Press.

Cross, D. (1973). The worker opinion survey: A measure of shop-floor satisfaction. *Occupational Psychology*, 47, 193–208.

Dunnette, M.D., & Borman, W.C. (1979). Personnel selection and classification systems. *Annual Review of Psychology*, 30, 477–525.

England, G.W. (1971). *Development and use of weighted application blanks* (rev. ed.). Minneapolis: University of Minnesota Industrial Relations Center.

England, G.W., & Paterson, D.G. (1960). Selection and placement—The past ten years. In H.G. Henneman, L.C. Brown, M.K. Chandler, R. Kahn, H.S. Parnes, & G.P. Shultz (Eds.), *Employment relations research: A summary and appraisal.* New York: Harper & Brothers Publishers.

Finkle, R.B. (1976). Managerial assessment centers. In M.D. Dunnette (Ed.), *Handbook of industrial and organizational psychology.* Chicago: Rand McNally.

Ghiselli, E.E. (1966a). *The validity of occupational aptitude tests.* New York: Wiley.

Ghiselli, E.E. (1966b). The validity of a personnel interview. *Personnel Psychology*, 19, 389–394.

Ghiselli, E.E. (1973). The validity of aptitude tests in personnel selection. *Personnel Psychology*, 26, 461–477.

Ghiselli, E.E., & Barthol, R.P. (1953). The validity of personality inventories in the selection of employees. *Journal of Applied Psychology*, 38, 18–20.

Ghiselli, E.E., & Brown, C.W. (1955). *Personnel and industrial psychology* (2nd ed.). New York: McGraw-Hill.

Guion, R.M. (1965). *Personnel testing.* New York: McGraw-Hill.

Guion, R.M., & Gottier, R.F. (1965). Validity of personality measures in personnel selection. *Personnel Psychology*, 18, 135–164.

Hackman, J.R., & Oldham, G.R. (1975). Development of the job diagnostic survey, *Journal of Applied Psychology*, 60, 159–170.

Hakel, M.D. (1982). Employment interviewing. In K.M. Rowland & G.R. Ferris (Eds.), *Personnel management.* Boston: Allyn & Bacon.

Hinrichs, J.R., Haanpera, S., & Sonkin, L. (1976). Validity of a biographical information blank across national boundaries. *Personnel Psychology*, 29, 417–421.

Hollon, C.J., & Chesser, R.J. (1976). The relationship of personal influence dissonance to job tension, satisfaction and involvement. *Academy of Management Journal*, 19, 308–314.

Hoppock, R. (1935). *Job satisfaction.* New York: Harper & Brothers.

Howard, A. (1974). An assessment of assessment centers. *Academy of Management Journals*, 17, 115–134.

Huck, J.R. (1973). Assessment Centers: A review of the external and internal validities. *Personnel Psychology*, 26, 191–212.

Huck, J.R., & Bray, D.W. (1976). Management assessment center evaluations and subsequent job performance of white and black females. *Personnel Psychology*, 29, 13–30.

Hunter, J.E., & Schmidt, F.L. (1982). Ability tests: Economic benefits versus the issue of fairness. *Industrial Relations*, 21, 293–308.

Jaffee, C.L., & Cohen, S.L. (1980). Improving human resource effectiveness through assessment center technology: Emergence, design, application and evaluation. In E.L. Miller, E.H. Burack, & M. Albrecht (Eds.), *Management of human resources.* Englewood Cliffs, NJ: Prentice-Hall.

Jaffee, C.L., Cohen, S.L., & Cherry, R. (1972). Supervisory selection program for disadvantaged or minority employees. *Training and Developmental Journal*, 26, 22–28.

James, L.R., & Jones, A.P. (1980). Perceived job characteristics and job satisfaction: An examination of reciprocal causation. *Personnel Psychology*, 33, 97–135.

Kahn, R.L., Wolfe, D.M., Quinn, R.P., Snoeck, J.D., & Rosenthal, R. (1964). *Organizational stress: Studies in role conflict and ambiguity.* New York: Wiley.

Klimoski, R.J., & Strikland, W.J. (1977). Assessment Centers—Valid or merely prescient. *Personnel Psychology*, 30, 353–361.

Kraut, A.I. (1976). New frontiers for assessment centers. *Personnel*, 53, 30–38.

Latham, G.P., Saari, L.M., Pursell, E.D., & Campion, M.A. (1980). The situational interview. *Journal of Applied Psychology*, 65, 422–427.

Lake, D.G., Miles, M.B., & Earle, R.B. (Eds.). (1973). *Measuring human behavior: Tools for the assessment of social functioning.* New York: Teachers College Press.

Landy, F.J., & Farr, J.L. (1980). Performance rating. *Psychological Bulletin*, 37, 72–107.

Latham, G.P., Wexley, K.N., & Pursell, E.D. (1975). Training managers to minimize rating errors in the observation of behavior. *Journal of Applied Psychology*, 60, 550–555.

Lent, R.H., Aurbach, H.D., & Levin, L.S. (1971). Predictors, criteria, and significant results. *Personnel Psychology*, 24, 519–533.

Linn, R.L. (1978). Single group validity, differential validity, and differential prediction. *Journal of Applied Psychology*, 63, 507–512.

Locke, E.A., & Hulin, C.L. (1962). A review and evaluation of the validity studies of activity vector analysis. *Personnel Psychology*, 15, 25–42.

Lodahl, T., & Kejner, M. (1965). The definition and measurement of job involvement. *Journal of Applied Psychology*, 49, 24–33.

Mayfield, E.C., Brown, S.H., & Hamstra, B.W. (1980). Selection interviewing in the life insurance industry: An update of research and practice. *Personnel Psychology*, 33, 725–739.

McCormick, E.J., & Winstanley, N.B. (1950). A fifteen-minute oral trade test. *Personnel*, 27, 144–146.

McMurray, R.N. (1947). Validating the patterned interview. *Personnel*, 23, 263–272.

Miles, R.H. (1975). An empirical test of causal influence between role perceptions of conflict and ambiguity and various personal outcomes. *Journal of Applied Psychology*, 60, 334–339.

Miller, D.C. (1977). *Handbook of research design and social measurement* (3rd ed.). New York: David MacKay.

Mosel, J.N., & Cozan, C.W. (1952). The accuracy of application blank work histories. *Journal of Applied Psychology*, 36, 365–369.

Moses, J.L., & Boehm, V.R. (1975). Relationship of assessment center performance to management progress of women. *Journal of Applied Psychology*, 60, 527–529.

Munsterberg, H. (1913). *Psychology and industrial efficiency*. Boston: Houghton Mifflin.

Newman, J.E. (1975). Understanding the organizational structure—job attitude relationship through perceptions of the work environment. *Organizational Behavior and Human Performance*, 14, 371–397.

Norton, S.D. (1977). The empirical and content validity of assessment centers vs. traditional methods for predicting managerial success. *Academy of Management Review*, 2, 442–453.

Owens, W.A. (1976). Background data. In M.D. Dunnette (Ed.), *Handbook of industrial and organizational psychology*. Chicago: Rand McNally.

Owens, W.A., & Schoenfeldt, L.F. (1979). Toward a classification of persons. *Jouernal of Applied Psychology*, 65, 569–607.

Pace, L.A., & Schoenfeldt, L.F. (1977). Legal concerns in the use of weighted applications. *Personnel Psychology*, 30, 159–166.

Paterson, D.G. (1957). The conservation of human talent. *American Psychologist*, 12, 134–144.

Parker, T.C. (1980). Assessment centers: A statistical study. *Personnel Administrator*, 25, 65–57.

Perlman, J., Schmidt, F.L., & Hunter, J.E. (1980). Validity generalization results for tests used to predict training success and job proficiency in clerical occupations. *Journal of Applied Psychology*, 65, 373–406.

Perloff, R. (1982). The case for life satisfaction counseling as a critical role for the counseling psychologist in industry. *The Counseling Psychologist*, 10, 41–44.

Porter, L.W. (1961). A study of perceived need satisfactions in bottom and middle management jobs. *Journal of Applied Psychology*, 45, 1–10.

Pursell, E.D., Campion, M.A., & Gaylord, S.R. (1980). Structured interviewing: Avoiding selection problems. *Personnel Journal*, 59, 907–912.

Quinn, R., & Cobb, W. (1971). *What workers want: Factor analyses of importance ratings of job facets*. Ann Arbor, MI: Institute for Social Research.

Quinn, R.P., & Shepard, L.J. (1974). *The 1972–73 quality of employment survey*. Ann Arbor, MI: Institute for Social Research, University of Michigan.

Quinn, R.P., & Staines, G.L. (1979). *The 1977 Quality of Employment Survey*. Ann Arbor, MI: Institute for Social Research.

Reilly, R.R., & Chao, G.T. (1982). Validity and fairness of some alternative employee selection procedures. *Personnel Psychology*, 35, 1–62.

Rice, R.W., Near, J.P., & Hunt, R.G. (1980). The job-satisfaction/life-satisfaction relationship: A review of empirical research. *Basic and Applied Social Psychology*, 1, 37–64.

Robinson, J.P., Athanasion, R., & Head, K.B. (1969). *Measures of occupational attitudes and occupational characteristics*. Ann Arbor, MI: Institute for Social Research.

Robinson, J.P., & Shaver, P.R. (1973). *Measures of social psychological attitudes*. Ann Arbor, MI: Institute for Social Research.

Roethlisberger, F.J., & Dickson, W.J. (1939). *Management and the worker*. Cambridge, MA: Harvard University Press.

Saal, F.E. (1978). Job involvement: A multivariate approach. *Journal of Applied Psychology*, 63, 53–61.

Sackett, P.D., & Hakel, M.D. (1979). Temporal stability and individual differences in using assessment information to form overall ratings. *Organizational Behavior and Human Performance*, 23, 120–137.

Schmidt, F.L., & Hunter, J.E. (1977). Development of a general solution to the problem of validity generalization. *Journal of Applied Psychology*, 62, 529–540.

Schmidt, F.L., & Hunter, J.E. (1981). Employment testing: Old theories and new research findings. *American Psychologist*, 36, 1128–1137.

Schmidt, F.L. (1977). Job sample vs. paper-and-pencil trades and technical tests: Adverse impact and examinee attitudes. *Personnel Psychology*, 30, 187–197.

Schmidt, F.L., Hunter, J.E., & Pearlman, K. (1981). Task differences and validity of aptitude tests in selection: A red herring. *Journal of Applied Psychology*, 66, 166–185.

Schmidt, N. (1976). Social and situational determinants of interview decisions: Implications for the employment interview. *Personnel Psychology*, 26, 79–101.

Schmitt, N. (1977). Interrater Agreement in dimensionality and combination of assessment center judgments. *Journal of Applied Psychology*, 62, 171–176.

Schmitt, N., Coyle, B.W., White, J.K., & Rauschenberger, J. (1978). Background, needs, job perceptions, and job satisfaction: A causal model. *Personnel Psychology*, 31, 889–901.

Schoenfeldt, L.F. (1974). Utilization of manpower: Development and evaluation of an assessment classification model for matching individuals with jobs. *Journal of Applied Psychology*, 59, 583–595.

Schrader, A.D., & Oburn, H.G. (1977). Biodata faking: Effects of induced subtlety and position specificity. *Personnel Psychology*, 30, 395–404.

Schriesheim, C.A., & Murphy, C.J. (1976). Relationships between leader behavior and subordinate satisfaction and performance: A test of some additional moderators. *Journal of Applied Psychology*, **61**, 634–641.

Schwab, D.P., & Heneman, H.G. (1969). Relationship between interview structure and inter-interviewer reliability in an employment situation. *Journal of Applied Psychology*, **53**, 214–217.

Scott, W.D., Clothier, R.C., & Spriegel, W.R. (1949). *Personnel management* (4th ed.) New York: McGraw-Hill.

Smith, F.J. (1962). *Problems and trends in the operational use of employee attitude measurements.* Paper presented at the annual meeting of the American Psychological Association.

Smith, F.J. (1977). Work attitudes as predictors of attendance on a specific day. *Journal of Applied Psychology*, **62**, 16–19.

Smith, P.C., Kendall, L.M., & Hulin, C.L. (1969). *The measurement of satisfaction in work and retirement.* Chicago: Rand-McNally.

Stahl, M.J., Manley, T.R., & NcNichols, C.W. (1978). Operationalizing the Muskos institution—occupation model: An application of Gouldner's Cosmopolitan—local research. *Journal of Applied Psychology*, **63**, 422–427.

Stead, W.H., Shartle, C.L., Otis, J.L., Ward, R.S., Osborne, H.F., Endler, O.L., Dvorak, B.J., Cooper, J.H., Bellows, R.M., & Kolbe, L.E. (Eds.). (1940). *Occupational counseling techniques.* New York: American Book Company.

Stone, E.F., Mowday, R.T., & Porter, L.W. (1977). Higher-order need strengths as moderators of the job scope—job satisfaction relationship. *Journal of Applied Psychology*, **62**, 466–471.

Task Force on Assessment Center Standards. (1980). Standards and ethical considerations for assessment center operations. *Personnel Administrator*, **25**, 35–39.

Taylor, J.C., & Bowers, D.G. (1972). *Survey of organizations: A machine scored standardized questionnaire instrument.* Ann Arbor, MI: Institute for Social Research.

Ulrich, L., & Trumbo, D. (1965). The selection interview since 1949. *Psychological Bulletin*, **63**, 100–116.

Valenzi, E.R., & Andrews, I.R. (1973). Individual differences in the decision process of employment interviewers. *Journal of Applied Psychology*, **58**, 49–53.

Viteles, M.S. (1932). *Industrial psychology.* New York: W.W. Norton.

Vroom, V.H. (1960). *Some personality determinants of the effects of participation.* Englewood Cliffs, NJ: Prentice-Hall.

Wagner, R. (1949). The employment interview: A critical review. *Personnel Psychology*, **2**, 17–46.

Wanous, J.P. (1974). A causal-correlational analysis of the job satisfaction and performance relationship. *Journal of Applied Psychology*, **59**, 139–144.

Warr, P.B., Cook, J., & Wall, T.D. (1979). Scales for the measurement of some work attitudes and aspects of psychological well-being. *Journal of Occupational Psychology*, **52**, 129–148.

Warr, P.B., & Routledge, T. (1969). An opinion scale for the study of managers' job satisfaction. *Occupational Psychology*, **43**, 95–109.

Weaver, C.N. (1978). Job satisfaction as a component of happiness among males and females. *Personnel Psychology*, **31**, 831–840.

Webster, E.D. (1964). *Decision making in the employment interview.* Montreal: Eagle.

Weiss, D.J., & Dawis, R.V. (1960). An objective validation of factual interview data. *Journal of Applied Psychology*, **40**, 381–385.

Weiss, D.J., Dawis, R.V., England, G.W., & Lofquist, L.H. (1967). *Manual for the Minnesota Satisfaction Questionnaire.* Minneapolis, MN: Industrial Relations Center, University of Minnesota.

Wernimont, P.F., & Campbell, J.P. (1968). Signs, samples, and criteria. *Journal of Applied Psychology*, **52**, 372–376.

AUTHOR INDEX

Marx, N., 282, 290
Masek, B.J., 370, 391, 399
Mash, E.J., 351, 353, 354, 361, 365, 367–369, 390, 392, 397, 398
Masters, J.C., 371, 399
Matarazzo, J.D., 79, 82, 83, 85, 86, 93–95, 97, 98, 111, 115, 151, 155, 238, 242, 244, 255, 276, 290, 383, 398
Mataya, P., 317, 330
Matson, J.L., 361, 367, 379, 380, 382, 398
Matthews, C.G., 192, 208, 249, 255
Mattis, S., 224, 233
Maultsby, M.C., 272, 274
Mavissakalian, M.G., 382, 383, 385, 398
Maxwell, A.E., 298, 303
Mayeux, R., 247, 253, 255
Mayfield, E.C., 131, 424, 438
Mayman, M., 261, 274, 339, 346
McAfee, R.D., 383, 395
McCall, R.B., 220, 233
McCall-Perez, F., 136, 155
McCarthy, C.E., 317, 330
McCarthy, D., 71, 75, 135, 155
McCarthy, F.D., 281, 289
McCarthy, J.J., 224, 232
McCormick, E.J., 427, 438
McCue, M., 205, 208
McDonald-Scott, P., 302, 303
McFall, R.M., 370, 373, 383, 390, 392, 398, 399
McFarling, D., 246, 255
McFie, J., 4, 15, 242, 255
McFillen, J.M., 131
MGonigle, J.J., 359, 368
McGough, W.E., 410, 420
McGovern, K., 382, 394
McGuire, J.M., 86, 97
McHugh, P.R., 5, 14, 270, 271, 274
McIntyre, T.J., 378, 387, 399
McIver, J.P., 46, 53
McKay, S., 202, 208
McKee, J., 247, 254
McKelpin, J.C., 109, 115
McKinley, J.C., 309, 313
McKnew, D., 271, 274, 285, 289
McLaren, S.M., 417, 419
McLean, P.D., 10, 15, 412, 419
McLean, R.S., 326, 327, 330
McMahon, R.C., 217, 233
McMahon, R.J., 356
McMurray, R.N., 425, 438
McNair, D.M., 308, 330, 409, 419
McNemar, O., 304
McNichols, C.W., 432, 439
McPherson, F.M., 417, 419
McReynolds, P., 330, 367
McReynolds. W.T., 412, 419
McVaugh, M., 292, 303
Meachum, J., 235

Mead, R.J., 50, 53
Meador, A.E., 365, 367
Meadows, J.C., 237, 253, 255
Meehl, P.E., 5, 7, 15, 19, 33, 36, 307, 308, 314, 330, 414, 418
Meeker, M.N., 63, 69, 75
Megargee, E.I., 314, 315, 330
Mehrens, W.A., 125, 129, 131
Meichenbaum, D.H., 218, 233, 353, 367, 412, 419
Meier, M.J., 188, 197, 209, 248, 249, 255
Meili-Dworetzki, G., 338, 346
Melamed, B.G., 370, 382, 398
Meltzer, H.Y., 271, 273
Melver, J.P., 46
Mendelson, M., 304
Mendlewicz, J., 234
Menninger, K.A., 5, 15, 261, 274, 293, 294, 303
Mercer, J., 134, 140, 142, 144, 145, 148, 151, 152, 155
Merluzzi, T.V., 370, 374, 381, 391, 398
Merrill, M.A., 53, 63, 64, 76, 78, 81, 98
Messick, S., 140, 149, 151, 154, 155, 373, 399
Mesthene, E.G., 307, 330
Mesulam, M.-M., 246, 255
Meyer, A., 260, 274, 294, 303, 414, 419
Meyer, E. III, 411, 419
Meyer, M.M., 346
Meyer, P., 271, 274
Meyers, A., 376, 391, 395
Meyers, C., 139, 155
Michael, J., 393, 399
Michael, W.B., 29, 37
Michelberg, J., 65, 75
Michels, R., 272, 274
Mikhael, M., 186, 208
Milby, J.B., 412, 418
Miles, J.E., 10, 15
Miles, M.B., 429
Miles, R.H., 432, 437, 438
Mille, M., 143, 146, 156
Miller, A.S., 337, 345
Miller, D.C., 429, 438
Miller, E.L., 437
Miller, J.W., 210, 216, 232
Miller, L.C., 156, 357, 358, 367
Miller, M.J., 174, 176, 414, 419
Miller, P.M., 14, 370, 371, 373, 380, 381, 384, 385, 390, 391, 395, 398, 399
Millman, J., 112, 115
Millon, T., 19, 37, 309, 330
Milner, B., 187, 209, 245, 255
Miner, J.B., 157, 176
Minskoff, E., 136, 155
Mirkin, P.K., 136, 153, 156, 271, 274
Mischel, W., 353, 367, 371, 373, 399
Miskimins, R.W., 414, 419
Mitchell, B.C., 101, 115
Mitchell, C., 393, 396
Mittman, B.L., 338, 344, 345

SUBJECT INDEX

ABOUT THE EDITORS
AND CONTRIBUTORS

The Editors

Gerald Goldstein (Ph.D., University of Kansas, 1962) is coordinator for Research and Development at the Highland Drive Veterans Administration Medical Center and Associate Professor of Psychiatry and Psychology at the University of Pittsburgh. He has authored and co-authored numerous articles, chapters and books in the area of clinical neuropsychology, which is his major research interest. He is on the editorial board of *Clinical Psychology Review*, *The Journal of Behavioral Assessment*, and *Clinical Neuropsychology*, and is Secretary of the Division of Clinical Neuropsychology of the American Psychological Association.

Michel Hersen (Ph.D., State University of New York at Buffalo, 1966) is Professor of Psychiatry and Psychology at the University of Pittsburgh. He is the Past President of the Association of Behavior Therapy. He has co-authored and co-edited 36 books including: *Single-Case Experimental Designs: Strategies for Studying Behavior Change (1st edition)*, *Behavior Therapy in the Psychiatric Setting*, *Behavior Modification: An Introductory Textbook*, *Introduction to Clinical Psychology*, *International Handbook of Behavior Modification and Therapy*, *Outpatient*

Behavior Therapy: A Clinical Guide, *Issues in Psychotherapy Research*, *Handbook of Child Psychopathology*, *The Clinical Psychology Handbook*, and *Adult Psychopathology and Diagnosis*. With Alan S. Bellack, he is editor and founder of *Behavior Modification* and *Clinical Psychology Review*. He is Associate Editor of *Addictive Behaviors* and Editor of *Progress in Behavior Modification*. Dr. Hersen is the recipient of several grants from the National Institute of Mental Health, the National Institute of Handicapped Research, and the March of Dimes Birth Defects Foundation.

The Contributors

James N. Butcher (Ph.D., University of North Carolina, 1964), is Professor of Psychology and the former Director of the Clinical Psychology Training Program at the University of Minnesota. Dr. Butcher is an Associate Editor of the *Journal of Consulting and Clinical Psychology*. He had written numerous articles on objective personality assessment, abnormal psychology and brief psychotherapy, and recently edited, with Philip Kendall, the *Handbook of Research Methods in Clinical Psychology*.

467

Anthony J. Costello (Medical Training at University College and University College Hopsital, London, 1962). His post-graduate training was at the Royal Free Hospital, The Institute of Psychiatry and the Maudsley Hospital, and The Hospital for Sick Children, all in London, England. He subsequently worked for the Medical Research Council Unit on the Study of Environmental Factors on Physical and Mental Disease, before coming to Pittsburgh where he is now Medical Director of the Child Psychiatric Treatment Service at Western Psychiatric Institute and Clinic. His main interests are in assessment and the recording of child behavior, and he has explored a wide range of techniques ranging from electronic recording of mother-infant interaction to structured interviewing.

James A. Craft (Ph.D., University of California, Berkeley, 1968) is Professor of Business Administration at the University of Pittsburgh. His major areas of teaching and research include human resources management, industrial relations, and organizational behavior. Dr. Craft is Coordinator of the Human Resources Interest Group in the Graduate School of Business, a member of the editorial board of *Human Resources Planning*, and the author of numerous articles and monographs relating to human resources management.

Craig Edelbrock (Ph.D., Oregon State University, 1976) is Assistant Professor of Psychiatry at the University of Pittsburgh School of Medicine. His major interests are developmental psychopathology and the assessment of children's behavior disorders. He serves on the editorial board of the *Journal of Consulting and Clinical Psychology* and the *Journal of Abnormal Child Psychology*. Among his recent publications are chapters in the *Handbook of Child Psychopathology* and the *Annual Review of Psychology*.

Joan G. Ehler (M.D., University of Pittsburgh, 1958) is Assistant Professor of Psychology in the Department of Psychiatry at the University of Pittsburgh School of Medicine and Western Psychiatric Institute and Clinic. Her major area of interest is in the treatment of mood disorders. She is also a consultant to the Vocational Rehabilitation Center in Pittsburgh.

Philip Erdberg (Ph.D., University of Alabama, 1969) is a diplomate in clinical psychology of the American Board of Professional Psychology. His professional interests are in the use of psychological assessment in treatment planning and evaluation, and he is a consulting psychologist for a variety of schools, agencies, and treatment facilities in the San Francisco area. He has taught in academic, clinical, and postdoctoral settings and, since 1977, has been an instructor for Rorschach Workshops.

John E. Exner, Jr. (Ph.D. Cornell University, 1958) is the Executive Director of the Rorschach Research Foundation and a Professor of Psychology at Long Island University. He is the author of six books concerning the Rorschach Test, including the three volume series, *The Rorschach: A Comprehensive System*, plus more than 50 articles covering a variety of issues in psychopathology and intervention.

Jack M. Fletcher (Ph.D., University of Florida, 1978) is Chief, Developmental Neuropsychology Section, Texas Research Institute of Mental Sciences. He is also an Associate Professor of Psychology at the University of Houston in the Neuropsychology and Developmental programs. Dr. Fletcher has published widely on the neuropsychology of learning disabilities and brain injuries in children.

Lynn H. Fox (Ph.D., The Johns Hopkins University, 1974) is a professor of education in the Evening College and Summer Session of The Johns Hopkins University. Her research interests are primarily in sex differences in mathematical achievement and education, particularly mathematics education for the academically gifted. She holds a B.S.Ed. with specialization in mathematics, and a M.Ed. in Educational Psychology from the University of Florida. Her M.A. and Ph.D. are in Developmental and Educational Psychology from The Johns Hopkins University. She has had research grants from the Spencer Foundation, The Robert Sterling Clark Foundation, the National Institute of Education and has served on the SAT advisory Committee for the College Board and as a consultant to the Ford Foundation. She is a co-editor of *Mathematical talent: Discovery, description and development*, the *Learning disabled/gifted: Identification and Issues*, and *Women and the Mathematical Mystique*. She is the author of numerous journal articles and book chapters including an article on the use of tests for the identification of the academically talented for a special issue of the *American Psychologist* and a chapter on educational programs for the gifted for a special publication on the gifted for the American Psychological Association.

Michael D. Franzen (Ph.D., Southern Illinois University at Carbondale, 1983) is a post-doctoral fellow in clinical neuropsychology at the University of Nebraska Medical Center. He has published several papers in the areas of psychophysiology, neuropsychology, and psychometric methodology. His current research interests are in scale construction and psychometric methodology in neuropsychological assessment.

Charles Golden (Ph.D.) is currently Professor of Medical Psychology at the University of Nebraska Medical Center. His work is primarily in the area of research and clinical work in neuropsychology, as well as supervision of interns and post-doctoral fellows in neuropsychology. He is best known for his work on the Luria-Nebraska Neuropsychological Battery. He is the author of a number of books including *Diagnosis and Rehabilitation in Clinical Neuropsychology*, *Interpretation of the Halstead-Reitan*, and *Item Interpretation of the Luria-Nebraska Neuropsychological Battery*. Dr. Golden is a 1975 graduate of the University of Hawaii.

Kerry deS. Hamsher (Ph.D., University of Iowa, 1977) is Assistant Professor of Neurology at the University of Wisconsin Medical School, Milwaukee Clinical Campus, and Director of Neuropsychology at Mount Sinai Medical Center, Milwaukee, Wisconsin. He was formerly a Research Scientist in the Benton Laboratory of Neuropsychology in the Department of Neurology at the University of Iowa. His major areas of interest include the development of neuropsychological assessment instruments, disorders of visuospatial perception, the aphasias, dementia, and related disorders. Dr. Hamsher has authored and co-authored many research articles and recently co-authored *Contributions to Neuropsychological Assessment: A Clinical Manual* describing some of the tests developed in the Benton Laboratory. He has been an ad hoc reviewer for scientific journals in psychology, neuropsychology, and neurology.

Jo-Ida C. Hansen (Ph.D., University of Minnesota, 1974) is Professor of Psychology and Director of the Center for Interest Measurement Research at the University of Minnesota. She has authored many articles in journals and has presented papers on vocational interest measurement at national and international meetings. She is co-author of the Strong-Campbell Interest Inventory, author of the *Interpretive Guide to the SCII*, and was project director for the 1981 and 1985 revisions of the SCII. Dr. Hansen received the E.K. Strong, Jr. Gold Medal award in recognition of her contributions to vocational interest measurement and interest inventory development in 1983 and was elected a Fellow in Division 17 (Counseling) of the American Psychological Association in 1984.

Stephen N. Haynes (Ph.D., University of Colorado, 1971) is Professor of Psychology at Southern Illinois University—Carbondale. He has authored numerous books, chapters, and articles in the areas of behavioral assessment, medical psychology, and experimental psychopathology.

Laura S. Keller (B.A., St. Olaf College, 1980), is a doctoral student in clinical psychology at the University of Minnesota. Before entering graduate school, she worked as a data analyst in the Department of Medical Statistics and Epidemiology at the Mayo Clinic. She is presently a Research Coordinator on the University of Minnesota's national MMPI Restandardization Project and is also employed as a Research Associate at Assessment Systems Corporation in St. Paul, Minnesota, developing automated psychological test interpretive reports. Her interest areas include test personality assessment, computer applications to psychological assessment, and behavioral medicine.

James E. Lindemann (Ph.D., The Pennsylvania State University, 1954) is Professor of Medical Psychology at the Crippled Children's Division of the Oregon Health Sciences University. His major interests are in physical disability, cognitive and social development, and rehabilitation planning. He is the author of *Psychological and Behavioral Aspects of Physical Disability*.

Joseph D. Matarazzo (Ph.D., Northwestern University, 1952) is Professor and Chair, Department of Medical Psychology, School of Medicine, Oregon Health Sciences University, Portland, Oregon. He is the author of the *Fifth Edition of Wechsler's Measurement and Appraisal of Adult*

Intelligence, has published many articles on psychology as a science and a profession, and serves on the editorial board of a number of scientific and scholarly journals.

Alice E. Meador (B.A., University of Virginia, 1979) is a doctoral student in clinical psychology at Virginia Polytechnic Institute and State University. She is currently completing her predoctoral internship at the University of New Mexico Medical Center. Her major areas of interest include social skills training with children, cognitive-behavioral procedures, and child behavioral assessment. Ms. Meador's most recent research has appeared in *Child and Family Behavior Therapy*.

Robert W. Motta (Ph.D., Hofstra University, New York 1975) is an Assistant Professor of Psychology. He is the Director of The Doctoral Program in School-Community Psychology at Hofstra and is the supervisor of Educational Counseling in Hofstra's Clinical and School Doctoral Program. Dr. Motta has authored and co-authored a number of articles in the area of childhood learning and behavioral difficulties and recently co-authored a chapter on the development and use of group intelligence test measures.

Thomas H. Ollendick (Ph.D., Purdue University, 1971) is currently Professor of Psychology and Associate Department Head at Virginia Polytechnic Institute and State University. He has held former positions at the Devereux Foundation, Indiana State University, and Western Psychiatric Institute and Clinic. He has co-authored *Clinical Behavior Therapy with Children* with Jerome Cerny and co-edited the *Handbook of Child Psychopathology* and *Child Behavioral Assessment* with Michel Hersen. The author of several research articles and chapters, he is currently on the editorial board of six journals and on the Executive Committee of APA's Division 12 Section I on Clinical Child Psychology.

Evelyn Perloff (Ph.D., Ohio State University) is Associate Professor of Nursing Research and of Psychology at the University of Pittsburgh. Her areas of expertise in psychological measurement include not only applications to business and industry but also those involving mental and physical health. She is currently developing an extensive Instrument File (checklist, interview protocols, questionnaires, rating skills, tests) in these areas.

Robert Perloff has been active on a number of fronts in the field of testing and measurement, including his position as Director of Research and Developments for Science Research Associates and the publication of a number of articles in testing and the field of program evaluation. A former President of the Eastern Psychological Association and of the Evaluation Research Society, he is currently President-Elect of the American Psychological Association and his current position is Professor of Business Administration and of Psychology at the University of Pittsburgh.

Mark D. Reckase (Ph.D., Syracuse University, 1972) is Assistant Vice President of the Assessment Programs Area of The American College Testing Program (ACT). Before coming to ACT, he was Associate Professor of Educational Psychology at the University of Missouri-Columbia. He has authored and co-authored many articles and book chapters on psychometric theory and statistical analysis, and for the past seven years has performed funded research on statistical models of test performance for the Office of Naval Research.

Daniel J. Reschly (Ph.D., University of Oregon, 1971) is Professor of Psychology and Professional Studies in Education and Director of School Psychology Graduate Program at Iowa State University. Reschly has authored numerous articles dealing with psychological testing, the mildly handicapped, minority students, and legal guidelines. He has edited the *School Psychology Review* and served as President of the National Association of School Psychologists in 1984–85.

Paul Satz (Ph.D., University of Kentucky) is Professor of Psychiatry at the University of California at Los Angeles and is a staff member at Camarillo State Hospital. He previously was Professor at the University of Florida, School of Medicine and was Visiting Professor of Psychology at the University of Victoria, British Columbia. Dr. Satz is renowned for his work in experimental neuropsychology with children suffering from dyslexia and other learning disabilities. Dr. Satz is past President of the International Neuropsychology Society. In 1977 he received the Albert J. Harris Award for research distinction in reading disabilities from the International Reading Association. He serves on a number of editorial boards, study sections, research advisory panels, etc., and is a member of several learned and professional societies.

Robert F. Sawicki (Ph.D., Kent State University, 1983) is a neuropsychologist at Community Hospital of Indianapolis. His research interests are in scale construction in neuropsychological assessment and the neuropsychology of neurological disorders.

Iradj Siassi (M.D., Indiana University Medical School, 1963) is Professor of Psychiatry at University of California at Los Angeles (UCLA). His major areas of interest include practice of Psychodynamic psychotherapy, and applications of psychoanalytive principles to working with patients from non-Western cultures. He has published and presented over 100 articles/papers and presently is on the Editorial Board of two major professional journals.

Duane G. Spiker (M.D., Ohio State University, 1971) is Associate Professor of Psychiatry at the University of Pittsburgh School of Medicine in Pittsburgh, Pennsylvania. He is Medical Director of the Mood Disorders Module at Western Psychiatric Institute and Clinic, Department of Psychiatry, University of Pittsburgh. He has authored, co-authored, and presented over 75 articles/papers; and is a reviewer for the *American Journal of Psychiatry*. His major research interests are in the diagnosis and treatment of Affective Disorders.

H. Gerry Taylor (Ph.D.) is an Assistant Professor of Pediatrics and Psychiatry at the University of Pittsburgh School of Medicine, and a pediatric neuropsychologist at Children's Hospital of Pittsburgh. After receiving his Ph.D. in developmental psychology from the University of Iowa, he worked as a fellow on the Florida Longitudinal Dyslexia Project with Dr. Satz. For the past several years, Dr. Taylor has been actively involved in the assessment of children with learning and neurological disorders. His research has focused on clarifying the neuropsychological deficits associated with these disorders as an aid to improved diagnosis and treatment.

Julia R. Vane (Ph.D., New York University, 1951) is Professor of Psychology at Hofstra University. She is Chair of the Department of Psychology and Director of the Doctoral Programs in Psychology at Hofstra. She is a Diplomate in Clinical and in School Psychology. She has published the Vane Kindergarten Test and Vane Language Test and has authored a number of articles in the area of behavioral and clinical assessment. She is past president of the Nassau County Psychological Assoc., past president of the Division of School Psychologists of the American Psychological Association, a member of the New York State Board for Psychology, and a member of the Commissioner's Task Force on Professional Education in New York State. She has been a consulting editor for the *Journal of Educational Research*, *Journal of School Psychology*, and the *Journal of Clinical Psychology*.

J. Richard Wittenborn (Ph.D., University of Illinois, 1942), University Professor of Psychology and Education at Rutgers University, has published numerous reports describing the conceptualization and quantification of various aspects of human behavior, including the development of rating scales and the design of clinical investigation. He has been active in the development of psychopharmacology at both the national and international levels and is currently engaged in the study of changes in human behavior.

James M. Woo-Sam (Ph.D., Purdue University, 1960) is Service Chief at the North Region Clinic Health Care Agency Children and Youth Services of Orange County, California. He is the coauthor of the *Clinical Interpretation of the WAIS*, as well as many articles and papers on assessment.

Irla Lee Zimmerman (Ph.D., University of California at Los Angeles, 1953) is a clinical psychologist in private practice in Whittier, California. For the last ten years she has been involved in a major longitudinal study of children being raised in alternative life styles. She is the coauthor of the *Clinical Interpretation of the WISC* and the *Clinical Interpretation of the WAIS*, as well as numerous articles/papers on assessment and child development.

Barbara G. Zirkin (M.A., M.S., The Johns Hopkins University, 1979) is a graduate student completing a dissertation in the Division of Education, The Johns Hopkins University. Her major areas of interest include education of the gifted child and research in testing and measurement. A former high school English teacher, she has served as an instructor and graduate research aide at Johns Hopkins University.